A Photographic Field Guide to the

BIRDS OF INDIA

Pakistan, Nepal, Bhutan, Sri Lanka, and Bangladesh

Princeton University Press
Princeton and Oxford

This edition published in North America, the United Kingdom, and Europe in 2017 by

Princeton University Press
41 William Street
Princeton, New Jersey 08540
press.princeton.edu

First published in 2016 by
Om Books International

Corporate & Editorial Office
A-12, Sector 64, Noida 201 301
Uttar Pradesh, India
Phone: +91 120 477 4100
Email: editorial@ombooks.com
Website: www.ombooksinternational.com

Editor: Ipshita Mitra

Library of Congress Control Number: 2016956133

ISBN: 978-0-691-17649-9

Printed in India

10 9 8 7 6 5 4 3 2 1

A Photographic Field Guide to the

BIRDS OF INDIA

Pakistan, Nepal, Bhutan, Sri Lanka and Bangladesh

CONTENTS

INTRODUCTION

BIRDS OF THE INDIAN SUBCONTINENT

AN OVERVIEW BY CAROL AND TIM INSKIPP

Dr. Salim Ali

Dr. S Dillon Ripley

Spotted Creeper

Pale Rockfinches

The Indian subcontinent has a great wealth of birds, making it a paradise for the birdwatcher. The classic *Handbook of the Birds of India and Pakistan* by Salim Ali and S Dillon Ripley, which covers the whole region and was first published in 1968-1975, lists over 1,200 species. With additional recording and following the more up-to-date nomenclature in the *Howard and Moore Complete Checklist of Birds of the World* edited by E. C. Dickinson (2003) the current species total for the subcontinent stands at 1,375 species – 13 per cent of the world's birds. A further relevant reference is *Birds of South Asia: the Ripley Guide* by Pamela Rasmussen and John Anderton, which has adopted much narrower species limits and, consequently, the latest edition (2012) recognises 1451 species in the region. Note that less than 800 species are found in all of North America.

The Indian subcontinent is species-rich partly because of its wide altitudinal range extending from sea level up to the summit of the Himalayas, the world's highest mountains. Another reason is the region's highly varied climate and associated diverse vegetation. The extremes range from the almost rainless Great Indian or Thar Desert, where temperatures reach over 55°C, to the wet evergreen forests of the Assam Hills where 1,300 cm of rain a year have bee recorded at Cherrapunji – one of the wettest places on Earth, and the Arctic conditions of the Himalayan peaks where only alpine flowers and cushion plants flourish at over 4,900 m.

The other major factor contributing to the subcontinent's species-richness is its geographical position in a region of overlap between three biogeographic provinces – the Indo-malayan (South and South-East Asia), Palearctic (Europe and Northern Asia), and Afro-tropical (Africa) realms. As a result, species typical of all three realms occur. Most species are Indo-malayan, for example the ioras and minivets; some are Palearctic, including the accentors, and a small number, such as the Spotted Creeper *Salpornis spilonotus*, originate in Africa.

New species are continually being added to the region's list. For example, J. K. Tiwari recently found a flock of Pale Rockfinches *Carpospiza brachydactyla* in Gujarat - a bird previously recorded only in the Middle East. Even more exciting, in 2006 Ramana Athreya first described for science the multi-coloured Bugun Liocichla *Liocichla bugunorum*, from the Himalayan forests of Arunachal Pradesh.

Two species from the subcontinent are probably now extinct. The Pink-headed Duck *Rhodonessa caryophyllacea* was formerly locally distributed in pools and swamps in the elephant grass jungles of north-eastern India, Bangladesh, Nepal and Myanmar. It was last definitely seen in Bihar in 1935, but there are more recent unconfirmed reports from hunters in Myanmar. The Himalayan

Himalayan Quail

Pink-headed Duck

Quail [Mountain Quail] *Ophrysia superciliosa* has not been recorded since the end of the last century, despite intensive searching, but some ornithologists think it might still be surviving. It was only found in Uttarakhand in the Western Himalayas, where it inhabited long grass and scrub. Rahul Kaul indicated that this habitat is similar to that occupied by the more widespread Cheer Pheasant *Catreus wallichii*, and advocated searches over a wider area. Another species that was long considered to be extinct is the Forest Owlet [Forest Spotted Owlet] *Athene blewitti*, because there had been no confirmed sightings since 1914. However, it was rediscovered in 1997 in the Satpura mountains in Central India, where it frequents moist deciduous forest and wild mango groves, usually near streams.

BirdLife International annually produce a world list of bird species threatened with extinction. In 2012 a total of 1,313 species has been listed (13 per cent of the world's avifauna), including 90 species which regularly occur in the Indian subcontinent. A book, the *Threatened Birds of Asia*, was published in 2001, which describes all Asian species at risk of extinction, highlighting the threats they face and the conservation measures proposed to save them. Similarly BNHS has recently published *Threatened Birds of India* edited by Dr. Asad Rahmani.

Forest Owlet

Overall, the subcontinent supports 164 (or 199 - Rasmussen & Anderton) endemic species, those found nowhere else, a total of over ten per cent of the region's avifauna. BirdLife International has identified eight centres of endemism lying within or mainly in the region, often called Endemic Bird Areas or conservation hotspots. These areas were identified throughout the world by analysing patterns of distribution of birds with restricted ranges, that is with breeding ranges below 50,000 sq.km. (about the size of Sri Lanka). The analysis showed that restricted range species tend to occur in places which are often islands or isolated patches of a particular habitat. These natural groupings of species are regarded as Endemic Bird Areas and are especially important for bird conservation. BirdLife published *Endemic Bird Areas of the World: Priorities for Biodiversity Conservation* in 1998.

Cheer Pheasant

The wet lowland and montane rainforests of the Eastern Himalayas in India, Nepal and Bhutan (also extending into Myanmar and south-west China), form one Endemic Bird Area in the subcontinent, as they are extremely species-rich. Other isolated endemic-rich areas of rainforest are on the coastal flanks of the Western Ghats and in south-western Sri Lanka. The other Endemic Bird Areas

Chestnut-breasted Partridge

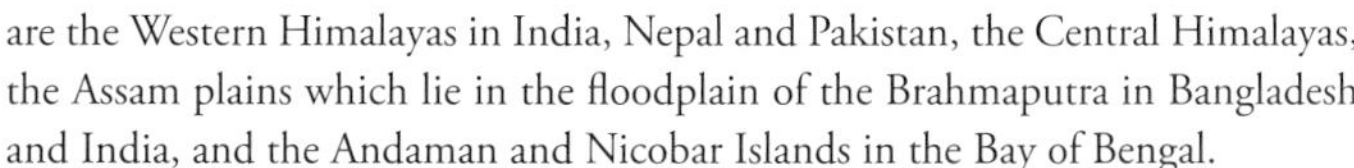

are the Western Himalayas in India, Nepal and Pakistan, the Central Himalayas, the Assam plains which lie in the floodplain of the Brahmaputra in Bangladesh and India, and the Andaman and Nicobar Islands in the Bay of Bengal.

A total of 19 restricted range species occur only in the Eastern Himalayas. Half of them are considered at risk from loss or fragmentation of their habitat, and some are also threatened by hunting. Many of the birds are relatively poorly known because much of the area has long been inaccessible for political and logistical reasons. More bird surveys have been made in recent years and it is perhaps the most exciting area in the region for future work. One threatened species which would certainly benefit from further study is the enigmatic Chestnut-breasted Partridge [Red-breasted Hill Partridge] *Arborophila mandellii* which has only been recently reported from two or three localities in Arunachal Pradesh and one in Bhutan. It frequents dense undergrowth in broad leaved evergreen forest, and its habits have never been recorded in the wild.

Western Tragopan

The Rusty-throated Wren Babbler [Mishmi Wren] *Spelaeornis badeigularis* was, until recently, only known from a specimen collected in 1947 from the wet subtropical forests of the Mishmi Hills in eastern Arunachal Pradesh. It was recently rediscovered in the same area and its song and habits are now being documented. The Dark-rumped Swift [Darkbacked Swift] *Apus acuticauda* is a threatened species which is a breeding endemic in the region (and there are other records from Myanmar and Thailand) It is only known to breed at two sites in the Khasi Hills, Meghalaya, in cliffs and gorges and is presumed to breed in Mizoram. The true status and threats to this species are unknown.

There are 11 restricted range species in the Western Himalayas, including the probably extinct Himalayan Quail and three which are thought to be at risk of extinction: Western Tragopan *Tragopan melanocephalus*, Cheer Pheasant and Kashmir Flycatcher [Kashmir Red-breasted Flycatcher] *Ficedula subrubra*. All three are threatened by habitat loss and deterioration, while the two pheasants also suffer from the effects of hunting. The rare and magnificent Western Tragopan inhabits dense undergrowth in temperate forests in Northern Pakistan and north-west India and occurs in at least seven protected areas. The Cheer Pheasant occurs very locally from Northern Pakistan and north-west India to west-central Nepal. It seems to favour early successional habitats, such as recently cleared areas with secondary scrub. It is found in several protected areas, but its future is by no means certain. The Kashmir Flycatcher breeds in mixed deciduous forests in Kashmir and the Pir Panjal range in north-west India and Pakistan, and winters in forest edges, gardens and tea estates in Sri Lanka and the Western Ghats. Once it was common in its breeding range, but it appears to have declined.

Hoary-throated Barwing

The Central Himalayas Endemic Bird Area supports three restricted range species: Hoary-throated Barwing [Hoary Barwing] *Actinodura nipalensis*, whose range extends into the Eastern Himalayas, Spiny Babbler *Turdoides nipalensis*, and Nepal Wren Babbler *Pnoepyga immaculata*, which was described in 1991 from Nepal but is now known to occur west to Himachal Pradesh.

Sri Lanka Whistling Thrush

Sri Lanka has more endemic species, 26 (-33) than any other area in the region. Forest loss and disturbance have resulted in two of these species becoming seriously threatened and a number of others are in significant decline. Two species are endangered – the Serendib Scops Owl *Otus thilohoffmanni* and the Sri Lanka Whistling Thrush [Ceylon Whistling Thrush] *Myophonus blighi*. The discovery of Serendib Scops Owl, which inhabits rain forests in the south-west of the island, was published in 2004 after several years of research by Deepal Warakagoda. The Sri Lanka Whistling Thrush is a shy bird inhabiting mountain streams running through fern-clad ravines and gorges in dense, moist hill forest. It is now rare and declining, and like a number of other Sri Lankan species has probably suffered from replacement of natural forests by monoculture plantations which lack the undergrowth it needs.

Nilgiri Wood Pigeon

The Western Ghats support 17 - 22 restricted range species, of which seven are thought to be at risk of extinction; most are suffering to some extent from habitat damage and loss, mainly of forests. These species include the Nilgiri Wood Pigeon *Columba elphinstonii* and Black-chinned Laughingthrush *Garrulax cachinnans*, which are threatened by forest loss; and Nilgiri Pipit *Anthus nilghiriensis* and Broad-tailed Grassbird *Schoenicola platyurus*, which are threatened by changes in the upland grasslands.

The Andaman and Nicobar Islands form two Endemic Bird Areas and possess 18 (- 26) endemic bird species. Based on the latter figure 15 are found only on the Andamans, eight on the Nicobars and three on both groups of islands. The main conservation concerns are settlement by people from the mainland, who have cleared forest to farm, the development of infrastructure for the main-landers and commercial exploitation of the islands. BirdLife International considers that there are three globally threatened species on the islands: Nicobar Megapode [Megapode] *Megapodius nicobariensis*, Narcondam Hornbill *Rhyticeros narcondami*, and Nicobar Sparrowhawk *Accipiter butleri*. The Nicobar Megapode is a terrestrial bird, about the size of a domestic hen, which lives in undergrowth in thick forest adjacent to sandy beaches, and now appears to be restricted to the Nicobar Islands. The only immediate threat facing the megapode is habitat loss on the Nancowry group of islands. The Narcondam Hornbill is only found in evergreen forests on Narcondam Island in the Andamans. The island is less than 7 km^2 in area and currently uninhabited. A recent proposal to build a radar surveillance station on the island would have been a serious threat to the survival of the species, but was thankfully averted. The Nicobar Sparrowhawk is only definitely known from a few records from Car Nicobar and Katchall, where it is threatened by forest destruction.

Narcondam Hornbill

Manipur Bush Quail

All three species endemic to the Assam lowlands Endemic Bird Area are threatened. There have been no fully accepted published reports of the Manipur Bush Quail *Perdicula manipurensis* since 1938, although a small group was reported in 2006. Formerly, this bush quail was described as "local" but not very rare in the tall damp grass and scrub of the foothills in Northeast India and Bangladesh. It may have suffered from drainage and destruction of its habitat and perhaps hunting. The other two species, the Marsh Babbler [Marsh Spotted Babbler] *Pellorneum palustre* and the Black-breasted Parrotbill [Gould's Parrotbill] *Paradoxornis flavirostris* both occur in reed beds and tall grass alongside rivers and marshes and must have suffered from damage and loss to their wetland and grassland habitats. Formerly, they were locally common, but there are very few recent records of either. The Assam lowlands are also a refuge for two globally endangered species: the Greater Adjutant [Adjutant] *Leptoptilos dubius*, a large stork, and the Bengal Florican *Houbaropsis bengalensis*, a bustard occupying wet grassland. Very few breeding sites of the stork are now known, the largest being in the Assam lowlands.

Black-breasted Parrotbill

The bird habitats of the Indian subcontinent can be roughly divided into forests, scrub, wetlands (inland and littoral), marine, grasslands and agricultural. There is overlap of some habitats, for example mangrove forests can also be considered as wetlands, as can seasonally flooded grasslands. Many bird species require mixed habitat types, for example the Black-necked Crane *Grus nigricollis* which requires marshy grassland. The forests of the region are vitally important for many of its birds. Seven of the subcontinent's eight Endemic Bird Areas are largely forested. Over half of the region's globally threatened birds and two-thirds of its endemic birds are dependent on forests.

Bengal Florican

There is an immense variety of forest types in the region. Tropical forests range from coastal mangroves to wet, dense evergreen, dry deciduous and open desert thorn forests. In the Himalayas temperate forests include those of mixed broadleaves, moist oak and rhododendron draped with epiphytic mosses and lichens and dry coniferous forests of pines and firs. Forest resources are significantly declining throughout most of the region. The major threats are overexploitation for fuel wood, timber and fodder, overgrazing, conversion to agriculture or monoculture tree plantations and dam construction. Both the extent and quality of forest have declined. Forest with a crown density of 40 per cent or more covered 12.3 per cent of India in 2012, although this figure is disputed. In 2005 25.4 per cent of Nepal was covered with forest. Bhutan, however, still retains much of its forests relatively intact, with 69 per cent of its land area under forest in 2010, including 12.7 per cent of primary forests. The country possesses some of the best forest habitats left in the Himalayas.

Black-necked Crane

Wetlands in the region are abundant and support a rich array of waterfowl, including grebes, pelicans, cormorants, ducks, geese, herons, egrets, storks, spoonbills, flamingos, cranes, rails, waders, gulls and terns. As well as providing habitats for breeding resident species, the subcontinent's wetlands include major staging and wintering grounds for waterfowl breeding in Central and

Northern Asia. The region possesses a wide range of wetland types distributed almost throughout, including mountain glacial lakes, freshwater and brackish marshes, large water storage reservoirs, village tanks, saline flats and coastal mangroves and mudflats. Wetland destruction and degradation in the region are reducing the diversity of wetlands and population numbers of many bird species. Major direct threats are over-exploitation of wetland resources, hunting, dam-building, and pollution from sewage and industrial effluents, siltation and agricultural fertilisers and pesticides. A total of 22 of the subcontinent's wetland bird species is globally threatened including the Spoon-billed Sandpiper *Eurhynorhynchus pygmeus* and Baer's Pochard *Aythya baeri*, which are Critically Endangered. Awareness of the problems facing wetlands is increasing. In India, for example, this has resulted in the setting up of a National Commission on Wetlands, Mangroves and Coral Reefs to advise the government on wetland conservation. A detailed directory of Indian wetlands compiled by WWF India and the Asian Wetland Bureau describing the values, threats and conservation measures was published in 1993.

Spoon-billed Sandpiper

Baer's Pochard

The subcontinent's most important wetland sites include Chilika Lake, a brackish lagoon in Odisha on the east Indian coast, which supports one of the largest concentrations of migrant waterfowl in the region. Wetlands in the Indus valley in Pakistan form another major wintering refuge and staging area for a wide variety of waterfowl, notably the Chashma Barrage reservoir and Haleji Lake. The Sundarbans in the Ganges-Brahmaputra delta in the Bangladesh and India include one of the largest contiguous areas of mangrove forest in the world. The mangroves support a rich and diverse avifauna. Although no data are available, the coastal mudflats and estuaries are thought to be of great importance as staging and wintering areas. The extensive seasonally flooded manmade lagoons of Keoladeo Ghana in Rajasthan are particularly diverse – at least 332 bird species have been recorded there. Keoladeo is internationally renowned, especially for its wintering flock of the endangered Siberian Crane *Grus leucogeranus*, where it was the only known site for the species in the region. Very sadly, this flock declined from 125 in the 1960s to just six birds in the winter of 1991/1992, and none has been reported in the region since. Hunting in Afghanistan may have caused the decline, although the species' feeding habitat at Keoladeo has been invaded by a thick growth of grasses. The vast saline flats of the Rann of Kutch in north-west India are important for migratory waterfowl and support breeding colonies of the Lesser Flamingo *Phoenicopterus minor*, herons and egrets. Wetlands in the moist tropical and subtropical forests of Assam and Arunachal Pradesh support two globally endangered species: the shy and little known White-bellied Heron [Great Whitebellied Heron] *Ardea insignis* for which there are very few records and the White-winged Duck [White-winged Wood Duck]

Siberian Crane

White-winged Duck

Lesser Florican

Cairina scutulata, which was formerly common in parts of Northeast India, but has suffered a major decline this century and is now rare. Other wetlands in the region valuable for birds include the extensive and largely untouched mangroves of the Andaman and Nicobar Islands; the marshes, *jheels* and Terai swamps of the Gangetic plain; Point Calimere and Pulicat Lake on India's east coast; the Haor Basin of Sylhet and east Mymensingh in north-east Bangladesh; and the Brahmaputra floodplain in the Assam lowlands.

The most important grasslands for birds in the subcontinent are the seasonally flooded ones occurring across the Himalayan foothills and in the floodplains of the Indus and Brahmaputra rivers; the arid grasslands of the Thar Desert, and grasslands in peninsular India. These lowland grasslands support distinctive bird communities with a number of specialist endemic species. They have been greatly reduced, fragmented and degraded by large scale expansion of agriculture, drainage, changes in land use and overgrazing. As a result most of the region's endemic grassland birds are seriously at risk.

Great Indian Bustard

These threatened species include two bustards: the Lesser Florican *Sypheotides indicus* and the Great Indian Bustard *Ardeotis nigriceps*. Once the Lesser Florican was the most common and widespread of Indian bustards, but it is now the most threatened; it is restricted as a breeding bird to Western India. The late Ravi Sankaran, who carried out extensive studies on its ecology, distribution and status, spearheaded conservation measures to save both the florican and its grassland habitat. He emphasised that the grasslands used by the breeding floricans are crucial to the rural economy. An action plan was developed with specific recommendations for the sustainable utilisation of grassland resources, reconciling human needs and conservation of the Lesser Florican.

Swamp Francolin

The stately great Indian bustard inhabits wide open grasslands and cultivated areas in semi-desert. A century ago it ranged from Pakistan east to West Bengal and south through the peninsula to Madras, but now it is confined to grasslands mainly in protected areas in Western India. A Bombay Natural History Society (BNHS) team carried out detailed studies of the status, ecology and needs of the species during the 1980s and made comprehensive recommendations for its conservation. Sadly, the Great Indian Bustard has continued to decline and by 2008 was reduced to about 300 individuals. The primary cause has been habitat destruction.

Another endemic grassland species is the Swamp Francolin [Swamp Partridge] *Francolinus gularis*, which is confined to the Ganges and Brahmaputra river basins, where it occupies tall wet grasslands and swamps.

The other threatened grassland birds restricted to the subcontinent are Bristled Grassbird [Bristled Grass Warbler] *Chaetornis striata* and Finn's Weaver [Finn's Baya] *Ploceus megarhynchus*. Both inhabit wet grasslands and are threatened by destruction and modification of their habitat.

Scrub has developed in the region where trees are unable to grow either because soils are poor and thin or because they are too wet, such as at the edges of wetlands or in seasonally inundated floodplains. Scrub also grows naturally in extreme climatic conditions, such as in semi-desert or at high altitudes in the Himalayas. In addition, there are now large areas of scrubland in the region where forests have been over-exploited by fodder and fuel collection or grazing.

Relatively few birds in the subcontinent are characteristic of scrub habitats alone, but many are found in scrub mixed with grasslands, in wetlands or at forest edges. Rather less than a third of endemic birds in the region occupies habitats wholly or partly comprising scrub. One of the most interesting is the endangered Jerdon's Courser *Rhinoptilus bitorquatus*, known historically from a few records in Andhra Pradesh. It was presumed to be extinct until it was rediscovered in 1986 by BNHS biologist Bharat Bhushan. Since then, small numbers have been located at sites in the Lankamalai and Veliconda hills in Andhra Pradesh, where it inhabits scrub on rocky foothills. Bharat Bhushan has highlighted the conservation issue facing the species. Development activities pose major problems. As a result of lobbying, a planned irrigation scheme which would have affected the courser's range has been diverted. Two protected areas have been gazetted there, but comprehensive management for the courser's habitat in these areas is needed.

Finn's Weaver

Jerdon's Courser

Stoliczka's Bushchat [Stoliczka's Whinchat] *Saxicola macrorhynchus* occupies scrub habitats in desert. It is virtually endemic to the region, with records from north-west India, Pakistan (where it may now be extinct) and two old records just over the border in Afghanistan. Systematic searches by a team led by Asad Rahmani in Rajasthan, in 1993 and 1994, showed that the species was fairly common in some areas, so it may not be as threatened as previously thought. However, it no longer occurs in semi-arid areas, and its stronghold is now the waterless sandy plains of the Thar Desert. The reasons for its range contraction are unclear, but could partly be due to habitat alteration, as improved irrigation has converted large tracts of semi-desert to cultivation; however, other factors must be involved, as uncultivated semi-desert areas are unoccupied by the bushchat. Asad Rahmani concluded that more work was needed to determine the species' ecological requirements and local movements (if any), to enable a conservation strategy to be developed.

Ferdinand Stoliczka

Seabirds in the region comprise the skuas, petrels, shearwaters, frigatebirds and boobies, most of which are passage migrants or vagrants, gulls (mainly winter visitors), terns and noddies (mainly resident, winter or summer visitors or passage migrants), tropicbirds (residents and passage migrants), and phalaropes (one winter visitor and one vagrant). As a result of increased watching several seabirds have been added to the region's avifauna in recent years, notably the threatened Barau's Petrel *Pterodroma baraui*, which was first described for science only in 1963. It is known only from the Indian Ocean, where it breeds on the Mascarene Islands. In recent years there have been sightings between the Maldives and Lakshadweep and off the Sri Lankan coast. Seabird breeding colonies in the subcontinent are chiefly concentrated in the Maldives and Lakshadweep but, sadly, intense persecution and egg collection is significantly reducing breeding success. Terns and noddies are by far the most numerous breeding species, with the commonest being the Brown Noddy [Noddy Tern] *Anous stolidus* and Sooty Tern *Onychoprion fuscatus* in Lakshadweep and Black-naped Tern *Sterna sumatrana*.

Barua's Petrel

Sooty Tern

Speckled Wood Pigeon

Grandala

Pied Thrush

European Bee-eater

The large majority of species in the region (about 1000 species) are resident, although the numbers of some of these are augmented by winter visitors breeding further north. Some residents are sedentary throughout the year, while others undertake irregular movements, either locally or more widely in the region depending on water conditions or food supply. The Speckled Wood Pigeon *Columba hodgsonii*, for example, appears wherever its favoured trees have ripe fruit. Many Himalayan residents are altitudinal migrants, the level to which they descend in winter frequently depending on weather conditions. For instance, the Grandala [Hodgson's Grandala] *Grandala coelicolor* summers up to 5,500 m and chiefly winters down to 3,000 m., but has been recorded as low as 1,950 m. in bad weather. A number of other residents in the subcontinent breed in the Himalayas and winter further south in the region, including the endemic Pied Thrush [Pied Ground Thrush] *Zoothera wardii* which spends the winter in Sri Lanka.

There are 18 species that are exclusively summer visitors to the region. Most of these, such as the Lesser Cuckoo [Small Cuckoo] *Cuculus poliocephalus* and Common Swift [swift] *Apus apus* winter in Africa. Several species breed chiefly to the north and west of the subcontinent and just extend into Pakistan and north-west India, for instance the European Bee-eater *Merops apiaster*. Some species move south-eastwards, perhaps as far as Malaysia and Indonesia, for example the White-throated Needletail [White-throated Spinetail Swift] *Hirundapus caudacutus* and Asian Emerald Cuckoo [Emerald Cuckoo] *Chrysococcyx maculatus*.

The subcontinent attracts about 150 winter visitors, some of which are also passage migrants. There is also a small number of species which are *only* known as passage migrants. The winter visitors originate chiefly in Northern and Central Asia and include grebes, ducks, geese, herons, storks, pelicans, birds of prey, cranes, waders, rails, gulls and terns. Passerines include pipits, wagtails, accentors, thrushes, shrikes, warblers, finches and buntings.

Information on migration routes in the region is still patchy but ringing recoveries have shown that the majority of winter visitors to the subcontinent enter via the Indus plains. The Indus valley has been internationally acknowledged as the fourth major migratory flyway for waterfowl in the world. There is less information about migration routes in the north-east of the region, but the Brahmaputra river and its tributaries are thought to form a flyway for birds from north-east Asia. There is increasing evidence suggesting that some birds breeding in the Palearctic, mainly non-passerines, migrate across the Himalayas to winter in the subcontinent. Birds have been seen flying over the highest regions of these ranges, for example a flock of Bar-headed Geese *Anser indicus* was recorded flying as high as 9,375 m. over Sagarmatha in Nepal. Other birds follow the main valleys, such as those of the Kali Gandaki, Dudh Kosi and Arun valleys in Nepal. Birds of prey, especially *Aquila* eagles have also been found to use the Himalayas as an east-west pathway in autumn. The wintering area of these birds is poorly known but is assumed to be the plains of north-west India and Pakistan. The Spot-winged Starling [Spotted-winged Stare] *Saroglossa spiloptera* also undertakes east-west movements along the Himalayas, and it is possible that other species undergo similar migrations. A number of pelagic and coastal passage migrants and wintering species travel by oceanic or coastal routes. One identified coastal flyway lies on India's east coast linking Point Calimere in Tamil Nadu and Chilika and Pulicat Lakes. Migration patterns of seabirds are especially poorly understood, but there is now evidence that some species occur more regularly than previously thought, especially around the time of the south-west monsoon. In Sri Lanka a mass migration of Bridled Terns [Brown-winged Tern] *Onychoprion anaethetus.* takes place in autumn; an estimated half a million or more move southwards off the south-west coast within sight of land every year. A few species which breed outside the region and winter in East Africa migrate through Pakistan and north-west India; for example, the Rufous-tailed Rock Thrush [Rock Thrush] *Monticola saxatilis* and Red-backed Shrike *Lanius collurio.* As they mainly occur on autumn passage; they presumably use a different route in spring. In addition to the subcontinent's residents, summer and winter visitors and passage migrants, about 100 species of vagrants have been recorded.

Asian Emerald Cuckoo

The numbers and distribution of bird populations in the Indian subcontinent are changing, largely because of pollution and land use changes, which have often resulted in the losses of natural habitats, such as forests and wetlands.

In Europe, such factors have been shown to cause widespread declines in numerous bird species, including many which were previously common. Could the same be happening in the Indian subcontinent? This seems likely, but we can only speculate on the changes. Apart from the annual waterfowl counts organised by Wetlands International and some studies on rare species, there is a lack of data for most birds, especially for common and widespread species. The Indira Gandhi Nahar Project, the largest irrigation canal system in the world, in the Thar Desert, has undoubtedly had a profound effect on many desert birds. Asad Rahmani has shown that the canal and associated seepage wetlands and plantations alongside canals have provided suitable habitats for generalist species such as some waterfowl, herons, babblers, munias and parakeets, but the specialist species of the desert such as the Great Indian Bustard and sandgrouse have been edged out.

Rufous-tailed Rock Thrush

The protection of wildlife has a long tradition in the history of much of the region. Indeed one of the world's first wildlife sanctuaries was established in the third century BC by King Devanampiyatissa in Sri Lanka. Despite the enormous pressures created by being the second most populated country on Earth, wildlife conservation in India is of great national concern. Particular emphasis is being given to protecting sites of high species diversity and endemism, such as the Western Ghats, as well as ecologically fragile areas. The recently revised protected areas system in Bhutan is especially impressive, covering 22 per cent of the country and representing all of the country's major ecosystems. Large proportions of Nepal (23 per cent) and Sri Lanka (14 per cent) are also covered by protected areas. The enlightened and benevolent attitudes to wildlife of Hinduism and Buddhism have undoubtedly helped to conserve the rich natural heritage of the Indian subcontinent, which still remains today.

Red-backed Shrike

Note: The English names used are those preferred by the authors; the alternative names in square brackets are from *Ripley's Synopsis of the Birds of India.*

The maps in the book give the range of the species in the subcontinent. The red areas indicate resident birds. The blue area denotes non-breeding winter visitors.

Red Avadavat

NICOBAR MEGAPODE

Megapodius nicobariensis Megapodiidae

Size 43 cm

Voice Call a loud gull-like screech; also a cackling *kuk...a...kuk*

Range Resident; Nicobar Islands

Habitat Near dense undergrowth of evergreen forests on sandy beaches

Stout, short-tailed bird with powerful legs and feet; small ashy-grey head; reddish face with exposed skin and small rufous crest. Largely dark brown, though underparts greyer than brown. Female greyer than brown. Immature birds lack bare red skin patch. Often found in pairs or mixed droves with young. Strong runners, mostly spending time on the ground, flying reluctantly to take shelter on nearby trees. Breeds all year round. Female lays eggs in mounds of rotting vegetation. Feeds on vegetation, seeds, insects and snails.

SNOW PARTRIDGE

Lerwa lerwa Phasianidae

Size 38 cm

Voice Loud call, similar to Grey

Range Resident; the Himalayas, 2,500–5,000 m

Habitat Alpine meadows; scrubby hillsides; rhododendron; fern undergrowth

Rather plump bird with prominent bright red bill and legs. Upperparts blackish-grey and finely barred with rufous and white. Underparts dark chestnut, broadly streaked white and deep chestnut breast. Upper half of legs feathered and spurred. Dark tail also barred with white, white tip to tail. Sexes alike, but male has blunt spur on tarsus. Juvenile has mottled underparts and less prominent barring. Found in small groups of about six to eight, and upto 30, in non-breeding season. Nests on ground under rock ledges. Feeds on lichens, mosses and shoots. Nests well concealed on hillsides under rocks.

TIBETAN SNOWCOCK

Tetraogallus tibetanus Phasianidae

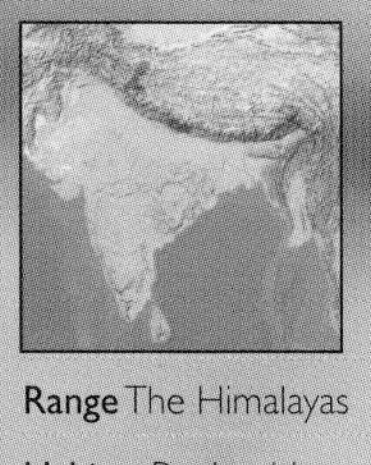

Size 51 cm

Voice Noisy. Call an accelerating bubbling, a whistle and loud *cur…lee*

Range The Himalayas

Habitat Rocky ridges; slopes and meadows above snowline

Largish partridge with strong, short, red legs. Distinguished from other snowcocks by extensive white underparts with heavy blackish streaks on sides and flanks. Adult has overall heavily streaked plumage, pale grey-buff upperparts streaked with dark grey. White forehead, ear-coverts and throat. White cheeks, chin, throat and breast, with some irregular dark grey-patches on upper breast and foreneck; dark grey bands on sides of neck and breast. Dark grey crown and upperparts; grey wing-coverts streaked white; white secondaries; reddish-brown rump and tail. Underparts white with black barring. Short tail with pale brown uppertail-coverts. Sexes alike, but female slightly smaller and duller.

HIMALAYAN SNOWCOCK

Tetraogallus himalayensis Phasianidae

Size 55–72 cm

Voice Noisy; cock utters loud whistle of several notes

Range Resident; the Himalayas; Kashmir to Kumaon and W Nepal; 3,800–5,500 m in summer; moves lower to 2,200 m in winter

Habitat Alpine meadows; rocky country above treeline

Largish bird, overall grey, black-and-white with some chestnut streaking that provides good camouflage among rocks and boulders. Sides of head and throat bordered chestnut. Dark reddish-brown band extends from behind eye, to neck, forming collar on white throat. Dark moustachial stripe from hindneck to collar. Upper breast barred with darker grey; white vent and undertail-coverts; white trailing edge on secondaries; rufous outer-tail feathers; yellow legs; dark grey bill, brown eyes surrounded by yellowish orbital skin. Legs and feet dark orange-yellow. Sexes alike but female smaller; male has tarsal spurs. Juvenile paler and less distinctly marked with conspicuous white supercilium.

CHUKAR PARTRIDGE

Alectoris chukar Phasianidae

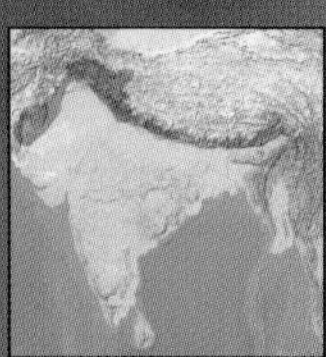

Size 38 cm

Voice Male utters a loud chuckle, of upto a dozen notes

Range Resident; W Himalayas to C Nepal; about 1,200-5,000 m

Habitat Scrub and rock-covered hills; cultivation

Plumpish, medium-sized partridge, overall greyish-brown with distinct black band running from eye to base of neck; whitish-buff face and throat; grey head and breast. Upperparts grey-buff, black gorget across forehead and eyes, white cheeks and throat. Flanks prominently barred black-and-white with tinge of buff; tail and lower back dark grey; buffish belly; chestnut outer-tail feathers; bright red bill and legs. Sexes similar, but female smaller with smaller knob on legs. Juvenile smaller and mottled brown-and-grey, with slight brown barring on flanks. Small groups forage on open barren grounds.

BLACK FRANCOLIN

Francolinus francolinus Phasianidae

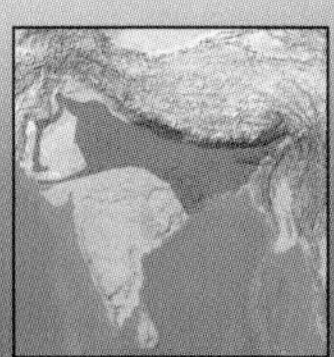

Size 34 cm

Voice Male utters a loud 3- to 6-noted crow

Range Locally resident; N subcontinent, along foothills; south to N Gujarat and C Madhya Pradesh; an eastern race *melanotus* occurs east of Nepal in Duars

Habitat High grass, cultivation; prefers wetter areas along canals and rivers

♀

Handsome, jet-black bird with stub-tail. Upperparts and flanks spotted white and fulvous; white-patch on cheeks; chestnut collar, belly and undertail-coverts; brownish-red legs. Black tail has narrow white bars. Female similar to male, but paler with wider brown bars on lower back, white cheek-patch and chestnut collar missing, small nuchal patch. Singly, or in small parties in high grass and edges of water; secretive; fast runners on ground. Nests in grass-lined depression in bare ground.

PAINTED FRANCOLIN

Francolinus pictus Phasianidae

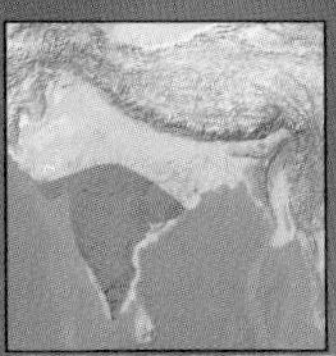

Size 31 cm

Voice Noisy when breeding (SW monsoon). Call a high-pitched, harsh grating 4- or 5-noted *khik...kheek...khee...khheeki*, quite similar to that of Black Francolin; may call every 20–30 seconds, for upto 40 minutes; often in duet

Range Most of India; south of range of Black Partridge; south of line from C Gujarat, N Madhya Pradesh, S Uttar Pradesh

Habitat Grasslands; scrubs; cultivation

Medium-sized, profusely marked bird. Distinguished from the female Black by lack of rufous hind-collar and white spots on underside. Rufous face; chestnut head and throat. Upperparts blackish-brown; neck and underparts densely spotted white; white rump and tail finely barred with black; yellowish orange legs. Female similar to male, but paler head and buff-white throat and no spurs on legs. Pairs or adults with young. Skulking, shy and secretive; not easily flushed. Rarely flies. Roosts in trees. Feeds on grain, grass and insects.

GREY FRANCOLIN

Francolinus pondicerianus Phasianidae

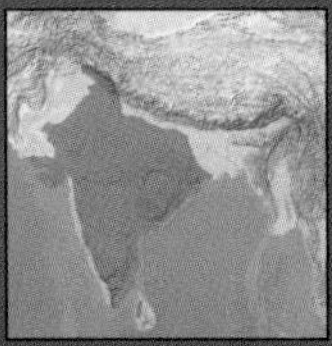

Size 34 cm

Voice Noisy. Call a very loud, high-pitched 2- to 3-noted *pat...ee...la*

Range Resident; all subcontinent, south of the Himalayan foothills

Habitat Open scrubs; grass; cultivation

Medium-sized, greyish-brown partridge with spear-shaped buff streaks. Pale face bordered with fine black gular-band; orange cheeks, throat and forehead. Upperparts grey-brown and rufous; buffy-rufous below; breast and abdomen greyish-buff with dark barring; mantle and wings chestnut with lighter streaking; fine cross-bars on throat and upper breast; fine black markings on abdomen and flanks.

SWAMP FRANCOLIN

Francolinus gularis Phasianidae

Size 37 cm

Voice Calls include vocal and loud *kyew…kyew…kyew…kaa…kaa* and *chukeroo…chukeroo…chukeroo.* Alarm a loud *kaw*

Range Globally threatened; breeding endemic resident restricted to Nepal, N India and Assam

Habitat Tall grasslands; swamp; sugarcane fields

Largest francolin with unusually long legs. Brown crown, beige supercilium and thin brown eye-stripes that extend to neck; upper throat and upper neck rusty-brown. Back and wings have mix of black and brown feathers with white flashes on the chest, chestnut flight feathers and outer-tail. Underparts brown longitudinally streaked with white. Blackish bill and dull brownish-red legs. Sexes alike, but female smaller and lacks spurs. Male has darker legs. Shy, seen in pairs or small groups near rivers and jheel edges in tall wet grasslands. Comes into open ground or cultivation to feed. Nests on a pad in shallow water amongst reeds.

TIBETAN PARTRIDGE

Perdix hodgsoniae Phasianidae

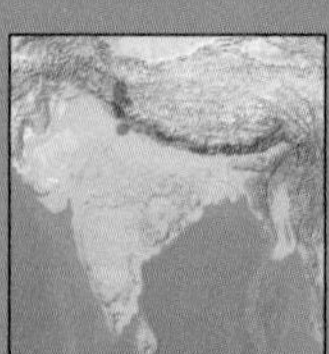

Size 31 cm

Voice Calls include strong, repeated *scherrrreck* and a high *chee…chee…chee*

Range Common breeding resident: N India, Nepal, Bhutan

Habitat High altitude semi-desert and rocky slopes with scattered low scrub

Medium-sized terrestrial bird of high altitude. Striking black-and-white facial markings contrasting with rufous nape. White throat and supercilium; black cheek patches; chestnut hind-collar and flanks, brown back, blackish belly. Underparts pale buff barred black on breast and belly; white lower belly. Rufous tail visible in flight. Female similar to male but duller. Juvenile a featureless buff-brown. Flies for short distances, glides downhill when disturbed. Feeds in pairs or small groups of 10-15, mainly on seeds, shoots and insects. Nests in grass-lined depression near rocks or scrub.

COMMON QUAIL

Coturnix coturnix Phasianidae

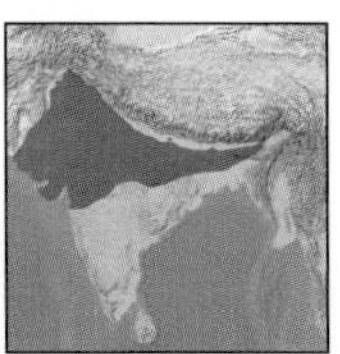

Size 20 cm

Voice Fluid, whistling *wet…me…lips* of male is common and familiar call

Range Resident; local migrant; breeds in Kashmir and parts of N and NE India; common in winter over the country

Habitat Cultivation; standing crop; grasslands

Smallish roundish bird, overall streaked brown with distinct white eye-stripe. Upperparts pale buff-brown, boldly marked; black to russet throat with stripe down throat centre and narrow stripe curving towards ear-coverts; black-and-white striped head. Rufous-buff breast with white shaft streaks; streaked flanks; long wings. Female has pale underparts, whitish belly, buffy throat; breast heavily streaked with black. Seen in pairs or small groups on ground, feeding on seeds, grain and small insects. Secretive; can only be seen when flushed. Usually located by its distinct call. Reluctant to fly. Nests in grass.

JAPANESE QUAIL

Coturnix japonica Phasianidae

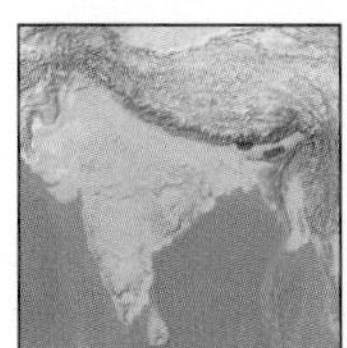

Size 20 cm

Voice Call a soft *chew…petree.* Also a rasping *chur…churk*

Range Winter visitor to NE India

Habitat Grasslands; crops

Overall tawny, brown bird mottled lighter buff. Breeding male has rufous face, dark moustachial and gular stripes; reddish cheeks; uniform rusty-brown upper throat and lower breast. Underparts uniform unmottled rufous-buff. Similar to Common, but rufous parts darker. Female slightly larger than male, with lighter cinnamon breast, stippled black and paler cheeks. Seen singly, or in pairs. Largely cultivated as a table bird.

RAIN QUAIL

Coturnix coromandelica Phasianidae

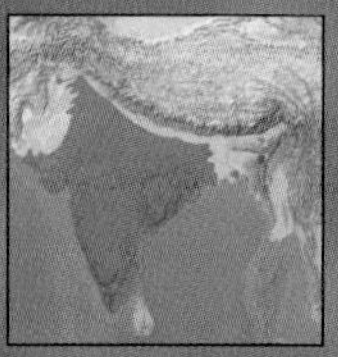

Size 18 cm

Voice Call a loud, high-pitched, repeated, *whit…whit*

Range Subcontinent

Habitat Grasslands; crops

Small quail with distinct black-and-white head pattern similar to European but bolder. The male has buff breast with black 'anchor' breast-patch; diagnostic stripe on the crown and supercilium; white neck bordered with black; flanks streaked with black. Female very similar to the female Common, minus barring on primaries. Found in small groups. Nervous and jumpy. Feeds on grass and weed seeds, small insects and insect larvae. Nests in standing crops. Cultivated as a table bird.

♀

KING QUAIL

Coturnix chinensis Phasianidae

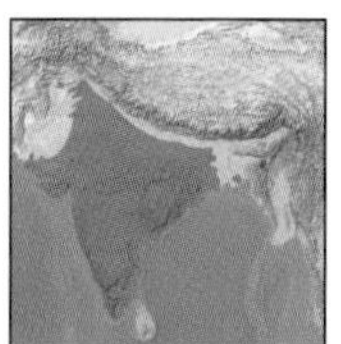

Size 14 cm

Voice High-pitched call of three descending notes

Range Widespread. Not found in the NW

Habitat Grasslands and scrub

♀

Overall dark brown bird with diagnostic slaty-blue breast and black throat-patch bordered with white band and black stripe; black eye-stripe; chestnut-red belly and undertail-coverts, black-and-white patterning on head, white lores, moustachial patch and crescent-shaped gorget, bordered in black, and bright yellow legs. Female smaller and more evenly brown with a rusty-brown belly and breast barred black, narrower crown-stripe; slaty-grey breast patch absent. Black beak and orangish-yellow legs. Shy, elusive and difficult to spot. Generally found in small coveys; flushes easily, but difficult to flush again. Nests on ground in sparsely-lined nests. Rarely seen.

JUNGLE BUSH QUAIL

Perdicula asiatica Phasianidae

Size 17 cm

Voice Call a trilling, musical *tirri…tirri…*

Range All over India, to about 1,200 m in the outer Himalayas

Habitat Dense grass; scrubs; edges of forests

Very small, heavily barred back with whitish underparts, slightly barred with brown, rufous head; crown slightly mottled with brown-and-white; white supercilium and moustache; dark eyebrow-stripe bordered white coming down to nape; variegated wings. Upperparts mottled black, brown-and-yellow. Brown beak, black tip; orangish-yellow legs and feet. Small spurs also present.

♀

ROCK BUSH QUAIL

Perdicula argoondah Phasianidae

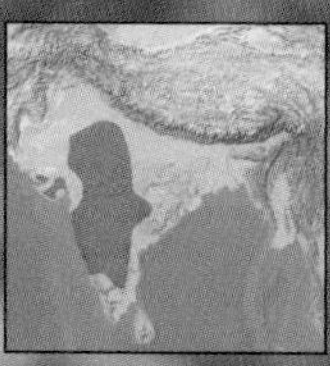

Size 17 cm

Voice Call a musical, ascending trill

Range W India from Haryana to S Kerala, Gujarat to Madhya Pradesh

Habitat Dry semi-desert; thorny scrubs

♀

Male similar to Jungle but with white underparts barred with black; rufous stripe above pale eyebrows; vermiculated beige and black underparts; pale undertail-coverts. Female has plain rufous face, whitish chin and pale supercilium. Small coveys feeding under vegetation. Nests under rock cover. Feeds on grain, seeds and leaves, sometimes insects.

PAINTED BUSH QUAIL

Perdicula erythrorhyncha Phasianidae

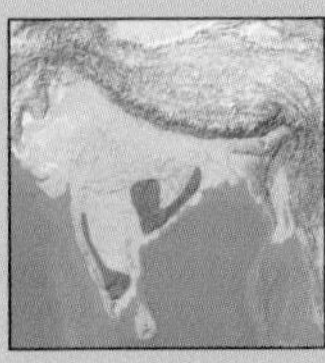

Size 17 cm

Voice Calls *kirikee...kirikee*

Range Endemic resident: Eastern and Western Ghats, hills of C India

Habitat Low, hilly scrubs along forest margins

♀

Distinct-looking bird, easily recognised by big bold spots on brown upperparts, black face and white throat; rufous underparts and flanks, white scapular line and wing-coverts; black around eyes, forehead and chin; bright red bill and legs. Female not as bright-coloured and no black-and-white markings on head and brick-red below. Seen feeding in small groups on grass, seeds, weeds, grains and insects in the open, early mornings or late afternoons. Subspecies *P. e. erythrorhyncha* occurs in the Western Ghats in Maharashtra, Kerala and Tamil Nadu. Subspecies *P. e. blewitti* occurs in Maharashtra, Madhya Pradesh, Bihar, West Bengal and Odisha.

RUFOUS-THROATED PARTRIDGE

Arborophila rufogularis Phasianidae

Little-known bird with distinct head and throat pattern; white half-collar and broad chestnut breast-band, rufous-orange ear-coverts, throat and foreneck; black spots on ear-coverts and neck sides. Sexes alike. Habits little known but said to breed on a cushion of grass under rocks in forests. Feed on insects, seeds, berries, shoots and invertebrates. *A. r. rufogularis* and *A. r. intermedia* are two subspecies found in the foothills of the Himalayas.

HIMALAYAN QUAIL

Ophrysia superciliosa Phasianidae

Presumed extinct, this mysterious quail was last recorded in 1890 and has not been seen since then. Old accounts record that it moved in small coveys and rarely left its habitat of long grass and brushwood on steep hillsides. Known only from the Kumaon and Garhwal regions of Uttarakhand.

MANIPUR BUSH QUAIL

Perdicula manipurensis Phasianidae

Small darkish grey quail with dark olive upperparts, finely marked with black; white eye-patch; golden-brown underparts with black cross-shaped markings; rich buff belly and vent, whitish loral patch, faint eyebrow. Male has chestnut forehead and throat. Not seen recently but said to be very secretive, keeping to dense cover. Habits and flight similar to other bush quails. Endemic. Confined to Assam, Manipur, Meghalaya and Nagaland. Globally threatened.

CHINESE FRANCOLIN

Francolinus pintadeanus Phasianidae

Easily confused with the female Black. Male has orangish-buff crown; white cheek-patch and white throat separated by black stripe. Strong moustachial stripe divides white throat from white ear-coverts. Overall body plumage mottled black-and-white. Little is known about this species in India but said to be a scarce breeding resident in SE Manipur. Few recent records. Sexes similar, although female paler in colour and lacks spurs.

WHITE-CHEEKED PARTRIDGE

Arborophila atrogularis Phasianidae

Medium-sized bird, identified by black mask and throat; throat both black and white; barred upperparts like Common; grey flanks instead of rufous streaks. Rare resident of E Himalayas, NE India and Bangladesh; inhabits bamboo thickets and forest undergrowth.

HILL PARTRIDGE

Arborophila torqueola Phasianidae

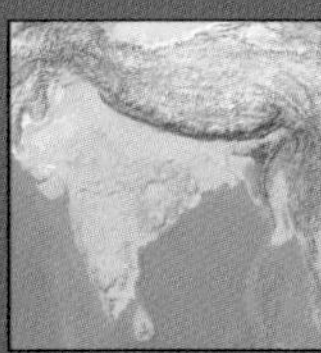

Size 28 cm

Voice Call a mournful whistle *po…eer…po…eer…*, the second syllable slightly longer

Range The Himalayas, east of Garhwal

Habitat Dense jungle undergrowth in hill country

Plump, medium-sized game bird with black barred brown upperparts and grey underparts with chestnut, white flank streaks. Male has bright chestnut head with white-streaked black eye-stripe, throat and neck, and white gorget. Female smaller, less colourful with brownish head and no white neck-collar. Secretive, prefers to run if disturbed. Expert flier through trees. Roosts in trees at night, huddled together. Nests on ground. More heard than seen.

♀

MOUNTAIN BAMBOO PARTRIDGE

Bambusicola fytchii Phasianidae

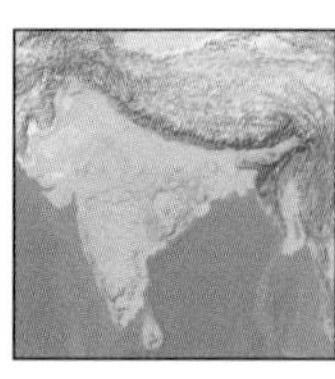

Size 35 cm

Voice Calls *che...chirree... che...chirree*

Range Resident: S Assam Hills

Habitat Rocky scrub and thickets on dry hillsides

Smallish bird with long tail. Characteristic black-and-white eye-stripe; buffish-white supercilium; distinctive patterning on the head; buff ear-coverts, throat and foreneck; rufous spotting on creamy-white breast, mantle and scapulars; strong blackish, heart-shaped spotting on flanks; displays rufous in primaries and sides of tail in flight. Sexes alike. Spends considerable time in undergrowth, feeding on seeds, berries, shoots, buds, grains, insects and worms. Secretive and difficult to flush.

SRI LANKA SPURFOWL

Galloperdix bicalcarata Phasianidae

Size 34 cm

Voice Series of whistles

Range Endemic to Sri Lanka

Habitat Dense forests

Partridge-sized secretive bird, difficult to spot, but located by its unmistakable cry. Male has deep maroon plumage bordered black with white spangled markings, vivid crimson red legs and bare facial skin; striking black-and-white dorsal plumage extending to head; extensive white ocellated chestnut wings and upper back. Female has chestnut underparts, plain brown back and wings, more prominently crested than the male. Extremely difficult to see. Rarely photographed.

RED SPURFOWL

Galloperdix spadicea Phasianidae

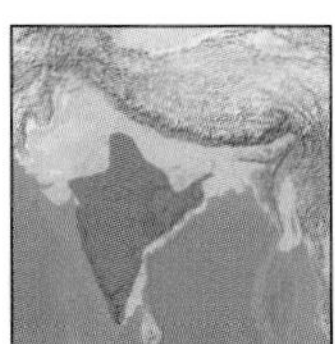

Size 36 cm

Voice Loud cackling notes. Calls when flushed

Range From Uttar Pradesh terai south across Gangetic plains through the peninsula

Habitat Scrub in forested, broken hilly country

stewarti

♀ *stewarti*

Reddish-brown bird with grey face, head and neck; red facial skin, eye patches, legs and feet; long tail and crown feathers. Sexes similar. Kerala race is deeper chestnut red. Male larger and darker with darker markings with one or two spurs. Shy; runs rapidly if disturbed, rarely taking to flight. Forages in small groups of two to five birds in open patches.

spadicea

PAINTED SPURFOWL

Galloperdix lunulata Phasianidae

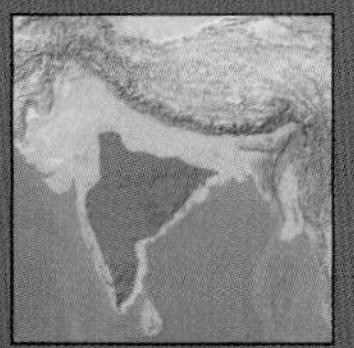

Size 32 cm

Voice Loud call of male reported

Range South of a line from Gwalior to Bengal; absent in Gujarat and Konkan; also Rajasthan

Habitat Dense thorn and bamboo jungles in broken hilly, rocky country

♀

Colourful, medium-sized bird with dark brown upperparts, dark bill and grey legs. Black head and neck have luminous green sheen. Black tail. Male has finely white-barred black head and neck, white-spotted chestnut upperparts; underparts ochre with black flecks; mantle, rump and wing-coverts chestnut. Female uniform brown with paler throat and belly and sparse spotting. Extremely shy and timid, runs swiftly away to hide in cover when disturbed. Seen in the shade of fruiting trees. Nests on ground.

BLOOD PHEASANT

Ithaginis cruentus Phasianidae

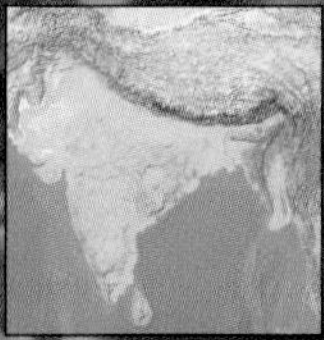

Size 38 cm

Voice Call a long-drawn squeal

Range High Himalayas, east of C Nepal

Habitat Steep hill forests

tibetanus

Dissimilar to other pheasant species, resembling partridge in size and shape. White crest; black stripe above and below the eye; red orbital skin. Upperparts white-streaked grey. Pale buff upper breast, rest of underparts, greyish-white streaked with red. Tail streaked with grey and buff. Female even brown with grey nape and crest. Colour varies according to race. Feeds on ground, scratching for food.

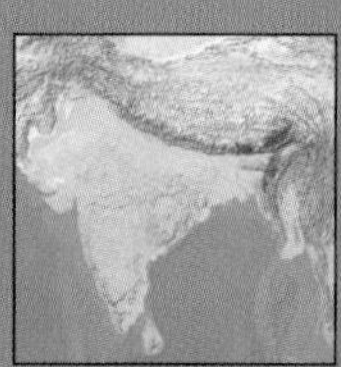
♀

cruentus

BLYTH'S TRAGOPAN

Tragopan blythii Phasianidae

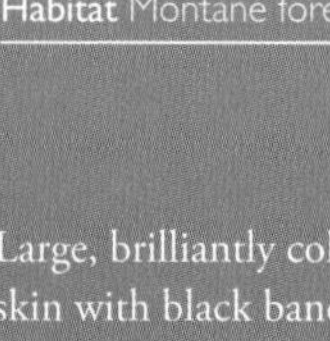

Size Male 68 cm; Female 59 cm

Voice Call a loud *hwaa…ouwaa…ouwaa*. Also *gock…gock…gock*

Range Globally threatened; rare breeding resident; Bhutan, S Assam Hills

Habitat Montane forest undergrowth on steep slopes

Large, brilliantly coloured game bird. Bare yellow facial skin with black band extending from base of bill to crown. Unmarked red head, rusty-red neck and breast. Pale blue horns. Upperparts brownish red with many white ocelli. Grey-red lower breast belly faintly spotted. Pinkish-brown legs; white-spotted red flanks. Female uniform brown with black buff and white mottling.

♀

SATYR TRAGOPAN

Tragopan satyra Phasianidae

Size Male 68 cm; Female 59 cm

Voice Call a loud mournful *guwaa... guwaah...guwaah*. Also, a *wak...wak* alarm

Range Scarce, very local breeding resident from Uttarakhand to Arunachal Pradesh. Relatively common in Bhutan

Habitat Montane forest undergrowth particularly on slopes or in ravines

Found in oak forests with an understorey of bamboo and rhododendrons or mixed coniferous and deciduous forests. Also found in rocky areas or gorges with small flowing streams.

♀

WESTERN TRAGOPAN

Tragopan melanocephalus Phasianidae

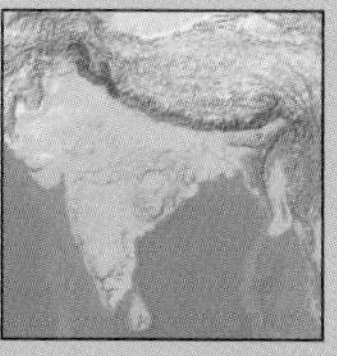

Size Male 71 cm; Female 60 cm

Voice Call notes rather goat-like *waa...waa ...wan...*; unmistakable once heard

Range W Himalayas, from W Pakistan, through Kashmir to Garhwal; rather uncommon and little-known over its entire range

Habitat Dense forest undergrowth; ringal bamboo

Male has black crown, red hindneck and cheeks; green throat; reddish-orange breast; grey-brown upperparts and black and red underparts, both heavily spotted with white. Female greyish-brown with white spots. Very skulking, but appears in open areas early morning or late evening. Male displays horns and lappets on head when breeding. Mostly vegetarian. Feeds on fresh leaves, bamboo shoots, acorns, berries, seeds and insects.

TEMMINCK'S TRAGOPAN

Tragopan temminckii Phasianidae

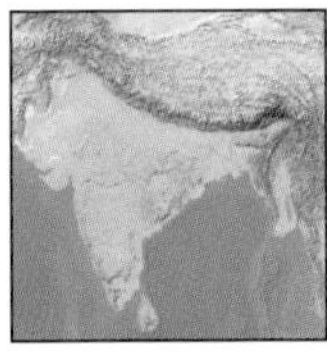

Size Male 64 cm

Voice Call a loud, moaning *whoah*, gets louder, longer

Range Rare resident: E Arunachal Pradesh

Habitat Deep forested hills

Medium-sized, extremely bright-coloured pheasant similar to Satyr. Upperparts orange, densely covered with cream ocelli; brilliant blue face surrounded with black; black-and-white spotted brown wings and uppertail-coverts and darker tail. Red underparts have grey spots. Black bill and pink legs. Female brown with white spots; has brown-and-blue circular eye skin.

♀

KOKLASS PHEASANT

Pucrasia macrolopha Phasianidae

Size Male 61 cm; Female 53 cm

Voice Call a loud *khok…kok…kok…kokha…*; vocal around dawn and dusk, but intermittently through the day

Range The Himalayas, hills of NE India; lower in winter. Several races

Habitat Steep forested hills; nullahs

♀

Silvery grey and brown bird with distinct backswept crest and elongated tail. Black head; white cheek-patches; bright orange breast; male has deep green head and ear tufts; golden-brown crest. Underparts chestnut; silver-grey flanks; dark pointed tail. Female paler with shorter crest. Feeds in pairs on steep slopes on seeds, insects and berries. Very shy and timid; running or flying when disturbed. Interesting display of courting male. Nests on ground; spends nights roosting on trees, or under rock overhangs.

HIMALAYAN MONAL

Lophophorus impejanus Phasianidae

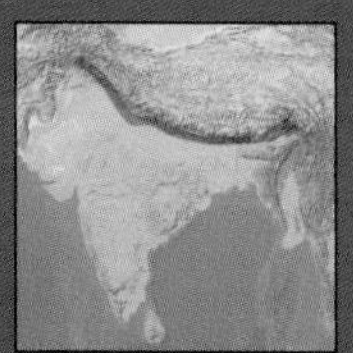

Size Male 72 cm; Female 63 cm

Voice Call a wild whistling, *cooooor…lew*, much like Curlew's

Range The Himalayas, west to east

Habitat High forest; glades; snow patches. Not uncommon

Sturdy bird with long luminous green crest. Male has overall iridescent purple-blue upperparts with chestnut tail and wings. Underparts, face and foreneck brown-black; patch of metallic purple behind ear-coverts. Rear neck coppery-yellow changing to green on mantle; purple shorter tail-coverts and longest tail-coverts irridiscent green. Female brown with black-and-white throat. Confiding; seen flying down hill at great speed.

SCLATER'S MONAL

Lophophorus sclateri Phasianidae

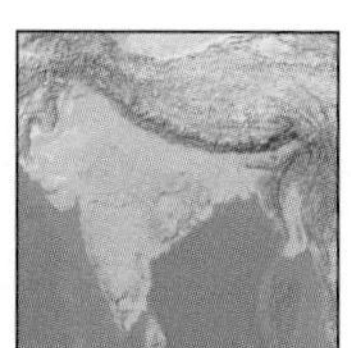

Size Male 68 cm; Female 63 cm

Voice Call a shrill, harsh cry

Range Arunachal Pradesh

Habitat Fir forests with dense undergrowth

Medium-sized bird similar to Himalayan but with blue and bronze colouring on head. Upperparts range from larger iridescent purplish-green to metallic green, blue, purple and black with white back patches; velvety-black underparts. Lacks the spatulate crest. Female dark brown with white throat and tail-tip.

RED JUNGLEFOWL

Gallus gallus Phasianidae

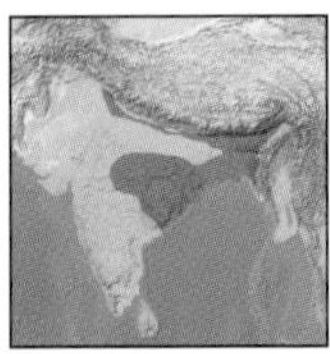

Size Male 65 cm; Female 42 cm

Voice Characteristic crow of male, shriller version of domestic. Other cackling sounds

Range The Himalayas, E Kashmir; E and C India, south to Narmada

Habitat *Sal* forests mixed with bamboo and cultivation patches

Both sexes resemble domestic bantam breeds. Male vibrant red-orange with combination of glossy blue-green, rich dark red, maroon-red, fiery orange, rufous and blackish brown feathers; deep red crown and neck; metallic green tail with long, drooping central feathers distinctive. Female has bright chestnut forehead, supercilium continuing to foreneck; reddish-brown plumage, vermiculated with fine black and buff. Seen in small parties, often several hens accompanying a cock; shy and skulking; emerges in clearings and on forest roads; flies up noisily when flushed.

SRI LANKA JUNGLEFOWL

Gallus lafayetii Phasianidae

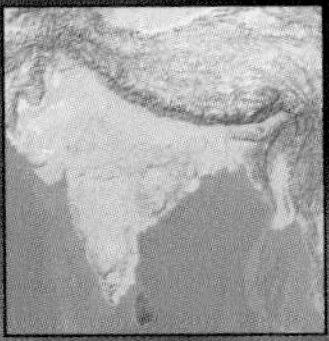

Size Male 66–70 cm; Female 35 cm

Voice Call a *chiok…chaw…. chowk*

Range Sri Lanka

Habitat Large forest patches. Locally plentiful in protected, less inhabited areas in lowlands and hills

Similar to Red except that the male has orange-red breast and belly, streaked with chestnut, oblong red comb with yellow centre, and elongated deep orange feathers covering mantle and back; face has bare, red skin and wattles; wings and tail purplish-black. Female similar to female Red. Endemic to Sri Lanka.

GREY JUNGLEFOWL

Gallus sonneratii Phasianidae

Size Male 80 cm; Female 40 cm

Voice Loud crow of male distinctive. Calls *kuk….kuk… kkura…kuk*; noisy in early mornings, but intermittently calls during day. Rather vocal when breeding

Range Peninsula and S India, range coinciding with teak country

Habitat Mixed deciduous forests; forest clearings

Silvery game bird with pink legs, long tail and elongated neck. Male larger but similar in shape to Red, with gold streaks restricted to neck and wing-coverts, silver belly and black flight feathers. Female overall brown above and black with bold white streaks below. Wings not barred like Red. Feeds in pairs; often seen on roads in morning and evening. Shy, but confiding.

KALIJ PHEASANT

Lophura leucomelanos Phasianidae

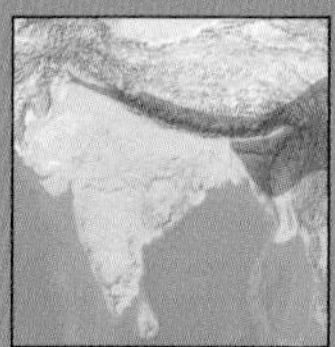

Size Male 65 cm; Female 60 cm

Voice Loud crowing by male. Chuckling calls on disturbance

Range The Himalayas, NE hill regions; foothills across country

Habitat Forest undergrowth; clearings; terraced cultivation; vicinity of hillside habitation

Male glossy black above, with steel-blue gloss; glossy tail, ending in sickle-like feathers; whitish edges to rump feathers; bare, scarlet around eyes; long, hairy white crest; brownish-grey underbody; lanceolate breast feathers. Female reddish-brown, scalloped paler; brown crest and bare scarlet patch around eye; brown tail, smaller than male's. Several races over the Himalayas and NE India; male varying in colour from glossy black to black and grey or white; crest black in other races. Pairs or small gatherings; spends day on ground, gleaning on forest roads and clearings during early mornings and late afternoons; good flier; roosts in trees at night.

♀

hamiltonii

melanota

leucomelanos

lathami

CHEER PHEASANT

Catreus wallichii Phasianidae

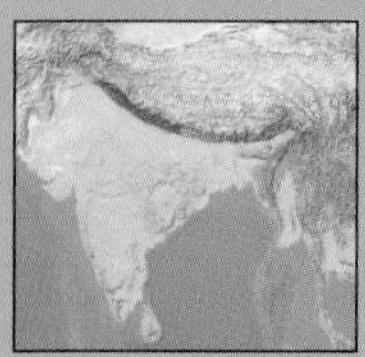

Size Male 118 cm; Female 76 cm

Voice Noisy before dawn and at dusk. Call a loud, distinct sounding *ehir… pir…ehir…pir*. Other cackling calls

Range The Himalayas between NW Pakistan and C Nepal

Habitat Grass-covered steep rocky hillsides with scattered tree cover

Male grey-brown; buff bar-tailed pheasant with long crest and red facial skin; large and very long-tailed; long backswept crest and red face; plain pale-grey upper neck. Male more boldly marked than female with black barring above and on white breast. Female smaller and more brown with greyish-brown rump. Feeds on roots, tubers, bulbs, seeds, insects and worms in pairs or groups on ground. Very wary and runs swiftly for cover when disturbed; hurtles downhill if flushed. Nests on ground. Roosts in trees.

MRS HUME'S PHEASANT

Syrmaticus humiae Phasianidae

Size Male 90 cm; Female 60 cm

Voice Distinctive crowing. Also utters cackling notes

Range S Assam Hills

Habitat Steep rocky slopes

Large pheasant with graduated tail barred black-and-brown. Male has greyish head, red facial skin, yellowish bill; metallic blue neck, upper breast and upper mantle and mainly chestnut underparts. Female brown with whitish throat and white-tipped tail. Little known. Recently recorded only in Mizoram. Globally threatened and seldom seen.

GREY PEACOCK PHEASANT

Polyplectron bicalcaratum Phasianidae

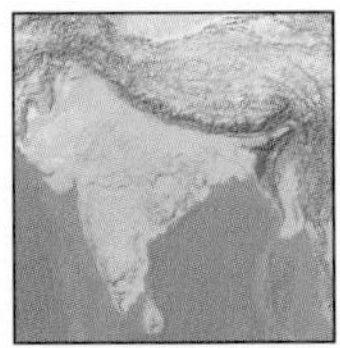

Size Male 64 cm; Female 48 cm

Voice Call a loud, guttural *hoo*

Range Sikkim to Arunachal Pradesh

Habitat Dense undergrowth in tropical forests

Small greyish-brown pheasant with short tufted crest and long broad tail. Male has striking iridescent purple and green ocelli, rimmed in white on mantle, wing and uppertail-coverts and tail; bare pink or yellow facial skin, white throat, and grey iris, bill and legs. Female similar though smaller and less ornamented. Found singly, in pairs or family groups. However, rarely seen, though not uncommon.

INDIAN PEAFOWL

Pavo cristatus Phasianidae

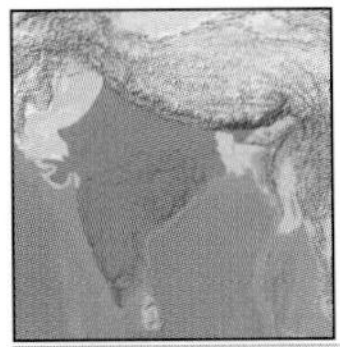

Size Male 110 cm (plus train); Female 95 cm

Voice Loud *may...yow* calls at dawn and dusk; also loud nasal calls and cackles. Very noisy during rains, when breeding

Range All subcontinent except Pakistan, upto about 2,000 m in the Himalayas

Habitat Forests; neighbourhood of villages and cultivated country

Best known for its exquisite train and plumage. Glistening blue neck and breast; wire-like crest and very long distinctive train an iridescent arrangement of multiple colours with ocelli; golden feathers on sides and back. When displayed, male's train spreads out in wide fan, showing off gold, brown, green, and black feathers. Female lacks blue neck and breast; more brown plumage; lacks long train. Familiar bird of India. Solitary or in small parties, several females with one or more males; wary in forested parts, rather tame and confiding.

GREEN PEAFOWL

Pavo muticus Phasianidae

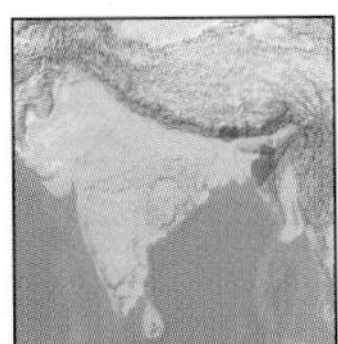

Size Male 80–300 cm; Female 100 cm

Voice Call a loud *ki...wao*

Range Earlier recorded from E and NE India, but now extirpated from subcontinent

Habitat Dense forest near streams or clearings

Large pheasant that resembles Indian superficially, except that long train has more vivid bronze, copper-and-purple hues. Male has green tufted crest, blue-and-yellow facial skin, green neck and underparts, green coverts and brown tertials and secondaries. Iridescent metallic green upperparts. Emerald green tail feathers with ocelli, seen in display. Long train and ocelli absent in female.

FULVOUS WHISTLING-DUCK

Dendrocygna bicolor Dendrocygnidae

Tawny-coloured duck with long neck, blue-grey legs and bill. Dark brown wings edged with pale grey; dark cinnamon crown; dark rear neck-stripe; white flank feathers. Larger in size than Lesser, but otherwise similar. Sexes similar, male slightly larger. Feeds at night, on seeds of aquatic plants and grasses, grain; particularly fond of rice. Forages both on land and in water. Swims on the surface sometimes tipping downward and sticking its head underwater. Extremely wary. Nests high in trees.

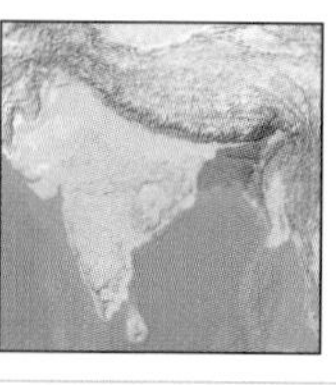

Size 51 cm

Voice Call a high-pitched *pe... wheeah*, usually when in flight

Range Scarce and declining breeding resident: NE India, Bangladesh. Rare elsewhere

Habitat Shallow freshwater or brackish marshes; flooded fields and pastures; irrigated rice fields

LESSER WHISTLING-DUCK

Dendrocygna javanica Dendrocygnidae

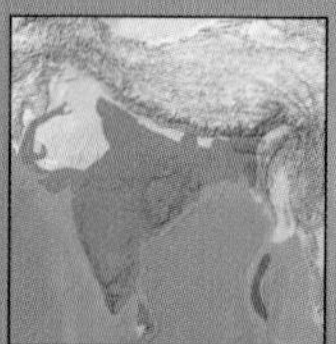

Size 35–45 cm

Voice Call a wheezy, whistling *seasick, seasick*, uttered in flight. Roosts can be quite noisy

Range Largely resident species distributed unevenly from the Pakistan lower river valleys eastwards across most of peninsular India, Nepal terai, Sri Lanka, Bangladesh

Habitat Still freshwater lakes, with plentiful vegetation. Occasionally seeks refuge in the ocean just outside surf area

Smallish overall pale buff duck, with maroon-chestnut upperparts; crown darker grey-brown with golden-orange feather margins; chestnut uppertail-coverts; scaly pattern on back, large head, thin neck and long legs, inconspicuous yellow eye-ring. Dark brown, rounded wings with chestnut lesser wing-coverts. Sexes alike. Juvenile duller and paler. Nests in treeholes, abandoned bird nests and platforms of sticks. Gregarious bird, seen perching on tree branches near waterbodies. Feeds on seeds and other vegetation.

BEAN GOOSE

Anser fabalis Anatidae

Size 66–84 cm

Voice Honking and cackling flight call. Also *hank…hank*

Range Vagrant

Habitat Marshes; lakes, during spring

Medium to large goose, slimmer and more slender than Greylag, with smaller head; orange legs and feet; long, black bill with orange stripe over upper mandible. Dark brown upperwing-coverts. Feeds on herbs, grasses, sedges and grain. Definite sightings recently in Harike in Punjab, Alwar in Rajasthan and Dibru-Saikowa in Eastern Assam. Possibly overlooked.

GREYLAG GOOSE

Anser anser Anatidae

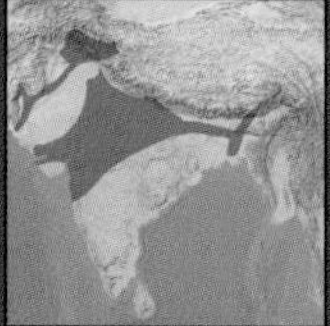

Size 74–84 cm

Voice Domestic goose-like single-note honk, often uttered several times, loud and ringing. Typical geese gaggles when feeding

Range Winter visitor; most common in N India, across the Gangetic plain to Assam, Odisha; S to N Gujarat; Madhya Pradesh; rarer south

Habitat Jheels; winter cultivation

Large goose with bluish-grey plumage with pale fringes to feathers; large darker head; thick long neck; thick pink bill, pink legs and feet; white uppertail-coverts; pale belly dotted black. Sexes alike, though male larger than female. Black-speckled belly, absent in juvenile. Feeds on grass, on grassy islets and shore meadows. Occasionally feeds in the water on algae. Gregarious and wary. Nests on heaps of plant material, lined with feathers.

GREATER WHITE-FRONTED GOOSE

Anser albifrons Anatidae

Size 70 cm

Voice Mostly silent

Range Very rare winter visitor. Possibly overlooked in large Greylag flocks

Habitat Large rivers and lakes; grasslands

Large, grey-brown goose with white band near eye; white patch at base of pink or orange bill. Similar to Greylag but with irregular black spotting on belly; orange legs and feet. White under and uppertail-coverts; dark tail. Sexes similar. Juvenile lacks black barring on belly. Habits similar to other goose species. Likely to be shy. Low nest built with plant material, lined with feathers. Sometimes nests in sparse colonies.

LESSER WHITE-FRONTED GOOSE

Anser erythropus Anatidae

Size 53–66 cm

Voice Call a squeaky *kyu-yu-yu*

Range Globally threatened. Rare winter visitor to N India

Habitat Little known

Plumpish goose with smallish head, long neck and wings. Almost uniformly brown; darker brown head and neck; flashes of white on face; sometimes black patches on belly of adult. Distinguished from other geese by prominent bright yellow eye-ring. White on face and black belly patches absent in juvenile. Usually seen with Greater White-fronteds and Greylags.

BAR-HEADED GOOSE

Anser indicus Anatidae

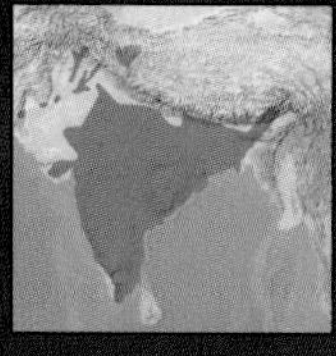

Size 75 cm

Voice Nasal, quite musical honking

Range Breeds only in Ladakh within Indian limits; winter visitor, commoner from Kashmir, S to C India and east across Gangetic plains to Assam; less common in south of Deccan

Habitat Rivers; large jheels

Silvery-grey and white bird with two horseshoe-shaped, brownish-black bars on back of white head. Body overall grey; dark hindneck and lower flanks; yellow legs, black-tipped yellow bill, white neck-stripe along back of neck, white tail-coverts and grey tail. Juvenile has black cap and lack head stripes. In flight, the silvery-grey forewings contrast with the dark flight feathers. Feeds on grasses, roots, stems and other plant matter. Very gregarious.

COMMON SHELDUCK

Tadorna tadorna Anatidae

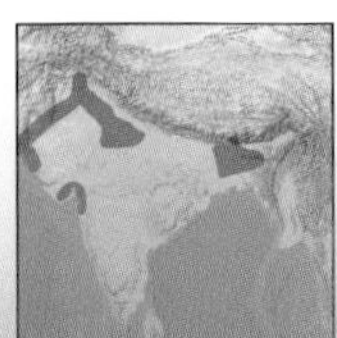

Size 61 cm

Voice Loud honks

Range Local, irregular winter visitor: Pakistan, NW, NE India

Habitat Rivers; lakes; salt pans and the coast

Large duck with white and chestnut body and glossy dark green head and neck. Broad chestnut breast-band that wraps around upper back; black flight feathers, back and belly-stripes; chestnut vent; green speculum; dark pink legs and bright red bill. Male and female look alike, but, female generally duller and smaller. Breeding male has swollen red bill knob. Generally feeds on larvae as well as aquatic animals, plant material, seeds, small fish, snails and crabs.

WHITE-WINGED DUCK

Asarcornis scutulata Anatidae

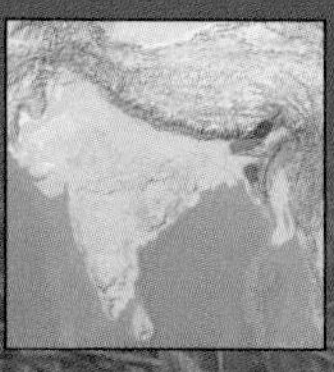

Size 65–80 cm

Voice Usually silent

Range Globally endangered breeding resident. Now restricted to few areas in NE India

Habitat Undisturbed, secluded pools and marshes adjacent to evergreen, deciduous or swamp forests

Large khaki, black-and-brown duck with whitish mottled head and neck. Lesser median coverts and inner edges of tertials whitish; secondaries bluish-grey. White edges of wings obvious in flight. Male larger than female with whiter heads. Roosts and nests on trees and tree holes. Rarely wanders from breeding grounds. Feeds on seeds, grain, rice, snails, small fish and insects.

KNOB-BILLED DUCK

Sarkidiornis melanotos Anatidae

♀

juvenile

Size 55–75 cm

Voice Usually silent, but may occasionally utter some low croaking sounds

Range Almost all over India; mostly resident, but moves considerably with onset of monsoons; uncommon in extreme S and NW India

Habitat Frequents wet areas such as swamps, rivers and lakes with scattered trees

Unmistakable because of fleshy knob (comb) on top of beak. White head and neck, speckled black; purple-green glossy back; bluish and greenish iridescence, especially prominent on the secondaries; white lower neck-collar and underbody; short black bars extend on upper breast sides and flanks. Female duller, smaller; lacks comb. Juvenile has dull buff underparts, face and neck, dull brown upperparts, crown and eye-stripe. Small parties, either on water or in trees over water. Nests in trees.

RUDDY SHELDUCK

Tadorna ferruginea Anatidae

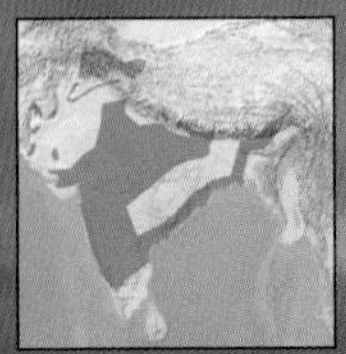

Size 66 cm

Voice Call a loud, goose-like honking, on ground and in flight

Range Breeds in Ladakh; winter visitor, all over India; less common in the south

Habitat Around freshwater, salty and brackish lakes and rivers in open country, avoiding areas with dense, tall vegetation

♀

Distinct rusty orange colouring with lighter head and white face. Stubby black bill; buff neck; rump, tail, primary and secondary feathers black. White wing-coverts conspicuous in flight; legs and feet black. Black collar on neck present in breeding bird. Female similar to male, but smaller, with more white on the face, no collar and buff wash on upperwing-coverts. Juvenile similar to female but duller and with more brown back. Pairs or small parties; nocturnal feeder; rather wary; rests on riverbanks, sandbars, edges of jheels during day; prefers clear, open water.

breeding

COTTON PYGMY-GOOSE

Nettapus coromandelianus Anatidae

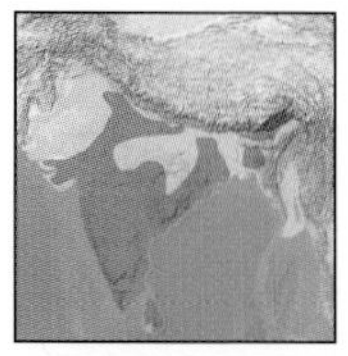

Size 32 cm

Voice Clucking noises, uttered in flight

Range Almost all over India; not common. Possibly absent over arid NW regions

Habitat Still freshwater lakes (jheels); rain-filled ditches; inundated paddy fields; irrigation tanks, etc.

Small duck with round head and short blackish bill. White head, neck and underparts; glossy dark green above; narrow dark breast-band. Breeding male has green-black upperparts and white underparts; black cap and breast-band; pale grey flanks. Striking white wing-bars visible in flight. Non-breeding plumage similar to female; drabber, more brown; dark stripe through eye and white eyebrow. Feeds in flocks on seeds and other vegetation, crustaceans, insects and vegetation.

GADWALL

Anas strepera Anatidae

Size 50 cm

Voice Single-noted, low call of male; loud quacking of female

Range Winter visitor, fairly abundant; all over India, but decreasing in numbers towards S India

Habitat Prefers marshes, sloughs, ponds, and small lakes with grasslands in both fresh and brackish water during breeding

Medium-sized dull, grey-brown duck. Male has distinct vermiculations on scapular and back feathers; grey and brown upperparts; grey bill and orange legs. Brown head; upper and lower tail-coverts black. Long, pointed, silver-grey tertials; white secondaries with black greater secondary coverts distinctive and obvious in flight. Female lacks vermiculation very similar to male with plumage but more brownish on back and buffy tan on breast.

FALCATED DUCK

Anas falcata Anatidae

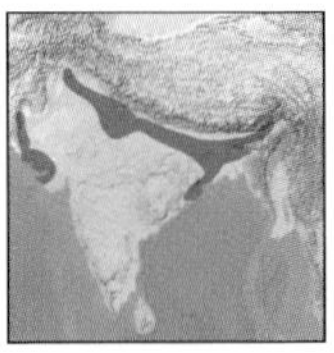

Size 45–55 cm

Voice Male utters a crisp low-pitched whistling note; female a rough *quack*

Range Very scarce but, regular winter visitor

Habitat Freshwater lakes; ponds; rivers and marshes that are surrounded by forests

♀

Striking duck with large head. Male has green head and high, chestnut crown; black-bordered white throat and neck and black-and-white speckled breast. Rest of the body grey with black rear and yellow vent patch. Elongated black and grey scapular wings, diagnostic. Female barred brown all over and has greyer head. Seen singly, or in small groups. Wary.

EURASIAN WIGEON

Anas penelope Anatidae

♀

Size 50 cm

Voice Male has a haunting *wheeo* whistle; female a gruff bark

Range Common winter visitor throughout. Most numerous in N India

Habitat Jheels, marshes and large rivers where there is access to short grass or cereals for grazing

Medium-sized, plump, large-headed and short-necked duck. Breeding male has grey backs, white bellies and pink chests, rusty red head with buff forehead, tail predominantly black. White shoulder patch; stubby, greyish-blue bill with black tip. Male in eclipse resembles female. Female dull, mottled greyish-brown. Juvenile very similar to female. Both sexes show white belly, long, pointed wings and pointed tail in flight. Very gregarious, often mixing with other ducks.

♀

MALLARD

Anas platyrhynchos Anatidae

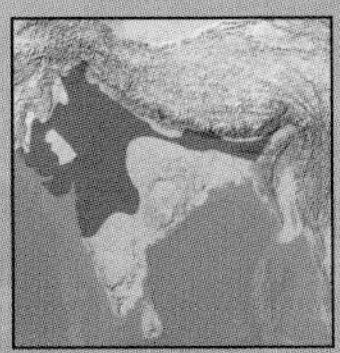

Size 60 cm

Voice Call a loud, wheezy *yheeep* of drake; female quacks loud, loudest when alarmed

Range Very small numbers breed in some of Kashmir's lakes. Winter visitor: N, C India. Rare in Deccan and further south

Habitat Marshes; lakes; swamps; rivers; streams; ponds

Large heavy-looking duck said to be the ancestor of most domestic ducks. Male has long, grey body and black stern. Head and neck are glossy deep green; white neck-ring and dark purplish-brown breast; whitish underparts; yellow bill. Diagnostic blue patch on top of wings bordered white; two curly feathers on tail. Female and eclipse male mottled brown; orange bill. Both sexes have orange feet and bluish-purple speculum, edged with white.

INDIAN SPOT-BILLED DUCK

Anas poecilorhyncha Anatidae

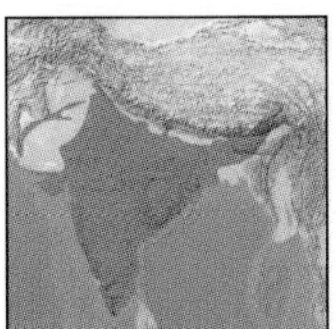

Size 65 cm

Voice Call a loud, duck-like quack

Range Resident; all over India, to about 1,800 m in Kashmir; local migrant in some areas

Habitat Wetlands; freshwater vegetation; covered jheels; reservoirs

Overall grey bird with paler head and neck; black bill with bright yellow tip. Whitish wings with black flight feathers below; whitish head; upperparts blackish-brown, feathers edged paler; black cap, dark, broad eye-stripe; green-blue speculum bordered above with white; coral-red legs and feet. Male has black bill tipped yellow; red spot on base of bill. Sexes alike. Juveline more brown and duller than adult. Pairs or small parties seen on marshy land, wet cultivation, or upending in shallow water.

EASTERN SPOT-BILLED DUCK

Anas zonorhyncha Anatidae

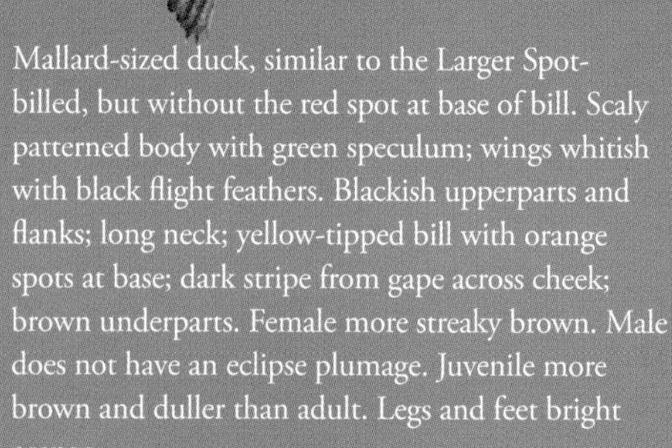

Size 61 cm

Voice Like Indian Spot-billed

Range Winter visitor to NE India

Habitat Shallow water with significant amounts of aquatic vegetation

Mallard-sized duck, similar to the Larger Spot-billed, but without the red spot at base of bill. Scaly patterned body with green speculum; wings whitish with black flight feathers. Blackish upperparts and flanks; long neck; yellow-tipped bill with orange spots at base; dark stripe from gape across cheek; brown underparts. Female more streaky brown. Male does not have an eclipse plumage. Juvenile more brown and duller than adult. Legs and feet bright orange.

NORTHERN SHOVELER

Anas clypeata Anatidae

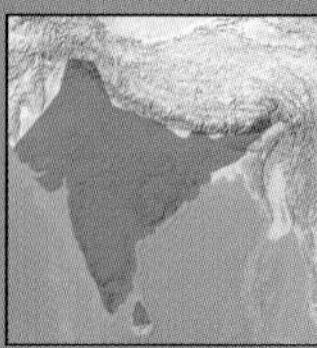

Size 50 cm

Voice Call a loud, 2-noted quacking of male

Range Abundant winter visitor across the subcontinent

Habitat Vegetation-covered jheels, lagoons

Broad, long beak diagnostic. Male: metallic-green head and neck; in flight, dark head, back-centre, rump and uppertail-coverts contrast with white of back and tail; also, dull-blue upperwing-coverts against dark flight feathers; metallic-green speculum and white wing bar; in overhead flight, dark head, thick white neck, dark chestnut belly and flanks. Female: mottled brown, but blue-grey shoulders (wing-coverts) and dull green speculum distinctive. Pairs or small flocks.

♀

ANDAMAN TEAL

Anas g albogularis Anatidae

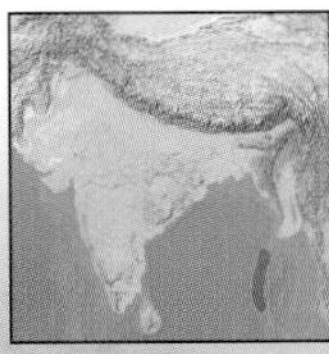

Size 37-47 cm

Voice Call a low whistle

Range Resident; Andaman Islands

Habitat Freshwater pools; marshes

Small brown duck that is restricted to the Andaman Islands. Face and throat pale; prominent white eye-ring and red iris. Uncommon and shy. Prefers paddy fields, small pools and mangroves. Feeds mostly at dusk.

NORTHERN PINTAIL

Anas acuta Anatidae

♀

Elegant, slim and long-necked duck with dark brown head and white breast and throat. White line extends up the neck; light grey body with black-edged feathers; white belly; black, long rump. Female mottled brown-and-black with pointed tail and dark bronze speculum on wing. Both sexes have grey legs and dark grey bill, although bill of the male lined with blue on sides. Male in eclipse plumage similar to female, but with more white-patches on neck sides. Wary and secrective when flightless. Forages on land.

♀

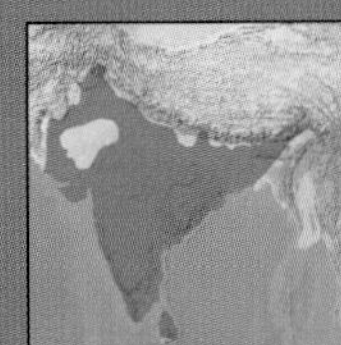

Size 60 cm (excluding tailpins)

Voice Usually quiet

Range Common winter visitor across the subcontinent

Habitat Shallow ponds and marshes in open areas

GARGANEY

Anas querquedula Anatidae

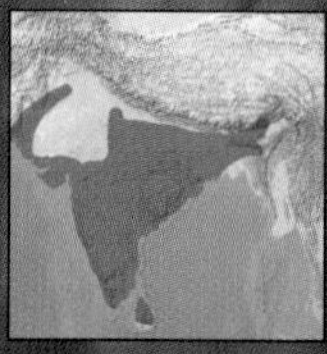

Size 40 cm

Voice Male's mating call a distinctive crackling call

Range Abundant winter visitor

Habitat Narrow or well-sheltered, and shallow standing freshwaters, merging into grasslands, floodlands, or other wetlands

Small, slight duck with large grey bill and flat crown. Dramatic broad, white supercilium crossing to the back of mottled brown head and curving downwards to neck; grey flanks; brown breast and spotted brown stern; white underparts; silvery-blue forewings seen in flight. Female similar to Common Teal, but paler, more patterned head, mottled brownish and distinct eye-stripe; pale supercilium; loral and chin spots and larger bill. Gregarious and social, seen often with other species.

BAIKAL TEAL

Anas formosa Anatidae

Size 39–43 cm

Voice Call a chuckling *wot...wot...wot*

Range Winter vagrant to N India

Habitat Recorded on large rivers

Male has distinct head patterned in green, buff, black and white. Pink breast spotted black; white stripe running down breast sides, black undertail-coverts; pointed brown-red scapulars. Breeeding male has vibrant plumage with golden cheek, black stripe on top of head bordered with white streaks. Female has more detailed head pattern and more reddish-brown.

COMMON TEAL

Anas crecca Anatidae

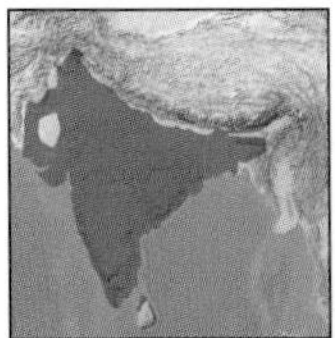

Size 34 cm

Voice Call a *krit...krit...* . Also, wheezy quack

Range Entire subcontinent in winter

Habitat Jheels; marshes; village ponds. Often hunted

Small pale-grey duck with chestnut head. Underparts finely streaked dark grey; creamy patch on chest has fine black spots. Dark russet-red head with bottle green eye-stripe bordered white. Both sexes display dark green, black-and-white wing-bar in flight. Female mottled dark and light brown; pale belly; black and green wing speculum. Most common migratory duck. Swift flier.

MARBLED DUCK

Marmaronetta angustirostris Anatidae

Size 39–42 cm

Voice Call a squeaking *jeep* uttered by displaying male; otherwise relatively silent

Range Said to breed in Pakistan. Rare winter visitor to N India

Habitat Mainly shallow, eutrophic wetlands, typically with dense emergent and submerged vegetation

Small, grey-brown dabbling duck with shaggy hood, dark eye patch and broad eye-stripe from eye to nape. Sandy-brown body finely spotted with creamy-brown. Juvenile more blotchy. Feeds in shallow water dabbling or upending, occasionally diving. In pairs with other dabbling ducks. Characteristic slow and low flight. Secretive.

PINK-HEADED DUCK

Rhodonessa caryophyllacea Anatidae

Unmistakable. Long-bodied and long-necked, with slightly tufted head in the male, and peculiar stiff-necked posture. Adult male has chocolate-coloured body; deep pink head and hindneck. Female and juvenile duller, appearing much like dark female Red-crested Pochard with pinkish tinge to the head. Presumed extinct.

RED-CRESTED POCHARD

Netta rufina Anatidae

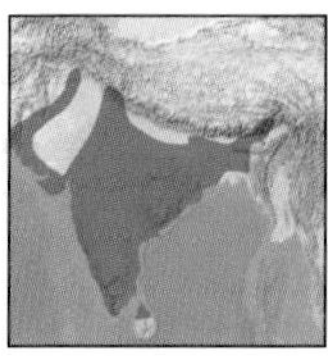

Size 55 cm

Voice Silent

Range Rather scarce winter visitor throughout lowlands

Habitat Well-vegetated large rivers and lakes

Large duck with deep orange-crested head and red bill. Black neck and breast; pale flanks; brown back and black stern. Female lighter brown with pale cheeks and darker crown, dark bill. Juvenile darker with multicoloured belly. In flight, both sexes display broad white wing-bars. Nests near slow-moving rivers and clearings of open water with shrubs. Feeds actively early morning and late evening. Feeds on aquatic plants and animals by diving and upending.

♀

COMMON POCHARD

Aythya ferina Anatidae

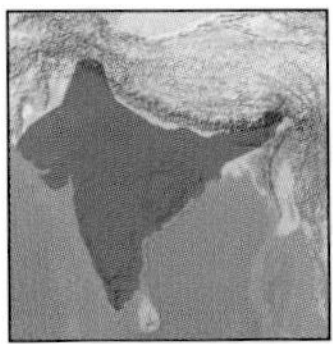

Size 45 cm

Voice Rather quiet. Female sometimes purrs in flight

Range Common winter visitor throughout lowlands. Less common in east

Habitat All types of open water including village ponds

Stocky, medium-sized with rich reddish-brown, wedge-shaped head, black breast, stern and tail. Grey body; large black bill with broad grey band; red eyes. Female more brown with pale cheeks and flanks. Both show black bordered grey wing-bars in flight. Feeds by diving or dabbling, on aquatic plants, aquatic insects and small fish. Gregarious; forming large flocks in winter, often mixed with other diving ducks.

BAER'S POCHARD

Aythya baeri Anatidae

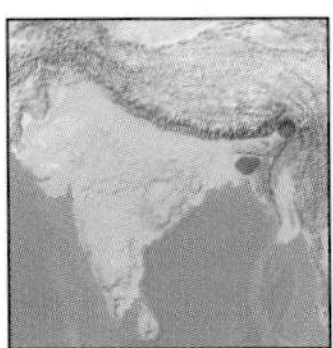

Size 41-46 cm

Voice Mostly silent

Range Winter vagrant mostly to NE India and Bangladesh

Habitat Large rivers; lakes

Dark grey to black head, neck and back, with light brownish-red and white sides. Head can be seen to have dark green sheen on it in sunlight, and at all times, white eyes contrast strongly with surrounding feathers. White band on upperwing can be seen in flight, but not when wings are folded at rest. Female can be distinguished by difference in colour between head and brown breast, and more domed head. Juvenile similar to female, except for light brown head.

FERRUGINOUS DUCK

Aythya nyroca Anatidae

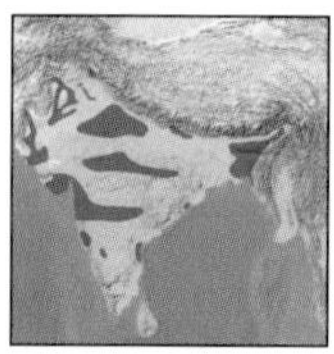

Size 40 cm

Voice Usually silent, although female sometimes makes burring sound in flight

Range Scarce and local winter visitor throughout lowlands. Commonest in NW India. Rarely in large numbers

Habitat Well-vegetated jheels, rivers, canals and ponds

Small, compact diving duck with peaked head. Both sexes are mahogany brown, darker on back and head. Large triangular patches of white under the tail. Male brighter, russet-brown; sharp white iris. Long white wing-bars and belly visible in flight. Not as gregarious as other diving ducks. Usually keeping in small groups. Cautious and wary.

TUFTED DUCK

Aythya fuligula Anatidae

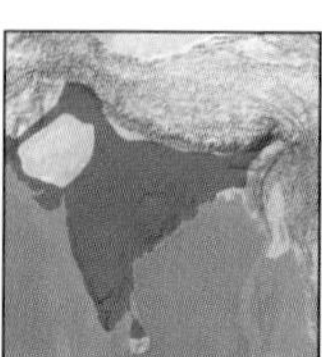

Size 45 cm

Voice Rather quiet. Male has high bubbling note; female croaks

Range Fairly common winter visitor throughout lowlands. Less common in E and S India

Habitat All kinds of open water including reservoirs

Round-bodied, medium-sized diving duck with round head and very obvious head tuft. Male glossy black with broad white flanks, while female dark brown with paler flanks; white under the tail, occasionally visible in flight. Both sexes have yellow irises and black-tipped grey bills. Feeds during day by diving.

WHITE-HEADED DUCK

Oxyura leucocephala Anatidae

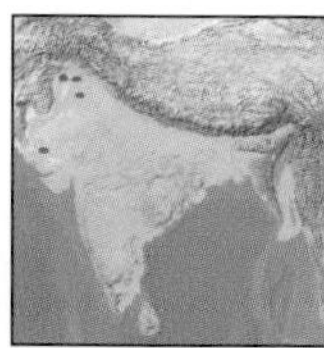

Size 45 cm

Voice Usually quiet; when displaying, low rattling noises produced

Range Globally threatened. Rare winter visitor

Habitat Open water, including reservoirs

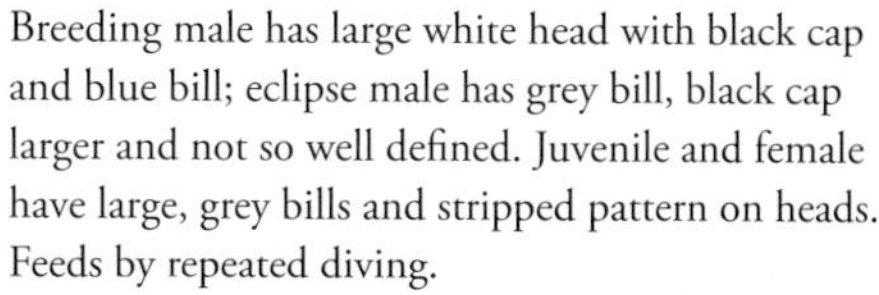

Breeding male has large white head with black cap and blue bill; eclipse male has grey bill, black cap larger and not so well defined. Juvenile and female have large, grey bills and stripped pattern on heads. Feeds by repeated diving.

SMEW

Mergellus albellus Anatidae

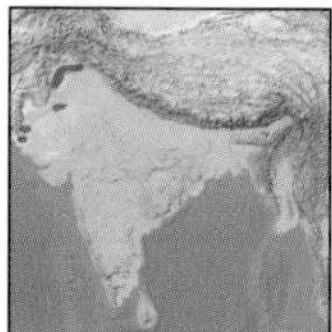

Size 45 cm

Voice Rather quiet. Male has a high bubbling note; female croaks

Range Rare winter visitor

Habitat Fish-rich lakes; slow rivers

Male has pristine white body with black marking on head, back and breast. Distinct white crest bordered black; pale grey flanks. Non-breeding male has grey tint to body and no crest. Female has dark grey body, chestnut cap and white cheeks. Both sexes display dark upperwings with white wing-covert patches in flight.

GREATER SCAUP

Aythya marila Anatidae

Size 40–50 cm

Voice Mostly silent

Range Rare winter visitor

Habitat Coastal bays; lagoons and estuaries. Winters on inland lakes

♀

Larger and bulky duck with no crest. Iridescent greenish-black head; barred, grey back; light blue-grey bill; black breast and rump. Female overall brownish with white collar. Feeds mainly by diving; spends days swimming around waterbodies. In large flocks outside breeding season. Gregarious. Few details about this duck are known in the subcontinent.

COMMON GOLDENEYE

Bucephala clangula Anatidae

Size 42–50 cm

Voice Quiet, occasionally emitting a faint *krrr* or a loud *zee-zee*. In flight, wings produce a whistling or rattling sound

Range Rare winter visitor

Habitat Uncommon. Sometimes seen in open freshwater such as rivers, avoiding shallow, heavily vegetated waters

♀

Attractive sea duck with distinct plumage. Breeding male has wedge-shaped, glossy green-black head, golden eye, peaked forehead, short bill with white patch at base, white patch on wing; longish tail; white body with white dorsal stripe. Female and non-breeding male have chocolate-brown head; white collar and grey body with white wing patch. Juvenile similar to female, but has more grey-brown head. Preys on invertebrates with short dive with wings closed and tail spread.

RED-BREASTED MERGANSER

Mergus serrator Anatidae

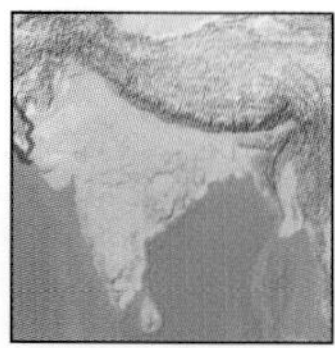

Size 52–58 cm

Voice Call a short *grak…grak…grak*

Range Afghanistan; Makran Coast to Karachi

Habitat Sea coasts

Breeding male has reddish-brown mottled breast; green head with white neck-collar; thin serrated, orange bill; red eyes; black-and-white back; white wings; grey flanks. Female has overall grey body; reddish-brown head, reddish eyes. Juvenile similar to female but with white bar on face. Non-breeding adult male similar to female. Swims low when foraging in fresh, brackish and saltwater wetlands and in sheltered bays. Nests in sheltered spot on ground.

♀

♀

GOOSANDER

Mergus merganser Anatidae

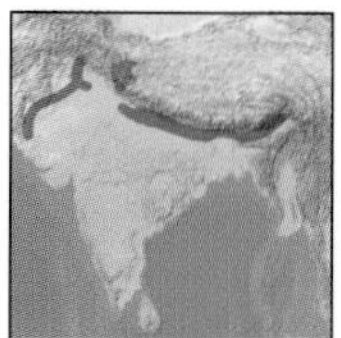

Size 58–72 cm

Voice Male has a deep *kruu…kra* call; female a shorter *praha* note

Range Rather scarce. Breeds in the Himalayas and NE mountains. Winters on N rivers

Habitat Rests on rocks. Flight path usually follows river course

Large, slender duck with streamlined body, big head and long, narrow, reddish-orange, serrated bill. Breeding male has glossy green domed head; bushy, mane-like feathers on back of neck; white lower neck, breast, belly and flanks; bright red feet and legs; pinkish tint to underparts; white patch on inner wing. Female has brown head and shaggy crest; grey and cream underparts. Juvenile similar to female, but duller with whitish throat, paler head and creamy-yellow bill. Feeds solely on fish by repeated diving. Often swims with head submerged to locate prey.

♀

CAPE PETREL

Daption capense

Broad-winged, black-and-white, stocky bird with black head, white upperparts messily marked with black, black tail-bands, black upperwings with bold white-patches. Vagrant in the region.

WEDGE-TAILED SHEARWATER

Puffinus pacificus

Big, broad-winged bird with long tail occurring in two colour morphs. The tail's wedge shape not usually visible in flight, as the shearwater folds its tail so that it appears long and pointed. Long dark bill. Flight action slow with lazy flapping followed by short glides. Can often be seen tagging behind fishing boats. Vagrant off the coast of Goa; also Lakshadweep.

SHORT-TAILED SHEARWATER

Puffinus tenuirostris

Brownish shearwater with steeply rising forehead; short bill; relatively short tail. Strong, deliberate flight action with comparatively fast, skip-winged flapping, followed by long glides. Vagrant in the region. Feeds mainly underwater, diving deep below the surface in pursuit of prey.

FLESH-FOOTED SHEARWATER

Puffinus carneipes

Large, dark brown bird. Flight action elegant and relaxed with slow, powerful flapping interspersed with leisurely stiff-winged glides. Catches prey by plunge diving underwater to follow its quarry. Vagrant off the southern Indian coast; Lakshadweep.

WHITE-FACED STORM-PETREL

Pelagodroma marina

Adult birds distinguished by white underparts and white underwing-coverts, white supercilium contrasting with dark crown and ear-coverts. Feet project noticeably beyond tail. Flight action rapid and jumpy, followed by glide. Vagrant.

STREAKED SHEARWATER

Calonectris leucomelas

Large, broad-winged bird with white head, with variable dark streaking. Flight action languid, relaxed, almost gull-like in calm conditions; strong winds force it to rise. Vagrant off Cape Comorin, southern Tamil Nadu and Sri Lanka.

WILSON'S STORM-PETREL

Oceanites oceanicus

White rump and dark underparts. Tail square-ended with yellow webbed feet projecting much beyond tail. Found in the southern Indian coast; commonest along the coast of Mumbai.

AUDUBON'S SHEARWATER

Puffinus lherminieri

Small shearwater with white underparts and head. Distinguished from other shearwaters by blackish-brown upperparts, rectrices, undertail-coverts and distal undersides of remiges and sometimes entire feathers. Dark, dull pink feet; grey bill, darker towards tip.

LITTLE GREBE

Tachybaptus ruficollis Podicipedidae

non-breeding

breeding

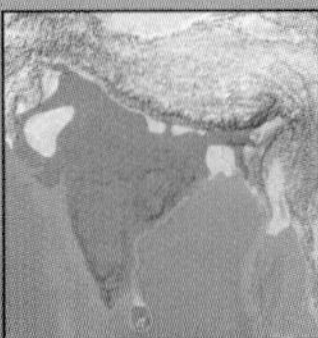

Size 23–29 cm

Voice Shrill trilling notes. Occasional click

Range Subcontinent, upto 2,000 m in Kashmir. Resident in most areas

Habitat Reasonably large waterbodies in lowlands, with plenty of vegetation

Very small grebe, with short neck; short, straight beak; plump, rounded body. Black head, nape, breast and back; dark reddish-brown cheeks, throat and neck; dark brown flanks. Diagnostic small yellow-patch at base of pale-tipped, black beak. Dark green legs; reddish-brown iris. Juvenile paler than adult, with dark cap, nape and back; yellowish-brown cheeks, neck sides and flanks, and reddish-brown lower neck and chest. Feeds on small fish, insects, crustaceans, shellfish and molluscs by diving or dabbling. Hard to spot as mostly concealed in vegetation. Floating nest built near shoreline, attached to aquatic plants or branches of waterside bushes; territorial, solitary nester. Performs a variety of elaborate courtship display.

RED-NECKED GREBE

Podiceps grisegena Podicipedidae

Size 30 cm

Voice Call includes loud, guttural croaks when breeding

Range Rare winter visitor: N Pakistan, N and NW India

Habitat Recorded on lakes in the region. Also occurs on coastal waters

Large, stocky grebe with long neck; straight long black bill with yellow at base. Breeding adult has dark brown-black upperparts; dark wings with two prominent white-patches; black cap extending below eye; small crest and large, pale grey cheek patch with whitish margins extending behind eye. Rusty-red neck in front and upper breast; pale belly, greyish flanks and sides; black legs and feet. Usually feeds in shallow water, diving underwater, or picking from vegetation.

GREAT CRESTED GREBE

Podiceps cristatus Podicipedidae

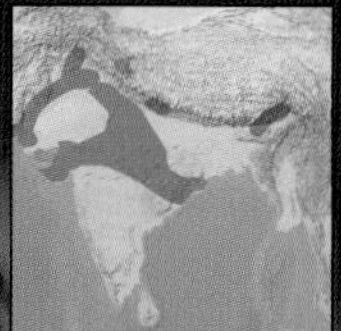

Size 46–51 cm

Voice Call includes loud, guttural croaks when breeding

Range Scarce breeder in N mountains and Gujarat. Winter visitor to N lowlands

Habitat Large, deep open bodies of freshwater, rivers, lagoons, lakes, swamps, reservoirs, saltfields, estuaries and bays

Medium to large-sized, graceful bird with long neck, long bill and distinctive black double crest. Black crown; white face; black line from base of bill to eye; dark brown wings with prominent white-patches; satiny-white underparts; dark olive-green feet prominent in flight. Breeding adult of both sexes has reddish-orange head plumes, tipped black. Sexes similar, but female slightly smaller than male. Juvenile can be distinguished by blackish stripes on cheeks. Both male and female take part in elaborate courtship display. Dives for fish, insects and invertebrate larvae, chasing prey underwater by propelling feet.

non-breeding

breeding

SLAVONIAN GREBE

Podiceps auritus Podicipedidae

Size 31–38 cm

Voice Call a long, squealing trill and loud, nasal *aaarrh*, which descends in pitch and ends in a rattle or trill

Range Rare winter visitor to Pakistan, India

Habitat Lakes; coasts

Small waterbird with distinctive golden-yellow patches of feathers behind eye in breeding plumage, that resemble short horns. Straight, stubby bill; large, flat-topped head. Breeding adult has glossy black head; chestnut neck and flanks; dark brown-black back; white belly; small white marking on shoulder and white secondary feathers visible in flight. Bright scarlet red eyes.

non-breeding

breeding

BLACK-NECKED GREBE

Podiceps nigricollis Podicipedidae

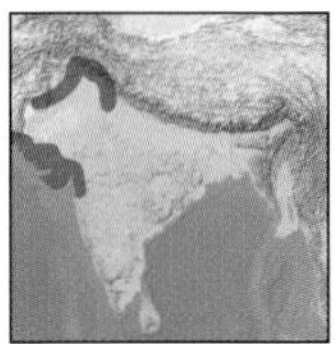

Size 30 cm

Voice Calls include trills and whistles when breeding

Range Scarce, very local breeding resident: Parts of NW, NE India. Wanders more widely in winter, but rare except in Pakistan

Habitat Well-vegetated wetlands; the coast in winter. Wanders more widely in the north in winter

Small grebe with upturned bill, short uptilted tail and fluffy rear end. Breeding adult has blackish upperparts and rusty-red underparts. Head and neck black with golden yellow feathers on cheeks. Non-breeding adult has dark upperparts, light, greyish-white belly and dirty grey neck; white crescent near ear. Sexes alike. Juvenile plumage buff-grey with white chin. Gregarious in nesting season; participates in elaborate courtship display.

non-breeding

breeding

GREATER FLAMINGO

Phoenicopterus roseus Phoenicopteridae

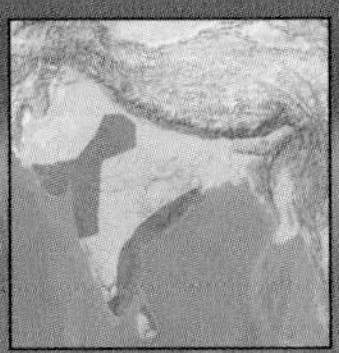

Size 120-145 cm

Voice Assortment of cackles. Also, goose-like honking *ka-haunk*

Range Breeds in Kutch. Wanders widely throughout the region particularly to E coast and NW India. Sporadic in appearance

Habitat Breeds on saline or brackish lagoons

Easily recognisable bird with long, thin curved neck long pink legs, and distinctive downward-bending pale pink beak with black tip. Rose-white plumage; red shoulders and black tips to wings; yellow eyes. Female smaller than male. Juvenile grey-brown with some pink in underparts, wings and tail, and brown legs and beak. Distinguished from Lesser by larger size, paler plumage, lighter beak, and pink rather than dark red legs. Characteristic flight with legs and neck stretched to full length. Feeds in any shallow water including estuaries, lakes, rivers and flooded fields. Feeds with head immersed; often rests on one leg, neck coiled and head tucked in feathers.

juvenile

LESSER FLAMINGO

Phoenicopterus minor Phoenicopteridae

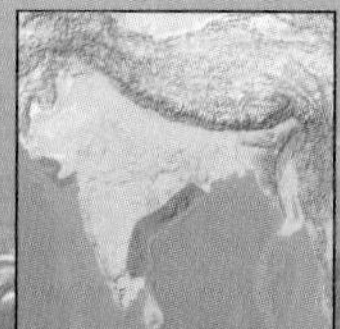

Size 80–90 cm

Voice Call a *murr-err, murr-err*. Feeding flocks may make goose-like honking sound, higher-pitched than Greater.

Range Breeds in Kutch. Some wander particularly to the E coast

Habitat Prefers salt and brackish lagoons and salt pans

ASIAN OPENBILL

Anastomus oscitans Ciconiidae

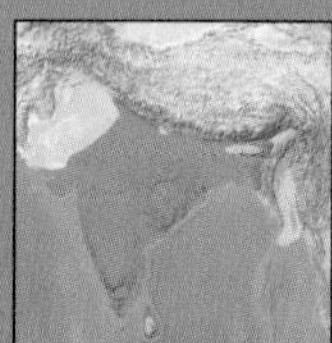

Size 76–81 cm

Voice Call a mournful *hoo-hoo*. Very noisy while flying in flocks

Range Locally common breeding resident throughout lowlands. Rare in Pakistan

Habitat Large wetlands. Rare on the coast

juvenile

breeding

Smallest stork in the region. Breeding adult has white plumage, lightly washed with smoky grey; glistening purplish-greenish black on wings and tail. Non-breeding adult grey; black scapulars, flight feathers and tail; white or grey head; characteristic open bill formed by hollow in lower mandible; pinkish-grey bill; greyish-pink lores; pink to red legs. Sexes similar. Juvenile has brownish tinge on plumage with dark grey bill and straighter lower mandible. Feeds in rice fields and marshes in freshwater.

Shorter and darker rose-pink than Greater, with light pink bill, tipped with black. Pale pink feathers with black primaries and secondaries, deep crimson legs; yellow-orange eyes with maroon ring. Male slightly taller than female. Juvenile has brown feathers and dark grey beak. Feeds with long neck bent over and bill upside down in water. Spectacular courtship takes place throughout the year. Very sociable.

juvenile

PAINTED STORK

Mycteria leucocephala Ciconiidae

Size 95 cm

Voice Characteristic mandible clattering of storks

Range Resident and local migrant, from Terai south through the region's well-watered areas

Habitat Inland marshes; jheels; occasionally riversides

juvenile

Fabulously coloured waterbird with long neck and striking wing pattern. White plumage; blackish-green and white wings; blackish-green breast-band and black tail; rich rosy-pink wash on greater wing-coverts; large, slightly curved orangish-yellow bill. Juvenile pale dirty brown, with neck feathers edged darker and lacks breast-band. Common and gregarious; feeds with beak partly submerged. When not feeding, settles hunched up outside water; regularly soars high on thermals.

BLACK STORK

Ciconia nigra Ciconiidae

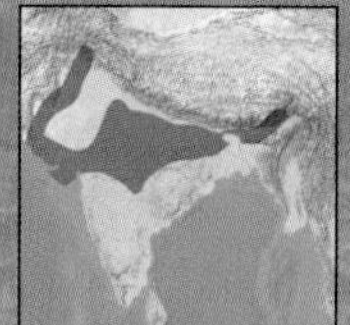

Size 95–100 cm

Voice Voiceless

Range Scarce winter visitor mainly to N India

Habitat Prefers undisturbed, open forests and woodlands, upto 2,000 to 2,500 m

Similar to White, but sturdier with wider wings. Long neck, bill, and legs; short tail; black upperparts with varying green and purple gloss; white breast and belly; scarlet red bill and legs, brighter in breeding and more brownish in non-breeding. Flies with neck and legs extended; white triangles on underwings visible in flight. Sexes alike, though male larger. Juvenile, less brightly-coloured. Secretive.

juvenile

WOOLLY-NECKED STORK

Ciconia episcopus Ciconiidae

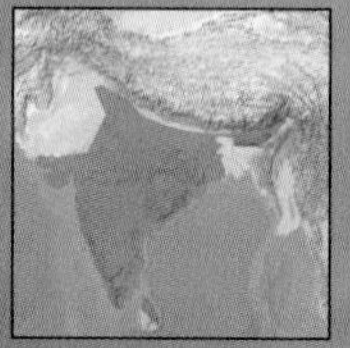

Size 86–95 cm

Voice Usually silent, but may give some croaking *honks*. Seldom heard

Range Locally common breeding resident; subcontinent, upto about 1,400 m in the Himalayas

Habitat Wetlands such as rivers, marshes, lakes, rice fields, flood plains and pastures; swamp forests

Large, glossy black-and-white stork with huge wing span. Bare grey face; red legs and deep red eyes; well-defined, glossy black forecrown and crown, back and breast (black parts have distinct purplish-green sheen); white lower back and rump; black forked-tail, concealed by long white undertail-coverts; white neck and lower abdomen, with pale purplish wash; long, stout, black bill, occasionally tinged crimson. Sexes alike. In juvenile, glossy black replaced by dark brown. Usually seen alone, walking slowly along water; sometimes, in pairs or small scattered parties, feeding along with other storks, ibises and egrets; stalks on dry land too; settles on trees.

WHITE STORK

Ciconia ciconia Ciconiidae

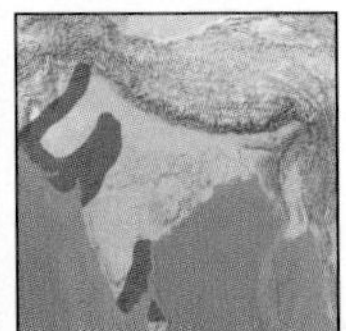

Size 100–115 cm

Voice Voiceless. Claps its bill

Range Scarce winter visitor mainly to S India

Habitat Cultivation and open, grassy marshes

Large long-necked wading bird with slender orangish-red legs and long, sharp, red bill. Upperparts mainly white, with black wing feathers. Dark iris; shadow around eye. Sexes alike, male little larger. Black parts replaced by brown in juvenile; brown bill and legs. Long, broad wings, suitable for soaring. Flies with outstretched neck. Feeds on amphibians, reptiles and insects, particularly grasshoppers. Sociable and not shy. Flocks often seen soaring high on thermals. Red bill and legs tell it apart from Openbill. Long feathers on lower neck and upper breast form ruff that extends during courtship display.

juvenile

BLACK-NECKED STORK

Ephippiorhynchus asiaticus Ciconiidae

juven

♀

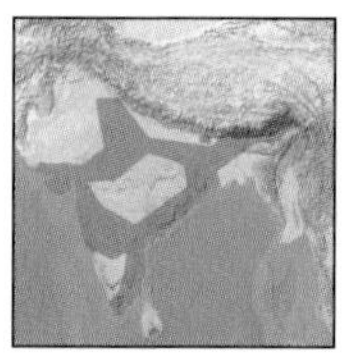

Size 140 cm

Voice Voiceless, but clatters mandibles

Range Increasingly rare breeding resident throughout Indian lowlands

Habitat Wetlands

Largest stork in the region. Unmistakable, massive black bill. Overall white with glossy greenish-black head, wing-bar and tail. Iridescent purple tinted green-blue neck; coral-red legs. White wings with broad band along length, conspicuous in flight. Sexes identical except for iris, which is yellow in female, brown in male. Singly, or in pairs; sometimes family group. Shy and wary.

juvenile

LESSER ADJUTANT

Leptoptilos javanicus Ciconiidae

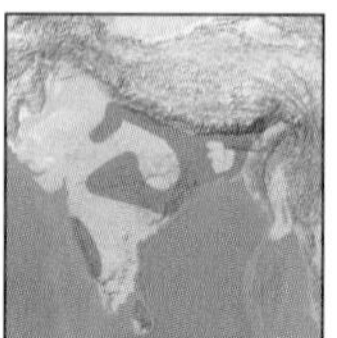

Size 110–120 cm

Voice Usually silent

Range Globally threatened, rare, but widespread breeding resident throughout lowlands. Most frequent in Nepal and NE India. Recently undergone rapid decline in number, rare throughout its range

Habitat Wet areas such as mangroves, mudflats, marshes, flooded grasslands, coastal swamps, lakes and rice fields

Adult has dark slaty blue-black upperparts and white underparts; white neck base spotted black. Black underwing and undertail; bare yellow head in non-breeding and red in breeding male; bare pinkish-orange neck, with sparse grey feathers; bony plate on top of head; long, thick beak greyish to horn-coloured; pale blue-grey eyes and legs. Juvenile has more feathering on neck and duller upperparts. Characteristic hunched posture. Solitary and shy. Feeds on aquatic animals and grasshoppers by walking slowly on ground or through shallow water. Small colonies or individual pairs. Breeds in wet habitats.

GREATER ADJUTANT

Leptoptilos dubius Ciconiidae

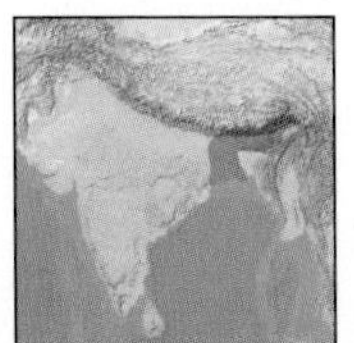

Size 150 cm

Voice Silent, apart from croaks and bill-clattering

Range Globally threatened and now very rare except in Assam, where locally common

Habitat Marshes; jheels; cultivation and urban garbage dumps

Tall, greyish-white stork with almost prehistoric appearance. Breeding male has bare red head and neck (yellowish-brown in non-breeding). Long, thick yellow bill; pendulous gular pouch; large pale pink bill. Silvery-grey wing-band and thick white neck ruff; white underparts. Dark legs. Juvenile similar to adult, but duller plumage and more feathery neck. Slow, measured gait, gives it its name. Heron-like flight with retracted neck. Nests of sticks in canopy of large trees. Sometimes eats injured ducks and carrion.

BLACK-HEADED IBIS

Threskiornis melanocephalus Threskiornithidae

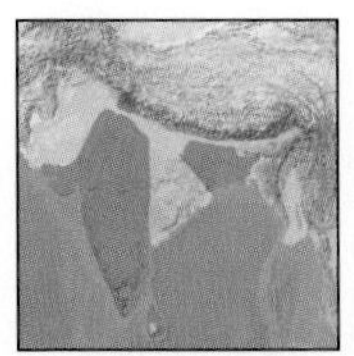

Size 75 cm

Voice Loud, booming call; nasal grunts reported during breeding

Range Resident; local migrant; subcontinent, from south of Terai

Habitat Marshes; riversides

juvenile

Large, white bird with prominent bare black head and neck, and long, down-curved bill. Grey ornamental tail feathers. Breeding adult has blood red-patches on underwings, blue tinge on head, glossy black legs and loose ruff of white feathers on lower neck and sometimes yellowish wash on breast and back. Sexes alike. Juvenile has grey feathers on head and white neck. Feeds actively in water; probing mud with partly open bill; can submerge entire head and neck while wading when necessary. Feeds and nests communally.

RED-NAPED IBIS

Pseudibis papillosa Threskiornithidae

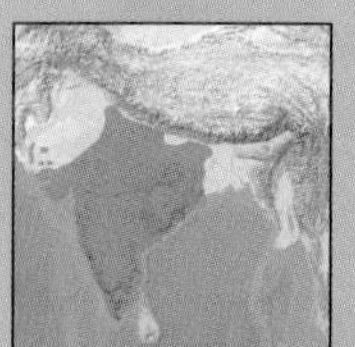

Size 70 cm

Voice Calls include loud 2- to 3-note nasal screams, uttered in flight

Range Scarce breeding resident; NW India, east through Gangetic plains; south to Karnataka

Habitat Lakes; marshes; riverbeds and irrigated farmlands

juvenile

Medium-sized bird with diagnostic triangular-patch of red warts on head and long downcurved bill. Glossy dark brownish-black plumage glazed blue; scapulars and back feathers, bronze green. Brown neck, mantle, lower back and rump; bright orange-red eye; black tail, richly glazed with blue green; short legs hidden beneath steel blue tail and lesser wing-coverts with white shoulder patch, visible in flight. Red or fleshy pink legs. Re-uses nest year upon year. Feeds in shallow water.

GLOSSY IBIS

Plegadis falcinellus Threskiornithidae

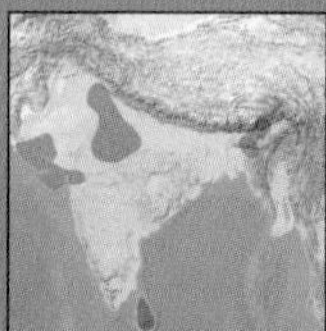

Size 60 cm

Voice Usually silent

Range Fairly common, but local breeding resident subject to wandering. Most frequent in N and W India

Habitat All types of shallow freshwater, particularly with floating vegetation

Dark wading bird with long legs and decurved bill. Breeding adult chestnut with green and purple gloss; naked, grey, facial skin; pale blue lines bordering the front part of face; brown eyes and bill; grey legs with red knee joints. Flies with neck and legs outstretched. Nests on ground, in reeds or low shrubs. Feeds in shallow water or marshy wetlands on small fish, aquatic insects, molluscs, frogs, and food sifted from water surface.

juvenile

EURASIAN SPOONBILL

Platalea leucorodia Threskiornithidae

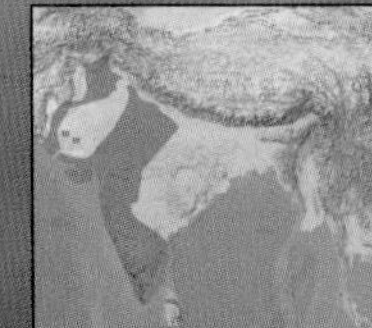

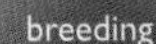

breeding

Size 80-93 cm

Voice Mandible clattering, short grunts when breeding

Range Locally common breeding resident, winter visitor: NW, W, S India and Sri Lanka

Habitat Shallow wetlands, marshes, rivers, large waterbodies with muddy, clay or fine sandy beds

Snowy-white bird, with long, spoon-shaped black bill and long, blackish legs. Breeding adult has orangish-yellow tip on bill, crest and yellow breast patch. Sexes alike. Immature has paler bill and black wing-tips. Flies with neck and legs outstretched, with flapping movements interspersed with gliding. Spends much of day sleeping on one leg. Feeds on aquatic animals by sweeping bill from side to side through water.

non-breeding

GREAT BITTERN

Botaurus stellaris Ardeidae

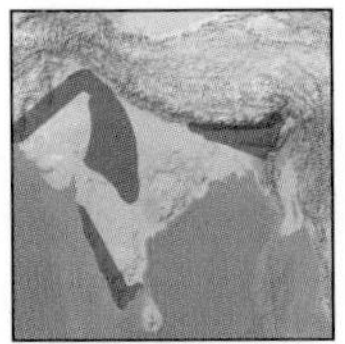

Size 75 cm

Voice Call a deep croak in flight. Far-carrying booming when breeding

Range Rare, but widespread winter visitor throughout lowlands of Pakistan, India and Nepal

Habitat Reeds in marshes

Overall golden brown with black crown and moustache; mottled above and dusky stripes below; thick neck; green legs; yellowish bill; brown cheeks and white throat. Upperparts intricately patterned with black; black stripes run down foreneck. Heavy owl-like flight with retracted neck. When startled, adopts camouflage by pointing bill upwards and stretching neck vertically. Secretive.

LITTLE BITTERN

Ixobrychus minutus Ardeidae

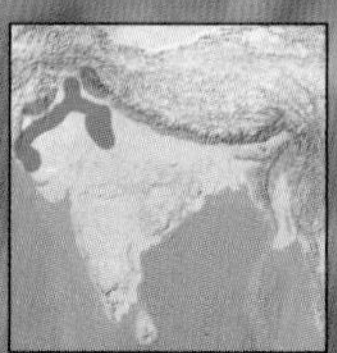

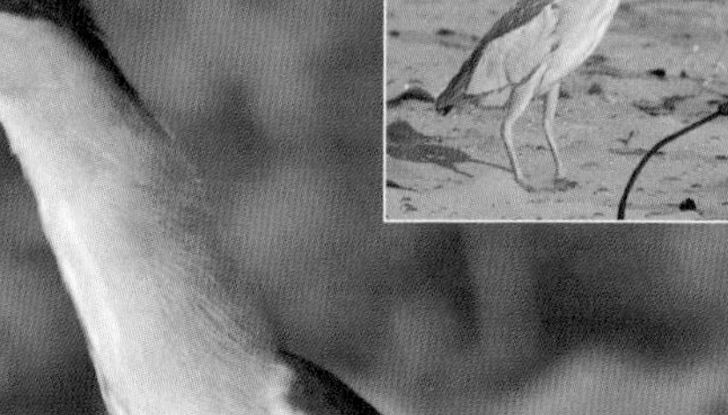

Size 25–35 cm

Voice Call a distinctive *kohr*

Range Very local breeding resident, mainly in Kashmir and Assam. Scattered records from elsewhere, mainly N India

Habitat Reed beds near rivers and jheels

Small heron with dark back and cap; buff-white neck and wing patches. Male has small green crest; yellowish-green bill and iris. Upper breast and sides have tufts of elongated black feathers. Buffy-white undersides streaked brown; white underwings; greyish-green legs. Solitary and crepuscular.

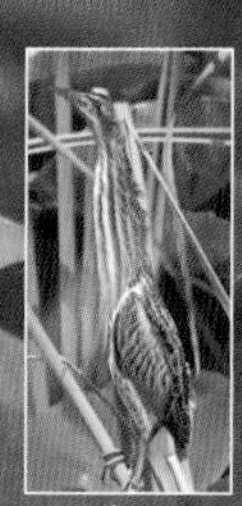
juvenile

YELLOW BITTERN

Ixobrychus sinensis Ardeidae

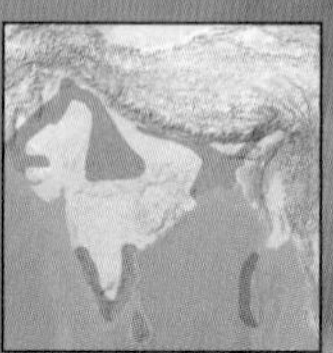

Size 35–38 cm

Voice Occassionally, a sharp *kark*. Male's breeding call a quiet *uu…uu*

Range Rather local breeding resident mainly in NE India, Bangladesh, Sri Lanka and Indo-Gangetic Plains. Monsoon breeding visitor to NW India

Habitat Reed beds and wet scrubs near rivers, jheels and wet paddy

Small bittern with dull yellowish-brown upperparts and whitish underparts streaked darker from chin to belly. Short neck; longish bill. Crown, short crest and nape black marked with buff; orangish-brown on side of face, head and neck; deeper rufous on hindneck, greyer on forehead and supercilium; white undertail- and underwing-coverts; black tail. Female has brown streaking on crown, neck, and breast. Juvenile similar, but heavily streaked brown below, and mottled buff above. Solitary; hunts quietly in reed beds and undergrowth. Solitary but breeding densities can be quite high. Usually seen in feeding flights.

juvenile

CINNAMON BITTERN

Ixobrychus cinnamomeus Ardeidae

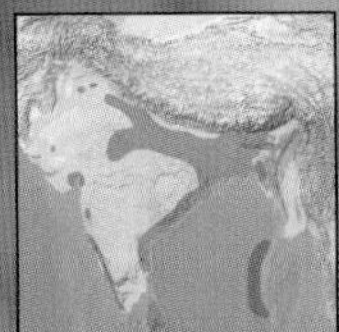

Size 36–38 cm

Voice Male's breeding call a loud *kok…kok*

Range Rather local breeding resident mainly to eastern coast, NE India, parts of the Indo-Gangetic Plains, Bangladesh and Sri Lanka

Habitat Reeds in marshes

juvenile

Solitary and crepuscular bittern, overall cinnamon in colour with darker crown. Sides of face, mantle, back and tail paler and tinged with pink; underparts rich buffy-brown with dark reddish-black central streaks down the middle from chin to belly. Chin and throat whitish. Flanks pale cinnamon; vent and undertail-coverts pale buffy-brown. Female has more brown crown and mantle, more streaked neck, while immature darker and more boldly streaked.

BLACK BITTERN

Dupetor flavicollis Ardeidae

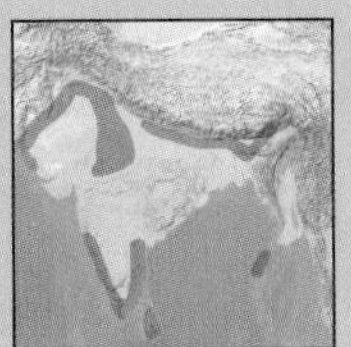

Size 58 cm

Voice Characteristic booming call mainly heard during breeding season, at day or night

Range Scarce breeding resident

Habitat Reed beds with bushes and bushy margins of canals, rivers and jheels

Medium-sized heron with diagnostic yellow neck-stripe. Male has dull black upperparts; buff streaks on the throat; rufous-streaked, black and grey belly. Female paler than male, with more yellowish wash on underparts. Immature more streaked; upperpart feathers have buff fringes. Nests on bed of sticks on branch overhanging water. Feeds on frogs, reptiles, fish and invertebrates. Crepuscular, solitary and extremely secretive. May fly quite high to feeding sites.

MALAYAN NIGHT HERON

Gorsachius melanolophus Ardeidae

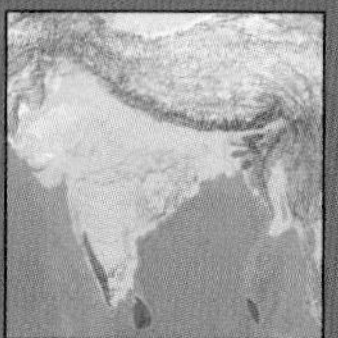

Size 47 cm

Voice Usually silent

Range NE India; S Western Ghats; Nicobar Islands. Winter visitor to Sri Lanka

Habitat Subtropical and tropical swamps, streams, marshes; especially regions with high rainfall

Reddish-brown heron with streaked underparts, black underwings, black crown and variable bluish lores; reddish-brown sides to head and neck; stout dark bill. Sexes similar, but male may have dark crest. Juvenile greyish-brown with black-and-white spots and streaked underparts. Immature greyish-brown above with black-and-white spots; underparts buff with brown spots and bars. Rarely seen. Nests in forest trees and bamboos.

BLACK-CROWNED NIGHT HERON

Nycticorax nycticorax Ardeidae

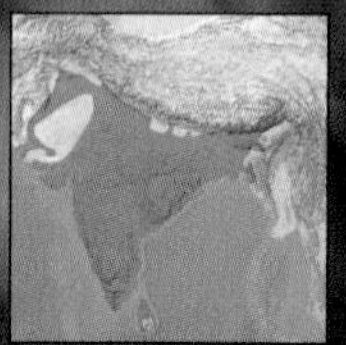

Size 58-72 cm

Voice Call a harsh raucous *quak quak*, mostly in flight

Range Locally common breeding resident throughout lowlands

Habitat All wetland types including paddy and mangroves

Stocky heron with short neck and legs. Black cap, upper back and scapulars; grey wings, rump and tail; stout, black bill; blood-red iris; pink legs in breeding; creamy-white underparts. Sexes alike. Juvenile buff-spotted and streaked brown. Social; nests colonially on trunks or forks of branches.

juvenile

juvenile

INDIAN POND HERON

Ardeola greyii Ardeidae

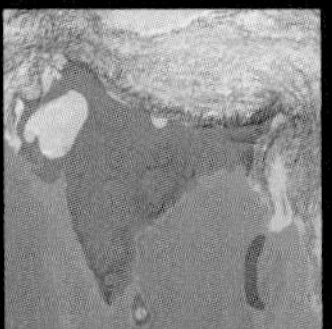

Size 45 cm

Voice Call a harsh croak, usually when flushed

Range Common resident throughout subcontinent

Habitat Marshes; jheels; riversides; roadside ditches; tidal creeks

Small heron, commonest of family in India; thick-set and earthy-brown in colour, with dull green legs; bill bluish at base, yellowish at centre with black tip; neck and legs shorter than in true egrets. Difficult to sight when settled; suddenly springs to notice with flash of white wings, tail and rump. In breeding, buffy-brown head and neck; white chin and upper throat, longish crest; rich maroon back; buff-brown breast. In non-breeding, streaked dark brown head and neck; grey-brown back and shoulders; more white in plumage. Sexes alike. Found around water, even dirty roadside puddles; ubiquitous in the plains; found in hills upto 1,200 m; remains motionless in mud or upto ankles in water, or slowly stalks prey. Hunts alone; roosts in groups with other pond herons.

breeding

non-breeding

CHINESE POND HERON

Ardeola bacchus Ardeidae

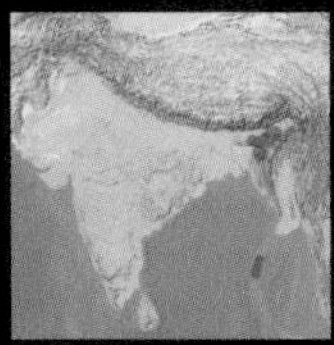

Size 42-45 cm

Voice Rather silent. Call a hard *croak* in flight, at dusk or when flushes

Range NE India; Andaman Islands

Habitat Wetlands; shallow water; fresh or saltwater; also ponds

Breeding adult has slaty-black mantle and scapulars. Dark brown head, neck and breast; slaty-patch in lower breast; white wings and belly. Legs and feet pinkish in breeding; yellow bill with black tip, pale blue on base of upper mandible; yellow lores and eyes.

non-breeding

GREY HERON

Ardea cinerea Ardeidae

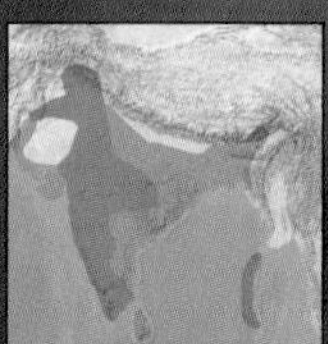

Size 100 cm

Voice Call a loud *quaak* in flight

Range Mostly resident; subcontinent; breeds upto 1,750 m in Kashmir

Habitat Marshes; tidal creeks; fresh waterbodies

Long-legged, long-necked bird of open marshes. Ash-grey above; white crown, neck and underparts; black stripe after eye continues as long, black crest; black-dotted band down centre of foreneck; dark blue-black flight feathers; golden-yellow iris at close range. Sexes alike. Mostly solitary except when breeding; occasionally enters shallow water; usually stands motionless, head pulled in between shoulders, waiting for prey to come close; characteristic flight, with head pulled back and long legs trailing.

WHITE-BELLIED HERON

Ardea insignis Ardeidae

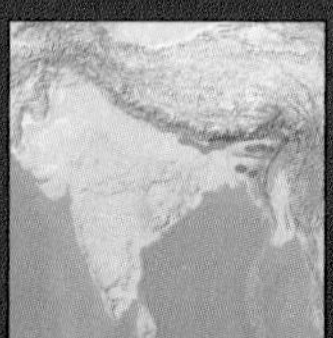

Size 127 cm

Voice Call a loud croaking *bray*

Range Small pockets in Bhutan, Assam and Arunachal Pradesh. Exceedingly rare and little known. Seldom seen

Habitat Undisturbed forested streams; rivers; marshes

Large, darkish grey, long-necked heron with white throat, belly and vent. Scapulars, foreneck and upper breast streaked white; large black bill, black legs. Breeding adult has greyish-whitish nape plumes and elongated grey breast feathers with whitish centres. Juvenile more brown, with smaller plumes. Similar to Grey, but larger. In flight, white belly and underwing linings diagnostic. Shy and rarely seen. Forages alone or in small groups. Feeds mainly during day on fish, frogs and reptiles.

STRIATED HERON

Butorides striata Ardeidae

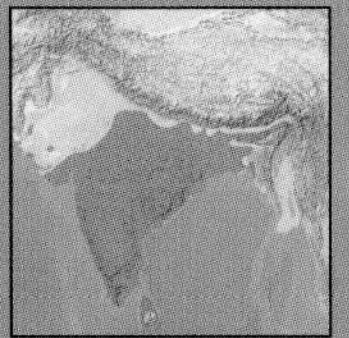

Size 45 cm

Voice Call a Redshank-like *tewn...tewn*

Range Uncommon resident, south of the Himalayas

Habitat Secluded pools. Found in mangroves, intertidal flats

Small, squat heron with longish drooping crest. Upperparts slaty-grey, washed green; underparts grey with pinkish tint; green wing feathers outlined with yellow; yellow eye has deep grey surround; deep green forehead; short legs, grey head and black crown. Orange feet in breeding. Juvenile darker, more heavily streaked and mottled. Characteristic hunched posture with head tucked into body.

GOLIATH HERON

Ardea goliath Ardeidae

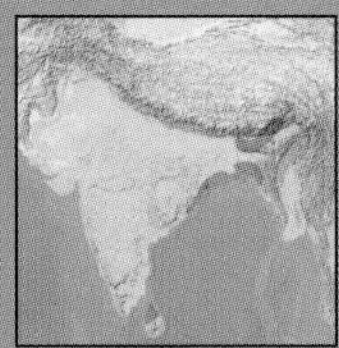

Size 147 cm

Voice Call a *kowoork* under normal circumstances, an *arrk* in response to a disturbance

Range Very rare, presumed breeding, resident or an occasional visitor from Africa, where common

Habitat Lakes; rivers; estuaries; mangroves

Huge greyish-purple heron with rufous-orange head, and long, bushy crest. Chestnut neck and breast; white throat and upper breast, streaked black; pale chestnut face and neck sides; slaty-grey back and upperwings. Similar to Purple, but lacks distinctive black markings on face and neck, and bigger with thicker head and neck. Female slightly smaller than male. Juvenile more rufous with mottled breast and belly, less distinct stripes. Nocturnal feeder; skittish. Nests on islands in low vegetation. Solitary and shy. Feeds on fish and other water animals.

PURPLE HERON

Ardea purpurea Ardeidae

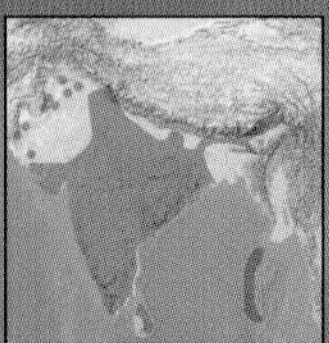

Size 78–90 cm

Voice Usually silent. Occasionally, a harsh croak

Range Mostly resident

Habitat Marshes and lakes with extensive reed beds. Prefers more open wetlands with fringing vegetation outside breeding season

juvenile

Slender-necked, lanky bird with slaty-purple upperparts, black crown with long, drooping black crest; rufous rear neck with prominent black stripe along length; white chin and throat; deep slaty-grey and chestnut below breast; almost black on wings and tail; pale yellow eyes; yellow bill; orange-yellow legs and feet. Crest and breast plumes less developed in female. Juvenile more brown and lacks crest; duller in colour and narrow steaks in neck and underparts. Solitary; crepuscular; extremely shy but master of patience; freezes and hides.

CATTLE EGRET

Bubulcus ibis Ardeidae

br

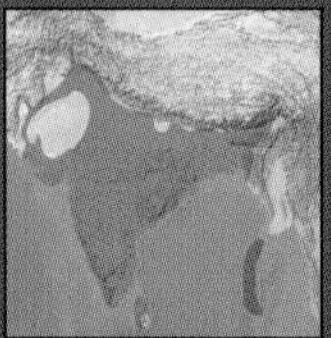

Size 50 cm

Voice Mostly silent except for some croaking sounds when breeding

Range Resident; subcontinent, upto 1,800 m in outer Himalayas. Rare in NW and NE India

Habitat Marshes; lakes; forest clearings; also, fields

Non br

breeding

Small snowy-white heron with characteristic hunch and relatively short legs and thick neck. Breeding adult white with orange-buff feathers on crown, neck and back; bright red bill, lores and legs; yellow eyes. Non-breeding adult very similar to Little, but told by yellow beak and from other egrets by size. White plumage, sometimes with pale reddish-buff wash. Sexes alike. Juvenile resembles non-breeding adult, has blackish bill, legs and feet. Eyes pale yellowish. Immature has black leg and bill. Very social. In large flocks; follows livestock, also farm equipments like tractors to catch insects that are disturbed. Nest of sticks in bushes or trees.

GREAT EGRET

Casmerodius albus Ardeidae

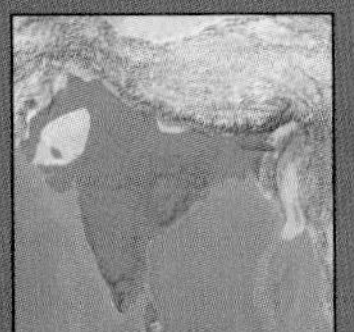

Size 94-104 cm

Voice Occasional croak

Range Resident, local migrant; not common but widespread across country

Habitat Marshes; jheels; rivers; tidal estuaries

Large, almost entirely white heron with contrasting black feet and long, black legs. Black tip to bright yellow bill; greenish-yellow patch between bill and eye; long S-shaped neck prominent in flight. Breeding adult displays beautiful plumes extending from back to beyond tail. In courtship display, bird spreads plumes into a fan shape. Juvenile similar but without plumes. Feeds actively at dawn and dusk, waiting motionlessly to catch prey.

INTERMEDIATE EGRET

Mesophoyx intermedia Ardeidae

Size 80 cm

Voice Usually silent

Range Locally common breeding resident throughout lowlands and the coast

Habitat Wetlands; the coast

As its name implies, intermediate in size between Great Egret and smaller white egrets. Overall striking white bird with dark legs and thickish, yellow bill. Breeding adult may have reddish or black bill, greenish-yellow gape skin, loose filamentous breast trails and back plumes, and dull yellow or pink upperparts. Sexes similar. Stalks prey in shallow water, including flooded fields. Feeds on fish, frogs, crustaceans, and insects. Nests in colonies with other herons, normally on platforms of sticks, trees, or shrubs.

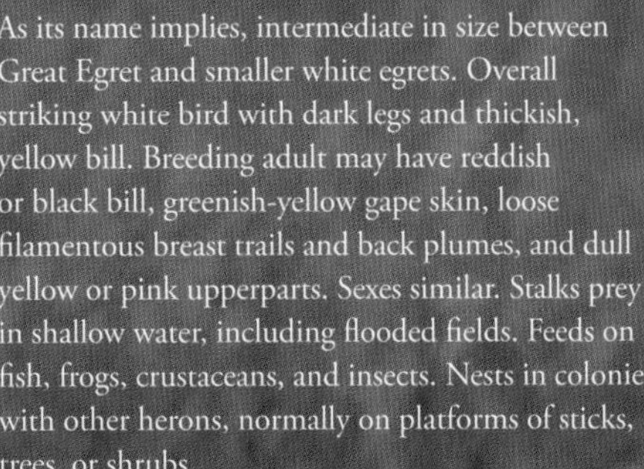

breeding

LITTLE EGRET

Egretta garzetta Ardeidae

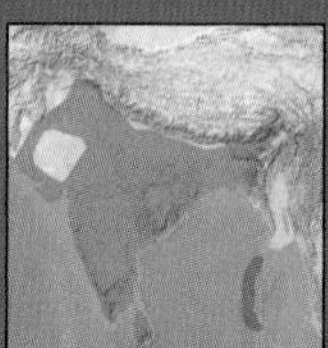

Size 65 cm

Voice Occasional croak

Range Fairly common breeding resident; subcontinent, upto 1,600 m in the outer Himalayas

Habitat Margins of coastal and inland water habitats, preferring open areas with shallow freshwater

Striking and elegant heron distinguished by pure white feathers, long sinuous neck, long, black legs and dark, pointed bill. Breeding adult has two long, nape plumes and light feathery plumage around breast and back. Juvenile similar in appearance to non-breeding adult, but has less striking colouration on feet and around eyes.

breeding

PACIFIC REEF EGRET

Egretta sacra Ardeidae

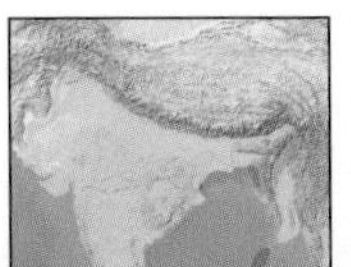

Size 60 cm

Voice Usually silent. Call a harsh *squak* when disturbed. Also grunts

Range Common breeding resident of Andaman and Nicobar Islands

Habitat Rocky and muddy coasts

dark morph

white morph

Medium-sized, purely coastal, dimorphic heron (some with an entirely white plumage while more birds charcoal-grey). Can be confused with Little, but much stockier, with thicker neck and shorter legs. Only toes protrude beyond tail when in flight. Colour ranges identical except, grey phase lacks obvious throat. Acquires short, bushy crest when breeding. Nests colonially in mangroves or among rocks.

WESTERN REEF EGRET

Egretta gularis Ardeidae

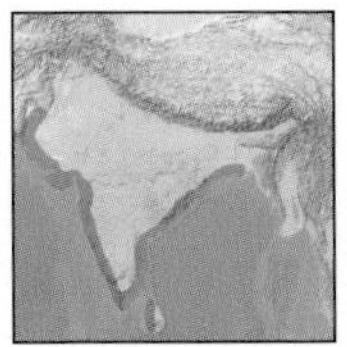

Size 65 cm

Voice Rasping croaks

Range W, E coasts; often inland

Habitat River deltas; coasts; mangroves

Slim, medium-sized heron with skinny neck. Thick, pale and heavy bill. Polymorphic and varies from all white to light to dark grey. Throat usually white. Breeding adult has red lores and plumes on head, breast and back. Sexes alike. Usually solitary or seen foraging with other egrets. More active at twilight. Often both phases seen feeding together.

intermediate morph

white morph

RED-BILLED TROPICBIRD

Phaethon aethereus Phaethontidae

Adult has bright red bill; white tail-streamers, black barring on mantle and scapulars and much black on primaries. Juvenile has yellow bill with black tip, black band across nape and shows more black on primaries, with black primary coverts when compared with juvenile Red-tailed and White-tailed.

RED-TAILED TROPICBIRD

Phaethon rubricauda Phaethontidae

Adult has red bill and red tail-streamers; lacks black barring on mantle, back and rump. Wings mainly white, with black primary shafts and marking on tertials. Juvenile has grey or black bill that becomes yellow with age; lacks black nape-band and shows less black on primaries, more strongly barred than juvenile Red-tailed and White-tailed.

BROWN BOOBY

Sula leucogaster Sulidae

Dark coffee-brown booby with white underbody and underwing-coverts, distinctly demarcated between brown head, neck and upper breast. Juvenile has dusky brown underbody with pale-panel across underwing-coverts, though overall appearance similar to adult.

RED-FOOTED BOOBY

Sula sula Sulidae

Smallish, graceful booby with red legs and feet. White, brown and intermediate morphs occur; white morphs most likely to be encountered in the Indian Ocean. Adult white morph smaller in size than Masked, and has variable yellow wash on crown and hindneck, bluish bill and no mask on chin.

GREAT FRIGATEBIRD

Fregata minor Fregatidae

Adult male almost overall black above, except for pale brown wing-bar; greenish-purple gloss on head, neck and upper back; scissor-shaped tail; large, red, distensible gular pouch in breeding male. Female larger, and less glossy; non-distensible gular pouch; white upper breast; light grey; pale brown wing-bar. Juvenile has reddish-brown patch on head and white underparts.

WHITE-TAILED TROPICBIRD

Phaethon lepturus Phaethontidae

Small tropicbird with very long tail streamers, extending from wedge-shaped tail. Mostly white with strong black eye-stripe, black wing-bar and black tips to wings; robust decurved bill. Long, pointed wings. Juvenile soft, downy grey. Strong flier, but moves awkwardly on land, as its short legs are set far back.

MASKED BOOBY

Sula dactylatra Sulidae

Large and robust booby. Adult predominately white with black mask and black flight feathers and tail; white head and neck, black tail and black tertials help distinguish it from the Red-footed.

LESSER FRIGATEBIRD

Fregata ariel Fregatidae

Smaller and more finely built than the other two frigatebirds. Adult male mostly black except for white spur extending from breast sides on to inner underwings. Adult female has black head and throat, white neck sides, white spur extending from breast, also white, on to inner underwings, black belly and vent. Juvenile has rufous or white head.

GREAT WHITE PELICAN

Pelecanus onocrotalus Pelecanidae

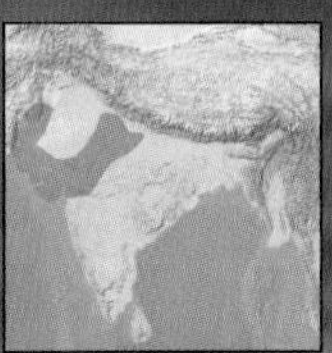

Size 175 cm

Voice Grunts and croaks. Rarely heard

Range Resident, Rann of Kutch. Winters in parts of N, S and SE India

Habitat Large jheels; lakes; coastal lagoons

Enormous bird with dramatic azure blue bill with central red stripe. Bright yellow, expandable pouch extends from lower jaw to base of throat. Bare, fleshy pink face; white, bushy crest; creamy white plumage with pale pinkish wash; pink feet and yellowish tuft on breast; black primaries and underside of secondaries. Social. Feeds on large fish early in the morning; rarely settles on land; strong flier.

SPOT-BILLED PELICAN

Pelecanus philippensis Pelecanidae

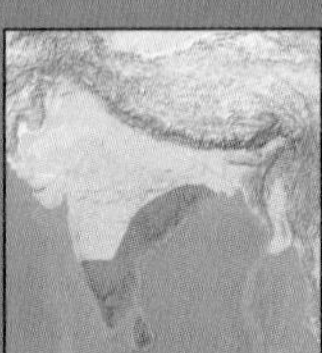

Size 125-152 cm

Voice Mostly silent

Range Breeds in the well-watered parts of S, SE and E India, but population spreads in non-breeding season

Habitat Large jheels; lakes

Relatively small pelican, mostly white with greyish-brown tint; pinkish rump and lower back; browny-grey crest; black primaries and dark brown secondaries visible in flight; large spotted bill has orange-yellow tip; pinkish elastic throat pouch with large pale spots. In breeding adult, skin at base of bill dark, pink orbital patch. Sexes alike. Juvenile lacks spots on bill. Purely aquatic. Breeds in colonies in tall trees. Feeds in open water, mostly on fish.

DALMATIAN PELICAN

Pelecanus crispus Pelecanidae Ardeidae

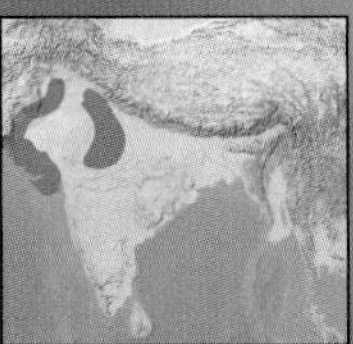

Size 170-190 cm

Voice Grunts and groans; hissing, and also explosive calls. Utters *wo-wo-wo* sounds when alarmed. Often silent

Range Globally threatened. Very local winter visitor mainly to Pakistan, NW India

Habitat Large waterbodies with fish

Largest pelican with curly nape feathers, grey legs and silvery-white plumage. Breeding adult has red lower mandible and pouch against yellow upper mandible; loose feathers on forehead form W-like shape above bill; bare skin around eye varies from yellow to purple; grey legs. Greyish-white underwings with black tips distinctive in flight. Elegant, soaring flight of flocks in graceful synchrony.

LITTLE CORMORANT

Phalacrocorax niger Phalacrocoracidae

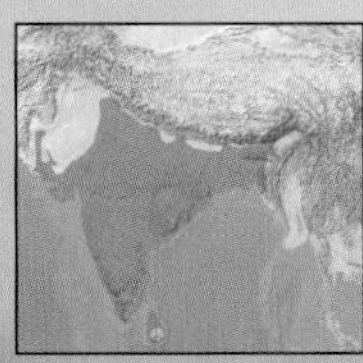

Size 50 cm

Voice Vocal, low roaring sounds near nest and roost

Range Subcontinent, south of the Himalayas

Habitat Village tanks; jheels; lakes; rivers and coastal areas

juvenile

Small, glossy black cormorant with few white head plumes. Short, thick neck. Breeding adult has some white spots and filoplumes on face; short silky white crest on back of head; dark eyes, gular skin and face. Non-breeding adult and juvenile more brownish with white throat patch and more crest. Sexes similar. Forages in small loose groups; swims underwater to capture fish. Roosts communally, often in the company of other waterbirds.

INDIAN CORMORANT

Phalacrocorax fuscicollis Phalacrocoracidae

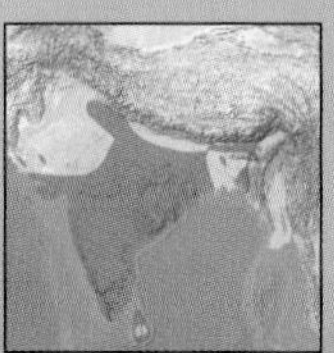

Size 63 cm

Voice Harsh croaks at nest

Range Throughout the region. Locally common breeding resident

Habitat Large freshwater wetlands; marshes; estuaries; brackish tidal creeks and mangrove swamps

Small to medium-sized slender cormorant mainly black in breeding season, with white neck plumes and whitish throat. Silvery wing-coverts; longish tail; white ear tufts, white-flecked feathers on neck, blackish gular pouch and no crest. Non-breeding adult more brown, with no ear tufts or white plumes and more yellow gular pouch. Sexes alikes. Juvenile more brown and lacks neck plumes. Gregarious, often found in larger bodies of water and rivers. Feeds in shallow water.

GREAT CORMORANT

Phalacrocorax carbo Phalacrocoracidae

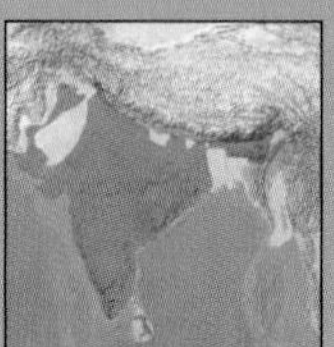

Size 80 cm

Voice Usually silent

Range Resident in most areas; subcontinent

Habitat Jheels; lakes; mountain torrents; occasionally coastal lagoons

Sexes alike. Breeding adult has black plumage with metallic blue-green sheen; white facial skin and throat; bright yellow gular pouch and white thigh patches; silky white plumes on head and neck. Non-breeding adult has no white thigh patches; gular pouch less bright. First year juvenile dull brown above, white below. Aquatic. Not gregarious outside breeding season; usually one or two birds feeding close by; dives underwater.

br

breeding

DARTER

Anhinga melanogaster Anhingidae

Size 90 cm

Voice Calls include loud croaks and squeaks

Range Subcontinent, south of the Himalayan foothills

Habitat Freshwater lakes; jheels

Long, snake-like neck, pointed bill and stiff, fan-shaped tail. Black upperparts, streaked and mottled with silvery-grey on back and wings; chocolate-brown head and neck; white stripe down sides of upper neck; white chin and upper throat; entirely black below. Juvenile brown with rufous and silvery streaks on mantle. Bird of deep freshwater; small numbers scattered along with Little. Highly specialised feeder, entire structure of bird modified for following and capturing fish underwater. Swims low in water with only head and neck uncovered; chases prey below water with wings half open, spearing fish with sudden rapier-like thrusts made possible by bend in neck at 8th and 9th vertebrae, which acts as spring as it straightens. Tosses fish into air and swallows it head-first. Basks on tree stumps and rocks, cormorant style.

immature

PIED FALCONET

Microhierax melanoleucos Falconidae

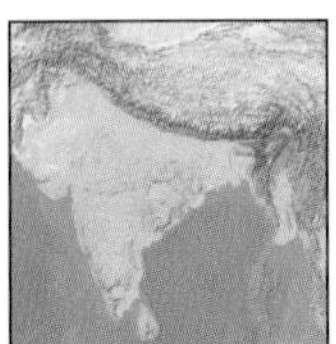

Size 20 cm

Voice Low, chattering call. Utters a shrill scream

Range Resident; E Himalayas and NE India

Habitat Forest clearings; tea plantations; wooded foothills

Smallest falcon in the world, only slightly larger than sparrow. Upperparts glossy black and underparts white, with black mottling on breast. Some have thin white line across base of cere, above eyes and down to breast giving the appearance of white face with large black eye patches. White spots on inner wing and narrow white bars on innertail.

COLLARED FALCONET

Microhierax caerulescens Falconidae

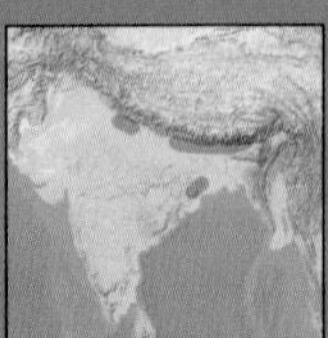

Size 18 cm

Voice Call a shrill whistle *killi…kill*

Range Scarce breeding resident: Himalayan foothills, Nepal

Habitat Clearings in, and edges of, broadleaved tropical forests and plantations

Very small pied falcon, with bold white supercilium and collar. Slaty-grey cheeks and crown; double-toothed bill, shortish wings, barred tail; underwings white with black bars; strong half-feathered legs, and powerful feet. Sexes similar. Juvenile has brownish-orange forehead and supercilium. Perches on top or edges of trees or bushes, frequently bobbing head and slowly moving tail up and down. The more northeasterly Pied Falconet, *M. melanoleucos,* is larger, black-and-white with no collar.

LESSER KESTREL

Falco naumanni Falconidae

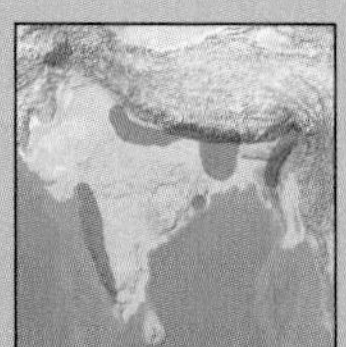

Size 30 cm

Voice Call a diagnostic harsh *chay-chay-chay*

Range Migrant mostly to N and W India

Habitat Open country

Small bird of prey, similar to Larger Common but more delicate-looking, with shorter wings and shorter tail. Rufous-brown back; barred grey underparts; grey head; grey-patches in wings; blue-grey greater coverts; wing-tips reach, or almost reach, the tip of the tail. In flight, underwings look whiter and darker trailing edges and wing-tips more clearly pronounced; tail looks more wedge-shaped; whitish-horn coloured talons. Female and juvenile slightly paler. Feeds on insects, small birds, reptiles and rodents. Nests colonially on cliffs, or in tree holes; like other falcons, no nest structure is built.

♀

COMMON KESTREL

Falco tinnunculus Falconidae

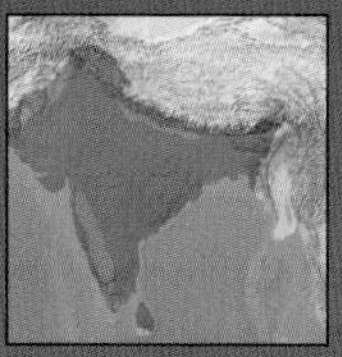

Size 32–39 cm

Voice Infrequent clicking sound. Also *kee-kee-kee*

Range Resident; local migrant; several races

Habitat Open country; cliffsides

Overall light chestnut brown falcon, with dark spotting on upperparts and buff underparts with narrow blackish streaking. Ash-grey crown, neck sides and nape; prominent black malar stripe; white tip to grey tail with black subterminal band. Bright yellow cere, feet and eye-ring; dark bill. Female has more black spots and streaking on pale rufous upperparts and pale buff underparts. Juvenile similar to female, but broader streaks on underparts and yellow parts paler. Solitary or in pairs; often hovers when hunting.

♀

RED-NECKED FALCON

Falco chicquera Falconidae

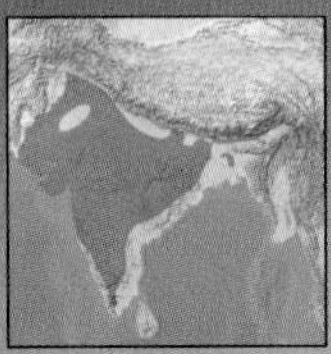

Size 35 cm

Voice Calls include shrill, trilling screams

Range Resident; all over India, south of Himalayan foothills

Habitat Avoids dense forests; prefers open country; wide cultivated plains with groups of trees

Smallish stout falcon, with short, blunt-ended wings, long, rounded tail and distinctive chestnut head and neck. Overall blue-grey plumage with black primary feathers; white-tipped grey tail, whitish underparts mottled and streaked black and rufous; black banding on belly. Sexes similar, but female slightly larger. Juvenile darker brown, with paler rufous-brown underparts. Hunts from sheltered perch. Rapid, direct flight; rarely hovers.

AMUR FALCON

Falco amurensis Falconidae

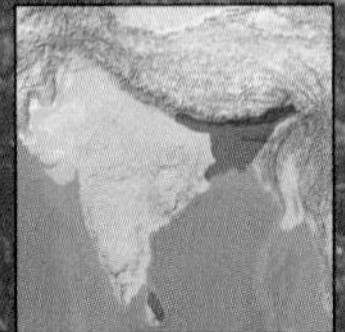

Size 26–30 cm

Voice Call a high-pitched *kew… kew… kew* at roost

Range Scarce passage migrant (mainly in autumn) between NE Asia and SC Africa

Habitat Open country; often near water

Small, slender falcon with long, pointed wings. Male overall dark grey, with rusty-cinnamon lower abdomen and thighs; white underwing, prominent in flight; bright orange-red legs and facial skin; orange base to beak; white claws. Female similar in size to male, with cream or rusty underparts, streaked and barred; grey upperparts; slaty-grey head with cream forehead; barred tail with dark tip; white cheeks and throat; dark eye patch and moustache. Juvenile similar to female, but paler, with rusty-brown or buff-edged feathers. Very sociable.

SOOTY FALCON

Falco concolor Falconidae

Medium-sized bird with long, slender wings and long tail. Upperparts almost uniform grey with bluish tint (female lacks tint); almost black flight feathers and darkish-patch below eye. Bright yellow ring around eye; yellow base of bill and legs; dark trailing edge to wings and tail. Female darker than male. Juvenile has brown-grey upperparts and heavily streaked brown underparts; dark stripe from base of bill; creamy throat and lower cheeks. Nests on ledge or on rocks; feeds mainly on birds, but also large insects which are eaten in flight.

MERLIN

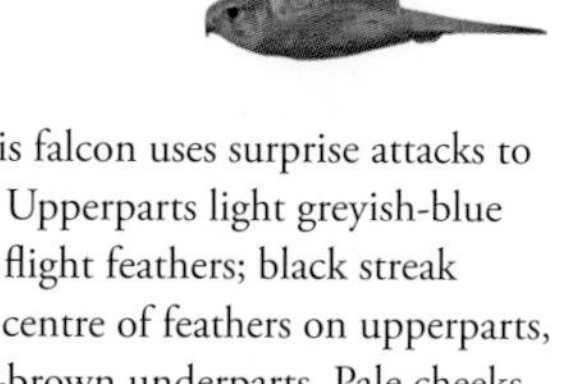

Falco columbarius Falconidae

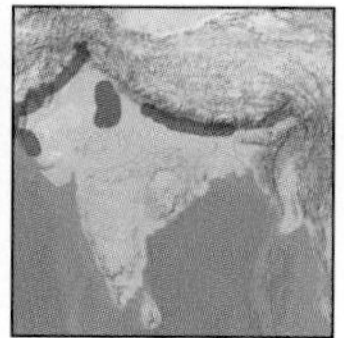

Size 29 cm

Voice Usually silent

Range Scarce winter visitor to N lowlands

Habitat Open country including cultivation and semi-desert. Frequently perches on ground and rarely in trees

Though small, this falcon uses surprise attacks to bring down prey. Upperparts light greyish-blue with black upper flight feathers; black streak running through centre of feathers on upperparts, and light reddish-brown underparts. Pale cheeks surrounded by grey, faint moustache; white throat; darkish underwings uniformly marked; long, square-cut tail with broad, black banding and narrow, blue-grey stripe near tip.

♀

EURASIAN HOBBY

Falco subbuteo Falconidae

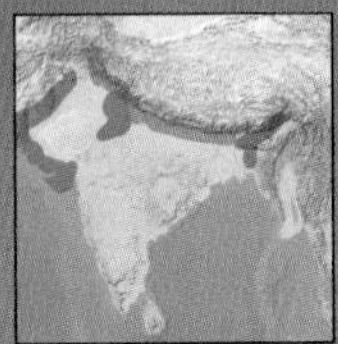

Size 33 cm

Voice Call a hurried *ki ki ki ki*

Range Breeds in the Himalayas; scarce passage migrant mainly in the NW India. Scattered records throughout lowlands

Habitat Open, wooded country often over or near water

juvenile

Small, slender falcon with long square-tipped tail. Upperparts and crown slaty-grey; creamy buff underparts heavily streaked black; chestnut thighs and vent; underwings and undertail barred; pale throat and cheeks; dark moustache; thin white line above eye. Sexes alike. Juvenile more brownish and mottled; creamish thighs and vent, and bluish-grey to greenish legs and facial skin. Aerial feeder, pursuing bats and small birds. The rarer Oriental Hobby, *F. severus*, is even darker with chestnut underparts.

ORIENTAL HOBBY

Falco severus Falconidae

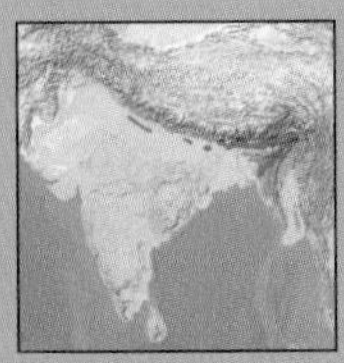

Size 27–30 cm

Voice Call includes a shrill trill of 3- to 4-notes

Range Resident to the Himalayas, NE India

Habitat Forested, hilly country

Small, robust falcon with slaty-grey upperparts; deep black head and cheeks; rich chestnut underparts, paler on throat. Long, pointed wings; short, powerful bill with 'tooth' on sides; black teardrop-shaped patch on sides of head. Juvenile has rufous breast, streaked black and some mottling on back. Fast flying birds attaining high speed as they dive from high altitudes to knock out birds; eats on wing or on perch. Nests in holes in trees or in nest of another species; in trees, building ledges or cliffs.

LAGGAR FALCON

Falco jugger Falconidae

Size 45 cm

Voice Call a 2-or 3-note scream, mostly when breeding

Range Resident, local migrant; all over India, to about 1,000 m in the Himalayas

Habitat Open country; scrubs

Overall dark greyish-brown falcon with white head; rufous crown; narrow, dark moustache. Whitish underparts streaked densely on flanks. In flight, pale breast contrasts with darker flanks and thighs; longish tail. Sexes alike, but female larger. In juvenile, underbody below throat dark brown. Juvenile similar to adult, but has more heavily streaked underparts. Usually in pairs, often seen in towns and cities; pair often hunts in concert, chasing prey; spectacular displays at onset of breeding season. Returns to favourite perch.

SAKER FALCON

Falco cherrug Falconidae

Size 55 cm

Voice Usually silent. Occasionally, a harsh *kerk…kerk…kerk*

Range Rare winter visitor: W Pakistan, NW India as far south as Delhi, Rajasthan and Gujarat

Habitat Dry, open country in mountains and plains

Large, powerful bird with wide wing span. Variations in colour make this a difficult bird to identify. Colour ranges from uniform chocolate-brown to pale buff with dark barring and streaking, to almost pure white. Pale head with long, thin moustache; sharp, curved talons; powerful, hooked beak; whitish underparts variably marked brown; long tail extends beyond wings; large feet. Female larger. Ferocious hunter that often attacks prey larger than itself.

PEREGRINE FALCON

Falco peregrinus Falconidae

♀

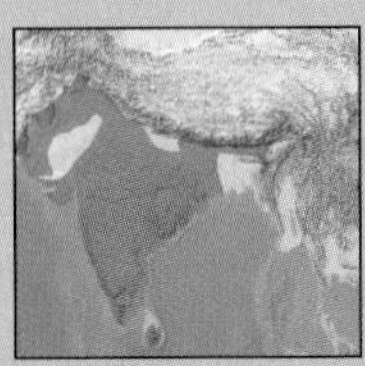

Size 42 cm

Voice Variety of calls including loud, harsh, persistent chatter, used against intruders

Range Resident; all over India, to about 3,000 m in the Himalayas; not found in semi-arid regions

Habitat Mostly rugged, mountainous areas; cliffs

calidus

One of the fastest fliers, the Peregrine is fairly large; stocky falcon with pointed wings and relatively short, square tail. Upperparts bluish-grey; underparts reddish-brown with variable dark spotting and barring; barred underwing and tail; pale throat and cheeks; broad, dark moustachial stripe. Yellowish-orange facial skin and legs; bluish beak, tinged yellow at base and black at tip. Sexes similar, but female substantially larger. Juvenile ore brown with heavily streaked underparts, and blue-grey or greenish legs and facial skin.

peregrianator

BARBARY FALCON

Falco pelegrinoides Falconidae

Medium to large-sized falcon similar to Peregrine, but slimmer. Bluish-grey upperparts; brown cap; rufous forehead, nape and sides of crown; slaty-grey-patch around eye extending down to thin moustache and eye-stripe; creamy cheek patch; whitish throat. Creamy underparts with darker spotting and streaking on belly. Dark primaries; undersides of wings, finely barred; short, square tail, broadly barred black. Sexes similar, but female substantially larger.

SHAHEEN FALCON

Falco f peregrinator Falconidae

Powerful, broad-shouldered falcon. Slaty-grey upperparts; black head; long dark moustache running down to neck sides; rufous crown and nape; creamish chest; pale rust underparts, barred black from abdomen to below tail; large yellow-patch around black beak. Yellow legs and feet. Sexes alike, but female much larger. Juvenile darker brownish-black above and more rufous below. Strong flight with stiff shallow beats. Hunts from lookout and can wait for hours to drop down on prey.

Size 40 cm

Voice Usually silent

Range Scarce breeding resident throughout the region

Habitat Open, usually rocky, country; sometimes urban areas

OSPREY

Pandion haliaetus Accipitridae

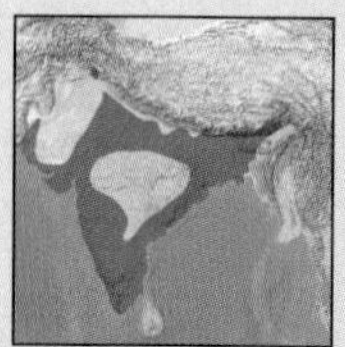

Size 55-58 cm

Voice Short, nasal scream. Calls rarely

Range In parts of the Himalayas, between about 2,000-3,500 m. Winter visitor all over India

Habitat Lakes; rivers; coastal lagoons

Large bird whose long wings have characteristic bend at carpal joints. Underparts sharp white, with dark brown-patches at carpal joints and mottled dark brown necklace. Dark eye-stripe; dark brown back; pale blue-grey feet; black beak. Female heavier and darker with more defined necklace. Solitary, or in scattered pairs; circles over water; hovers characteristically; dives with feet dangling; often splashes into water; carries fish on to perch.

JERDON'S BAZA

Aviceda jerdoni Accipitridae

Size 48 cm

Voice Calls include a *kip… kip… kip* and *keeya…keeya* during breeding. Also *pee…ow*

Range Rare breeding resident to hills of NE India, Bangladesh. Also, Sri Lanka and S peninsular hills

Habitat Evergreen forests and plantations; crepuscular

Medium-sized raptor characterised by short, stout legs and feet and well-developed talons; unfeathered lower tarsus and thin white-tipped black crest usually held erect; brown upperparts; rufous barred underparts; three black tail-bands tipped white. Long, paddle-shaped wings reach almost till tail-tip. Sexes alike. Perches well concealed in tall trees. Feeds on snakes, lizards, frogs, and insects. Insects captured by sallying from perch.

BLACK BAZA

Aviceda leuphotes Accipitridae

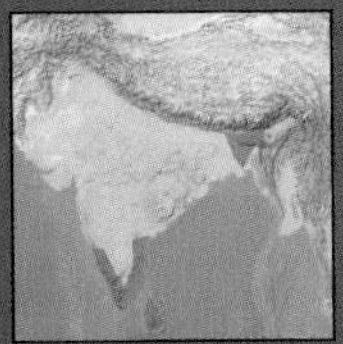

Size 32 cm

Voice Vocal in flight and when perched. Utters soft, quavering, plaintive or whistling notes

Range Uncommon resident; Kerala and some parts in adjoining Karnataka; NE India, east of E Nepal

Habitat Evergreen forests; clearings; streams; foothills

Small raptor with black head, neck, upperparts and tail. Black head with long, black crest; black throat; dark blue-grey cere; snowy white breast-band bordered black and chestnut; rufous belly barred with buff. Secondary flight feathers show chestnut and white-patches; chestnut markings on lower back, scapulars and greater wing-coverts. Black vent, undertail-coverts and thighs. Groups of several birds often perch on same tree. Feeds on large insects, lizards, tree frogs, and occasionally small mammals, bats and birds.

ORIENTAL HONEY-BUZZARD

Pernis ptilorhynchus Accipitridae

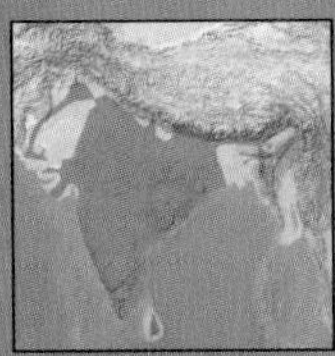

Size 65 cm

Voice Call a high-pitched, long-drawn *weeeeeu…*

Range Resident and local migrant; subcontinent to about 2,000 m in the Himalayas

Habitat Forests; open country; cultivation; vicinity of villages

Highly variable buzzard. Upperparts greyish-brown; grey head, underparts range from cream to blackish-brown and marked and streaked; slender head; longish neck distinctive; tail rarely fanned; crest rarely visible; pale underside of wings barred; broad dark subterminal tail-band; two or three more bands on tail; tarsus unfeathered. Scale-like feathers around eyes and forehead protect from stings of wasps, bees and hornets the bird preys upon. Specialises in feeding on larvae and honey of bees and wasps.

BLACK-WINGED KITE

Elanus caeruleus Accipitridae

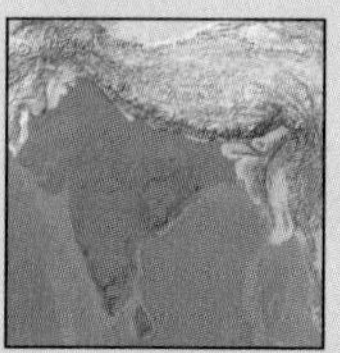

Size 32 cm

Voice Generally silent. Call a weak *weeet...weeet... weeet* when agitated

Range All over India, to about 1,500 m in the outer Himalayas

Habitat Open scrub and grass country; light forests

Striking bird of prey with pure white head and breast and ruby-red eyes surrounded by black-patches. Grey crown, back of neck and upperparts; black-patch on upper edges of wings. Juvenile similar but with more brown upperparts and dusky streaks on crown; yellowish-brown breast and head. Solitary, or in pairs; sits on exposed perch or flies over open scrub and grass country; mostly hunts on wing.

BLACK KITE

Milvus migrans Accipitridae

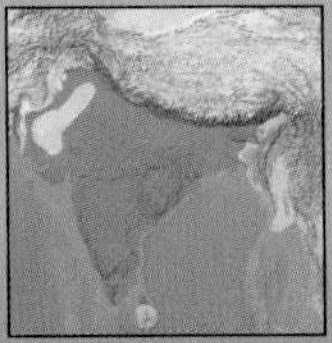

Size 47–60 cm

Voice Call a loud, musical whistle

Range Resident; subcontinent upto about 2,200 m in the Himalayas, co-existing with Black-eared in some localities

Habitat Mostly neighbourhood of humans

Medium-sized raptor; overall very dark brown plumage with light brown and rufous markings, particularly on head, neck and underparts. Light brown bar on shoulder; tail forked and barred darker brown; edges of wings appear 'fingered', dark brown eye; black bill with yellow cere. Sexes similar. Juvenile lighter brown with less pronounced fork in tail.

BLACK-EARED KITE

Milvus m lineatus Accipitridae

Overall dark brown kite with variable whitish crescent at primary bases on underwing and pale band across median coverts on upperwing. Juvenile has whitish or buffish streaking on head and underparts. Shallow fork-tail; much movement of arched wings and twisting of tail in flight.

BRAHMINY KITE

Haliastur indus Accipitridae

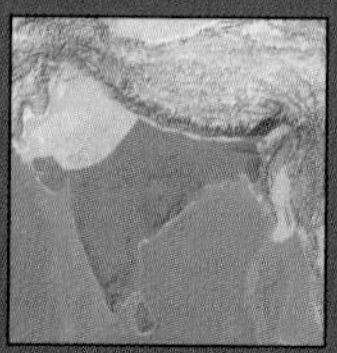

Size 50 cm

Voice Loud scream

Range Resident and local migrant; subcontinent

Habitat Margins of lakes; marshes; rivers; sea coasts

juv

White head, neck, throat, upper belly and flanks diagnostic. Chestnut wing-coverts, thighs and tail; black outer flight feathers; white-tipped tail. Sexes similar in appearance; female tends to be slightly larger. Juvenile various shades of brown, with darker upperparts and lighter head and underparts and rounder tail. Solitary, or in pairs, scavenging; also hunts for live food including crabs, crustaceans, amphibians, small reptiles, fish, insects, small mammals and birds.

juvenile

WHITE-BELLIED SEA EAGLE

Haliaeetus leucogaster Accipitridae

Size 70 cm

Voice Call a loud goose-like honking *hank...hank...hank* typically heard during breeding season

Range Resident; coast of Bombay and all along the E coast; flies many miles inland to freshwater lakes, rivers

Habitat Islands; rocky coasts; large inland waterbodies; wetlands

Ash-brown and white bird with pure white head, neck and short white tail. Black flight feathers; white underwing-coverts; pale blue-grey hooked bill with dark tip and grey cere; dark brown eyes; pale greyish yellow legs and feet. Sexes similar, but female larger. Juvenile has dark brown upperparts and wings, white-edged feathers on back and wing-coverts; white tail with brown subterminal band.

PALLAS'S FISH EAGLE

Haliaeetus leucoryphus Accipitridae

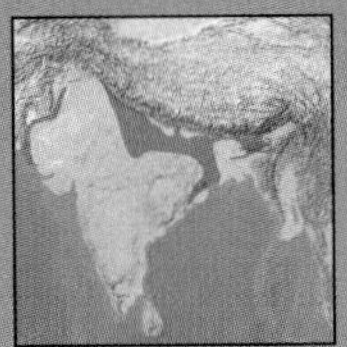

Size 76-84 cm

Voice Call a loud, creaky *kha… kha…kha…kha.* Noisy during breeding season

Range Resident; local migrant; N India, along Gangetic plains to E India; Chilka Lake

Habitat Jheels; large rivers

Upperparts dark brown with pale brown-grey head and neck and brown underparts; dark grey beak and cere; long, rounded tail and contrasting broad, white band diagnostic. Juvenile brown from above and below with white markings on underwing. Sexes alike; female larger. Feeds mostly on fish caught close to surface of water. Known to hunt in pairs and sometimes steal food from other birds.

WHITE-TAILED EAGLE

Haliaeetus albicilla Accipitridae

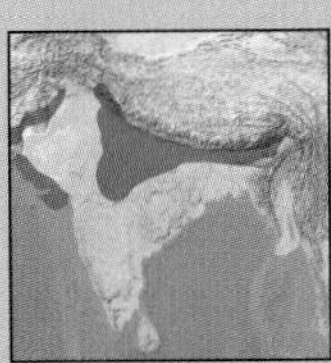

Size 90 cm

Voice Call a loud *klee…klee…klee*

Range Rare winter visitor: India, Pakistan. Records throughout

Habitat Large rivers and lakes; only rarely on coast in this region

Impressive-sized bird with broad club-ended wings. Relatively short, wedge-shaped tail; large head and beak. Feathers mottled shades of brown with paler head and neck and pale areas on both upperwing and underwing. Reddish-brown tail feathers, and pale stripes running down to tail-tip. Immature has brown tail and very dark head. Head and neck protrude in flight, edges of wings appear 'fingered'. Hunts for fish, mammals and birds.

LESSER FISH EAGLE

Ichthyophaga humilis Accipitridae

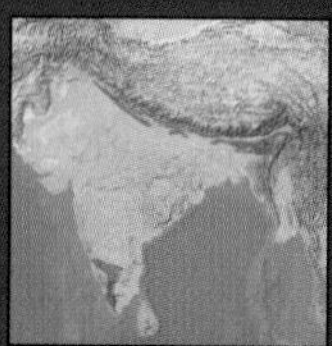

Size 64 cm

Voice Loud excitable shrieks include wavering *kleeeuee*

Range The Himalayas; SW India

Habitat Forested streams; lakes

Medium-sized bird; overall grey-brown plumage. Blunt, broad wings; featherless legs. Similar to Grey-headed but smaller and has brown breast, white thighs and belly and grey tail with slightly darker subterminal tail-band. Short, rounded tail; long neck and small head; large, curved talons specialised for catching fish. Juvenile similar to adult, but has brown eyes as opposed to yellow in adult, has more brown head and neck, more brown upperparts, and pale mottling on underwing-coverts. Feeds on fish, snatched from water.

GREY-HEADED FISH EAGLE

Ichthyophaga ichthyaetus Accipitridae

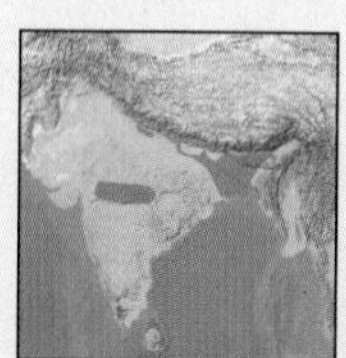

Size 61-75 cm

Voice Calls include *awh-awhr* and *chee-warr* repeated

Range Resident; from E Delhi to Assam; south through the peninsula

Habitat Lakes, rivers in forested country

Striking bird with relatively small head, longish neck and powerful, grey beak. Upperparts brownish-grey and white underparts. Rounded tail; sandy-yellow eyes; long, black talons; relatively short legs; and tail with broad, black terminal band. Female larger and heavier than male. Juvenile has white belly mottled with brown.

juvenile

BEARDED VULTURE

Gypaetus barbatus Accipitridae

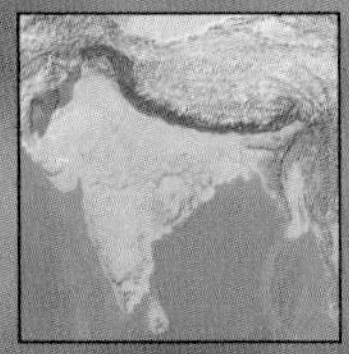

Size 125 cm

Voice Usually silent. Sometimes, a deep croak

Range The Himalayas, W to E, 1,000–5,000 m. Soars higher

Habitat High mountain slopes

immature

Large, majestic vulture, with enormous wings that enable it to soar easily above the mountains. Long, diamond-shaped tail distinctive in flight. Creamy-yellow head; black eye patches that extend below bill; short, narrow bill; black bristles under chin creating a 'beard'. Neck and underparts rusty-orange; back, wings and tail dark grey-blue to black. Juvenile patchy brown. Known for its unusual habit of dropping bones on to rocks to smash them open and get at the marrow.

EGYPTIAN VULTURE

Neophron percnopterus Accipitridae

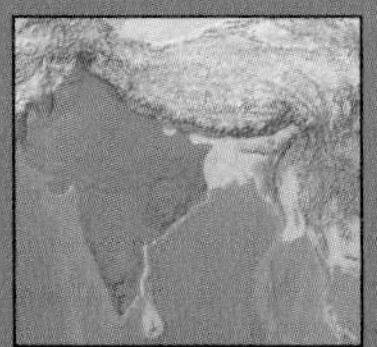

Size 60-70 cm

Voice Usually silent

Range All over India; plains to about 2,000 m in the Himalayas

Habitat Open areas or semi-open areas

ginginianus

rubripersonatos

Small vulture with mostly bare head that shows yellow to orange coloured skin. Ruff long whitish feathers on hindneck; brownish neck and back. Long pointed wings and long wedge-shaped tail; dark flight feathers; long, slender bill with curved tip; blood red iris; yellow or light grey legs. Immature uniformly brown. Nests solitarily, sometimes in loose colonies. Seen in small numbers on ground or gliding downhill slopes.

juvenile

INDIAN VULTURE

Gyps indicus Accipitridae

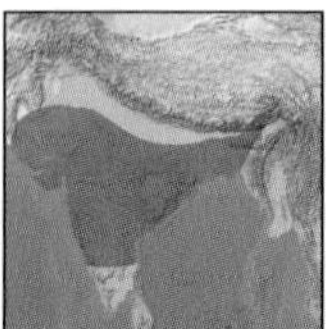

Size 90 cm

Voice Quieter than White-rumped

Range Formerly common breeding resident except in extreme south and Sri Lanka. Now globally threatened and very local. Most frequent in large wildlife sanctuaries

Habitat As White-rumped. Nests colonially exclusively on cliff ledges and buildings

Scruffy-looking bird with bald head, very broad wings, and short tail feathers. Pale yellow bill; pale eye-rings; white neck-ruff, black neck and head. Brown upperwings graduating to cream below. Dark flight feathers and tail form striking contrast to pale underparts. Cream feathered thighs. Juvenile has dark bill with pale culmen, pinkish head and neck with pale below; brown and cream-streaked undersides.

WHITE-RUMPED VULTURE

Gyps bengalensis Accipitridae

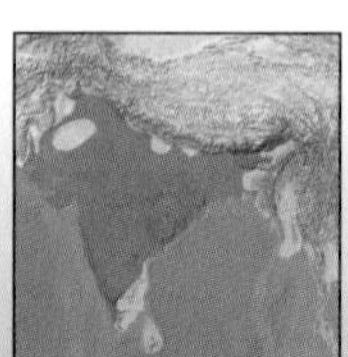

Size 85 cm

Voice Utters sounds mainly at carcass, when disputes and interactions occur

Range Formerly very common breeding resident throughout. Now globally threatened

Habitat Open country

juvenile

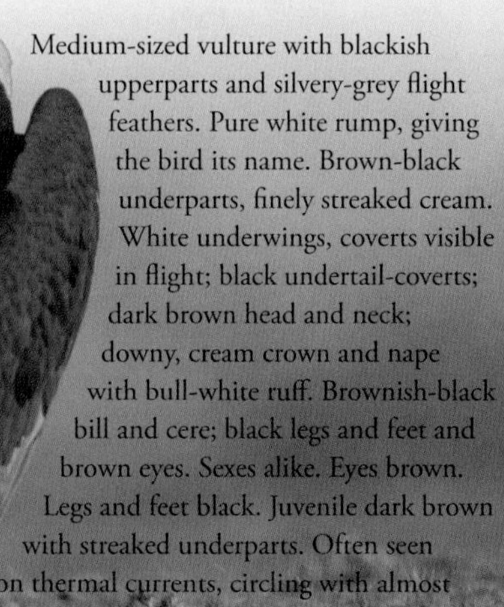

Medium-sized vulture with blackish upperparts and silvery-grey flight feathers. Pure white rump, giving the bird its name. Brown-black underparts, finely streaked cream. White underwings, coverts visible in flight; black undertail-coverts; dark brown head and neck; downy, cream crown and nape with bull-white ruff. Brownish-black bill and cere; black legs and feet and brown eyes. Sexes alike. Eyes brown. Legs and feet black. Juvenile dark brown with streaked underparts. Often seen on thermal currents, circling with almost motionless wings.

SLENDER-BILLED VULTURE

Gyps tenuirostris Accipitridae

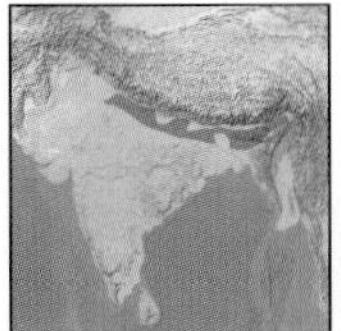

Size 93-100 cm

Voice Cackling screeches

Range Resident; lower Himalayas, from NW India through Nepal; NE India and Ganges delta

Habitat Similar to White-rumped. Cities; towns; villages. Globally threatened

Overall greyish-brown vulture, with sharply accentuated dome. Rather scruffy, ill-kempt appearance. Generally slimmer and more elongated body than Indian. Slender snake-like neck; thin elongated dark bill; dark cere with pale culmen; bare head and neck with wrinkled skin; dark eye-ring; Underparts streaked pale. White thigh patches visible in flight. Dark underside to flight feathers. Juvenile similar to adult, but with whitish downy feathers on nape and upper neck.

HIMALAYAN VULTURE

Gyps himalayensis Accipitridae

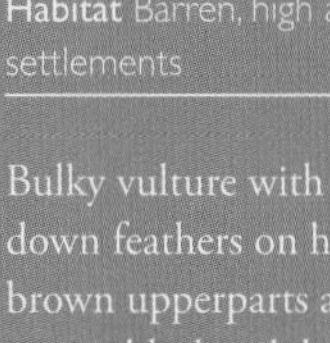

Size 125 cm

Voice Cackling screeches at carcass site

Range The Himalayas, between about 600-3,000 m; forages much higher. Recorded over 5,000 m

Habitat Barren, high altitude country; around mountain settlements

Bulky vulture with huge wing span. Soft white down feathers on head and upper neck; sandy-brown upperparts and ruff on lower neck; short, square black tail; buffy-white coverts; dark brown flight feathers. Tawny underparts streaked white; large heavy yellow bill, yellow eyes; fleshy pink legs. Sexes similar. Juvenile dark brown with whitish streaks; brown neck; black beak. Wary and shy; takes flight if disturbed while feeding. Soars solitary, or in small flocks over mountain slopes and cliffs.

GRIFFON VULTURE

Gyps fulvus Accipitridae

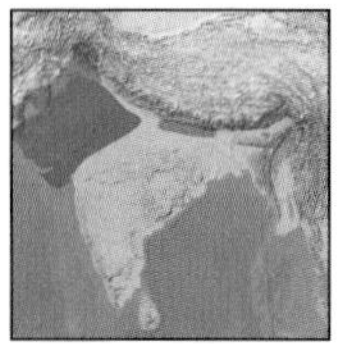

Size 100 cm

Voice Quiet. Grunts and hisses when feeding

Range Common breeding resident to W Pakistan hills, N India and Nepal to E Sikkim. Winters widely in lowlands of Pakistan and NW India, south to Gujarat and Madhya Pradesh

Habitat Mountains and semi-desert, wandering into nearby dry plains in winter

Large, carnivorous scavenger, with impressive creamy-white ruff. Plain pale reddish-brown upperparts; white head and neck; yellow bill; dark flight feathers on rest of wings and tail; pale underwing-coverts with bands of white. Juvenile has very pale upperwing feathers and grey bill. Breeds colonially containing 15 to 20 pairs. Builds nest on cliff-face, preferably in protected ledge or cave. Usually in pairs or small groups, often with other vultures.

RED-HEADED VULTURE

Sarcogyps calvus Accipitridae

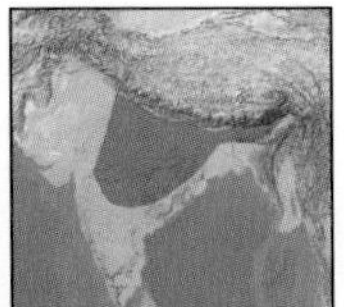

Size 85 cm

Voice Call a hoarse croak

Range Scarce resident; all over India, upto about 2,800 m in the Himalayas

Habitat Open country; village outskirts

Medium-sized, bulky vulture with wing span of over two metres. Unmistakable with its black feathers and bald red head. Two lappets attached to neck; thin, white margin on underside of wings at base of remiges; white-patches on thigh. Sexes similar, male has white or yellow eyes while female has dark. Juvenile overall paler with more mottled plumage and dark eyes. Usually found alone, or in breeding pair.

CINEREOUS VULTURE

Aegypius monachus Accipitridae

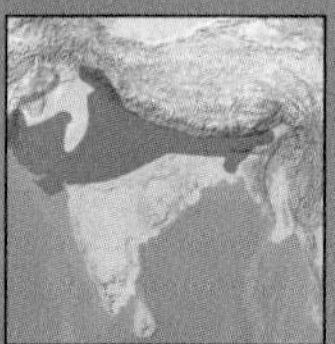

Size 115 cm

Voice Usually silent

Range Mainly scarce winter visitor; N mountains, river valleys

Habitat Open country, ranging widely and solitary while singly looking for carcass, often near rivers. Dominant over other species at carcass

Large bird with long and broad parallel wings that have prominently indented trailing edge and splayed wing-tips. Short, wedge-shaped tail; bare, buff head; dark eyes; dark facial mark; whitish legs; chocolate brown plumage and ruff; bluish neck; blackish throat and large, dark eye patches. Powerful horn-coloured bill; pale blue cere. Juvenile has blackish face, black bill and pink cere; and often fluffy tuft on back of head. Nests on small trees growing out of cliffs.

SHORT-TOED SNAKE EAGLE

Circaetus gallicus Acciptridae

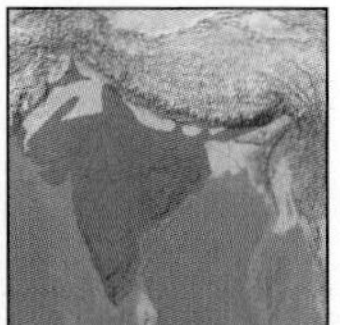

Size 65 cm

Voice Call a loud *kee yo*

Range Scarce breeding resident in lowlands, more common and widespread winter visitor except in NE India, Bangladesh and Sri Lanka

Habitat Open country with preference for scrubby grasslands

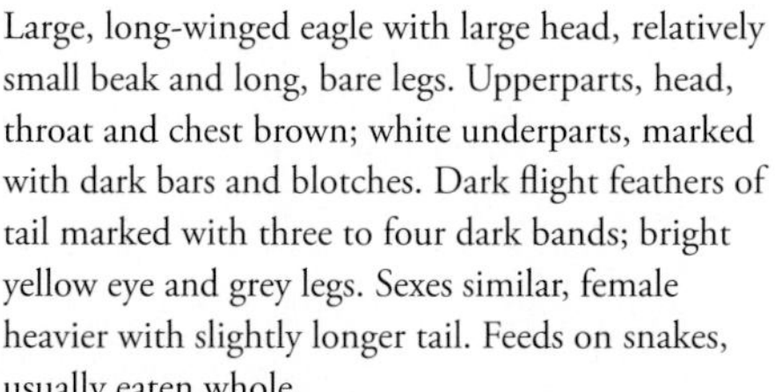

Large, long-winged eagle with large head, relatively small beak and long, bare legs. Upperparts, head, throat and chest brown; white underparts, marked with dark bars and blotches. Dark flight feathers of tail marked with three to four dark bands; bright yellow eye and grey legs. Sexes similar, female heavier with slightly longer tail. Feeds on snakes, usually eaten whole.

EURASIAN MARSH HARRIER

Circus aeruginosus Accipitridae

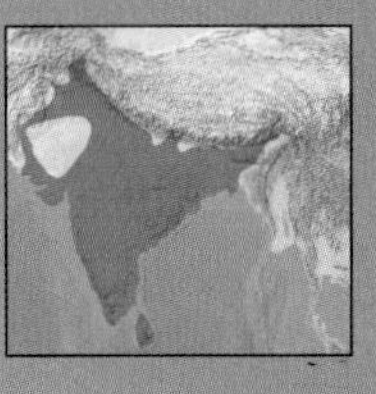

Size 55 cm

Voice Usually silent

Range Winter visitor; common; subcontinent, south of the Himalayan foothills; most common in N India

Habitat Marshes; jheels; wet cultivation

Large broad-winged harrier, with sexes dissimilar. Male overall dark reddish-brown with buff-yellow streaks, more dense on breast; dull rufous head and breast; silvery-grey wings, tail; black wing-tips visible in flight; legs, feet, iris and cere yellow; black bill. Female and juvenile uniform chocolate brown; throat, crown and shoulders have yellowish wash; lack grey tail and wing patch.

juvenile

juvenile

♀

juvenile

EASTERN MARSH HARRIER

Circus a spilonotus Accipitridae

Variable harrier with blackish upperparts, streaked paler. Rest of wing grey with black wing-tips and white front edge; grey tail; rump and underparts white; tail has dark bars. Similar to Pied, but larger. Sexes similar, but female larger. Juvenile dark brown; buff head and pale underwing patch. Hunts, glides low over open ground, searching for prey with wings held in shallow V-shape and often with legs dangling.

CRESTED SERPENT EAGLE

Spilornis cheela Accipitridae

Size 65-75 cm

Voice Call a loud whistling scream *keee…kee…ke…*

Range Subcontinent, to about 3,000 m in the Himalayas

Habitat Forested country

juvenile

Medium-sized eagle with brown upperparts and light brown underparts. Wing-coverts and scapulars heavily streaked and mottled; black flight feathers with broad bands; black crown and nape; brown crest barred white; rusty orange thighs and belly barred and mottled white; short, broad wings; bright yellow eyes. Fans crest when alarmed. Solitary, or in pairs; flies high over forests and swoops down on prey.

ANDAMAN SERPENT EAGLE

Spilornis elgini Accipitridae

Almost entirely dark brown eagle with bright yellow face and legs. Breast, belly and scapulars speckled white; black primary feathers finely edged white; undertail banded black and white; short, bushy crest; long wings. Juvenile paler with whiter head and dark-streaked throat; wing-coverts spotted; underparts barred buff; barring on belly; thinner bars on undertail.

GREATER NICOBAR SERPENT EAGLE

Spilornis klossi Accipitridae

Small raptor that has cinnamon scaling to black crown and crest; grey sides of heads with dark grey malar stripe; whitish throat with black mesial-stripe and yellowish-brown collar and underparts. Unlike other serpent eagles, undertail more narrowly banded with black. Juvenile has beige tips to crown and upperparts; no black banding on underwing and undertail.

HEN HARRIER

Circus cyaneus Accipitridae

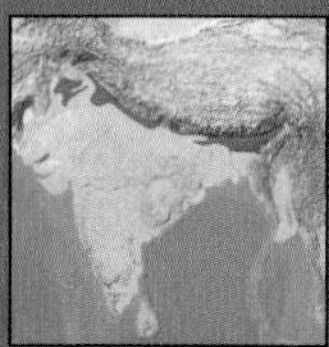

Size 40 cm

Voice Usually silent

Range Winter visitor to mainly Pakistan, the Himalayas and N India

Habitat Open country, grasslands and cultivation in plains and foothills

Slender, medium-sized raptor with flat owl-like face and broad wings. Long, rounded tail; sharp, hooked bill. Upperparts grey; underparts whitish; black wing-tips, dark trailing edge to wing; black-banded tail; white-patch on rump, conspicuous in flight. Female brown, with black bands on tail; whitish underparts streaked brown. Juvenile also brown, but more buffy and less streaked. Roosts gregariously on ground. All Northern Harriers have white rump patch obvious in flight, with wings held in V-shape.

♀

PALLID HARRIER

Circus macrourus Accipitridae

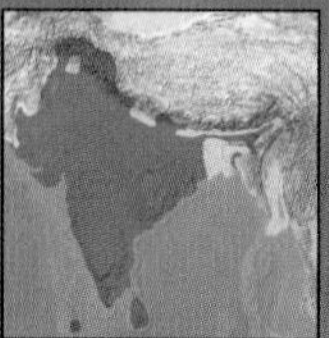

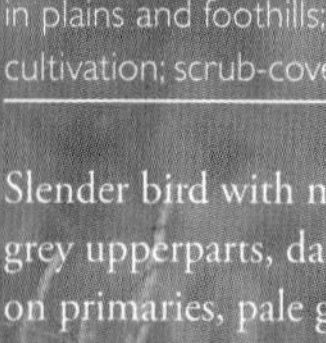

Size 40-48 cm

Voice Usually silent

Range Widespread winter visitor. Unrecorded in parts of NE India and W Pakistan

Habitat Open country in plains and foothills; semi-desert; grassy slopes; cultivation; scrub-covered plains and marshes

Slender bird with narrow wings and tails. Light grey upperparts, dark wedges on primaries, pale grey head and underbody; lacks black secondary bars. Female has distinctive underwing pattern; pale primaries, irregularly barred and lacking dark trailing edges. Immature male may display rusty breast-band and juvenile facial markings.

♀

♀

PIED HARRIER

Circus melanoleucos Accipitridae

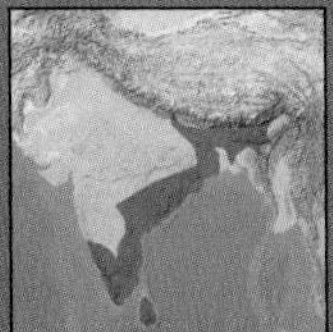

Size 45-49 cm

Voice Usually silent

Range Resident: Manas and adjoining areas in Assam. Winter visitor over parts of E India and erratically in parts of C and S India

Habitat Grassy areas; cultivation; reedy edges of jheels

♀

Slim and long-winged raptor, overall white and grey. Black head, back, throat and breast; grey tail, wings; black primaries; black band across median coverts. Female dark brown above; pale white nape patch, rump; pale buffy-rufous below; marked underside of flight feathers. Juvenile has pale marking on head, rufous brown underparts, dark upperwings; pale-patch on primaries, white uppertail-covert patch. Solitary, or in pairs.

MONTAGU'S HARRIER

Circus pygargus Accipitridae

Size 48 cm

Voice Usually silent; alarm a high-pitched chatter

Range Rather scarce winter visitor throughout peninsula. Passage migrant through NW India. Rare in the east

Habitat Open country including cultivation; often in scattered groups

♀

♀

Slender, medium-sized, slim bird with long narrow wings and long tail. Extensive black marking on wing-tip; distinct black band on both lateral and dorsal sides of wing. Head, breast, back and inner wing dark grey; rest of wing and tail lighter grey; narrow white rump; chestnut streaking on belly and underwing. Female and immature streaked brown with flat owl-like faces and white rumps. Juvenile similar to female but has reddish-brown underparts. Roosts communally in long grass. Hunts birds, rodents and large insects.

CRESTED GOSHAWK

Accipiter trivirgatus Accipitridae

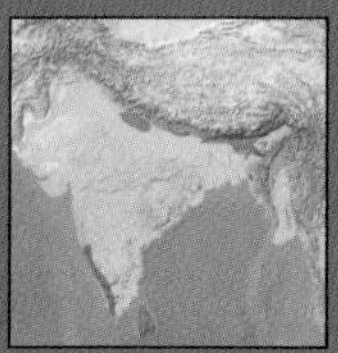

Size 42 cm

Voice Call a high-pitched scream *ke…ke…ke…ke*

Range Fairly common breeding resident

Habitat Forests

Large dark brown hawk with diagnostic black mesial-stripe from chin to breast. Long, brown tail has four wide black bands; brownish-black head with slight crest; black neck and white throat. White undertail; breast vertically streaked rufous; belly marked with horizontal dark brown bands. Iris, legs and feet yellow. Watches prey from perch, capturing it in rapid attack.

SHIKRA

Accipiter badius Accipitridae

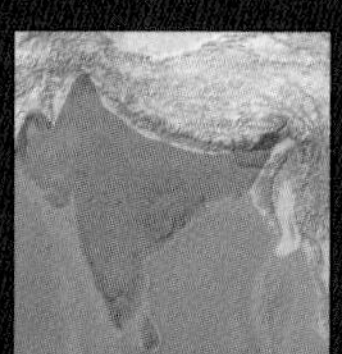

Size 35 cm

Voice Call a loud, drongo-like *titew…titew*

Range Subcontinent, upto 1,600 m in the Himalayas

Habitat Light forests; open country; neighbourhood of villages. Also in cities

Adult male has uniform grey upperparts, with faint rufous half-collar. Dark grey primaries tipped black. Underparts white, with narrow black streak from chin to throat centre; greyish red face and neck sides; breast and belly finely barred chestnut; grey tail has five dark bands and dark tip. Underwings rufous to buff; orange to red eye; yellowish-orange legs. Female larger, more slaty-brown and boldly barred.

♀

juvenile

JAPANESE SPARROWHAWK

Accipiter gularis Accipitridae

Small raptor with darkly barred underwings, lightly barred pale grey to underparts, dark grey upperparts and red eyes; yellow orbital rings and cere; indistinct supercilium. Similar to Eurasian but with more narrow and pointed wings. Female larger and has yellow eyes and dark barred underparts. Juvenile has brown upperparts and streaked breast; yellow iris, streaked throat and breast, barred belly and brown hood.

NICOBAR SPARROWHAWK

Accipiter butleri Accipitridae

Medium-sized hawk with pale blue-grey upperparts. Underparts and underwing-coverts pale; rusty breast; barred flanks; dark primaries; dark subterminal band. Female has more brown upperparts and more barring on breast. Juvenile rich rufous brown with dark bands on uppertail; dark bands on rufous-cinnamon secondaries and tail. Primarily forest-dwelling.

CHINESE SPARROWHAWK

Accipiter soloensis Accipitridae

Overall slaty blue-grey bird. Outer-tail feathers barred dark grey and black. Pale grey head sides and neck; white chin and throat with black shaft streaks; grey upper breast and belly washed pale rufous; whitish belly and undertail-coverts; white underside of tail graduating to grey with narrow black bands. Pale rufous underwing-coverts; white-patch under the wing. Brownish-red eyes; yellow cere and legs. Female similar to male but, larger.

BESRA

Accipiter virgatus Accipitridae

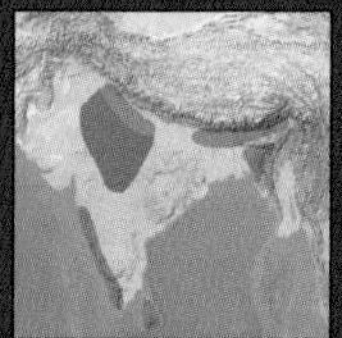

Size 32 cm

Voice Quite noisy. Call a high-pitched *chew…chew…chew*, when perched and in flight

Range Scarce breeding resident: The Himalayan foothills, Nepal, NE India, Western Ghats, Sri Lanka. Winters in N plains

Habitat Forests; open woodlands

Medium-sized raptor with short broad wings and long tail. Similar to Shikra, but darker and distinct dark vertical throat-stripe. Upperparts dark bluish-grey and whitish underparts barred rufous. Female larger and more brown. Juvenile has dark brown upperparts and white underparts barred brown with barred tail.

EURASIAN SPARROWHAWK

Accipiter nisus Accipitridae

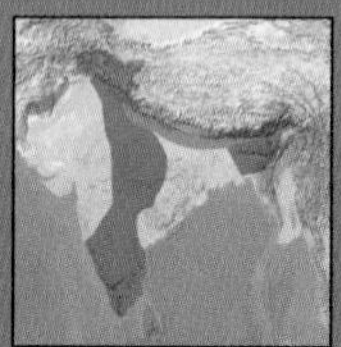

Size 35 cm

Voice Rather quiet. Call a rapid *kew…kew…kew…kew* when nesting

Range Fairly common breeding resident

Habitat Open wooded country, including cultivation. Probably overlooked

Smallish sparrowhawk with long legs and short, rounded wings. Upperparts dark grey with pale underparts finely barred reddish-brown. Hooked beak; pale line above eye; white chin patch. Female significantly larger, with darker, more brown upperparts and white underparts barred. Juvenile similar to female, but more brown upperparts, with rusty feather margins, broader barring on underparts; yellow iris. The Himalayan resident, *A.n. melaschistos*, is blackish-grey above.

NORTHERN GOSHAWK

Accipiter gentilis Accipitridae

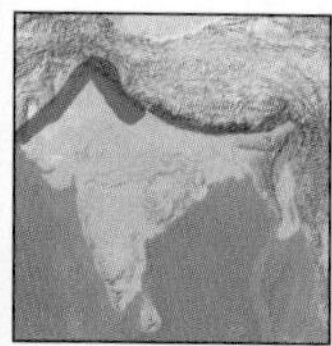

Size Male 50 cm; Female 61 cm

Voice Usually quiet. Pairs call a chattering *yek…yek…yek*; female a high *kee…aw*

Range Scarce winter visitor

Habitat Often soaring high over oak and coniferous forests

Large, powerful bird with short, strong wings and long tail. Upperparts brown-grey; black cap on head; distinct white supercilium; orange-red eyes; light grey underparts, finely barred on breast; throat, vertically streaked. Female has more brown upperparts and less-defined markings on breast. Juvenile brown above and pale buff to whitish below, with heavy streaking. Usually solitary, or in pairs.

WHITE-EYED BUZZARD

Butastur teesa Accipitridae

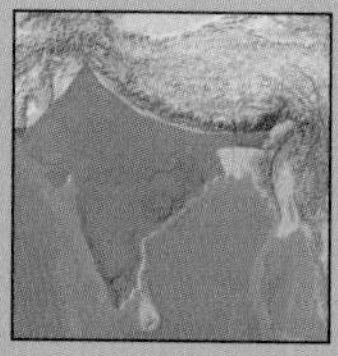

Size 45 cm

Voice Musical, plaintive *te…twee*. Calls frequently when breeding

Range Subcontinent, upto about 1,200 m in the Himalayas

Habitat Open and dry forests; cultivated country. Moves considerably

juvenile

juvenile

Ash-brown hawk with white throat, two dark cheek-stripe. Underparts brown-and-white; orange-yellow cere; whitish eyes with white and nuchal patch; buff shoulders. Solitary, or scattered pairs; seen on exposed perches, trees, poles or telegraph wires; seems to prefer certain sites; soars high and does aerial displays when breeding. Feeds on locusts, grasshoppers, crickets and other large insects as well as mice, lizards and frogs. Nests in loose, unlined cup of twigs in fork of thickly foliaged trees.

COMMON BUZZARD

Buteo buteo Accipitridae

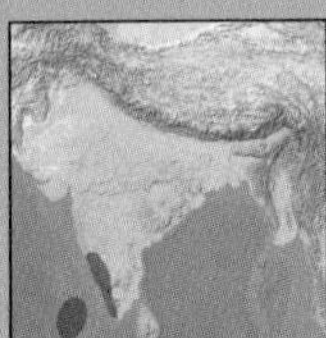

Size 51 cm

Voice Mostly silent in winter

Range Widespread winter visitor but status uncertain

Habitat Open wooded or cultivated areas

Large buzzard with broad, rounded wings, and short neck and tail. Plumage highly variable, ranging from darkish-brown to russet to pale buff. Upperparts darker; wing-tip and trailing edge of wing also darker than rest of wing feathers. Barred tail and flight feathers; streaked throat and breast. Wings held in shallow V-shape and tail fanned when gliding and soaring.

Steppe Buzzard

HIMALAYAN BUZZARD

Buteo b burmanicus Accipitridae

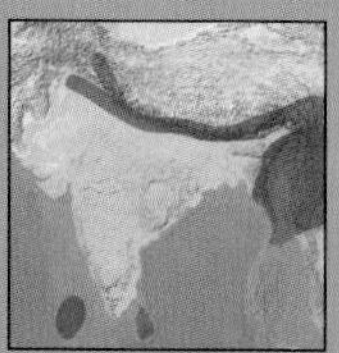

Size 51-57 cm

Voice Call a loud *peee…ooo* similar to that of *buteo buteo* but clearer, higher-pitched

Range Resident and winter visitor to the Himalayas. Winter visitor to NE India

Habitat Mountains; cultivated slopes

Recently split from Common to which it is very similar. Resident but numbers augmented in winter.

LONG-LEGGED BUZZARD

Buteo rufinus Accipitridae

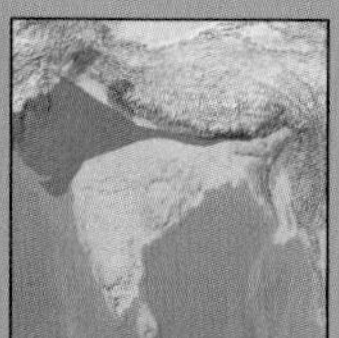

Size 43-58 cm

Voice Rather quiet

Range Breeds in a few site N India. Winters commonly in NW India, particularly Pakistan. Rare elsewhere

Habitat Open, uncultivated areas with high bushes, trees, cliffs or hillocks favoured nesting areas

Largest of buteo species with many colour morphs from pale white to dark brown but with clear orangish tint to plumage. Tail reddish and head pale. Underwings whitish; rump mostly dark brown. Hunts mostly small and medium-sized mammals. Often seen sitting on electricity posts, pylons and other vantage points.

rufous morph

UPLAND BUZZARD

Buteo hemilasius Accipitridae

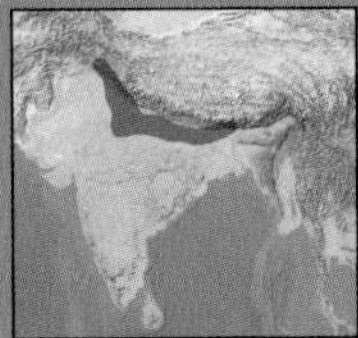

Size 70 cm

Voice Call a nasal *pee…ou*

Range Scarce, probably breeding resident of N mountains, but status unclear

Habitat Open, often rocky country, frequently soaring

Very large buzzard with pale head, and broad, brown moustachial streak. White edge to head, culminating in white-patch on nape. White chin and brown throat. Upperparts light brown edged pale rufous; white spotting on uppertail-coverts; brown tail with two or three bars towards tip; black primaries. Underparts whitish, washed rufous; rusty-red underwing-coverts; upper breast, flanks blotched brown; brown thighs have pale bars. Greenish-yellow cere; yellowish-grey legs and feet. Feeds mainly on rodents.

GREATER SPOTTED EAGLE

Aquila clanga Accipitridae

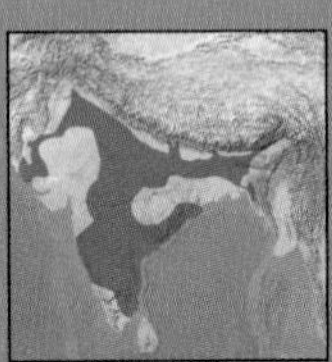

Size 62-74 cm

Voice Call a loud, shrill *kaek… kaek…* often from perch

Range Globally threatened. Breeds in parts of NW India; spreads south in winter

Habitat Tree-covered areas in vicinity of water

fulvescens

Large eagle with massive wing span. Adult almost entirely blackish except for some white in wings and base of tail. Immature has broad white bars on wings and white rump. Huge wings hold out straight from body when soaring. Seen mostly in open country, near freshwater. Often perches on low trees. Regularly seen on carcass; impressive master of the air.

BLACK EAGLE

Ictinaetus malayensis Accipitridae

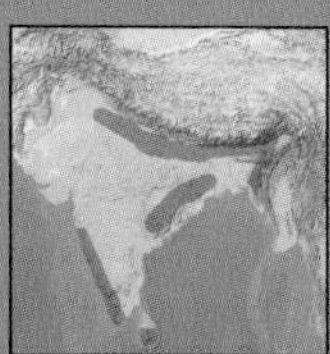

Size 69-81 cm

Voice Rather quiet. Call a loud *kee… kee…kee* when courting

Range Local breeding resident to N hills from E Punjab to Myanmar border, Bangladesh, and hills of Eastern and Western Ghats, Sri Lanka

Habitat Hills; mangrove forests

Almost entirely black eagle with yellow cere and yellow feet. Brown eyes; yellow-grey beak tipped black; white-patches at base of primary feathers; extended primary feathers; long wings reach tail-tip at rest. Wings held in shallow V-shape with long upturned fingers when gliding. Juvenile has dark brown crown, nape, back, and wings, speckled buff-yellow; tail barred with grey; heavily streaked underparts. Normally seen soaring alone, or in pairs over canopy.

INDIAN SPOTTED EAGLE

Aquila hastata Accipitridae

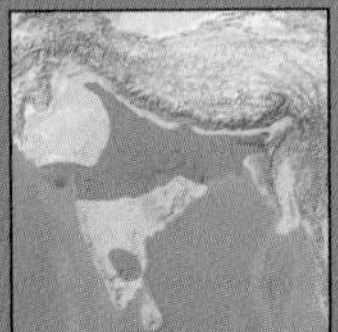

Size 59–67 cm

Voice Very high-pitched cackling call

Range N subcontinent; largely unrecorded in Pakistan

Habitat Wooded areas interspersed with cultivation in lowlands. Globally threatened

Medium-sized eagle with short, broad wings and short tail. Adult overall brown. Broad head with wide mouth. Flesh gape extending to middle of eye. Upperparts medium-brown; uppertail-coverts light brown barred white; large creamy spots on median coverts. Wings angled down at shoulder. In flight, shows rounder wings, lighter and slimmer than Greater Spotted. Seizes prey from ground whilst quartering over areas within, or near forests.

TAWNY EAGLE

Aquila rapax Accipitridae

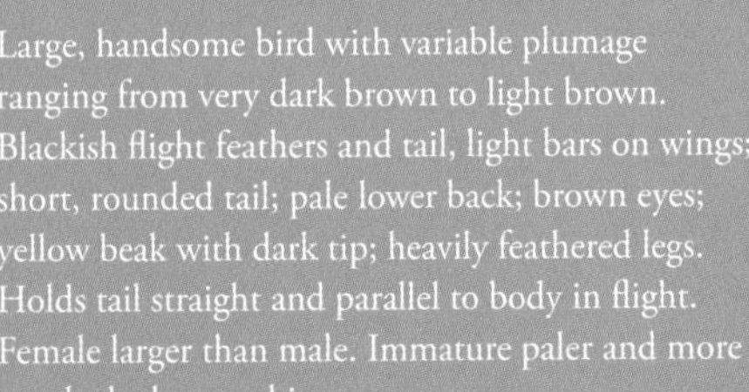

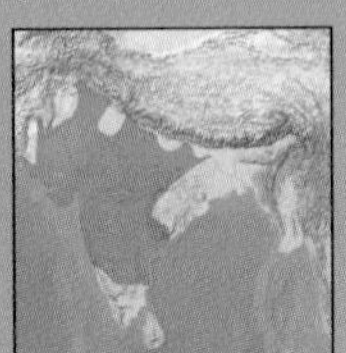

Size 70 cm

Voice Loud crackling notes; high-pitched call

Range Sporadically over parts of the country; *nipalensis* is a winter visitor

Habitat Open country; vicinities of villages; towns and cultivation

Large, handsome bird with variable plumage ranging from very dark brown to light brown. Blackish flight feathers and tail, light bars on wings; short, rounded tail; pale lower back; brown eyes; yellow beak with dark tip; heavily feathered legs. Holds tail straight and parallel to body in flight. Female larger than male. Immature paler and more streaked, almost white.

juvenile

STEPPE EAGLE

Aquila nipalensis Accipitridae

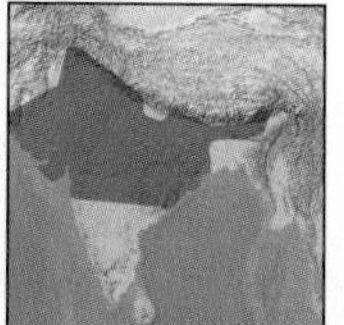

Size 80 cm

Voice Usually silent

Range Fairly common winter visitor

Habitat Lightly wooded and open country. Also villages and towns

juvenile

Adult overall dark brown, with well-defined bars on flight and tail feathers; pale-tipped secondaries; reddish-brown patch on nape of neck; long, wide gape; small head; pale throat; dark iris; yellow legs. Juvenile resembles adult, but paler brown, with characteristic broad white band running along underside of wing.

EASTERN IMPERIAL EAGLE

Aquila heliaca Accipitridae

juvenile

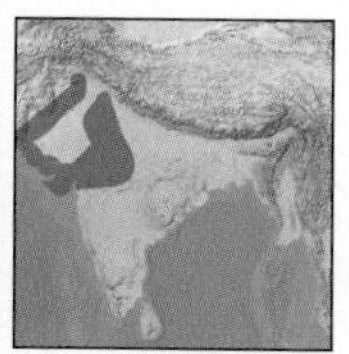

Size 85 cm

Voice Usually silent. Gruff barking occasionally

Range Globally threatened, scarce winter visitor mainly to NW India. Very rare elsewhere

Habitat Wetlands; other open country

Entirely brown eagle with light gold crown and neck sides. Dark grey tail with subterminal band tipped white; white-patch on shoulder; wing-coverts also edged white. Pale, rusty-cream undertail; yellow eyes and feet; grey beak with black tip. Long tail; large head and large feet. Juvenile light brown with dark streaked head, breast, scapulars and wings; wing-coverts tipped white; buff underparts. Spends much time in high soaring or sitting on ground or bare trees.

GOLDEN EAGLE

Aquila chrysaetos Accipitridae

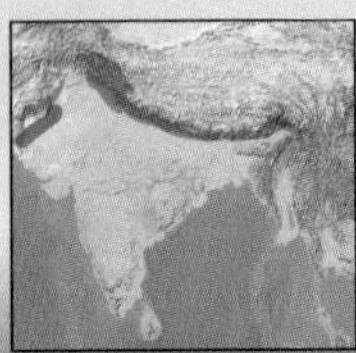

Size 90 cm

Voice Usually silent

Range Scarce breeding resident of N mountains. Rarely wandering to plains in winter

Habitat Mountains above treeline and near steep cliffs; open country in plains

juv

Huge bird of prey with very long wings and long tail. Almost entirely dark brown with massive bright yellow talons. Golden or reddish-brown head, nape and neck; dark-tipped tail; protruding head and neck; legs, densely feathered. Flies in V-shape with wings lifted. Solitary, or in pairs. Captures prey on or near ground, locating it by soaring, flying low over ground, or hunting from perch.

BONELLI'S EAGLE

Aquila fasciata Accipitridae

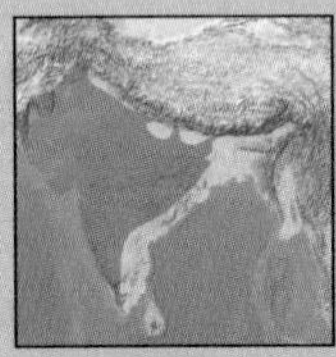

Size 70 cm

Voice Call a shrill scream of 3- to 6 notes

Range All over India, sporadically from about 2,400 m in the Himalayas

Habitat Forests

juvenile

♀

Large brown-and-white eagle with short, rounded wings and long tail. Dark brown back and wings; white belly and underparts mottled brown; white trailing edge to wing; black terminal band; grey-patch at carpal joint; long, feathered legs; yellow-orange eyes; yellow feet and cere. Juvenile has pale chestnut underside and hazel eyes.

BOOTED EAGLE

Hieraaetus pennatus Accipitridae

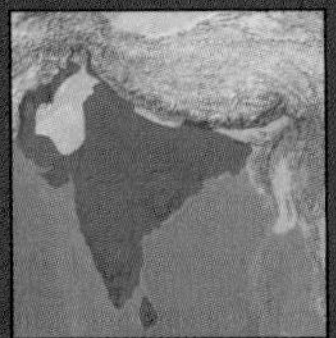

Size 52 cm

Voice Call a loud scream of several notes

Range Breeds in the Himalayas

Habitat Open forests; scrubs

pale morph

dark morph

Has two distinct colour phases. In lighter phase, head paler as uppertail and upperwing-coverts. Buffy white wing linings, underbody and tail with blackish flight feathers distinctive. In darker phase, chocolate-brown below. Pale-banded tail makes it easily identifiable in flight. Often seen alone, or sometimes in pairs hunting in concert. Often roosts together at night.

pale morph

RUFOUS-BELLIED EAGLE

Lophotriorchis kienerii Accipitridae

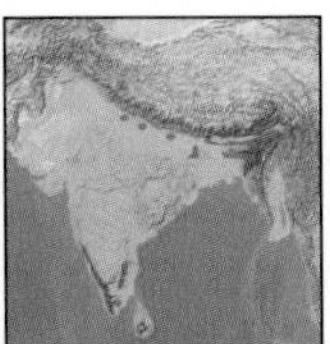

Size 60 cm

Voice Normally silent, but has plaintive scream when breeding

Range Rare breeding resident: Western Ghats, Sri Lanka, Nepal, Bangladesh, NE India and the Himalayan foothills

Habitat Humid forests

Medium-sized raptor with black hood and short crest. Black upperparts; white to rufous throat and chest; rufous belly and legs streaked black; brown, square tail; undertail barred black-and-white; barred wings; white base to primary feathers; red-brown eyes; yellow cere and feet; feathered legs. Juvenile has dark brown upperparts, brown crown and nape, and two black eye patches; white underparts and grey tail with dark, narrow barring and white tip. Normally seen soaring over canopy.

CRESTED HAWK EAGLE

Nisaetus cirrhatus Accipitridae

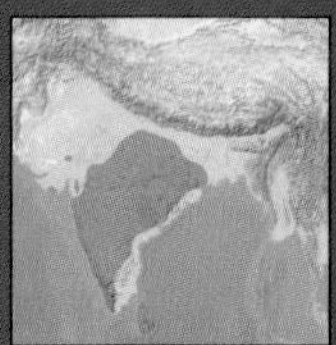

Size 70 cm

Voice Call a loud, screaming cry, usually long-drawn

Range S Gujarat and Rajasthan; peninsular India; NE India

Habitat Semi-evergreen and deciduous forests; clearings

Large, slender, crested forest eagle. Brown upperparts and white underparts longitudinally streaked brown; prominent occipital crest; streaked whitish body, broad wings and long, rounded tail distinctive in flight. Sexes alike, but female larger. Solitary, occasionally pair circles high over forests, especially when breeding; surveys for prey from high, leafy branches near forest clearings.

CHANGEABLE HAWK EAGLE

Nisaetus c limnaeetus Accipitridae

Size 70 cm

Voice Similar to Crested, but slower

Range The Himalayan foothills; NE India, Andaman Islands and Bangladesh

Habitat Well-wooded country

Recently split from Crested Hawk to which it is very similar. Mostly distinguished by its prominent crest. Also, lacks dark morph. Tail more heavily barred. Usually solitary, or in pairs; soars infrequently.

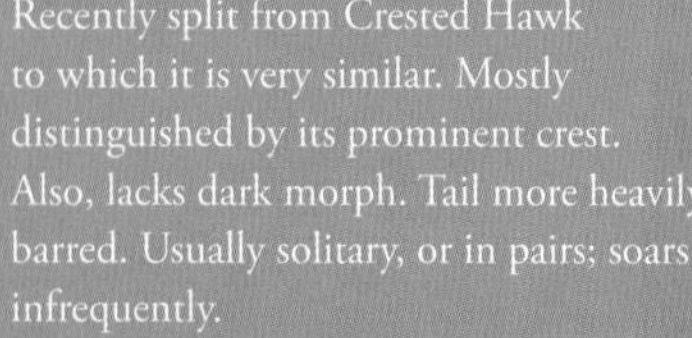

MOUNTAIN HAWK EAGLE

Nisaetus nipalensis Accipitridae

Size 72 cm

Voice Call a high whistling *peeo... peeo* during breeding season

Range Locally common breeding resident: N mountains, Western Ghats and Sri Lanka

Habitat Upland forests

Large brown-and-white raptor with brown upperparts, rufous head and black, pale-tipped crest. Belly and underwing-coverts barred dark brown; tail has three bands and grey-brown from above and white below. Juvenile dark brown with buff to tawny underparts, barred tail and white legs. Broad wings with curved trailing edge, held in shallow V-shape in flight.

juvenile

GREAT INDIAN BUSTARD

Ardeotis nigriceps Otididae

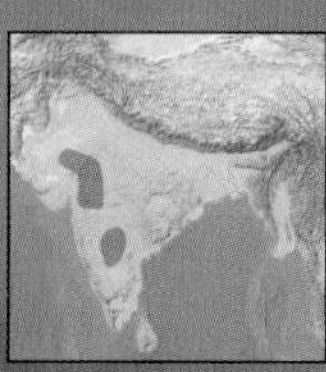

Size Male 120 cm; Female 92 cm

Voice Call a loud *whonk*... often audible for over a mile

Range Resident and local migrant; distant areas of Rajasthan, Gujarat, Maharashtra, Karnataka; numbers and erstwhile range much reduced today

Habitat Open grasslands and scrubs; semi-desert

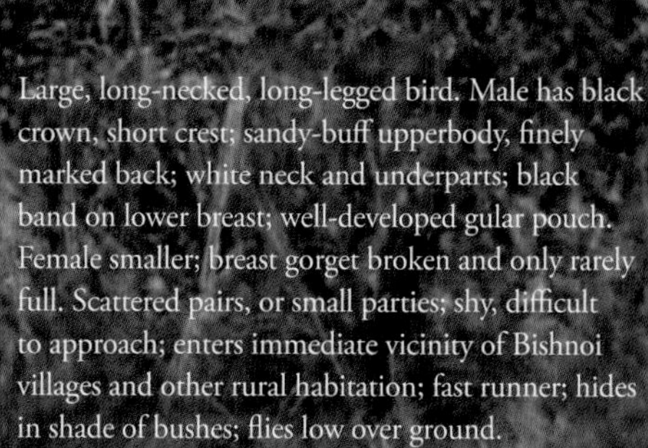

Large, long-necked, long-legged bird. Male has black crown, short crest; sandy-buff upperbody, finely marked back; white neck and underparts; black band on lower breast; well-developed gular pouch. Female smaller; breast gorget broken and only rarely full. Scattered pairs, or small parties; shy, difficult to approach; enters immediate vicinity of Bishnoi villages and other rural habitation; fast runner; hides in shade of bushes; flies low over ground.

BENGAL FLORICAN

Houbaropsis bengalensis Otididae

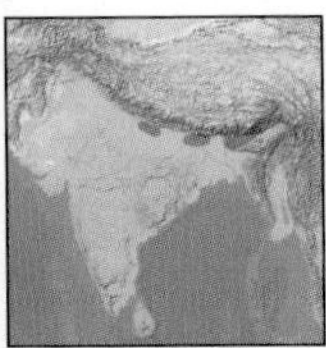

Size 66 cm

Voice Clicking sound in display and when flushed

Range Globally threatened; breeding resident, now restricted to few sites in the Terai and Assam

Habitat Wet grasslands

Very reclusive bird known for courtship display where male shows off black-and-white plumage in aerial displays. Overall black with white wings conspicuous in flight. Long, black feathers on head and neck, upright during display. Female larger than male with brownish plumage; white wing patch visible in flight. Young birds have pale brown head and neck, breast and white belly.

MACQUEEN'S BUSTARD

Chlamydotis macqueenii Otididae

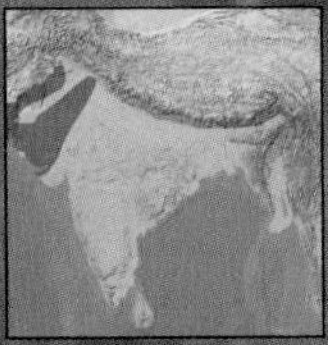

Size 65 cm

Voice Nothing recorded

Range Now, mainly a rare winter visitor to semi-desert areas of Pakistan and NW India. Also occurs in W and C Asia

Habitat Semi-desert and associated cultivation, particularly mustard fields

Overall brown bustard with prominent black stripe on neck sides. Long wings show black and brown on flight feathers, visible in flight. Sexes similar but female smaller and greyer above, smaller with indistinct crest. Macqueen slightly larger and paler than Houbara. Female has less black on neck; also less white in wings. Raises white feathers of head and throat, withdraws head in flamboyant courtship display. Extremely wary; lurks under low cover with neck outstretched.

LESSER FLORICAN

Sypheotides indicus Otididae

Size 45 cm

Voice Call a rattling click in display; whistles when flushed

Range Globally threatened endemic breeding visitor to few sites in NC India. Reportedly moves to SE India after breeding, but rarely recorded there

Habitat Dry, scrubby grasslands; tall crops

Small, slender bustard, with long, curved neck and long, thin legs. Adult male has distinct, black head plumes with spatulate tips. Black head, neck and belly; brown back and wing feathers brown edged black; whitish collar and white coverts. Female larger and more sandy brown with black streaks on head, neck and underparts. Juvenile similar to female. Jumps suddenly out of grass, into air in courtship display. Solitary, or in pairs. Lays eggs on ground in small patch of grass. Omnivorous, eats both invertebrates as well as plant shoots.

SLATY-LEGGED CRAKE

Rallina eurizonoides Rallidae

Size 25 cm

Voice Noisy mix of double-notes

Range All over India

Habitat Well-watered areas

Rich brown bird with short, rounded wings. Rufous head and breast, reddish-brown iris, bold, strong black-and-white barring on flanks, underparts and undertail; small white throat patch, yellowish or greyish bill, greenish-grey legs. Sexes similar. Walks through leaf litter, foraging on berries, insects, worms and molluscs.

ANDAMAN CRAKE

Rallina canningi Rallidae

Size 34 cm

Voice Deep croak. Alarm call a sharp *click*

Range Andaman Islands

Habitat Forests

Adult bird has glossy chestnut plumage, with strongly barred underparts and unbarred undertail-coverts; pale barring on outer primaries and greater and medium coverts; bright green bill; long and fluffy tail; olive-green legs and feet.

SPOTTED CRAKE

Porzana porzana Rallidae

Size 22 cm

Voice Silent in winter

Range Winter visitor over most of the country

Habitat Reed-covered jheels, vegetation in and around marshes

Adult brown above, with rufescent wash, streaked black; grey supercilium, sides of head and neck; whitish chin, throat; greyish breast spotted white; white barring on grey-brown flanks. Sexes alike. Solitary, or in pairs; crepuscular.

SLATY-BREASTED RAIL

Gallirallus striatus Rallidae

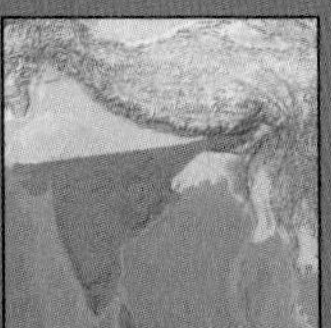

Size 27 cm

Voice Call a harsh, repeated *gelek*

Range Scarce but overlooked resident throughout peninsula, NE India, Bangladesh and Sri Lanka. Also occurs in China and SE Asia

Habitat Well-vegetated freshwater marshes and adjacent scrubs

Medium-sized bird with longish, straight bill. Chestnut forehead, hindneck and neck sides; rest of upperparts olive-brown, spotted and barred white; blackish underparts, barred white; white chin and throat; grey breast; red iris. Female has duller head and neck; paler upperparts and whitish belly. Extremely shy and somewhat crepuscular. Feeds on insects and seeds. Nests well-hidden on ground.

WATER RAIL

Rallus aquaticus Rallidae

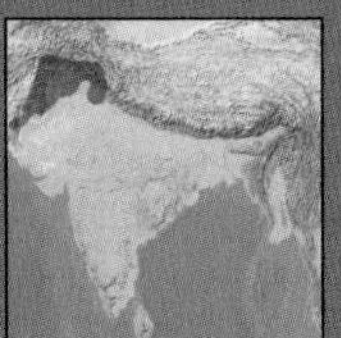

Size 25-28

Voice Shrill squeal

Range Breeds in Kashmir

Habitat Marshes; reed beds; paddy cultivation; ponds

Similar to Brown-cheeked Rail, from which it has recently been split.

BROWN-CHEEKED RAIL

Rallus indicus Rallidae

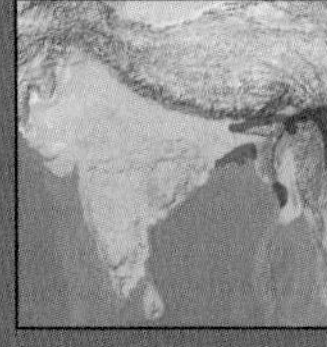

Adult has brown upperparts streaked with black; dirty-white throat and chin with grey breast and belly barred black-and-white. Long red bill diagnostic. Young has distinct white barring on wings. Mostly solitary though mates usually nearby; unobtrusive, secretive and cautious.

BROWN CRAKE

Amaurornis akool Rallidae

Size 28 cm

Voice Mostly silent, but a plaintive note and long-drawn, vibrating whistle

Range Local migrant; south from Kashmir lowlands down through the peninsula, at least to Karnataka and Odisha

Habitat Reed-covered marshes; irrigation channels; dense growth on jheels

Overall olive-brown crake with white chin and throat that fade into ash-grey underparts; more brown on breast, flanks and abdomen. Sexes alike, but female slightly smaller. Solitary, or in pairs; mostly crepuscular; extremely elusive and secretive; feeds in early mornings and late evenings on edges of jheels, flicking stub tail and generally moving very suspiciously.

BLACK-TAILED CRAKE

Porzana bicolor Rallidae

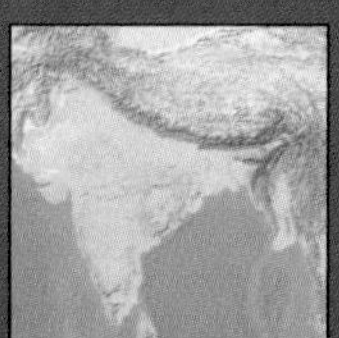

Size 25 cm

Voice Call a low, hoarse *hraaa…hraaa…waak…waak; keck…kik;* then an extended trilling

Range Isolated pockets in Nepal, Bhutan, Assam and Arunachal Pradesh. Often found in high altitudes

Habitat Forests and dense undergrowth surrounding paddy fields; marshy streams; pools in or near forests, secondary growth

Small, red-legged, jungle-dwelling crake with sooty-grey head, neck and underparts, whitish chin, rufous-chestnut mantle and wings; charcoal-black rump, vent, tail and undertail-coverts. Pale green bill, sometimes with red base. Red iris. Generally shy.

RUDDY-BREASTED CRAKE

Porzana fusca Rallidae

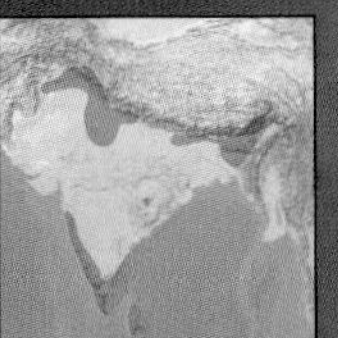

Size 22 cm

Voice Rather quiet, but makes soft crake calls, sometimes accelerated into trill

Range Scarce breeding resident, local migrant. Most often recorded from N Pakistan, Nepal, Bangladesh, Sri Lanka and Western Ghats

Habitat Secretive; crepuscular and thus easily overlooked. Well-vegetated marshes; jheels and riverbanks

Medium to small, uniformly reddish-brown crake. Upperparts brown; deep chestnut forehead, forecrown and sides of head; pale throat, deep red underparts and white-barred black undertail-coverts; bright pink legs and feet. Sexes similar, but female paler. Juvenile more brown with faint white barring on underparts.

BAILLON'S CRAKE

Porzana pusilla Rallidae

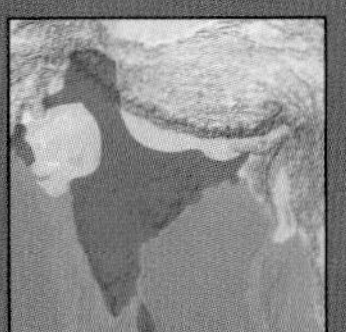

Size 19 cm

Voice Call a frog-like or grasshopper-like dry rattling *trrr…, trrr.* Unlikely to be heard unless breeding

Range Common breeding visitor to Kashmir. Scarce passage migrant and winter visitor throughout the region

Habitat Marshes; reedy jheel edges; small ponds; wet paddy. Much overlooked

Very small crake with streaked black-and-white upperparts. Pale grey underparts that stretch from breast to around eyes. Pale green bill and legs. Sexes similar in appearance, but female often has reddish-brown streak over ear and paler grey upperparts; stout, well-muscled legs with three forward-facing toes and one hind toe. Juvenile has mottled-white breast and more barred. Walks with bobbing head and flicking tail.

WHITE-BREASTED WATERHEN

Amaurornis phoenicurus Rallidae

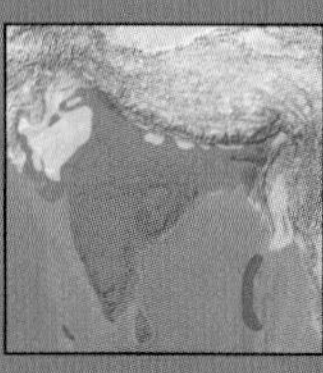

Size 32 cm

Voice Very noisy when breeding during rains, series of loud croaks and chuckles, the commonest being a harsh *krr…khwakk…*. Often calls through the night; silent during dry season

Range South from the Himalayan foothills

Habitat Reed-covered marshes; ponds; tanks; monsoon cultivation; streams

midnicobarica

juvenile

Large, distinctive-looking bird with white forehead and sides of head and dark slaty-grey upperparts. Underparts silky white; slaty-grey sides of breast and flanks; rufous on vent and undertail-coverts; stump-like tail. Sexes alike. Solitary, or in small groups; often around village ponds and tanks. Walks with long strides; climbs trees easily, especially when breeding.

WATERCOCK

Gallicrex cinerea Rallidae

♀

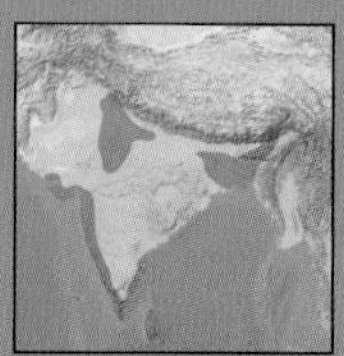

Size 36 cm

Voice Booming call when breeding

Range Scarce local migrant throughout lowlands, breeding mainly in NE India, Bangladesh and Sri Lanka. Also occurs in E and SE Asia

Habitat Extensive reed beds, marshes and wet paddy. Also tidal estuaries when migrating.

Mainly blue-black bird; conical red bill an extended 'frontal shield'; green legs. Female smaller with dark brown upperparts and paler below with streaked and barred plumage; yellow bill and green legs. Probes mud for insects, small fish and seeds, but also picks food by sight. Secretive, but sometimes seen in the open. Crepuscular; secretive, sometimes seen in flight.

COMMON COOT

Fulica atra Rallidae

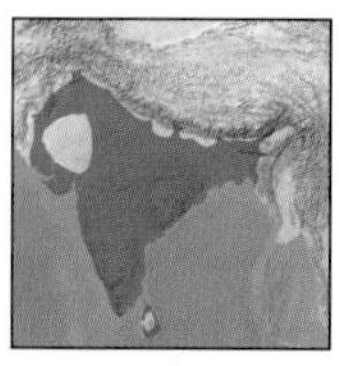

Size 40 cm

Voice Quite noisy. Calls include abrupt *towk*, sharper *pseek*; various conversational chucklings

Range Common winter visitor throughout lowlands but rather sporadic breeder

Habitat Large swimming flocks on open water of jheels and rivers, often mixing with duck. Walks on floating vegetation

Roundish bird with greyish body, black head, neck and white bill. Has distinct white 'frontal shield'; almost no tail; white-tipped secondary flight feathers; pale grey underwing; pale pinkish-white bill; deep red eyes. Greenish-yellow legs with grey, lobed feet. Breeding male shows broader white shield than female. Juvenile has whitish head sides, breast and foreneck; brownish-grey body; no white frontal shield. Gregarious in non-breeding season when it forms large flocks. Weak and reluctant flier.

COMMON MOORHEN

Gallinula chloropus Rallidae

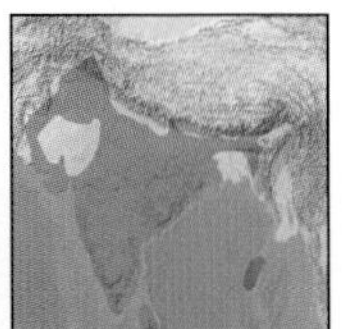

Size 32 cm

Voice Extremely vocal; capable of bizarre, distinctive sounds, including a variety of clucks and chattering calls

Range All over India, upto about 2,400 m in the Himalayas; breeds commonly in Kashmir

Habitat Vegetation and reed-covered ponds; tanks; jheels

Medium-sized, striking looking water bird. Distinctive red shield; short, yellow bill; dark olive-brown upperparts; grey underparts; white centre of abdomen; bright yellowish-green legs; white trim on undertail. Sexes alike but female slightly larger. Juvenile has brown-grey crown, neck and back, paler and whitish throat and belly. In small feeding groups in marsh vegetation. Jerks head and tail while swimming.

juvenile

GREY-HEADED SWAMPHEN

Porphyrio poliocephalus Rallidae

Size 45 cm

Voice Noisy when breeding, a mix of cackling and hooting notes

Range Mostly resident throughout the subcontinent, upto about 1,500 m in Kashmir

Habitat Vegetation and reed-covered jheels; tanks

Large rail with dusky black upperparts, broad, dark blue collar, and dark blue to purple underparts. Strong, red bill and frontal shield; orange-red scaly legs and feet. Long legs and elongated toes trail behind body in flight. Strong flier, readily takes to wing when threatened. Flicks revealing white undertail. Proficient swimmer, but prefers to wander on edges of water, among reeds and on floating vegetation.

MASKED FINFOOT

Heliopais personatus Heliorithidae

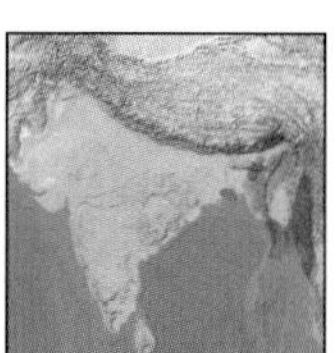

Size 56 cm

Voice Call a high-pitched bubbling sound, loud grunting quack

Range Rare resident. Assam and Bangladesh

Habitat Pools in dense forests and mangrove creeks. Globally threatened

Beige-brown bird with long neck; large yellow beak and lobed green feet. Black mask and eyebrow; white eye-ring; lateral cervical-stripe; grey neck; pale breast; rich brown back, wings and tail. Male has black chin while female has white chin. Breeding male has small yellow horn at base of bill. Immature similar to female, but has grey forehead and dull bill.

SIBERIAN CRANE

Grus leucogeranus Gruidae

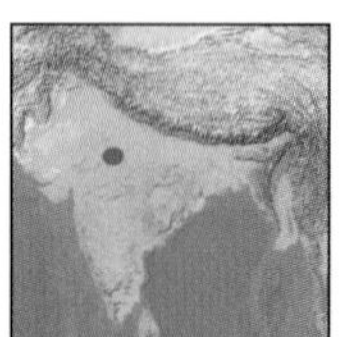

Size 140 cm

Voice Vocal; loud trumpeting calls; musical *koonk…koonk…*in flight. Flute-like calls unique amongst cranes

Range Was winter visitor to Bharatpur, Rajasthan. Not seen since 2002

Habitat Open marshes; jheels

Striking bird with snow-white plumage. Serrated bill; black in-flight feathers. Unique red-coloured mask covering forecrown, forehead, face and sides of head, ending at back of pale yellow eyes; reddish toes and legs. Lives in pairs or small flocks. Sexes alike, but female little larger. Juvenile has feathered mask and more buffy-cinnamon body. Nests in freshwater bogs and marshes.

DEMOISELLE CRANE

Grus virgo Gruidae

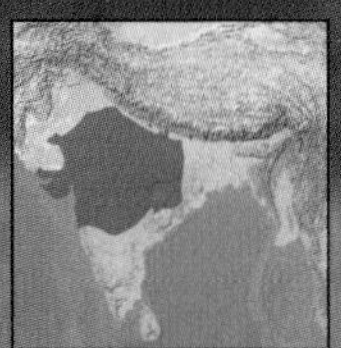

Size 95 cm

Voice Call a high-pitched, sonorous *kraak…kraak…*

Range Winter visitor; most common in NW India and over E Rajasthan, Gujarat and Madhya Pradesh, though sporadically over much of area

Habitat Winter crop fields; sandy riverbanks; ponds

Overall grey bird with black head and neck, prominent white ear tufts. Long black feathers of lower neck fall over breast; brownish-grey secondaries sickle-shaped and drooping over tail. Juvenile has grey head and much shorter drooping secondaries over tail than adult. Sexes alike. Huge flocks in winter, often many thousands. Feeds early mornings and early evenings in cultivation; rests during hot hours on marsh edges and sandbanks; flies en masse when disturbed.

juvenile

SARUS CRANE

Grus antigone Gruidae

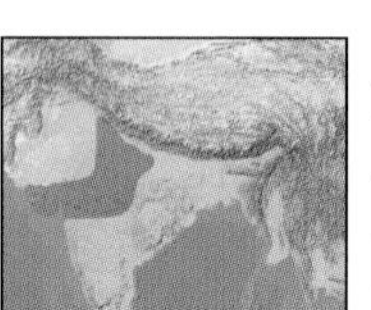

Size 165 cm

Voice Call includes a very loud, far-reaching trumpeting, often a duet between pair; elaborate dancing rituals

Range Most common in N and C India (E Rajasthan, Gujarat, N and C Madhya Pradesh, Gangetic Plain)

Habitat Marshes; jheels; well-watered cultivation; village ponds

Grey crane with naked red head and upper neck. Small pale grey ear patch on head sides; sparse black feathers on chin and upper neck; pale brown to orange eyes. Long, pointed, grey bill; pinkish-red legs. Sexes alike, but female slightly smaller than male. Juvenile brownish-grey, with rusty-brown on head. In pairs, family parties or flocks; also feeds along with other waterbirds; known to pair for life and usually well-protected in Northern and West-Central India, but habitat loss continues to be a grave threat; flies under 12 m off ground.

juvenile

COMMON CRANE

Grus grus Gruidae

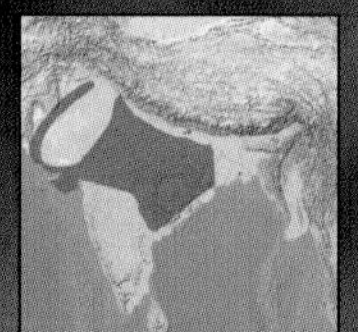

Size 140 cm

Voice Call a loud, strident trumpeting *krr…oohk…*; calls on ground and from high in sky; also other harsh, screeching notes

Range Winter visitor; commonest in NW India, progressively less towards the east, rarely straying south of S Maharashtra and N Andhra Pradesh

Habitat Cultivation of wheat, gram, groundnut; also riverbeds

Large, impressive crane with pale slaty-grey plumage; slight red on crown; black face, throat and white stripe on sides of head, neck; black flight-feathers and dark, drooping tail plumes diagnostic; bright red or reddish-brown eye. Sexes alike. Juvenile has yellowish-brown tips to feathers; lacks drooping wing feathers neck pattern; fully-feathered crown. Gregarious in winter; feeds in mornings and evenings in cultivation; rests during day; rather shy and suspicious, ever alert; slow, but strong flight.

BLACK-NECKED CRANE

Grus nigricollis Gruidae

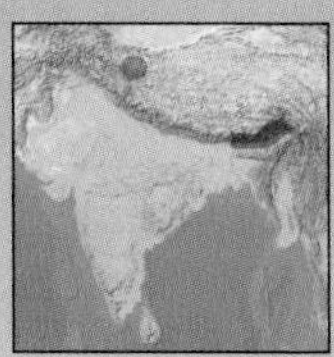

Size 150 cm

Voice Loud, trumpet-like call, higher-pitched than Sarus's

Range Breeds only in Ladakh within Indian limits; possibly in parts of Arunachal Pradesh

Habitat High-altitude marshes; lakesides; open cultivation

Ash-grey crane with black head, neck; dull-red lores, complete crown; small white-patch around eye; black wing-tips, drooping plumes; whitish underparts. Sexes alike. Female slightly smaller. In pairs or small flocks; upto 100 birds seen together in Bhutan, where much revered by locals. Barely three to five pairs breeding in Indian region (Ladakh). Dancing displays commence around March, flies high during afternoons, calling loudly.

juvenile

YELLOW-LEGGED BUTTONQUAIL

Turnix tanki Turnicidae

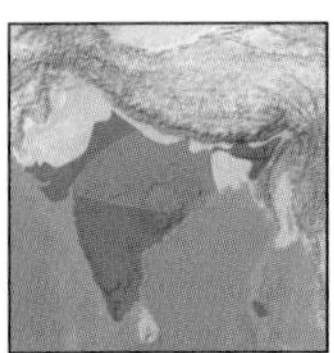

Size 15-16 cm

Voice Loud, drumming call

Range All over India, from about 1,200 m in the Himalayas

Habitat Damp grasslands; scrubs; cultivation

Grey-brown bird. Blackish crown has rufous and buff; pale stripe through centre of crown; white chin, throat; buffy underparts with dark spots on sides of breast; yellow legs and beak; beak reddish-brown above and chrome-yellow below. Female slightly larger than male.

BARRED BUTTONQUAIL

Turnix suscitator Turnicidae

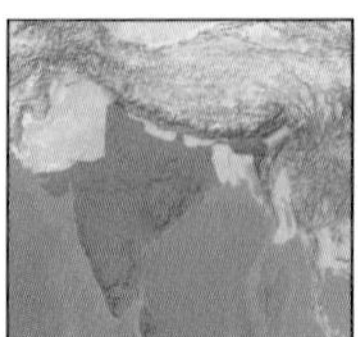

Size 15 cm

Voice Loud, drumming call of female during breeding

Range All over India, south of the Himalayas

Habitat Grass; scrubs

Distinctive white eye; dark brown crown; black specks on white sides of head; back speckled with white, black and brown. Pale buff on wing shoulders seen in flight diagnostic. Sexes alike. Female slightly larger and more brightly coloured.

♀

♀

SMALL BUTTONQUAIL

Turnix sylvaticus Turnicidae

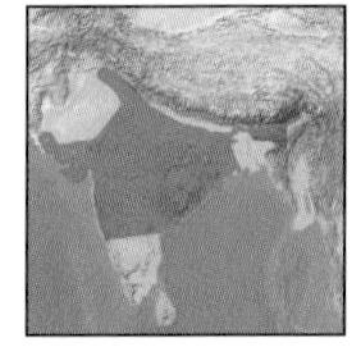

Size 13 cm

Voice Female has a far-carrying, low-pitched, intermittent hoot at dusk and dawn

Range Probably fairly common resident throughout lowlands, but much overlooked

Habitat Scrubby, dry grasslands

Small bird with round body, small head and short, pointed wings, small grey bill, yellowish legs and white iris. Mostly brown with broad buff feather edgings above; paler, speckled head with crown-stripe. Orangish-buff below with black spotting on flanks. Female slightly larger.

♀

♀

INDIAN THICK-KNEE

Burhinus o indicus Burhinidae

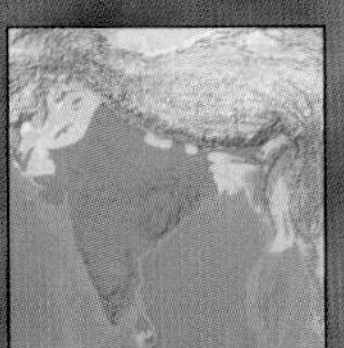

Size 41 cm

Voice Plaintive, curlew-like call at dusk; also sharp *pick…pick…* notes

Range Drier parts of the subcontinent, upto about 1,200 m in the outer Himalayas

Habitat Light, dry forests, scrubs, dry riverbanks; ravinous country; orchards; open *acacia* clad areas

Sandy-brown bird streaked darker; whitish underparts; thick head, long, bare, yellow legs and large goggle-eyes diagnostic; white wing patch in flight; black-tipped bill with yellow base. Sexes alike. Solitary, or in pairs; strictly a ground bird; crepuscular and nocturnal.

GREAT THICK-KNEE

Esacus recurvirostris Burhinidae

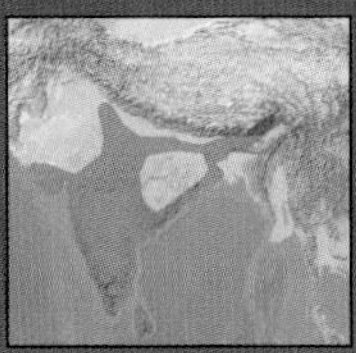

Size 50 cm

Voice Harsh call-note, somewhat whistle-like; wild, piping calls at night

Range Almost all over India, south of the Terai; uncommon in NE regions

Habitat Dry, open country; barren lands; riverbanks; rocky areas; islands; jheels

Sandy-grey bird with large head and large upturned, black and yellow beak; large goggle-eyes surrounded by white, two black bands on face; white below, washed grey on neck, breast; white in-flight feathers, visible at night. Sexes alike. Solitary, or in pairs on open barren land, riverbanks or rocks in mid-river; mostly crepuscular and partly nocturnal; spends day under strong sun resting; usually very difficult to spot; extremely wary.

BEACH THICK-KNEE

Esacus neglectus Burhinidae

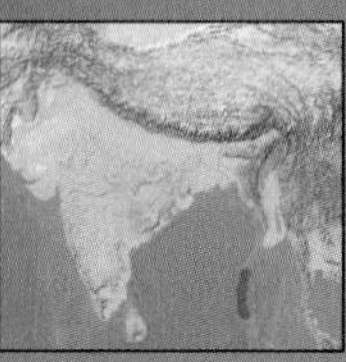

Size 49-54 cm

Voice Call a harsh, wailing *wee…loo…*; alarm call a *quip* or *peep*

Range Andaman Islands

Habitat Sandy and muddy shores; coral reefs

Large, distinctive shorebird with massive, thick, slightly upturned beak and large head. Head strikingly marked with white stripes across black face; mainly black forehead and lores; black on sides of crown and ear-coverts; white supercilium and throat. Grey-brown upperparts; paler grey-brown underparts and whitish belly. Long, broad wings with 'finger-like' edges. Juvenile has duller beak, eyes and legs; buff fringes on wing feathers. Mainly nocturnal.

EURASIAN OYSTERCATCHER

Haematopus ostralegus Charadriidae

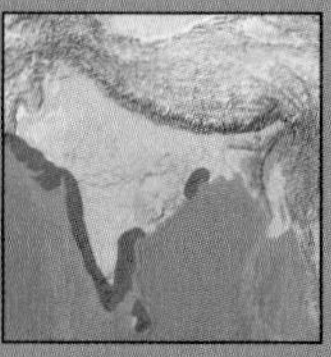

Size 42 cm

Voice Call a piping *kleeeep…* in flight; also a shrill whistle, often double-noted, uttered on ground as well as in flight

Range Winter visitor, especially to the coastal regions; most common on western seaboard

Habitat Rocky and sandy coastal areas

Large oystercatcher with distinct pied plumage. Black head, upperparts and breast; white underparts; long orange beak and pinkish legs distinctive. White on throat in winter. White rump and broad wing-bar conspicuous in flight. Juvenile more brown than adult. Sexes alike. Most common on sea coasts; frequently associates with other shorebirds; runs and probes mud; beak highly specialised for feeding on molluscs.

IBISBILL

Ibidorhyncha struthersii Charadriidae

Size 41 cm

Voice Call a high *ti… ti…, kluklu; wicka… tik…tik*

Range Rare breeding resident in N mountains; moves lower in winter

Habitat Pebble beds in fast-flowing rivers, blending well among stones

Grey wader with white belly, crimson, long downcurved bill, black face and black breast-band. Short orange legs. Upperparts sandy-grey with short white wing-bars. Head, neck and breast lavender-grey with white-edged black crown and face, white and black breast-bands. White below. Juvenile has grey bill and pale face. Usually solitary, or in small groups. Wary, but loyal to favoured spots. Bobs when alarmed. Feeds on invertebrates by probing and turning over stones.

CRAB PLOVER

Dromas ardeola Glareolidae

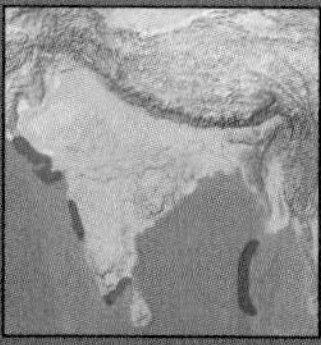

Size 41 cm

Voice Call a goose-like honking *qurk…qurk…qurk*

Range Very local winter visitor to most coasts

Habitat Sandy coasts; reefs

Distinctly-patterned, large, ungainly wader. Overall black-and-white with long, bluish legs; heavy, straight black bill; large, white head with black-edged eye; short, grey tail. Juvenile more uniform grey-brown. Feeds in plover-like manner, scattered over flats or among exposed reefs, mainly on crabs but also mudskippers. Nests in deep burrows in sandbanks. Feeds at low tide. Often confiding.

BLACK-WINGED STILT

Himantopus himantopus Charadriidae

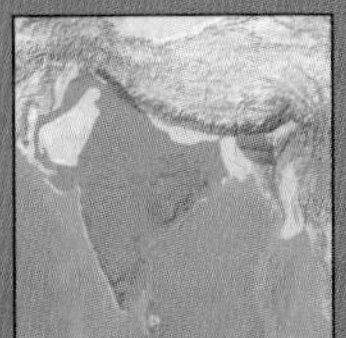

Size 35 cm

Voice Calls include shrill notes in flight, very tern-like. Noisy when breeding

Range Resident and local migrant all over India, south from about 1,800 m in W Himalayas

Habitat Marshes; salt pans; tidal creeks; village ponds; also riversides

Characterised by long, red legs and black-and-white plumage. Jet-black mantle has greenish iridescence; rest of plumage glossy white. Underparts white, sometimes with pale pinkish wash on breast. Pointed wings. Female dark brown with black spots on head; duller overall in winter. Gregarious; seen in large numbers, often along with other waders in wetlands; long legs enable to enter relatively deep water; clumsy walk; submerges head when feeding.

♀

juvenile

NORTHERN LAPWING

Vanellus vanellus Charadriidae

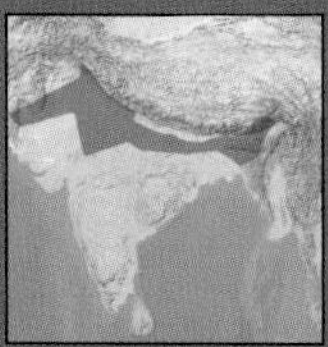

Size 31 cm

Voice Characteristic shrill call has given rise to the imitative local name *peewit*

Range Rather scarce winter visitor mainly to N lowlands

Habitat Wet grasslands; jheels; river margins; fallow

Striking black-and-white wader with black wispy crest, and black crown, face and cheek-stripe. Glossy upperparts with purplish-green iridescence. Orange undertail-coverts; black breast; pinkish legs and short dark bill. Rounded wings have white tips and white underwing-coverts. White tail has black tips. Sexes similar but female has white-patches in black areas. Juvenile similar to adult but scalier with shorter crest. Rarely mixes with other waders. Usually appears in parties, feeds by running and stopping to pick up surface invertebrates. Relaxed, low, flapping flight.

PIED AVOCET

Recurvirostra avosetta Charadriidae

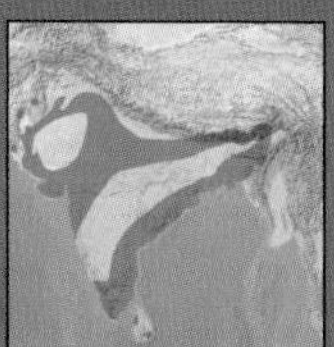

Size 45 cm

Voice Call a loud, somewhat fluty *klooeet* or *kloeep*, mostly on wing; also some harsh, screaming notes

Range Breeds in Kutch, N Balochistan; winter visitor, sporadically over most parts of the country; most common in NW regions

Habitat Freshwater marshes; coastal tidal areas; creeks

Long-legged, black-and-white wader with slender upcurved beak, long bluish-black, long legs extend much beyond tail in flight. Black head, upper neck and inner scapulars; dark brown greater coverts; rest of plumage pure white. Sexes alike. Usually gregarious, frequently enters shallow water; characteristic sideways movement of head when feeding with head bent low as upcurved beak sweeps along bottom mud; also swims and upends. Nests in colonies on sandbanks.

YELLOW-WATTLED LAPWING

Vanellus malabaricus Charadriidae

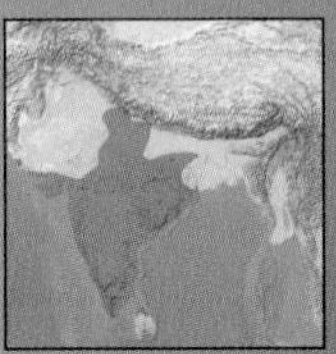

Size 27 cm

Voice Quiet. Calls include short, plaintive notes; quick-repeated notes when nest site intruded upon

Range From NW India, south through the area; does not occur in extreme NE India

Habitat Dry, open country

Medium to large wader with jet-black crown, bordered with white. Upperparts sandy-brown; black trailing edge to secondaries. In flight, white bar in black wings; black chin and throat; sandy-brown breast; white belly; black band on lower breast; white below; lemon-yellow wattles above and in front of eyes and yellow legs diagnostic. Sexes alike.

juvenile

GREY-HEADED LAPWING

Vanellus cinereus Charadriidae

Size 37 cm

Voice Rather quiet. Call a high-pitched *chee…e…it*, similar to that of Red-wattled

Range Local winter visitor to lowland Nepal, NE India and Bangladesh. Rare elsewhere in N India

Habitat Open, usually wet grasslands, jheel and river edges and fallow. Seeks out recently burnt, damp grasslands. Feeds in typical plover fashion

Large, sandy-brown wader, striking in flight with extensive black wing-tips, white secondaries and black-banded white tail. Pale grey head, neck and breast; black breast-band; black-tipped yellow bill; long spindly yellow legs; red iris and bare yellow lores. Sexes alike, but male slightly larger. Juvenile has less distinct breast-band and pale fringes to wing-coverts. Feeds in shallow water on insects, worms and molluscs.

SOCIABLE LAPWING

Vanellus gregarius Charadriidae

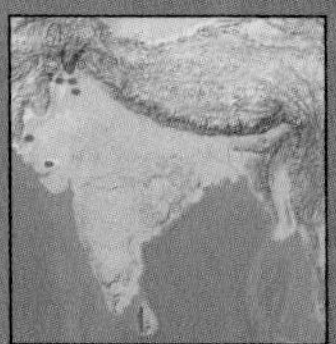

Size 27-30 cm

Voice Rather quiet

Range Winter visitor, now mainly to Pakistan, N and NW India

Habitat Dry fallow fields, stubbles and scrub desert.

Globally threatened

Distinctly marked plover with olive-brown upperparts, throat and breast. Olive-brown head with conspicuous white supercilium from forehead to neck; black crown and lores; fine black eye-line extending to rear of eye; white chin; black and chestnut belly; white vent and undertail-coverts; white rump and uppertail feathers; subterminal white crescent-shaped patch visible in flight. Black bill; dark brown eyes; blackish feet. Female duller than male. Juvenile similar to adult, but has heavily streaked face, crown and breast. Feeding behaviour similar to that of Red-wattled.

RED-WATTLED LAPWING

Vanellus indicus Charadriidae

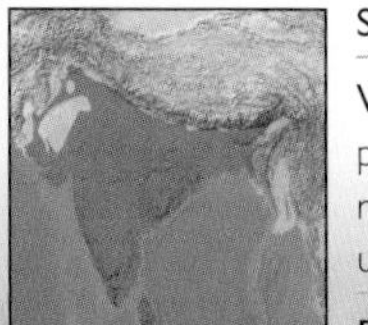

Size 35 cm

Voice Quiet. Calls include short, plaintive notes; quick-repeated notes when nest site intruded upon

Range From NW India, south through country; does not occur in extreme NE India

Habitat Dry, open country

atronuchalis

indicus

juvenile

Jet-black head, neck, breast; bronze-brown upperbody; white below, continuing to broad bands up the neck-sides towards eyes; fleshy crimson facial wattles diagnostic. Solitary or pairs when breeding; often large flocks in winter; moves on open ground, feeds during mornings and evenings; vigilant species, its loud cries heraldng any new activity in an area; feeds late into evening.

WHITE-TAILED LAPWING

Vanellus leucurus Charadriidae

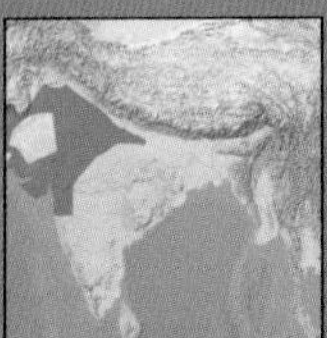

Size 28 cm

Voice Mostly silent in winter except for an occasional soft, double-noted whistle

Range Winter visitor, NW India; smaller in number east to Uttar Pradesh, parts of Bihar, C India

Habitat Open marshy areas; edges of lakes and jheels

Elegant looking bird with unusually long, bright yellow legs. Upperparts greyish-brown tinged with pink and streaked black; pinkish-brown head and back; long, dark bill; grey-white forehead, supercilium; ash-grey chin, throat, turning dark-grey on breast; rusty-red ring around eye. Sexes alike. Juvenile has mottled, grey-brown neck and breast, dark-centred feathers on upperparts. In small to medium-sized flocks, often with other waders.

RIVER LAPWING

Vanellus duvaucelii Charadriidae

Size 30 cm

Voice Rather like that of Red-wattled, only bit softer and less shrill; also sharp *deed…did…did…*

Range Breeds in parts of E and C India, including Odisha, Andhra Pradesh and E Madhya Pradesh; may disperse in winter

Habitat Stony riverbeds, sandbanks; sometimes collects around jheels in winter

Striking bird in flight with black primaries, white underwings and upperwing secondaries, and brown upperwing-coverts. Black crest, crown, face and central throat and greyish-white nape and neck sides. Underparts white; grey-brown breast-band; black belly patch; brown back; white rump, black tail. Sexes alike, but male slightly larger. Juvenile has brown tips to black head feathers, sandier brown back, pale fringes to upperpart and wing-covert feathers. Usually pairs in close vicinity; may collect into small parties during winter, sometimes with other waders.

PACIFIC GOLDEN PLOVER

Pluvialis fulva Charadriidae

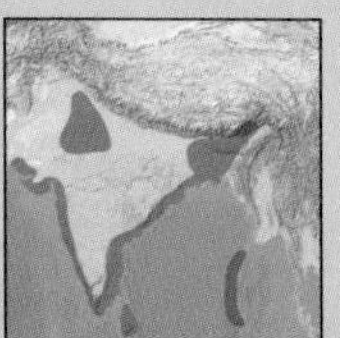

Size 25 cm

Voice Distinct *tu…leep* like a soft Spotted Redshank

Range Locally common winter visitor to all coasts and inland in Bangladesh and NE India. Most common in SE India and Bangaldesh. Scarce but regular passage migrant to inland and elsewhere

Habitat Coastal mudflats; salt pans and grasslands. Inland on marshes, jheels

breeding

non-breeding

Medium-sized to large shorebird with short neck and fairly long, grey legs. Overall golden-brown, speckled back. Dark head and ear-coverts. Non-breeding adult has buff head, neck and breast streaked darker. Breeding adult has black face, neck, breast and belly; creamy-white forehead and supercilium. Juvenile similar to non-breeding adult, but with light barring on chest sides, and flanks, has more distinct yellow edges and spots on feathers of crown, back and wings.

GREY PLOVER

Pluvialis squatarola Charadriidae

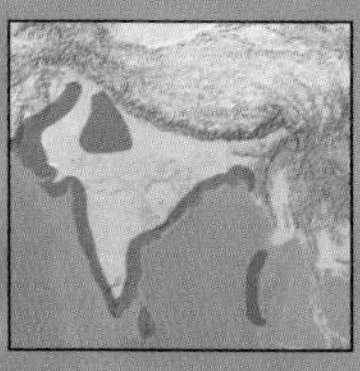

Size 30 cm

Voice Call a loud, penetrating *pee-ou ee*

Range Uncommon winter visitor to most coasts. Rare inland on passage

Habitat Coastal, open mudflats. Inland on open jheels, floods and rivers

Medium-sized, long-legged plover distinguished by large head and sturdy, black beak. Upperparts dark greyish-brown with white edges; distinctive black axillaries visible beneath wings in flight. Upperparts pale grey above with fine mottling; whitish forehead and eyebrow; strongly barred white tail. Whitish underparts. Breeding adult boldly marked black-and-white.

breeding

non-breeding

COMMON RINGED PLOVER

Charadrius hiaticula Charadriidae

Small, plump bird with sandy-brown upperparts, white underparts and short orange or orange-yellow legs and short orange bill with black tip. Broad black neck-band; black eye mask; black stripe across forehead. Juvenile duller; often incomplete grey-brown breast-band, dark bill and dull yellowish-grey legs. Known for 'broken wing display' where it feigns a broken wing to draw predators away from nesting chicks.

juvenile

Size 19 cm

Voice Call a rising disyllabic *poo…eep*

Range Rare winter visitor to Pakistan, Sri Lanka and Indian E coast

Habitat Muddy and sandy margins of lakes, rivers and the coast. Mixes with other waders

LONG-BILLED PLOVER

Charadrius placidus Charadriidae

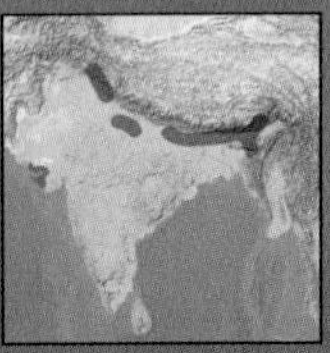

Size 22 cm

Voice Call a high *pee…wee*

Range Rare winter visitor: N rivers, Gujarat coast. Also occurs in China, N, SE and C Asia. Probably overlooked in winter

Habitat Shingle banks on rivers, muddy banks

Largest of the ringed-plovers, with long black bill, black breast-band, brown cheeks and yellowish-brown legs. Upperparts and crown muddy-brown; white forehead and rear eye-stripe; black forecrown bar and narrow breast-band, brownish cheeks. Displays thin white wing-bar and trailing edges and black subterminal tail-band in flight. Sexes alike. Solitary and unobtrusive.

LITTLE RINGED PLOVER

Charadrius dubius Charadriidae

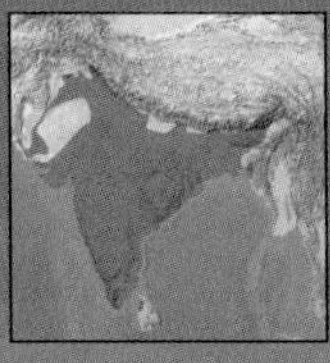

Size 16 cm

Voice Call a *few…few…* whistle, high-pitched but somewhat plaintive, uttered mostly on wing. Warning or attention-seeking call a loud *piuu*

Range Resident and local migrant; all over India

Habitat Shingle-covered riverbanks; tidal mudflats; estuaries; edges of lakes

non-breeding

breeding

Similar to Ringed, but has yellow eye-ring and almost non-existent wing-bars. Upperparts sandy-brown; white forehead; brown cap; black eye masks and breast, white neck-ring diagnostic; white chin and throat; white belly; short, dark bill; flesh-coloured legs. Sexes alike. Walks with fast steps, stopping suddenly, then runs a small stretch again. Tramples around on sand or mud to flush prey out of hiding places. Flies rapidly, low over ground; zigzag flight.

KENTISH PLOVER

Charadrius alexandrinus Charadriidae

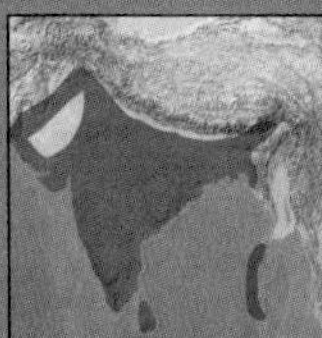

Size 17 cm

Voice Call a soft *dri…ip…*; alarm a *whi…it* on ground. In flight, an abrupt *tit…tit*

Range Fairly common winter visitor, local breeding resident to most coasts and throughout lowlands

Habitat Coastal sandflats, salt pans but inland on river sandbars, open lakeshores and drying floods

breeding

One of the smallest plovers, paler than Ringed with longer legs and thinner bill. Pale grey-brown upperparts, crown and cheeks; incomplete breast-band; white underparts. Breeding male has small white forehead, black forecrown-band, and slightly reddish hindcrown; black eye-band below slim white brow. Forages in a 'run-and-pause' rather than steady probing.

LESSER SAND PLOVER

Charadrius mongolus Charadriidae

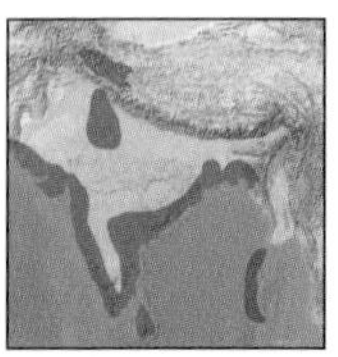

Size 19 cm

Voice Call a hard, repeated *tri… ip*. Also a trilling *trrp*. Flight call a hard trill

Range Common winter visitor to most coasts. Scarce on passage inland

Habitat Coastal sand and mudflats. River and jheel margins and flooded inland fields

Small wading shorebird with greyish-brown upperparts, white belly and throat, and black forehead. Dark partial breast-band; brown face with slight pale eyebrow-stripe. White underwing and upperwing have prominent white wing-bars. Breeding adult has rusty-red feathers on head and black cheeks; thin, black line separating reddish breast from white neck. Female duller. Breeding female has peachy breast-band. Juvenile lacks chestnut, only hint of rufous on head. Bill short and dark, and long and greenish-brown legs.

non-breeding

breeding

GREATER SAND PLOVER

Charadrius leschenaultii Charadriidae

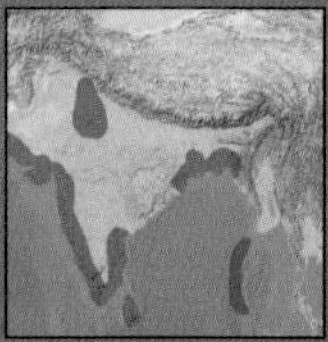

Size 22 cm

Voice Call a trilling *trrr…t*

Range Rather scarce winter visitor to most coasts. Commonest in NW India. Rare on inland

Habitat Behaviour as Lesser Sand, with which it often mixes

Relatively dull looking in non-breeding plumage. Dark lores, bill and upperwing; dusky ear-coverts; prominent white plumage on forehead, chin, throat and underparts, including underwing.
In breeding, crown and breast turn dull brick-red, and area around ear changes to black. Chin and throat remain white throughout the year, while nape and forehead greyish-brown colour all year round. Greenish legs distinguish it from Lesser.

breeding

GREATER PAINTED-SNIPE

Rostratula benghalensis Rostratulidaet

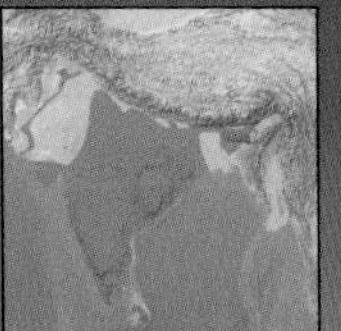

Size 25 cm

Voice Common call a long-drawn, mellow note that can be likened to the noise made by blowing into a bottle mouth

Range All over India, upto about 2,000 m in the Himalayas

Habitat Wet mud; marshes; areas where there is a mix of open water and heavy low cover

♀

♀

Medium-sized water bird, polyandrous. Breeding female metallic-olive above, marked buff and black; buff stripe down crown centre; white-patches around eyes; chestnut throat, breast and sides of neck; white below breast. Breeding male duller overall; lacks chestnut. Sexes difficult to distinguish when not in breeding plumage. Crepuscular and nocturnal. Solitary, or a few scattered birds; feeds in squelchy mud but also moves on drier ground; runs on landing.

EUROPEAN GOLDEN PLOVER

Pluvialis apricaria Charadriidae

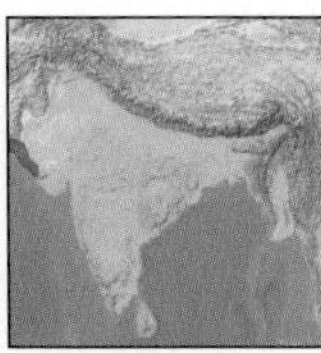

Size 27 cm

Voice Call a plaintive whistle *tu...lee*

Range Very rare winter visitor or passage migrant recorded from Pakistan and N India east to Assam

Habitat Damp grasslands; jheels; muddy coasts

Medium-sized plover with short bill, white supercilium and white belly. Breeding adult spotted gold and black on crown, back and wings; face and neck black with white border; black breast and dark rump; black legs. In winter, black replaced by buff and white. Stands upright and runs in short bursts. Very wary in breeding.

PHEASANT-TAILED JACANA

Hydrophasianus chirurgus Jacanidae

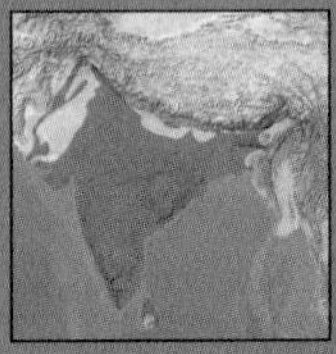

Size 30 cm

Voice Loud, mewing call when breeding, two birds often calling in duet

Range All over India, upto about 1,500 m in Kashmir; occasionally seen much higher

Habitat Ponds and jheels covered with floating vegetation

non-breeding

juvenile

Male in breeding plumage chocolate-brown and white; golden-yellow hindneck; dull brown-and-white when not breeding, also has blackish necklace and lacks long tail; very long toes diagnostic. Sexes alike. Solitary, or in pairs when breeding; small flocks in winter; purely aquatic, moves on vegetation-covered pond surfaces; unusually long toes enable walk on lightest of floating leaves; quite confiding on village ponds.

BRONZE-WINGED JACANA

Metopidius indicus Jacanidae

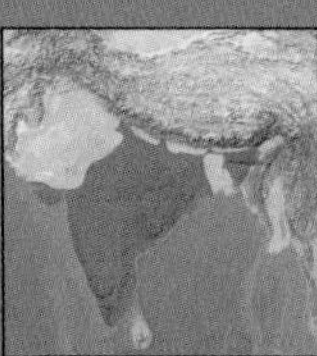

Size 30 cm

Voice Loud harsh notes; also a shrill piping call

Range Most of India, except some NW regions

Habitat Vegetation-covered jheels, ponds

Glossy black head, neck, breast; glistening bronze-green back, wings; broad white stripe over eyes; chestnut rump, tail; long legs with massive toes distinctive. Immature has rufous-brown crown; black terminal band to tail and whitish underbody, tinged rufous-buff around breast. Sexes alike. Female slightly larger. Small gatherings during winter and summer, keeps to leafy, floating growth on jheel beds, village tanks; wary, moves slowly and silently; flies low with long legs trailing.

juvenile

EURASIAN WOODCOCK

Scolopax rusticola Scolopacidae

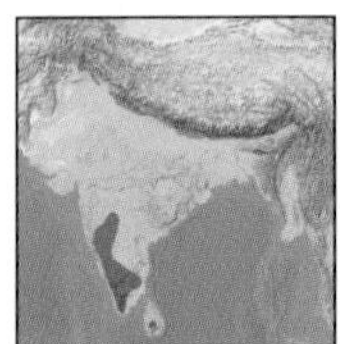

Size 33–38 cm

Voice Usually silent in winter

Range Breeds in the Himalayas

Habitat Dense forests

Medium to small wader with intricately patterned reddish-brown upperparts and buff underparts; long straight bill; head barred black; eyes set far back on head to give 360° vision; rounded wings; base of bill flesh-coloured with dark tip; legs vary from grey to pinkish. Probes ground for food with long bill. Crepuscular; rarely active during the day unless flushed.

JACK SNIPE

Lymnocryptes minimus Scolopacidae

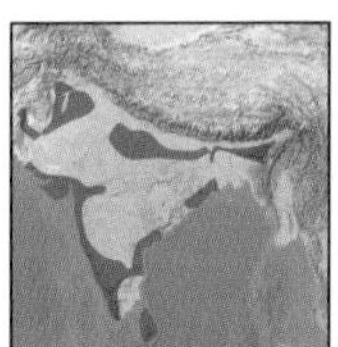

Size 21 cm

Voice Invariably silent when flushed

Range Winter visitor: Plains of N Afghanistan, Indus Valley

Habitat Marshes; paddy fields

Extremely small, secretive bird and exceptionally well-camouflaged within habitat. Lacks central crown-stripe; two pale lateral crown-stripes separated from supercilium by dark patch; dark eye-stripe. Mottled brown upperparts and pale underparts; streaked breast; narrow, pointed wings; conspicuous long straight golden scapular and mantle-stripes; short, wedge-shaped tail; yellow back-stripes visible in flight. Forages in soft mud for insects, earthworms and plant material. Feeds in characteristic bouncing motion. Crouches in undergrowth. Low and rapid zigzag flight when flushed. Male performs an aerial display during courtship.

SOLITARY SNIPE

Gallinago solitaria Scolopacidae

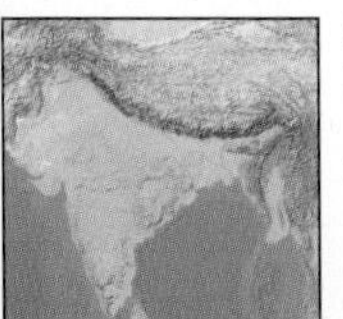

Size 30 cm

Voice Rather quiet. Loud, deep *pench* on flushing. Hoarse *kensh* call when taking off; far-carrying *chok-a-chok-a* call when displaying

Range Rare breeding resident of N mountains moving down to foothills in winter. Very rarely seen elsewhere

Habitat Alpine bogs and streams with thick cover

Small, stocky wader, with long, slender bill and pale face. Relatively short legs; heavily streaked head, neck and upperparts; fine barring on underparts; distinct warm ginger-brown wash on upper breast; white belly; olive-yellow to brownish-yellow legs; brown barring on flanks. Sexes similar, but female larger. Like other snipes, uses long bill to probe deeply in mud. Bobs up and down constantly as it feeds. Solitary and unobtrusive.

WOOD SNIPE

Gallinago nemoricola Scolopacidae

Size 28-32 cm

Voice Invariably silent when flushed

Range Breeds in the Himalayas and winters in the foothills and in S India and Sri Lanka

Habitat Marshes; paddy fields

Large, relatively short-billed snipe with broad wings. Dark-tipped pale yellow bill; distinct chestnut and black head-stripes; dark upper back with chestnut stripes running down towards tail; chestnut neck and breast; buff underparts streaked brown; creamish belly; dense barring on underwing; pale green-yellow legs. Heavy, direct flight.

PINTAIL SNIPE

Gallinago stenura Scolopacidae

Size 28 cm

Voice Call said to be *squik* or *chef*

Range Winter visitor to peninsula from about Mumbai south and to EC India and S Nepal to Arunachal Pradesh, Assam Valley

Habitat Marshes; paddy fields

Small, stocky wader with short greenish-grey legs and long, straight dark bill. Upperparts mottled brown with linear cream markings down back. Underparts pale with streaked buff breast and white belly; dark stripe through eye with lighter stripes above and below. Sexes similar. Wings less pointed than Common, lacks white trailing edge. Distinguished by shorter tail and flatter flight path when flushed.

SWINHOE'S SNIPE

Gallinago megala Scolopacidae

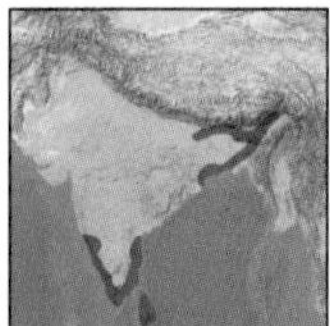

Size 28 cm

Voice In flight, a sudden *chrek* with abrupt ending. Pintail has more subdued *tesch;* coarse shriek

Range Probably fairly common but overlooked winter visitor mainly to E and S of the region

Habitat Marshes; wet paddy

Cryptically-patterned black, brown buff and white snipe, with extremely long bill. Very similar to *Pintail G. stenura* but distinguished by proportionately longer bill. Pale, dull upperparts. Greyish legs extend just beyond tail. Greyish flight feathers contrast with heavily barred white wing-coverts. Sexes alike. Lumbering flight. Feeds by deep, vertical probing.

COMMON SNIPE

Gallinago gallinago Scolopacidae

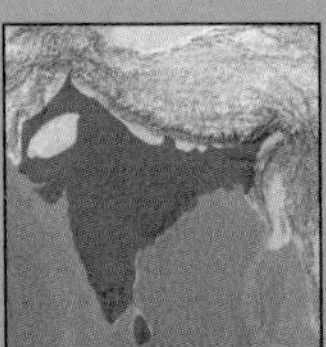

Size 28 cm

Voice Call a loud *scaaap* when flushed

Range Breeds in parts of W Himalayas; mostly winter visitor over the subcontinent, most common in N and C India

Habitat Marshlands; paddy cultivation; edges of jheels

Well-camouflaged bird, usually seen when flushed. Mottled-brown upperparts, with pale stripes on back and dark streaks on chest; paler underparts. Short legs; long wings; short tail and very elongated beak. Sexes alike, female may have slightly longer bill. Juvenile's wing feathers fringed with cream. Fast, zigzag flight. Probes with long beak in mud, often in shallow water; feeds mostly during mornings and evenings, often continuing through the night.

ASIAN DOWITCHER

Limnodromus semipalmatus Scolopacidae

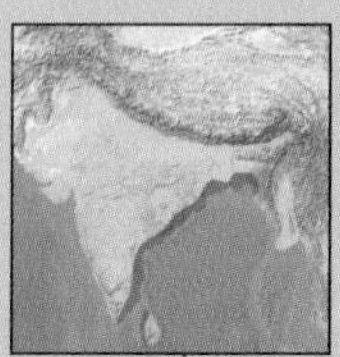

Size 34 cm

Voice Usually silent. Sometimes a soft *maou*

Range Rare passage migrant: E, S coasts. Rarer inland

Habitat Mudflats and if inland, jheels and flooded fields. Mixes with other waders

Medium to large-sized wader similar to Bar-tailed Godwit but distinguished by straight, completely black bill. Upperparts brown; breeding adult reddish from crown to belly; barred black-and-white tail; dark legs and long straight dark bill. Non-breeding adult overall grey; obvious white supercilium and barred flanks. Feeds on insects, molluscs, crustaceans and marine worms, and some plant material by probing in shallow water or on wet mud.

WHIMBREL

Numenius phaeopus Scolopacidae

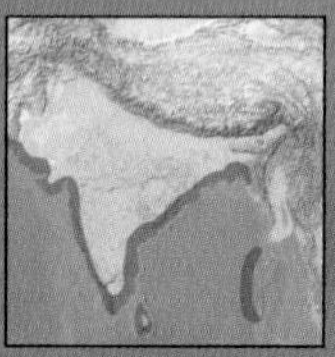

Size 43 cm

Voice Noisy. Call a trilling, usually 7-note whistle *tee…tee…tee…tee…tee…tee…tee*

Range Fairly common winter visitor to most coasts. Rare inland

Habitat Coastal muddy and rocky shores, particularly favouring mangroves on which it perches at high tide

Large shorebird with long downcurved bill, long neck and long legs. Streaked brown upperparts, neck, and breast; white belly and rump; dark brown crown; greyish line above eye, and dark brown line on eye mask. Immature similar to adult, but with light spotting on back and has less distinct crown-stripe. Uses bill to probe deep in sand for invertebrates; also feeds on berries and insects. Aggressive nest protectors.

EURASIAN CURLEW

Numenius arquata Scolopacidae

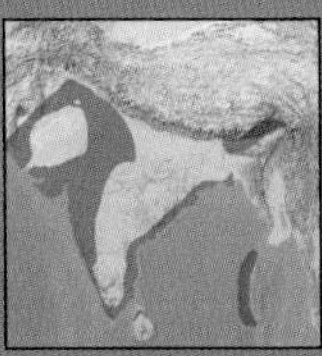

Size 58 cm

Voice Famed scream; wild, rather musical *cour…leeor…cooodee…*, first note longer

Range Winter visitor: Sea coast, W to E; large inland marshes; rivers

Habitat Estuaries; creeks; large remote marshes

Breeding adult has pale buff-brown head and neck streaked darker; darkish spots on upper mantle; white lower back and rump; dark brown, barred tail; pale brown upperwing spotted dark; black-brown flight feathers. Underparts whitish, with heavily streaked belly; white underwing with variable spotting and streaking. Head finely streaked; indistinct white supercilium. Long, grey downcurved bill; bluish-grey legs and feet. Non-breeding adult duller and overall greyer. Sexes similar, but female larger with longer bill. Juvenile has more buff on breast, flanks less streaked.

non-breeding

BAR-TAILED GODWIT

Limosa lapponica Scolopacidae

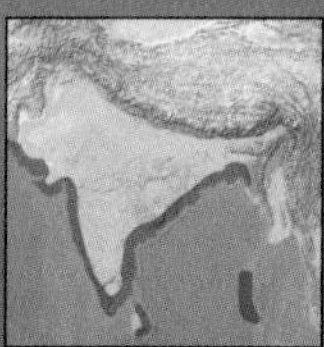

Size 35 cm

Voice Rather quiet. Call a soft *kik…kik…kik* in flight

Range Rather scarce winter visitor. Commoner on NW coasts. Rare inland

Habitat Coastal. Favours open mudflats

Large wader with long neck, bill and legs. Has wedge-shaped white rump patch and no wing-bars. Stockier than Black-tailed with shorter, slightly upturned bill and shorter legs. Size varies; female and eastern race larger. Non-breeding adult finely streaked brown above and on head and neck; latter turns rich orange, as do all underparts, when breeding. Back turns darker and wing-coverts silvery-grey.

non-breeding

breeding

BLACK-TAILED GODWIT

Limosa limosa Scolopacidae

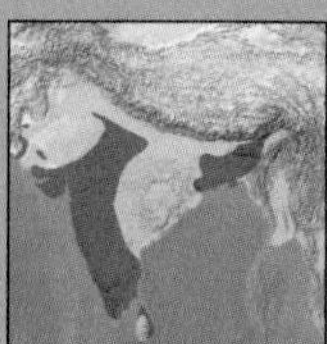

Size 35 cm

Voice Occasional, fairly loud *kwika…kwik*

Range Winter visitor, fairly common over N India; lesser numbers towards E and S India. Bar-tailed most common along Western seaboard, south to between Goa and Mumbai

Habitat Marshes; estuaries; creeks

non-breeding

Large, graceful bird with rather small head, long neck, very long, straight or slightly curved bill and very long legs. Distinguished from Bar-tailed by straighter and blunter bill, longer neck, shallower forehead, slimmer body and longer legs. In flight, broad white wing-bars, white rump and black tail-tip distinctive. Female slightly larger with longer bill, but overall duller. Solitary, or in groups, often with other waders. Feeds in sea-edge flocks. Fast, low flight.

breeding

SPOTTED REDSHANK

Tringa erythropus Scolopacidae

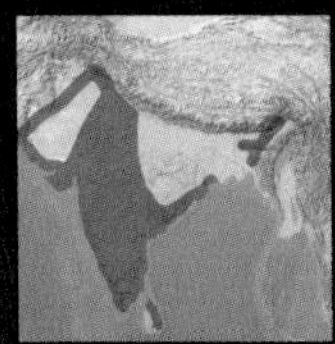

Size 33 cm

Voice Noisy. Call an explosive *chew it*

Range Fairly common winter visitor throughout lowlands. Scarce on the coast, NE India

Habitat Marshes; jheels; rivers

Slightly larger, slimmer and longer-legged than Common. No wing-bars; long cigar-shaped white-patch on back between wings, extending to rump; long red legs. Non-breeding adult has light grey, speckled upperparts and whitish underparts; paler head and neck with short, white supercilium. Red lower mandible, downcurved. Breeding adult has black underparts, head and neck; dark grey upperparts, spotted white. Juvenile resembles pale Redshank.

COMMON REDSHANK

Tringa totanus Scolopacidae

Size 28 cm

Voice Quite musical, fairly loud and shrill *tleu…ewh…ewh*

Range Breeds in Kashmir, Ladakh; winter visitor all over India. Fairly common

Habitat Marshes; creeks; estuaries

Elegant-looking bird with greyish-brown upperparts, spotted dark brown and black. Whitish underparts streaked and spotted dark brown on breast, flanks and belly. White secondary flight feathers, rump, lower back and barred tail visible in flight. Breeding adult more brown above, marked black and fulvous, and more heavily streaked below. Brown head streaked and spotted darker. Orange-red legs and base of beak; long, straight bill with red base and black tip; dark brown eyes with white eyelids. Legs and feet bright red.

breeding

COMMON GREENSHANK

Tringa nebularia Scolopacidae

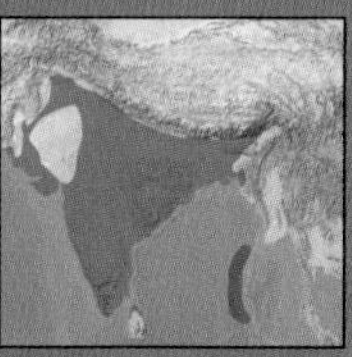

Size 32 cm

Voice Call a wild, ringing *tew… tew…tew…*

Range Winter visitor, fairly common over most of the region

Habitat Marshes; estuaries

Medium-sized slim wader with dark grey back and white underparts. Diagnostic long; greyish-green legs, slightly upturned, blackish-grey bill. Long neck; white rump extending into distinctive white wedge up the back, visible in flight; grey streaking on head and neck; whitish tail. Breeding adult heavily streaked, spotted darker on upperparts, head, neck and upper breast. Juvenile similar to non-breeding adult, but upperparts more brown and feathers edged buff; neck and breast more heavily streaked.

NORDMANN'S GREENSHANK

Tringa guttifer Scolopacidae

Size 30 cm

Voice Call a full, piercing *kyew* and a higher, shriller *sklee*

Range Rare winter visitor to coasts of SE Bangladesh

Habitat Coasts

Medium-sized wader with slightly upturned bill and relatively short yellow legs. Breeding adult has boldly marked blackish upperparts with whitish spotting and spangling; head and upper neck also heavily streaked; broad blackish crescent-shaped spots on lower neck and breast; dark lores; white axillaries and underwing-coverts; grey flight feathers. Grey tail extends beyond tips of toes, conspicuous in flight. Juvenile more brown than adult, with pale brown breast and wing edges. Similar to Common, but larger head; shorter, thicker neck and yellow base to stouter bill.

MARSH SANDPIPER

Tringa stagnatilis Scolopacidae

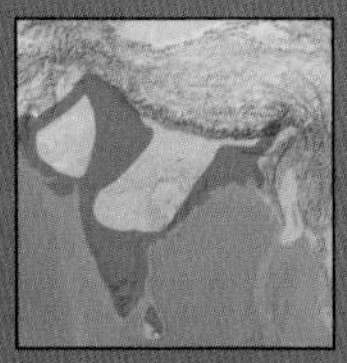

Size 23 cm

Voice Rather quiet. Call a briefly repeated *klew*, rather like first note of Common Redshank

Range Fairly common winter visitor throughout lowlands. Less common on coasts

Habitat Shallow freshwater jheels; village ponds; wet paddy; river shoals

breeding

Distinctive wader with long needle-like bill and very long greenish legs, often mistaken for Common Greenshank. Non-breeding adult has greyish-brown upperparts and white underparts; grey crown and hindneck; white eyebrow. Breeding adult has heavily streaked head and neck; flanks and lower breast show bars or chevrons. Juvenile has more heavily patterned upperparts than non-breeding adult; dark outer wing and slightly lighter inner wing, white wedge on lower back and rump visible in flight. Feeds upright with slow graceful movements breaking into quick dashes.

non-breeding

GREEN SANDPIPER

Tringa ochropus Scolopacidae

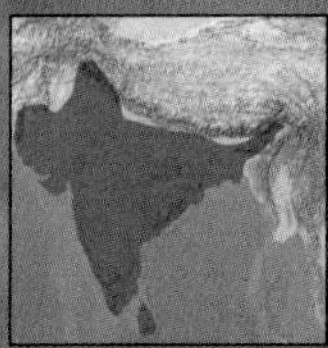

Size 23 cm

Voice Call a ringing *tlu… eet…weet*

Range Widespread but rather scarce winter visitor

Habitat Well-vegetated pools; streams; mangroves; village ponds

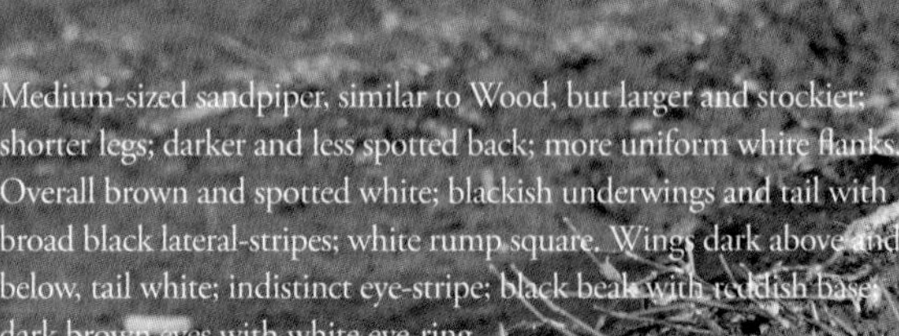

Medium-sized sandpiper, similar to Wood, but larger and stockier; shorter legs; darker and less spotted back; more uniform white flanks. Overall brown and spotted white; blackish underwings and tail with broad black lateral-stripes; white rump square. Wings dark above and below, tail white; indistinct eye-stripe; black beak with reddish base; dark brown eyes with white eye-ring.

WOOD SANDPIPER

Tringa glareola Scolopacidae

Upperparts greyish-brown, spotted white; breast and neck white and striped brown. White supercilium, extending from behind eye to back of ear-coverts; short, straight beak with deep olive-green base; long yellow to greenish-yellow legs; brownish tail contrasts with white rump patch. Breeding adult more olive-brown, spotted white and bill has pale base. Juvenile similar to non-breeding adult, but upperparts much darker, warmer brown; more spotting and streaking on breast.

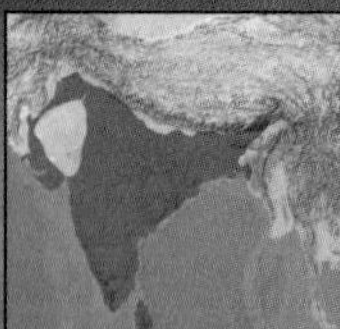

Size 21 cm

Voice Quite noisy; sharp, trilling notes on ground. Call a shrill, somewhat metallic *chiff…chiff* when flushed; sometimes loud, sharp *tluie…*

Range Winter visitor throughout the region

Habitat Wet cultivation; marshes; tidal creeks; mudflats

breeding

COMMON SANDPIPER

Actitis hypoleucos Scolopacidae

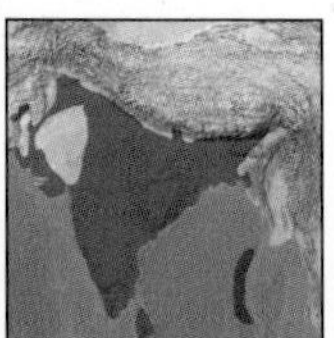

Size 20 cm

Voice Vocal in flight. Call includes a 3-note sound with distinctive 3-note, piping-like cry; often represented as *twee-wee-wee*

Range Breeds in the Himalayas, Kashmir to Uttarakhand to about 3,000 m; winter visitor all across the region

Habitat Freshwater marshes; lakes; tidal areas; creeks

Small to medium-sized bird, with relatively long legs. Upperparts olive-brown, streaked on head and neck sides; white underparts; lightly streaked, brown breast; narrow white wing-bar, brown rump; white 'hook' at shoulder conspicuous in flight. Breeding adult has darker and more speckled upperparts. Active; feeds on ground on crustaceans, insects, worms, and other coastal creatures; makes short dashes, bobbing and wagging short tail; stiff-winged flight.

breeding

TEREK SANDPIPER

Xenus cinereus Scolopacidae

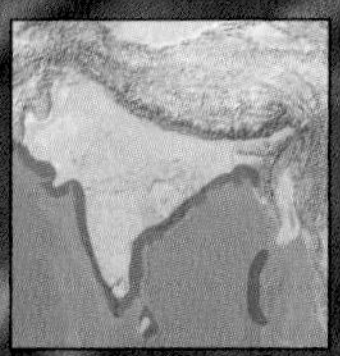

Size 24 cm

Voice Call a ringing *twoot…wee…wee*

Range Rather scarce winter visitor to most coasts. Most numerous on Arabian Sea coast. Rare inland

Habitat Muddy coasts and mangroves. When inland, mostly on sandy rivers or muddy jheels

non-breeding

Resembles Common, but has long bill with dull yellow to orange base, visibly upcurved. Brownish-grey upperparts; grey face; neck and breast speckled pale grey, but other underparts white. Breeding adult has stronger and increased streaking across head and prominent irregular dark stripes on upper scapulars. White trailing edge to wings; black lengthwise stripe over each wing. Orange legs; blackish-brown eyes. Sexes alike. Juvenile similar to breeding adult but upperpart feathers have buff fringes and dark subterminal marks; yellow legs.

RUDDY TURNSTONE

Arenaria interpres Scolopacidae

Size 22 cm

Voice Call a rapid *tuka…tuk…tuk* in flight

Range Scarce winter visitor to most coasts. Commonest in the NW. Rare inland

Habitat Mainly rocky coasts. Also sandy flats and by large rivers

breeding

Medium-sized, attractively-patterned stocky shorebird. Short, thick and dark bill has slight upturn; black-and-white or black and grey clown-like patterning on face; bold wing pattern visible in flight; white lower back; short, orange legs. Adult turns rich chestnut in breeding. Juvenile resembles winter adult, but overall more brownish and paler head.

GREAT KNOT

Calidris tenuirostris Scolopacidae

Size 28 cm

Voice Rather quiet. Call a low *chukka… chukka*

Range Rare winter visitor, could occur on any coast and even inland

Habitat Coastal mudflats; salt pans

Easily confused with Red, but distinguished by longer bill and whitish rump that is conspicuous in flight. Non-breeding adult has bolder chevron-shaped markings on sides, darker streaks on breast and forehead, less obvious supercilium, heavier streaking on forehead, and feathers of upperparts more brown with darker centres than Red. Breeding adult easily identified by gorget of black spots across breast, large red spots and patches on scapulars. Sexes alike.

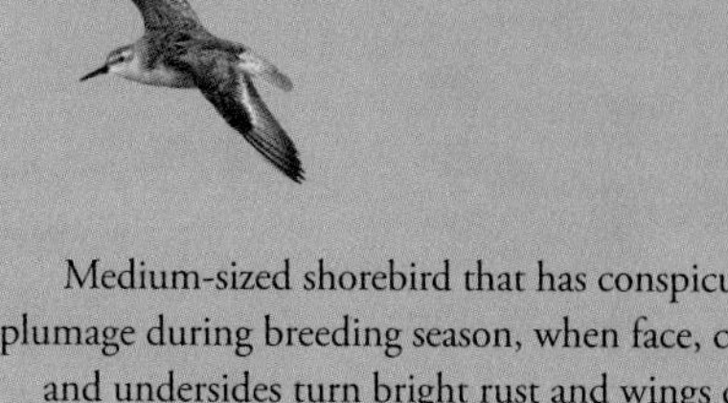

RED KNOT

Calidris canutus Scolopacidae

Size 24 cm

Voice Rather quiet. Sometimes a soft *chuk…chuk*

Range Rare winter visitor to E coast and particularly Sri Lanka

Habitat Coastal mudflats

Medium-sized shorebird that has conspicuous plumage during breeding season, when face, chest and undersides turn bright rust and wings dark brown; tail develops dark stripe. Non-breeding adult has grey head, chest and upperparts; white belly; blackish primaries and white stripe across wing; white-patch above throat and eye. Long greenish legs; pointed black bill. Sexes alike. Juvenile variable grey; feathers edged darker; dark grey primaries and white wing-stripe.

breeding

RED-NECKED STINT

Calidris ruficollis Scolopacidae

Size 15 cm

Voice Call a hoarse *chrit…it…it*

Range Scarce but overlooked winter visitor, most regular in Bangladesh, Tamil Nadu and Sri Lanka

Habitat Coastal mudflats; salt pans. Also inland in Bangladesh

Rather small shorebird with small head, round forehead, short legs and attenuated rear end. Longish body; short, very slightly decurved bill; white wing-bars, white sides to black-centered rump visible in flight. In breeding plumage, head turns russet, crown acquires brown streaks and breast gorget. Sexes alike. Juvenile plainer and duller. Forages by walking, on shore edge rapidly picking food from surface. Sometimes probes mud. Highly sociable; often found in mixed flocks.

breeding

TEMMINCK'S STINT

Calidris temminckii Scolopaidae

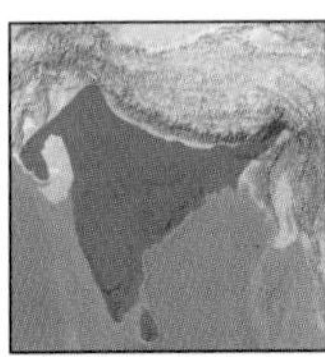

Size 14 cm

Voice Call a dry, high-pitched trilling in flight

Range Common winter visitor throughout lowlands. Scarce on the coast

Habitat Vegetated freshwater habitats favouring flooded short grass and paddy fields

Small, uniform brown sandpiper, similar in size to Little, but darker and greyer. Greyish-brown head and chest; blackish-brown bill and brown iris; thin, downcurved bill; well-defined line between breast and white belly; greenish-brown legs. Uniform chest patch and greyish upperparts similar to Common Sandpiper. V-shaped white mark on back; extensive white edge to black-centered tail conspicuous in flight.

breeding

non-breeding

LONG-TOED STINT

Calidris subminuta Scolopacidae

Size 14 cm

Voice Call a trilling, slightly throaty *krrrt*

Range Mainly E, NE India and Bangladesh

Habitat Marshes; riverbanks; mudflats

Tiny, delicate wader with distinctive shape, small head, and long slim neck. Variegated rufous, black and buff upperparts; brown scapulars and tertials with broad rufous fringes; roundish belly, short rear-end, long legs and long toes, short, pointed bill; yellow-green legs and feet, pale-brown or yellow base to lower mandible. Brown crown and white supercilium; brown spots on cheek and brown forehead. Similar to Red-necked, but has darker and brighter upperparts.

LITTLE STINT

Calidris minuta Scolopacidae

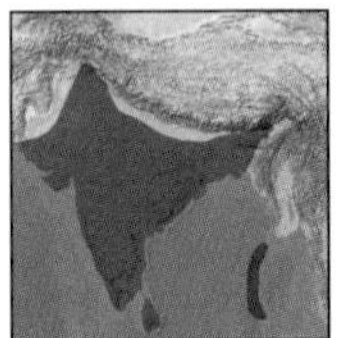

Size 14 cm

Voice Call a piercing, repeated *stit...it*

Range Abundant winter visitor throughout lowlands; all coasts

Habitat Coastal mudflats; salt pans; shallow open freshwater; muddy lakes; river margins

Tiny wader. In breeding plumage, edges of back feathers, flanks and cheeks turn rusty-red with darker mottling, and white underparts. Dark and split cap; white supercilium. Short, straight and narrow-tipped beak. Thin wing-bars and distinct white V on back, prominent in flight. White lengthwise stripes on backs and grey on tail feathers diagnostic. Black legs, beak and iris. Sexes similar. Juvenile similar to Temminck but with pale forehead and pale eyebrow-stripe split into two. Swift flight with extremely rapid wingbeats.

breeding

CURLEW SANDPIPER

Calidris ferruginea Scolopacidae

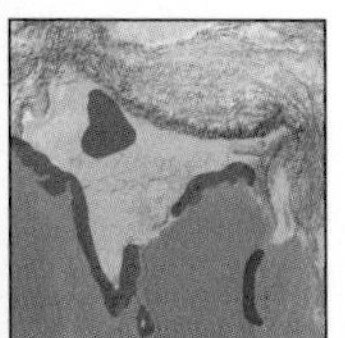

Size 21 cm

Voice Call a trilling *chirrup* in flight

Range Common winter visitor to most coasts, particularly in S and E. Scarce passage migrant inland

Habitat Coastal mud, sandflats, salt pans. Inland on floods, muddy jheels, sandy rivers

Very similar to Dunlin, but larger, more slender with longer bill, neck and legs and divided eyebrow-stripe. Obvious downcurved bill. Breeding adult has deep chestnut head, neck and belly (paler in female) and black, white and reddish patterning on upperparts; bright white rumps and white wing-stripe and white chin. Non-breeding adult greyer with distinct white supercilium. Toes extend beyond tail-tip in flight. Juvenile has greyer underparts and pale red breast. In mixed flocks with other waders. Feeds mainly on insects and small invertebrates and worms, occasionally feeds on seeds and other plant material.

breeding

SANDERLING

Calidris alba Scolopacidae

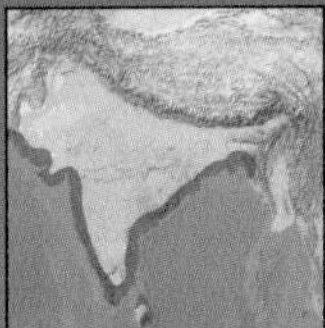

Size 20 cm

Voice Call a metallic *plit*

Range Local winter visitor to most coasts. Very rare inland

Habitat Almost entirely restricted to sandy coasts

Small, active shorebird with short, stout, black beak and black legs that lack hind toe. Breeding adult has cinnamon-red upperparts, head and breast mottled black-and-white. Non-breeding adult largely white; pale grey upperparts; pure white underparts; distinct, dark shoulder patch; broad, white wing-bar bordered black; Sexes similar, but female larger and paler, less reddish-brown. Juvenile similar to non-breeding adult, but more streaked black; buff breast and head; back more darkly marked with black-and-white.

breeding

SPOON-BILLED SANDPIPER

Eurynorhynchus pygmeus Scolopacidae

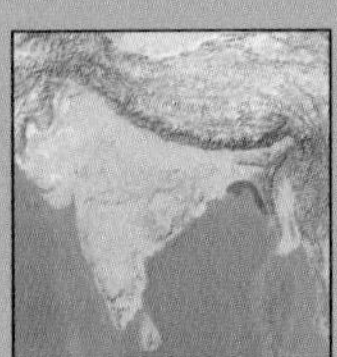

Size 15 cm

Voice Call includes a series of short *zhree…zhree…zhree…*

Range Rare winter visitor to coastal Bangladesh, West Bengal

Habitat Usually found in small numbers among stint flocks, at water's edge or in wettest parts of mudflats

Sparrow-sized wader with unique spoon-shaped bill. Non-breeding adult has pale brown-grey upperparts, with edge to feathers; white underparts. Breeding adult has russet-red head, neck and breast streaked brown, and dark upperparts with pale brown-and-red trim to feathers. Strongly territorial; returns year after year to breed at the same nest site.

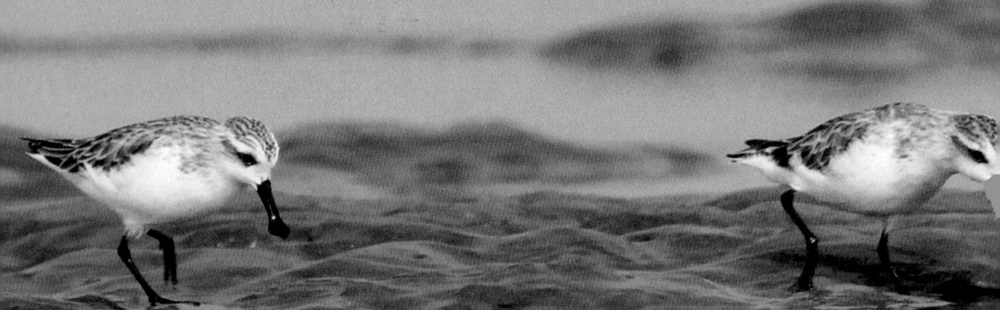

DUNLIN

Calidris alpina Scolopacidae

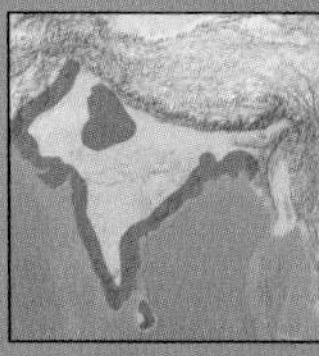

Size 19 cm

Voice Call a trilling *creep* in flight

Range Locally common winter visitor to most coasts. Most common in NW. Rare inland

Habitat Coastal mudflats. Inland: occurs on sandy rivers, muddy jheels

breeding

non-breeding

Medium-sized sandpiper with bright reddish upperparts, black belly, and long, drooping bill. Relatively short neck and long, blackish legs. Breeding adult has black belly, rufous back and crown. Non-breeding adult overall dull brownish-grey with whitish belly; black bill and legs. Juvenile has more red on back and brownish-black markings on belly. Slightly hunched appearance.

BROAD-BILLED SANDPIPER

Limicola falcinellus Scolopacidae

Size 18 cm

Voice Call a buzzing, metallic *brr…eet* in flight

Range Scarce winter visitor to most coasts, most regular in Tamil Nadu. Rare inland

Habitat Mudflats; sandbanks; salt pans

Small wader, slightly smaller than Dunlin, but with longer, straighter bill and shorter legs. Breeding adult has patterned dark grey upperparts and white underparts with blackish markings on breast; pale crown-stripe and supercilium. Non-breeding adult has pale grey upperparts and white underparts; neck, breast, and belly intensely speckled darker. Dark grey legs and dark brown iris. Juvenile similar to adult but duller with rusty-brown edges to back feathers and faint streaking on underparts.

RUFF

Philomachus pugnax Scolopacidae

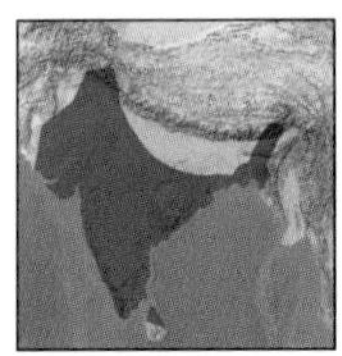

Size Male 30 cm; Female 23 cm

Voice Silent. No call recorded

Range Abundant winter visitor mainly to W and S parts of the region

Habitat Marshes; jheels; stubble; cultivation; mudflats; salt pans

Medium-sized wader with long neck, small head, rather short, slightly droopy bill and medium-long orange or reddish legs. Non-breeding adult has scalloped brown-grey upperparts. Breeding male has striking ruff ranging from black or brown to orange or white with pronounced black stripes and ear tufts. Female (known as Reeve) and male in non-breeding plumage similar, with orange bills and white feathers at bill base, but male much larger; upper flanks marked with dark spots. Shows white U on tail, separating dark rump and dark tail-tip in flight.

♀

breeding

breeding

breeding

RED PHALAROPE

Phalaropus fulicarius Scolopacidae

Size 27 cm

Voice Silent. No call recorded

Range Vagrant

Habitat Marshes; mudflats; salt pans

Female larger than male with more flamboyant breeding plumage, large white cheek patch, black crown; chestnut-red neck and chestnut underparts. Breeding male similar but less vibrantly-coloured and mottled crown. Non-breeding adult has black bill, white head and neck, white underparts.

breeding

RED-NECKED PHALAROPE

Phalaropus lobatus Scolopacidae

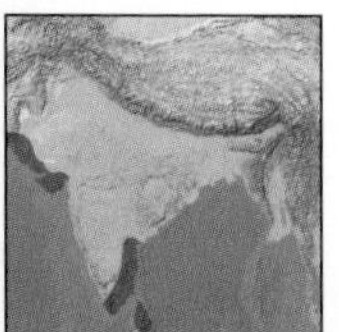

Size 20 cm

Voice Call a husky *chet*

Range Scarce winter visitor to Arabian Sea and Sri Lankan coast. Rare inland

Habitat Marine. Inland, prefers salt lakes

Female more brightly-coloured than male, especially on neck. In breeding, both sexes have distinct white cheek patch, dark grey head and back. Male has whitish underparts; female has grey breast. Non-breeding adult more drab with greyish upperparts and white below; strong, black eye-stripe; thin, black, needle-like bill; narrow wing-bar visible in flight. Juvenile darker brown. Feeds by swimming rapidly.

CREAM-COLOURED COURSER

Cursorius cursor Glareolidae

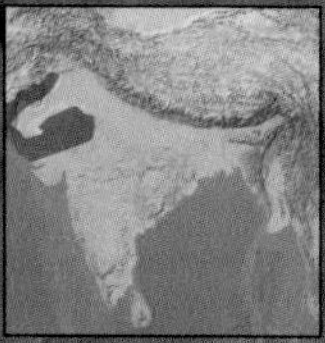

Size 23 cm

Voice Calls include liquid *whit… whit* and *whek…whek*

Range Scarce breeding resident, winter visitor to Pakistan, the Thar Desert in India

Habitat Desert and semi-desert including dry grass flats. Sociable, sometimes mixing with Indian

Tall, slender bird with longish, pointed, downcurved beak. Uniform sandy-cream upperparts; white lower belly; black underwings and wing-tips; distinct black eye-stripe running to back of neck, bordered narrow white; blue-grey hindcrown; long, pale legs and feet; pale lores and short tail. Sexes alike. Juvenile has scaly, mottled back and less-marked head. Strong flight on short wings, with legs trailing; chases insects afoot.

INDIAN COURSER

Cursorius coromandelicus Glareolidae

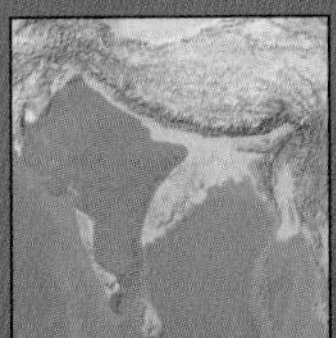

Size 23 cm

Voice Soft, hen-like clucking call in flight, when flushed

Range Most of the area south of the Himalayas, but distribution rather patchy; absent in NE India

Habitat Open scrub; fallow lands; dry cultivation

Similar to Cream-coloured, but brighter and with broader eye-stripe. Bright chestnut crown; white and black stripes above and through eyes to nape; sandy-brown above; chestnut throat and breast and black belly; long, whitish legs; in flight, dark underwings. Sexes alike. Juvenile has dull buff, irregularly barred with blackish-brown upperparts and has pale supercilium; breast dull rufous, more or less barred with blackish; chin and abdomen white. In small parties in open country; strictly ground bird, runs in short spurts and feeds on ground; flies strongly for a short distance and lands; can fly very high.

JERDON'S COURSER

Rhinoptilus bitorquatus Glareolidae

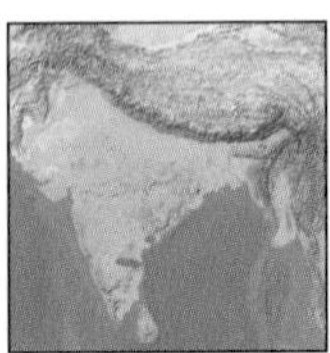

Size 27 cm

Voice Call a clear *tuick…ttuuu… tuick…tuuu…tuickt…* notes

Range Resident; foothills of S Andhra Pradesh

Habitat Scrubs

Small bird, with cryptic sandy-brown plumage. White underparts with banded lower breast; distinct rufous neck patch; dark brown hindneck and crown; broad, cream eye-stripes joined to form V; straight, yellow bill with black tip; black tail with white base. Walks with upright stance. Thought to be extinct, it was rediscovered in 1986, after a lapse of 86 years since the previous sighting.

COLLARED PRATINCOLE

Glareola pratincola Glareolidae

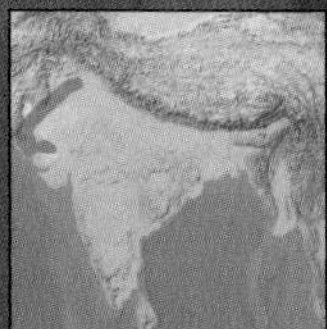

Size 25 cm

Voice Call a tern-like *kirrik* in flight

Range Breeds in lower Pakistan; rare winter visitor elsewhere in the region

Habitat Open, bare mud usually near drying jheels, rivers or near the coast

Attractive; with fine black collar which outlines cream throat patch and bright red base of bill. Long, narrow wings and long forked tail; short, black, hooked bill; black lores; white partial eye-rings. Sandy brown with sharp demarcation from white lower breast. Darker brown outer wings, white trailing edges, black tail extending to or beyond wing-tips. White outer-tail feathers, uppertail-coverts and rump. Sexes alike.

ORIENTAL PRATINCOLE

Glareola maldivarum Glareolidae

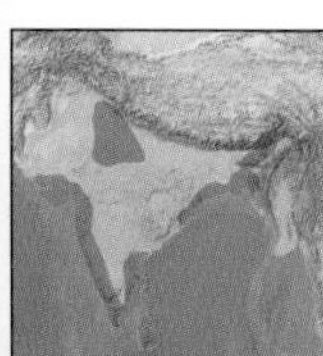

Size 25 cm

Voice Call a tern-like *krek…krek* in flight

Range Resident, local migrant; common breeding resident. Most frequent in N and extreme S, including Sri Lanka

Habitat As Collared; more tolerant of dry fallow away from water. Favours river sandbanks

Very similar to Collared, but distinguished by brown breast extending down to belly and merging into white; long, narrow wings and short, forked tail; much less contrast above and no white trailing edges seen in flight. Short bill; brown back and head; wings brown with black flight feathers. Sexes alike.

SMALL PRATINCOLE

Glareola lactea Glareolidae

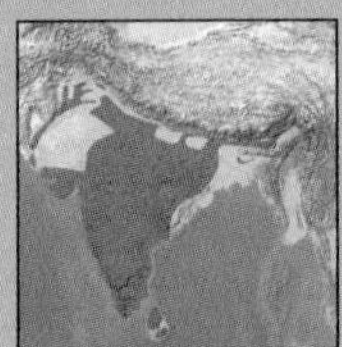

Size 17 cm

Voice Call a sharp *tirrit tirrit tirrit*

Range Resident and local migrant; subcontinent south of outer Himalayas, from about 1,800 m

Habitat Large and quiet riversides, sandbars, marshy expanses, coastal swamps, tidal creeks

Similar, but much smaller and paler than Oriental. Brown forehead; pale sandy-grey mantle and grey crown. Breeding adult has black stripe from eye to beak; white, squarish tail, tipped black; smoky-brown underbody has rufous wash; whiter on lower breast and abdomen; long, narrow wings; pale grey wing-coverts, white base to secondaries, black flight feathers and short legs. Sexes alike. Gregarious; large, loose flocks over open expanse, close to water; very swallow-like in demeanour; strong and graceful flight over water surface, catching insects on wing; flies high during late evening.

SOOTY GULL

Ichthyaetus hemprichii Laridae

Size 39 cm

Voice Call musical but nasal, fairly high-pitched

Range Resident; Balochistan to Sind Coast

Habitat Follows offshore fishing boats

Exceptionally long, thick beak. Heavy looking with broad pointed wings and dull yellowish legs; prominent crescent above eye and sometimes faint crescent below; dark hood forming bib on chest, bordered above by white partial collar. Breeding adult has distinct red-tipped mustard bill and black subterminal ring; inconspicuous white spot above eye and tiny indistinct one below; white trailing edge of wings inconspicuous owing to lack of dark band on secondaries.

MEW GULL

Larus canus Laridae

Size 35 cm

Voice Calls include a nasal *keow* and long shrill *glieeoo, gleeu...gleeu...gleeu* in alarm; high-pitched 'laughing' cry

Range Winter vagrant

Habitat Wooded lakes and rivers when on summer breeding grounds. In winter, found along coastline, especially near river mouths and brackish lagoons

Small gull with unmarked yellow bill and white head and underparts. Back medium-grey, outer primaries speckled white; greenish-yellow legs. Juvenile has dirty grey-brown head, back, and chest. Back feathers have pale tips, giving scaly appearance. Light brownish-grey underparts, barred on flanks; dark brown tail, with paler base; blackish wing-tips; black bill; dark eyes and pinkish legs. Breeds colonially near water or marshes, making lined nest on ground or in trees.

CASPIAN GULL

Larus cachinnans Laridae

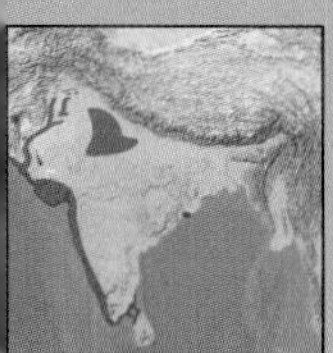

Size 41 cm

Voice Nasal, ringing

Range Rare vagrant

Habitat Coasts; inland waters

Slender gull with elongated body and yellow legs; dark wings; pale iris with red ring. Large white head; deep yellow bill with distinctive bright red spot. White upperparts merge into grey back and wings, with black-and-white wing-tips. Sexes alike, but male slightly larger. First-winter bird has dark bill and dark eyes; pink-grey legs; mottled grey-brown plumage; white back and wings. Opportunistic feeder, follows fishing boats, as well as forages on rubbish. Nests under bushes.

HEUGLIN'S GULL

Larus heuglini Laridae

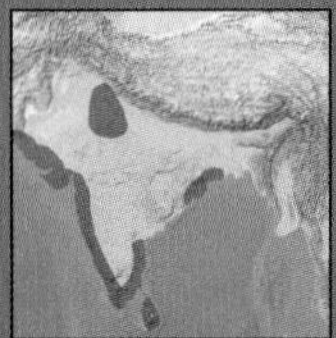

Size 65 cm

Voice As Yellow-legged

Range Scarce winter visitor to W and S coasts from Pakistan to Andhra Pradesh. Also Sri Lanka

Habitat As Yellow-legged but probably even more coastal

Elongated gull with small rounded head, relatively fine bill, slender legs and short tail. Male has flatter crown and bulbous tip to bill. Very similar to Black-headed and almost indistinguishable in field, but for slimmer bill, smaller head and more slender legs. Breeding adult has white head. Non-breeding adult streaked slightly dark, particularly on hindneck; duller bare parts. Juvenile has paler bill and less darkly marked head and body.

STEPPE GULL

Larus h barabensis Laridae

Recently split from Heuglin's. Status still uncertain due to identification problems.

BROWN-HEADED GULL

Chroicocephalus brunnicephalus Laridae

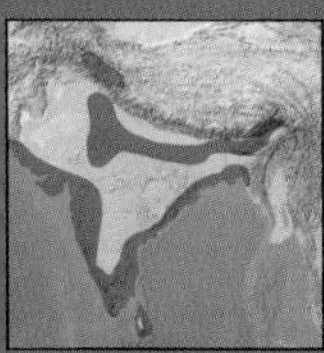

Size 42 cm

Voice Call a deep *kraaa*

Range Breeds in Ladakh. Common winter visitor to most coasts, sometimes inland

Habitat Coasts, rivers and lakes. Very gregarious, often with Black-headed

Slightly larger than Black-headed; summer adult has pale brown head, pearl-grey body, chocolate-brown partial hood, red bill and legs. In non-breeding adult, mask reduced to brown ear patch. Black-tipped primary wing, feathers have large, conspicuous white spots; grey underwing; black flight feathers. Juvenile has brownish tinge to wings, black tail-bars, pale iris and white eye-rings. Sexes alike. Light, easy flight. Swims buoyantly, often among ducks and coots. Breeds colonially in high-altitude bogs.

BLACK-HEADED GULL

Chroicocephalus ridibundus Laridae

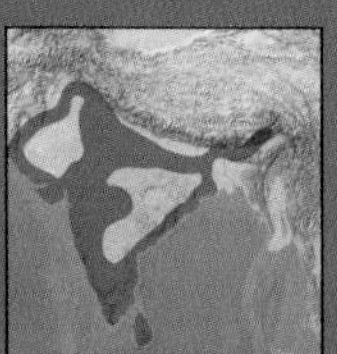

Size 38 cm

Voice Noisy. Call includes querulous *kree…ah…* screams

Range Common winter visitor; most common on W seaboard; also strays inland, both on passage and for short halts

Habitat Sea coasts; harbours; sewage outflows; refuse dumps. Disciplined skeins

Greyish-white plumage; dark ear patches; white outer flight feathers, with black tips. Breeding adult has coffee-brown head and upper neck. Sexes alike. Highly gregarious; large flocks on sea coasts, scavenges in harbours; wheels over busy seaside roads or beaches; large numbers rest on rocky ground and sand; follow boats in harbours.

SLENDER-BILLED GULL

Chroicocephalus genei Laridae

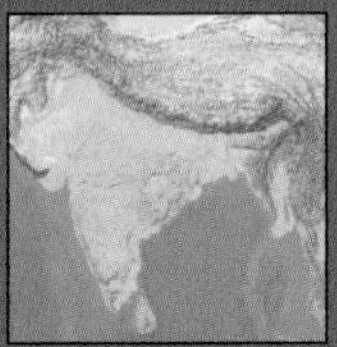

Size 43 cm

Voice Slightly deeper than that of Black-headed

Range Resident: Pakistan; winter visitor: Nepal, India, Bhutan and Sri Lanka

Habitat Coastal waters; lagoons; estuaries; large tidal creeks; salt pans

Distinguished by remarkably long and slender blood-red bill, very flat forehead, pale iris and long neck. Breeding adult usually has strong pink wash on underparts. Very similar to Black-headed, but lacks black hood in summer. Pale grey body, white head and breast; black tips to primary wing feathers. Dark red legs; yellow iris. First-year immature has black terminal tail-band, and dark areas on wings. Flies above water surface diving on prey; probes mud for invertebrates.

breeding

PALLAS'S GULL

Ichthyaetus ichthyaetus Laridae

juvenile

juvenile

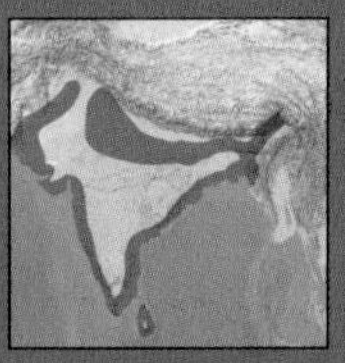

Size 69 cm

Voice Rather quiet. Call a nasal *argh*

Range Rare winter visitor to most coasts, inland

Habitat Coasts; large rivers; lakes

Large, striking-looking, long-winged gull with long-sloping forehead and strong black and orange-tipped yellow bill. Breeding adult has velvety-black hood and white eye-rings. Non-breeding adult has duskier head. Upperparts pale grey; whiter outer wing with black speckling near tips. Orangish-yellow bill; greenish-yellow legs with orange web. Immature pale grey-brown; grey mantle and wing panel. Solitary; mixes with smaller gulls and turns where fish is in abundance. Displays heavy buoyant heron-like flight.

breeding

BLACK-LEGGED KITTIWAKE

Rissa tridactyla Laridae

Size 43 cm

Voice Call a nasal *kitti-wake*; short harsh *kwark* or *kewack* when foraging

Range Rare visitor; Arabian coast

Habitat Graceful, aerially adapted

Small, graceful, 3-toed gull (hind toe reduced to small bump), with short, black legs. White head and underparts; blue-grey upperparts and wings; black wing-tips; slightly forked tail; yellow bill; orangish-red inside mouth. Breeding adult has narrow ring of red around eye. Non-breeding adult has darkish-grey marking on crown and hindneck; dark mark behind eye. Sexes alike, but female smaller. Juvenile has distinguishing black zigzag pattern on wings, and black collar, dark patches on neck and behind eyes; black tip to tail, and yellow beak; normal flight light, in high winds careens like shearwater, and may hover.

GULL-BILLED TERN

Gelochelidon nilotica Laridae

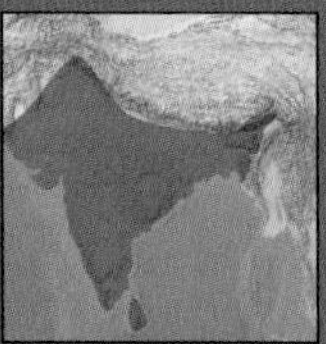

Size 38 cm

Voice Normally rather quiet but occasionally, call a guttural *ger…erk*

Range Common winter visitor; coasts; inland. Local breeder

Habitat Rivers; jheels; coasts

Medium-sized tern with broader wings and thicker bill than most other terns and long, black legs. Tail short and notched; sleek, black cap when breeding. Non-breeding adult has white head and dark smudge behind eyes. Pale grey, black-tipped wings; white body; black legs; dark trailing edge to primaries visible in flight. Sexes alike. Hawks for flying insects, often over dry land but also picks fish from water surface. Nests on ground.

CASPIAN TERN

Hydroprogne caspia Laridae

juvenile

juvenile

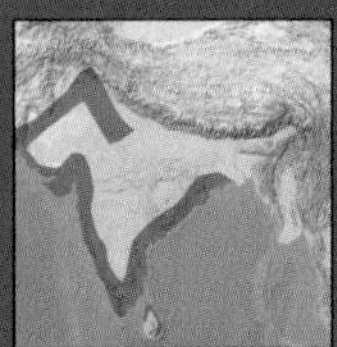

Size 53 cm

Voice Call a deep heron-like *kaarrh* in flight

Range Scarce winter visitor to some coasts and inland. Most frequent in W and S. Breeds in Gujarat and Pakistan

Habitat Coasts; large rivers; lakes

Large, gull-like tern, with white body and black cap. Large, thick brilliant red bill with black band near yellow tip. Breeding adult has black crown becoming speckled white in non-breeding season. Pale grey upperparts; blackish outer primaries visible in flight. Juvenile has blackish crown, black edging to back feathers. Sexes alike.

LESSER CRESTED TERN

Thalasseus bengalensis Laridae

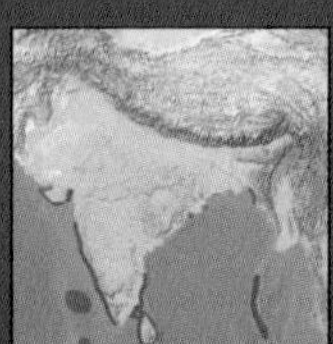

Size 35-37 cm

Voice Call a high-pitched *krrreeep…*

Range Over the entire Indian sea coast in winter; possibly breeds in parts of W Pakistan coast, and some islets off the W coast of India

Habitat Open sea; coastal regions

Typical-looking tern with greyish upperparts washed lilac; jet-black forehead, crown and nuchal crest in summer; whitish forehead and white-streaked crown diagnostic in winter. Blackish primaries, bright orange-yellow beak and black feet diagnostic. Sexes alike. Small parties out at sea, sometimes coming into coastal waters; flies leisurely between 2 and 8 metres over water, hovering occasionally; dives headlong for fish.

SANDWICH TERN

Thalasseus sandvicensis Laridae

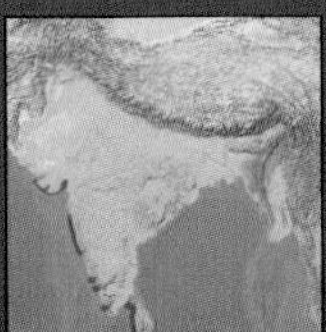

Size 36–41 cm

Voice Call an upward-inflected, hoarse *kree…it*

Range Visitor to mainly W coasts

Habitat Frequents coasts, tidal creeks and open sea

breeding

Medium-sized marine tern with long, thin, black bill with pale yellow tip and short black legs. Overall almost uniformly plain grey; small shaggy crest behind head; white rump and tail; white forehead and crown. Breeding adult has black cap which turns pale in winter plumage. In flight, grey wedges on wing-tips and short-forked tail noticeable. Similar to Gull-billed but wings narrower and more pointed and sharply angled. Juvenile similar to non-breeding adult, except for dusky crown and dark markings on back, bill may lack yellow tip.

GREATER CRESTED TERN

Thalasseus bergii Laridae

Size 47 cm

Voice Call a coarse *kerrick*

Range Local resident. Most regular off Pakistan coast; Sri Lanka, W and S Indian coasts

Habitat Seen mainly offshore or around archipelagos, where it nests on islets

Large, grey-backed marine tern with distinctive black cap and long crest. Upperparts dark grey; blackish wing-tips; white forehead in all plumages; large greenish-yellow bill; black legs. Non-breeding plumage, black cap reduced. Dark legs. Sexes alike. Juvenile has more heavily mottled or barred brown upperparts. Smaller and slimmer; Lesser Crested Tern *S. bengalensis* paler grey above and has thinner orange bill.

RIVER TERN

Sterna aurantia Laridae

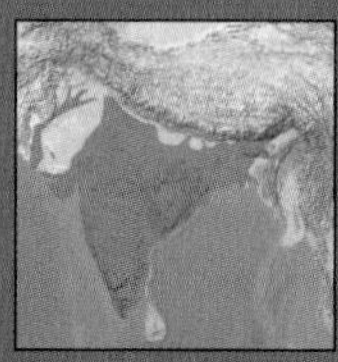

Size 42 cm

Voice Occasional harsh, screeching note

Range All over India; most common in N and C India

Habitat Inland waterbodies, rivers, tanks; almost completely absent on the sea coast

br

Graceful bird with pearly-grey upperparts; jet-black cap and nape, when breeding; white below; narrow, pointed wings; deeply-forked tail; bright yellow, pointed beak and red legs diagnostic. In winter, black on crown and nape reduced to flecks. Sexes alike. Solitary or small flocks, flying about erratically; keeps to riversides, calm waters, large tanks; scans over water, plunges if possible prey in sight; rests on riverbanks, noisy and aggressive, especially at nesting colonies (March to mid-June).

juvenile

ROSEATE TERN

Sterna dougallii Laridae

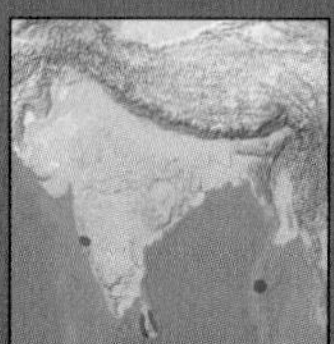

Size 41 cm

Voice Typical call a *chivy* or *cherr…rrick*

Range Summer visitor to Vengurla Rocks on W coast. Sri Lanka

Habitat Flocks with similar tern species; often follows fishing boats

Called so for its pinkish tint on underparts. Very similar to Common, but distinguished by long streamer tails and less black on wing-tips. Paler grey upperparts, long fine bill with extensive black tip, longish legs. Breeding adult has extensive black forehead, crown and nape. Non-breeding adult has white forehead. Feeds by plunge-diving.

BLACK-NAPED TERN

Sterna sumatrana Laridae

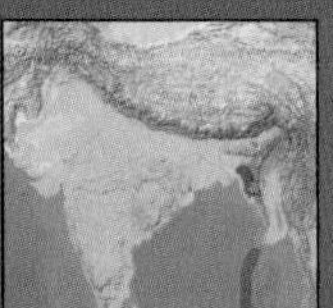

Size 33 cm

Voice Call a sharp *kik*

Range Local breeding resident; restricted to Maldives; Andaman and Nicobar Islands. Very rare off coasts of Bangladesh, S India and Sri Lanka

Habitat Strictly maritime

Crisply-marked, slim tern white with narrow black lines from eyes to black nape and deep-forked tail. Upperparts washed very pale grey with dark shafts to outer primary only. May show pink flush below when breeding. Black legs and bill. Sexes alike. Juvenile black-flecked above. Looks whiter than Roseate, which is similar in non-breeding plumage.

COMMON TERN

Sterna hirundo Laridae

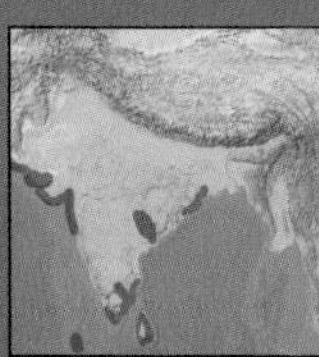

Size 35 cm

Voice Call a loud, harsh *kirrah… kirrah*

Range Breeds in Ladakh. Local winter visitor; most coasts and sometimes inland. Most common: Pakistan, S India and Sri Lanka

Habitat Coasts; rarely, inland lakes and rivers

Similar to Roseate, but distinguished by shorter tail, red bill with black tip and more black on wing-tips. Greyish wash to underparts; mantle and wings pale grey contrasting with white rump and white deeply-forked tail. In flight, shows darker tips to primaries. Non-breeding and juvenile have mottled head. Sexes alike. Feeds by plunge-diving.

WHITE-CHEEKED TERN

Sterna repressa Laridae

Size 32-34 cm

Voice Similar to Common's; also has diagnostic hoarse *kee…err* or *kee…ceek*

Range Breeds off Maharashtra coast; offshore waters of Pakistan, W India

Habitat Offshore waters

Very similar to Common but distinguished by darker grey upperparts and uniform grey rump and tail with back; underwing has darker trailing edge and pale central panel. Breeding adult has dirty-grey back, wings, rump, tail and underparts; black crown; white cheeks. Non-breeding adult has almost completely white head with brownish-patch around eye and nape. Brownish-red legs and feet; bill graduates from dark red base and black towards pale tip. Juvenile similar to non-breeding adult, but has more brown upperparts.

SAUNDERS'S TERN

Sternula saundersi Laridae

Size 23 cm

Voice Call a penetrating, wiry, nasal worried *ker…wick*

Range W coasts

Habitat Coastal waters

Often confused with Little. Pale grey upperparts; white underparts, rump and tail; black streaks on outer primaries, conspicuous in flight. Legs and feet vary from olive-brown to reddish-brown or pinkish-brown. Breeding adult has black cap, white-patch on forehead; yellow bill with black tip. Non-breeding adult has white head, with black plumage extending from hindneck through eye; black bill. Juvenile has sandy-buff plumage, with each feather having darker centre.

LITTLE TERN

Sternula albifrons Laridae

Size 23 cm

Voice Call a high, hurried *kink…kink*

Range Local breeder in N, S coasts and Sri Lanka. Disperses widely, mainly to coasts in non-breeding season

Habitat Sandy coasts; large rivers; lakes

non-breeding

Tiny tern with short tail and fast flight. Distinctive yellow bill with black tip and yellow legs; white forehead; pale grey back and wings with dark outer primaries. Forehead patch extends like a point above eye. Non-breeding has black bill and smaller black cap. Sexes alike. Hovers over surface of water with fast wingbeats; plunges to catch fish. Male's aerial display involves calling and carrying fish to attract female, which soars high before descending by gliding with wings in a V. Juvenile has black on grey upperparts and wings.

ARCTIC TERN

Sterna paradisaea Laridae

Size 41 cm

Voice Similar to Common's and may only be told with comparative experience

Range Vagrant; recorded only in Kashmir

Habitat Oceans

Smallish tern, similar to Common, but has shorter beak, legs and neck, and narrower wings. Soft, grey upperparts and white throat, neck and breast; long, pointed, forked-tail and pointed wings edged with dark line; very short legs, and looks like it is crouching down when standing. Mature has bright red beak, seldom with black tip. Flight similar to Common's, but little more graceful; rounder crown. Breeding adult has longer tail-streamers and extensive black cap. Sexes alike. More aerially adept than Common, with deep steady wingbeats.

BLACK-BELLIED TERN

Sterna acuticauda Laridae

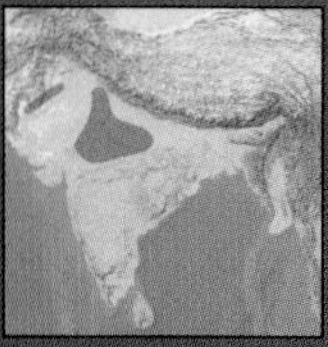

Size 33 cm

Voice Calls include a shrill *krek… krek* and fast *kek…kek…kek*

Range Globally threatened, local resident; now very local breeding resident throughout most of the region

Habitat Inland rivers; lakes

Small, slender tern with very long tail and black underparts. Similar to River, but distinguished by deep orange bill with variable black tip. Black cap; darkish-grey upperparts, white face, neck. Breeding adult has black from lower breast to vent. Non-breeding adult white, streaked on crown. Sexes alike.

BRIDLED TERN

Onychoprion anaethetus Laridae

Similar to Sooty, but smaller and less pied, with paler upperparts and black nape and crown; narrower white forehead patch. In flight, has prominent white leading edge to wings and whiter outer rectrices. Variation, as many as three races once recognised in the region.

juvenile

Size 33 cm

Voice Call low-pitched, includes a robust yapping *wup…wup*

Range Breeding visitor; (or resident), Vengurla Rocks

Habitat Flocks regularly; gathers where fish shoal near surface, or near fishing boats

adult

SOOTY TERN

Onychoprion fuscata Laridae

Size 33-36 cm

Voice Call a loud, piercing *wide…a…wake*

Range Breeds off Maharashtra coast, Lakshadweep and Maldives, seas adjacent to breeding islands in non-breeding season

Habitat Pelagic

Largish black tern with white underparts, forehead and tail-streamers and thin white leading edge to inner wing; extensive blackish underside to primaries, black tail with white outer-tail feathers; white forehead patch with narrower black loral-stripe. Non-breeding adult may show white spotting on crown and white fringed-upperparts; upperparts may appear brownish and white feather bases may be visible. Juvenile similar but greyer with white scallops above and grey breast.

WHISKERED TERN

Chlidonias hybrida Laridae

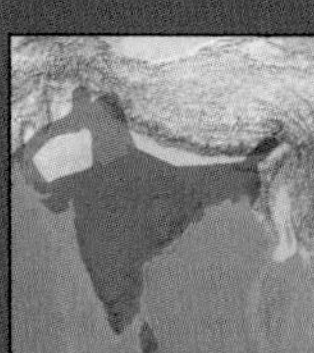

breeding

Size 25 cm

Voice Sharp, wild notes

Range Breeds in Kashmir and Gangetic plain; common in winter over the area

Habitat Inland marshes; wet cultivation; coastal areas; tidal creeks

Slender tern with black markings on crown; silvery-grey-white plumage; long, narrow wings and slightly forked, almost squarish tail; short red legs and red beak distinctive. Breeding adult has jet-black cap and snow-white cheeks; black belly. At rest, closed wings extend beyond tail. Sexes alike. Large numbers fly about marshes or tidal creeks, leisurely but methodically, beak pointed down; dives from about 5 m height, taking turn when just about to touch ground, picking up insects in the process; also hunts flying insects over standing crops.

non-breeding

WHITE-WINGED TERN

Chlidonias leucopterus Laridae

Size 23 cm

Voice Quiet. Call a rasping *chree*

Range Scarce passage migrant, winter visitor

Habitat Rivers, lakes and estuaries. Feeds by surface-dipping. Does not dive

Breeding adult has velvety-black head, neck, breast and belly; almost white tail and rump; pale grey upperwings with broad, white leading edge; red bill and short, red legs. Non-breeding adult has largely grey upperparts and tail; white rump; white head and neck, and black-and-white streaked cap. Juvenile similar in appearance to non-breeding adult, but has an entirely black cap.

BLACK TERN

Chlidonias niger Laridae

Size 23 cm

Range Vagrant

Small, graceful tern with distinct breeding plumage. Black head, neck and underparts; slaty-grey upperparts and wings; grey tail; grey undersides to wings; white undertail; black beak; short, blackish-red legs. Sexes alike, but female more greyish. Non-breeding adult has pale grey upperparts and white underparts; white head; dark patch on either side of breast; dark crown attached to dark patch behind eye; dark spot in front of eye. Juvenile similar to non-breeding adult, but has pale brownish wash on forehead; greyish-brown back and pale edges to feathers.

WHITE TERN

Gygis alba Laridae

Size 29 cm

Voice Call a harsh *grich…grich*

Range Common resident; only in Maldives. In non-breeding season, wanders Indian Ocean and could be storm-blown to mainland coasts

Pristine white, elegant seabird with slender body and long tapering wings. Short, deeply forked-tail; black bill, curves slightly upwards and tapers to sharp point; blackish legs with yellow webs between toes, small eyes surrounded by black rings. Sexes alike. Juvenile has brownish-grey back; grey neck; black mark behind eye. Feeds offshore on small fish shoals, usually catching them in air as they jump to escape predators. Flies with deliberate, slow wingbeats in undulating pattern for long periods. Extremely confiding at nest.

BROWN NODDY

Anous stolidus Laridae

Size 42 cm

Voice Call a dry growling *hrrrrarrhh*

Range Resident: Lakshadweep, Maldives

Habitat Pelagic. Breeds in huge colonies

Tropical seabird and largest of the noddies, distinguished from the closely-related Black by larger size and dark brown plumage and greyish-white cap. Broadish wings and longish wedge-shaped tail; white forehead, narrow white half-ring below eye; black lores. Juvenile has narrower, often brown-mottled white forehead and pale edges on upperparts; pale grey underwings and dark brown tail visible in flight. Known to perch on heads of brown pelicans to capture fish that escape from the bill of pelican.

BLACK NODDY

Anous minutus Laridae

Size 37 cm

Voice Call includes varied short rattles, perhaps drier and shriller than in Lesser

Range Vagrant

Habitat Pelagic

Medium-sized tern with uniformly dark, sooty plumage and white cap. White cap graduates into grey body. Small, white markings on lower and upper rims of eyelids; black lores; black eye patch continues to form broad patch above and behind eye; black face sides and black underparts; white half-ring below eye; strong, black bill; reddish-brown to orange legs and feet; mouth lining and tongue orange-yellow; wedge-shaped tail. Sexes similar. Juvenile also similar, but slightly paler; white cap sharply differentiated from grey body. Forages in large flocks.

LESSER NODDY

Anous tenuirostris Laridae

Size 33 cm

Voice Call includes varied short rattling notes; generally squeakier and more cackling than in the other two noddies

Range Non-breeding visitor; Sri Lanka

Habitat Similar to Brown's

Similar to Black, but distinguished by smaller size and paler, greyer body and shorter bill. Distinguished from Brown by longer, thinner bill and darker brownish-black colour; shorter and broader wings and shorter tail. Non-breeding adult has whiter forehead and crown. Pale grey cap grading evenly into grey face sides; white half-ring below eye; pale grey lores; dark brown underwings and belly visible in flight. Flight somewhat faster and more fluttery than Brown's. Juvenile whiter on head than adult and shows pale fringes to upperparts. Distinguished from juvenile Brown by slimmer shape, dark underwing and overall darker colour.

INDIAN SKIMMER

Rynchops albicollis Laridae

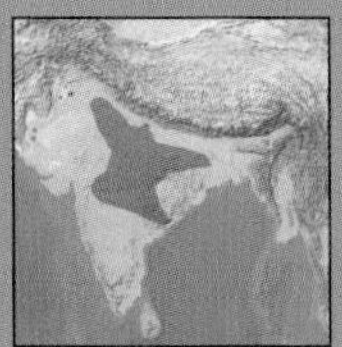

Size 40 cm

Voice Call a shrill scream; twittering cries at nest colony

Range Most common in N and C India, east to Assam. Less common in S Maharashtra, N Andhra Pradesh

Habitat Large rivers; fond of placid waters

Diagnostic yellowish-orange beak, much longer lower mandible; slender, pointed-wings and tern-like pied plumage, blackish-brown above, contrasting with white underbody; white forehead, neck-collar and wing-bar; red legs. Sexes alike, but female slightly smaller. Juvenile has dusky orange bill with blackish tip, dull orange legs, paler, brownish-grey upperparts and white-buff fringes to mantle and wing-coverts. Solitary, or loose flocks fly over water; characteristic hunting style to skim over calm waters, beak wide open, longer projecting lower mandible partly submerged at an angle to snap up fish on striking; many rest together on sandbars.

BROWN SKUA

Stercorarius antarcticus Stercorariidae

Size 63 cm

Range Rare visitor to India, Sri Lanka and Maldives

Habitat Pelagic

Large, broad-winged skua showing wide white areas at base of upper- and underside of primaries. Larger and more powerful than South Polar, with broader-based wings and larger bill. Adult distinguished from dark-morph South Polar by warmer brown hues to upperparts and underparts, and pale streaking and reddish-brown mottling on mantle and scapulars, which often show fairly large white blotches. Some can be paler brown on upper- and underparts, but lack contrast between head, underbody and mantle shown by intermediate morph South Polar. Juvenile warmer brown on upperparts and underparts.

SOUTH-POLAR SKUA

Stercorarius maccormicki Stercorariidae

Size 53 cm

Range Vagrant to Lakshadweep

Habitat Coastal waters

Large and powerfully built bird. Smaller than Brown with shorter bill. Shows white 'flashes' at base of upper- and underside of primaries. At rest, primaries usually extend beyond tail. Pale morph has pale buff head and body quite different from brown. Dark morph more similar to Brown, but has pale buff collar.

ARCTIC SKUA

Stercorarius parasiticus Stercorariidae

Size 45 cm

Voice Usually quiet at sea

Range Probably regular off Pakistan coast in non-breeding season

Habitat Pelagic

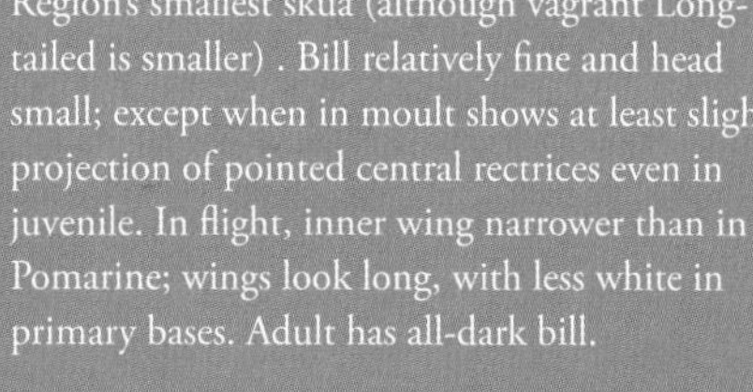

Region's smallest skua (although vagrant Long-tailed is smaller) . Bill relatively fine and head small; except when in moult shows at least slight projection of pointed central rectrices even in juvenile. In flight, inner wing narrower than in Pomarine; wings look long, with less white in primary bases. Adult has all-dark bill.

POMARINE SKUA

Stercorarius pomarinus Stercorariidae

Size 56 cm

Range Occurs as vagrant in the region's seas

Habitat Pelagic

Small skua with short and thick bill, with prominent dark tip. Breeding adult paler grey than other skuas, and bears unusual spoon-shaped central tail feathers. Non-breeding adult lacks streamers. Dark morph generally dark brown all over and has dark cap, while pale morph has dark wings, dark cap and pale breast. Powerful, steady flight.

PALLAS'S SANDGROUSE

Syrrhaptes paradoxus Pteroclidae

Size 40 cm

Voice Call a melodic, resonant *ten…ten*

Range Vagrant specimen in W Rajasthan

Habitat Barren, sandy desert and arid stony foothills

Heavily barred bird with elongated primary feathers giving a characteristic look. Rufous-orange face, back and rump, and post-ocular streak, and unmarked upper breast; distinctive black belly patch and white vent. Male has unmarked grey crown, narrow breast-band, and buff wing with large black spots on lower coverts and tertials. Female has fine black barring on mantle, coverts and tertials. Normally highly sociable and tame; flight unusually graceful for sandgrouse.

SPOTTED SANDGROUSE

Pterocles senegallus Pteroclidae

Size 30-35 cm

Voice Call a distinctive and far-carrying *quitoo…quitoo*

Range Breeds in S Pakistan and Rajasthan; winters in Pakistan and NW India

Habitat Barren, sandy desert and arid stony foothills

Diagnostic longitudinal black stripe on belly, mostly visible in flight. Throat and head sides ochre or orange-yellow, paler in female; yellow orbital ring; blue-grey bill. Male has khaki-brown upperparts with spotting on wing-coverts, and plain unmarked underparts; grey supercilium. Female has spotted upperparts and upper breast and plain lower breast; pale upperwing with dark trailing edge and black line down centre of whitish belly. Regularly flies to water about two hours after sunrise, also during evening in hot weather.

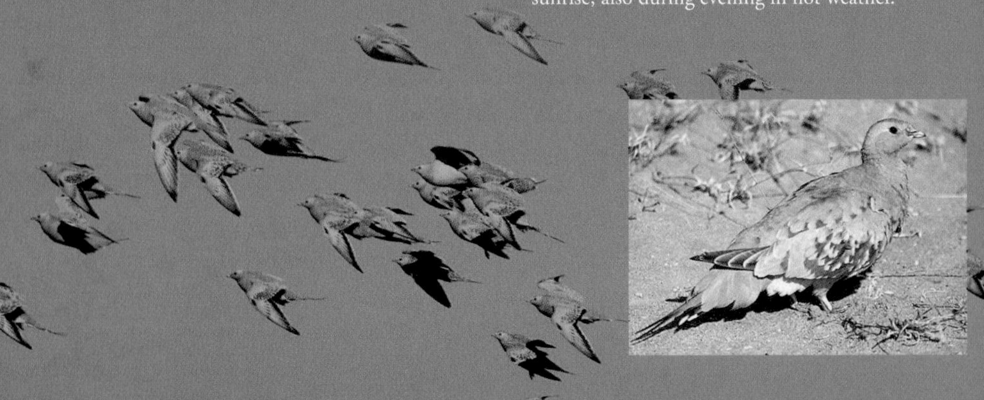

CHESTNUT-BELLIED SANDGROUSE

Pterocles exustus Pteroclidae

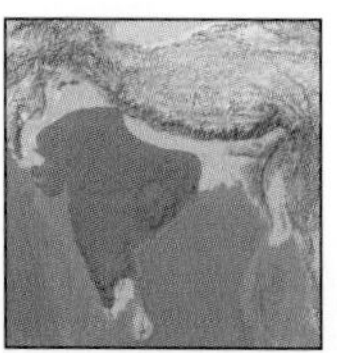

Size 28 cm

Voice Call note a deep, clucking *kut…ro…*, uttered mostly on wing

Range All over India except NE and extreme S; most common in NW, C India

Habitat Open areas; semi-desert; fallow lands

More plain-looking sandgrouse. Male has sandy-buff upperparts speckled brown and dull yellow; black gorget and chocolate-black belly. Female buffy above, streaked and barred darker; black-spotted breast; rufous and black-barred belly and flanks. Pointed central tail feathers and black underside of wings distinctive in flight. Large flocks at waterholes in dry season; regularly arrives at water; prefers to stay on ground.

PIN-TAILED SANDGROUSE

Pterocles alchata Pteroclidae

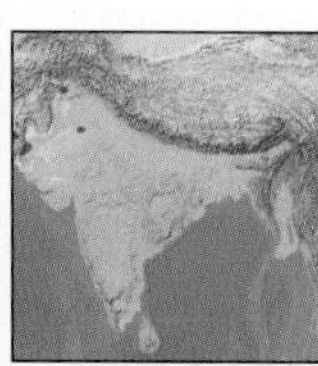

Size 31-39 cm

Voice Calls include ringing *catar… catar*, nasal *ga…ga…ga* and abrupt guttural *gang…gang*

Range Probably breeds; winter visitor to Pakistan and NW India

Habitat Arid, sandy desert, scrub desert and fallow lands in partly cultivated semi-desert

Medium to large-sized bird with small head and long pointed wings. Uppperparts and head ochre-green; white underparts with strong dull orange breast-band, bordered black; white underwings visible in flight; long tail. Sexes more or less similar, but female has shorter tail. Gregarious; nests in dry, open ground. Seen in flocks near waterholes.

BLACK-BELLIED SANDGROUSE

Pterocles orientalis Pteroclidae

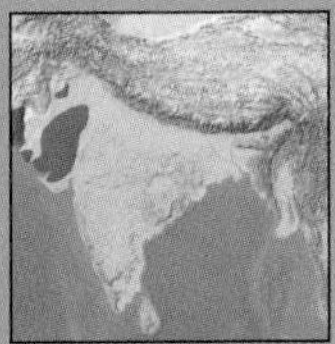

Size 40 cm

Voice Clucking call-notes; noisy on arrival on ground

Range Abundant but erratic winter visitor to NW India; sporadically in Gangetic plain and C India

Habitat Semi-desert areas, fallow lands

Rounded bird with stocky appearance. Male has mottled sandy-grey upperparts; rufous-brown neck sides, and upper throat; black throat, belly and flanks; narrow black breast-band defines upper breast and buff-brown band between gorget and belly. Female has mottled dull peach plumage; black line below yellow throat; black belly, flanks. Whitish underside of wings. Gregarious, regularly seen at waterholes. Breeds in Baluchistan.

TIBETAN SANDGROUSE

Syrrhaptes tibetanus Pteroclidae

Size 48 cm

Voice Call a deep, musical *guk…guk*

Range Locally common breeding resident in Ladakh, Himachal Pradesh and Sikkim. Also occurs in C Asia

Habitat High altitude, stony pastures and semi-desert where it is the only sandgrouse

Large sandgrouse with pigeon-shaped body that can be identified by white belly and dark underwing. Small head and bill; feathered legs and feet; long, pointed wings. Adult male overall pale sandy-brown. Orangish face; fine black barring on breast; scapular spots. Sexes similar, but female has shorter tail and barred upperparts. Feeds on plant material. Nests on bare ground. Fast flight.

PAINTED SANDGROUSE

Pterocles indicus Pteroclidae

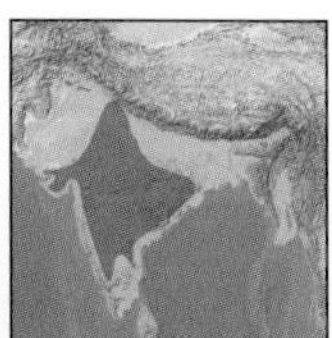

Size 28 cm

Voice Call a thick, clucking *wuko… wuko* in flight

Range Scarce breeding, endemic resident mainly in dry parts of N and C India

Habitat Dry, open woodlands and thorn scrub usually on hillsides

Small, blunt-tailed sandgrouse. Male has broad black-and-buff and chestnut breast-bands and black-and-white crown pattern; plain sandy head and neck; intensely barred black-and-white; plain, sandy wing-coverts; plain underwings. Both sexes have barred upperparts and foreneck. Female has plainer face and finer barring on body and plain greyish throat. Feeds mainly on seeds. Gregarious; flocks congregate at waterholes.

HILL PIGEON

Columba rupestris Columbidae

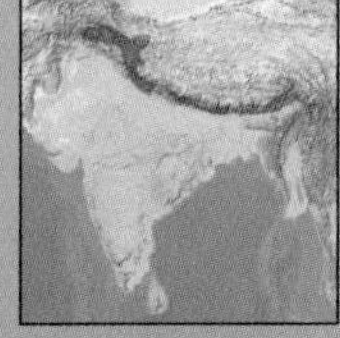

Size 33 cm

Voice Call a rather high-pitched *guk… guk…guk*

Range Common resident in the Himalayas from Kashmir to Nepal

Habitat High rocky country; village cultivation

High-altitude, pale grey pigeon with greenish-purple iridiscence on neck and breast. White back; grey rump; dark bars on inner wing; dark tail with striking, broad, white subterminal band. Very similar to Common Pigeon but paler, with white band on tail and dark terminal band. Sexes alike. Juvenile more brown and lacks metallic sheen on body. Feeds on grains.

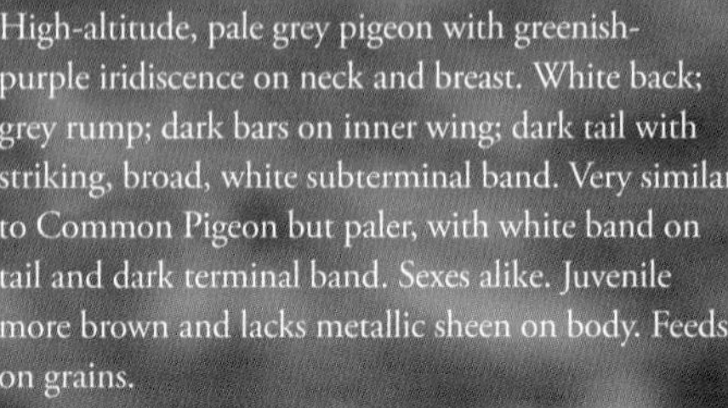

SNOW PIGEON

Columba leuconota Columbidae

Size 35 cm

Voice Call a high *coo…coo…coo*

Range The Himalayas, 2,800-5,000 m, may descend to about 1,000 m in winter

Habitat Open meadows; cultivation; mountain habitation; cliff-faces

Blackish-brown head separated from dull brown back by whitish collar; extensive white on lower back and three dark bands in grey wings, seen both at rest and in flight; very dark tail with white subterminal band; black beak and red feet. Sexes alike. Flocks of variable size gleaning on ground, frequently around mountain habitations, freshly-sown cultivations and vicinities of melting snow; flight very strong; breeds in large colonies on cliffs and in rock-caves.

YELLOW-EYED PIGEON

Columba eversmanni Columbidae

Size 33 cm

Voice Usually silent

Range Winter visitor, passage migrant; Pakistan and N India

Habitat Lightly-wooded areas in plains or cultivation

Small, grey pigeon with white back, two partial black wing-bars and small patch of iridescent green and purple on neck sides. Similar to Common, but smaller and paler and has distinct yellowish bill tip; distinguished by short, black bars on inner wing, yellow eye-ring and pinkish crown. Yellowish iris and orbital skin; grey mantle with diffused greyish-brown fringes; upperparts can, sometimes, be more uniform grey. Short tail with dark band diffusely demarcated. Large pale areas on primaries, narrow black trailing edge. Juvenile duller with fawn breast. Nests in hole in tree or bank. Flight fast and direct.

COMMON WOOD PIGEON

Columba palumbus Columbidae

Size 43 cm

Voice Call a deep crooning *dooh…doo…daw…daw doo.* Wings clatter on take off

Range Local breeding resident: N hills of Pakistan and Kashmir. Erratic but sometimes numerous winter visitor further south in hills of NW India east to Nepal

Habitat Hill scrub and woodlands; also cultivation

Plump grey dove with white wing flashes, small head and long, black-tipped tail. Green and whitish neck marks on head, pinkish breast, small red-and-yellow bill, pink legs. Bold, white band on upperwing visible in flight, diagnostic. Often in flocks. Feeds mainly on seeds, grain, acorns and buds. Climbs about in foliage. On ground, crouches low when feeding. Wary, especially where hunted. Nests in trees. Slow, heavy flight.

SPECKLED WOOD PIGEON

Columba hodgsonii Columbidae

Size 38 cm

Voice Utters a deep *whock… whr…ooooo…whroo*

Range Resident: The Himalayas, hills of NE India

Habitat Oak-rhododendron forests

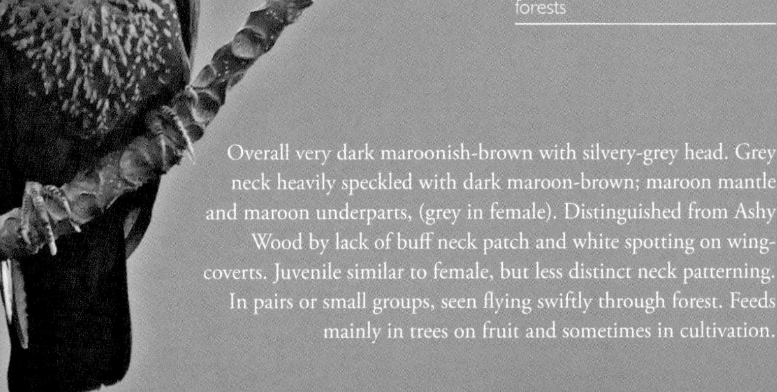

Overall very dark maroonish-brown with silvery-grey head. Grey neck heavily speckled with dark maroon-brown; maroon mantle and maroon underparts, (grey in female). Distinguished from Ashy Wood by lack of buff neck patch and white spotting on wing-coverts. Juvenile similar to female, but less distinct neck patterning. In pairs or small groups, seen flying swiftly through forest. Feeds mainly in trees on fruit and sometimes in cultivation.

ASHY WOOD PIGEON

Columba pulchricollis Columbidae

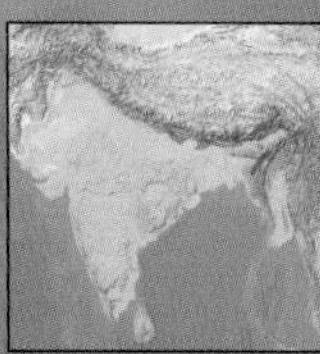

Size 36 cm

Voice Call a slightly booming, repeated *whuoo…whuoo…whuoo*

Range Resident: The Himalayas, hills of NE India

Habitat Dense foliage in broadleaved forests

Creamy-buff collar, pale grey head and blackish-grey mantle diagnostic. Similar to Speckled but distinguished by slate-grey upperparts, lack of white speckles on wing-coverts and uniform dark slate-grey breast. Iridescent green-and-purple on lower neck and back. Juvenile has more brown upperparts, with less distinct patterning on neck, and rufous fringes to feathers of breast and belly. Singly, or in pairs; sits quietly in tree canopy; disappears swiftly when flushed. Nests in flimsy structures of intertwined twigs. Feeds mostly on fruit.

NILGIRI WOOD PIGEON

Columba elphinstonii Columbidae

Size 42 cm

Voice Call a loud *who*, followed by 3-to-5 deep and eerie sounding *who…who…who…* notes

Range Western Ghats south from Mumbai

Habitat Evergreen forests; sholas; cardamom plantations

Strikingly beautiful bird with reddish-brown upperparts and metallic purple-green sheen on upper back. Grey head and underbody; whitish throat; black-and-white chessboard on hindneck diagnostic. Sexes alike. Solitary, or in small gatherings; arboreal but often descends to forest floor to pick fallen fruit; strong flier, wheeling and turning amidst branches at fast speed; occasionally along with other frugivorous birds.

PALE-CAPPED PIGEON

Columba punicea Columbidae

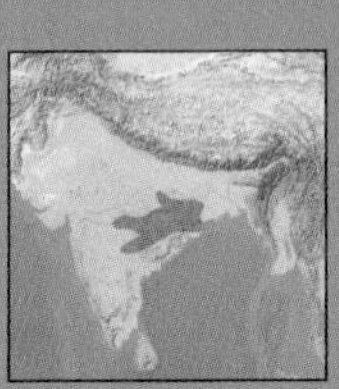

Size 36 cm

Voice Unknown

Range Rare breeding resident Odisha and Assam

Habitat Tall trees

juvenile

Rich chestnut-maroon upperparts, pale vinous-chestnut underparts. Pale bluish-grey cap; maroon-brown mantle and wing-coverts with green-and-purple sheen. Sexes similar, but female darker with dark grey crown. Juvenile lacks cap; upperparts more brown, with chestnut fringes, and underparts mixed grey and rufous-buff.

♀

ROCK PIGEON

Columba livia Columbidae

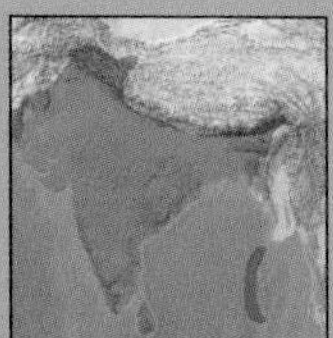

Size 33 cm

Voice Call a deep *tru…troo…tru*

Range Abundant feral and wild breeding resident throughout

Habitat Urban areas; cultivation

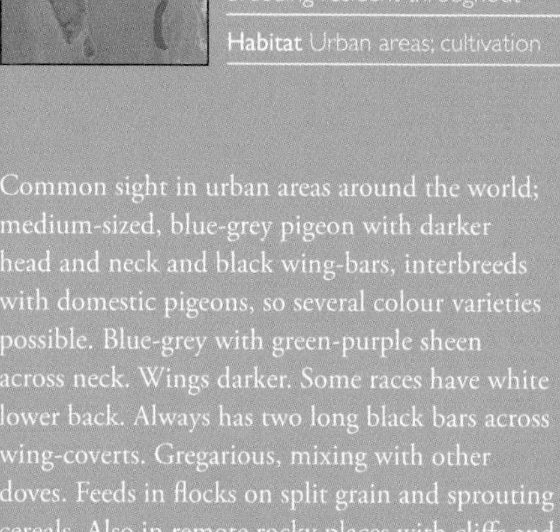

intermedia

neglecta

Common sight in urban areas around the world; medium-sized, blue-grey pigeon with darker head and neck and black wing-bars, interbreeds with domestic pigeons, so several colour varieties possible. Blue-grey with green-purple sheen across neck. Wings darker. Some races have white lower back. Always has two long black bars across wing-coverts. Gregarious, mixing with other doves. Feeds in flocks on split grain and sprouting cereals. Also in remote rocky places with cliffs and ruins. Nests colonially in cavities and on ledges in buildings and cliffs.

SRI LANKA WOOD PIGEON

Columba torringtoniae Columbidae

Size 36 cm

Voice Call a deep owl-like *hoo* in courtship display

Range Resident; Sri Lanka

Habitat Plains, cultivation. Globally threatened

Medium-sized pigeon with dark grey wings tinged green. Upperparts slaty-grey while underparts dark vinous; nape has prominent black-and-white 'chessboard' pattern; broad tail. Distinguished from Speckled Wood by lack of white spotting on wing-coverts and uniform dark breast. Sexes alike. Juvenile duller with barely noticeable 'chessboard'. Strong flier. Feeds on ficus fruits, rarely descending to ground. In pairs, or small groups. Shy and wary. Difficult to see as often concealed amidst deep foliage of dense forest.

ORIENTAL TURTLE DOVE

Streptopelia orientalis Columbidae

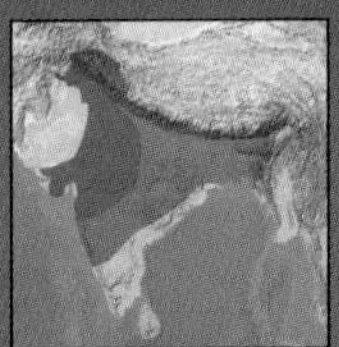

Size 32 cm

Voice Call a deep and grating *ghur…ghroo…goo…*

Range Several races, resident and migratory, distributed over much of the Indian region

Habitat Mixed forests; vicinity of cultivation; orchards

Large, stocky dove with grey-and-black spotted patch on neck sides. Rufous-brown back and scapulars, with black markings diagnostic; slaty-grey lower back, rump; whitish border to roundish tail, best seen when tail fanned during landing. Sexes alike. In pairs or loose parties, occasionally solitary birds; feeds mostly on ground; rests during hot hours in leafy branches; perches on overhead wires.

meena

erythrocephala

EURASIAN COLLARED DOVE

Streptopelia decaocto Columbidae

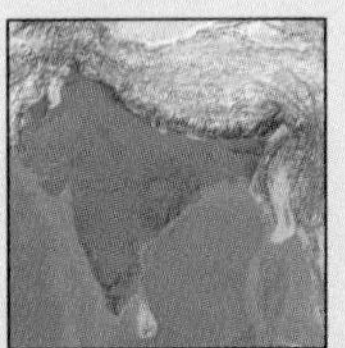

Size 32 cm

Voice Call a characteristic *kukkoo…kook…*

Range Most of the region, except extreme NE Himalayas; resident and local migrant; most common in NW, W and C India

Habitat Cultivation; open scrub; dry forests

Similar to Red Collared female but larger with different tail pattern. Greyish-brown plumage; lilac wash about head and neck; black half-collar on hindneck distinctive; broad whitish tips to brown tail feathers, seen as terminal band when fanned during landing; dull lilac breast and ash-grey underbody. Sexes alike. Small parties, when not breeding; often associates with other doves; large gatherings glean in cultivated country; strong flier, chases intruders in territory.

RED COLLARED DOVE

Streptopelia tranquebarica Columbidae

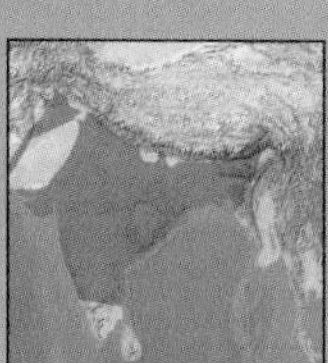

Size 23 cm

Voice Call a quick repeated *gru... gurgoo...*, with more stress on first syllable

Range Throughout the region, south of the Himalayan foothills

Habitat Cultivation; scrubs; deciduous country

Male has deep ash-grey head; black hindneck-collar; rich wine-red back; slaty grey-brown lower back, rump and uppertail; whitish tips to all but central tail feathers. Female much like Eurasian Collared, but smaller size and more brownish colouration distinctive. Solitary, in pairs or small parties; associates with other doves but less common; feeds on ground, gleaning on harvested croplands; perches and suns on leafless branches and overhead wires.

SPOTTED DOVE

Stigmatopelia chinensis Columbidae

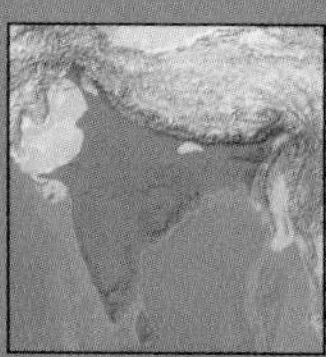

Size 30 cm

Voice Familiar bird sound of India, a soft, somewhat doleful *crook...cru...croo or croo...croo...*

Range Subcontinent, upto about 3,500 m in the Himalayas

Habitat Open forests; scrubs; habitation; cultivation

Slender dove with long wedged tail. Grey and pink-brown above, spotted white; white-spotted black hindneck-collar (chessboard) diagnostic; dark tail with broad white tips to outer feathers seen in flight; vinous-brown breast, merging into white on belly. Sexes alike. Juvenile barred above and lack chessboard. In pairs or small parties on ground; frequently settles on paths and roads, flying further on intrusion; quite tame and confiding in many areas; drinks often; at harvest times, seen along with other doves in immense gatherings.

LAUGHING DOVE

Stigmapelia senegalensis Columbidae

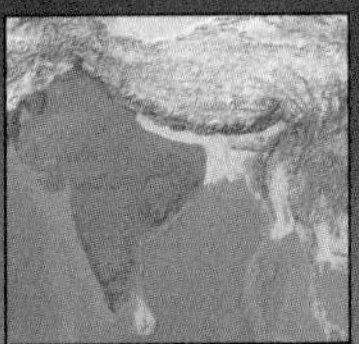

Size 27 cm

Voice Call a somewhat harsh but pleasant *cru… do…do…do…do*

Range Almost across India upto about 1,200 m in the outer Himalayas; uncommon in NE states

Habitat Open scrub; cultivation; neighbourhood of habitation

Pinkish grey-brown plumage with black-and-buff chessboard on sides of foreneck; white tips to outer-tail feathers and broad grey wing patches best seen in flight; small size distinctive. Sexes alike. In pairs, or small flocks; associates freely with other doves in huge gatherings at harvest time; feeds mostly on ground, walking about silently.

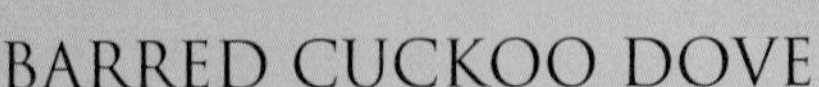

BARRED CUCKOO DOVE

Macropygia unchall Columbidae

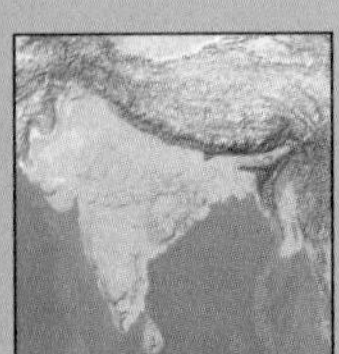

Size 41 cm

Voice Call a deep *croo…umm*

Range C Nepal east to entire NE Indian region

Habitat Dense broadleaved evergreen, tropical, subtropical and temperate forests; secondary growth

Large and distinctive dove with slim body and long graduated tail; reddish-brown upperparts and tail heavily barred with brown; male has paler unbarred buff head and underparts; iridescent green on nape and crown; some barring on sides of neck and upper breast; female has barring on underparts and some iridescence on nape and sides of neck. Forest-dwelling, often acrobatic in effort to reach food. Most often glimpsed flying between trees. Feeds mostly on small fruits and berries.

ANDAMAN CUCKOO DOVE

Macropygia rufipennis Columbidae

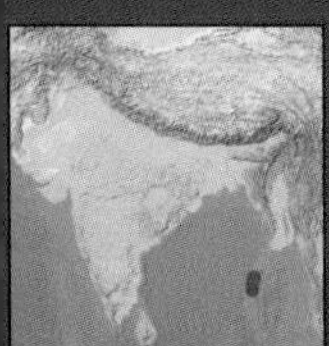

Size 41 cm

Voice Call a repeated, hoarse, deep, subdued croaking *o…o…o…oh*

Range Andaman and Nicobar Islands; only cuckoo dove in these islands

Habitat Dense forests

Large cuckoo dove with smallish head and slim body and long, graduated tail. Head and underparts reddish-brown in colour. In flight, shows rufous flashes across inner webs of primaries and rufous underwing-coverts. Male has brown barring across breast and belly, and unmarked rufous head.

EMERALD DOVE

Chalcophaps indica Columbidae

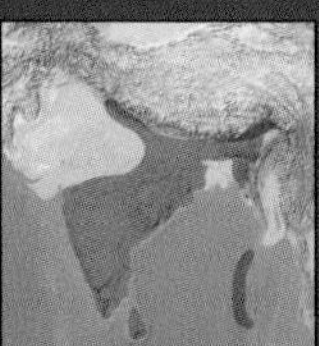

Size 26 cm

Voice Call a deep, plaintive *hoo…oon…hoo…oon…*, many times at a stretch

Range Almost throughout the subcontinent upto about 2,000 m. Absent in Pakistan

Habitat Forests, bamboo clearings; foothills

Bronze emerald-green upperbody; white forehead and eyebrows; grey crown and neck; white on wing shoulder and across lower back; whitish rump diagnostic in flight; rich pinkish-brown below; coral-red beak and pink-red legs. Sexes similar with female duller. Solitary, or in pairs; moves on forest paths and clearings or darts almost blindly through trees, usually under 5 m off ground; difficult to spot on ground.

NICOBAR PIGEON

Caloenas nicobarica Columbidae

Size 41 cm

Voice Usually silent; occasionally croaks

Range Rare endemic breeding resident of Nicobar Islands, sometimes visits Andaman Islands

Habitat Undisturbed wet evergreen forests

Said to be the closest living relative of the extinct dodo. Iridescent slaty blue-grey and green upperparts with coppery wash. Male has diagnostic neck and back hackles; red legs; short white tail; dark eyes, bill and feet. Female smaller than male and identified by white iris. Juvenile has no hackles, dark tail and lacks iridescence. Often flies between islands. Feeds on fruits and seeds on forest floor. Flies noisily up into tree-tops when disturbed. Nests in forest trees, sometimes colonially.

ORANGE-BREASTED GREEN PIGEON

Treron bicinctus Columbidae

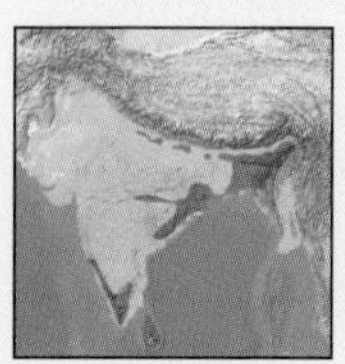

Size 33 cm

Voice Call a typical green pigeon whistle; quiet gurgle

Range Throughout the region

Habitat Subtropical moist deciduous broadleaved evergreen forests; secondary growth; well-wooded country

Smallish green pigeon with blue eyes. Male has distinctive bright orange breast with lilac border above; face and forehead yellowish green; nape and hindneck bluish-grey; unmarked plain green mantle. Female has yellower wash on underparts. Both have dark uppertail-coverts; central tail feathers grey; light grey banding on tail; yellow bordered wing-coverts. Gregarious; in small flocks; often in large groups or mixed feeding parties with other frugivores; arboreal; in fruiting trees; quiet; hard to detect; acrobatic.

GREY-FRONTED GREEN PIGEON

Treron p affinis Columbidae

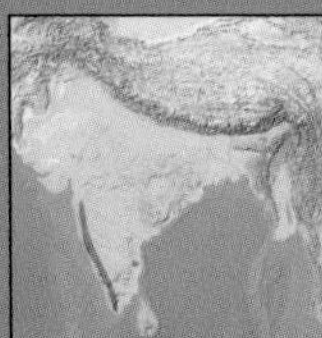

Size 28 cm

Voice Call includes fluty whistles

Range Western Ghats

Habitat Foothills of evergreen and moist-deciduous forests

The only similar species in western peninsular India is the Orange-breasted. Small, dark green pigeon with whitish forehead and pronounced grey crown. Face and brow greenish yellow. Male has maroon mantle, uniform green breast, pale blue-grey cap, yellowish face and throat, and darker chestnut undertail-coverts. Female has green mantle, and is distinguished from female Orange-breasted by yellowish face and throat, pale blue-grey cap and green scaling on whitish undertail-coverts. Juvenile similar to female, but slightly duller overall. In small flocks, but large concentrations in fruiting periods.

ASHY-HEADED GREEN PIGEON

Treron p phayrei Columbidae

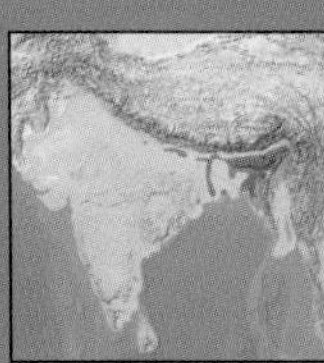

Size 28 cm

Voice Call includes fluty whistles

Range NE India

Habitat Foothill, evergreen and moist-deciduous forests

Similar to Thick-billed Green but distinguished by distinct grey crown, thin blue-grey bill; lacks red base to bill and greenish orbital skin. Male has maroon mantle; broad orangish breast-band on yellowish underparts; buffy-orange thighs; dark brown undertail-coverts. Female has dull grey mantle and white undertail-coverts. Often found in company of Orange-breasted. Mostly arboreal, descending only to drink or at salt-licks.

SRI LANKA GREEN PIGEON

Treron pompadora Columbidae

Size 28 cm

Voice Song a low-pitched mellow whistling

Range Sri Lanka

Habitat Forests and open areas with trees

Only similar species in Sri Lanka is Orange-breasted. Male has grey-blue rear crown and nape which turns green on hindneck; maroon mantle; green central uppertail. The outer feathers pale-tipped. Female very similar to female Orange-breasted, but has strongly marked vent and undertail.

♀

THICK-BILLED GREEN PIGEON

Treron curvirostra Columbidae

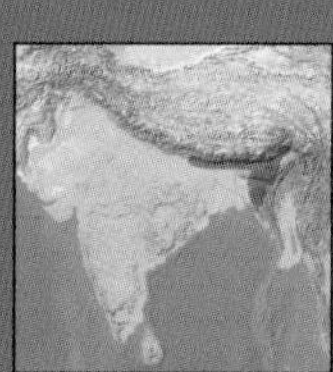

Size 27 cm

Voice Calls include musical whistles and throaty *kloo…kloo*

Range Scarce resident: NE India, parts of Bangladesh and Nepal

Habitat Forests; groves

Medium-sized green pigeon. Male has greyish nape and crown; maroon mantle; brown undertail-coverts; broad bluish-green orbital skin; heavy, large bill with scarlet red base. Female has greyish crown and nape while mantle and underparts green. Gregarious, and often found with other green pigeons. Primarily forest bird, but often seen in forest fringes, gardens and plantations.

YELLOW-FOOTED GREEN PIGEON

Treron phoenicopterus Columbidae

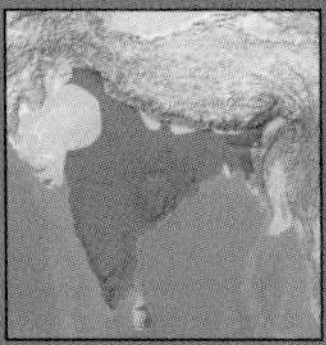

Size 33 cm

Voice Call includes rich, mellow whistling notes

Range South roughly of line from S Rajasthan to N Odisha to Sri Lanka; rarer in Pakistan

Habitat Forests; orchards; city parks; cultivated village vicinities

Male ash olive-green above; olive-yellow collar, dark, slaty tail has band; lilac-red shoulder patch (mostly absent in female); yellow legs and underbody. Female slightly duller than male. The nominate (northern) race has grey lower breast and belly. Small flocks; mostly arboreal, rarely coming to salt-licks or cropland; remains well hidden in foliage but moves briskly; has favourite feeding trees.

PIN-TAILED GREEN PIGEON

Treron apicauda Columbidae

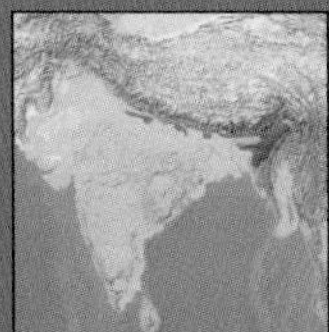

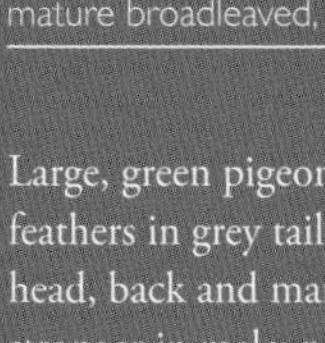

Size 42 cm

Voice Call a soft, winding *ko… kla…oi…oi…oi…oilli…illio…kla*

Range Uttarakhand eastwards through entire NE Indian region

Habitat Tropical, subtropical mature broadleaved, usually evergreen forests

Large, green pigeon with long, pointed central feathers in grey tail; vivid yellow-green rump; green head, back and mantle; grey cast on upper mantle, stronger in male; pale yellow edges to wing-coverts; male also has light orange wash to breast, lacking in female; both sexes have blue-grey around base of bill and eye. Strong flier. In small flocks, sometimes in mixed feeding parties.

WEDGE-TAILED GREEN PIGEON

Treron sphenurus Columbidae

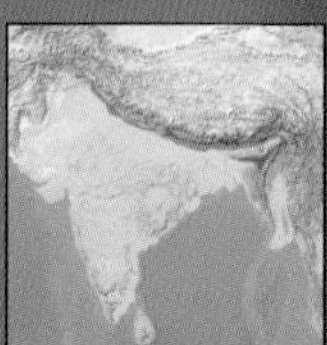

Size 33 cm

Voice Call a melodious whistling *hoo …whoo…huhuhu…*

Range Himachal Pradesh east to the entire NE Indian region

Habitat Subtropical broadleaved mixed forests; edges of forests

Largish pigeon with distinctive wedge-shaped tail; dark grey-green plumage on upperparts; maroon-patch of male restricted to shoulders and lower mantle; grey upper mantle; pale orange crown and breast; only faint, narrow yellow edges to wing-coverts; yellowish green face, throat, underparts. Often associates with other green pigeons.

GREEN IMPERIAL PIGEON

Ducula aenea Columbidae

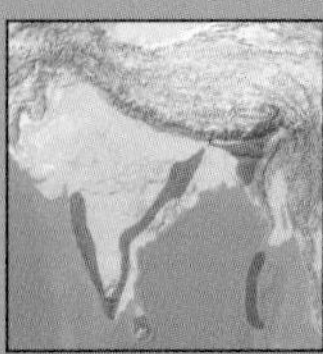

Size 43 cm

Voice Deep chuckling notes, quite pleasant-sounding and somewhat ventriloquistic

Range Forested parts of N India, from Garhwal Terai eastwards; forested regions of C and E India, Western Ghats south of Mumbai; resident in many areas but also moves considerably

Habitat Evergreen forests

Large forest pigeon, often confused with similar Mountain Imperial, but much smaller. Greyish head, neck and underbody with distinct pinkish wash; metallic bronze-green upperbody, unbanded tail; chocolate-maroon undertail; reddish legs. Sexes alike. Juvenile overall duller. Known for aerial display, repeatedly rises to dive with half-closed wings. In pairs, or small parties on fruiting trees, not infrequently with other species; chiefly arboreal but comes to ground, at salt-licks and water; strong flight; has favourite feeding spots. Several regional variations.

MOUNTAIN IMPERIAL PIGEON

Ducula badia Columbidae

Size 45 cm

Voice Call a booming *oomp…oomp*

Range Fairly common breeding resident: Western Ghats, NE India, parts of Nepal

Habitat Closed forests

Very large pigeon with grey head and neck tinged with pink. Wings and mantle brownish-maroon, throat and chin white. Pinkish-grey underparts; dark-based tail with broad, pale terminal band. Red-based bill and red eye-rings with pale iris. Pinkish feet. Sexes alike.

PIED IMPERIAL PIGEON

Ducula bicolor Columbidae

Size 41 cm

Voice Calls include deep *kru…kroo*, chuckling *hu…hu…hu*

Range Common breeding resident on Nicobar Islands. Visits Andaman Islands rarely

Habitat Forests, particularly mangroves

Large pigeon, overall white with flight feathers and tail-tip black. Bluish-grey bill and legs. Restricted to certain islands in Andaman and Nicobar. Moves in small groups, flying above coastal coconut and mangrove forests. Feeds on fruiting trees. Difficult to distinguish against pale blue sky.

RED-BREASTED PARAKEET

Psittacula alexandri Psittacidae

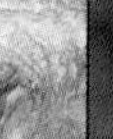

Size 38 cm

Voice Rather quiet. Call a sharp *quawnk*

Range Scarce breeding resident in N foothills east from Uttarakhand

Habitat Foothill forests

Adult has green upperparts; green or yellow median wing-coverts forming large patch on wing; grey head, with varying tinges of blue, and around eyes washed with green; black narrow line from forehead to eyes, black wide band across lower cheeks; salmon/pink throat to upper abdomen duller in female; green lower abdomen to undertail-coverts with blue suffusion; blue central tail feathers tipped with yellow/green. Bill coral red. Eye pale yellow. Juvenile has green crown and underparts; dark brown lower cheeks; brown/grey wash on green sides of head; green median wing-coverts margined with yellow/green. Tail short. Bill pale red. Eye grey.

VERNAL HANGING PARROT

Loriculus vernalis Psittacidae

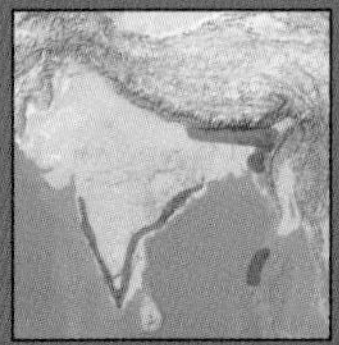

Size 15 cm

Voice Quiet but distinctive and rapid *zzit…zzit* in flight

Range Scarce breeding resident of lower hills of SW, E India and Bangladesh, subject to local movements

Habitat Forests

Small short-tailed and primarily emerald green-plumaged bird with blue-patch on throat; red rump and uppertail-coverts; red bill; white eye. Female similar to male but with little or no blue on throat. Juvenile similar to adult but has dull greyish-green on forehead and cheeks; no blue on throat; dull red rump washed green; pale orange bill; brown eye. Unique for its ability to sleep upside down. Very arboreal.

SRI LANKA HANGING PARROT

Loriculus beryllinus Psittacidae

Size 14 cm

Voice As Vernal's

Range Sri Lanka

Habitat Broadleaved evergreen and moist deciduous forests

Very similar to Vernal Hanging, but has larger bill, crimson forehead and crown, golden-orange cast to nape and mantle, turquoise wash on throat (like Vernal). Immature has greyish-green forehead, orange cast to green crown (with few splashes of red), and faint turquoise wash to throat.

ALEXANDRINE PARAKEET

Psittacula eupatria Psittacidae

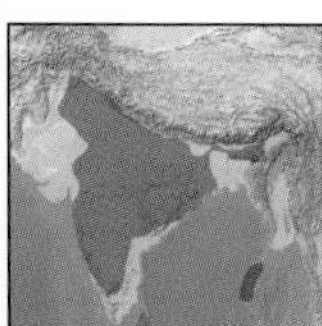

Size 53 cm

Voice Call a high-pitched *kreeak*... scream, on wing as well as on perch; popular cage bird, learning to imitate some notes and few human words

Range Almost throughout the region, south of the Himalayan foothills

Habitat Forests; orchards; cultivated areas; towns

Rich, vibrant-coloured bird. Male has rich grass-green plumage; hooked, heavy red beak; deep red shoulder patch; rose-pink collar and black stripe from lower mandible to collar distinctive. Female smaller and lacks collar and black stripe. Yellow undertail in both sexes. Seen in small flocks and large gatherings; feeds on fruiting trees in orchards and on standing crops; strong flier; roosts along with other birds at favoured sites.

ROSE-RINGED PARAKEET

Psittacula krameri Psittacidae

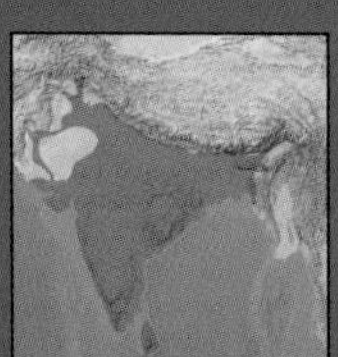

Size 42 cm

Voice Call a shrill *keeak*...; screams

Range Subcontinent, south of the Himalayan foothills

Habitat Light forests; orchards; towns; villages

♀

Male has grass-green plumage; short, hooked, red beak; rosy-pink and black collar distinctive (attained only during third year). Female lacks pink-and-black collar; instead, pale emerald-green around neck. Gregarious; large flocks of this species familiar sight in India; causes extensive damage to standing crops, orchards and garden fruit trees; also raids grain depots and markets; large roosting colonies, often along with mynas and crows.

SLATY-HEADED PARAKEET

Psittacula himalayana Psittacidae

Size 40 cm

Voice Noisy. Call a distinctive high-pitched, musical *tool...tool*

Range Common breeding resident of N hills; resident in the Himalayas (600-2,500 m) from Pakistan to Arunachal Pradesh in forests, well-wooded areas

Habitat Hill forests and cultivation; descends much lower in winter

Adult of both sexes overall green, washed blue; bluish-grey head; blackish chin; wide stripe across lower cheeks; blue-green band around hindneck bordered with fine black line; base of tail green graduating to deep blue, tipped with bright yellow; red upper mandible and lower pale yellow; pale yellow eyes. Male has prominent maroon-patch on inner median wing-coverts and long central tail feathers. Female lacks maroon-patch, has central tail feathers. Juvenile has greyish-green face; dull green head; faint pale green stripe below cheeks to hindcrown; maroon wing patch absent; short tail; orange bill; grey eye.

GREY-HEADED PARAKEET

Psittacula finschii Psittacidae

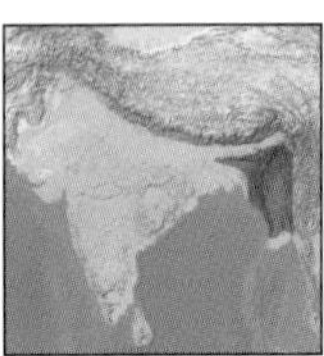

Size 33 cm

Voice Call includes steeply upturned, clear prolonged whistles

Range Resident of extreme NE Himalayas. S Assam Hills

Habitat Forests and open woodland; city gardens

Adult of both sexes overall yellowish-green; dark grey head; black chin; wide stripe across lower cheek narrowing to thin line around hindneck; small purplish-red patch on inner median wing-coverts; central tail feathers long (shorter in female); bluish-purple uppertail tipped with yellow or white. Female lacks maroon shoulder patch of male. Immature has dark bill similar to Slaty-headed's; greyish-green face; faint pale green band below cheeks to hindcrown; wing patch absent. Short tail, orange bill; orange-and-grey eye.

PLUM-HEADED PARAKEET

Psittacula cyanocephala Psittacidae

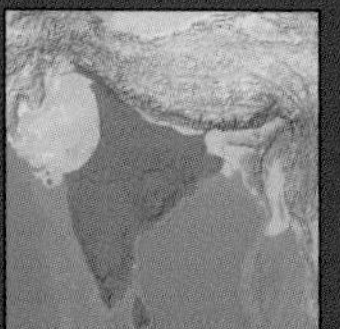

Size 36 cm

Voice Call includes loud, interrogative *tooi…tooi…* notes in fast flight; also other chattering notes

Range Subcontinent, south of the Himalayan foothills

Habitat Forests; orchards; cultivation in forest

Male has yellowish-green plumage; plum-red head washed purplish-blue on hindcrown; black chin strap; black and bluish-green collar; maroon-red wing shoulder patch; dark red spot on inner median wing-coverts; white tips to central tail feathers distinctive. Female dull, greyer head; yellow collar; almost non-existent maroon shoulder patch. In pairs, or small parties; arboreal, but descends into cultivation in forest clearings and outskirts; sometimes huge gatherings in cultivation; strong, darting flight over forest.

♀

BLOSSOM-HEADED PARAKEET

Psittacula roseata Psittacidae

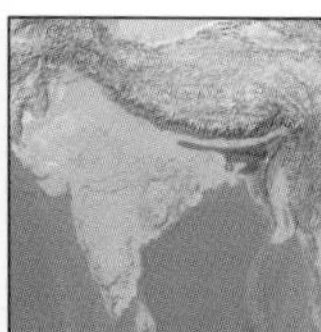

Size 36 cm

Voice As Plum-headed's

Range Mainly hills of NE India and Bangladesh

Habitat Open forests

Male has rosy-pink cheeks, forehead and ear-coverts; pale purplish-blue nape and crown; black chin strap graduating to fine stripe around hindneck; dark reddish-brown spot on inner median wing-coverts. Central tail feathers blue-tipped with pale yellow; side tail feathers greenish-yellow, tipped pale yellow. Orangish-yellow upper mandible; dark grey lower mandible; pale yellow eye. Female has dull blue-grey head, dull yellowish-green collar and smaller shoulder spot. Juvenile has green head, shorter tail, pale yellow bill and grey eye. Gregarious and noisy.

♀

MALABAR PARAKEET

Psittacula columboides Psittacidae

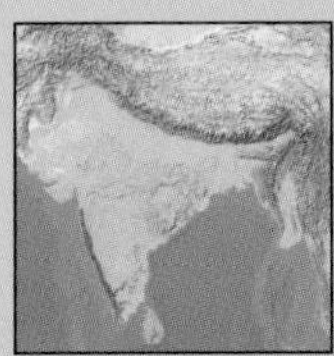

Size 38 cm

Voice Call a hard squeaky *screet…screet*, harsher than Plum-headed

Range Fairly common endemic breeding resident restricted to Western Ghats

Habitat Mainly evergreen hill forest, feeding high in canopy on fruits and flowers

Long-tailed, mainly blue and grey parakeet with bluish-grey head, breast and mantle, blue flight feathers and yellow-edged blue tail. Green-patch around eyes. Both sexes have black collar but male's edged with blue-green band; pale iris. Bluish-green collar band absent in female and has less green on face and forecrown. Juvenile has greenish head, bluish-green band under black stripe absent. Very sociable. Nests in tree holes.

LAYARD'S PARAKEET

Psittacula calthropae Psittacidae

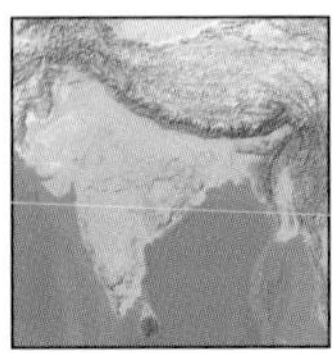

Size 31 cm

Voice Call a loud, harsh chattering scream

Range Sri Lanka

Habitat Edges of forests; plantations; gardens

Lovely looking parakeet identified by lavender-grey head and mantle, broad emerald green collar and deep cobalt blue tail. Broad, black chin-stripe; blue tail tipped yellow. Male has scarlet red upper mandible and brown lower beak. Female has black beak and deep green cheek-stripe; lacks pink nape-band, yellow-green collar, and bluish tint on head; mid tail feathers tinged blue. Immature similar to female, but with shorter tail feathers, with mainly green plumage and dark red bill.

DERBYAN PARAKEET

Psittacula derbiana Psittacidae

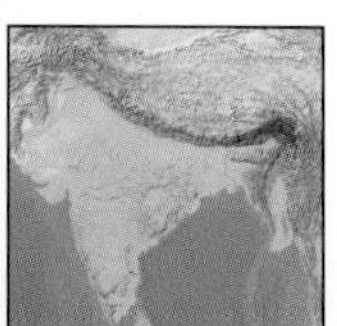

Size 46 cm

Voice Loud call, very nasal

Range Evidently common in border regions of NE Arunachal Pradesh

Habitat Little known; typically in small flocks. Seen in Mishmi Hills in September

Very large Tibetan parakeet with purple head and underparts; large bill; with black broad moustache. Male has red upper mandible; black in female. Juvenile duller, with mostly greyish head and duller, paler lore-line and moustache; some green feathers on face and some rusty-brown feathers below. In flight, blue wing-lining visible. Frequently visits nest-holes in tall trees.

♀

NICOBAR PARAKEET

Psittacula caniceps Psittacidae

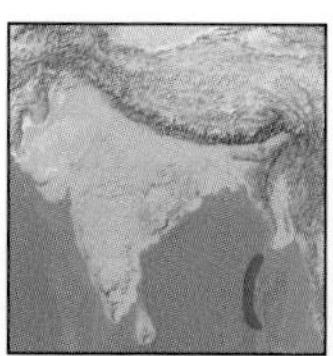

Size 61 cm

Voice Call a loud, raucous corvid-like *kroon…kroon*

Range Nicobar Islands

Habitat Tall forests

Male mainly yellowish-green in colour, with buffish-grey head, black forehead and broad black chin-stripe, and blackish flight feathers with bluish edges. Female has bluish-grey tinge to crown and nape, and black (rather than red) upper mandible.

LONG-TAILED PARAKEET

Psittacula longicauda Psittacidae

Size 47 cm

Voice Similar to Rose-ringed's, but less screeching

Range Common breeding resident in, and restricted to, Andaman and Nicobar Islands

Habitat Forests; plantations

Typical parakeet with pinkish cheeks, green crown and broad black chin-stripe. Back often with bluish wash and very long blue tail. Lower mandible black, upper red in male, black in female. Female more green above. Immature uniform green with fainter chin-stripe. Raids fruits and cereal crops. Acrobatic and very fast flight. Nests in tree holes.

JACOBIN CUCKOO

Clamator jacobinus Cuculidae

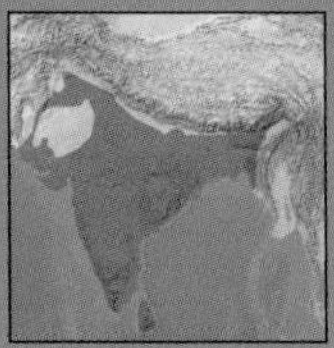

Size 33 cm

Voice Noisy; loud, metallic *plew…piu…* call notes

Range Chiefly SW monsoon breeding visitor

Habitat Open forests; cultivation; orchards

Earlier known as Pied Crested Cuckoo, this summer visitor has black upperparts; noticeable crest; white in wings and white tip to long tail feathers diagnostic in flight; white underbody. Juvenile, seen in autumn, dull sooty-brown with indistinct crest; white areas dull fulvous. Sexes alike. Solitary, or in small parties of four to six; arboreal; occasionally descends to ground to feed on insects. Brood-parasite, laying eggs in other birds' nests (usually bulbuls), arrives just before SW monsoon by end of May. Noisy and active, chasing one another; mobbed by crows on arrival.

CHESTNUT-WINGED CUCKOO

Clamator coromandus Cuculidae

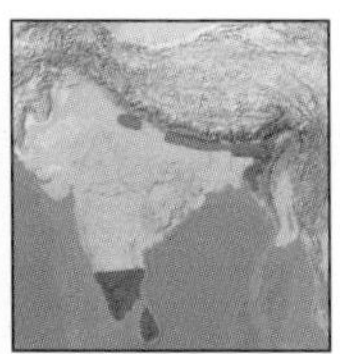

Size 45 cm

Voice Call a whistling *peep… peep* in breeding season. Also, hoarse screech

Range Scarce, local breeding summer visitor to N foothills

Habitat Forests; thick scrub

Slender, long-tailed cuckoo with chestnut wings, white collar and long, black, erect crest. Top of head and upperparts to tail of adult glossy metallic black, pale orange-brown throat to upper breast, breast and upper belly; white belly; blackish undertail-coverts; tail tipped white. Juvenile has dark brown head and upperparts, feathers edged paler, smaller crest; white underparts; rufous-edged wing-coverts and buff edge and tip of tail. Swift direct flight with rapid wingbeats.

LARGE HAWK CUCKOO

Hierococcyx sparverioides Cuculidae

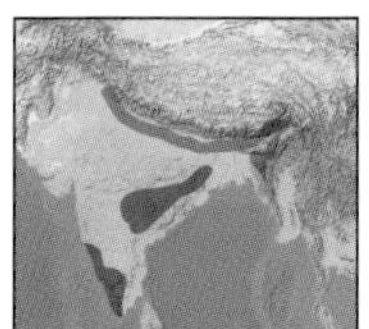

Size 38 cm

Voice Call a measured *kee… keeah…kee…keeah* usually without crescendo. Heard at night as well as day

Range Fairly common breeding summer visitor: Himalayas and hills of NE India. Winters sparsely in lowlands

Habitat Broadleaved evergreen forests

Large greyish-brown bird with rufescent subterminal bar to white-tipped tail; rufous-washed belly, barred brown-and-white; black chin; orange iris; pale yellow feet; bill black above and greenish-yellow below. Immature has chestnut-brown upperparts, barred with rufous; buff underparts with black streaks.

COMMON HAWK CUCKOO

Hierococcyx varius Cuculidae

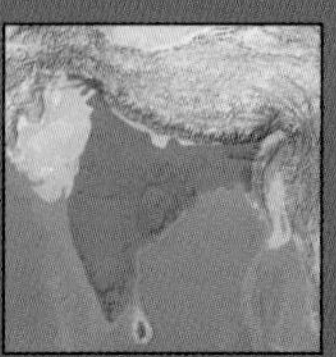

Size 34 cm

Voice Famous call notes; interpreted as brain-fever, uttered untiringly in crescendo; also described as *pipeeha…pipeeha…*; very noisy in overcast weather

Range Subcontinent, south of the Himalayan foothills; uncommon, even during rains, in arid zones

Habitat Forests; open country; near habitation

juvenile

Popularly known as the Brainfever bird; medium-sized cuckoo with ash-grey upperparts; dark bars on rufescent-tipped tail; dull white below, with pale ash-rufous on breast; barred below. Juvenile broadly-streaked dark below; pale rufous barrings on brown upperbody. Sexes alike. Solitary, rarely in pairs; strictly arboreal; noisy during May–September; silent after rains. Brood-parasite, laying eggs in nests of babblers.

HODGSON'S HAWK CUCKOO

Hierococcyx fugax Cuculidae

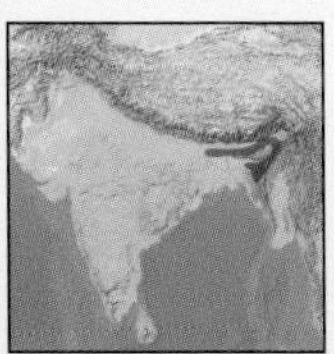

Size 31 cm

Voice Call includes a series of paired, thin, sharp, high-pitched gee…*whiz*

Range Summer visitor: E Himalayas from E Nepal to Assam

Habitat Deciduous forests; winters in evergreen forests

Medium-sized slaty-grey cuckoo with barred tail and rufous breast with white streaks; black chin; white throat; yellow or red iris; black bill with yellow tip and base. Similar to Large Hawk, but smaller in size and distinguished by grey upperparts, whitish belly, grey head sides and lacks moustachial-stripe and white band on nape. Shy and difficult to locate, but may sing incessantly in breeding season.

INDIAN CUCKOO

Cuculus micropterus Cuculidae

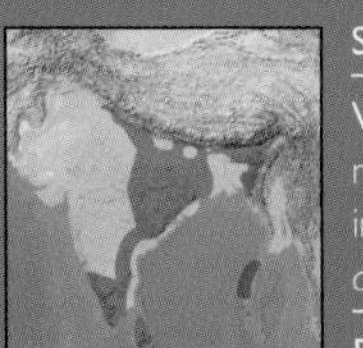

Size 33 cm

Voice Very distinct call; 4-noted mellow whistle, variously interpreted, *bo…ko…ta…ko or crossword…puzzle* best known

Range Subcontinent, south from the Himalayas to about 2,500 m, excepting drier and arid parts of NW India; absent in Pakistan

Habitat Forests; orchards

Medium-sized, solitary and shy bird. Slaty-brown above; greyer on head, throat and breast; whitish below, with broadly spaced black cross-bars; broad subterminal tail-band (characteristic of the non-hawk cuckoos of genus *Cuculus*); female often has rufous-brown wash on throat and breast; call notes most important identification clue. Sexes alike. Arboreal, not easy to see; overall appearance very hawk-like, but distinctly weaker-looking flight.

EURASIAN CUCKOO

Cuculus canorus Cuculidae

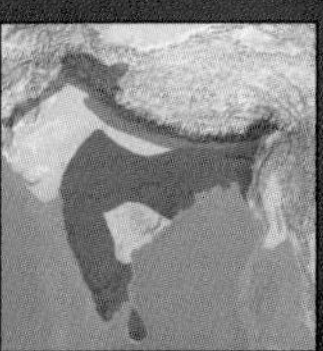

Size 33 cm

Voice Well-known, repetitive *cuc…koo.* Also, rapid bubbling, mainly by female

Range Common breeding summer visitor to N mountains. Scarce winter visitor elsewhere in lowlands

Habitat Woodlands and scrubs, where brood-parasites. Winters in wooded country and cultivation. Typically flies with wings held low and rather humped back

♀

hepatic

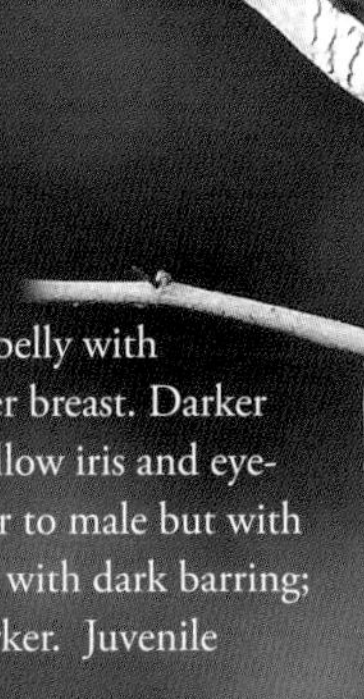

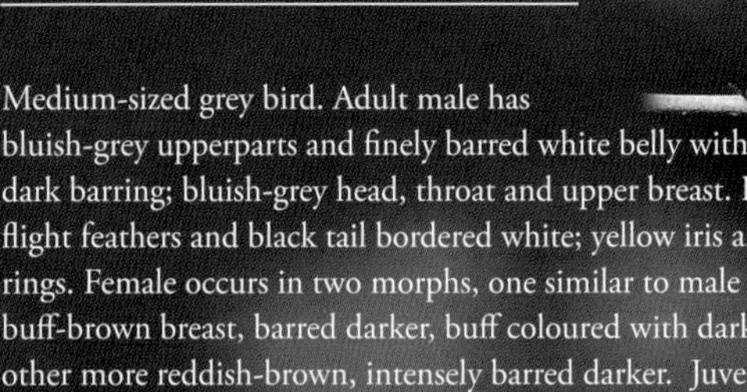

Medium-sized grey bird. Adult male has bluish-grey upperparts and finely barred white belly with dark barring; bluish-grey head, throat and upper breast. Darker flight feathers and black tail bordered white; yellow iris and eye-rings. Female occurs in two morphs, one similar to male but with buff-brown breast, barred darker, buff coloured with dark barring; other more reddish-brown, intensely barred darker. Juvenile slaty-grey with hints of reddish-brown.

HIMALAYAN CUCKOO

Cuculus saturatus Cuculidae

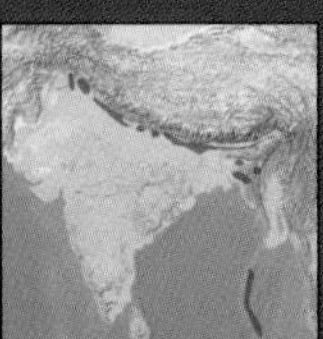

Size 31 cm

Voice Call a distinctive, repetitive *po…po…po…po* in series of 4- to 8-notes. Often calls at night

Range Breeding summer visitor to N hills. Scarce winter visitor to lowlands

Habitat Hill forests

hepatic

Very similar to Eurasian, but smaller in size, and distinguished by darker back and more strongly barred underparts; plain vent and beige wash to undertail-coverts; yellow to brown iris and eye-rings. Female and juvenile occur as grey and rufous morphs, grey morph and rufous morph difficult to see except when calling from tree-tops. Flight and shape as Eurasian. Brood-parasites in warbler's nests.

LESSER CUCKOO

Cuculus poliocephalus Cuculidae

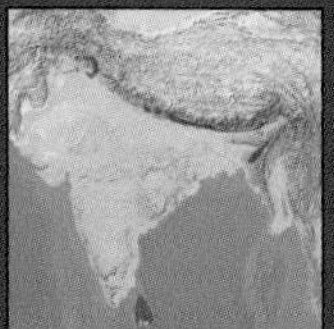

Size 25 cm

Voice Strong, cheerful song, rendered as pretty-*peel*...*lay*...*ka*

Range Breeds in the Himalayas from N Pakistan east to Arunachal Pradesh

Habitat Forests; well-wooded country

hepatic

Adult male has slaty-grey upperparts, pale slaty-blue head, neck, throat and upper breast; white lower breast and rest of underparts, boldly-barred black. Grey morph female similar to male, but has rufous wash on upper breast; hepatic morph has rufous upperparts with blackish barring except on rump, white underparts barred black, tail barred rufous and black with white tip. Juvenile has dark grey-brown upperparts with variable, narrow whitish to rufous barring and broadly barred underparts.

BANDED BAY CUCKOO

Cacomantis sonneratii Cuculidae

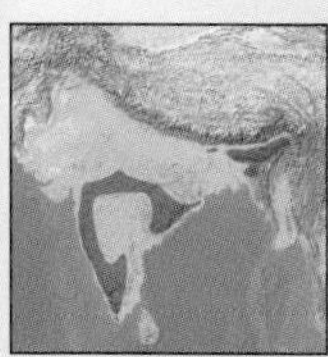

Size 24 cm

Voice Call a shrill whistle

Range From N Uttar Pradesh east to Assam and Bangladesh

Habitat Dense broadleaved forests in Nepal; lightly wooded country in India; edges of forests, patches of shifting cultivation and open forests in Sri Lanka

Small cuckoo with longish, curved bill. Upperparts rufous-brown, strongly barred, uniformly and regularly, dark brown. Adult male has broad white supercilium (cross-barred with black), which encircles brown ear-coverts; dark eye-stripe; whitish cheeks; white-tipped tail. Whitish underparts, washed pale buff from belly to flanks, finely and uniformly barred; central tail feathers barred and darker on each side of shaft. Juvenile similar to adult, but whiter on head and upper mantle; less barring on underparts.

GREY-BELLIED CUCKOO

Cacomantis passerinus Cuculidae

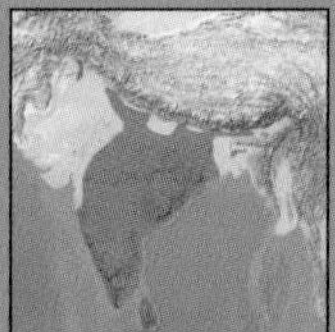

Size 23 cm

Voice Noisy, with good range of calls. Call a mournful (plaintive) single-noted *piteeer...*; sometimes 3-noted, second note shortest, third long-drawn

Range India, south from the Himalayas to about 2,500 m, except arid NW regions

Habitat Open forests, orchards and gardens in vicinity of habitation

hepatic

Grey head; grey-brown glossy upperparts; white tail-tip and patch under the wing seen in flight; grey throat, upper breast; paler, almost white below. Female also has hepatic (reddish) phase. Bright chestnut upperparts and throat, with reddish-brown wash; cross-barred black on back; white below throat, narrowly cross-barred black. Sexes alike. Mostly solitary; keeps to foliage.

PLAINTIVE CUCKOO

Cacomantis merulinus Cuculidae

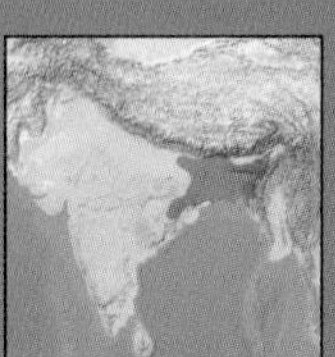

Size 23 cm

Voice Mournful, rising 'play to *tee*' often in a trailed-off crescendo

Range Generally scarce breeding resident in NE India, most frequent in Bangladesh

Habitat Wooded country including parks and gardens

Small, palish cuckoo with grey upperparts, buff-grey chin and upper breast, rest of underparts warm orange. Pale grey head and throat; some rufous on wing-coverts and rump; black tail, tipped white. Grey morph similar to male but with whitish barring on belly. Hepatic female dark rufous, heavily barred above; throat, breast and tail uniform rufous; rest of underparts whitish, barred black. Calls actively in rapid restless flights; brood-parasites in warbler's nests.

ASIAN EMERALD CUCKOO

Chrysococcyx maculatus Cuculidae

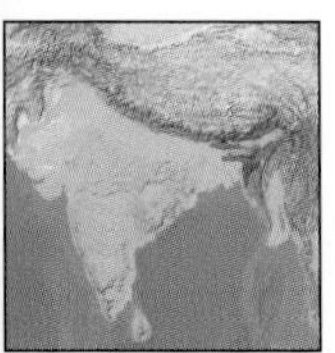

Size 18 cm

Voice Call a loud *kee... kee...kee*; in flight, sharp *chweek*; whistle; trill

Range Uttarakhand east to Assam, Arunachal Pradesh and S Assam Hills

Habitat Primary broadleaved evergreen forests; secondary growth

♀

Tiny cuckoo with distinctive iridescent emerald green head, neck, breast and upperparts; white underparts barred prominently metallic green; orange orbital skin; black-tipped yellow bill; female similar to female Violet, but brighter rufous crown and upper mantle; glossy bronze-green wash on lower mantle and wings; rufous wash on face. Juvenile overall paler. Arboreal; mainly in canopy, venturing out occasionally to pursue insects.

VIOLET CUCKOO

Chrysococcyx xanthorhynchus Cuculidae

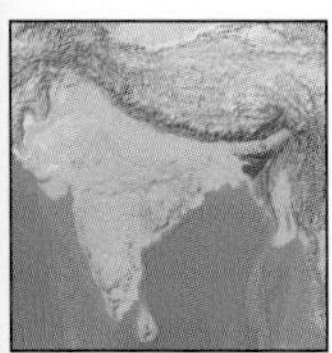

Size 17 cm

Voice Calls *che wick* in flight; shrill trilling

Range Assam; Arunachal Pradesh; S Assam Hills; Bangladesh

Habitat Broadleaved evergreen forests; secondary growth

Tiny, distinctive forest bird with iridescent dark purple head, upperparts and upper breast. White underparts strongly barred deep purple, bright orange bill; white-spotted dark undertail. Female similar to female Asian Emerald, but dark bronze-brown above and white underparts barred brown; rufous outer-tail feathers; dull orange-yellow bill. Female like female Asian Emerald, but dark bronze-brown above with green tinge, rufous outer tail feathers and orange-yellow bill with black tip. Juvenile is more rufous.

DRONGO CUCKOO

Surniculus lugubris Cuculidae

Size 23 cm

Voice Diagnostic; noisy during monsoon. Call a short whistled *pee…pee…pee…pee*

Range Hills of C and SW India. Summer visitor to the Himalayas, hills of NE India

Habitat Open forests; orchards; shade trees

Smallish, mainly glossy black cuckoo, similar to drongo but with smaller, slimmer, downcurved bill, long, black, square-cut tail, with only slight fork or notch; tail and vent white-barred, unlike those of true drongos; white thighs; sometimes, white nape spot; no white rictal spot of Black Drongo. Juvenile duller, white-spotted; quieter, shyer, more inconspicuous than the bolder and more active drongos; cuckoo-like flight; mostly arboreal; sometimes in lower growth or ground; sings from bare branches. The square-tailed and forked-tailed forms are sometimes considered to be separate species.

square-tailed

forked-tailed

ASIAN KOEL

Eudynamys scolopaceus Cuculidae

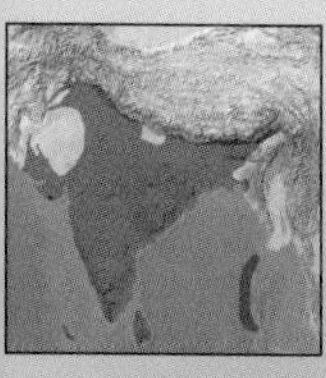

Size 43 cm

Voice Familiar call of Indian countryside. Very noisy between March and June, coinciding with breeding of crows; loud *kuoo...kuooo...* whistling calls in crescendo by male koel, first syllable longish; water-bubbling call of female

Range Subcontinent, upto about 1,800 m in the outer Himalayas; uncommon in drier areas

Habitat Light forests; orchards; city parks; cultivation; open areas

Large cuckoo with metallic, bluish-greenish black plumage; greenish beak and crimson eyes. Female dark brown, thickly-spotted and barred white; whitish below, dark-spotted on throat, barred below. Solitary, or in pairs; arboreal; mostly silent between July and February; fast flight.

♀

GREEN-BILLED MALKOHA

Rhopodytes tristis Cuculidae

Size 51 cm

Voice Rather silent, sometimes croaks quietly

Range Scarce breeding resident: N foothills, NE India, Eastern Ghats

Habitat Forests; scrub undergrowth

Large, long-tailed bird with pale green, robust bill. Overall greenish-grey with paler head and underparts; grey underparts, darker on breast; glossy green, graduated tail, black with white feather-tips; red facial skin; black bristles around gape. Juvenile duller than adult with shorter retrices and narrower white tail-tip. Narrow white border surrounding red orbital skin. Holds tail straight when running through tangled vegetation.

BLUE-FACED MALKOHA

Rhopodytes viridirostris Cuculidae

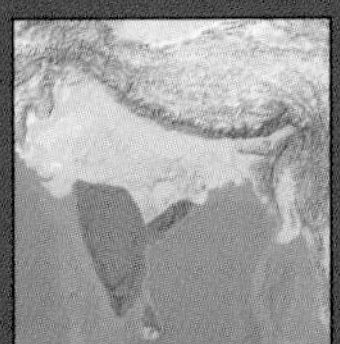

Size 39 cm

Voice Rather silent; sometimes croaks quietly

Range Scarce, but overlooked endemic breeding resident in S India, Sri Lanka

Habitat Thick thorn scrub and open forest undergrowth

Large, dark greenish-grey cuckoo with diagnostic blue, bare and warty orbital skin. Head and upperparts dark grey; iridescent greenish-grey wings and tail; dark grey underparts, washed rufous on abdomen; bluish streaked throat; very long black-and-white tail. Deep brown to red iris with white eye-ring. Sexes alike. Juvenile duller and less glossy. Soliary, or in pairs. Scrambles in tangled vegetation, foraging. Seldom seen in open.

SIRKEER MALKOHA

Taccocua leschenaultii Cuculidae

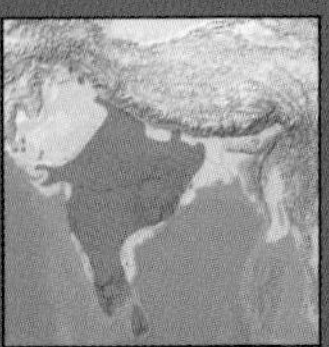

Size 43 cm

Voice Fairly loud and sharp clicking notes; mostly vocal when breeding

Range Most of the subcontinent, upto about 1,800 m in the Himalayas; absent in NW India and Kashmir

Habitat Open jungles, scrubs, ravines, dense growth around habitation. Endemic resident of thorn scrub and semi-desert regions

Sandy-brown head, hindneck and upperparts; shiny black shaft streaks on head and nape. Long, graduated tail, with broad white tips to blackish outer feathers distinctive in flight; cherry-red beak, with yellow tip. Sexes alike. Solitary, or in pairs; sometimes four or five birds in neighbourhood; moves mostly on ground, in dense growth; may clamber out on some bush-tops or low trees. Laboured and flapping flight. Shy. Runs low and rat-like when disturbed.

RED-FACED MALKOHA

Phaenicophaeus pyrrhocephalus Cuculidae

Size 40 cm

Voice Usually silent

Range Sri Lanka

Habitat Frequents tree canopy. Typically threads its way through foliage, creepers and branches

Very large, boldly patterned, dark green malkoha; large red facial patch with broad, white band, speckled with black below; iridescent bluish-green upperparts, black throat and breast; stout green bill; long, black tail with broad, white tail-tip. White lower breast, flanks, abdomen and undertail-coverts. Male has dark eyes, female has white. Juvenile duller with smaller, red face patch and shorter tail. Shy and restless, forages in small groups.

LESSER COUCAL

Centropus bengalensis Centropodidae

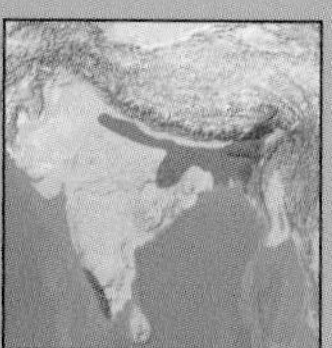

Size 33 cm

Voice Call a deep, rapid *oop… oop…oop* varying in tone. Also *kutook…kutook* and variants

Range Local breeding resident and summer visitor: N foothills from Uttarakhand east to Myanmar border, throughout NE India, south to Odisha and including Bangladesh. Also SW India

Habitat Grasslands; open country

Small coucal with short decurved beak. Breeding adult glossy bluish-black. Bright buff shaft streaks on scapulars and lesser wing-coverts; wings mottled dark brown and rufous. Non-breeding adult has dark brown head and mantle, dark brown rump barred rufous; pale buff throat and breast streaked darker. Juvenile similar to non-breeding adult, but has dark and light buff streaking on head and upperparts. Usually solitary, or in pairs. Feeds mainly on grasshoppers.

juvenile

BROWN COUCAL

Centropus andamanensis Centropodidae

Size 48 cm

Voice Song much like that of Greater

Range Resident, Andaman Islands

Habitat Nest placed well up in trees or bushes, breeding during monsoon

Large grey-brown coucal. Adult has dark chestnut-red back and wings; dark brown tail; pale tawny-brown head, mantle and breast grading to dark brown on belly and vent; iris pale brown. Sexes similar. Juvenile slightly barred on body, darker supercilium, sides of head and underparts. Nests in trees. Feeds on insects, small frogs, crabs and lizards.

GREEN-BILLED COUCAL

Centropus chlororhynchos Centropodidae

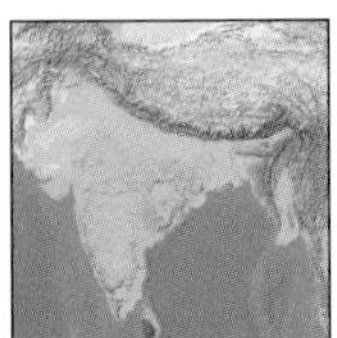

Size 45 cm

Voice Similar to Greater Coucal, but deeper and shorter

Range Endemic to SW Sri Lanka

Habitat Wet forests; bamboos

Overall purple-black, except for wings, which are maroonish-brown on top and black underneath; head and underparts paler; long, dark tail glossed purplish; curved, light green bill; dark reddish eye. Sexes alike. Juvenile duller and barred blackish on chestnut wing-coverts; grey eye. Very shy and difficult to see. Feeds, creeping with surprising manoeuvrability, low down in vegetation tangles. Eats insects and reptiles. Flies poorly and usually only for short distances. Builds own nest.

GREATER COUCAL

Centropus sinensis Centropodidae

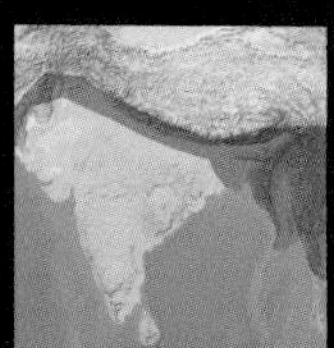

Size 50 cm

Voice Loud and resonant *coop... coop...coop...* call familiar; occasionally a squeaky call

Range Subcontinent, from outer Himalayas to about 2,000 m

Habitat Forests; scrubs; cultivation; gardens; derelict patches; vicinity of habitation

Beautiful terrestrial bird with glossy bluish-black plumage; chestnut wings; blackish, glossy dark green, long, graduated tail; strong, heavy, darkish bill; deep red eyes; dark grey feet. Female somewhat larger than male. Sexes alike. Solitary, or in pairs; moves amidst dense growth, fanning and flicking tail often; clambers up into trees, but poor flier, lazily flying short distances.

SOUTHERN COUCAL

Centropus s parroti Centropodidae

Size 50 cm

Voice Call a resounding and repeated *poop... poop...poop*, often fading away. Croaks and chuckles

Range Common breeding resident throughout. Also occurs in S China and SE Asia

Habitat Grasslands, cultivation, scrubs, open woodlands, edges of forests

Recently split from Greater. Very large, black and chestnut cuckoo with long, broad black tail. All glossy black with chestnut mantle and wings. Red iris. Strong bill. Female similar but larger. Juvenile barred white. Often looks shaggy-headed.

BARN OWL

Tyto alba Tytonidae

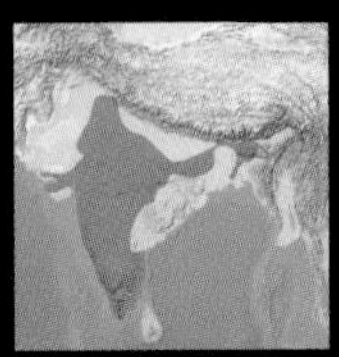

juvenile

Size 35 cm

Voice Call a long-drawn, wild shriek; variety of snoring, hissing notes

Range Almost all over India, south of the Himalayan foothills

Habitat Grasslands; cultivation; human habitation; town-centres

Dull golden-buff above, finely speckled black-and-white; white below, often with fine, dark spots; heart-shaped, white facial disc with brown edge; brownish wash between lower edge of eyes and base of pale pink bill. Sexes alike. Solitary, or in pairs; nocturnal, but sometimes hunts during day; normally rests during day, mostly in tree-cavity, dense creepers or some dark loft; perches upright; flies silently, mostly under 4 m from ground; pounces on prey.

ANDAMAN BARN OWL

Tyto a deroepstroffi Tytonidae

Size 36 cm

Voice Call a high-pitched abrupt screech

Range Resident, Andaman Islands

Habitat Cultivation, along coasts

Adult has vinaceous brown facial disc bordered rufous; dark brown upperparts marked with darker brown-patches and spotted buffish orange; shortish narrowly barred tail and wings; orangish-gold breast, graduating to whitish abdomen. Feathered legs buffy white; dark pinkish-grey feet; purplish-grey claws. Distinguished from Barn by reddish-brown face and extensive, darkly-spotted underparts, and darker upperparts, strongly marked with rufous and dark brown. Nocturnal; leaves daytime roost at dusk. Little-known about food, but possibly feeds on rats and mice.

EASTERN GRASS OWL

Tyto longimembris Tytonidae

Size 36 cm

Voice Hissing scream, similar to that of Barn, though tends to be more silent than Barn

Range Resident; NE and SW India, and S Nepal

Habitat Tall grasslands

Similar to Barn in size but distinguished by darker eyes and whitish face and underparts. Adult male has white facial disc, while female has more beige facial disc. Dark brown upperparts mottled with fine white and ochre spots; creamy-white underparts blotched darker; long wings; three dark bars on primaries; shortish tail has three or four bars. Feathered legs with blackish-brown claws and yellowish-grey toes. Female similar, but slightly larger. Mainly nocturnal, but ocassionally seen during day; ground bird; hides in grass. Breeds colonially; several birds hunt in same area.

ORIENTAL BAY OWL

Phodilus badius Tytonidae

Size 29 cm

Voice Calls include a series of eerie, upward-inflected whistles

Range Resident; NE India

Habitat Dense evergreen broadleaved forests

Sri Lanka Bay Owl

Medium-sized owl with whitish-vinaceous, elongated facial disc, short, rounded wings and short tail. Pale V-shaped, brownish-grey forehead and dark brown vertical eye patches. Long legs feathered to feet. Large dark eyes; white necklace; rich chestnut and buff upperparts spotted and barred with black. Pale yellow-brown underparts, speckled with blackish-brown and buff. Chestnut tail has few narrow bars. Nocturnal bird, roosts in holes and hollows in tree trunks. The similar Sri Lanka Bay Owl *P. b. assimilis* is found in SW India and Sri Lanka.

MOUNTAIN SCOPS OWL

Otus spilocephalus Tytonidae

juvenile

Size 27 cm

Voice Song an eerie, gliding whistle *whi…whoo…ee…yo*

Range The Himalayas, NE and Bangladesh

Habitat Dense forests; mangrove edges

Seen in many morphs and individually variable. Adult has reddish-brown facial disc with pale base and dark-tipped bristles; yellow eyes; blackish cheeks and ear-coverts; paler head sides and forehead. Dark tawny or rufous brown upperparts, darkly vermiculated. Whitish underparts, barred rufous with small triangular paired, black-and-white spots. Like other scops owls, completely nocturnal and difficult to spot.

SERENDIB SCOPS OWL

Otus thilohoffmanni Tytonidae

Size 17 cm

Voice Call a short, soft but far-carrying musical *whoo…oh*

Range Sri Lanka

Habitat Large, dense rainforests

Discovered in 2001 in rainforests. Small owl with short tail and no ear tufts. Upperparts overall rufous speckled black; unmarked rufous facial disc; lighter rufous underparts mottled black; whitish bill; pinkish-white legs; iris orangish in male and yellow in female. When alert, vertical compression of facial disc forms two shorter projections of 'false' ear tufts. Endemic, fairly rare and local. In pairs. Nocturnal and territorial. Roosts near ground, where colouration, size and shape camouflage the bird well amongst dry leaves.

ANDAMAN SCOPS OWL

Otus balli Tytonidae

Size 19 cm

Voice Call an abrupt *hoot…hootcoorroo*

Range Andaman Islands

Habitat Humid primary forests

Seen in two morphs: brown morph has white eyebrows, and throat lores and blotch-white underparts. Rufous morph has less-marked back and underparts have smaller, paler blotches. Poorly-defined facial mask; small stubby ear tufts; crown, nape and mantle have sparse and indistinct buff and dark brown markings. Has weaker legs and feet than Oriental, and tarsus partly bare. Bill and claws yellow.

INDIAN SCOPS OWL

Otus bakkamoena Tytonidae

Medium-sized buffy brown owl with large, prominent ear tufts; buff nuchal-collar edged with dark brown, finely streaked underparts, and buffish scapular spots; dark orange or brown eyes, although can be yellow. Very variable in colouration: can be pale grey-brown or warm rufous-brown; legs feathered to base of toes.

juvenile

Size 23-25 cm

Voice Call a subdued, frog-like *whuk*

Range Widespread resident, south of the Himalayas

Habitat Forests, well-wooded areas

COLLARED SCOPS OWL

Otus b lettia Strigidae

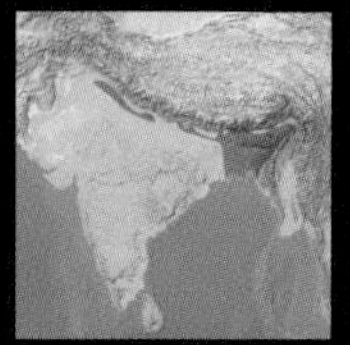

Size 23 cm

Voice Call fluty and questioning. Calls throughout the night

Range Resident of the Himalayas, NE India

Habitat Forests; cultivation; orchards; trees in vicinity of habitation

Small owl with buff and brown 'imitation face' on nape. Small ear tufts and upright posture. Greyish-brown above; buffy nuchal-collar diagnostic; buffy-white underbody, streaked and mottled dark. Sexes alike. Solitary, or in pairs; remains motionless during day in thick, leafy branches or at junctions of stems and branches; very difficult to spot; flies around dusk.

PALLID SCOPS OWL

Otus brucei Strigidae

Size 21 cm

Voice Resonant, extended *hoop…hoop…hoop*. Soft dove-like call

Range Little-known resident of N Pakistan mountains east to Ladakh. Some winter in NW India

Habitat Dry mountain ranges. Highly nocturnal

Small, cryptically plumaged owl. Overall sandy-grey plumage very sparsely streaked; small, often depressed ear tufts; narrow, well-defined black border to pale facial disc. Underparts finely streaked with black. Large eyes with yellow iris. Tail extends marginally beyond wing-tips, with tail-bands diffusing towards tip; legs feathered till base of toes. Similar to Oriental, but paler, less distinct scapular spots and darker and narrower streaking on underparts. Sexes alike. Juvenile has completely barred underparts. Nests in tree holes.

EURASIAN SCOPS OWL

Otus scops Strigidae

Size 19 cm

Voice Call a single *took*, repeated

Range Summer visitor to N and W Pakistan mountains; winters in S Pakistan and NW India

Habitat Similiar to Oriental. Scrub in dry rocky hills and valleys

Greyish, heavily-marked owl, well-camouflaged against tree trunk. Grey-brown facial disc, finely mottled with diffused edge; paler underparts, streaked and vermiculated blackish-brown, similar to that of tree bark; flight feathers and tail barred dark and pale; prominent ear tufts; bright yellow eyes; grey bill. Occurs as grey and brown morphs. Nocturnal bird, most active after sunset till midnight. Roosts by day in trees, normally close to trunks or rock holes.

ORIENTAL SCOPS OWL

Otus sunia Strigidae

Size 19 cm

Voice Distinctive call of slowly repeated *wug-chug-chug*

Range Locally common breeding resident in plains and lower hills mainly in north from N Pakistan, east to Myanmar border, Bangladesh, Sri Lanka, Western Ghats and S peninsular India

Habitat Forests; groves; orchards

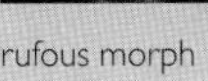

rufous morph

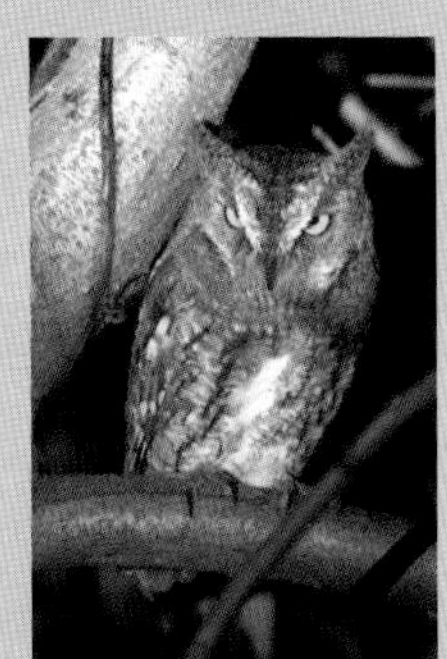

Small mottled brown owl with short ear tufts. Breast heavily streaked with black; orange-yellow iris; greyish bill and feet. Cryptic, mottled plumage in three morphs: rufous (shown), brown and grey. Latter two not readily separable from rarer Eurasian *O. Scops* and call only reliable identification factor. Well-streaked crown and underparts distinguish it from Mountain and Pallid. Prominent white scapular lines. Large vertical ear tufts often suppressed. Strictly nocturnal, roosts in day close to trunks in thickly-foliaged trees. Hunts in smaller trees on forest edge, clearings and secondary growth. Nests in holes.

INDIAN EAGLE OWL

Bubo b bengalensis Strigidae

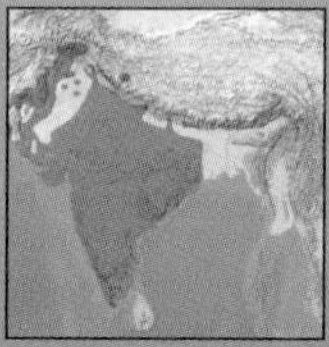

Size 48.5 cm

Voice Call a deep, booming *bu…boo…*; snapping calls at nest

Range Throughout the region, upto about 1,500 m in the Himalayas

Habitat Ravines; cliffsides; riversides; scrubs; open country

Brown plumage, mottled and streaked, dark and light; prominent ear tufts; orange eyes; legs fully-feathered. Sexes alike. Solitary, or in pairs; mostly nocturnal; spends day in leafy branch, rock-ledge or old well; flies slowly but maintains considerable distances when disturbed; emerges to feed around sunset, advertises arrival with its characteristic call.

EURASIAN EAGLE OWL

Bubo bubo Strigidae

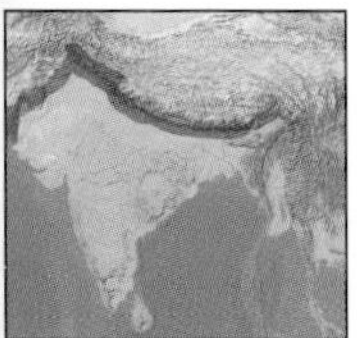

Size 60 cm

Voice Call a deep, booming *bu…boo…*; snapping calls at nest

Range Northern hills of Pakistan and Himalayas, from about 1500m

Habitat Ravines; cliffsides; riversides; scrubs; open country

Large owl with conspicuous ear tufts and heavily feathered, powerful talons; tawny-buff facial disc, mottled blackish-brown; blackish bill; greyish-olive cere; bright orange-red to golden-yellow eyes; white chin and throat, continuing down to centre upper breast. Brownish-black and tawny-buff upperparts; tawny-buff underparts except for chin, throat finely-barred.

SPOT-BELLIED EAGLE OWL

Bubo nipalensis Strigidae

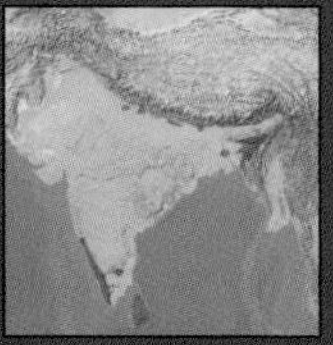

Size 63 cm

Voice Low, blood-curdling moan and scream

Range Uttarakhand eastwards, throughout NE Indian region; also in Western Ghats and Sri Lanka

Habitat Dense broadleaved evergreen forests

Large, dramatic-looking bird of prey. Pallid, overall stark, greyish-brown with prominent horizontally-held ear tufts; characteristic dark heart or chevron-shaped markings on white underparts diagnostic; dark brown primaries striped lighter; heavily-barred secondaries; plain white facial discs; white supercilium; large, pale yellow bill, dark brown eyes. Juvenile overall whiter with distinctive crown and mantle. Nocturnal; roosts by day in thickly-forested areas; hunts deep in forests, but sometimes ventures to edges at dusk; formidable strength allows to take on large prey.

juvenile

DUSKY EAGLE OWL

Bubo coromandus Strigidae

juvenile

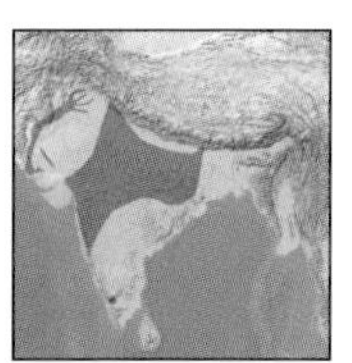

Size 58 cm

Voice Call a deep, hollow, somewhat eerie hoot of 5- to 8-notes fading towards end; interpreted as *woo...wo...wo...wo...o...o...o*

Range Throughout the region, south of outer Himalayas; status in extreme south of country unclear. Also spotted in Myanmar and Malaysia

Habitat Groves; light forests; roadside leafy trees; vicinity of habitation

Pale grey-brown plumage, profusely spotted, streaked and marked with white; pale buffish-grey underparts with dark shaft stripes and brown cross-bars; prominent ear tufts, erect when alert and dull yellow eyes diagnostic. Feathered tarsus and bristled toes. Sexes alike. Mostly in pairs, sometimes three to four scattered; has favoured roost sites in large, leafy trees; may call and fly during daytime.

BROWN FISH OWL

Ketupa zeylonensis Strigidae

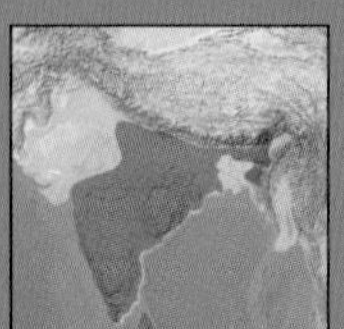

Size 56 cm

Voice Call a deep *whom...whom*. Also, an undulating *cur...ree*

Range Scarce breeding resident throughout lowlands

Habitat Well-wooded areas with water, including village groves near fish-rich ponds

Large owl with flat-head and outward-facing ear tufts; tawny ill-defined facial disc; conspicuous white-patch on throat and foreneck. Dark rufous-brown upperparts, heavily streaked darker; paler underparts with dark streaking; blackish-brown back and mantle with buff margins and pale spots near tips. Dark brown primaries and secondaries banded with white or fulvous; very short tail with white tips and three to four buff-white bands; yellow iris; greyish-black bill. Sexes alike. Mainly nocturnal, roosting in leafy trees. Hunts fish, crabs and frogs.

TAWNY FISH OWL

Ketupa flavipes Strigidae

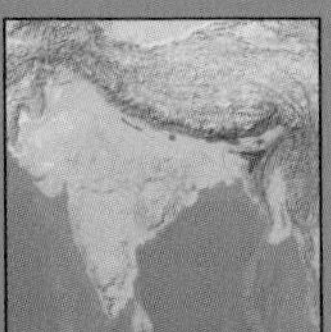

Size 61 cm

Voice Call a low, resonant *whoo… hoo; buh…huh…woo;* cat-like mewing

Range Uttarakhand eastwards to NE India

Habitat Primary broadleaved tropical forests near water; riverbanks, streams, pools; deep, well-wooded gorges

Similar to Buffy, but more unmarked. Rufous-brown with prominent flattened ear tufts, smallish facial disc; rich tawny plumage; white-patch on front of neck, black bill; short white supercilium; heavy black and tawny mottling, streaking on upperparts; broad black streaking below; generally in pairs; partly diurnal; roosts by day in dense foliage trees, earthen banks; actively hunts by dusk; will hunt and fish in daylight, in breeding season.

BUFFY FISH OWL

Ketupa ketupu Strigidae

Size 50 cm

Voice Call a monotonous *bup…bup…bup…bup… bup…bup…bup*

Range NE India; Bangladesh

Habitat Forested streams in plains and mangroves

Medium to large owl with prominent, outward-facing ear tufts. Rich brown upperparts, more blackish on back and mantle. Dark brown primaries and secondaries with whitish bands; dark brown tail feathers tipped and banded whitish. White forehead and eyebrows; yellow eyes and black-lined eyelids; blackish-grey bill; similar to Tawny, but much smaller and with finer streaking on underparts. Distinguished from Brown by white forehead, more rufous-orange upperparts with thicker and more prominent black streaking, orange-buff underparts with more clearly defined black streaking on breast, and lack of black cross-barring on feathers of underparts.

MOTTLED WOOD OWL

Strix ocellata Strigidae

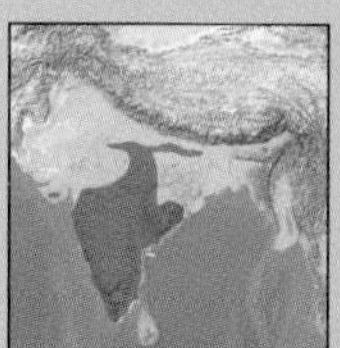

Size 48 cm

Voice Call a loud, hooting note

Range All over India, south from the Himalayan foothills; absent in arid NW parts and much of NE India

Habitat Forests; orchards; vicinity of habitation; cultivation

Medium-sized owl with no ear tufts. Yellowish-red upperparts, profusely mottled and vermiculated red-brown, black, white and buff; whitish facial disc with narrow chocolate-black barrings forming concentric circles; white spots on crown, nape; chestnut and black throat, stippled white; rest of underparts whitish, barred golden-buff to orange-buff. Yellowish-brown toes, blackish talons. Sexes alike. Solitary, or in pairs; nocturnal, spends day in dense foliage of large trees; roosts after sunset.

BROWN WOOD OWL

Strix leptogrammica Strigidae

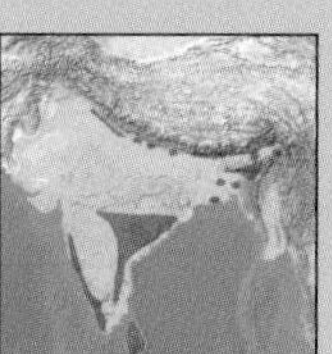

Size 47-53 cm

Voice Calls include *hoo… hoohoohoo…(hoo)* and loud eerie scream

Range The Himalayas, NE India, Eastern and Western Ghats, Bangladesh and Sri Lanka

Habitat Dense broadleaved subtropical or temperate forests

Medium-sized owl with warm-brown plumage; no ear tufts; fulvous or rufous-brown facial disc with narrow but distinct black rim. The Himalayan *S.l. newarensis* has dark brown face, with prominent white eyebrows, and striking white band across foreneck. Underparts greyish-white, heavily barred with brown.

juvenile

TAWNY OWL

Strix aluco Strigidae

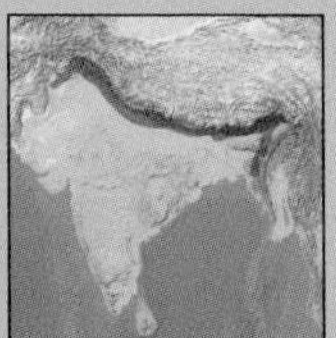

Size 46 cm

Voice Calls include wavering *tu…who…oo* and sharp *ker wik*. Sometimes, combined to sound like *tu… wit…to woo*

Range Fairly common breeding resident: N, NE mountains

Habitat Mountain broadleaved, coniferous forests

Now split into Himalayan Wood Owl by some authorities, which is similar to Tawny, but distinguished by unstreaked upperparts, white-patch on throat and arrow-shaped spotting on breast. Overall colouration ranges from greyish to rufous-brown. Dark streaking on upper and underparts and well-barred wings and tail. Whitish scapular lines and V-mark on forehead. Large, pale dark-rimmed facial disc. Nocturnal, roosts high and close to tree trunk. Both forms occur in the region.

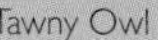

Tawny Owl

Himalayan Wood Owl

COLLARED OWLET

Glaucidium brodiei Strigidae

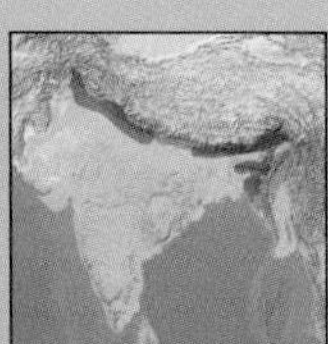

Size 17 cm

Voice Noisy when breeding. Call a liquid *poop…po…poop…poop*

Range Locally common breeding resident: N mountains from N Pakistan, east to Myanmar border. Moves lower down in winter

Habitat Thick forests at lower-levels

Smallest owl in Asia; short-tailed, dark, barred owlet with distinctive 'face' marks on hindneck; rufous or greyish upperparts; dark brown barring on mantle, wings, tail and on sides of upper breast; relatively large, rounded head with tiny buffy spots and bright yellow eyes; white underparts have brown bar across throat and rufous-brown 'droplet'-shaped spots along sides. Sexes alike.

ASIAN BARRED OWLET

Glaucidium cuculoides Strigidae

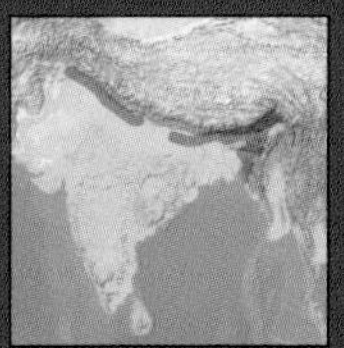

Size 23 cm

Voice Call a bubbling *wowowowowowo* which gets deeper and louder. Also, abrupt *kao…kuk*

Range Locally common breeding resident in N hills

Habitat Hill forests

rufescens

Smallish, heavily-barred owl with bright lemon yellow eyes; white eyebrows; white moustache; yellowish-green bill; greyish-green cere. Upperparts overall olive-brown; nape and head finely speckled pale buff; faintly barred mantle. Underparts plainer with indistinct markings; white-patch on throat; whitish barring on dark brown breast. Yellow feet. Sexes alike. Eastern race more rufous. Hunts during day.

cuculoides

JUNGLE OWLET

Glaucidium radiatum Strigidae

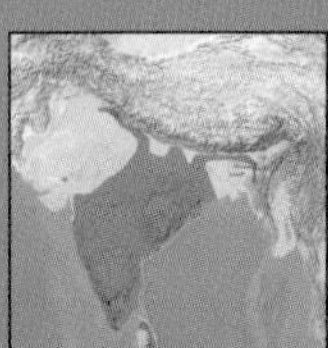

Size 20 cm

Voice Noisy; musical *kuo…kak…kuo…kak…* call-notes, rising in crescendo for few seconds only to end abruptly, other pleasant bubbling notes

Range All over India, from about 2,000 m in the Himalayas; probably absent in extreme NE states

Habitat Forests; partial to teak and bamboo mixed forests

Darkish-brown above, barred rufous and white; flight-feathers barred rufous and black; white moustachial stripe, centre of breast and abdomen; remainder of underbody barred-dark rufous-brown-and-white. Sexes alike. Solitary, or in pairs and sometimes in small groups; crepuscular, but sometimes also active and noisy by day; otherwise spends day in leafy branch; flies short distance when disturbed.

radiatum

malabaricum

CHESTNUT-BACKED OWLET

Glaucidium castanonotum Strigidae

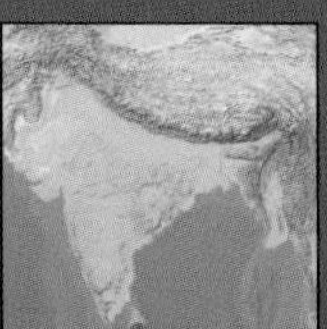

Size 19 cm

Voice Call a slow, resonant *kraw…kraw*

Range Sri Lanka

Habitat Dense forests

Small, stocky owlet, similar to Jungle, but distinguished by bright chestnut back and wing-coverts that are narrowly and diffusely barred with brown and buff. Round, dark grey head, barred black. Heavily-barred upper breast forms collar; white lower throat; abdomen shaft-streaked dark brown. Greenish-yellow bill has rictal bristles at base; legs feathered black-and-white. Diurnal, shy and wary. Seen on top of tall trees on steep hillsides; also frequents plantations.

LITTLE OWL

Athene noctua Strigidae

Size 23 cm

Voice Calls include repeated kee…*u* and low bark

Range Scarce and very local breeding resident in NW mountains east to Nepal

Habitat Rocky desert areas with cliffs and ruins

Diminutive, brown owl with flat crown and plump-round body. Two subspecies: western (east to Ladakh); smaller, paler Ludlow's Owl *A. n. ludlowi*. Eastern (from Ladakh eastwards); darker Hutton's Owl *A.n. bactriana*. Both have extensive white marking on head. Underparts have large white spots and blotches, breast has larger white-patches. Wings and tail broadly barred. White collar and eyebrows and pale facial disc. Juvenile paler and more uniformly patterned.

FOREST OWLET

Heteroglaux blewitti Strigidae

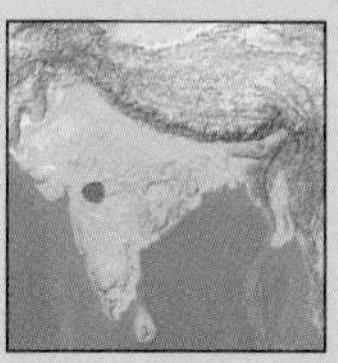

Size 23 cm

Voice Not well-known but *oh…hu* and *kweek…kweek* calls reported

Range Rare endemic breeder rediscovered in extreme NW Maharashtra in 1997 after no sightings for over a century. Also, now known from sites in Madhya Pradesh

Habitat Open, dry deciduous forests on low hills

Thought to be extinct for over a hundred years till rediscovered in 1997. Small, overall dark, greyish-brown bird with fairly small, round head. Tail and wings, heavily-banded; almost completely white underparts; white face; unspotted, brown crown; broad brown breast-band; barred flanks. Similar to Spotted but darker brown with whitish spotting and broader, but paler barring on tail and wings. Underparts white with large claws. Diurnal, shy and wary.

SPOTTED OWLET

Athene brama Strigidae

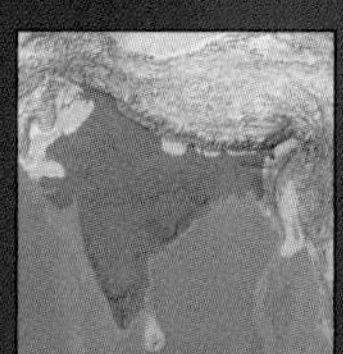

Size 21 cm

Voice Assortment of scolding and cackling notes, screeches and chuckles

Range Throughout the region, upto about 1,800 m in outer Himalayas

Habitat Open forests; orchards; cultivation; vicinity of habitation

Small, stocky owlet with greyish-brown upperparts, spotted white; no ear tufts; yellowish eyes; broken whitish-buff nuchal-collar. Juvenile more thickly-marked white; darkish streaks below breast. Sexes alike. In pairs, or small parties; roosts during day in leafy branches, tree cavities or cavities in walls; active in some localities during daytime; when disturbed flies to nearby tree or branch and bobs and stares at intruder.

BOREAL OWL

Aegolius funereus Strigidae

Size 24-26 cm

Voice Calls include repeated *po...po...po* and squirrel-like smacking *yiop* or *chink*

Range Rare resident or visitor to NW Pakistan, NW India and Bhutan. Status unknown

Habitat Subalpine scrub

Small, nocturnal owl with relatively large, squarish-shaped head; no ear tufts; greyish-white facial discs circled black and finely speckled white; spotted white forehead and crown; blackish-patch between eyes and base of bill; pale yellow eyes; bill and cere yellowish-grey; creamy white underparts, with broad streaks of darkish brown, denser on breast and trailing off at lower belly; short brown tail, with four to five white cross-bars; legs and feet feathered white; darkish claws with sharp tips.

BROWN HAWK OWL

Ninox scutulata Strigidae

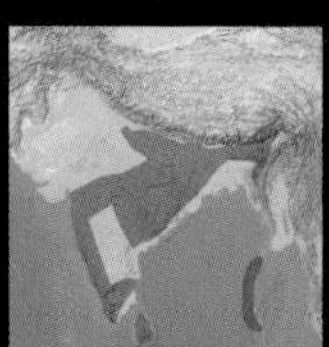

Size 32 cm

Voice Call includes an extended, liquid *oowup... oowup...oowup*

Range Locally common breeding resident mainly in lower hills from Uttarakhand east to Myanmar border, Bangladesh, peninsular India and Sri Lanka

Habitat Well-wooded country, usually near water

Slender, dark owl. Dark brown facial disc has white radial streaks; chocolate-brown crown and nape with ochre streaks; mantle and wing-coverts plain chocolate-brown; some white on back and wings; underparts have intense, drop-shaped streaks, becoming chevron-shaped towards flanks; long, grey-banded tail with whitish tip; no ear tufts; yellow eyes; feathered legs. Andaman and Nicobar race all dark. Sexes alike, male larger than female. Hunts singly, or in pairs, insects, birds and other animals from favoured perch. Hawk-like flight with flaps and long glides. Crepuscular or nocturnal. Roosts during day in thick canopy.

HUME'S HAWK OWL

Ninox (scutulata) obscura Strigidae

Size 32 cm

Voice Call a fluty, interrogative 2-noted *coo…whuk*

Range Andaman Islands

Habitat Edges of forests and well-wooded areas

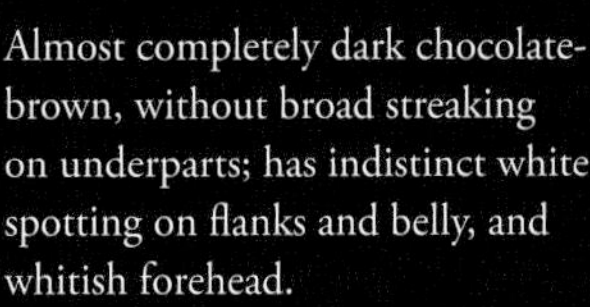

Almost completely dark chocolate-brown, without broad streaking on underparts; has indistinct white spotting on flanks and belly, and whitish forehead.

ANDAMAN HAWK OWL

Ninox affinis Strigidae

Size 25 cm

Voice Call a loud, resounding *craw*

Range Andaman Islands

Habitat Forests, secondary woodlands and mangroves

Small to medium-sized brown owl with round head, greyish facial disc and no ear tufts; yellow eyes; dull green cere; yellowish-grey bill; plain brown crown and mantle finely vermiculated ochre. Upperparts pale buffy-brown and underparts longitudinally streaked with chestnut from neck to abdomen. Smaller in size than Hume's, and distinguished by reddish-brown spotting on white underparts, paler brown colouring to upperparts, unmarked undertail-coverts and more broadly barred tail. Distinguished from Brown Hawk by paler bill, and more pronounced white forehead and throat, paler grey-brown upperparts, and rufous-streaking on underparts.

LONG-EARED OWL

Asio otus Strigidae

Size 35-37 cm

Voice Territorial call of male a long drawn, subdued *os* or *flu*

Range Winter visitor to Pakistan and NW India

Habitat On passage, in winter frequents stunted trees and poplar plantations

Medium-sized owl with distinct, erect ear tufts that sit in middle of forehead. Pale ochre-brown facial disc bordered black; short creamy-white eyebrows. Upperparts ochre-brown, finely speckled darker; crown finely mottled with dark grey; hindneck and nape have grey shaft streaks; ochre-brown tail is washed grey with seven or eight dark, narrow bands. Underparts pale ochre-brown, more streaked towards upper breast, graduating to cross-bars near belly. Noiseless, gliding flight.

SHORT-EARED OWL

Asio flammeus Strigidae

Size 38 cm

Voice Usually silent

Range Scarce but widespread winter visitor throughout lowlands

Habitat Dry, open country with scattered bushes

Medium-sized owl with cat-like face and tiny ear tufts set in middle of forehead; bold facial disc; black mask around small yellow iris. Buff upperparts and breast streaked blackish; yellowish-ochre upper primaries with black tips and white trailing edge; whitish underwing with black tips and carpal crescents; long wings; slightly wedge-shaped tail. Sexes alike. Moth-like flight with slow, deep, rowing wingbeats; glides on stretched wings. Rests in grass clumps. Will perch on posts. Roosts communally outside breeding season.

SRI LANKA FROGMOUTH

Batrachostomus moniliger Batrachostomidae

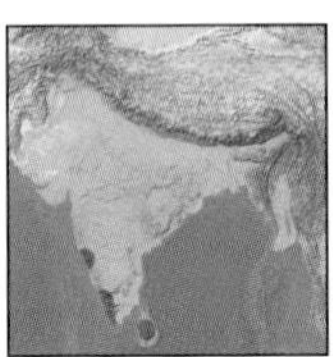

Size 23 cm

Voice Calls include harsh *chaak*; decelerating whistle *klok-klok...*

Range Scarce endemic breeding resident of Western Ghats and Sri Lanka, where it is the only frogmouth

Habitat Thick, wet evergreen forests

Large-headed nightjar with huge frog-like gape and flat, hooked, and feathered bill. Male grey-brown, heavily-mottled white with white neck bar. Female plainer orange-rufous, lightly spotted white. Hunts insects at night; roosts in thick undergrowth; perches vertically, camouflaged by its cryptic plumage. Points bill upwards when disturbed. Nests on branch. Secretive. Lays single white egg which is incubated by both parents, male during the day and female at night.

HODGSON'S FROGMOUTH

Batrachostomus hodgsoni Batrachostomidae

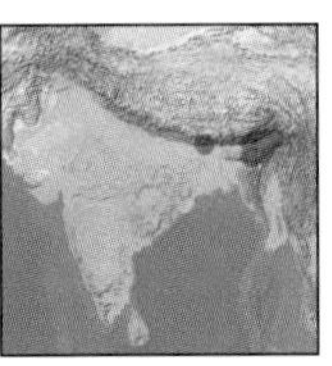

Size 26 cm

Voice Calls include slightly trilled whistles; *wheeow*; *whurree*; soft *gwaa* notes

Range Pockets in E Bhutan and Arunachal Pradesh

Habitat Primary subtropical broadleaved evergreen forests; pine

Medium-sized frogmouth with large head; wide gape; very broad, hooked bill; long facial bristles; slit-like nostrils, and forward-facing eyes. Male mottled grey-rufous with washed rufous-buff, with white collar made up of large spots; large white spots on scapulars; blackish crown. Rufous underparts roughly barred with black-and-white. Female more rufous with white-spotted collar, scapulars, breast; nocturnal. Assumes alarm posture when disturbed; head and neck stretched and bill pointing upwards and freezing.

GREAT-EARED NIGHTJAR

Eurostopodus macrotis Caprimulgidae

Size 40-41cm

Voice Call a clear, wailing *pee…wheeeu*

Range Mainly NE India, Bangladesh and Western Ghats

Habitat Tropical and subtropical broadleaved moist forests; secondary growth

Very large and vividly coloured nightjar. At rest, shows prominent ear tufts, and generally more richly-marked with golden buff and rufous than other nightjars.

JUNGLE NIGHTJAR

Caprimulgus indicus Caprimulgidae

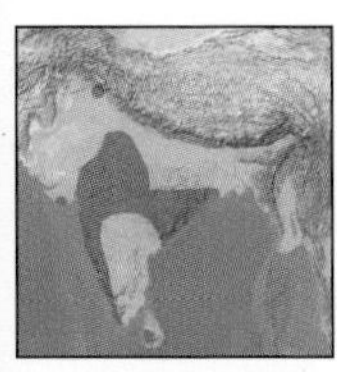

Size 30 cm

Voice Somewhat whistling *chuckoo…chuckoo*, upto 7 minutes at a stretch, with pauses in-between; quick-repeated, mellow *tuck…tuck…tuck* call, eight to 50 at a stretch; occasionally pleasant *uk…kukrooo…*; vocal between dusk and dawn

Range Resident and summer visitor from E Rajasthan to Bihar and Odisha, W peninsula

Habitat Forest clearings; broken scrubby ravines

Large greyish-brown nightjar. Upperparts grey-brown streaked darker; white tip to tail in male; cream sub-moustachial stripe; large white-patch on throat sides; brownish bill, legs and feet; dark brown iris. Underparts also grey-brown, barred darker and becoming more buff towards belly and flanks; calls highly diagnostic. Flies around dusk, hawking insects in zigzag flight; settles on cart tracks and roads.

GREY NIGHTJAR

Caprimulgus i jotaka Caprimulgidae

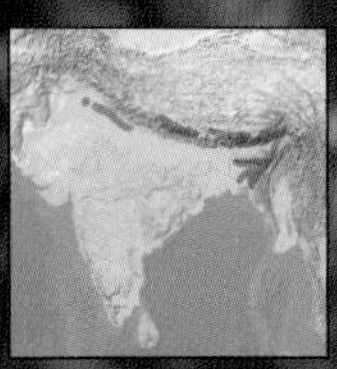

Size 32 cm

Voice Song a *kowrr…kowrr…kowrr*; guttural *tuk…tuk*

Range Himalayas and NE India

Habitat Forest clearings

Medium-sized nightjar with long pointed tail; short legs; short bill with rectal bristles larger than Sykes's, with longer wings and tail. Small dark arrowhead-shaped markings on crown, and irregular buff spotting on nape forms indistinct collar. Roosts on the tree along length of branch.

SYKES'S NIGHTJAR

Caprimulgus mahrattensis Caprimulgidae

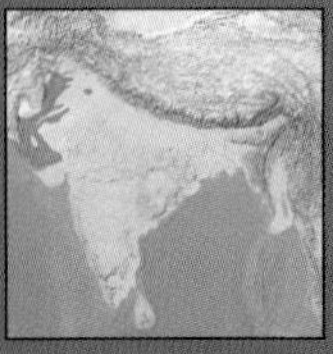

Size 23 cm

Voice Continuous churring song; low, soft *chuck…chuck*

Range Breeds in Pakistan and parts of NW India; winters in S to C India

Habitat Breeds in semi-desert; wide variety of habitats in winter

Similar to Indian, but distinguished by less-marked crown, less-defined buff collar and plainer scapulars; central tail feathers more strongly barred. Overall grey; large white-patches on throat sides and blotchy buff markings on nape forming half-collar; finely streaked crown; black 'inverted anchor-shaped' marks on scapulars.

JERDON'S NIGHTJAR

Caprimulgus atripennis Caprimulgidae

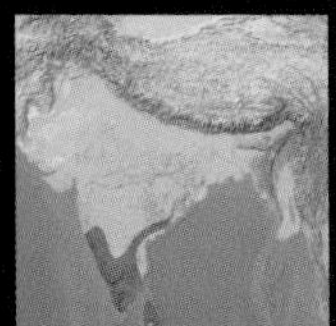

Size 28 cm

Voice Call a series of liquid, tremulous *ch…wo…wo*

Range C and S peninsula; Sri Lanka

Habitat Edges of forests

Larger than Indian, distinguished by barred tail, rufous rear neck, and wing-bars. Male has white wing patch; plumage mainly variegated buff and brown; buff edges to scapulars; unbarred brown breast, rufous neck-band; unbroken white gorget similar to Long-tailed's, but has a shorter tail. Roosts in bushes.

EUROPEAN NIGHTJAR

Caprimulgus europaeus Caprimulgidae

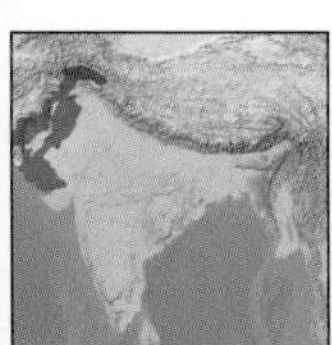

Size 25 cm

Voice Rhythmic churring like a distant motorcycle sound. Soft *quoit… quoit* flight call

Range Locally common breeding summer visitor to hills of W and N Pakistan. Also scarce passage migrant probably en route to E Africa. Mainly in Indus Valley and W Gujarat. Very rare elsewhere

Habitat Rocky, bushy hillsides

Plumage cryptically-patterned like bark of tree providing excellent camouflage; flat, wide head, small bill; large eyes. Male has distinct white wing patch; small, white throat patch; broad creamy-white malar stripe. Upperparts brownish-grey, streaked darker; prominent buff scapular and covert spots. Belly and flanks buff with brown-bars. Female lacks white in wing. Crepuscular and nocturnal. Roosts on ground in daytime or along branch. Difficult to find in day unless flushed. Feeds on flying insects. Nests on ground.

LARGE-TAILED NIGHTJAR

Caprimulgus macrurus Caprimulgidae

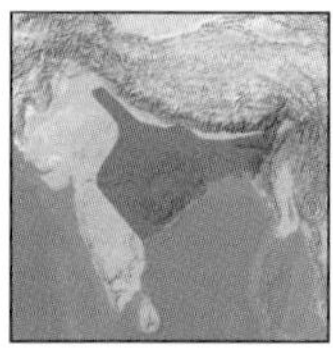

Size 30 cm

Voice Call a resounding, rather slow *chunk…chunk…chunk*

Range Fairly common resident along Gangetic Plain and throughout NE India, south to Andhra Pradesh

Habitat Lowland forests; woodlands

Large, long and broad-tailed nightjar. Grey-brown upperparts streaked darker; more broadly on crown; indistinct buff collar; bright buff-edged black scapular lines; white moustache and breast patch; small bill. Male has broad white (female buff) apical tips to tail and primary patches. Roosts on ground well-camouflaged by dead leaves. Hunts flying insects at night. Erratic, stiff-winged flight.

INDIAN NIGHTJAR

Caprimulgus asiaticus Caprimulgidae

Size 24 cm

Voice Call a far-carrying *chuk… chuk…chuk…cli…uk…tukoroo*

Range Widespread resident; unrecorded in NW and most of NE India

Habitat Open-wooded country in plains and foothills

Medium-sized sandy-grey to brownish-grey nightjar with shortish wings and tail; boldly streaked crown; rufous-buff markings on nape forming distinct collar; bold black centres and broad buff edges to scapulars; bold rufous-buff or buff spotting on wing-coverts, and pale, relatively unmarked central tail feathers. Similar to Large-tailed, but with shorter tail.

SAVANNA NIGHTJAR

Caprimulgus affinis Caprimulgidae

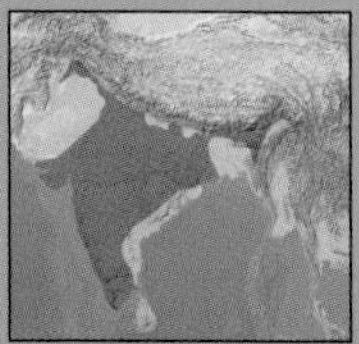

Size 23 cm

Voice Calls on wing as well as on perch, fairly loud, penetrating *sweeesh…* or *schweee*

Range Throughout the region, south of outer Himalayas to about 2,000 m; moves considerably locally

Habitat Rocky hillsides, scrub and grass country, light forests, dry streams and riverbeds, fallow land, cultivation

Male has grey-brown plumage, mottled dark; buffy V on back, from shoulders to about centre of back; two pairs of white outer-tail feathers, with pale dusky tips; white wing patches. Female similar to male, but lacks white outer-tail feathers, which are barred; conspicuous rufous-buff wing patches; call most important identification clue. Solitary, or sometimes several scattered over open expanse; overall behaviour like that of other nightjars; remains motionless during day on open rocky, grass or scrub-covered ground; sometimes roosts on trees, along length of branches; flies around dusk, often flying high; drinks often.

ANDAMAN NIGHTJAR

Caprimulgus andamanicus Caprimulgidae

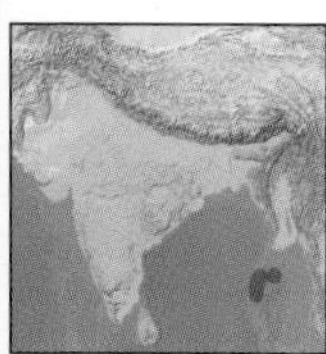

Size 28 cm

Voice Calls include a series of *tyuk* notes, rather weak and rapidly repeated

Range Andaman Islands

Habitat Open forests and open country with scattered trees

Once considered a subspecies of the Large-tailed, however, song and morphology distinct. Medium-sized; distinguished from Large-tailed, scapulars lack prominent pale edgings, coverts comparatively uniform, has rufous barring at base of primaries, and lacks prominent nuchal-collar.

GLOSSY SWIFTLET

Collocalia esculenta Apodidae

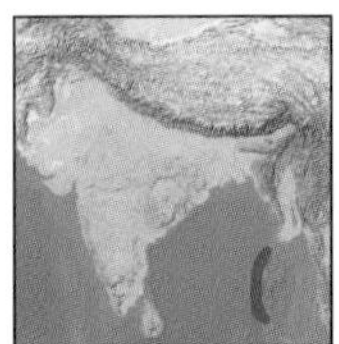

Size 10 cm

Voice Soft twittering call

Range Common breeding resident in Andaman and Nicobar Islands

Habitat Nests in buildings

Tiny swiftlet with square, notched tail. Upperparts glossy blue-black; dark grey throat and breast; white from belly to flanks, finely speckled at margins; black underwing; rounded wing-tips; white panels on tail. Distinguished from Edible-nest by white belly. Smaller in size than Indian. Fast-flying. Feeds on tiny insects high in sky. Often seen flying over forests as well as towns. Difficult to observe closely when away from nest.

INDIAN SWIFTLET

Collocalia unicolor Apodidae

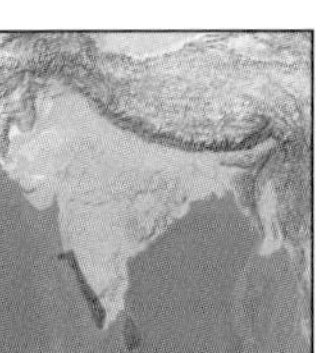

Size 12 cm

Voice Roosting birds keep up incessant, faint chatter

Range Western Ghats, south of Ratnagiri; associated hill ranges

Habitat Caves; cliffs on rocky; offshore islands

Dimunitive blackish-brown swiftlet with slightly forked-tail visible in flight. Gregarious and colonial; huge numbers on cliffsides and caves; swarms leave before dawn in a rush of wings; spends day high over mountains and countryside, hawking insects, often along with other swifts and martins; arrives back to caves and cliff roosts around dusk, when bats are leaving.

HIMALAYAN SWIFTLET

Collocalia brevirostris Apodidae

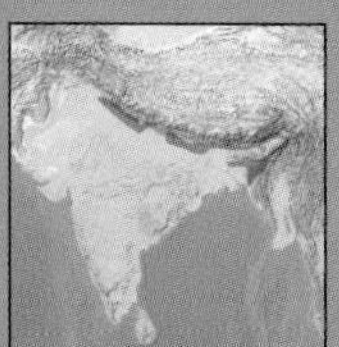

Size 14 cm

Voice Call a low, rattling and twittering *chit…chit* at roost

Range The Himalayas; NE India

Habitat Similar to Indian's

Large swiftlet with very obvious forked-tail and looks boomerang-shaped in flight with back-swept wings. Slightly glossed upperparts. Underparts paler grey-brown; distinct pale grey rump-band; rounded wings; lightly feathered legs; small, rounded beak with bristles; short legs let the bird cling to vertical surfaces. Sexes similar. Juvenile has indistinct rump-band. Distinguished from Edible-nest by larger size, more forked-tail, less distinct rump-band. Larger than Indian. Roosts in caves; forages over forest.

EDIBLE-NEST SWIFTLET

Collocalia fuciphaga Apodidae

Medium-sized swiftlet with overall dark brown plumage; uniform grey-brown underparts; narrow, greyish rump-band; moderately forked-tail; unfeathered legs. Duller blackish-brown above than Glossy. Very similar to the Himalayan, but smaller. Indian paler with no rump contrast. Roosts and nests in caves which it navigates by echolocation. Large numbers cling to walls like bats. Enters and leaves roost in rushing cascades. White nest made of saliva affixed to cave wall. Much prized for birds' nest soup and some colonies frequently and illegally raided for nests.

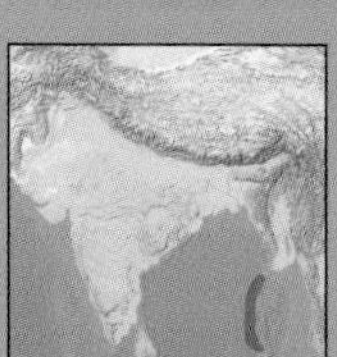

Size 12 cm

Voice Call a loud, metallic *zwing*

Range Common breeding resident on Andaman Islands, less common on Nicobar

Habitat Feeds aerially on insects over mangroves, coasts and towns. More coastal than Glossy

WHITE-RUMPED SPINETAIL

Zoonavena sylvatica Apodidae

Size 11 cm

Voice Call a twittering *chick…chick*, uttered on wing

Range The Himalayas from N Uttar Pradesh, east to Sikkim

Habitat Broadleaved evergreen and moist deciduous forests

Small, stocky, broad-winged needletail. Has bulging secondaries, with wings pinched in at base and pointed at tip. Typically, flight action fast with rapid wingbeats, and banking from side-to-side, interspersed with short glides on slightly bowed wings. Upperparts mainly blue-black with contrasting white rump; throat and breast grey-brown, merging into whitish lower belly and undertail-coverts. From below, long white undertail-coverts contrast with black of sides and tip of undertail. 'Spines' at tip of tail visible at close range.

WHITE-THROATED NEEDLETAIL

Hirundapus caudacutus Apodidae

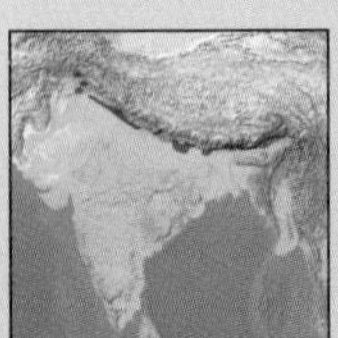

Size 20 cm

Voice Utters feeble, rapid metallic chittering, audible only at close range

Range Summer visitor; the Himalayas and NE India

Habitat Often seen over ridges, cliffs, forest, upland grasslands and river valleys

Like other needletails, strong flier combining very strong flapping with swooping, gliding and soaring, often at very high speeds. Like other species has pale 'saddle' on upperparts, and dramatic white 'horseshoe' crescent at rear-end. Distinguished from Silver-backed and Brown-backed by clearly demarcated white throat, and white inner webs to tertials (showing as white-patch, although may be obscured). Additional differences from Brown-backed include smaller size, dark lores, and more contrasting pale 'saddle'. Also shows shorter, square-ended tail projection beyond white undertail-coverts, and tail 'spines' less distinct. Juvenile has less clear-cut white throat (more similar to Silver-backed); has black streaking and spotting on white of hind flanks, and dark fringes to white undertail-coverts. Usually occurs solitary, or in loose parties. Roosts colonially on cliffs and trees.

BROWN-BACKED NEEDLETAIL

Hirundapus giganteus Apodidae

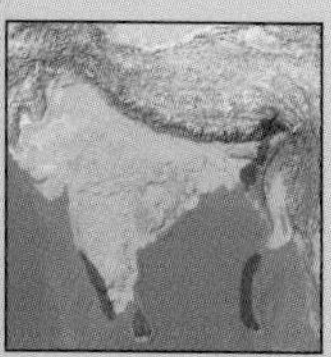

Size 23 cm

Voice Rather quiet. Calls include various soft squeaks and trills

Range Scarce breeding resident of Western Ghats, Sri Lanka and NE India

Habitat Forested areas

Large, dark, extremely fast-flying swift with white vent crescent and pointed tail. All sooty-brown with paler back, distinct white vent extending as crescent up the flanks. Needles in tail feathers visible and long enough to form pointed tail. Flapping of wings often audible in low flight. Roosts and breeds in large hollow trees. Flight exceptionally powerful and flexible; quite difficult to follow with binoculars. Hunts aerial insects low over forest in loose parties.

ASIAN PALM SWIFT

Cypsiurus balasiensis Apodidae

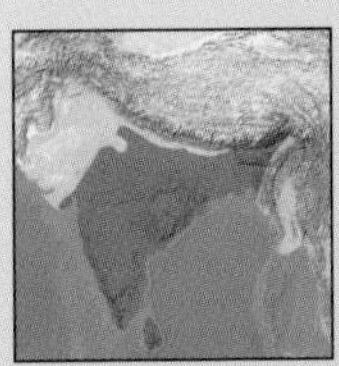

Size 13 cm

Voice Call a 3-note shrill scream, uttered very fast and always on wing

Range All over peninsular India, south of the Himalayan foothills (except NW); also in NE hill states

Habitat Open country, cultivation; this bird's life revolves around palms

Sooty-brown plumage; typical swift wings, long and sickle-like; deeply forked-tail distinctive, specially in flight. Sociable; small parties in open, palm-dotted country; strong in flight, and uttering lively screaming notes on wing; hawks insects all day, occasionally rising very high; roosts on underside of palm frond (leaf).

ALPINE SWIFT

Tachymarptis melba Apodidae

Size 23 cm

Voice Calls include shrill *chrrrr... chee...chee...* screams in fast flight; twittering notes at roost sites

Range All over India, from about 2,500 m in the Himalayas; uncommon over N Indian plains

Habitat Hill country; cliffsides

Very long, sickle-shaped, pointed wings; dark sooty-brown above; white underbody; broad, brown band across breast diagnostic in flight; dark undertail-coverts. Loose 'parties' dashing erratically at high speed in skies; extremely strong flier; seen high in skies around dusk, many birds wheeling and tumbling, their shrill screams rending the air; drinks at ponds and puddles by skimming over water surface. Sexes alike.

COMMON SWIFT

Apus apus Apodidae

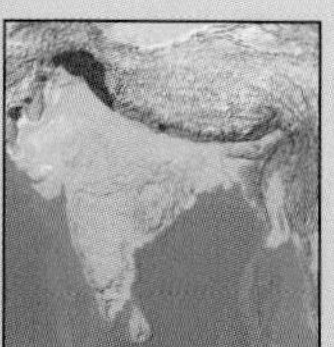

Size 17 cm

Voice Call a high-pitched scream *screee...screee...screee*

Range Summer visitor to Balochistan, Pakistan, and the Himalayas from N Pakistan east to Nepal; Maldives

Habitat Chiefly in mountains, but can occur fleetingly over any habitat

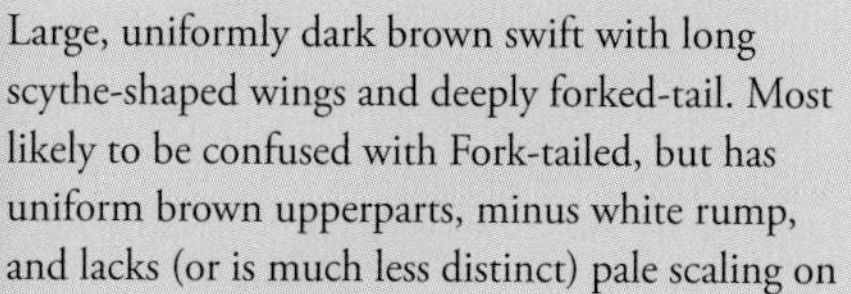

Large, uniformly dark brown swift with long scythe-shaped wings and deeply forked-tail. Most likely to be confused with Fork-tailed, but has uniform brown upperparts, minus white rump, and lacks (or is much less distinct) pale scaling on underparts. Distinguished from the very similar Pallid and Dark-rumped. Juvenile has whiter forehead and more extensive white throat, and extensive pale scaling on underparts (although not so prominent as on Fork-tailed).

PALLID SWIFT

Apus pallidus Apodidae

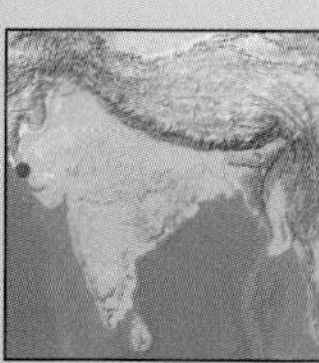

Size 17 cm

Voice Call a disyllabic *cheeu...eet* or *chumic*

Range Winter visitor to coastal regions; status unknown, but probably frequent in extreme W

Habitat Similar to those of Alpine

Large, uniformly grey-brown swift, very similar in shape and appearance to Common, and with similar flight, but has slower wingbeats than latter. Paler grey-brown in colouration than Common, appearing almost pale in bright light, with more extensive pale throat and forehead, which contrasts with dark eye patch. Has dark outer primaries and leading edge to wing, contrasting on both upperside and underside with rest of wing, which is pale. Also, has pale fringes to feathers of underparts, giving scaly appearance.

SALIM ALI'S SWIFT

Apus (pacificus) salimali Apodidae

Very similar to Fork-tailed Swift, with which it is usually considered conspecific. Breeds from the eastern Tibetan plateau eastwards, but wintering range unknown; may occur in NE as breeder or migrant. Larger than Fork-tailed with a deeper tail-fork and a small white throat patch.

FORK-TAILED SWIFT

Apus pacificus Apodidae

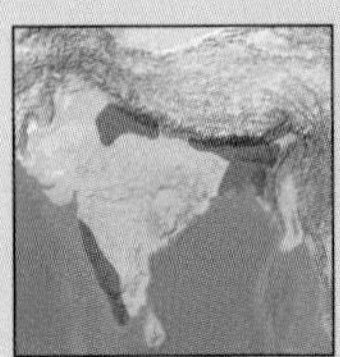

Size 15 cm

Voice Call a hard *shkree* in flight

Range Locally common breeding summer visitor to N mountains. Wintering areas unknown

Habitat Open skies

Medium-sized, blackish, long-winged and fork-tailed swift with narrow white rump-band, its most striking feature. Blackish-brown with small white throat patch. Deep and obvious tail-fork; sickle-shaped wings. Best chance of seeing the bird when flying low before weather front or passing thunderstorm. Very fast, lucid flight without fluttering, distinguishes it from House Martin. High aerial feeder (often out of sight) in loose flocks or singly with other aerial feeders.

DARK-RUMPED SWIFT

Apus acuticauda Apodidae

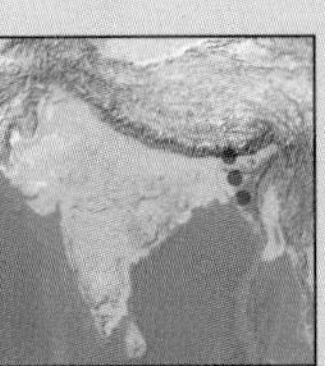

Size 17 cm

Voice Very high-pitched call uttered by flocking birds in vicinity of breeding cliffs

Range Resident, endemic to the subcontinent

Habitat Rocky cliffs, gorges

All-dark swift, similar to Fork-tailed. Distinguished from that species by all-dark rump, and lack of clearly-defined white throat. Greyish-white throat, with dark streaking, patterning merging with rest of underparts. Does not appear as slim and long-winged as Fork-tailed; sharper tail-fork, with narrower and more pointed outer-tail feathers. Very similar in shape to Common.

LITTLE SWIFT

Apus affinis Apodidae

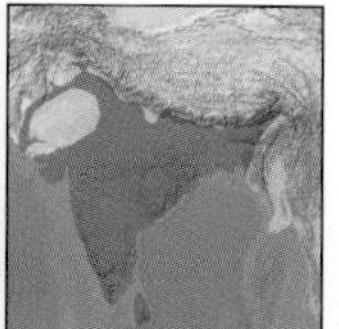

Size 15 cm

Voice Musical squeals on wing; very vocal at sunset, but also through the day

Range Throughout the region, upto about 2,400 m in the Himalayas

Habitat Human habitation; cliffs; ruins

Overall dark swift with white rump and throat distinctive; short, square tail. Highly gregarious; on wing during day, hawking insects, flying over human habitation, cliffs and ruins; strong flier, exhibiting great mastery and control in fast-wheeling flight; frequently utters squealing notes on wing; retires to safety of nest colonies in overcast weather.

CRESTED TREESWIFT

Hemiprocne coronata Hemiprocnidae

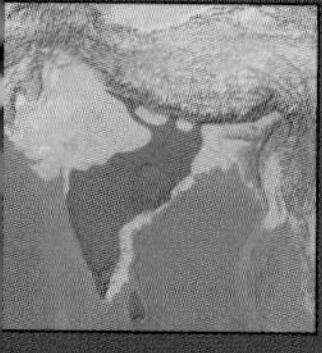

Size 23 cm

Voice Call a parrot-like *kea… kea…*; double-noted faint scream

Range Subcontinent, south of the Himalayan foothills; absent in arid parts of NW India

Habitat Open, deciduous forests

Male bluish-grey above, with faint greenish wash; chestnut sides of face and throat; ash-grey breast, whiter below. Female similar to male, but lacks chestnut on head. Backward-curving crest and long, deeply forked-tail diagnostic. In pairs or small, scattered parties; flies during day, hawking insects; has favourite foraging areas; flight graceful, not as fast as other swifts, but displays typical swift mastery; calls from perch and in flight; unlike other swifts, perches on bare, higher branches; drinks in flight from surfaces of forest pools.

MALABAR TROGON

Harpactes fasciatus Trogonidae

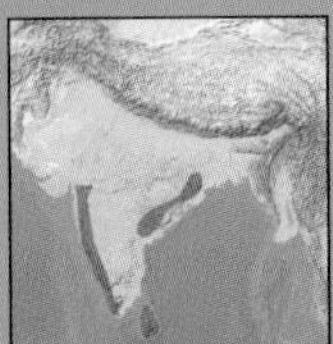

Size 30 cm

Voice Diagnostic, often a giveaway to bird's presence in forest; 3- to 8-noted, somewhat whistling *cue…cue…* calls

Range Forested areas of peninsular India; Satpura range, Western Ghats, east to Odisha and parts of Eastern Ghats. Also Sri Lanka

Habitat Forests

Male has sooty-black head, neck and breast; yellow-brown back; black wings narrowly-barred white; rich crimson underbody; white breast gorget. Female duller overall; lacks black on head and breast; orange-brown underbody. Long, squarish tail distinctive. Solitary, or in pairs; strictly arboreal; difficult to see because duller back mostly turned towards observer or intruder; hunts flycatcher-style or flits among taller branches; flicks tail and bends body when disturbed.

RED-HEADED TROGON

Harpactes erythrocephalus Trogonidae

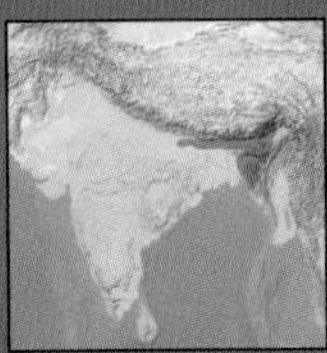

Size 35 cm

Voice Call includes a scaled sequence of *chaup…chaup…chaup* notes

Range Scarce breeding resident in NE India including parts of Nepal and Bangladesh

Habitat Dense broadleaved forests

Brilliantly-coloured bird with long, square-ended tail. Head and neck bright crimson, white crescent-shaped breast-band; underparts more pinkish. Golden-orange back; dark grey wings and black closely barred with white. Tail edged with black with slim white outer borders; broad bill; weak legs. Female has ruddy-brown head and breast. Hawks insects. Nests in tree cavities or termite mounds. Shy but inquisitive. Habits as Malabar Trogon. Equally difficult to see.

WARD'S TROGON

Harpactes wardi Trogonidae

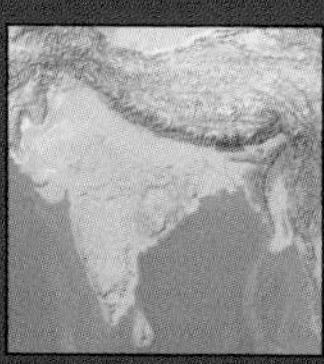

Size 38 cm

Voice Call includes dull, rapid rising, then dropping notes *klew… klew…klew*

Range E Bhutan and Arunachal Pradesh

Habitat Dense broadleaved evergreen montane forests; bamboos

Large, vividly-coloured trogon. Male has deep pink forehead and supercilium; pale blue orbital skin; slaty-grey hindneck, maroon upper breast; rest of underparts pinkish-red; short, broad, pink beak, and long, broad pink tail; upperparts, head and upper breast maroon. Female has olive-brown head; bright yellow forehead; and pale yellow underparts. Can sit still for long periods; prefers lower or middle forest storeys. Solitary, or in pairs; agile in hawking insects.

♀

INDIAN ROLLER

Coracias benghalensis Coraciidae

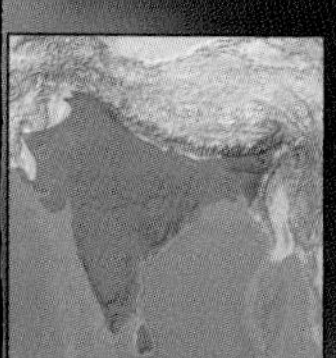

Size 31 cm

Voice Usually silent; occasionally harsh *khak…kak…kak…* notes; exuberant screeching notes and shrieks during courtship display, diving, and screaming wildly

Range Almost entire subcontinent, south of outer Himalayas, where found upto about 1,500 m

Habitat Open country; cultivation; orchards; light forests

Pale greenish-brown above; pinkish-brown breast; deep blue tail has light blue subterminal band; in flight, bright blue wings and tail, with Cambridge-blue bands distinctive. Sexes alike. Solitary, or in pairs; perches on overhead wires, bare branches, earthen mounds and small bush-tops; either glides and drops on prey or pounces suddenly; batters prey against perch. Elaborate courtship display, performs startling aerobatics including a series of 'rolls'.

affinis

EUROPEAN ROLLER

Coracias garrulus Coraciidae

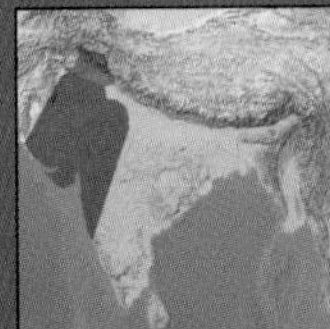

Size 31 cm

Voice Call a loud, harsh *rack…rack*

Range Breeding resident in N Pakistan and Kashmir. Scarce winter visitor

Habitat Open, dry country and cultivation

Crow-sized bird with large head, and crow-like bill. Pale blue head, neck and underparts; orangish-brown upperparts; azure scapulars. Black eye-stripes and black apical tips to tail; cinnamon rump. Juvenile greyer. Feeds on large insects, reptiles and rodents, usually catching them on ground in shrike-like pounce. Solitary. Seen perched on poles or wires.

DOLLARBIRD

Eurystomus orientalis Coraciidae

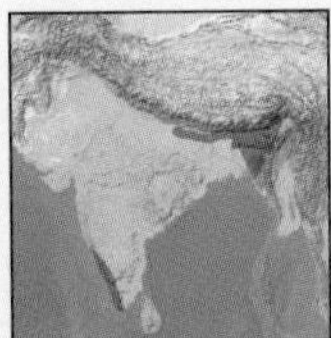

Size 31 cm

Voice Call a rasping *drak…drak*

Range Scarce breeding resident, partial migrant to NE India, Western Ghats

Habitat Forest edges and clearings, also nearby cultivation

Dark greenish-brown upperparts, washed bluish-green on back and wings. Brown breast; throat and undertail glossy blue; silvery-blue 'coin' on primaries, visible in flight; pale belly and undertail-coverts; stout red bill with black tip; red legs and eye-rings. Perches high in trees on bare branches from where it launches itself to catch large-flying insects. Crepuscular and sociable, groups often hunt after dusk. Nests in tree holes.

STORK-BILLED KINGFISHER

Pelargopsis capensis Halcyonidae

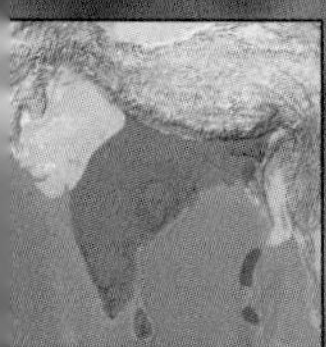

Size 38 cm

Voice Noisy. Call a *kee…kee…kee*, repeated many times

Range Subcontinent, except drier parts of NW India

Habitat Canals, streams, coastal backwaters in well-wooded country

Large kingfisher with blue-green back, blue wings and blue tail. Enormous red bill diagnostic; red legs. Dark grey-brown head with yellowish and blue collar on back of neck. Brownish-yellow underparts. Sexes alike. Solitary, more heard than seen. Does not normally hover. Laboured flight.

intermedia

capensis

BROWN-WINGED KINGFISHER

Pelargopsis amauroptera Halcyonidae

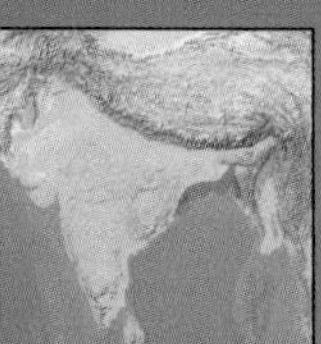

Size 36 cm

Voice Calls include laughing, descendent *cha…cha…cha* and low, whistling *chow…chow…chow*

Range Globally near-threatened. Scarce breeding resident, winter visitor to NE India, Bangladesh

Habitat Coasts with mangroves and wooded estuaries. Very rarely on inland wetlands

Large, brown kingfisher with bright orange head and underparts; huge red bill. Brown upperparts; blue rump and lower back. Feeds by plunging into water or onto mud from favoured perch. Will feed in sea-surf, often resting within breaking waves. Rather sluggish but has powerful high flight. Sits on bare twigs in the middle-storey while calling.

RUDDY KINGFISHER

Halcyon coromanda Halcyonidae

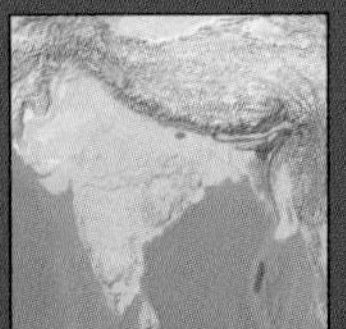

Size 25 cm

Voice Call a descending and high-pitched *tititititititi*

Range E Himalayan foothills, NE India, Bangladesh

Habitat Pools and streams in dense broadleaved tropical and subtropical evergreen forests; also mangrove swamps

Overall orange-rufous bird with large coral-red bill; rufous-orange upperparts washed violet, and lighter rufous underparts; bluish-white rump, conspicuous in flight. Juvenile has darker and more brown upperparts, bluer rump, faint blackish barring on rufous underparts, and blackish bill. Solitary, or in pairs. Secretive; more heard than seen; perches in understorey dropping to capture prey.

WHITE-THROATED KINGFISHER

Halcyon smyrnensis Halcyonidae

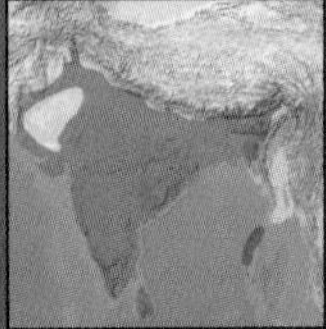

Size 28 cm

Voice Noisy, loud, crackling laugh, often audible over crowded urban areas; song a longish, quivering whistle, sounding *kilililili*... characteristic feature of hot season, in breeding; fascinating courtship display

Range Subcontinent, south of outer Himalayas

Habitat Forests, cultivation, lakes, riversides; also coastal mangroves and estuaries

Chestnut-brown head, neck and underbody below breast; bright turquoise-blue above, often with greenish tinge; black flight feathers with white wing patch visible in flight; white chin, throat and breast distinctive; coral-red beak and legs. Sexes alike. Solitary, or scattered pairs atop overhead wires, poles and tree-tops; frequently found far from water; drops on to ground to pick up prey.

BLACK-CAPPED KINGFISHER

Halcyon pileata Halcyonidae

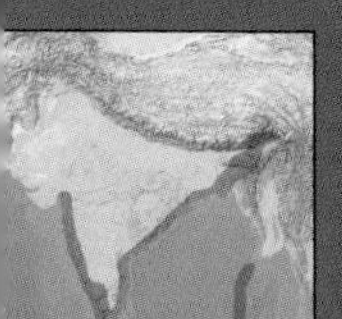

Size 30 cm

Voice Call a shrill, fairly loud cackle, quite like the Commoner White-Breasted, but unmistakable once heard

Range The coast, from around Mumbai south along entire W seaboard and all along the E coast, Sri Lanka

Habitat Chiefly coastal areas, mangroves, estuaries; may wander inland, especially along rivers

Black cap, white collar and deep blue upperbody; white throat, upper breast and dull rufous below; in flight conspicuous white wing patch; deep, dagger-like, coral-red beak. Sexes alike. Mostly solitary; coastal bird; has favoured feeding sites; dives for fish but also takes insects from ground.

COLLARED KINGFISHER

Todiramphus chloris Halcyonidae

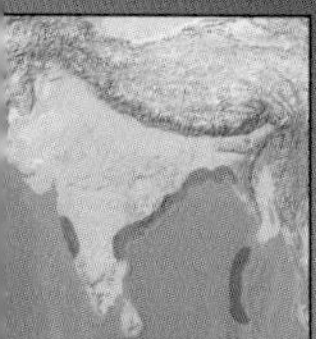

Size 24 cm

Voice Call a hard *krerk… krerk… krerk*

Range Scarce breeding resident sporadically along the coast from Bangladesh to Goa. Commoner in NE India and on Andaman and Nicobar Islands

Habitat Tidal creeks, mudflats and mangroves where feeds mainly on small crabs and skippers

Medium-sized, heavy-billed kingfisher with broad, white collar. White underparts, sometimes washed buff; turquoise head, wings and tail. Variable dark and white markings depending on race. Upperparts bright turquoise-green, bluer on wings. Sexes alike. Juvenile has faint buff scaling on upperparts, and indistinct dark scaling on underparts and collar. Solitary, or in pairs.

ORIENTAL DWARF KINGFISHER

Ceyx erithaca Alcedinidae

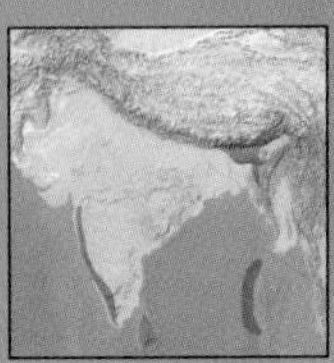

Size 13 cm

Voice Call a sharp, squeaky *chicheee... or chcheee...*

Range Apparently disjunct. From E Garhwal through NE states; Western Ghats south from around Mumbai; Nilgiris. Appears in many areas only with the onset of SW monsoons

Habitat Forest streams; nullahs

Brownish-chestnut crown; iridescent purple back, rump; deep purplish-blue of closed wings often hides the back; deep blue and white spots on neck sides and short, chestnut tail; orangish-yellow underbody and large, bright coral-red beak striking. Sexes alike. Solitary, or in pairs; tiny forest bird, usually overlooked when perched on stumps or tangled roots along nullahs and mud walls, often by forest path or road.

BLUE-EARED KINGFISHER

Alcedo meninting Alcedinidae

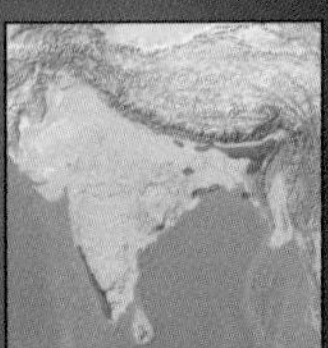

Size 17 cm

Voice Call a shrill *chichee... chichee*

Range C Nepal eastwards in lowlands

Habitat Rivers, pools, streams in dense tropical and subtropical evergreen forests, bamboo thickets, or near shady vegetation

juvenile

Small, short-tailed and vividly-coloured kingfisher. Brilliant ultramarine blue upperparts and rufous-red underparts; rufous loral spot; bright blue line down centre of back; stronger blue and black barring on crown; blue ear-coverts; creamy-white throat and neck patch; wing-coverts spangled lighter blue. Dark wings. Solitary and very shy; sits patiently near pools, bobs head and flicks tail; dives to catch prey.

COMMON KINGFISHER

Alcedo atthis Alcedinidae

Bright blue above, greenish on wings; top of head finely-banded black-and-blue; ferruginous cheeks, ear-coverts and white-patch on neck sides; white chin and throat and deep ferruginous underbody distinctive; coral-red legs and blackish beak. Sexes alike. Solitary, or in scattered pairs; never found away from water; perches on pole or overhanging branch; flies low over water, brilliant blue streak, utters shrill notes; sometimes tame and confiding; dives for fish from perch; occasionally hovers over water before diving.

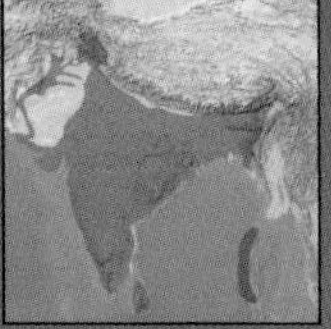

Size 18 cm

Voice Call a shrill *chichee…chichee*

Range Subcontinent, south of 2,000 m in the Himalayas; various races differ in shade of blue-green upperbody

Habitat Streams, lakes, canals; also coastal areas

BLYTH'S KINGFISHER

Alcedo hercules Alcedinidae

Larger than Common with brilliant blue upperparts and rufous underparts; long, robust bill; pale blue spangling on crown and nape; orange lores; blue ear-coverts; creamy-white chin and throat. Perches on overhanging branches near water. Shy and averse to disturbance.

Size 22 cm

Voice Call a surprisingly loud and strong *cheee*

Range E Nepal eastwards in lowland forests. S Assam Hills

Habitat Shady streams in dense broadleaved tropical forests

CRESTED KINGFISHER

Megaceryle lugubris Cerylidae

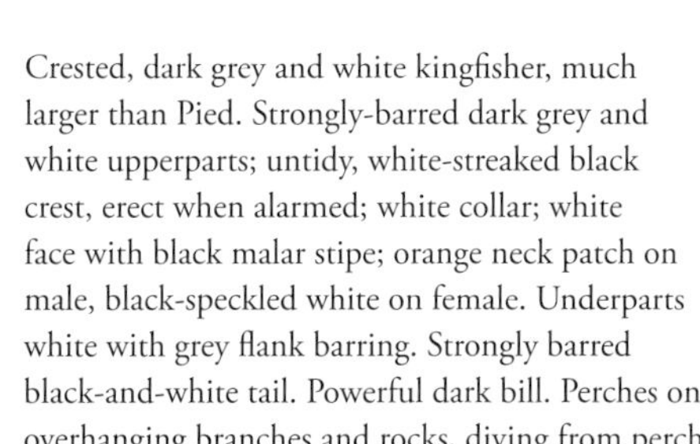

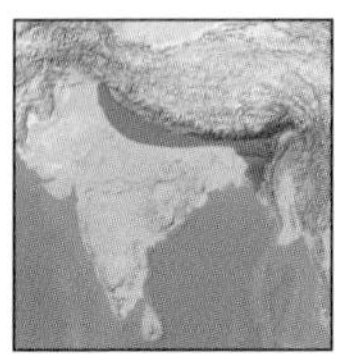

Size 41 cm

Voice Quiet; occasional *kik* note

Range Scarce breeding resident of N and NE uplands

Habitat Fast-flowing rivers

Crested, dark grey and white kingfisher, much larger than Pied. Strongly-barred dark grey and white upperparts; untidy, white-streaked black crest, erect when alarmed; white collar; white face with black malar stipe; orange neck patch on male, black-speckled white on female. Underparts white with grey flank barring. Strongly barred black-and-white tail. Powerful dark bill. Perches on overhanging branches and rocks, diving from perch for fish. Solitary and very loyal to favoured perches.

PIED KINGFISHER

Ceryle rudis Cerylidae

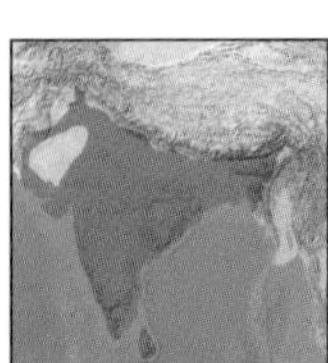

Size 25 cm

Voice Call includes piercing, twittering *chirrruk...chirruk...* cries in flight, sounding as if the bird is complaining

Range Subcontinent, upto about 2,000 m in the Himalayas

Habitat Streams, rivers, ponds; sometimes coastal areas

Kingfisher with black-and-white plumage; long dagger-like bill; untidy black crest on hindcrown; irregular black eye-band, continuing to back of head; black-and-white speckled underparts; white underwing; double black gorget across breast in male. Female has single, broken breast gorget. Solitary, in pairs or in small groups. Noisy and gregarious; hovers with flayed wings.

travancoreensis

lecucomelanura

GREEN BEE-EATER

Merops orientalis Meropidae

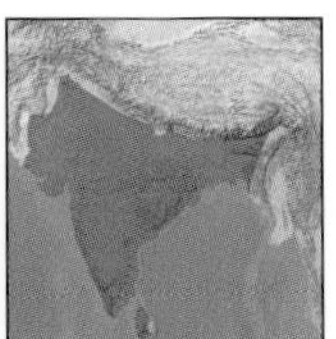

Size 21 cm

Voice Noisy; cheerful trilling notes, chiefly uttered on wing

Range Subcontinent, south of about 1,800 m in outer Himalayas

Habitat Open country and cultivation; light forests

orientalis

Small bee-eater with bright green plumage; red-brown wash about head; pale blue on chin and throat, bordered below by black gorget; slender, curved black beak; rufous wash on black-tipped flight feathers; elongated central tail feathers distinctive. Sexes alike. Small parties; perches freely on bare branches and overhead telegraph wires; attends to grazing cattle, along with drongos, cattle egrets and mynas; also seen in city parks and garden; launches graceful sorties after winged insects; batters prey against perch before swallowing. Large flocks of upto 300 birds roost communally.

beludschius

BLUE-BEARDED BEE-EATER

Nyctyornis athertoni Meropidae

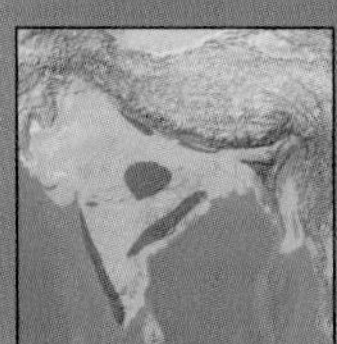

Size 34 cm

Voice Harsh *korrr...korrr* croaking notes, often followed by softer chuckling call

Range Outer Himalayas to about 1,800 m, from Himachal to extreme E; Western Ghats and Nilgiris; forested parts of Madhya Pradesh, Eastern Ghats through Andhra Pradesh, Odisha, Bihar and West Bengal

Habitat Edges of forests, clearings

Unmarked grass-green above, bluer on forehead; elongated, blue feathers along centre of throat to breast appear beard-like, prominent when bird is calling; buffy-yellow below breast, streaked green; tail lacks long central pins; long sickle-shaped tail. Sexes alike. In pairs, or in groups; arboreal, rarely descending low; makes short aerial sallies after winged insects; batters prey on perch; usually not an easy bird to observe from close.

non-breeding

BLUE-CHEEKED BEE-EATER

Merops persicus Meropidae

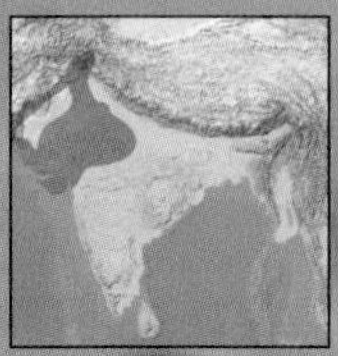

Size 27 cm

Voice Noisy. Call a liquid, disyllabic *priit…priit* mainly in high flight

Range Locally common breeding summer visitor: Pakistan, NW India

Habitat Dry, open country near water

Large, emerald green bee-eater with vividly-coloured face. Prominent black eye-stripe with pale blue above and below; yellow throat; rufous upper breast; chestnut underwings; two long central tail pins. Juvenile duller with pointed or square-ended tails. Sexes alike. Nests in colonies in sandy banks. Feeds largely on dragonflies in flight.

BLUE-TAILED BEE-EATER

Merops philippinus Meropidae

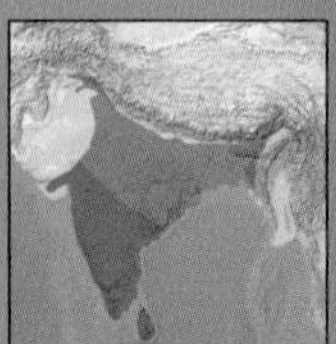

Size 30 cm

Voice Musical, ringing notes, chiefly uttered in flight

Range Exact range not correctly known; breeds in parts of NW and N India, and perhaps patchily through E and SC India; spreads wide during the rains and winter

Habitat Open country, light forests, vicinity of water, cultivation; may occasionally be seen in coastal areas

Elongated central tail feathers. Greenish above, with faint blue wash on wings; bluish rump, tail diagnostic; yellow upper throat patch with chestnut throat and upper breast; slightly curved black beak, broad black stripe through eye. Sexes alike. Usually small flocks, frequently in vicinity of water; launches short, elegant flights from wire or tree perch; characteristic flight, few quick wingbeats and stately glide.

CHESTNUT-HEADED BEE-EATER

Merops leschenaulti Meropidae

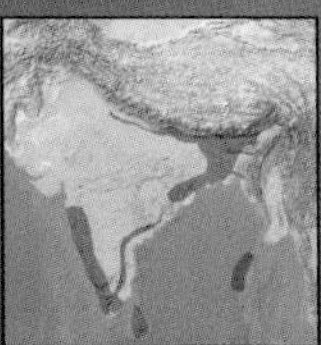

Size 21 cm

Voice Musical twittering notes, mostly uttered on wing, and sometimes from perch

Range Disjunct; the Himalayan foothills, from Uttarakhand to extreme NE; Western Ghats south of Goa; also, Sri Lanka. Occasionally may be encountered elsewhere in the peninsula, especially during monsoon

Habitat Vicinity of water in forested areas

Grass-green plumage; chestnut-cinnamon crown, hindneck and upper back; yellow chin and throat; rufous and black gorget. Sexes alike. Small gatherings on telegraph wires or bare upper branches of trees from where it launches short aerial sallies; fast, graceful flight; noisy when converging at roosting trees.

EUROPEAN BEE-EATER

Merops apiaster Meropidae

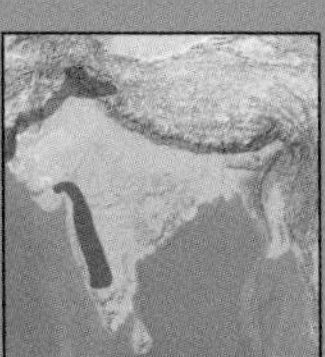

Size 27 cm

Voice Noisy. Call a liquid monosyllabic *prut…prut*, given mostly in flight

Range Common breeding summer visitor: Pakistan, Kashmir. May be encountered elsewhere in the peninsula

Habitat Dry, open country and cultivation

Extremely vividly-coloured, unmistakable bee-eater. Breeding adult has warm chestnut crown merging into golden yellow back; yellow throat bordered with black. Green and chestnut wings; emerald green tail and underparts; red eyes. Adults have short tail pins. Male has chestnut-patch in underwing; small or absent in female. Juvenile much duller and blunt-tailed with brown eyes. Pale orange underwings. Sexes alike. Feeds mainly on bees.

COMMON HOOPOE

Upupa epops Upupidae

Size 31 cm

Voice Call a pleasant, mellow *hoo…po…po…*

Range Subcontinent, upto about 5,500 m in the Himalayas; several races; spreads considerably in winter

Habitat Meadows, open country, garden lawns, open-light forests

Fawn-coloured plumage; black-and-white markings on wings, back and tail; black-and-white-tipped crest; longish, gently curved beak. Sexes alike. Solitary, or in scattered pairs; small, loose flocks in winter; probes ground with long beak, sometimes feeding along with other birds; flits among tree branches; crest often fanned open.

BROWN HORNBILL

Anorrhinus austeni Bucerotidae

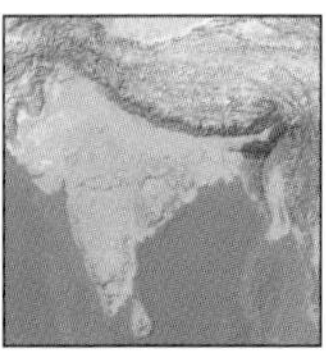

Size 60-75 cm

Voice Noisy; normal call a shrill squealing note; also other squeals and screams

Range Almost throughout India, upto about 1,500 m in the Himalayas; absent in arid NW regions and heavy rainfall areas of S Western Ghats

Habitat Forests; orchards; tree-covered avenues; vicinity of habitation

Medium-sized hornbill with dark brown upperparts and bright rufous-brown underparts. Male white on head and neck sides; large, pale bill; small, keel-shaped casque; pale blue orbital patch; whitish cheeks, throat and upper breast, white tips to tail and primaries, visible in flight. Female has paler underparts, pale brown tips to wing-coverts, and pinkish orbital skin.

MALABAR GREY HORNBILL

Ocyceros griseus Bucerotidae

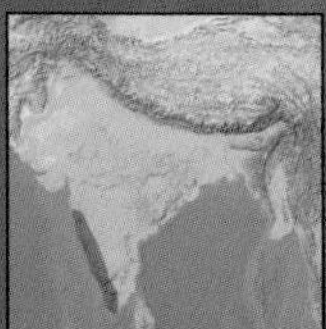

Size 45 cm

Voice Noisy, with squealing, laughing cry

Range Local endemic breeding resident in Western Ghats

Habitat Restricted to open, broadleaved Western Ghat forests

Medium-sized hornbill with dark grey upperparts and paler grey, streaked underparts. Distinct, very pale grey supercilium; blackish crown and eye-stripes; rufous bill graduating to yellow tip. Greyish-brown wings; white carpal patch; white-tipped primaries and tail; cinnamon vent. Female has black bill base. Immature has more brown upperparts and yellow bill. Similar to Indian Grey but distinguished by darker grey and no casque on bill. Feeds high in trees on fruits and small invertebrates. Nests in tree holes.

SRI LANKA GREY HORNBILL

Ocyceros gingalensis Bucerotidae

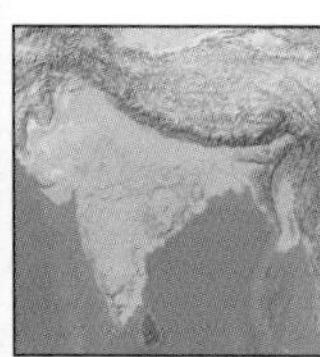

Size 45 cm

Voice Call a loud *kaa…kaa… kakakaka…* or *kuk…kuk…kuk… kuk…ko…ko…kokoko*

Range Endemic resident; lowlands and lower hills, more frequent in lowlands and in dry zone

Habitat Forests; well-wooded areas

Large hornbill with dark grey upperparts and scaly effect on back. Male has cream-coloured bill while female has dark grey pattern on bill. Head, forehead, crown and nape brownish-grey, finely streaked paler; slight bushy crest, hanging over nape; pale grey neck, chin and throat; greyish-white underparts, except pale buff vent and undertail-coverts. Primaries and tail have white tips. Similar to Malabar Pied, but lacks casque and has white throat and foreneck. Outer-tail and underparts turn whiter with age.

INDIAN GREY HORNBILL

Ocyceros birostris Bucerotidae

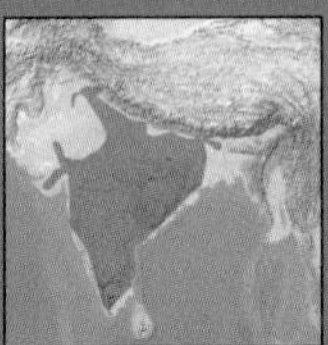

Size 50 cm

Voice Noisy; normal call a shrill squealing note, also other squeals and screams

Range Almost throughout India, upto about 1,500 m in the Himalayas; absent in arid NW regions and heavy rainfall areas of S Western Ghats

Habitat Forests; orchards; tree-covered avenues; vicinity of habitation

Smallest of the Indian hornbills. Overall grey-brown plumage; large, curved beak with casque diagnostic; long, graduated tail, tipped black-and-white. Male has reddish-brown eyes and black orbital skin. Female has dark brown eyes and red-brown orbital skin. Casque smaller in female. In pairs, or small parties; sometimes large gatherings; mostly arboreal, but descends to pick fallen fruits or lizards; feeds along with frugivorous birds on fruiting trees; noisy, undulating flight.

MALABAR PIED HORNBILL

Anthracoceros coronatus Bucerotidae

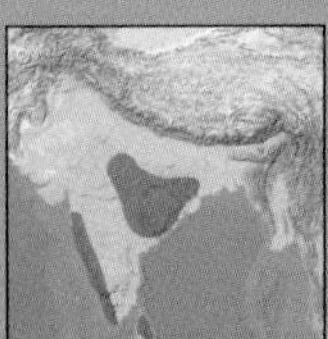

Size 65 cm

Voice Call a loud *kek...kek...kek...*

Range Scarce endemic breeding resident in foothills of Western and Eastern Ghats and Sri Lanka, where commoner. Probably overlaps in NC India with the Oriental Pied

Habitat Open forests and groves, particularly ficus and other fruiting trees on hillsides

Striking, medium-sized, with large creamish bill and very prominent black and yellow casque. Black head and neck; black orbital skin; white eye-ring; black white-tipped wings; white underparts. Female smaller with pale blue orbital skin that turns pinkish in breeding. Very similar to Oriental Pied but distinguished by broad white outer-tail feathers and broader wing-tips.

ORIENTAL PIED HORNBILL

Anthracoceros albirostris Bucerotidae

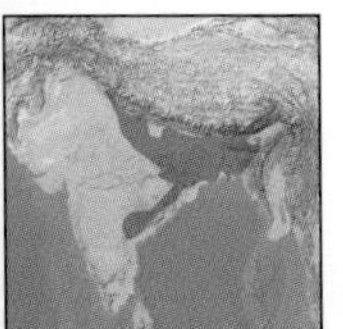

Size 60 cm

Voice Calls include loud cackles and screams; also rapid *pak…pak…pak*

Range Haryana and Uttarakhand to extreme NE; Eastern Ghats, south to Bastar and N Andhra Pradesh

Habitat Forests; orchards; groves

Similar to Malabar Pied, but tail much black; white face patch, wing-tips (seen in flight) and tips to outer-tail feathers; black throat and breast; white below. Black and yellow beak with large casque. Sexes alike, female slightly smaller. Small parties, occasionally collecting into several dozen birds on favourite fruiting trees; associates with other birds; arboreal but often feeds on ground, hopping about.

GREAT HORNBILL

Buceros bicornis Bucerotidae

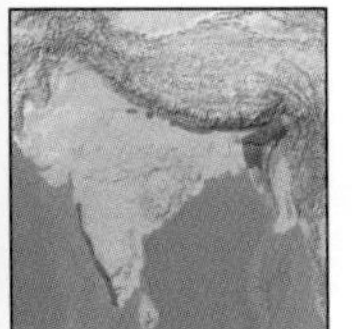

Size 100 cm

Voice Calls include loud and deep barking; loud *tokk* at feeding sites, audible from considerable distance

Range Lower Himalayas east of Uttarakhand, upto about 1,800 m; another population exists in Western Ghats

Habitat Forests

Black face, back and underbody; two white-bars on black wings; white neck, lower abdomen and tail; broad black tail-band; huge black and yellow beak with enormous concave-topped casque distinctive. Female slightly smaller. Sexes alike. In pairs, or small parties; occasionally large flocks; mostly arboreal, feeding on fruiting trees, plucking fruits with tip of bill, tossing it up, catching it in the throat and swallowing; may settle on ground to pick up fallen fruits; noisy flight; alternation of flapping and gliding, less undulating than in other hornbills.

RUFOUS-NECKED HORNBILL

Aceros nipalensis Bucerotidae

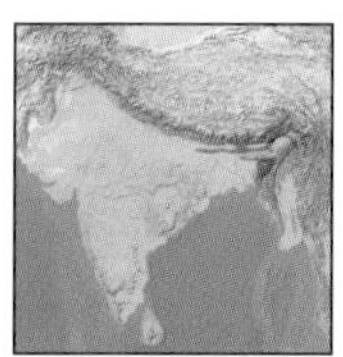

Size 100 cm

Voice Call a deep, single, far-carrying staccato *wok*

Range Globally threatened. Rare breeding resident in NE hill forests

Habitat Primary forests

Large impresive hornbill with dramatic downward curved bill. Male has rufous head and underparts; bright turquoise orbital skin; red chin pouch. Terminal half of tail white. Immature has rich rufous head, neck and most of underparts. Female has black head and underparts. Arboreal, feeding mainly on fruit. Nests as other hornbills.

♀

NARCONDAM HORNBILL

Rhyticeros narcondami Bucerotidae

Size 50 cm

Voice Call a cackling *ka...ka...ka...kaka*

Range Resident, endemic to Narcondam Island, Andaman Islands

Habitat Mature forests

Largish hornbill with green-glossed black body and white tail. The only hornbill occurring on Narcondam Island. Like small version of Rufous-necked but lacks black at base of tail and has bluish-white pouch. Male has rufous head and neck, yellowish-white bill with crimson at base. Female has all-black head and neck, and iris dark olive-brown (rather than reddish as in male). Immature similar to adult male, but initially lacks casque; has less red at base of bill, and pale grey iris. Casque grown, but not wreathed, by end of first year.

WREATHED HORNBILL

Rhyticeros undulatus Bucerotidae

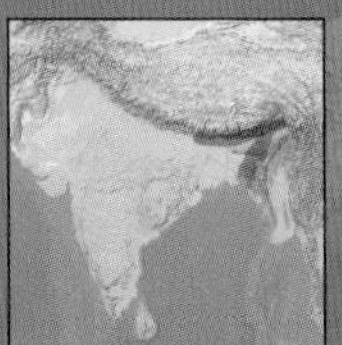

Size 80 cm

Voice Call a loud *kuk...kwek*; wings make whooshing sound in flight

Range Fairly common breeding resident: NE plains, foothills

Habitat Forests with fruiting trees

Black hornbill with completely white tail. Male has white face, chestnut crown and nape, red orbital patch; yellow pouch with black stripe. Female has blue pouch and black head. Female seals itself into tree holes while male hornbill feeds female and chicks through narrow slit. Feeds mainly on fruits, travelling in, sometimes, large parties to favoured sites. Roosts communally.

GREAT BARBET

Megalaima virens Megalaimidae

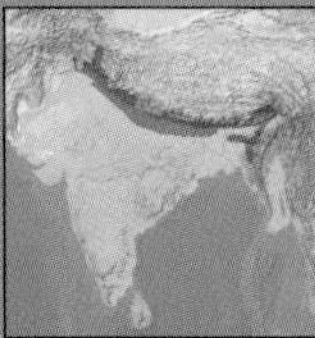

Size 33 cm

Voice Very noisy, especially between March and July; loud, if somewhat mournful *pi...you* or *pi...oo*

Range The Himalayas, 800-3,200 m

Habitat Forests; orchards

Bluish-black head and throat; black bristles at base of nostrils, on front of lores and chin; black orbital skin; reddish-brown eye; brown forehead, nape, lores, chin and throat maroon-brown back; yellowish hind-collar; green on lower back; green tail; deep brown upper breast; pale yellow below, with thick, greenish-blue streaks; red undertail-coverts distinctive. Long, broad, yellowish beak; olive-grey legs and feet. Female similar to immature with duller colour, sooty-brown head and pinkish undertail-coverts. Either solitary, or in small bands; arboreal, but comes into low-fruiting bushes; difficult to spot and mostly heard.

YELLOW-FRONTED BARBET

Megalaima flavifrons Magalaimidae

Size 21 cm

Voice Similar to Brown-headed's

Range Sri Lanka

Habitat Foothill forests, parks and gardens. Well-wooded gardens, broadleaved forests

Medium-sized plump barbet, endemic to Sri Lanka. Overall green, with scaly upper breast; heavy, greenish-horn-coloured bill surrounded by bristles; yellow forehead and forecrown; yellow malar stripe; light blue ear-coverts, throat and upper breast; dark legs and feet. Distinguished from Brown-headed by yellow and blue on head; and from Crimson-fronted and Coppersmith by absence of red on forehead. Sexes alike. Dipping flight interspersed with glides. Feeds on fruits. Not shy.

LINEATED BARBET

Megalaima lineata Magalaimidae

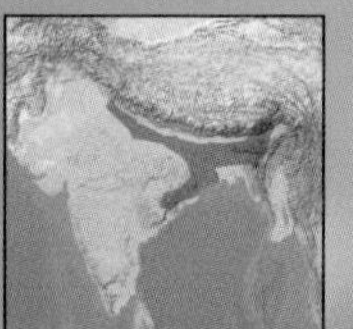

Size 28 cm

Voice Call a persistent, rather subdued *kuruk… kuruk*, usually with long guttural start-up note

Range Locally common breeding resident in the NE, Bangladesh and the Himalayan foothills west to Himachal Pradesh

Habitat Foothill forests, parks and gardens

Large green and brown barbet with light brown head streaked buff; pale yellow orbital patch; large yellowish- horn-coloured bill; bight green body with unmarked wings; heavy white streaking on head, neck, mantle and underparts to upper belly; white throat. Sexes alike. Similar to Green-eared, but lacks green rear-coverts. Strictly arboreal. Feeds on fruits. Very well camouflaged and rather secretive. Nests in tree holes. Calls from open branches.

WHITE-CHEEKED BARBET

Megalaima viridis Megalaimidae

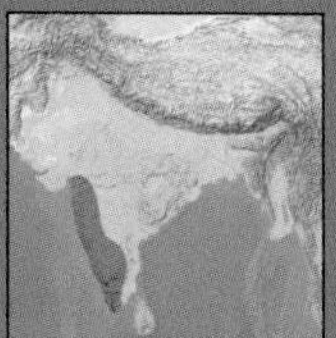

Size 23 cm

Voice Call a start-up *burring* followed by repeated, penetrating, rather high-pitched *putruk… putruk*

Range Common endemic breeding resident in SW foothill forests north to Gujarat

Habitat Hill forests; groves; gardens

Medium-sized, green and brown barbet with short white supercilium and broad stripe below eye. Brown head and paler brown upper breast, darker crown and nape; pale pink bill; white throat; heavy white streaking on breast. Rest of body unmarked grass-green. Sexes alike. Strictly arboreal feeding on fruits. Well camouflaged and often difficult to spot. Nests in tree holes.

MALABAR BARBET

Megalaima malabarica Megalaimidae

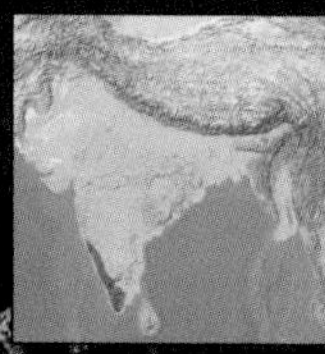

Size 17 cm

Voice Similar to Coppersmith's

Range Western Ghats

Habitat Endemic resident, common in wet lowlands and lower hills

Small barbet found in Western Ghats. Formerly treated as a race of the Crimson-fronted Barbet. Overall leaf-green wth crimson forehead, face and throat; dark streaking on breast; unmarked belly. Overlaps in some places with range of the Coppersmith Barbet from whom it is distinguished by its crimson face and throat.

GOLDEN-THROATED BARBET

Megalaima franklinii Megalaimida

Size 23 cm

Voice Start-up call *krrr* followed by monotonous *pukwok…pukwok*

Range Locally common breeding resident in N plains and hills from C Nepal east to Myanmar border

Habitat Forest trees, particularly fruiting figs

Plump, medium-sized, green barbet with distinct head pattern; yellow upper throat and greyish lower throat; red forehead and hindcrown and yellow crown centre; broad black stripe through eye; whitish cheeks. Mainly green upperparts and greenish-yellow underparts; bluish wing shoulders. Short tail. Sexes alike. Juvenile duller with weaker head pattern. Feeds mainly on fruits. Solitary, in pairs or small parties. Difficult to see in foliage. Nests in tree holes.

BROWN-HEADED BARBET

Megalaima zeylanica Megalaimidae

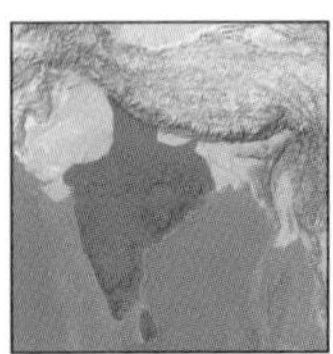

Size 28 cm

Voice Noisy; *kutroo…kutroo or pukrook…pukrook* calls one of the most familiar sounds of the Indian forests; call often begins with a guttural *kurrrr*

Range Most of India, south of the Himalayan foothills (Himachal Pradesh to Nepal)

Habitat Forests, groves; also city gardens

Overall green bird with brownish head, neck and upper back, streaked white; bare yellowish-orange-patch around eye; thick reddish-pink bill; short, green tail with brown-black shafts; wing-coverts tipped whitish; uniform green underparts. Sexes alike. Solitary, or in pairs; occasionally small parties; strictly arboreal; keeps to fruiting trees, often with other frugivorous birds; difficult to spot in canopy; noisy in hot season; strong, undulating flight.

BLUE-EARED BARBET

Megalaima australis Megalaimidae

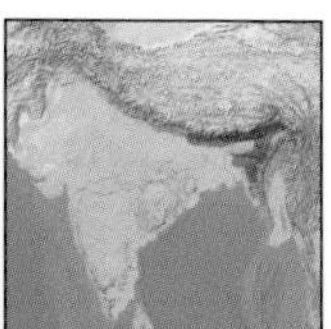

Size 17 cm

Voice Call a rapidly repeated *koo…trrk*

Range Scarce breeding resident in plains from E Nepal east to Myanmar border and Bangladesh

Habitat Forest trees, particularly fruiting figs

Small, green barbet with distinct marking on face and head; blue cheeks broadly bordered red; blue throat; blackish forecrown; black spot in centre of breast. Juvenile mainly green with hints of blue on face and neck; red-and-black absent on head. Sexes similar. Difficult to see in foliage. Nests in tree holes. Solitary, in pairs or in small parties.

BLUE-THROATED BARBET

Megalaima asiatica Megalaimidae

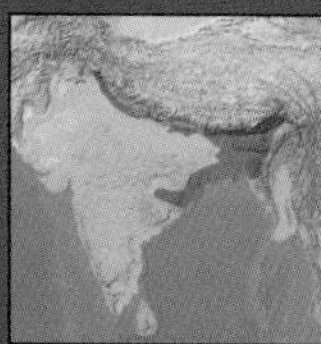

Size 23 cm

Voice Call similar to that of Brown-headed of plains; on careful hearing, sounds somewhat softer and there is a short note between the two longer ones; can be interpreted as *kutt…oo…ruk…*; also 4-note song when breeding

Range The Himalayas east from Pakistan and Kashmir; found upto about 2,250 m; also found in West Bengal, including Kolkata

Habitat Forests; groves

Medium-sized barbet with grass-green plumage; black, crimson, yellow-and-blue around head; blue chin and throat diagnostic; crimson spots on throat sides. Sexes alike. Solitary, or in pairs; sometimes small parties on fruiting trees, along with other fruit-eating birds; strictly arboreal; keeps to canopy of tall trees; difficult to spot but loud, monotonous calls indicator of its presence. Secretive. Nests in tree holes.

COPPERSMITH BARBET

Megalaima haemacephala Megalaimidae

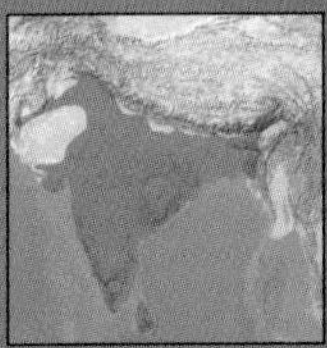

Size 17 cm

Voice Noisy between December and end of April; monotonous *tuk…tuk…* one of the best-known bird calls of India, likened to a coppersmith working on his metal

Range All over India, upto about 1,800 m in the outer Himalayas

Habitat Light forests; groves; city gardens; roadside trees

Small, vividly-coloured bird. Grass-green plumage; yellow throat; crimson breast and forehead; dumpy appearance. Sexes alike. Solitary, in pairs or small parties; strictly arboreal; feeds on fruiting trees, often with other birds; visits flowering *Erythrina* and *Bombax* trees for flower nectar; often spends early morning sunning itself on bare branches.

juvenile

CRIMSON-FRONTED BARBET

Megalaima rubricapillus Megalaimidae

Size 17 cm

Voice Call a slow, repeated *pop…pop…pop…* and rapidly repeated *popo…popo…popo…pop*

Range Sri Lanka

Habitat Similar to Coppersmith's. Open wooded country

Small barbet with bright orange supercilium; cheeks, throat and upper breast; small distinct red-patch on breast; unstreaked green belly and flanks; sides of neck and head, blue; black crescent marking behind eye; heavy bill, fringed with bristles. Gregarious; lives in large, loose flocks outside breeding season; extremely vocal.

YELLOW-RUMPED HONEYGUIDE

Indicator xanthonotus Indicatoridae

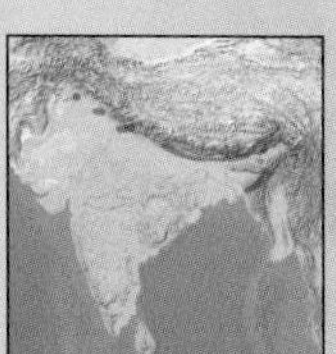

Size 15 cm

Voice Call note a sharp *cheep…*, mostly uttered on wing, and rarely on perch

Range The Himalayas, from Pakistan to Bhutan. Overlooked species

Habitat Rock faces and cliffs in forests; in some areas above treeline

Olive-brown plumage; bright orangish-yellow forehead, cheeks and rump (lower back) diagnostic, seen also when perched, with wings drooping slightly; finch-like beak; overall appearance sparrow-like. Sexes alike. Solitary, or in small scattered parties; keeps to cliffs and rock faces around honeybee colonies; no indication of guiding humans or any other mammal to honeycomb sites.

EURASIAN WRYNECK

Jynx torquilla Picidae

Size 17 cm

Voice Call a high-pitched *pee… pee… pee*. Hisses in nest

Range Breeds in Kashmir. Scarce but widespread winter visitor mainly to N areas

Habitat Breeds in edges of forests in N mountains. Elsewhere in scrubs and cultivation

Small, rather reptilian-looking woodpecker, the colour of tree bark. Basically grey-and-brown with dark eye-stripes and dark stripe running from crown to rump. Underparts barred and throat warm buff. Tail long and barred, making it look rather shrike-like in flight. Bill short and pointed. Twists neck round and often raises crown feathers. Unobtrusively feeds with long tongue on ants on ground and tree branches (shown). Does not drill holes or use tail as support. Nests in tree holes.

SPECKLED PICULET

Picumnus innominatus Picidae

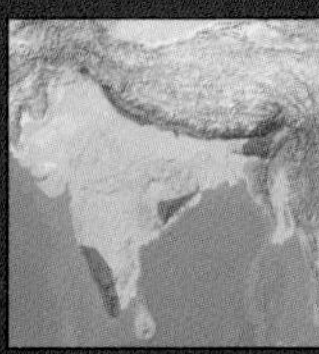

Size 10 cm

Voice Call a sharp, rapid *tsip... tsip...*; also loud drumming sound

Range The Himalayas, W to E, foothills to at least 2,500 m

Habitat Mixed forests, fondness for bamboo jungles

♀

Sexes alike. Olive-green above (male has some orange-and-black on forecrown); two white stripes on head sides, upper one longer; dark-olive band through eyes, moustachial stripe; creamy-white below, boldly spotted with black. Usually in pairs; moves around thin branches, or clings upside-down; taps with beak, probes crevices; exhibits typical woodpecker behaviour.

WHITE-BROWED PICULET

Sasia ochracea Picidae

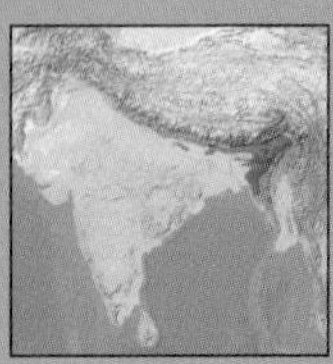

Size 9-10 cm

Voice Calls include a series of rapid *tseek... tseek* notes, high-pitched trills, also drumming and tapping, usually on bamboos

Range Restricted to NE regions of the subcontinent

Habitat Dense broadleaved forests, secondary growth with bamboos

Very tiny, almost sparrow-like bird with almost negligible tail, giving tail-less appearance. Olive-brown upperparts, rufous underparts; characteristic gold-yellow forehead and short white supercilium behind eye distinguishing features; red orbital patch. Solitary, in pairs, or small groups, also in mixed hunting parties, exhibits typical woodpecker behaviour while moving along branches.

BROWN-CAPPED PYGMY WOODPECKER

Dendrocopos nanus Picidae

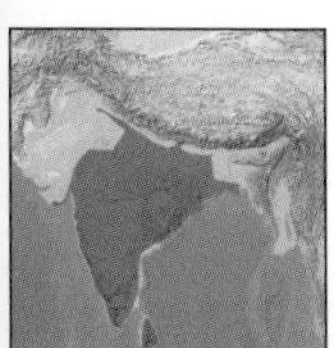

Size 13 cm

Voice Call a faint but shrill squeak, sounds like *clicck…rrr*

Range Almost all over India, including some of the drier regions of N India

Habitat Light forests, cultivation, bamboos, orchards; also vicinity of habitation

Small woodpecker. Male barred brown-and-white above; paler crown with short, scarlet streak (occipital); prominent white band from just above eyes extends to neck; pale dirty brown-white below, streaked black. Female similar to male but lacks scarlet streaks on crown sides. Mostly in pairs; often part of mixed bird parties in forests; seen more on smaller trees, branches and twigs, close to ground and also high in canopy; quite active.

GREY-CAPPED PYGMY WOODPECKER

Dendrocopos canicapillus Picidae

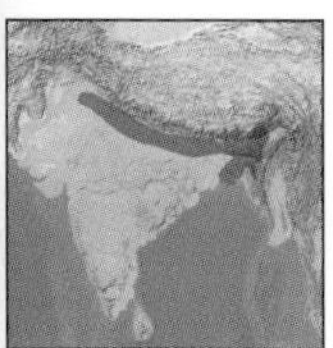

Size 14 cm

Voice Call a high rattling *trill* and weak *pik*

Range Fairly common breeding resident in N foothills including parts of Bangladesh

Habitat Unobtrusive inhabitant of forests and open woodlands in N plains

Small, dark woodpecker with dark iris. Barred black-and-white above with, usually, unbarred central tail feathers. Dark buff below with very bold dark streaking. Grey crown (red nape on male) and black eye-stripes contrasting with broad white supercilium and cheeks. Slight malar stripe. Often in pairs with mixed-species flocks feeding acrobatically high in canopy on smallest branches but also low on small trees. Feeds on insects and grubs in bark. Uses tail as prop. Nests in self-made holes.

FULVOUS-BREASTED WOODPECKER

Dendrocopos macei Picidae

Size 18 cm

Voice Call a hard *tik*, sometimes extended into chatter

Range Common breeding resident in N hills, NE India, Bangladesh and Eastern Ghats

Habitat Open, broadleaved and coniferous forests; edges of forests

Medium-sized, pied woodpecker with heavily barred black-and-white underparts. Male has distinct red crown, orange forehead, while black in female. Buff belly with light barring and streaking on flank; red undertail; whitish cheeks partially bordered black. Feeds on invertebrates. Often props itself on tail. Can be seen with other species in mixed flocks. Locally common. Nests in self-made tree holes.

STRIPE-BREASTED WOODPECKER

Dendrocopos atratus Picidae

Size 21-22 cm

Voice Calls include explosive *tchick* and whinnying rattle

Range Hills of NE India and Bangladesh

Habitat Open forests, also edges of evergreen and broadleaved forests

Medium-sized woodpecker with heavily streaked underparts; narrow white barring on black mantle; white head and neck sides. Underparts, dull olive-yellow; red head extending to nape. Easily confused with Fulvous-breasted. Male has white nasal tufts beneath dark lower forehead. Female has all-black crown. Juvenile male has dull red tinge on upper crown. Nests in holes excavated high in trees. Status uncertain and unknown, but certainly uncommon.

BROWN-FRONTED WOODPECKER

Dendrocopos auriceps Picidae

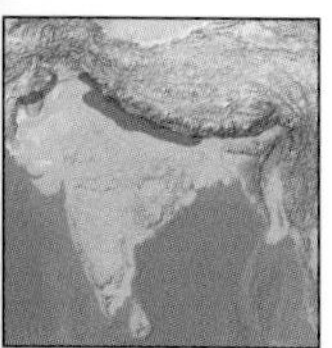

Size 20 cm

Voice Calls include fast chattering *chik…chik chik…rrr* and short *chik*

Range Locally common endemic breeding resident in N hills from Balochistan, east to Nepal. Moves lower down in winter

Habitat Deciduous, coniferous hill forests

Medium-sized Himalayan woodpecker. Overall pied; yellow crown; black upperparts barred white; black moustache extends to breast; black-streaked white underparts; deep pink vent. Male has brown forecrown with yellow centre; red rear crown; red vent. Female has entirely yellow crown. Often with mixed hunting groups. Uses tail as prop. Feeds on invertebrates and seeds in trees and bushes. Nests in self-made holes.

YELLOW-CROWNED WOODPECKER

Dendrocopos mahrattensis Picidae

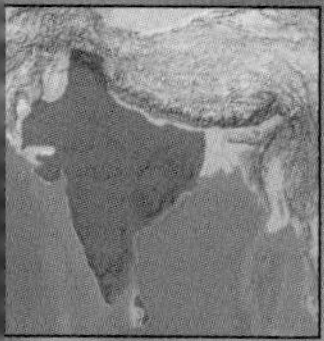

Size 17 cm

Voice Call a soft but sharp *clic…click…clickrrr…*; drums when breeding

Range Common and widespread; subcontinent, from the Himalayan foothills south; uncommon in NE regions

Habitat Open forests; scrubs; cultivation; vicinity of habitation; gardens

Male brownish-black above, spotted all over with white golden-brown forehead and crown; small scarlet crest; pale fulvous below throat, streaked brown; scarlet-patch in centre of abdomen distinctive. Female lacks scarlet crest. Solitary or in pairs; sometimes small bands of upto six birds; occasionally seen with mixed hunting parties; moves in jerks along tree stems and branches; hunts in typical woodpecker manner; rather confiding in some areas; birds keep in touch with faint, creaking sounds.

♀

DARJEELING WOODPECKER

Dendrocopos darjellensis Picidae

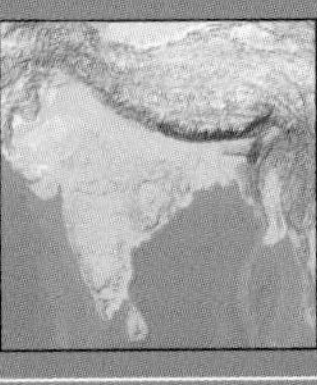

Size 25 cm

Voice Call a short *tsik*, rattling *di…di…di…di…dtttttt…dit*

Range Locally common breeding resident in N mountains from C Nepal east

Habitat High forests

Medium-sized woodpecker with creamy-white lower forehead, black upper forehead; black crown, broad red band on nape, black hindneck; white lores, white head sides washed-buff; white cheeks and long black moustache extending to upper breast. Upperparts mostly black, with large white, scapular patches and white-barred flight feathers and tail sides; red vent. Red nape-band absent in female. Feeds on invertebrates on and in upper branches and mossy trunks. Solitary, or in pairs.

HIMALAYAN WOODPECKER

Dendrocopos himalayensis Picidae

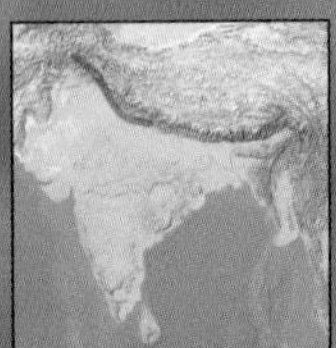

Size 24 cm

Voice Fairly loud calls, uttered in night

Range The Himalayas, from Kashmir to W Nepal; 1,500–3,200 m

Habitat The Himalayan forests

Male has black back and upperbody; white shoulder patch; white spots and barring on wings; crimson crown and crest; white lores, cheeks and ear-coverts; broad, black moustachial stripe; yellowish-brown underbody, darker on breast; crimson under tail. Female has black crown and crest. Mostly in pairs, moves about in forest; jerkily moves up and around tree stems or clings on under sides of branches; like other woodpeckers, often moves few steps back, as if to re-examine; sometimes seen in mixed hunting parties of Himalayan birds.

CRIMSON-BREASTED WOODPECKER

Dendrocopos cathpharius Picidae

Male has white forehead, chin and throat; black crown; buffy-white ear-coverts; black malar stripe extends to hindneck. Plain black back, mantle and scapulars; black wing with white-patch on coverts; primaries spotted or barred whitish; buff-washed white underparts streaked black; pinkish-red vent. Male has variable red-patch on nape, absent in female. Juvenile has less streaked underparts and less crimson on breast.

Size 18 cm

Voice Call a loud, monotonous *tchick*, higher-pitched and less sharp than Darjeeling's; shrill *kee…kee*

Range The Himalayas, NE India

Habitat Broadleaved forests

RUFOUS-BELLIED WOODPECKER

Dendrocopus hyperythrus Picidae

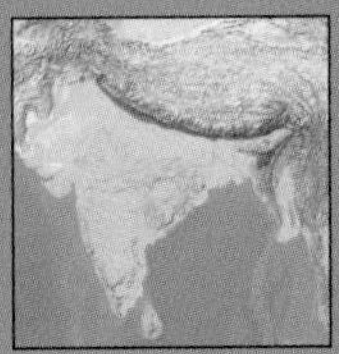

Size 24 cm

Voice Call a short *kit*, sometimes extended excitedly

Range Common breeding; endemic resident in NW mountains

Habitat Montane forests with preference for coniferous trees

Distinct woodpecker with rufous underparts and strongly barred black-and-white upper mantle; white face and chin; black rump and central tail. Male has red crown while female has black crown spotted white. Juvenile black above, boldly spotted white. The west Himalayan race is larger than the nominate east Himalayan. Singly, or in pairs; probes bark for sap. Nests in self-made tree holes. Confiding and approachable.

♀

♀

SPOT-BREASTED PIED WOODPECKER

Dendrocopos analis Picidae

Size 16 cm

Voice Call a distinctive staccato *chu-ik*

Range Resident, Andaman Islands

Habitat Open and secondary forests; plantations with scattered trees; scrubs

Exceedingly rare and seldom seen in the region. Smaller than the more common Fulvous-breasted, but distinguished by strongly spotted breast; rest of underparts greyish-buff. Bold white streaking on tail; peach vent; pale bill.

GREAT SPOTTED WOODPECKER

Dendrocopos major Picidae

Size 24 cm

Voice Call a resonant creaking

Range Scarce breeding resident in NE India only

Habitat Oak and pine forests

Medium-sized pied woodpecker with white neck and face sides. Diagnostic black band forms Z from base of beak to neck and back to breast. Male has distinct crimson-patch on back of head. Glossy black upperparts with broad white-patches from shoulder to lower back and white barring on flight feathers and tail edgings. Underparts buff with extensive bright red vent. Juvenile male has red crown and black nape. Distinct bouncing flight.

♀

BAY WOODPECKER

Blythipicus pyrrhotis Picidae

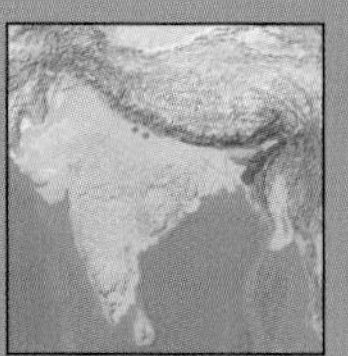

Size 27 cm

Voice Call a loud, cackling laugh *keek…kik…kik…kik…kik*; chattering *kerere…kerere…kerere*

Range E Nepal to Myanmar; S Assam Hills

Habitat Thick primary broadleaved and montane forests, dense secondary undergrowth, bamboos

Rare and seldom seen woodpecker, often confused with Rufous. Conspicuous, long, yellow bill. Tufted hindcrown; pale cinnamon face and nape; chestnut above with bold black and red-brown barring; faint barring on rusty-brown flanks; lightly barred rufous tail; brown iris with blue orbital-ring; greyish-olive legs. Sexes similar, but female lacks crimson-patch on lower neck sides. Juvenile overall duller with heavier barring on mantle. Secretive; most often seen in flight.

♀

RUFOUS WOODPECKER

Micropternus brachyurus Picidae

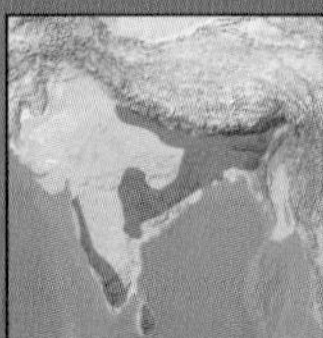

Size 25 cm

Voice Rather vocal between January and April; call a loud, high-pitched 3- or 4-noted *ke…ke…kr…ke…*; drums when breeding

Range Subcontinent, south of outer Himalayas, found upto 1,500 m

Habitat Mixed forests

Plumage mixture of different shades of brown; fine black cross-bars on upperbody, including wings and tail; paler edges to throat feathers; crimson-patch under eye in male, absent in female. Sexes alike. Usually in pairs; sometimes four or five scattered birds close by; mostly seen around ball-shaped nests of tree ants; clings to outside of nests and digs for ants; plumage often smeared with gummy substance.

WHITE-BELLIED WOODPECKER

Dryocopus javensis Picidae

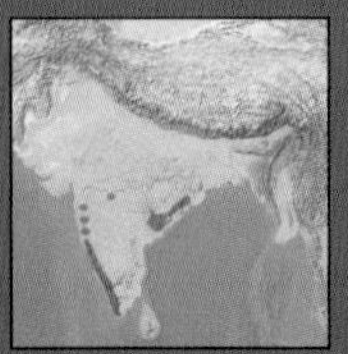

Size 48 cm

Voice Call a loud, metallic *chiank* note, often while clinging onto tree stems; loud drumming sound during December-March

Range Forested areas of Western Ghats, south of Tapti River; present range reduced due to habitat destruction and the bird, perhaps, no longer exists in N parts of Western Ghats; also Bastar and perhaps across C Indian hills

Habitat Tall evergreen forests

Male has black head, upperbody, breast; white rump and underparts below breast; bright, crimson crown (including forehead), crest and cheeks. Crimson restricted to nape in female. Pairs, sometimes four or five birds in tall forests; moves up along tree stems, jerkily and slowly, inspecting bark-crevices for lurking insects; strong, lazy flight; chuckling note in flight.

♀

ANDAMAN WOODPECKER

Dryocopus hodgei Picidae

♀

Size 38 cm

Voice Call a loud, chattering *kuk…kuk…kuk* ending in whistling *kui*

Range Andaman Islands

Habitat Tropical and subtropical, moist lowland forests

Large blackish woodpecker, endemic to Andaman Islands. Male has red crown, crest and moustachial stripe; red restricted to hindcrown and crest in female. Confused with White-bellied, but without white on belly. Habits very similar to those of White-bellied.

♂

LESSER YELLOWNAPE

Picus chlorolophus Picidae

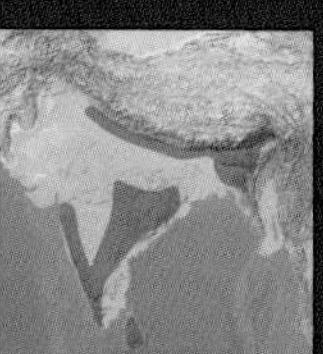

Size 27 cm

Voice Noisy. Call a loud, sad *pee…oo* and descending *ke…ke…ke…ke*

Range Locally common breeding resident in N foothills from Himachal Pradesh to Myanmar border and peninsular hills, Sri Lanka and Bangladesh

Habitat All types of open forests and plantations

Medium-sized woodpecker with green upperparts; bright yellow, tufted nape. Olive-green neck and breast; whitish belly, finely barred green; black rump and tail. Adult male has green head and white throat; red markings above eye and nape; red moustachial stripe. Female has red-patch above ear-coverts. Juvenile similar to female, but duller. Feeds on invertebrates at lower levels, including ground, and often in mixed hunting groups.

chlorigaster

chlorolophus

GREATER YELLOWNAPE

Picus flavinucha Picidae

Similar to Lesser, but larger. Lesser has smaller, dark bill, red markings on head, red stripe on whitish chin, smaller crest and barred underparts; prominent yellow-crested nape and throat. Underparts dark olive-green and grey. Brownish crown; flight feathers chestnut-barred black. Feeds on invertebrates from ground to canopy often with mixed-species parties. Shy, flushes readily if disturbed. Uses tail as prop. Nests in tree holes.

♀

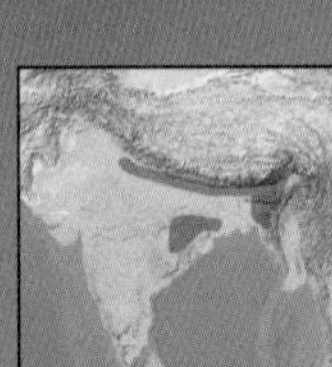

Size 33 cm

Voice Calls include loud, plaintive *keeyu* and hard *chep* note. Also, an accelerating trill *quee… quee…quee*

Range Fairly common breeding resident of N foothills, NE India, Bangladesh and Eastern Ghats

Habitat Upland broadleaved forests

STREAK-THROATED WOODPECKER

Picus xanthopygaeus Picidae

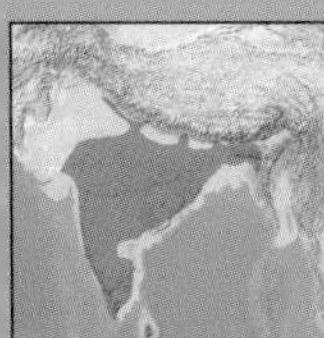

Size 30 cm

Voice Call an occasional faint *pick*... mostly silent; also drums on branches

Range Subcontinent; found upto 1,500 m in outer Himalayas

Habitat Mixed forests; plantations

Male grass-green above; crimson crown and crest; orange and black on nape; white supercilium and malar stripe; yellow rump; bold, black scaly streaks on whitish underbody, with tawny-green wash on breast; throat greyer, also streaked. Female has black crown and crest. Solitary, or in pairs; works up along tree stems; moves either straight up or in spirals; taps with beak for insects hiding in bark; also settles on ground.

♀

SCALY-BELLIED WOODPECKER

Picus squamatus Picidae

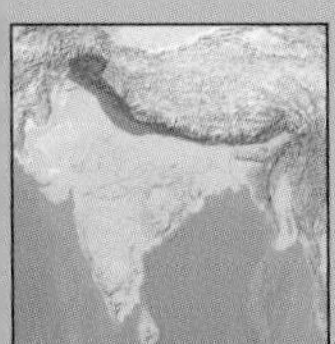

Size 35 cm

Voice Contact call a hard, repeated *quik*. Also musical, repeated *peeko...peeko*

Range Fairly common breeding resident in N mountain forests east to E Nepal

Habitat Upland coniferous and broadleaved forests; also open, dry and cultivated country with scattered trees

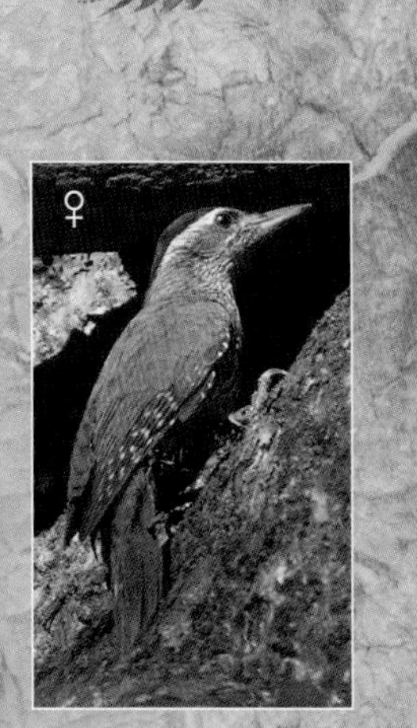

♀

Similar to Streak-throated, but larger with unstreaked throat and upper breast. Strong, black moustachial stripe; white supercilium speckled black; large pale bill; distinct scaling from breast to vent; strongly barred tail. Male has red forehead, crown and nape, while female has dark slaty-grey crown. Feeds on ants and termites and also berries. Forages solitary, or in pairs. Nests in self-made tree holes.

GREY-HEADED WOODPECKER

Picus canus Picidae

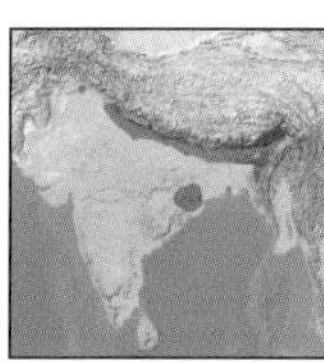

Size 32 cm

Voice Loud, chattering alarm; common call a high-pitched *keek...keek...* of 4- or 5-notes; drums often between March and early June

Range The Himalayas, from the lower foothills country to about 2,700 m

Habitat Deciduous and temperate forests

Male darkish-green above; crimson forehead; black hindcrown, faint crest and nape; dark sides of head and black malar stripe; yellow rump, white-barred dark wings and blackish tail; unmarked, dull greyish-olive underbody diagnostic. Female black from forehead to nape; no crimson. Solitary, or in pairs; typical woodpecker, moving on tree stems and larger branches, hunting out insects from under bark; descends to ground, hopping awkwardly; also digs into termite mounds.

HIMALAYAN GOLDENBACK

Dinopium shorii Picidae

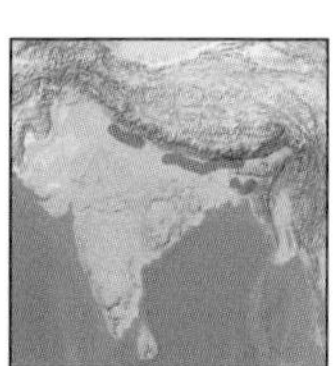

Size 30-32cm

Voice Call a rapid repeated *klok...klok...klak...klok...klak*

Range The Himalayas; locally in hills of peninsula and Bangladesh

Habitat Mature forests

Largish woodpecker with golden upperparts. Male has black hindneck; brownish-buff throat centre with irregular border of black spots; indistinctly divided moustachial stripe; brownish-buff centre, with small red-patch; reddish or brown eyes; blackish bill; greenish-brown feet. Underparts boldly streaked and scalloped black, and on some, almost unmarked. Three-toed. Female has black crest, streaked white. Confiding. Often seen in mixed feeding flocks. Locally common.

COMMON GOLDENBACK

Dinopium javanense Picidae

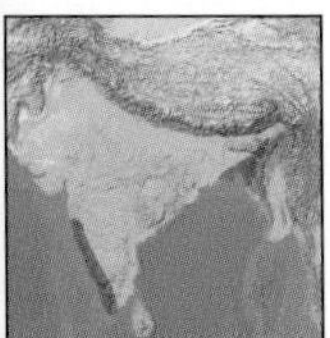

Size 30 cm

Voice Similar to, but higher-pitched than Black-rumped's

Range Locally common breeding resident in foothills of Western Ghats and hills of NE India

Habitat Damp woodlands; mangroves

Medium-sized woodpecker with golden mantle and wings; white face with two malar stripes; black hindneck; red lower back and rump. Male has red crown, while female has black crown. White underparts with strong black scaling; black tail; small bill and only three toes. In pairs, foraging in tree trunks. Very vocal.

LESSER GOLDENBACK

Dinopium benghalense Picidae

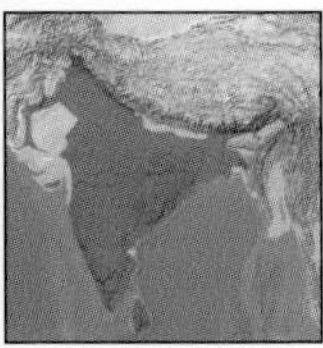

Size 30 cm

Voice Noisy. Call a loud, high-pitched cackle, like laughter; drums often

Range Subcontinent, upto about 1,800 m in outer Himalayas; also found in drier areas of NW India

Habitat Forests, both dry and mixed deciduous; orchards; gardens; also neighbourhood of villages and other habitation

Male has shining golden-yellow and black above; crimson crown and crest; black throat and sides of head, with fine white streaks; white underbody, streaked black, boldly on breast. Female has black crown spotted with white; crimson crest. In pairs, sometimes half a dozen together; widespread and common; moves jerkily up and around tree stems or clings on undersides of branches; taps out insects; often associates in mixed hunting parties; may descend to ground, picking off ants and other insects.

psarodes

GREATER GOLDENBACK

Chrysocolaptes lucidus Picidae

Size 33 cm

Voice Noisy. Loud, grating scream; calls mostly in flight

Range Uttarakhand to NE India; parts of Eastern Ghats, SE Madhya Pradesh; Western Ghats, Kerala to Tapti River; plains to about 1,500 m

Habitat Forests

Male has crimson crown and crest; golden-olive above; white and black sides of face and throat; whitish-buff below, profusely spotted with black on foreneck, and speckled over rest of underbody; extensive crimson rump and black tail and flight feathers distinctive. Female has white-spotted black crown and crest.

WHITE-NAPED WOODPECKER

Chrysocolaptes festivus Picidae

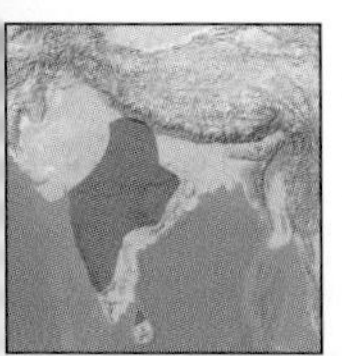

Size 29 cm

Voice Call a thin, repeated *tee... tee... tee*

Range Scarce breeding endemic resident mainly restricted to peninsular India, dry zone Sri Lanka and far-W Nepal

Habitat Dry open woodlands, plantations and scrubs

Diagnostic black V-shape surrounds conspicuous white nape and mantle. Striped head and face; broad, bold white supercilium extending to nape; broad black ocular-stripe running across ear-coverts to neck sides; prominent, white moustachial and malar stripes. Male has red, peaked crest, yellow in female. Feeds on lower parts of tree trunks and ground.

PALE-HEADED WOODPECKER

Gecinulus grantia Picidae

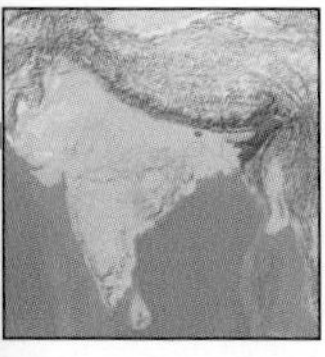

Size 25 cm

Voice Drumming loud, full, fairly short in duration and evenly pitched

Range Local resident in the Himalayas from E Nepal and E Arunachal Pradesh

Habitat Chiefly in bamboo jungles; also moist broadleaved secondary forests

♀

Arguably India's rarest woodpecker. Golden-brown or green head; unmarked face; maroon-brown mantle and back; mainly brownish wings with pink barring on primaries; dusky-olive underparts; red iris; pale bill with greenish base; olive-green legs with three toes. Female lacks reddish-pink central crown. Juvenile resembles female, but head duller and upperparts more brown. Numbers rapidly declining due to loss of bamboo forests. Wary and difficult to circumvent. Feeds lower down, though seldom descending to ground.

GREAT SLATY WOODPECKER

Mulleripicus pulverulentus Picidae

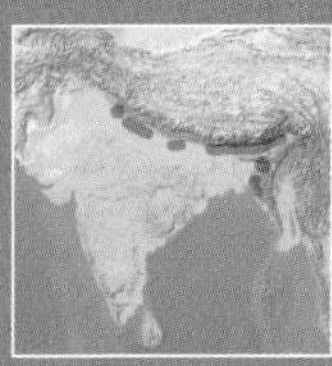

Size 51 cm

Voice Call a loud bleating, like a goat; very loud cackle in flight

Range The Himalayas

Habitat Mature trees in tropical forests and forest clearings

Probably the largest living woodpecker, with reptilian look, due to its thin serpent-like neck, rounded head and long tail. Overall grey with bluish wash; ear-coverts and neck speckled white; paler underparts; breast faintly speckled white; cream to golden throat and upper neck; darker tail and wings. Brown iris and grey orbital-ring. Male has pinkish-red-patch on malar region and pink on lower throat. Long, robust bill with grey-yellow lower mandible and grey upper mandible; bluish-grey legs. Juvenile overall duller with brown cast to upperparts. Forages chiefly on trunks and major branches in large trees. Often seen in large flocks.

HEART-SPOTTED WOODPECKER

Hemicircus canente Picidae

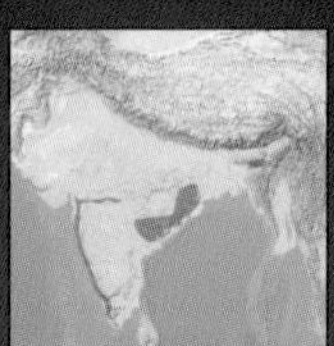

Size 16 cm

Voice Quite vocal, especially in flight; call a somewhat harsh *chur…* note; other sharp clicking and squeaky notes

Range Western Ghats from N Kerala to Tapti River; across E Satpura to SE Madhya Pradesh, Odisha, NE states

Habitat Forests

♀

♂

Male has black forehead (speckled white), crown and crest; black back; broad, pale buff wing patch (inner secondaries and wing-coverts) with heart-shaped spots; black flight feathers; whitish-buff, olive-and-black below. Female has extensive buff-white on forehead, otherwise like male. Pairs, or small parties; active and arboreal; perches across branches and calls often as it flies from one tree to another.

LONG-TAILED BROADBILL

Psarisomus dalhousiae Eurylaimidae

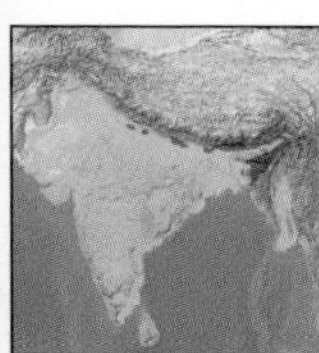

Size 28 cm

Voice Calls include loud, repeated whistles; *tseeay...pseeuw*

Range Uttarakhand eastwards to the entire NE Indian region

Habitat Tropical, subtropical semi-evergreen, evergreen forests; bamboos, *sal*

Gregarious, noisy forest-dwelling bird with vivid plumage. Long, thin, blue tail; black head; yellow face and throat sides; blue-patch on crown; yellowish blue ear-covert patch; yellow-green bill; large eyes; bright green upperparts; blue-green underparts. Diagnostic white-patch on blue underwing visible in flight. Juvenile duller, mostly green. Arboreal and crepuscular; feeds on insects. Perches upright.

SILVER-BREASTED BROADBILL

Serilophus lunatus Eurylaimidae

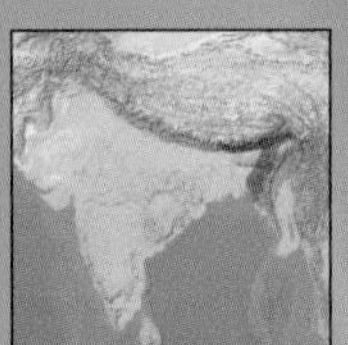

Size 19 cm

Voice Call a mostly squeaky *pee...ou*

Range Scarce breeding resident, now restricted to extreme NE India along Myanmar border

Habitat Lowlands; foothill forests

Adult male has red lores; rusty head sides and ear-coverts; greyish forehead; broad black eyebrow continuing through to neck; yellow eye-ring. Black wings with blue-and-white wing patches; ash-brown mantle; chestnut lower back; brown rump; black tail with white border. Silvery-grey throat and chest graduating to white belly; black thighs. Iris varies from emerald-green to sapphire blue. Female identified by thin silver band running through upper chest.

♀

BLUE-NAPED PITTA

Pitta nipalensis Pittidae

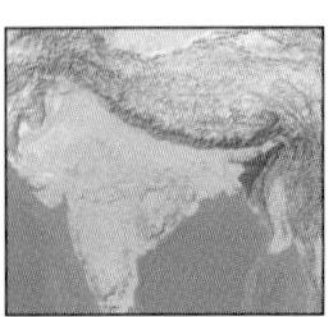

Size 25 cm

Voice Powerful double whistle

Range Rather local resident

Habitat Tropical and subtropical moist broadleaved evergreen forests; bamboo-dominated secondary growth in deserted forest clearings

Olive-green pitta with striking blue hindcrown and nape. Fulvous head sides, forehead and ear-coverts; black-patch behind eye. Plain, uniform fulvous underparts; brownish-green wings; brown tail washed green. Brown iris and bill. Female has rufous-brown crown and smaller, greenish-blue-patch on nape. Forages on forest floor amidst fallen leaves.

BLUE PITTA

Pitta cyanea Pittidae

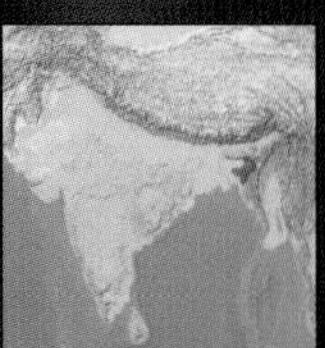

Size 23 cm

Voice Song a liquid *pleoow…whit*

Range Rare resident; NE India and Bangladesh

Habitat Broadleaved evergreen forests; moist ravines

Medium-sized, distinctly azure blue pitta. Pinkish-red hindcrown; broad, black eye-stripe and moustachial stripe. Bright blue tail. Pale underparts tinted blue, with bold black spotting and barring. Small white-patch in wing visible in flight. Female has dark olive upperparts with variable blue tinge; buffish breast. Juvenile overall dark brown, streaked and spotted rufous-buff; prominent buff supercilium and dark eye-stripe.

HOODED PITTA

Pitta sordida Pittidae

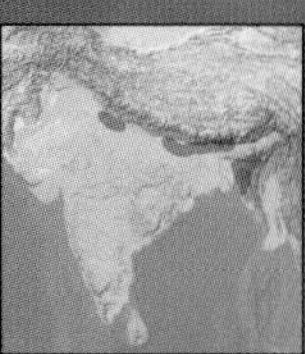

Size 19 cm

Voice Calls include explosive, double whistle *whee…whee* and harsh *skyew*

Range Rare and very local breeding; summer visitor to N foothills from Himachal Pradesh to Myanmar border including Nepal and Bangladesh

Habitat Forest undergrowth and thick scrub. Favours dark, damp, leaf-strewn areas

Unmistakable bright emerald-green pitta with black face and rusty-brown forehead, crown and nape; blue rump and shoulders; bright red rump; brown iris; black bill; strong, longish, flesh-coloured legs. Paler green underparts; short tail. Large white-patches on dark wings prominent in flight. Feeds on wet forest floor on invertebrates with bounding hops. Calls and roosts in trees. Solitary and secretive. Nests low down.

INDIAN PITTA

Pitta brachyura Pittidae

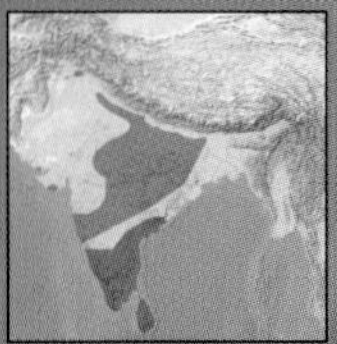

Size 19 cm

Voice Call a loud, lively whistle, *wheeet…peu*; very vocal when breeding (during rains); also longish single-note whistle

Range Almost entire subcontinent, with considerable seasonal movement

Habitat Forests, orchards; also cultivated country

Multicoloured, stub-tailed, stoutly built bird; bright blue, green, black, white, yellowish-brown and crimson; white chin, throat and patch on wing-tips and crimson vent distinctive. Sexes alike. Solitary, or pairs; spends much time on ground, hopping about, hunting for insects amidst leaf litter and low herbage; quietly flies into tree branch if disturbed; shows fondness for shaded, semi-damp areas.

MANGROVE PITTA

Pitta megarhyncha Pittidae

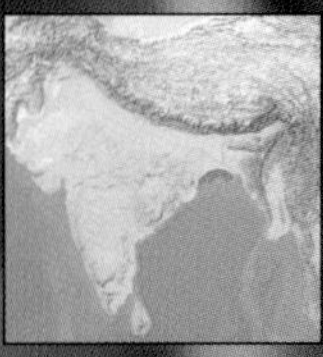

Size 20 cm

Voice Call a loud, but slurred *tae…laew*, repeated regularly, and alarm call a *skyeew*

Range Probably very local resident in the Sunderbans and Odisha coast

Habitat Mangroves

Closely resembles Indian with typical black stripe around eye. White throat; buff breast and flanks; red belly. However, has longer, heavier beak and dark brown crown without the characteristic black, coronal-stripe; larger, white wing patch and distinctively different call. Usually seen hopping in exposed mud among mangrove roots and adjacent drier land vegetation. Builds dome-shaped nest of twigs and leaves on banks or in vegetation close to ground, near high-tide line.

LARGE WOODSHRIKE

Tephrodornis virgatus Tephrodornithidae

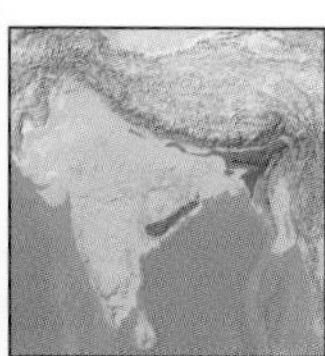

Size 23 cm

Voice Call a tuneful *kew… kew…kew*

Range Lowlands; E Nepal

Habitat Moist evergreen, broadleaved forests; glades

Plain, thickset, shrike-like bird with drab plumage; heavy, black bill; distinct nasal tufts. The Himalayan and eastern race *pelvicus* have grey crown and nape; brown mantle, upperparts; fairly broad, dark mask; black bill; usually, yellow eyes; breast, flanks have pale pink-grey wash. Female duller, with brown upperparts and ill-defined mask; paler bill. Juvenile has spotted, scaly crown. Fairly confiding, but quiet and inconspicuous.

♀

COMMON WOODSHRIKE

Tephrodornis pondicerianus Tephrodornithidae

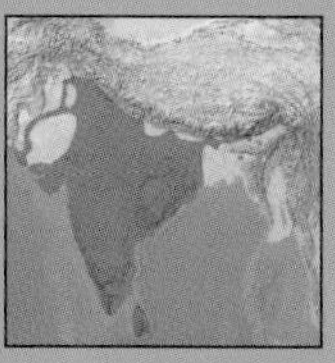

Size 16 cm

Voice Calls include whistling *wheet…wheet…* and interrogative, quick-repeated *whi…whi…whi…whee* afterwards; other trilling, pleasant notes when breeding

Range Across the country, S Himalayan foothills; most common in low country

Habitat Light forests; edges of forests; cultivation; gardens in and around habitation

Greyish-brown plumage; broad whitish supercilium and dark stripe below eye distinctive; grey-brown lores; white outer-tail feathers seen when bird flies. Dark stripe may be slightly paler in female. Sexes alike. In pairs, or small parties; quiet for greater part of year, vocal when breeding (February–May); keeps to middle levels of trees, hopping about, sometimes coming to ground. Nest is a small cup of moss and lichen.

Sri Lanka Woodshrike

MALABAR WOODSHRIKE

Tephrodornis (virgatus) sylvicola Tephrodornithidae

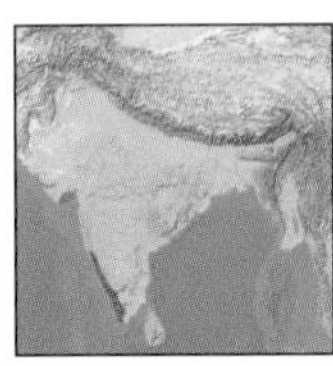

Size 23 cm

Voice Call a quick-repeated *wittoo... wittoo... wittoo... wittoo*

Range SE Gujarat and S Western Ghats

Habitat Broadleaved forests; well-wooded areas

Recently separated from Large, but told apart by more slaty-grey crown, nape and mantle; pinkish-grey throat and breast; well-defined, white sub-moustachial stripe. Female similar to male but has darker brown on upperparts and less-defined mask.

ASHY WOODSWALLOW

Artamus fuscus Artamidae

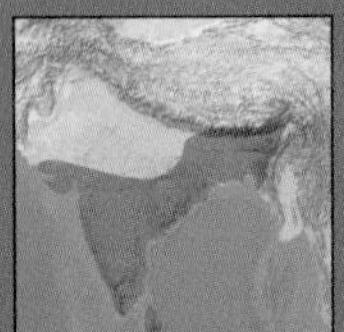

Size 19 cm

Voice Call a harsh *chey...chey...* or *chaek...chaek...*, often uttered in flight; short song occasionally when breeding, mix of harsh and melodious notes

Range Roughly towards east and south from W Gujarat to Shimla; widespread but not continuously distributed; upto about 1,800 m in outer Himalayas

Habitat Open country; edges of forests

Slaty-grey plumage, greyer on head; paler on rump, underbody; short square tail, tipped white; white undertail-coverts; somewhat heavy-looking bird, rather swallow-like in appearance, but wings much shorter and broader. Sexes alike. Small numbers in open country; perches on leaf stalks, overhead wires or flies characteristically, few wingbeats and glide; hunts flying insects; quiet during hot hours, feeds mostly in mornings and evenings.

WHITE-BREASTED WOODSWALLOW

Artamus leucorynchus Artamidae

Small woodswallow with largish head and relatively short, broad tail. Dark grey upperparts, hood and throat; white rump and uppertail-coverts. Creamy-white underparts; blackish primaries; flight feathers and tail narrowly-tipped white. Dark brown iris; bluish-grey legs. Sexes alike. Juvenile similar to adult, but darker brown.

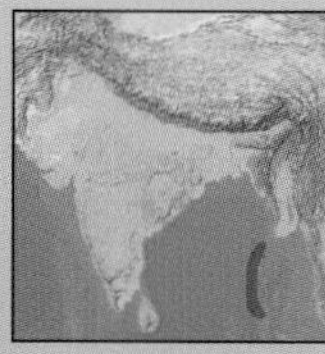

Size 18 cm

Voice As Ashy's

Range Common breeding; resident in Andaman Islands

Habitat As Ashy's, but mainly in forest clearings

COMMON IORA

Aegithina tiphia Aegithinidae

Male greenish above (rich black above, with yellowish rump, in some races); black wings and tail; two white wing-bars; bright yellow underbody. Female has yellow-green plumage; white wing-bars; greenish-brown wings. Pairs keep to leafy branches, often with other small birds; moves energetically amidst branches in hunt for insects, caterpillars; rich call notes often a giveaway of its presence in an area.

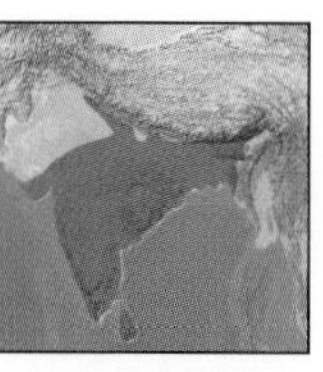

Size 14 cm

Voice Renowned vocalist; wide range of rich, whistling notes; common call a single or 2-note long-drawn *wheeeeeee* or *wheeeeeee...chu*; another common call a 3-note whistle

Range Subcontinent, upto about 1,800 m in the Himalayas; absent in arid NW India, desert regions of Rajasthan, Kutch

Habitat Forests; gardens; orchards; tree-dotted cultivation; habitation

tiphia

multicolor

humei

MARSHALL'S IORA

Aegithina nigrolutea Aegithinidae

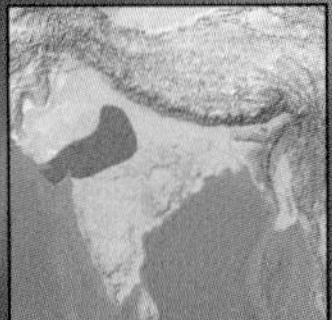

Size 14 cm

Voice Similar to Common's but also diagnostic nasal *tzee…cheert*

Range Now, rare and apparently declining endemic breeding resident confined to NW India. Earlier records from further south and east

Habitat Open woodlands and thorn scrub, often drier habitats than Common

Similar to Common but broad white edgings to tertials and extensive white in tail diagnostic. Breeding male has black crown and nape. Non-breeding male has greenish-yellow upperparts. Female similar to non-breeding male.

LARGE CUCKOOSHRIKE

Coracina macei Campephagidae

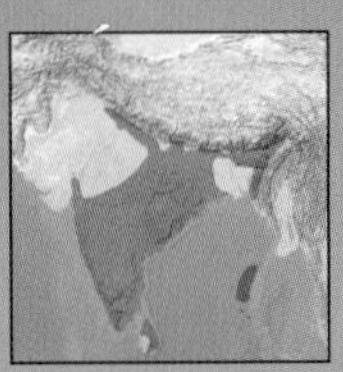

Size 28 cm

Voice Noisy. Call a 2-noted ringing whistle, *ti…treee…* second note long-drawn and higher; somewhat like Blossom-headed Parakeet's call

Range Most of India, from about 2,200 m in the Himalayas; absent in the drier, semi-desert regions of Kutch, C and N Rajasthan and much of NW India

Habitat Forests; gardens; tree-dotted cultivation

nipalensis

macei

Male grey above; broad, dark stripe through eyes to ear-coverts; black wings, tail; greyish breast, whitish below. Female barred grey-and-white below; paler stripe through eyes. In pairs, or small bands of four to six birds; characteristic flight over forest, few wingbeats and glide, often calls in flight; flicks wings on perching; keeps to upper branches, but may descend into bushes; very active and noisy when breeding (March-June).

BAR-BELLIED CUCKOOSHRIKE

Coracina striata Campephagidae

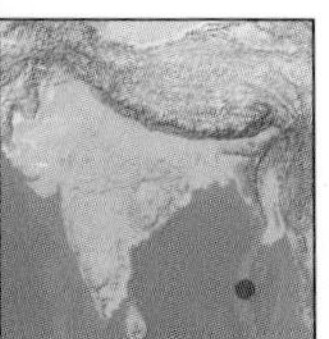

Size 26 cm

Voice Calls include clear, whinnying whistles *kliu…kliu…kliu…klis*; also grating *gree…ew gree…ew*

Range Andaman Islands

Habitat Forests

Similar to Large but smaller and deeper grey. Male has dark grey throat and breast; broad charcoal-grey, regular barring on rest of underparts. Female entirely barred below from chin to vent. Crimson iris. Juvenile scaly above with pale rufous tips and fringes to greater coverts and tertials, barred underparts, and rufous cast to throat and breast. Immature similar to female but with rufous throat and breast.

BLACK-WINGED CUCKOOSHRIKE

Coracina melaschistos Campephagidae

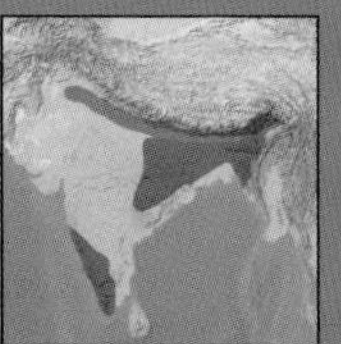

Size 22 cm

Voice Calls include loud, descending *twit…twit to…we* and *peeo…peeo…peeo*

Range Local breeding resident in N mountains from N Pakistan, east to Myanmar border. Winters lower down in foothills and plains mainly in Bangladesh and NE India south to Odisha. Scattered winter records throughout peninsular India

Habitat Open forests; edges of forests, groves

Medium-sized, dark cuckooshrike with unbarred, grey underparts. Male dark grey above with contrasting black wings and tail. Underside of tail shows broad white feather-tips. Female paler with very faint barring on underparts. Feeds on invertebrates in canopy and undergrowth; singly or in pairs. Joins mixed hunting groups. Undulating flight. Nests in trees.

BLACK-HEADED CUCKOOSHRIKE

Coracina melanoptera Campephagidae

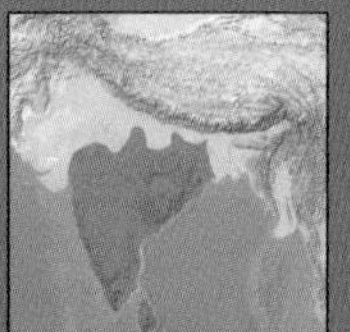

Size 20 cm

Voice Silent for most of the year; breeding male has a whistling song, upto a dozen notes, frequently uttered

Range Across E and S India from Mt. Abu to W Uttar Pradesh; a Himalayan race is found in parts of Punjab, Himachal and hill regions of Uttar Pradesh, to about 2,000 m. Undergoes considerable seasonal migration

Habitat Forests; gardens; groves

Male grey plumage; black head, wings, tail, latter white-tipped, except on middle feathers; pale grey below breast, whiter on abdomen, vent. Female has brown plumage; whitish-buff below barred dark brown till abdomen; lacks black head. Solitary, or in pairs, only occasionally several together; often part of mixed hunting bands; keeps for most part to leafy, upper branches, probes foliage for insects; methodically checks foliage before flying off.

PIED TRILLER

Lalage nigra Campephagidae

Size 18 cm

Voice Call a disyllabic whistle, second note lower

Range Uncommon or rare resident; occurs in the subcontinent only in the Andaman and Nicobar Islands

Habitat Edges of forests; secondary growth

Boldly-patterned pied triller with whitish underparts, tinged grey. Male has white face, black eye-stripe, and white supercilium; black crown, nape and mantle; black tail with white tip; white edges to wing-coverts; grey rump. Female has greyer and faintly barred underparts. The race *Lalage nigra davisoni* is found in the Andaman and Nicobar Islands.

ROSY MINIVET

Pericrocotus roseus Campephagidae

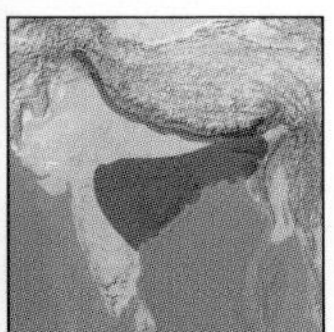

Size 18 cm

Voice Not well-known. Squeaky, trilling note recorded

Range Scarce and very local breeding resident, summer visitor: N mountains from N Pakistan, east to Myanmar border. Winter in Bangladesh and India south to Kerala but records very sporadic. Most frequently, recorded in NE India and Eastern Ghats

Habitat Poorly known species. Forests; woodlands; gardens

Has grey-brown upperparts. Male has pinkish-red patch on wings and tail; reddish rump; silvery-white face; pale grey crown and nape; blackish-brown wings and long tail. Pale buffy-pink underparts. Female has yellow underparts with yellow-olive rump. Behaviour similar to other minivets. Feeds in canopy on invertebrates. In small parties and less active than other minivets. Nests in trees in open broadleaved forests.

♀

ASHY MINIVET

Pericrocotus divaricatus Campephagidae

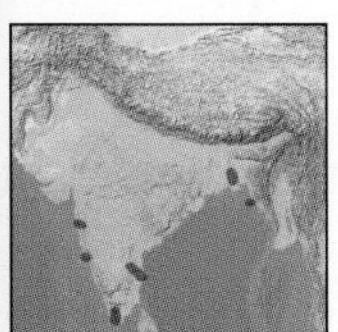

Size 20 cm

Voice Call a somewhat hesitant, *tchue...de...tchue-dee-dee...tchue...dee...dee*, slightly ascending

Range Winter visitor; regular but scarce near Madras, Tamil Nadu, rarely recorded in Maharashtra, Andhra Pradesh, Goa, Kerala and Andaman Islands

Habitat Canopy of light forests

Grey-and-white bird. Male has black head; white forehead and forecrown; black ear-coverts; whitish underparts and dark grey tail; whitish crown and forehead. Whitish wing-bar, visible in flight. Female similarly coloured as male, unlike other minivets with dark slaty-grey stripe across forehead.

Swinhoe's Minivet

SMALL MINIVET

Pericrocotus cinnamomeus Campephagidae

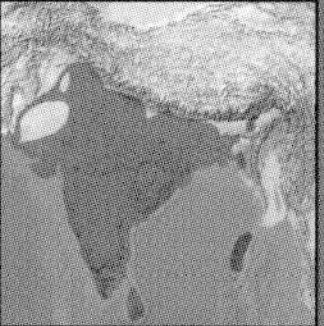

Size 15 cm

Voice Call a soft, low *swee… swee…* notes uttered as birds hunt in foliage

Range Most of India, upto about 900 m in outer Himalayas; absent in arid parts of Rajasthan

Habitat Forests; groves; gardens; tree-dotted cultivation

Male has dark grey head, back and throat; orange-yellow-patch on black wings; black tail; flame-orange breast, graduating to yellow on belly and undertail; strong dark beak; long tail. Female paler above and overall duller; orange rump; dusky-white throat, breast tinged with yellow; yellowish belly and undertail. Juvenile has more brown upperparts than female with faint barring and scaling; faintly speckled underparts. In pairs, or small flocks; keeps to tree-tops, actively moving amidst foliage; flutters and flits about in untiring hunts for small insects, often in association with other small birds; also hunts flycatcher-style.

WHITE-BELLIED MINIVET

Pericrocotus erythropygius Campephagidae

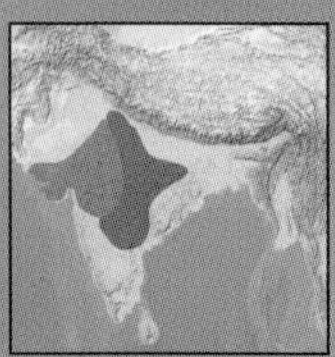

Size 15 cm

Voice Calls *tseep…tseep* in flight

Range Rare breeding resident of NC Indian lowlands and Gujarat

Habitat Open dry woodlands, thorn scrub

Small minivet, mostly black above with white markings on wing. White underparts with orange on breast and rump; long tail. Female greyish-brown above, with white underparts and grey breast. Juvenile similar to female but has some scaling and barring, particularly on crown and some mottling on breast and white tips on wing-coverts.

LONG-TAILED MINIVET

Pericrocotus ethologus Campephagidae

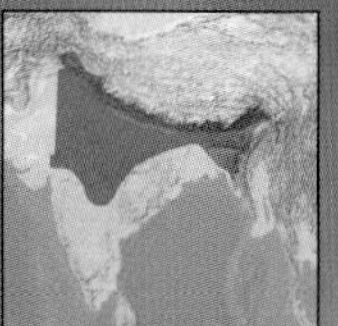

Size 18 cm

Voice Call a distinctive descending whistle *pee…ru*

Range Common breeding resident and summer visitor to N hills from W Pakistan, east to Myanmar border and Bangladesh. Winters widely in plains south to Maharashtra

Habitat Broadleaved and coniferous hill forests when breeding. Winters in open woodlands and groves. Nomadic in winter

Male has glossy blue-black upperparts, hood, chin and throat; scarlet rump; scarlet underparts; black wings with bright scarlet-patches on secondaries and inner greater coverts forming U shape; long tail with red outer-tail feathers. Female has yellow on forehead and supercilium; grey cheeks; greenish-yellow-grey, mantle, back and rump; pale yellow throat graduating to orange-yellow on breast and flanks.

GREY-CHINNED MINIVET

Pericrocotus solaris Campephagidae

Size 17 cm

Voice Call a thin *tsee…sip*

Range Local breeding resident in the mountains east from C Nepal to Arunachal Pradesh and Myanmar border hills. Also occurs in China and SE Asia

Habitat Hill forests

Small, brightly-plumaged minivet with dark grey face, head and mantle; pale grey chin; orange-yellow throat, washed grey; short, black bill. Male has bright to dull orange underparts; orange lower back and rump; orange tips on greater coverts. Female duller grey with bright yellow underparts, and in wings and tail. Dark mid-wing-bar visible in flight. Feeds actively, mainly in tree canopy in small, calling parties. Sometimes briefly descends to eye level.

SHORT-BILLED MINIVET

Pericrocotus brevirostris Campephagidae

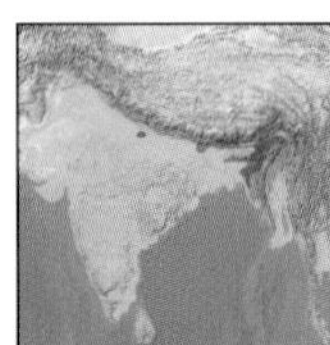

Size 19 cm

Voice Call a high whistled *tsee…tup*

Range C Nepal eastwards. S Assam Hills

Habitat Open broadleaved forests; edges of forests; secondary growth

Adult male has black hood, throat, mantle, wings; deep red underparts; similar to Long-tailed; shorter tail, like Scarlet, but smaller, more slender; wings lack red spots or 'drops' on tips of tertials, secondaries. Female brighter yellow below, including on throat; no wing spots; more yellow on forehead, including forecrown; yellower cheeks.

SCARLET MINIVET

Pericrocrotus (flammeus) speciosus Campephagidae

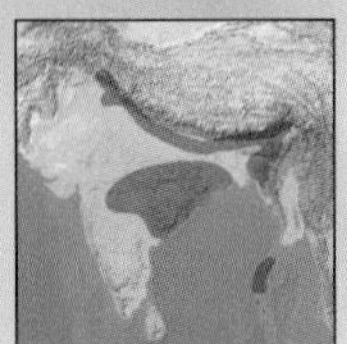

Size 20 cm

Voice Call a pleasant, 2-note whistle; also longer, whistling warble

Range Disjunct; several isolated races

Habitat Forests; gardens; groves

Male has glossy bluish-black head and upper back; deep scarlet lower back and rump; black-and-scarlet wings and tail; black throat, scarlet below. Female has rich yellow forehead, supercilium; grey-yellow above; yellow-and-black wings and tail; bright yellow underbody. In pairs, or small parties; sometimes several dozens together; keeps to canopy of tall trees; actively flits about to hunt for insects; also launches aerial sallies after winged insects; often seen in mixed hunting parties of birds; spectacular sight of black, scarlet and yellow as flock flies over forests.

ORANGE MINIVET

Pericrocotus flammeus Campephagidae

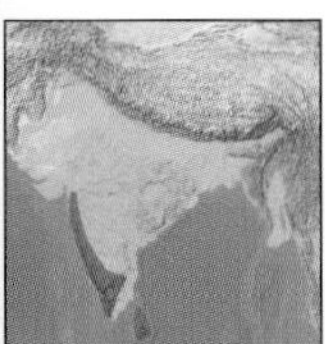

Size 20-22 cm

Voice Call a piercing, whistled *sweep...sweep*

Range Mainly the Himalayas, from E Jammu and Kashmir to Arunachal Pradesh

Habitat Open tropical, subtropical and lower temperate forests, usually of broadleaved, also coniferous

♀

Large and stock minivet with bright orange underparts. Male has black upperparts; bright orange outer-tail feathers and uppertail-coverts; orangish-scarlet rump; black throat. Female has grey-brown upperparts, bright yellow underparts and yellow-patch on wing and yellow-patch on forehead. Hawks on insects while perched on tree-tops. Highly active in small mixed flocks. Nests in fork of branches, high in trees.

BAR-WINGED FLYCATCHER-SHRIKE

Hemipus picatus Tephrodornithidae

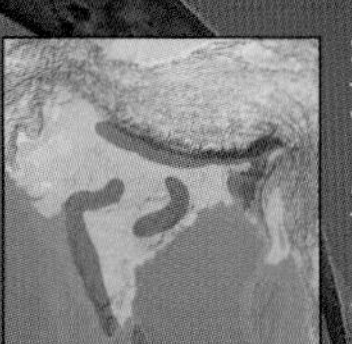

Size 14 cm

Voice Noisy. Calls include persistent *tsit...it...it...tsit...it...it...,si...* and short *chip*

Range Fairly common breeding resident in foothills from E Himachal Pradesh to Myanmar border, Eastern and Western Ghats and Sri Lanka. Makes attitudinal and other local movements

Habitat Open forests, edges of forests including adjoining scrubs

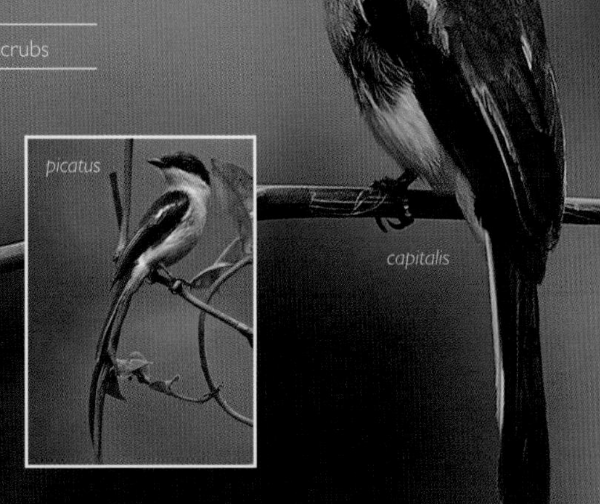

picatus

capitalis

Pied shrike with distinct black cap and hindneck. Brown mantle in the Himalayan race (shown). Black in southern races. Long white-patches on black wings showing V in rear views. Tail black with white borders. Throat white, contrasting with pinkish-grey underparts. Female more brown. Feeds on insects in noisy, active flocks, often in mixed hunting groups in canopy and lower down. Often flycatches. Nests high in trees.

MANGROVE WHISTLER

Pachycephala cinerea Pachycephalidae

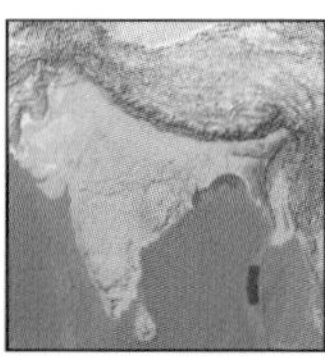

Size 17 cm

Voice Variable phrase with 2-4 introductory notes, last note louder, shriller and more explosive

Range Sunderbans in India; Bangladesh; Andaman Islands

Habitat Mangroves

Medium-sized bird with uniform grey-brown upperparts. Greyish-white throat; grey breast; white belly; white undertail-coverts; light grey lores; thick black bill; bark brown, reddish-brown iris; grey legs. Sexes alike. Solitary, in pairs or in mixed flocks; calls from high, open perch.

BROWN SHRIKE

Lanius cristatus Laniidae

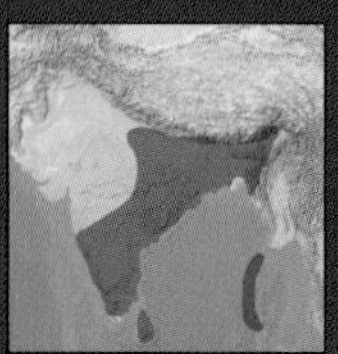

Size 19 cm

Voice Calls include harsh chattering, grating; sometimes sings in low chirruping tone with bill closed

Range Winter visitor to peninsular India

Habitat Open country; cultivation; edges of forests; scrubs; gardens

Adult male has uniform rufous-brown upperparts and darkish-brown crown; Broad, black 'bandit-mask' through eye; white brow over. Pale creamy underparts, washed buff; rufous flanks; rufous tail; brown wings; Female has less contrast and faint scalloping on underside. Immature has stronger scalloping on underparts. Solitary; perches in open or tree stumps and returns to same perch repeatedly; territorial.

juvenile

RED-BACKED SHRIKE

Lanius collurio Laniidae

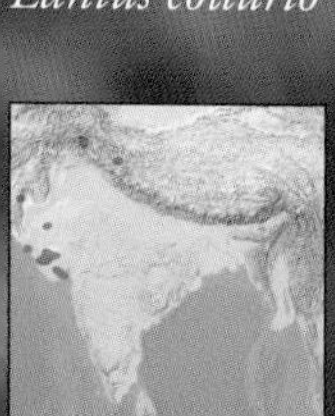

Size 17 cm

Voice Grating call

Range Southward passage migrant. Pakistan and NW India

Habitat Conspicuous when feeding; more secretive at other times. Bushes and cultivation in dry country

juvenile

Smallish shrike with pale bluish-grey head; black eye mask; chestnut back; black tail with white outer-tail feathers; buffy-pink underparts; short tail. Female lacks black eye mask and duller brown. Juvenile has barred back, no eye mask and more rufous tail. Flicks and swings tail on perch.

ISABELLINE SHRIKE

Lanius isabellinus Laniidae

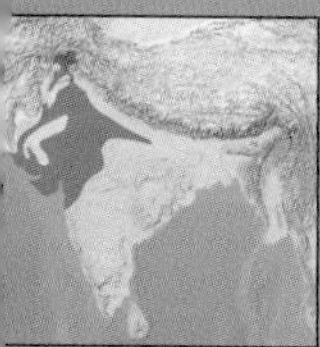

Size 17 cm

Voice Can be noisy. Call a grating *kerishk…kerishk*

Range Breeds in W Pakistan. Common winter visitor to Pakistan and NW India, vagrant further south and east

Habitat Dry thorn scrub and edges of fields, often near water

Small shrike, with rather plain sandy-brown plumage. Adult male has rufous lower rump and tail; dark face patch; fine white supercilium; white-patch on primaries; buff underparts. Adult male of *L. i. phoenicuroides* darker. *L. i. isabellinus* paler. White wing patch absent in female and juvenile. Sits on prominent perch, in open. Catches insects, small reptiles, mammals and birds from perch. Sometimes, impales prey on thorns.

RED-TAILED SHRIKE

Lanius phoenicuroides Laniidae

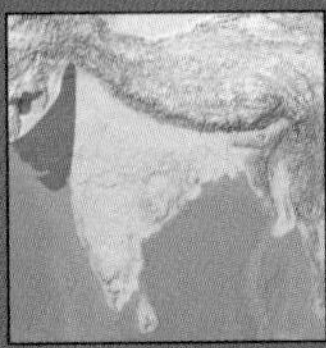

Size 17 cm

Voice Call a harsh repeated *tsch… ef, tsch…ef… or zech…zeck…*; mate attraction call *zautzat…zautzat…* or *ko…ick*

Range Summer visitor throughout Afghanistan and W Pakistan

Habitat Thorny scrub

Adult male has rufous crown, nape and hindneck; fairly dark sandy-brown mantle, scapulars and back; prominent white supercilium; black eye mask. Pale creamy-buff underparts; rich rufous rump usually richer in colour than *isabellinus*. Female duller above; faint rufous brown mask, restricted to lores and less distinct primary patch; fine barring on malar area, breast and flanks.

BAY-BACKED SHRIKE

Lanius vittatus Laniidae

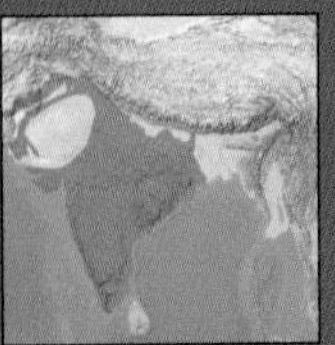

Size 18 cm

Voice Call a harsh, *churr*; lively warble of breeding male; sometimes imitates other bird calls

Range Subcontinent, upto about 1,800 m in the Himalayas; absent in the NE

Habitat Open country; light forests; scrubs

Deep chestnut-maroon back; broad black forehead-band, continuing through eyes to ear-coverts; grey crown and neck, separated from black by small white-patch; white rump distinctive; black wings with white in outer flight feathers; white underbody, fulvous on breast and flanks. Sexes alike. Solitary, or in scattered pairs in open terrain; keeps lookout from perch on some tree stumps, overhead wire or bush-tops, usually under 4 m off ground; pounces once potential prey sighted; usually devours prey on ground, tearing it; sometimes carries it to perch; keeps to fixed territories, defends aggressively.

juvenile

BURMESE SHRIKE

Lanius collurioides Laniidae

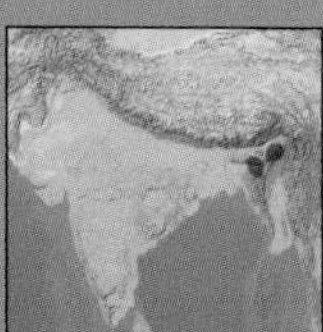

Size 20 cm

Voice Alarm call a loud, rapid, harsh chattering, *chikachikachitchit, chekoochekoochitititititit, chetetetetet*

Range Locally common passage migrant, mainly in Assam and Manipur

Habitat Subtropical or tropical moist lowland forests; subtropical or tropical moist montane forests

Medium-sized shrike with long slender tail. Adult male has black forehead and ill-defined face mask; slaty-grey hindneck; dark grey crown; chestnut mantle, rump and uppertail-coverts; white wing patch; white sides to tail. Adult female has whitish forehead and paler chestnut mantle.

LONG-TAILED SHRIKE

Lanius schach Laniidae

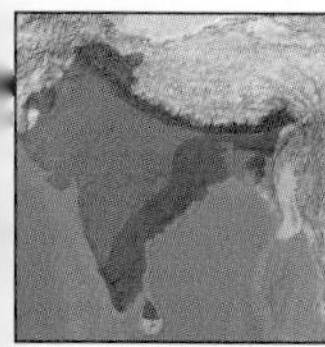

Size 25 cm

Voice Noisy. Calls include a harsh mix of scolding notes, shrieks and yelps; excellent mimic. Rather musical song of breeding male

Range Three races; undergo considerable seasonal movement; subcontinent, from about 2,700 m in the Himalayas

Habitat Open country, cultivation, edges of forests, vicinity of habitation, gardens; prefers neighbourhood of water

Pale grey from crown to middle of back; then bright rufous till rump; black forehead, band through eye; white 'mirror' in black wings; whitish underbody, tinged pale rufous on lower breast and flanks. Sexes alike. Mostly solitary; boldly defends feeding territory; keeps lookout from conspicuous perch; pounces onto ground on sighting prey; said to store surplus in 'larder', impaling prey on thorns; nicknamed Butcher-bird.

erythronotus

tricolor

caniceps

GREY-BACKED SHRIKE

Lanius tephronotus Laniidae

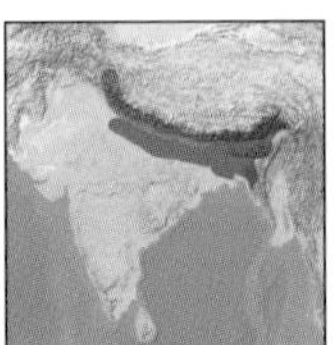

Size 25 cm

Voice Call a grating *shrek*; mimics other birds

Range Locally common breeding summer visitor to the Himalayas from Ladakh, eastwards to hills of NE India. Winters lower down to plains including Bangladesh

Habitat Open areas, usually with trees, but also in open high altitude steppe

Large shrike with dark grey upperparts; black mask; yellowish flanks; long tail; rufous uppertail-coverts and belly. Similar to Long-tailed but has darker grey, no rufous on upperparts and grey forehead; larger head and bill. Usually lacks white primary patch on blackish wings. Breeds at high altitudes.

SOUTHERN GREY SHRIKE

Lanius meridionalis Laniidae

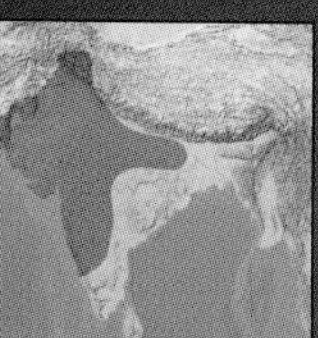

Size 25 cm

Voice Call a harsh, grating *khreck*...; mix of other harsh notes and chuckles; pleasant, ringing song of breeding male

Range Drier areas of NW, W and C India, across Gangetic Plain to West Bengal; south to Tamil Nadu

Habitat Open country; semi-desert; scrubs; edges of cultivation

Bluish-grey above; broad black stripe from beak through eye; black wings with white 'mirrors'; black-and-white tail; unmarked white underbody. Sexes alike. Mostly in pairs, in open areas; remains perched upright on bush-tops or overhead wires or flies low, uttering harsh scream; surveys neighbourhood from perch and pounces on prey; batters and tears prey before swallowing it; said to maintain 'larder', impaling surplus prey on thorns; keeps feeding territories year round; wild and wary bird.

INDIAN GOLDEN ORIOLE

Oriolus (oriolus) kundoo Oriolidae

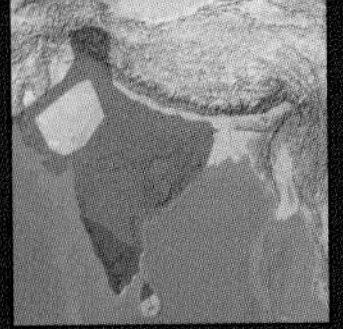

Size 25 cm

Voice Call includes a fluty whistle of 2- or 3-notes, interpreted *pee...lo...lo*

Range Summer visitor to the Himalayan foothills, spreads in winter to plains; breeds in many parts of peninsula

Habitat Forests; orchards; gardens around habitation

Male has bright golden-yellow plumage; black stripe through eye; black wings and centre of tail. Female yellow-green above; has brownish-green wings; dirty-white below, streaked brown. Juvenile similar to female. Solitary, or in pairs; arboreal, sometimes moving with other birds in upper branches; regularly visits fruiting and flowering trees; hunts insects in leafy branches; usually heard, surprisingly not often seen, despite bright colour; seen only when emerges on bare branch or flies across.

juvenile

SLENDER-BILLED ORIOLE

Oriolus tenuirostris Oriolidae

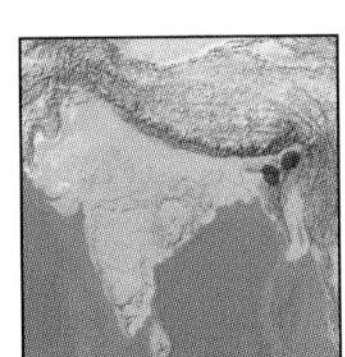

Size 27 cm

Voice Utters mellow fluty notes, *wheeow* or *chuck...tarry...you*

Range Breeds in the Himalayas from E Bhutan to Arunachal Pradesh

Habitat Well-wooded areas, groves, large trees in open country. Winters lower in broadleaved forests

Adult male has golden-yellow head; broad black band extending from lores around eye and across back of head. Very similar to Black-naped, but distinguished by longer and more downcurved bill and call and narrower nape-band. Olive-yellow wing-coverts and panel across tertials/secondaries. Female has more olive tinge to yellow in plumage and some indistinct barring in underparts. Juvenile hard to distinguish from Black-naped except by longer bill.

BLACK-NAPED ORIOLE

Oriolus chinensis Oriolidae

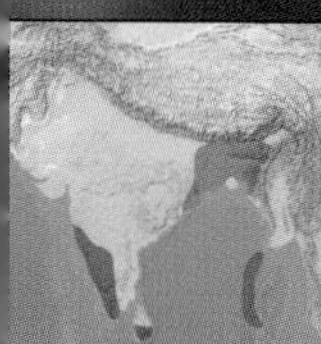

Size 25 cm

Voice Call similar to Indian's but less musical

Range Breeds on Andaman and Nicobar Islands. Scarce winter visitor to Kerala and SE Bangladesh. Scattered records elsewhere in peninsula

Habitat Rubber plantations

Easily differentiated from Golden by broad black eye-stripe continuing to join on nape (and much stouter bill). Female more greenish or olive on mantle. Overall yellow with black in-flight feathers and black tail with yellow-patches. Female more greenish-yellow. Juvenile has some streaking on underparts and more diffused eye-stripe. Indulges in high-speed aerial chases. Raids nests of other birds, taking their eggs and chicks.

BLACK-HOODED ORIOLE

Oriolus xanthornus Oriolidae

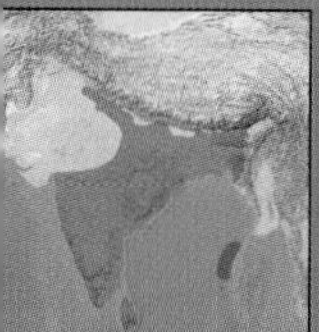

Size 25 cm

Voice Assortment of melodious and harsh calls; fluty 2- or 3-noted *tu…hee or tll…yow…yow…*more common; also single, mellow note

Range Subcontinent, upto about ,000 m in the Himalayan foothills

Habitat Forests, orchards, gardens, often amidst habitation

Golden-yellow plumage; black head diagnostic; black-and-yellow wings and tail; deep pink-red beak seen at close quarters. Sexes alike. In pairs, or small parties; strictly arboreal, only rarely descending into lower bushes or to ground; active and lively; moves a lot in forests and birds chase one another, rich colours striking against green or brown of forests; very vocal; associates with other birds in mixed parties, frequently joins mixed hunting groups. visits fruiting and flowering trees.

MAROON ORIOLE

Oriolus traillii Oriolidae

Size 28 cm

Voice Most commonly a cat-like squawking *meow*. Also, fluty *pi… lio…ilo*

Range Locally common breeding resident in N hills from E Himachal Pradesh to Myanmar border. Moves lower down to foothills and nearby plains, including Bangladesh, in winter

Habitat Subtropical or tropical moist lowland forests

Adult male has maroon body and black head and wings. Deep scarlet-red tail; strong, decurved grey-blue bill; startling white iris. Female has blackish upperparts, dull maroon back; white underparts heavily streaked maroonish-brown. In pairs, or singly, often in mixed hunting groups. Well-hidden in canopy; feeds on invertebrates, nectar and fruits.

♀

BLACK DRONGO

Dicrurus macrocercus Dicruridae

Size 31 cm

Voice Call a harsh *tiu…tiu;* also *cheece…cheece*

Range Subcontinent, upto about 1,800 m in the outer Himalayas

Habitat Open country; orchards; cultivation

Glossy black plumage; long, deeply forked-tail. Diagnostic white spot at base of bill. Sexes alike. Usually solitary, sometimes in small parties; keeps lookout from exposed perch; most common bird seen on rail and road travel in India; drops to ground to capture prey; launches short aerial sallies; rides atop grazing cattle; follows cattle, tractors, grass cutters, fires; consumes vast numbers of insects; bold and aggressive species, with several birds nesting in same tree.

ASHY DRONGO

Dicrurus leucophaeus Dicruridae

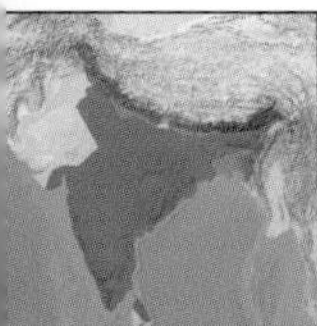

Size 30 cm

Voice Noisy and varied. Calls include *cha…ke wip…kit…whew* and *cheece…cheece…chichuk…*

Range Fairly common breeding summer visitor to N foothills from Pakistan, east to Myanmar border. Winters in plains and peninsula, including Sri Lanka

Habitat Forests and more open woodlands in winter

Adult has ash-grey upperparts; slightly lighter underparts, paler towards belly; red or reddish-brown iris; black legs and bill; black chin. Juvenile more brown than adult, with white edge on underside of tail and brown iris. Sexes similar, but male slightly larger. Agile flier, executing remarkable twists and turns in air with skill and speed. Mimic calls of other birds. Forages near edges of forests; perches on high, open branch to detect prey; swoops down to catch insects on ground or in mid-flight.

WHITE-BELLIED DRONGO

Dicrurus caerulescens Dicruridae

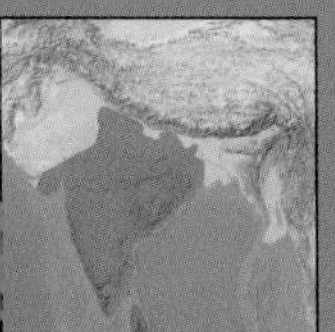

Size 24 cm

Voice Assortment of pleasant, whistling calls and some grating notes

Range Most of S India and east of a line from SE Punjab to around Kutch; east to Bengal; occurs to about 1,500 m

Habitat Open forests and well-wooded habitats

Adult has bluish-black upperparts; long, deeply forked-tail; greyish-brown throat and breast; white belly and undertail-coverts; short legs. Sexes alike. In pairs, or small groups of four birds, sometimes with other birds. Noisy; makes short flights; often hunts till very late in evenings; sits upright while perched prominently in shrike-like pose.

CROW-BILLED DRONGO

Dicrurus annectans Dicruridae

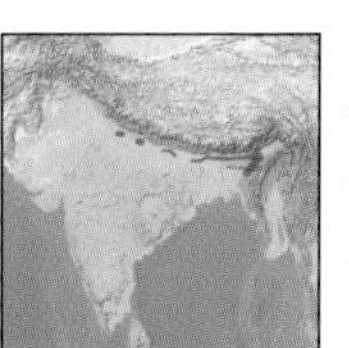

Size 28 cm

Voice Calls include loud, musical whistle and *churr*, characteristic descending series of harp-like notes

Range Winters in NE India and Bangladesh. Seen east of Almora upto 800 m

Habitat Dense broadleaved evergreen and moist deciduous forests

Stout drongo with thick, squat bill, covered at base by dense rictal feathers. Black plumage glossed bluish-green. Easily confused with Black, but distinguished by habitat. Short, broad tail with shallow fork but widely splayed and upcurved at tip. Immature has white speckled breast, belly and flanks, and undertail-coverts. Hawks from perch. Locally common.

LESSER RACKET-TAILED DRONGO

Dicrurus remifer Dicruridae

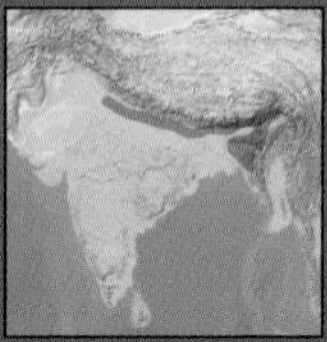

Size 25 cm

Voice Noisy like Greater. Musical whistle and screech. Mimics other birds

Range Locally common breeding resident in N foothills from Uttarakhand east to Myanmar border. Winters lower down and in Bangladesh

Habitat Shady understoreys of forests often near streams

Medium-sized, glossy black drongo with short crest and long streamers that end in feather-shaped rackets; square-ended rather than forked-tail. Juvenile duller, with flat-ended tail and no extentions. Sexes alike. Usually in pairs, or in mixed hunting groups or bird waves, feeding on invertebrates. Sits on perch waiting to swoop on prey, but often flycatches. Nests in trees.

immature

SRI LANKA DRONGO

Dicrurus p lophorinus Dicruridae

Size 33 cm

Voice As Greater's

Range Sri Lanka wet zone

Habitat Wet zone forests and nearby hills

Earlier considered a race of the Greater Racket-tailed Drongo which occurs in drier areas. Easily identified by frontal crest, glossy black plumage and long, deeply forked-tail without rackets. Vocal mimic, imitating variety of birds. Sexes alike. In pairs. Distinguished from Greater Racket-tailed, by longer and more deeply forked-tail, slightly decurved at tip, and lack of terminal rackets, shorter crest and more rounded tuft. Immature has white barring on belly and flanks similar to Greater Racket-tailed.

BRONZED DRONGO

Dicrurus aeneus Dicruridae

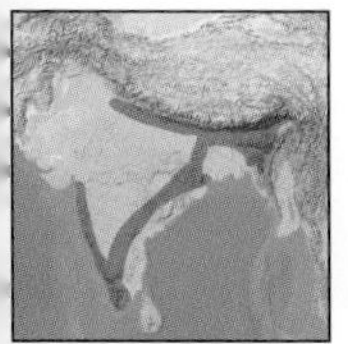

Size 24 cm

Voice Noisy. Varied whistles and grating calls. Also *cheet… chi… chew*

Range Fairly common breeding resident in foothills from E Punjab to NE India, including Bangladesh, then south through Eastern Ghats and throughout the length of Western Ghats. Makes some local movements

Habitat Clearings in thick forests, usually near streams

Smallish drongo with glossy, black plumage, and bluish-green/purple iridescence. Relatively short, spade-shaped tail with shallow fork, splayed at tips; short and heavy black bill; spiky rictal feathers give whisker-like appearance. Dark underparts, with more gloss over breast. Sexes alike. Perches high on exposed branch, hawking for insects. Very vocal and conspicuous; territorial. Pairs perform noisy displays.

SPANGLED DRONGO

Dicrurus hottentottus Dicruridae

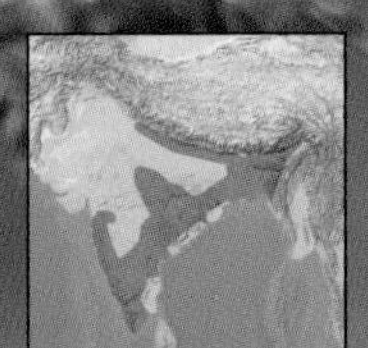

Size 32 cm

Voice Noisy; mix of whistling, metallic calls and harsh screams

Range Lower Himalayan foothills, east of Uttarakhand; down through NE India, along Eastern Ghats, Odisha, Bastar through to Western Ghats, up north to Mumbai, occasionally even further north

Habitat Forests

Glistening blue-black plumage, fine hair-like feathers on forehead; longish, downcurved, pointed beak; diagnostic tail, square-cut and inwardly bent (curling) towards outer ends. Sexes alike. Solitary, or scattered pairs, strictly arboreal forest bird; small numbers may gather on favourite flowering trees; rather aggressive; often seen in mixed hunting parties of birds. Selects exposed branch and flies out to prey.

ANDAMAN DRONGO

Dicrurus andamanensis Dicruridae

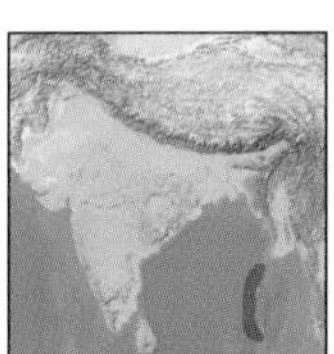

Size 35 cm

Voice Noisy. Various hard, metallic calls and *chyu* note

Range Common endemic breeding resident restricted to Andaman Islands where it is the only common drongo

Habitat Forests

Brownish-black bird with deeply-forked, recurved tail. Overall glossy, black plumage, except for brownish mantle. Long, heavy, decurved black bill. Similar to Black but distinguished by larger bill and brownish iridescence to feathers and diagnostic recurved fork on tail. Slight hair-like crest on forehead. Sexes similar, but female smaller with more shallow fork in tail. Often, in quite large groups and sometimes in mixed hunting parties. Feeds on insects, often by flycatching. Nests high in tree fork.

WHITE-SPOTTED FANTAIL

Rhipidura albogularis Rhipiduridae

Size 19 cm

Voice Call includes a scratchy *check* repeated irregularly, often in rapid series

Range Resident in peninsula north to Rajasthan and Gangetic Plain

Habitat Wooded areas, secondary forests

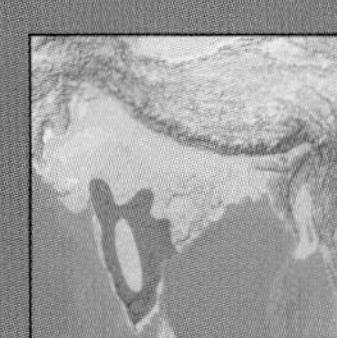

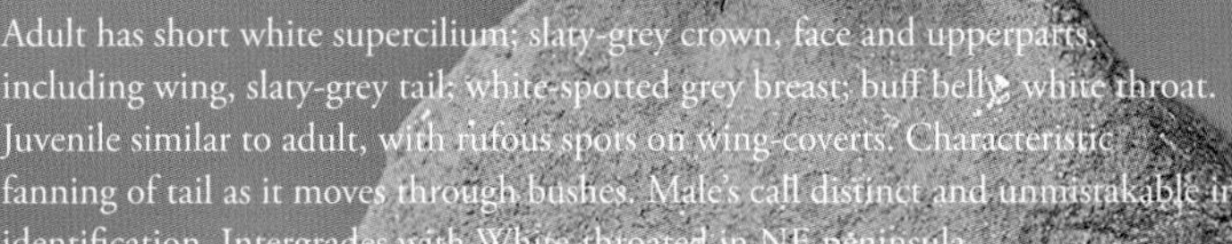

Adult has short white supercilium; slaty-grey crown, face and upperparts, including wing, slaty-grey tail; white-spotted grey breast; buff belly; white throat. Juvenile similar to adult, with rufous spots on wing-coverts. Characteristic fanning of tail as it moves through bushes. Male's call distinct and unmistakable in identification. Intergrades with White-throated in NE peninsula.

BLACK-NAPED MONARCH

Hypothymis azurea Monarchidae

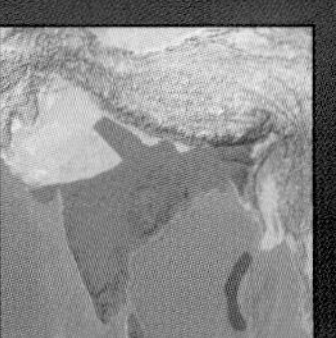

Size 16 cm

Voice Common call a sharp, grating, high-pitched *chwich… chweech* or *chwae…chweech*, slightly interrogative in tone, two notes quickly uttered; has short, rambling notes when breeding

Range India, south of outer Himalayas, to about 1,200 m, east of W Uttarakhand; absent in arid NW and N India

Habitat Forests; bamboos; gardens

Male has lilac-blue plumage; black-patch on nape, gorget on breast; slight black scaly markings on crown; sooty on wings and tail; white below breast. Female ash-blue, duller; lacks black on nape and breast. Solitary, or in pairs in forests, often amidst mixed hunting parties; extremely active and fidgety, flits and flutters about, often fans tail slightly; calls often as it moves about, calls are often first indication of its presence.

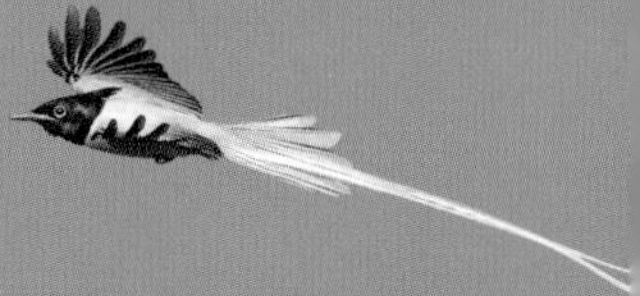

INDIAN PARADISE-FLYCATCHER

Terpsiphone paradisi Monarchidae

intermediate phase

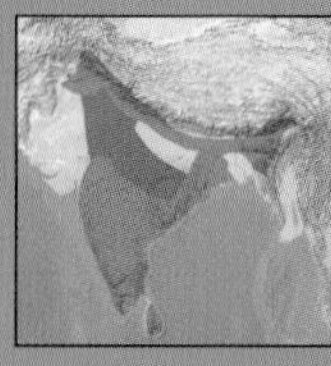

Size 20 cm (male's tail 30 cm more)

Voice Call a sharp, grating *chwae* or *chchwae*…; melodious warbling song and display of breeding male

Range The Himalayas, foothills to about 1,800 m, rarely 2,500 m; N India, south to Bharatpur; absent in broad belt across Gangetic Plain; widespread in peninsular India

Habitat Light forests; gardens; open country

Glossy blue-black head, crest and throat; black in wings; silvery-white body, long tail-streamers. Male occurs in two morphs: rufous phase has white parts replaced by rufous-chestnut with white underparts. White phase more variable, but has predominantly white plumage. Female and juvenile have no tail-streamers; shorter crest; rufous above; ash-grey throat and nuchal-collar; whitish below. Short legs; tends to sit upright on perch. Solitary, or in pairs; makes short sallies; flits through trees, tail-streamers floating; strictly arboreal, sometimes descending into taller bushes; cheerful disposition.

♀

rufous phase

white phase

BLACK-HEADED JAY

Garrulus lanceolatus Corvidae

Size 33 cm

Voice Usually, single harsh *kraaa*

Range Locally common endemic breeding resident in N mountains from W Pakistan, east to Nepal. Some move lower in winter

Habitat Mixed temperate forests, particularly oaks, but often in more open areas than Eurasian

Similar to Eurasian, but range restricted to W Himalayas. Adult has black head with crest; pinkish-buff body, washed grey on rump and mantle. Wings regularly patterned black, blue-and-white; tail black-barred blue. White-streaked throat contrasting with black head; yellow bill. Sexes alike. Less shy than Eurasian, and often around human habitation.

EURASIAN JAY

Garrulus glandarius Corvidae

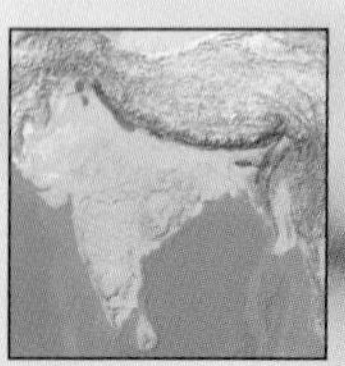

Size 33 cm

Voice Noisy; guttural chuckles, screeching notes and whistles; good mimic

Range Across the Himalayas, 1,500-2,800 m, somewhat higher in the east; may descend low in winter

Habitat Mixed temperate forests

Pinkish-brown plumage; velvety-black malar stripe; closely black-barred, blue wings; whitish crown streaked black; rufous lesser and median coverts; pinkish-brown underparts; white rump contrasts with jet-black tail. Sexes alike. Juvenile similar to adult, but darker body, greyer bill, bluish eyes, brighter legs. In small, noisy groups, often along with other Himalayan birds; inquisitive and aggressive; mostly keeps to trees, but also descends into bushes and onto ground; laboured flight.

SRI LANKA BLUE MAGPIE

Urocissa ornata Corvidae

Dramatically-coloured magpie with deep blue, long tail, chestnut head, breast and lower-wings; and bright coral-red bill, eye-ring and legs; white-tipped tail conspicuous in flight. Juvenile duller and greyer, with brown eye-ring; duller, soft parts. Usually shy and in small flocks, often with babblers and woodpeckers.

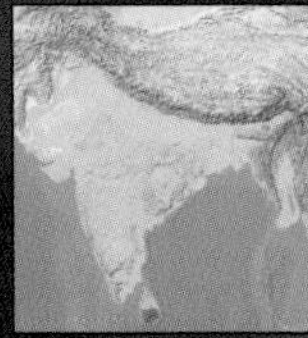

Size 47 cm

Voice Varied. Several calls loud and harsh, including jingling, metallic *chlink…chlink*, rasping *crakrakrakrak*, loud *whee*

Range Resident, Sri Lanka

Habitat Hill forests

YELLOW-BILLED BLUE MAGPIE

Urocissa flavirostris Corvidae

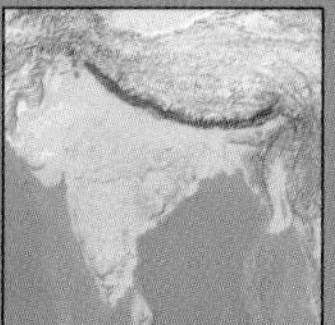

Size 66 cm

Voice Noisy. Calls include a great mix of metallic screams, loud whistles and raucous notes, often imitating other birds

Range The Himalayas, west to east; 1,500-3,600 m; may descend low in winter

Habitat Forests; gardens; clearings

Purple-blue plumage; black head and breast; white nape patch and underbody; very long, white-tipped tail; yellow beak and orange legs. Sexes alike. In pairs or small bands, often associating with jays, laughing thrushes and treepies; wanders a lot in forests, flying across clearings, entering hill station gardens, one bird following another; arboreal, but also hunts low in bushes; even descends to ground, long tail cocked as bird hops about.

RED-BILLED BLUE MAGPIE

Urocissa erythrorhyncha Corvidae

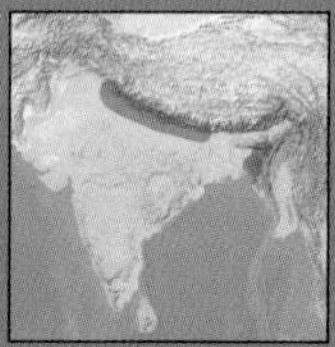

Size 70 cm

Voice Calls include loud *pit* and sharp *kwerer...pig...pig*. Other calls similar to Yellow-billed's

Range Locally common breeding resident in foothills of N mountains from Himachal Pradesh

Habitat Mixed forests; cultivation and gardens at lower altitude than Yellow-billed

Slaty-blue bird with very long-tail and robust, red bill, black head, neck and breast with bluish spotting on crown. Creamy-grey underparts. Larger than Yellow-billed and bluer above (purplish in eastern race). White nape patch larger. Black subterminal band to white-tipped tail. Red legs. Sexes alike. Juvenile has greyish bill, brownish head and back, very similar to Yellow-billed's.

COMMON GREEN MAGPIE

Cissa chinensis Corvidae

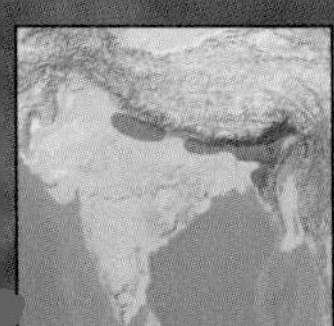

Size 47 cm

Voice Very variable. Call a loud *kik…*wee note. Complex mixture of whistles, squeals and wails. Also mimics

Range Locally common breeding resident in N mountains from Uttarakhand to Myanmar border, and also Bangladesh

Habitat Dense broadleaved forests, particularly ravine sides

Large green magpie with vivid red bill. Brilliant emerald-green upperparts; paler green underparts. Bold, broad black stripe extending from bill through eyes to short crest onto rear crown. Red legs. Wings black and white-tipped chestnut. Long, graduated, white-tipped tail. Sexes alike. Feeds low down in foliage or ground in pairs or small groups. Joins mixed hunting groups.

RUFOUS TREEPIE

Dendrocitta vagabunda Corvidae

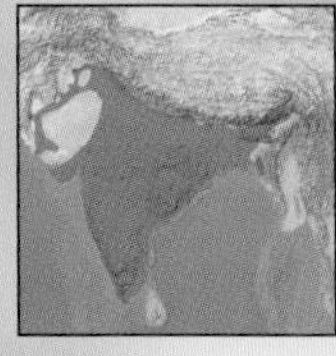

Size 50 cm

Voice Common call a fluty 3-note *goo…ge…lay* or *ko…ki…la;* harsh, guttural notes often uttered

Range Almost all over India, upto about 1,500 m in outer Himalayas

Habitat Forests; gardens; cultivation; habitation

pallida

vagabunda

Sexes alike. Rufous above; sooty grey-brown head and neck; black, white and grey on wings, best seen in flight; black-tipped, grey tail, long and graduated. In pairs, or small parties; feeds up in trees, but also descends low into bushes and onto ground to pick up termites.

GREY TREEPIE

Dendrocitta formosae Corvidae

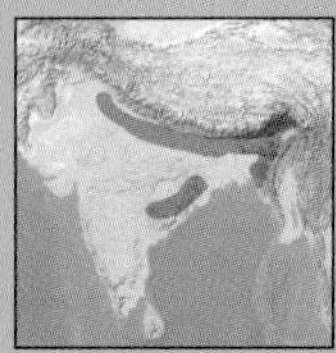

Size 40 cm

Voice Noisy and variable. Call a loud, clanking *klok…ti…klok…ti…ti*

Range Locally common breeding resident in N hills from extreme NE Pakistan to Myanmar border; Eastern Ghats

Habitat Forests; secondary growth

Duller and less rufous than the Rufous; long tail; grey-and-brown plumage; dusky grey face and grey head, neck and underparts; rufous vent; radiated grey tail black-edged and tipped; brownish back; black wings with small white-patch. Sexes alike. Less often near human habitation than Rufous. Behaviour and food as Rufous but shyer. Arboreal, often in groups or mixed hunting groups. Seems to seek company of drongos.

WHITE-BELLIED TREEPIE

Dendrocitta leucogastra Corvidae

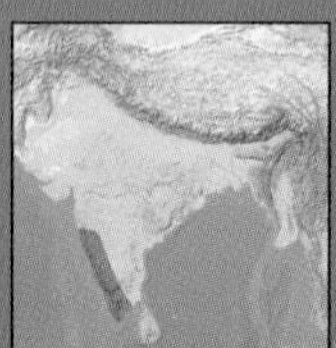

Size 50 cm

Voice Noisy. Calls include various loud, harsh and metallic notes, including *tikituk…tikituk* and *kreah…kreah*

Range Local breeding endemic resident in S Western Ghats

Habitat Evergreen hill forests; thick scrub; plantations

White, grey and chestnut crow with very long, black-tipped and pale grey-edged tail. Black face contrasts with white head and underparts. Chestnut mantle and black wings with white-patches. Sexes alike. Sociable, often with Greater Racket-tailed Drongos, which they imitate freely as well as other forest species. Feeds mainly on invertebrates at lower and middle levels. Nests in shrubs.

COLLARED TREEPIE

Dendrocitta frontalis Corvidae

Size 38 cm

Voice Various loud calls, similar to other treepies'

Range Patchy distribution in extreme E Nepal, Bhutan and Arunachal Pradesh

Habitat Thick tropical, subtropical, temperate moist evergreen, semi-evergreen forests; bamboos

Smaller treepie with compact body and long tail. Similar to Grey, Rufous, but distinctly separated by black forecrown, face, throat contrasting with pale grey hindcrown, nape, breast, upper belly; rufous mantle, lower belly, rump, vent; long black, not grey, tail; black wings have grey panels on coverts, no white-patch. In flight, black tail, rufous vent, rump, distinguish it from Rufous. Singly, or in small groups; like all treepies, joins mixed feeding parties with other forest species; mainly arboreal; not as noisy as Rufous, Grey.

ANDAMAN TREEPIE

Dendrocitta bayleyii Corvidae

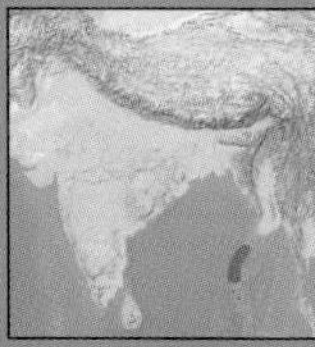

Size 36 cm

Voice Noisy and variable. Fluty *ke chew* and a rasping call

Range Fairly common breeding endemic resident of the Andaman Islands

Habitat Subtropical or tropical moist lowland forests

Long-tailed, dark crow with startlingly yellow iris; black face, wings and tail; dark grey head and neck; deep brown back and chestnut underparts; contrasting white wing patches. Smaller and slighter than other treepies. Sexes alike. Behaviour as other treepies and seems to seek company of Andaman Drongos.

EURASIAN MAGPIE

Pica pica Corvidae

Pied bird with glossy black head, neck, upper back, wings; tail glossed bronze-green and purple-blue; white scapulars, lower back (rump), belly; black undertail. Sexes alike. Tibetan race *bottanensis* can be identified by black rump. Usually, several in vicinity; moves on ground, perches on fence-posts, trees, house-tops; frequents high-mountain villages; typical crow, bold and aggressive, but also extremely alert; flicks tail often.

Size 52 cm

Voice Call a loud, grating *chak…chak*; also other piping notes

Range High NW, the Himalayas, Chitral, N Kashmir, Ladakh, Himachal Pradesh; Tibetan race found in Bhutan and Arunachal, 1,500-4,700 m

Habitat Open valleys; cultivation; habitation

SPOTTED NUTCRACKER

Nucifraga caryocatactes Corvidae

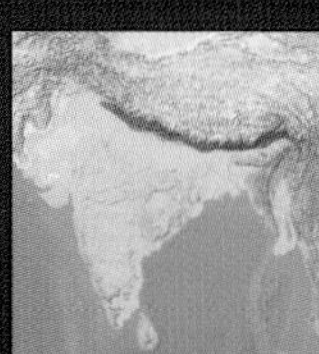

Size 32-35 cm

Voice Noisy. Call a guttural *kharr…kharr*

Range The Himalayas. 1,800-4,000 m, sometimes descending to about 1,200 m in winter

Habitat Coniferous, oak, rhododendron forests

Chocolate-brown plumage, thickly-speckled with white; dark central tail feathers, tipped white; white outer-tail and undertail-coverts; heavy, pointed beak distinctive. Sexes alike. The race *hemispila*, found between Kangra and CE Nepal, has smaller white spots; rump lacks white spots. Small parties in temperate forests; keeps to tree-tops but readily descends onto ground; rather wary; flies short distances across glades; rather noisy, usually attracting attention by its calling.

Large-spotted Nutcracker

ALPINE CHOUGH

Pyrrhocorax graculus Corvidae

Size 38 cm

Voice Less noisy than Red-billed. Calls include high rolling *krerrr*, high *kee…u* and deep *kruu*

Range Common breeding resident of N mountains from W Pakistan, east to Arunachal Pradesh. Many move lower in winter

Habitat As Red-billed's, with which it sometimes mixes, but usually at higher altitudes

Glossy black crow with diagnostic short, yellow, decurved bill. Similar to Red-billed, but shorter wings with bulging trailing edges and longer tail with rounded edges. Overall black plumage with bluish-green gloss on wings; short and inconspicuous nasal tuft; orangish-yellow bill, more greenish at base. Confiding. Large flocks often seen performing aerial displays, sweeping down mountainsides.

RED-BILLED CHOUGH

Pyrrhocorax pyrrhocorax Corvidae

Size 45 cm

Voice Call a melodious, high-pitched *cheeao… cheeau…*

Range High in the Himalayas

Habitat Cliffsides; alpine pastures; cultivation; vicinity of mountain habitation

Velvety black crow with characteristic coral-red decurved beak and red legs; upper mandible slightly overlaps lower; inconspicuous nasal tuft; square-ended tail. Sexes alike. Highly gregarious; feeds in cultivation; probes ground and dung for insects; does not hesitate to rob corn stored in attics of upland houses; flocks often fly high into skies, rising on thermals, playing and dancing in air currents in wild splendour; tame and confiding in some areas.

EURASIAN JACKDAW

Corvus monedula Corvidae

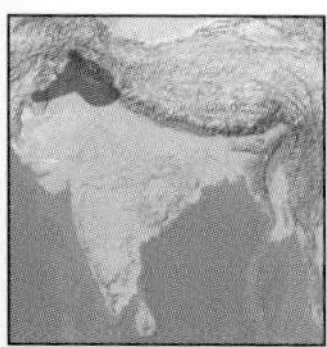

Size 33 cm

Voice Noisy. Commonest calls include abrupt *jack* and repeated *kyaa*

Range Locally common breeding summer visitor to N Pakistan, Kashmir. Winters in Pakistan plains in variable numbers, individuals sometimes occurring as far south and east as Uttar Pradesh

Habitat Mountain cultivation and pastures usually near cliffs. Also cultivation in winter in plains

Smallish black and grey crow; black crown and face; white iris; small, short beak; black legs. Distinguished from House Crow by smaller size and smaller bill. In flight, looks short-headed and stocky. Juvenile has dark eye, darker grey parts and lacks pale silvery-grey ear-coverts. Very gregarious; large flocks often wheel around cliffs. Runs on ground.Nests in holes.

HOUSE CROW

Corvus splendens Corvidae

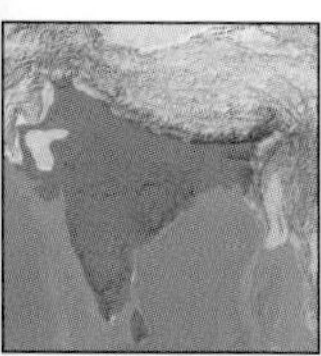

Size 43 cm

Voice Call a familiar *caw*; occasionally pleasant *kurrrrr* note; several other notes

Range Subcontinent, reaching about 2,500 m in the Himalayas

Habitat Rural and urban habitation; cultivation, edges of forests; wide range of habitats

Sleek-looking crow with glossy black plumage; grey collar, upper back and breast; glossy black on forehead, crown and throat; long, prominent, arched bill; black feet; brown eyes. Sexes alike. Mobs other birds, even large raptors; performs important scavenging services; occasionally flies very high into skies, either when flying long distance, or simply for fun; roosts communally.

zugmayeri

splendens

protegatus

ROOK

Corvus frugilegus Corvidae

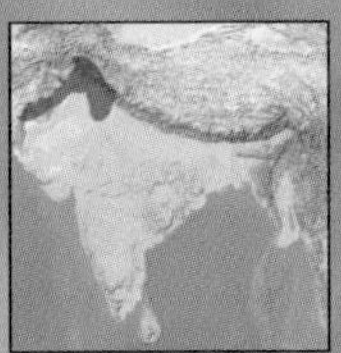

Size 48 cm

Voice Call a hoarse *karrh…karrh*

Range Locally common winter visitor to W and N Pakistan, Kashmir. No recent substantiated records from elsewhere in India

Habitat Cultivation; pastures

Large crow with long, pointed bill and whitish face and peaked crown. Long, slim unfeathered bill also has whitish base. Often has small throat pouch. Fingered, straight-edged, narrow-based wings and slightly wedge-shaped tail give different flight shape. Very gregarious, feeding and roosting in flocks, often with Eurasian Jackdaws. Walks rather cockily about fields feeding on invertebrates, for which it probes deeply. Also eats young shoots and seeds.

CARRION CROW

Corvus corone Corvidae

Size 48 cm

Voice Call a deep harsh *karr…karr*

Range Scarce breeding resident: N Pakistan, Kashmir. Hooded Crow is scarce winter visitor to same area but common in Ladakh

Habitat Open country and cultivation, often near human habitation

Similar to Rook and Large-billed, but distinguished by much stouter bill, feathered at base and slightly decurved; flatter head; shorter, more rounded tail; Hooded Crow *C. c. cornix* grey with black head and breast patch, wings and tail. Broad, even-edged wings and square-ended tail. Sexes alike. Lazy flight with steady wingbeats; soars and glides. Shy and wary. Solitary, or in pairs but roosts communally; feeds with other species, especially on carrion; eats almost anything. Inquisitive feeder, searching methodically.

BROWN-NECKED RAVEN

Corvus ruficollis Corvidae

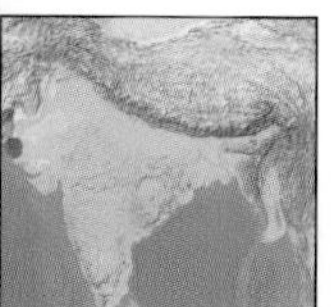

Size 52-56 cm

Voice Call a dry, rising *aarg... aarg...aarg*

Range Resident along Makran coast, where frequent, and in S Baluchistan; spreads north in winter, occasionally to Quetta, and west to Chagai

Habitat Desert

Similar to Northern, but has less massive and heavy bill; shorter nasal feathers; throat feathers longer and more pointed. Head, neck and breast brownish-black with purplish gloss; neck sides and crown more brown with copper gloss; rest of plumage glossed bluish-purple; long tail strongly graduated; fingered primaries; wedge-shaped tail; black bill, legs and feet. In pairs, or small parties feeding; roosts in large communities.

NORTHERN RAVEN

Corvus corax Corvidae

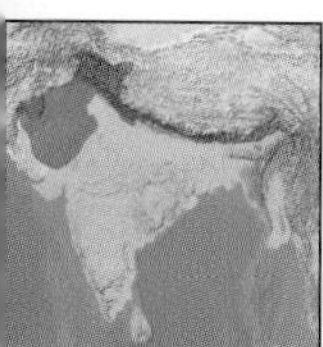

Size 58-69 cm

Voice Call a deep, resounding *kraa... kraa; gonk...gonk...; wock...wock*

Range Kashmir to Bhutan (Northern) and in NW (Punjab Raven)

Habitat High-altitude Trans-Himalayan stony desert; alpine meadows (Northern), deserts and semi-deserts (Punjab).

Impressively-sized, glossy black crow. Long, decurved bill with distal culmen; prominent nasal bristles. Similar to Large-billed, but has larger, less domed head; beard-like throat feathers, pale brownish-grey, less curved bill; distinct wedge-shaped tail conspicuous in flight. Flight feathers and tail more brown. Juvenile duller and less glossy with bluish-white iris. Powerful flight; soars on thermals; pairs indulge in aerial rolling displays. Singly, in pairs or small groups; sometimes larger flocks; roosts communally.

Punjab Raven

Northern Raven

LARGE-BILLED CROW

Corvus macrorhynchos Corvidae

Size 48 cm

Voice Call a harsh *khaa…khaa*; several variations among various races

Range The Himalayas

Habitat Forests, rural habitations; small numbers in towns and cities

Glossy black plumage; heavy beak, with noticeable culmen-curve. Relatively broad wings, particularly primaries; long tail, slightly wedged, obvious only in flight; nasal tufts; black bill and legs; dark iris. Sexes alike. Solitary, or in groups of two to six; most common around villages and only small numbers in urban areas; overall not as 'enterprising' as familiar House; in forested areas, behaviour often indicates presence of carnivore kills. Large nest, untidy assembly of twigs.

EASTERN JUNGLE CROW

Corvus (m.) levaillantii Corvidae

Size 42 cm

Voice Identical to Indian Jungle's

Range NE India, from Nepal eastwards and Andaman Islands

Similar to Large-billed, but shorter, more pointed, slender bill; flatter forehead profile and shorter, square-ended tail.

INDIAN JUNGLE CROW

Corvus (m.) culminatus Corvidae

Size 42 cm

Voice Similar to House's

Range South of the Himalayas; peninsular (except NW) India and Sri Lanka

Difficult to tell apart from Indian Jungle and Large-billed. Recently split.

BOHEMIAN WAXWING

Bombycilla garrulus Bombycillidae

Size 25 cm

Voice Call a high, dry, metallic, rapid clattery even-tempo *trill*

Range Winter vagrant: Hills of Balochistan, to Karachi (once), the Himalayas of N Afghanistan-Pakistan frontier to C Nepal

Habitat Mixed coniferous, deciduous forests

Grey, rust, black, yellow, red, white bird with narrow, sharply-defined black face mask finely bordered with white; black chin; rusty wash to forehead and cheeks; wings slightly darker grey; whitish lower abdomen; dull orange undertail-coverts; grey wings marked white, bordered red-and-yellow with dark tips; tail grey to black with broad bright yellow terminal band. Sexes similar. Juvenile similar but lacks red-and-yellow tips on wing feathers; facial markings less defined. Highly gregarious; dense, nervous flocks gather in trees.

HYPOCOLIUS

Hypocolius ampelinus Hypocoliidae

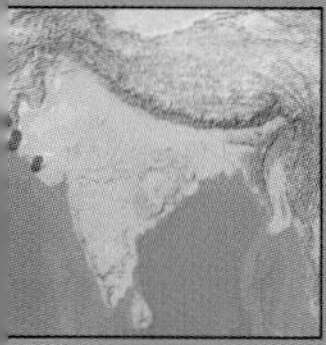

Size 25 cm

Voice Said to give whistled notes *wheew…whee…di… du…di…di…du…* etc.

Range Winter visitor to S Pakistan, Gujarat

Habitat Lowland wooded areas

Long-tailed and short-winged bird with diagnostic black face mask extending to hindneck. Overall bluish-grey. Slightly hooked bill. Often raises crown feathers, giving rise to crested appearance. In flight, shows black primaries with prominent white tips. Female and immature duller, brownish-grey and lack black mask; well-defined creamy-white throat, less white in primaries and indistinct black tail-tip.

CINEREOUS TIT

Parus major Paridae

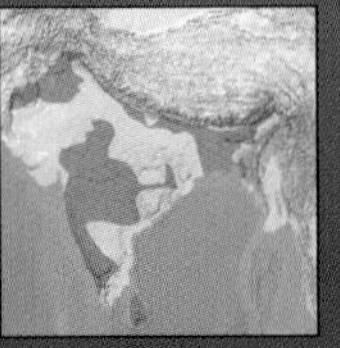

Size 13 cm

Voice Call a loud, clear whistling *whee...chi... chee...*; other whistling and harsh notes

Range Widespread in the Himalayas, foothills to about 3,500 m; peninsular India

Habitat Open forests; gardens; habitation

Adult has grey back; black crown continuing along neck sides to broad black band from chin along centre of underbody; white cheeks, nape patch, wing-bar and outer feathers of black tail; ashy-white sides. Sexes alike. In pairs or small bands, often with other small birds; restless, clings upside down, and indulges in acrobatic displays while hunting among leaves and branches; holds food fast between feet and pecks at it noisily; tame and confiding.

GREEN-BACKED TIT

Parus monticolus Paridae

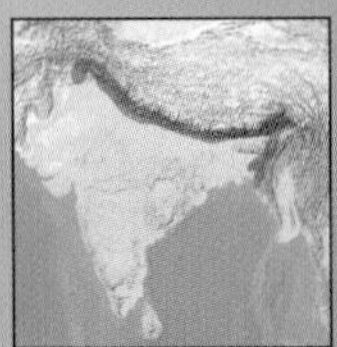

Size 13 cm

Voice Similar to Great's. Calls include loud *teacher... teacher*-note and repeated *whitee... whittee*

Range Locally common breeding resident to N mountains from N Pakistan east to Myanmar border. May move lower down in foothills during winter

Habitat Deciduous, coniferous mixed forests and tropical moist lowland forests

Yellow-green, and black tit distinguished by two white wing-bars, bright green upperparts and blue leading edges on wing feathers. White cheeks. Similar to Great but has brighter green mantle and back-and-yellow underparts. Sexes similar. Feeds mainly near ground on invertebrates and fruits.

BLACK-LORED TIT

Parus xanthogenys Paridae

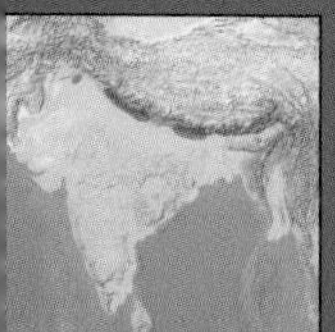

Size 14 cm

Voice Cheerful, musical notes. Call a loud tailorbird-like *towit… towit* near nest; other 2- to 4-noted whistling calls; whistling song. Also, harsh *charrr* and some chattering notes

Range The Himalayas to E Nepal; 1,200-2,500 m, widespread in parts of C, E and W India

Habitat Forests; gardens

Large tit with diagnostic bushy, black crest. Olive-green back; black crest, faintly-tipped yellow; stripe behind eye, broad central band from chin to vent; bright yellow nape patch, supercilium and sides of underbody. Sexes alike. In pairs or small flocks, often with other small birds; arboreal, active; feeds in foliage; sometimes enters gardens. Female and juvenile like male, but may have black replaced by olive.

YELLOW-CHEEKED TIT

Parus spilonotus Paridae

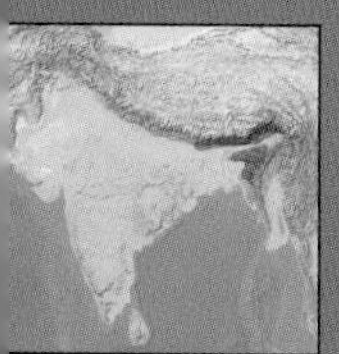

Size 14 cm

Voice Calls include *sit, si…si… si* and *chrrrr*. Great Tit-like song *chee…o…chee…pui*

Range Locally common breeding resident in N mountains from E Nepal east to Myanmar border. Moves lower down in winter

Habitat Open forests

Black-and-yellow tit with unmistakably erect and pointed black crest, tipped yellow, yellow forehead. Regional variations: yellow and green in the Himalayan region; greyer and black with yellow cheeks in rest of the region. Short, black lines behind eye; heavily streaked greenish mantle; grey rump; white wing-bars. Sexes similar, but female duller. Forages low down.

INDIAN YELLOW TIT

Parus (xanthogenys) aplonotus Paridae

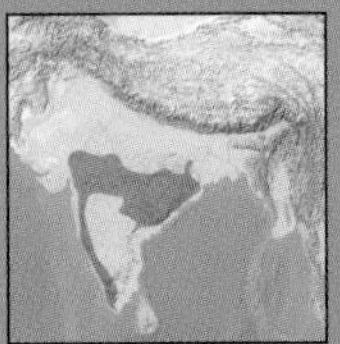

Size 14 cm

Voice Call resembles Great's. Song comprises 3-ringing notes rapidly repeated upto 6 times, *chee…thee…pui;*

Range E Himalayas; hills of NE India

Habitat Open forests

Adult has yellow forehead and lores; yellow cheeks; greenish mantle streaked black; white wing-bars. Juvenile similar to adult, but duller, with shorter blackish crest, yellowish-white wing-bars. Sexes similar in the nominate *E Himalayan* subspecies. Female *P. s. subviridis* of NE India south of the Brahmaputra River has olive bib and ventral line, and mantle less heavily marked with black.

RUFOUS-VENTED TIT

Periparus rubidiventris Paridae

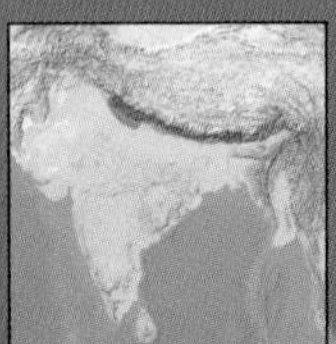

Size 10 cm

Voice Noisy. Calls include thin *seet* and *psst*. Rattling song

Range Common breeding resident in N mountains from Himachal Pradesh east to Nagaland. Moves lower down in foothills during winter

Habitat Open, coniferous and broadleaved forests, particularly rhododendron

Black-crowned bird with spiky crest and black bib. *Western Himalayan* race has olive-washed, dark grey upperparts, reddish-rufous underparts, pinkish-rufous belly, pale rufous-washed nuchal patch, white cheek patch, greyish flanks. *Eastern Himalayan* race *R. beavani* has whitish nuchal spot, blue-washed, dark grey underparts, buff-grey bib, and only rump has hint of cinnamon. Sexes similar, male darker. Juvenile duller with smaller crest.

COAL TIT

Periparus ater Paridae

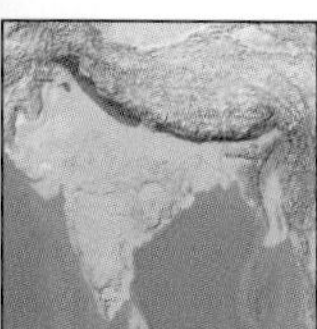

Size 11 cm

Voice Call includes thin *tsi… tsi.* Song a low-pitched, slow *wee…tsee…wee…tsee… wee…tsee*

Range Common breeding resident in Himalayas: western race *melanolophus* (Spot-winged Tit) from NW Pakistan to W Nepal, and *aemodius* in C and E Himalayas

Habitat Coniferous forests

Slender-billed small tit with largish head and floppy crest. Black crown and upper mantle; large, white nuchal and cheek patches; extensive black bib continuing to black nape. Underparts mainly buffy-white (*aemodius*) or grey with rufous breast sides (*melanolophus*). Slaty-bluish grey upperparts graduating to buffy olive-brown towards rump; two distinct white-spotted wing-bars and white-tipped tertials. Sexes alike. Very active; sometimes shy. Solitary, or in pairs; in flocks outside breeding.

aemodius

melanolophus

RUFOUS-NAPED TIT

Periparus rufonuchalis Paridae

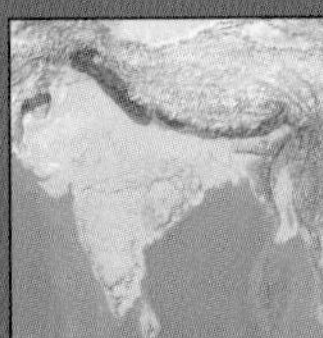

Size 13 cm

Voice Noisy. Calls include *tsee… tsee… peeou…*, *peep* and *seep*

Range Fairly common breeding resident in N mountains from E Balochistan to W Nepal. Moves lower down in foothills during winter

Habitat Open, coniferous forests

Dark tit with upright crest and large creamy-white cheek patch. White nuchal patch finely bordered rufous; extensive black bib, covering entire breast; dark grey upperparts and belly; rufous nape, sides of breast and vent. Sexes similar, but female has less extensive bib. Juvenile has much paler bib, less demarcated from lower breast and belly. Gregarious; appears often with other tit species or mixed hunting groups.

WHITE-NAPED TIT

Parus nuchalis Paridae

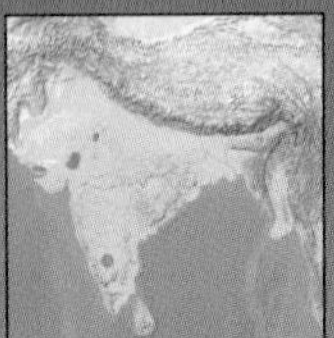

Size 12 cm

Voice Vocabulary very similar to Great's

Range Gujarat, Rajasthan. Isolated records from S India

Habitat Thorn-scrub forests. Globally threatened

Black-and-white tit with large white nuchal patch. Male has glossy black mantle and wing-coverts; extensive white on wing; white cheeks. Underparts white, with strong black ventral-band from throat to vent. Sexes similar, but female has bluish gloss to black parts and small, white tips to primaries. Juvenile duller and lacks gloss, smaller white nuchal patch and less white in tail and wings. In pairs, or family parties; shy; restless. More heard than seen; located through musical call. Feeds in canopy and shrub level.

GREY-CRESTED TIT

Lophophanes dichrous Paridae

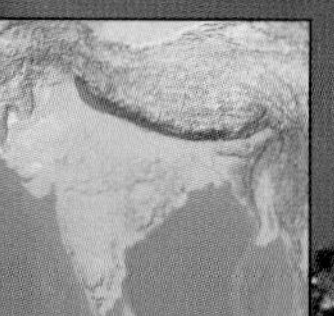

Size 12 cm

Voice Calls include thin *zai* and *ti…ti…ti…ti* and *chea…chea* alarm. Song *wee…wee tz…tz…tz*

Range Locally common breeding resident in N mountains from E Kashmir to Bhutan. Commonest in E. Moves lower down in foothills during winter

Habitat Hill forests

Adult has dull brownish-grey upperparts; similarly coloured upright crest; dirty whitish sub-moustachial stripe extending around neck to form collar; decurved eye-stripe; mottled-grey cheeks; lighter grey-brown throat. Underparts washed pale cinnamon. Sexes alike. Juvenile similar to adult with shorter crest and less uniform underparts. Often in mixed hunting groups. Rather quiet and inconspicuous; acrobatic behaviour.

SULTAN TIT

Melanochlora sultanea Paridae

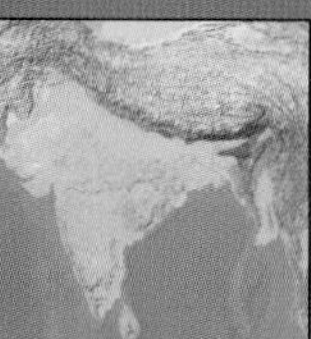

Size 20 cm

Voice Noisy. Call a loud, whistling *cheerie…cheerie*; other shrill whistling notes, often mixed with harsh *churr* or *chrrchuk*; varied chattering notes

Range The Himalayan foothills, east from C Nepal; NE; foothills to about 1,200 m, sometimes ascending to 2,000 m

Habitat Mixed forests; edges of forests

Male black above; yellow crown and crest; black throat and upper breast; yellow below. Female has deep olivish wash to black upperbody and throat; crest similar to male; some yellow also visible on throat. Small bands seen often along with other birds in mixed hunting flocks; active and inquisitive; clings sideways and upside down; checks foliage and bark crevices; feeds in canopy but also descends to tall bushes.

WHITE-CROWNED PENDULINE TIT

Remiz coronatus Paridae

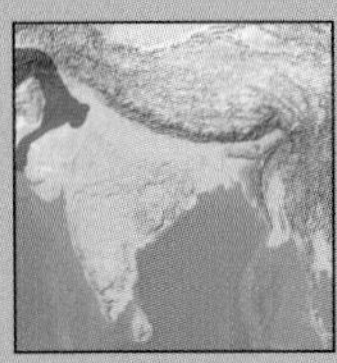

Size 10 cm

Voice Call a thin, high-pitched *tsee…*, *tseeuh* or repeated *tee… tsee…tsee*

Range Winter visitor to Pakistan and Punjab, India

Adult male has pinkish wash to cream head; blackish mask continuing behind head; variable nape-band (absent fresh plumage); whitish collar; large chestnut-patch on mantle; cinnamon wing-coverts and chestnut greater coverts. Female and first-year male duller with pale grey crown and collar, mask browner. Juvenile has beige upperparts and buffish underparts, no mask and band.

YELLOW-BROWED TIT

Sylviparus modestus Paridae

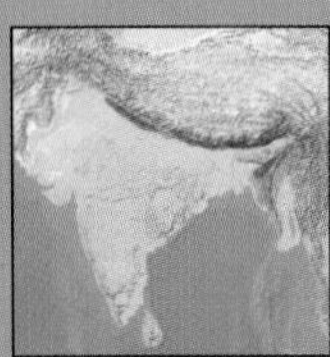

Size 10 cm

Voice Calls *psit…sisisi*

Range Pakistan to Myanmar; S Assam Hills

Habitat Oak, broadleaved, mixed forests; orchards; scrub

Tiny tit with olive-grey upperparts and pale greyish-yellow underparts. Narrow yellowish eye-ring; thin bright yellow indistinct supercilium; worn plumage more dull grey-brown above; slight crest; olive-green, ill-defined wing-bar; pale bluish-grey legs. Sexes alike. Juvenile very similar to adult. Solitary, or in pairs; seen in foraging parties; often overlooked; arboreal; mostly canopy feeder, sometimes descends to lower storeys; quiet, inconspicuous; restless with typical tit-like acrobatics. Raises crest when alarmed.

WHITE-THROATED TIT

Aegithalos niveogularis Aegithalidae

Small tit with distinct white forehead and forecrown and whitish throat. Black lores, head sides and cheeks; pure white sub-moustachial patch and neck sides; blackish mask merges with cinnamon-brown hindcrown and ear-coverts. Greyish-brown upperparts; pinkish-rufous patch on rump; greyish-brown tail, edged and tipped white. Underparts cinnamon, darker cinnamon band between throat and breast; pale grey chin and throat. Juvenile similar to adult, has dull pinkish throat, darker and more prominent breast-band (with paler lower breast and belly), and brown upperparts.

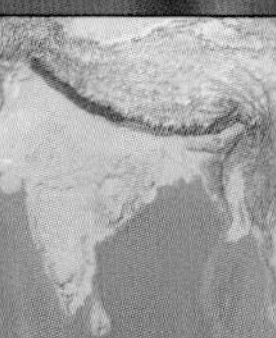

Size 11 cm

Voice Call a frequently uttered *t…r…r…r…r…t*. Song longer and more elaborate than that of other *Aegithalos* tits; has rapid chattering *tweet…tweet* interspersed with high-pitched *tsi…tsi* notes and short warbling phrases

Range The Himalayas from E Pakistan to NW Nepal

Habitat Bushes in mixed birch and coniferous forests

RUFOUS-FRONTED TIT

Aegithalos iouschistos Aegithalidae

Size 11 cm

Voice Calls include *trrr…trrr; trrup; si…si…si*

Range Nepal to Arunachal Pradesh

Habitat Broadleaved and coniferous forests; rhododendron; scrubs

Distinguished by extensive black head sides and lores. Cinnamon forehead, centre of nape, crown-stripe and cheeks; narrow rufous sub-moustachial stripe extends to breast sides; black chin and malar border; prominent white throat; silver-grey breast and rich rufous-buff on rest of underparts. Grey upperparts washed buff on upper mantle; pale cinnamon-patch on rump. Appears in groups of upto 40 outside breeding. Forages in canopy as well as in shrubs. There have been several recent sightings of the Black-browed Tit in Arunachal Pradesh.

Black-browed Tit

PLAIN MARTIN

Riparia paludicola Hirundinidae

Size 12 cm

Voice Calls *brret...*, rather harsh in tone, usually on the wing around nest colony. Twittering song

Range NW and N India, from the outer Himalayas, south at least to line from vicinity of Mumbai-Nasik to C Odisha; moves considerably locally

Habitat Vicinity of water, sandbanks, sandy cliffsides

Long wings and slightly forked-tail. Grey-brown above, slightly darker on crown; dark brown wings and tail; dull grey below, whiter towards abdomen. Sexes alike. Gregarious species, always in flocks, flying around sandbanks along water courses; individual birds occasionally stray far and high; hawks small insects in flight; flocks perch on telegraph wires.

SAND MARTIN

Riparia riparia Hirundinidae

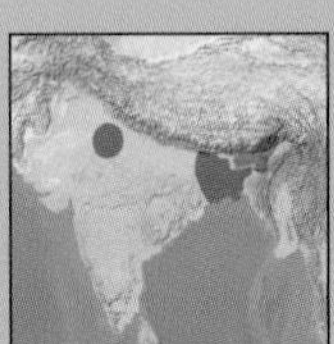

Size 13 cm

Voice Call a dry, quiet *trass*

Range Scarce breeding resident in Assam. Local winter visitor to Bangladesh. Scarce and irregular passage migrant, perhaps winter visitor in NW India

Habitat Vicinity of water

Adult has greyish-brown upperparts; darker tail and wings; long wings; slightly notched tail; dark underwings, white throat and underparts; contrasting brown chest-band sometimes extending to centre of belly; small, black beak; blackish or dark brown legs and feet. Sexes similar. Juvenile has buff or cream wash on belly, pale rust wash on face, neck, chin and breast. Gliding swallow-like flight. Northwestern Pale, similar in flight but much paler. Feeds on aerial insects close to surface of water. Sociable. Nests in tunnels in sandbanks.

PALE MARTIN

Riparia diluta Hirundinidae

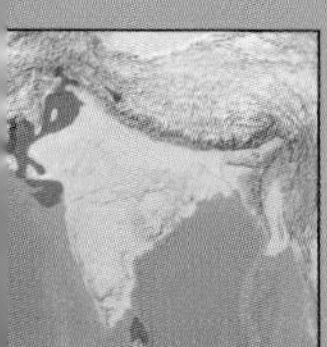

Size 13 cm

Voice Undocumented

Range Breeds in the Himalayas; winters in Pakistan and probably farther E

Habitat Large waterbodies

Treated as conspecific with Pale Sand. However, smaller and slimmer with shallower tail-fork; paler upperparts; greyish-brown; breast-band paler, more greyish-brown and less distinct with diffuse lower border. In some, the breast-band only slightly darker than rest of underparts, gives impression of broken breast-band with paler centre merging to darker sides; paler head, particularly crown and ear-coverts, contrasting with dark eye and darker lores; pale (often almost pure white, or buffish) throat.

BARN SWALLOW

Hirundo rustica Hirundinidae

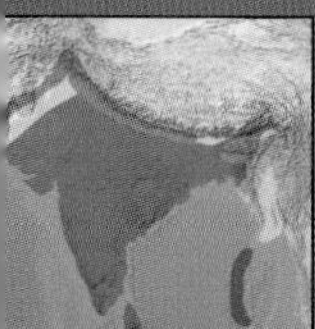

Size 18 cm

Voice Calls vary with object of alarm. Hard *vit* in flight and twittering rambling song

Range Common breeding resident to N mountains from W Pakistan east to Myanmar border. Common winter visitor throughout rest of the region

Habitat Cultivation, towns and villages usually near or over water

Slender bird with long, narrow, pointed wings, and deeply forked-tail with long streamers; spends most of its life on wing. Steel bluish-black upperparts; black wings and tail; pale underparts; red throat; steel-blue breast-band. Sexes alike, but male may have longer streamers. Juvenile has paler underparts and less deeply forked-tail. Agile flier; low, fast, powerful in flight. Constructs nest under eaves of buildings. Gregarious.

HILL SWALLOW

Hirundo (tahitica) domicola Hirundinidae

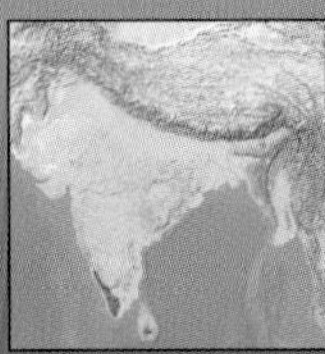

Size 12.5 cm

Voice Call an abrupt, high-pitched *chit*. Song a pleasant twittering

Range Western Ghats and Sri Lanka hill zone, wandering to foothills

Habitat Grassy hills around tea and coffee plantations, bungalows and factory sheds

Similar to Pacific but smaller with longer tail and metallic green iridescence to upperparts. Feeds on small flying insects on wing; in small flocks, sometimes with red-rumped swallows, barn swallows; nest a cup of mud and straw lined with feathers and bracketed on wall, road-bank or earth-slips. Less gregarious than Barn. Often perches on telegraph wires.

PACIFIC SWALLOW

Hirundo tahitica Hirundinidae

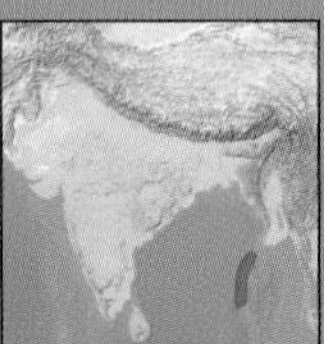

Size 13 cm

Voice Call a hard *qwik…qwik*

Range Resident in Andaman Islands

Habitat Open country and along coasts and rivers

Distinguished from Barn by lack of blue breast-band and streamers. Blue-black upperparts; short, forked-tail. Rufous from forehead to breast; greyish-white belly; dark grey vent with white scalloping; grey underwing-coverts. Hunts alongside Barn, but does not associate with them otherwise. Feeds sociably on aerial insects. Flight less sweeping than Barn. Often perches on wires and bare branches. Nests against wall in building or against bank or culvert.

WIRE-TAILED SWALLOW

Hirundo smithii Hirundinidae

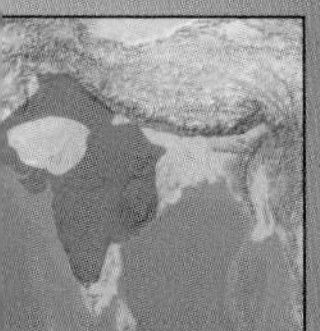

Size 14 cm

Voice Call a soft twittering note; pleasant song of breeding male

Range Common breeding (summer) visitor to N ndia, to about 1,800 m in the Himalayas; breeds n many other parts of India; widespread over the rea, excepting arid zones

Habitat Open areas; cultivation; habitation, mostly n vicinity of canals, lakes, rivers

Glistening steel-blue above; chestnut cap; unmarked, pure white underbody distinctive; two long, wire-like projections (tail-wires) from outer-tail feathers diagnostic. Sexes alike. In solitary, or small parties; almost always seen around water, either perched on overhead wires or hawking insects in graceful, acrobatic flight, swooping and banking; often flies very low, drinks from surface; roosts in reed beds and other vegetation, often with warblers and wagtails.

EURASIAN CRAG MARTIN

Ptyonoprogne rupestris Hirundinidae

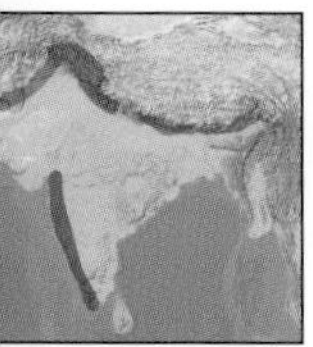

Size 15 cm

Voice Calls include short *plee*, musical *weeeh* and harsh *tshrr*

Range Fairly common but local breeding resident and summer visitor in W Pakistan and N nountains from N Pakistan to Bhutan. Winter visitor to Western Ghats

Habitat Rocky gorges; cliffs; old hill forts

Dusky-brown upperparts and crown; dark brown vings; dark, wedge-shaped tail spotted white on underside; pale chin and throat speckled darker graduating to pale buff-brown on breast and greyish-brown on belly. Pale chevron-shaped scalloping on ides of vent. Sexes similar. Juvenile has lighter throat nd indistinct mottling on underparts. Less slender han other species in this family. Feeds close to cliff aces; seen in pairs, or small groups.

DUSKY CRAG MARTIN

Ptyonoprogne concolor Hirundinidae

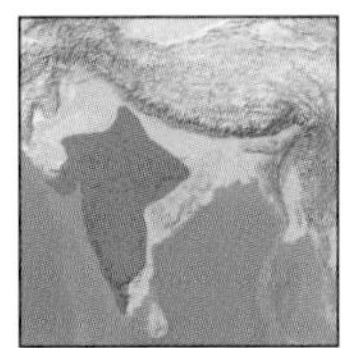

Size 13 cm

Voice Call a faint *chip…*, uncommonly uttered

Range Nearly, all over India, south of the Himalayan foothills, to about 1,500 m

Habitat Vicinity of ruins; old stone buildings in towns

Dark sooty-brown above; square-cut, short tail, with white spot on all but outermost and central tail feathers; paler underbody; faintly rufous chin and throat, with indistinct black streaking. Sexes alike. In small parties; flies around ruins, crags and old buildings, hawking insects in flight; acrobatic, swallow-like flight and appearance; rests during hot hours on rocky ledges or some corner.

RED-RUMPED SWALLOW

Cecropis daurica Hirundinidae

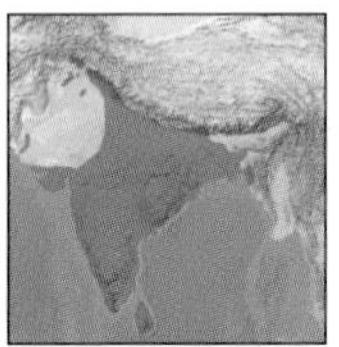

Size 18 cm

Voice Call a mournful chirping note. Pleasant twittering song of breeding male

Range Six races over the subcontinent, including Sri Lanka; resident, migratory

Habitat Cultivation; vicinity of human habitation; town centres; rocky hilly areas

Glossy steel-blue above; chestnut supercilium, head sides, neck-collar and rump; dull rufous-white below, streaked brown; deeply forked-tail diagnostic. Sexes alike. Small parties spend much of day on wing; migrant, winter-visiting race *nipalensis* highly gregarious; hawks insects along with other birds; freely perches on overhead wires, thin branches of bushes and trees; hunts insects amongst most-crowded areas of towns, over markets and refuse heaps, flying with amazing agility, wheeling, banking and stooping with remarkable mastery.

STRIATED SWALLOW

Cecropis striolata Hirundinidae

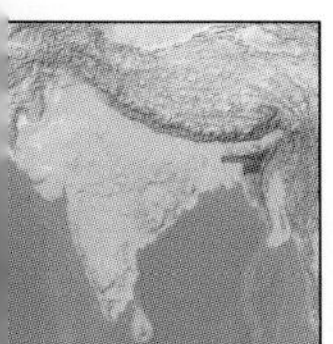

Size 19 cm

Voice Call a *pin* or long drawn-out *quitsch*, and *chi…chi… chi* when alarmed. Song a soft twittering

Range Hills of NE India and Bangladesh

Habitat Little information from the region; around steep cliffs in hills

Glossy steel-blue crown and back; indistinct, rufous hind-collar; narrowly streaked chestnut rump; deeply forked-tail; dark chestnut face and underwing-coverts. Similar to Red-rumped, but distinguished by larger size, stronger streaking on underparts and broader, blacker streaking on rump. Juvenile less glossy with paler rump. Feeds singly, or in small groups. Nest enclosed, with long tunnel, made of mud.

STREAK-THROATED SWALLOW

Petrochelidon fluvicola Hirundinidae

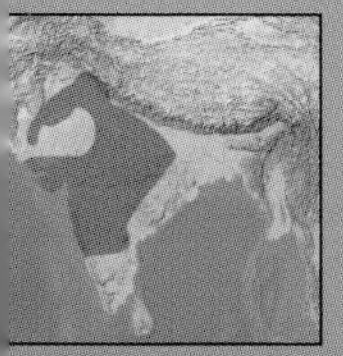

Size 12 cm

Voice Calls include *chrrp* and *trr…trr*

Range Locally common breeding resident in Indo-Gangetic Plains from E Pakistan to Uttar Pradesh and south through W peninsula to Karnataka. Mainly summer visitor to N areas

Habitat Open country, cultivation near water

juvenile

Glossy black upperparts; some whitish edges to dorsal feathers; dark-rufous crown; brownish rump; white underparts with black mesial streaks to feathers from throat to breast; pale brown underwing; tail slightly furcate, small whitish spot towards tip of inner web of each feather. Upto 200 birds nest communally on cliff faces.

COMMON HOUSE MARTIN

Delichon urbicum Hirundinidae

Size 14 cm

Voice Noisy. Calls include soft twittering chirps and short *prrit…prrit*

Range Local breeding summer visitor to N mountains from N Pakistan east to Himachal Pradesh. Scarce passage migrant throughout India, but perhaps overlooked because it flies so high. Some winter in Western Ghats

Habitat Mountain valleys with cultivation, cliffs and gorges

Adult has steel-blue upperparts and white underparts. Glossy bluish-black head; white rump and underwings conspicuous in flight; short legs with downy feathers; brown eyes; small black bill; deeply forked-tail. Sexes alike. Juvenile sooty-black, and wing-coverts, quills edged and tipped white. Sociable. In groups of several hundreds or even thousands of individuals. Spends time in open country. Cup-shaped nest made of mud and grass.

ASIAN HOUSE MARTIN

Delichon dasypus Hirundinidae

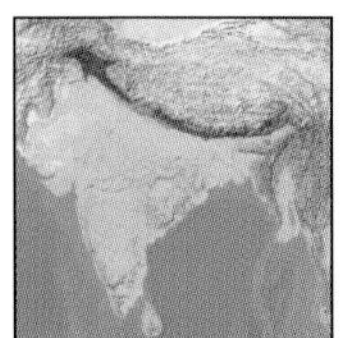

Size 12 cm

Voice Calls *jeep…jeep.* Twittering, trilling song

Range Pakistan to Myanmar; S Assam Hills

Habitat Mountain cliffs, gorges; steep, grassy hillsides; forest; cultivation; near watercourses; mountain settlements

Distinguished from Nepal by shallow fork to tail, blackish underwing-coverts, dirty-white rump and vent. Adult has blue cap, dark eye patch, dusky wash on whitish underparts; throat and vent whiter than breast and belly; duskier underparts; white vent; unmarked whiter throat; whiter, less marked rump. Feeds gregariously on aerial insects, often high in sky. Mixes with swifts and other swallows.

NEPAL HOUSE MARTIN

Delichon nipalense Hirundinidae

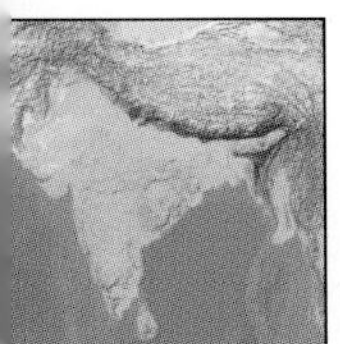

Size 12 cm

Voice Call a shrill *chee...ee.* Short song

Range Uttarakhand to Myanmar. S Assam Hills

Habitat Mountain cliffs, gorges, valleys, ridges; forest; hillside cultivation; along mountain rivers; villages

Smallish martin with square tail, dark underwings, black throat and vent. Blue cap; cheeks, chin and throat, upper breast streaked dark; dark underwing-coverts; white belly and breast. Similar to Asian House, but distinguished by no fork in tail, whiter underparts, darker chin, vent, undertail-coverts, underwing-coverts, and smaller white rump with black markings.

WHITE-BROWED TIT WARBLER

Leptopoecile sophiae Sylviidae

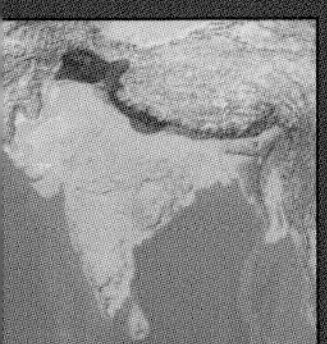

Size 10 cm

Voice Call a soft *teet* and hard *tzrit.* Loud chirping song

Range Locally common breeding resident in high mountains from N Pakistan east to W Nepal. Moves lower down in winter

Habitat Montane scrub, bushes by streams

One of the most difficult birds to see in the region. Very small, but distinctive, with obvious white supercilium. Rufous crown; greyish underparts, washed pinkish-blue; white outer-tail feathers; grey-brown mantle and wings; rump and flanks bluish; Female paler overall with greyish-brown head sides. Eastern race *sophiae* different from that of the west Himalayan *obscura.* Feeds on invertebrates in small parties or mixed hunting groups. Very active; rather shy. Cocks tail. Nests low down in bushes.

♀

JERDON'S BUSH LARK

Mirafra affinis Alaudidae

Stocky lark with large bill, short tail and wings, and relatively long legs. Narrow supercilium; buffish-grey-brown crown and nape with dark streaking; distinct yellow nape-band; pale grey ear-coverts, also streaked darker; rufous-buff upperparts; paler underparts, heavily spotted breast, rufous-patch on wing; rufous-buff outer webs to outer-tail feathers, and dark-centered-coverts and tertials.

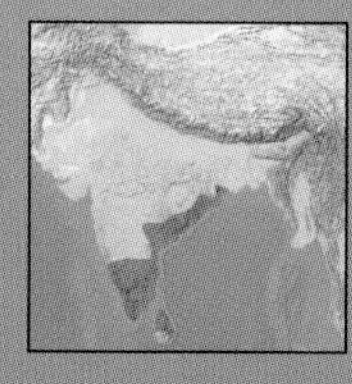

Size 14 cm

Voice Call a short, high-pitched trill. Dry, metallic rattle delivered from perch or during short song flight

Range Peninsular India and Sri Lanka

Habitat Dry open areas with bushes and trees

BENGAL BUSH LARK

Mirafra assamica Alaudidae

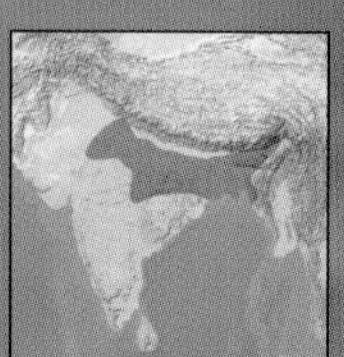

Size 15 cm

Voice Call a thin, high *p…zeee* or *tzee…tzee* delivered in high, circling song flight

Range Locally common breeding resident in N Indian plains from E Punjab to NE India and Bangladesh

Habitat Open grasslands, irrigated cultivation

Adult has weakly streaked, grey-brown crown and nape; pale indistinct supercilium; brownish ear-coverts; rufous-buff underparts, with diffused streaking on breast. Similar to Jerdon's Bush which is more brown and paler on belly. Nests on ground. Feeds on invertebrates and seeds on ground. Solitary, or in pairs.

SINGING BUSH LARK

Mirafra cantillans Alaudidae

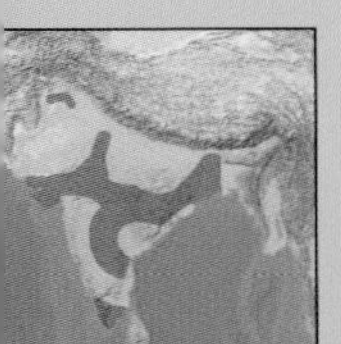

Size 14 cm

Voice High-pitched, Skylark-like song in air or from perch

Range Very local and patchily distributed breeding resident mainly in N and C peninsular India and parts of Pakistan and Bangladesh

Habitat Dry, open scrub, fallow and grasslands

Smallish lark with relatively short, stubby bill; prominent, pale supercilium and slight crest. Overall buff-brown; heavily streaked upperparts; brownish-buff ear-coverts; long tail with white outer-tail feathers; light rufous wing edgings. Buff underparts; white throat; fine streaks on breast sides; relatively long tail. Rufous wing patches visible in flight. Sexes alike. Feeds singly, or in pairs. Flies rapidly into cover when flushed. Often perches on top of low bushes if disturbed, or to sing. Nests on ground.

INDIAN BUSH LARK

Mirafra erythroptera Alaudidae

The word erythroptera i.e. red-winged in its Latin name, is for its prominent rufous-coloured primaries. Overall brown lark with prominent dark streaks and heavily spotted breast; cheek patch bounded by white supercilium; dark buff outer-tail feathers; whitish, unstreaked belly; stout bill and shortish tail. Sexes alike. Feeds on invertebrates and seeds on ground; in pairs, or small groups, when disturbed. Nests on ground.

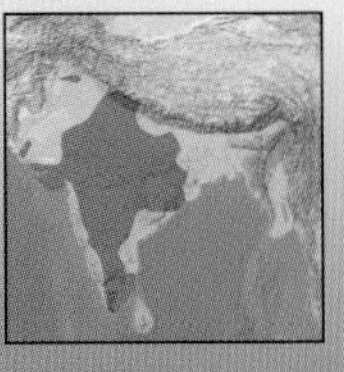

Size 14 cm

Voice Calls include *sweee* and *trrr… weet*. Song a whistling *tit… tit…tit tsweeh… tsweeh…tsweeh*, starts from top of bush and continues in parachuting song flight. Often sings at night

Range Locally common endemic breeding resident in plains of N and C India from S Punjab to Odisha and in W, N Tamil Nadu. Also in parts of Pakistan. Absent from SE, NE, Nepal, Bangladesh and Sri Lanka

Habitat Sparse rocky scrub and barren flats

GREATER HOOPOE LARK

Alaemon alaudipes Alaudidae

Size 19 cm

Voice Song a series of flute-like whistles

Range Pakistan and Rann of Kutch, Gujarat

Habitat Extensive areas of arid desert, especially low sand dunes and barren clay flats

Overall sandy-brown lark with elongated body and long legs. Long decurved bill; prominent white supercilium, black eye-stripe and moustachial stripe; faint black malar stripe. Creamy white underparts with darkly spotted breast. Striking wing pattern, white at base and tips of black primaries and secondaries showing as bands across wings, visible in flight. Sexes similar, but male smaller with shorter bill. Juvenile similar to adult but with less-defined markings on head; shorter, pinkish beak.

BIMACULATED LARK

Melanocorypha bimaculata Alaudidae

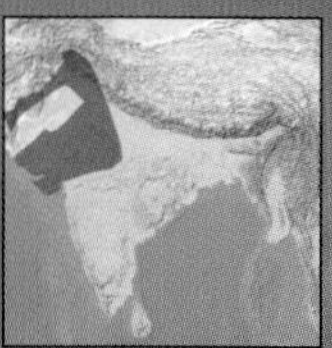

Size 17 cm

Voice Call a guttural *prrp* or *chirp*

Range Mainly Pakistan, also NW and N India (from Jammu and Kashmir south to N Maharashtra and east to Uttar Pradesh)

Habitat Semi-desert; paddy stubbles; fallow fields; edges of jheels and dry coastal mudflats

Large, stout-billed and stocky lark with long, broad-based wings and relatively short tail; prominent white supercilium and eye-ring. Grey-brown heavily streaked upperparts; pale brown to creamy underparts; blackish-brown, crescent-shaped patch on side of breast, dark grey underwing lacking white trailing edge, whitish tip to tail. Sexes similar, but female slightly smaller. Juvenile appears scalier above. Crouches motionless on ground; forages for seeds and invertebrates.

TIBETAN LARK

Melanocorypha maxima Alaudidae

Large brown lark, with small head, long neck and long, pale decurved bill. Upperparts mottled and streaked dark brown with dark-centred median coverts and variable blackish-patches on breast sides. Greyish-buff below with breast streaking. White trailing edges to secondaries and white tail-tip. Sexes alike. Feeds on invertebrates and seeds on ground. Twitches wings when singing. Confiding.

Size 21 cm

Voice Calls *tchu lip*. Song slow and hesitant

Range Local breeding resident on high plateaux of Ladakh and Sikkim

Habitat Montane grassy marshes

RUFOUS-TAILED LARK

Ammomanes phoenicura Alaudidae

Dark brown upperparts; rufous-brown underparts, with brown streaks on throat, breast; rich rufous tail with black band across tip diagnostic. Sexes alike. Pairs when breeding in small flocks during winter, occasionally with other larks; difficult to locate because of dull colouration; mostly keeps to ground, running about erratically; flies short distance if disturbed; as with several other larks, sudden appearance and disappearance of this species in many localities.

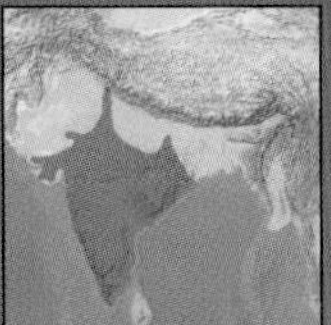

Size 16 cm

Voice Song a mix of rich whistling notes and chirps; sings on wing and from perch on earth mounds, stones or low bush

Range Commoner east from Kutch to around Delhi; east to West Bengal and south to N Andhra Pradesh

Habitat Cultivation; fallow ground; open riversides

DESERT LARK

Ammomanes deserti Alaudidae

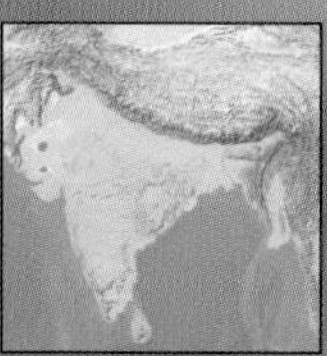

Size 17 cm

Voice Song comprises well-spaced, rising and falling, flute-like whistles

Range Mainly Pakistan and W Rajasthan

Habitat Low, very arid, rocky foothills, nullahs; also fallow land in desert-canal cultivation

Medium-sized, robust lark with relatively large head, rather thick yellow bill, longish wings with long primaries. Adult has brownish-grey upperparts and pinkish-brown upperparts. Diffuse streaking on breast; rufous on wings and uppertail-coverts; reddish-brown tail with diffused dark terminal band. Sexes alike. Juvenile lacks blackish centre on tail. Male attracts mate by singing in flight. Nests on ground. Forages for small seeds and insects on ground.

GREATER SHORT-TOED LARK

Calandrella brachydactyla Alaudidae

Size 15 cm

Voice Soft, dry rippling *chirip* and *dyu* often combined. Flocks call constantly in flight

Range Locally common, often numerous, winter visitor to lowlands of Pakistan, Nepal, Bangladesh and India south to Madhya Pradesh

Habitat Dry pasture; stubble; fallow; semi-desert; dry mudflats

Medium-sized, heavily streaked lark, without crest. Sandy-brown and sometimes brownish-black upperparts. Fine streaks on forehead; flattish head; dark cap; pale lores; short, pointed, pale pinkish bill; two black breast patches. Whitish underparts; short dark tail. Sexes alike. Juvenile has dark brown feathers edged buff. Bold, undulating flight. Imitates calls of other birds.

HUME'S SHORT-TOED LARK

Calandrella acutirostris Alaudidae

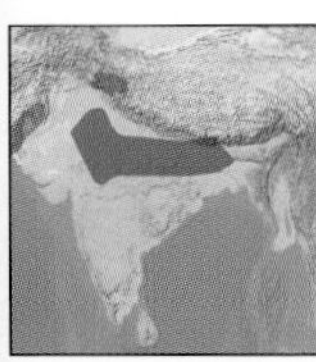

Size 14 cm

Voice Call a rolling *tyrrr*

Range Locally common breeding summer visitor to N hills from E Balochistan to Sikkim

Habitat Montane semi-desert, rocky hills to breed

Similar to Greater Short-toed, but with darker, greyer upperparts and breast and remaining underparts white; finer bill with more black culmen and tip; less prominently streaked crown and forecrown; less-defined supercilium and pale crescent below eye. Dark loral-stripe; rufous-washed uppertail-coverts; dark neck patch; unstreaked buff-grey breast. Sexes alike. Winters on open grass flats, river sandbanks, fallow and semi-desert. Feeds on seeds and insects on ground in large flocks.

SAND LARK

Calandrella raytal Alaudidae

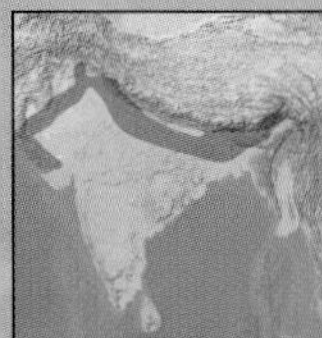

Size 12 cm

Voice Call a deep *prrr…prrr*. Song delivered from ground or in flight, a rapid, undulating and repeated series of warbles

Range Locally common breeding resident along rivers of Pakistan and N India east to Assam and Bangladesh. Also NW coasts

Habitat Sandy, muddy rivers; lake banks, islands. Also coastal flats and sand dunes

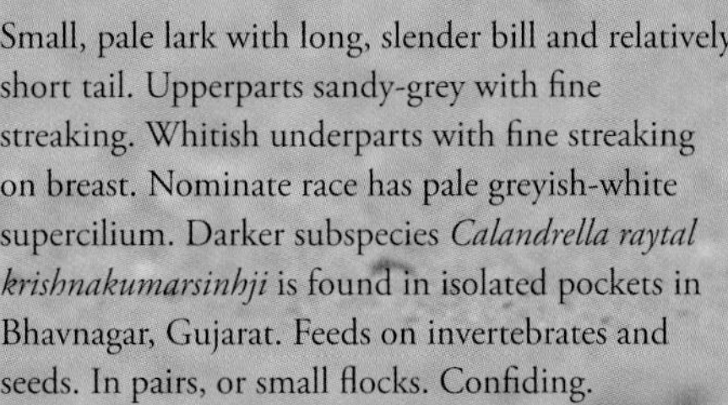

Small, pale lark with long, slender bill and relatively short tail. Upperparts sandy-grey with fine streaking. Whitish underparts with fine streaking on breast. Nominate race has pale greyish-white supercilium. Darker subspecies *Calandrella raytal krishnakumarsinhji* is found in isolated pockets in Bhavnagar, Gujarat. Feeds on invertebrates and seeds. In pairs, or small flocks. Confiding.

♀

ASIAN SHORT-TOED LARK

Calandrella cheleensis Alaudidae

Size 13 cm

Voice Songs highly variable

Range Winters to lowland Pakistan, straying to W India

Habitat As Greater's, but less gregarious in winter

Recently split from the Lesser Short-toed, almost impossible to tell them apart in field. Also confused with the Greater and Hume's. Little known but supposedly rare to our region. Small, nondescript, stocky lark. Pale underparts with light streaking on head, breast and flanks; short, heavy bill. Long primaries. Juvenile has white-spotted upperparts.

CRESTED LARK

Galerida cristata Alaudidae

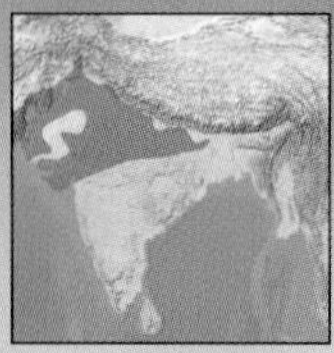

Size 18 cm

Voice Ordinary call note a pleasant *tee…ur…* . Short song of male during soaring display flight

Range N, NW India, Gangetic Plain; Rajasthan, Saurashtra, N Madhya Pradesh

Habitat Semi-desert; cultivation; dry grassy areas

Similar to Eurasian, but paler and weaker streaking on plumage. Sandy-brown above, streaked blackish; pointed, upstanding crest distinctive; brown tail has dull rufous outer feathers; whitish and dull yellowish-brown below, breast streaked dark brown. Sexes alike. In small flocks, breaking into pairs when breeding; runs briskly on ground, pointed crest carried upstanding; also settles on bush-tops, stumps, wire fences and overhead wires.

MALABAR LARK

Galerida malabarica Alaudidae

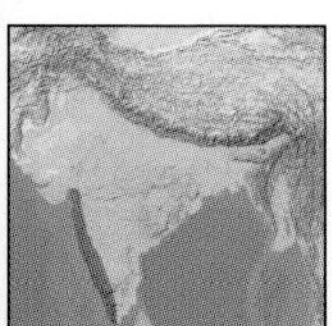

Size 15 cm

Voice Calls *chew…chew…yu.* Song similar to Crested's

Range Locally common endemic breeding resident in plains and hills of Western Ghats and W coast from Gujarat south to Kerala

Habitat Dry open habitats, preferably with some scrubs and rocks; cultivation; grassy hillsides and open scrub

Sturdy, medium-sized lark with prominent, long, spiky crest and short tail. Similar to Sykes's, but smaller. Reddish-brown upperparts boldly streaked black. Underparts pale rufous-buff with black streaking on breast. Pale rufous outer-tail feathers and large bill. Sexes similar. Very confiding, usually crouching if alarmed. Sings from perch or in short song flight. Nests on ground. Feeds on seeds and invertebrates on ground. In pairs, solitary or in small flocks.

SYKES'S LARK

Galerida deva Alaudidae

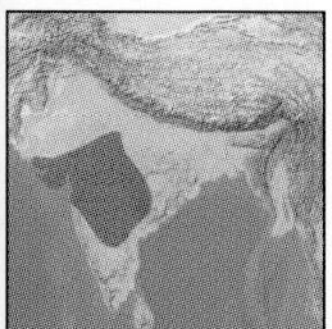

Size 14 cm

Voice Call a nasal *dwezee*. Song similar to Indian Bushlark's

Range Local endemic breeding resident in Deccan from Gujarat and S Uttar Pradesh south to N Karnataka and Andhra Pradesh

Habitat Dry stony grasslands; open scrub, arable cultivation. Often on dark soils

Small lark with spiky crest, inconspicuous when folded. Overall buff plumage, heavily streaked with black; pale buff supercilium. Underparts tawny-brown with some streaking on breast; rufous-buff outer feathers; short bill. Sexes alike. Feeds on invertebrates and seeds singly, in pairs or small parties. Fairly approachable. Nests on ground.

ORIENTAL SKYLARK

Alauda gulgula Alaudidae

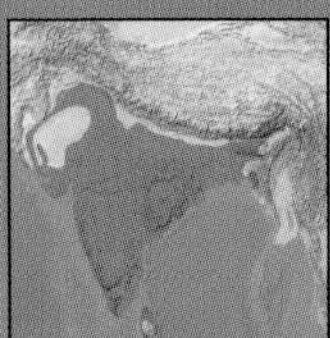

Size 16 cm

Voice Longish, pleasant warble of male, often imitations of other bird calls thrown in. Sings usually when soaring high

Range All over India

Habitat Grasslands; cultivation; mudflats; fallow lands

Similar to Eurasian; brownish above, feathers edged yellow-brown with black centres; short, indistinct crest, not often visible; dark brown tail with pale-buff outer feathers; dull-buff below; more yellowish-brown on breast, faintly streaked and spotted darker. Sexes alike. Pairs, or small parties on ground, runs in short spurts; squats when approached and flies low at the last moment.

EURASIAN SKYLARK

Alauda arvensis Alaudidae

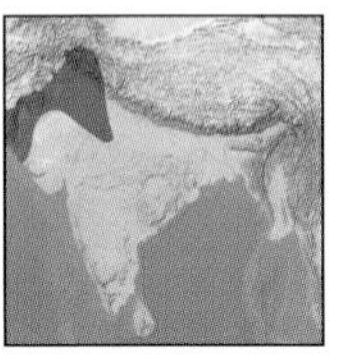

Size 18 cm

Voice Call a loud, dry *chirrup* or musical *truee*, often repeated with variants. Famous, continuous song delivered in towering song-flight

Range Locally common but rather erratic winter visitor to lowlands of Pakistan and N India east to Uttar Pradesh and south to Rajasthan

Habitat Fallow, stubble and young cereal cultivation

Medium to large lark, with short crest streaked brown. Seasonal and geographic colour variation on upperparts, ranging from rust-brown to buff grey. Stocky body; long tail; short, stout bill; heavily streaked plumage; pale, indistinct supercilium. Distinctive white outer-tail feathers. Sexes similar. Sociable. In large flocks, including other larks, finches and pipits. Fast runner, when alarmed. Feeds on invertebrates and seeds on ground. Frequently dust-bathes. Often in large flocks. Rather shy and flighty.

BLACK-CROWNED SPARROW LARK

Eremopterix nigriceps Alaudidae

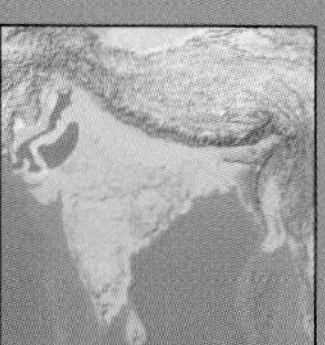

Size 13 cm

Voice Song a short, repeated, warbled *dwee…di…ul…twee…eh* followed by lower-pitched *de…e…e…e…h, de…e…e…e…h*

Range Pakistan and NW India

Habitat Arid regions, sandy deserts

Small, short-tailed and broad-winged lark with short bill. Adult male has sandy-brown upperparts, large white-patch on ckeeks and forehead; black underwing-coverts distinct in flight. Unmistakable black throat, centre of crown, and entire underparts; unstreaked belly. Female and juvenile indistinct sandy-brown with weak streaking on crown, nape and breast. Sociable; in small flocks outside breeding.

ASHY-CROWNED SPARROW LARK

Eremopterix griseus Alaudidae

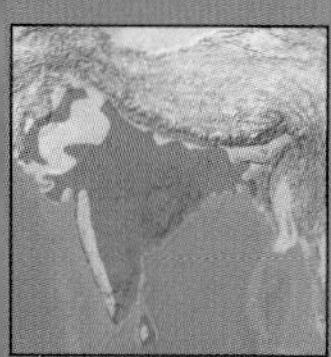

Size 12 cm

Voice Pleasant, monotonous trilling song by male; sings on wing and on ground

Range Almost across India, south of the Himalayan foothills; moves during rains; uncommon in heavy rainfall areas

Habitat Open scrub; semi-cultivation; fallow river basins; tidal mudflats

Adult male has pale greyish-brown forehead and crown; sandy-brown upperparts; white cheeks and breast sides; dark chocolate-brown sides of face and most of underbody; dark brown tail with whitish outer feathers. Female sandy-brown overall; dull rufous sides of face and underbody. Mostly loose flocks, scattered over area; pairs, or small parties when breeding. Feeds on ground; fond of dusty areas, where large numbers may squat about. Sandy colouration makes it impossible to spot birds, but when disturbed, large numbers suddenly take wing; striking display flight of male.

HORNED LARK

Eremophila alpestris Alaudidae

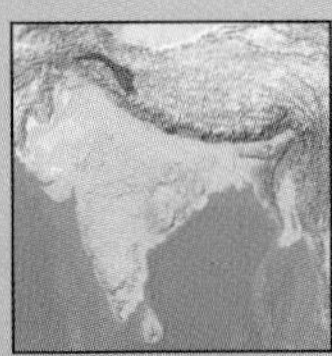

Size 19 cm

Voice Call a somewhat plaintive, soft *tsee…n…* . High-pitched, squeaky song of breeding male (May-August)

Range High mountain bird; from Chitral, Gilgit east through Ladakh, Lahaul, Spiti to Bhutan and E India

Habitat Open barren areas; scrub; meadows

Adult male has pinkish-brown upperparts and white underparts; black crown-band with conspicuous black 'horns' on either side; dull yellow-white face, throat; black cheeks and breast-band (gorget) separated by narrow white band distinctive; western race *albigula* of Gilgit and Chitral has black cheeks continuous with black gorget. Female has crown streaked black; overall less black, duller-black cheeks, gorget; tiny 'horns'. Juvenile duller and has spotted plumage.

ZITTING CISTICOLA

Cisticola juncidis Cisticolidae

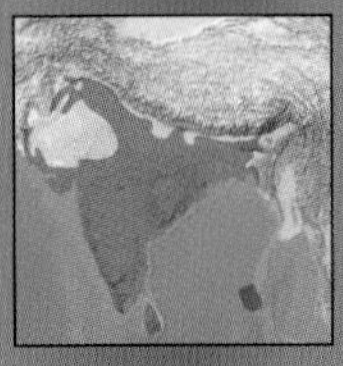

Size 10 cm

Voice Call a sharp, clicking *zit… zit*, continuous during display in air

Range Subcontinent, south of the Himalayan foothills; absent in extreme NW Rajasthan

Habitat Open country; grass; cultivation; reed beds; also coastal lagoons

Rufous-brown upperparts, prominently streaked darker; rufous-buff, unstreaked rump; white tips to fan-shaped tail diagnostic; buffy-white underbody, more rufous on flanks. Diagnostic calls. Sexes alike. Seen in pairs, or several birds over open expanse; great skulker, lurking in low growth; usually seen during short, jerky flights, low over ground; soon dives into cover; most active when breeding, during rains; striking display of male, soaring erratically, falling and rising, incessantly uttering sharp, creaking note; adult arrives on nest in similar fashion.

non-breeding

BRIGHT-HEADED CISTICOLA

Cisticola exilis Cisticolidae

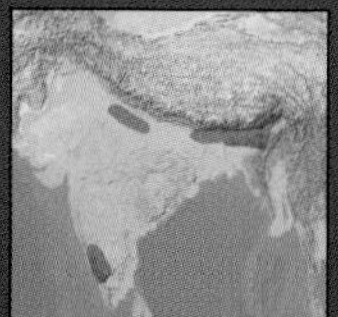

Size 10 cm

Voice Calls *nyaae*. Sings from perch or in rapid display flight, *bzzeee…joo…ee*

Range Scarce and local breeding resident in N Terai from Uttarakhand east to Arunachal Pradesh, NE plains and hills including parts of Bangladesh and SW hills

Habitat Tall, dry grasslands and scrubs, usually on hillsides. Drier habitat than Zitting's

Small cisticola with short, rounded tail in breeding and slightly longer in non-breeding. Similar to Zitting, in non-breeding plumage, but unstreaked, chestnut hindneck, supercilium and rump and indistinct brownish tips to tail diagnostic. Breeding male has bright golden-orange head, throat and breast (unstreaked, creamy crown in the NE, chestnut in Western Ghats). Sexes alike. Behaviour and food as Zitting's but display flight less bouncy and ends with steep dive. Low flight more direct. Nests in grass. Uses spiders' threads to stitch together nest.

RUFOUS-VENTED PRINIA

Prinia burnesii Cisticolidae

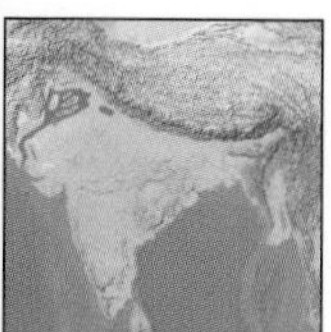

Size 17 cm

Voice Song a rising and falling, clear, high-pitched warbling, very different from other prinias except Swamp

Range Indus plains in Pakistan, N India and SE Nepal

Habitat Tall grasslands; reed beds

Large, long-tailed prinia. Streaked upperparts; greyish wash to crown; warm rufous-brown wash to nape and upper mantle; whitish throat, breast, lores and eye-ring; indistinct collar; rufous undertail-coverts; dark streaking on flanks. Juvenile an even sandy grey-brown, with indistinct streaking. *Prinia burnesii nipalensis* is a resident of Koshi Tappu Wildlife Reserve in Nepal. Other subspecies *Prinia burnesii burnesii* is found in Pakistan and Harike in Punjab.

SWAMP PRINIA

Prinia b cinerascens Cisticolidae

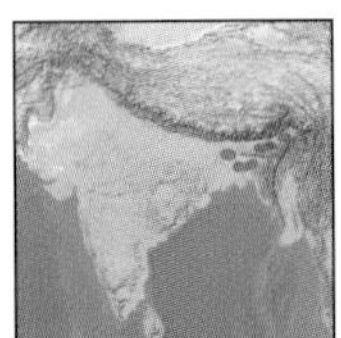

Size 15 cm

Voice Song an elaborate warble, resembling Rufous-vented's, but longer, more varied and faster

Range Brahmaputra plains in NE India and Bangladesh

Habitat Elephant grass in swamps and by large rivers

Recently separated from Rufous-vented. Olive-grey streaked upperparts; bold streaking on forehead; narrow, whitish eye-ring and dirty-white lores. Less distinct collar than Rufous-vented. Greyish-white underparts, largely unstreaked; grey flanks, and undertail-coverts; greyish-brown flight feathers. Larger than similar Graceful, but has broader tail with no white tips or dark subterminal spots.

BLACK-THROATED PRINIA

Prinia atrogularis Cisticolidae

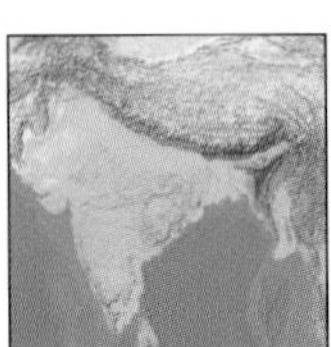

Size 17 cm

Voice Call includes buzzing, scraping notes

Range E Nepal, Bhutan, Arunachal Pradesh and S Assam Hills

Habitat Forest edges; clearings; grassy hillsides; scrubs; hillside cultivation

Large, plain prinia, with very long tail. Breeding adult has black throat and upper breast; black-and-white spotting on breast; prominent, long, white moustachial stripe; greyish face; grey-brown upperparts; fulvous-buff flanks; whitish centre of belly. Non-breeding adult has unstreaked upperparts; white supercilium; paler buff below, with varying degrees of dark streaking and mottling. Typical prinia-like skulking behaviour; very active ascending, than descending. In bushes, and undergrowth; breeding male sings from exposed perches.

khasiana

STRIATED PRINIA

Prinia crinigera Cisticolidae

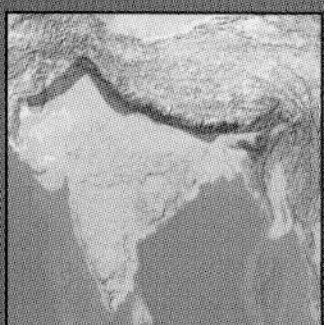

Size 16 cm

Voice Calls include grating *chitzweet… chitzweet* and hard *chak*

Range Common breeding resident in N hills from Pakistan east to Myanmar border. Moves lower down to foothills in winter

Habitat Grassy and scrub-covered hillsides and terraced cultivation

Fairly large, drab-looking hill warbler with long, graduated, pointed tail. Breeding male greyish-brown with dark streaking; darker lores. Underparts dirty-white, speckled dark. Non-breeding male more rufous-brown with light streaking on head, breast and upperparts; buffish lores and eye-ring. Indistinct dark tips to tail, dark strong bill and flesh-coloured legs. Sexes alike, but female slightly smaller. Juvenile overall more olive-brown above and yellowish wash to underparts. Usually solitary, or in pairs; feeds low down on insects and quite skulking. Male sings openly from bush-tops and wires. Nests low down in cover.

GREY-CROWNED PRINIA

Prinia cinereocapilla Cisticolidae

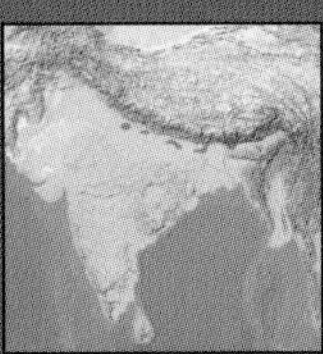

Size 11 cm

Voice Song a squeezed-out *cheeeeeeeesum… zip…zip…zip*

Range The Himalayan foothills and Assam

Habitat Bushes at forest edges and secondary growth. Globally threatened

Medium to small grass prinia with short, rounded wings. Ashy-grey crown; rufous wash to forehead; thin, rufous supercilium (absent in breeding); dark grey lores; ashy-grey ear-coverts. Warm rufous upperparts; fulvous underparts. Long, thin, slightly decurved bill; pale yellowish-brown legs; graduated tail with subterminal bands. Considered rare, numbers in rapid decline due to habitat loss. No longer found in many earlier breeding areas.

RUFOUS-FRONTED PRINIA

Prinia buchanani Cisticolidae

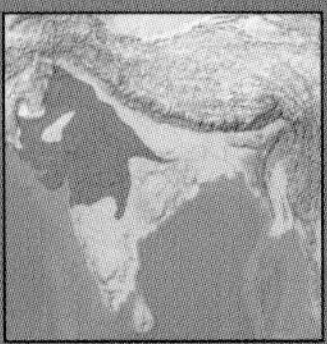

Size 12 cm

Voice Song a *chid-le-weest* followed by repetitive *chidle… ee…chidle…ee*

Range Pakistan and NW, C India

Habitat Scrubs in semi-desert

Medium to small-sized, overall pale-looking prinia with short, rounded wings. Long, dark brown, graduated tail with broad, white tips to outer feathers, conspicuous in flight. Greyish-brown upperparts (greyer in non-breeding); rufous-washed forehead and crown; dark brown flight feathers. Underparts almost completely white with slight rufescent wash on flanks, undertail-coverts and vent. Juvenile similar to adult, but rufous on crown absent.

RUFESCENT PRINIA

Prinia rufescens Cisticolidae

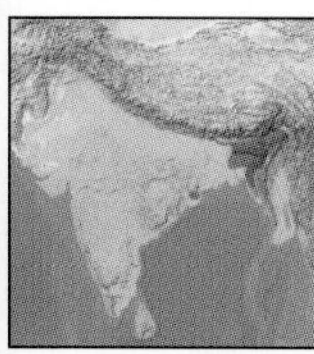

Size 11 cm

Voice Call a buzzing *peez… eez…eez…eez.* Song a rhythmic *chewp…chewp…chewp*

Range The Himalayas in Nepal and from Sikkim east to Arunachal Pradesh; hills of NE India and Bangladesh; Simlipal hills, Odisha and Andhra Pradesh

Habitat Tall grasslands; grass under deciduous forests; bushes around terraced cultivation; open wooded areas; secondary growth and edges of forests

Rather plain-looking, dull-coloured prinia. Short, rounded wings; white lores and supercilium; medium-sized, graduated tail with buffish-white tips and subterminal band on outer feathers; uppertail more chestnut brown. Breeding adult has rufous brown upperparts; greyish-brown nape and ear-coverts. Underparts dirty-white with yellowish-beige wash on belly, undertail-coverts and flanks. Thin, longish, decurved bill. Non-breeding adult has rufous-brown crown and ear-coverts and longer tail.

GREY-BREASTED PRINIA

Prinia hodgsonii Cisticolidae

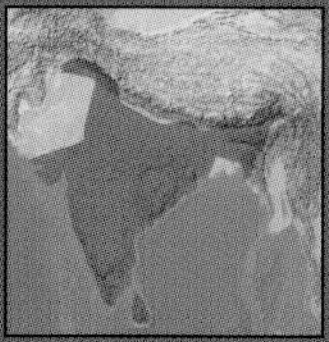

Size 11 cm

Voice Noisy when breeding. Longish, squeaky song; contact calls, almost continuous squeaking

Range All over India, S Himalayan foothills upto about 1,800 m; absent in arid W Rajasthan

Habitat Edges of forests; cultivation; gardens; scrub, often in and around habitation

Grey-brown, with some rufous above; long grey tail, tipped black-and-white; white underbody; when breeding, soft grey breast-band diagnostic. Sexes alike. Small bands always on the move; keeps to low growth but often clambers into middle levels; singing male may climb to tops of trees; few nearly always present in mixed hunting parties. Confiding.

GRACEFUL PRINIA

Prinia gracilis Cisticolidae

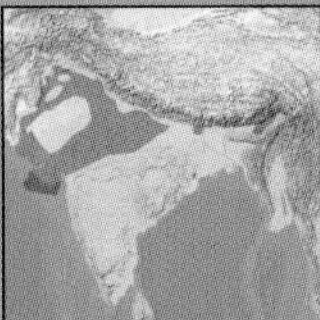

Size 13 cm

Voice *Szeep…szip…* call note. Longish warble when breeding; wing-snapping and jumping display of male

Range NW Himalayan foothills, Terai, south to Gujarat, across Gangetic Plain

Habitat Scrub; grass; canal banks; semi-desert

Dull grey-brown above, streaked darker; very pale around eyes; long, graduated tail, faintly cross-barred, tipped white; whitish underbody, buffy on belly. Plumage more rufous in winter. Sexes alike. Small parties move in low growth; usually does not associate with other birds; restless, flicks wings and tail often; occasionally hunts like flycatcher.

JUNGLE PRINIA

Prinia sylvatica Cisticolidae

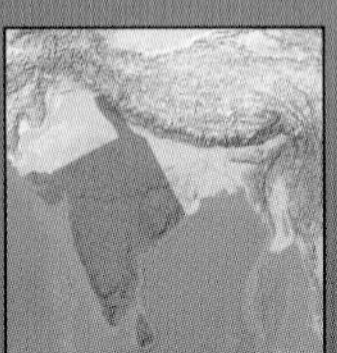

Size 15 cm

Voice Song a loud, rhythmic *zee…tu…zee…tu*

Range Locally common endemic breeding resident in lowlands and hills throughout most of India and Sri Lanka. Rare in NW India

Habitat Dry scrub and grass, often in rocky areas

Medium to large-sized, plain-looking prinia with long, graduated tail and a long, stout bill. Short supercilium; red iris. Breeding adult has dark grey-brown upperparts and creamy white underparts. Prominent white tips and whitish outer feathers on tail. More rufous-brown in non-breeding plumage. Sexes similar. Short supercilium and voice distinguish it from similar, but smaller, Plain. In pairs, or small parties. Feeds on insects low down but sings from high perch. Secretive but will appear in open briefly. Nests low down. Often seen with other prinias and babblers.

ASHY PRINIA

Prinia socialis Cisticolidae

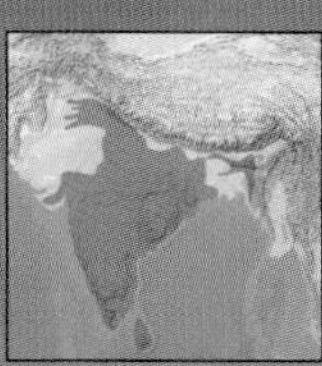

Size 13 cm

Voice Nasal *pee…pee…pee…* song. Loud and lively *jivee… jivee…jivee…* or *jimmy…jimmy…*, rather like Common Tailorbird's in quality, but easily identifiable once heard

Range Subcontinent south of the Himalayan foothills, upto about 1,400 m; absent in W Rajasthan

Habitat Cultivation; edges of forests; scrubs; parks; vicinity of habitation

Adult has rich, ashy-grey upperparts and rufous wings. Long, graduated, white-tipped tail with black subterminal spots; short, black bill; whitish lores; grey crown. Underparts dull rufous. In winter, less ashy, more rufous-brown; longer tail; whitish chin and throat. Sexes alike. Solitary, or in pairs. Common and familiar as Common Tailorbird in some areas; actively moves in undergrowth; hops on ground foraging for insects. Often flicks and erects tail; typical jerky flight when flying from bush to bush; noisy and excited when breeding. Delivers song from perch on bush. Nests close to ground, on shrubs or tall grass.

YELLOW-BELLIED PRINIA

Prinia flaviventris Cisticolidae

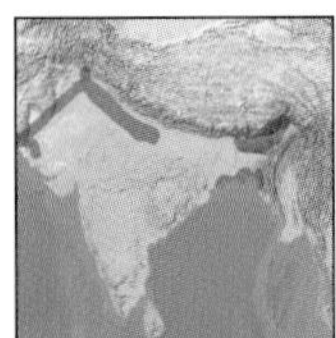

Size 13 cm

Voice Calls include *tzee* and *chink… chink.* Song a musical *twee…dulu…lu…lee*, often from high reed. Snaps wings

Range Locally common breeding resident in N river valleys in Indo-Gangetic Plain and the NE including Bangladesh coast

Habitat Reed beds; tall grass and tamarisk scrub near water

Small to medium-sized warbler with short, rounded wings and long, graduated tail (shorter in breeding). Upperparts olive-grey; grey crown; distinct white supercilium and eye-ring; creamy white chin and breast; yellow belly and vent. Sexes alike. Active, inquisitive and confiding, often appearing high on reed stem to look around and call. Feeds on insects low in cover; usually solitary, or in pairs. Nests low down.

PLAIN PRINIA

Prinia inornata Cisticolidae

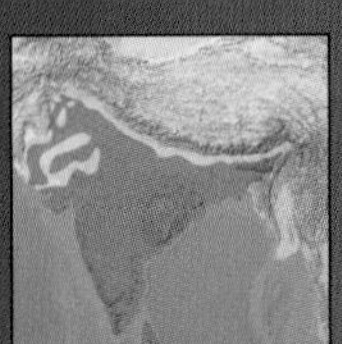

Size 13 cm

Voice Call a plaintive *tee…tee;* also *krrik…krrik* sound. Wheezy song, very insect-like in quality

Range Subcontinent, from Terai and Gangetic Plain southwards; absent in W Rajasthan

Habitat Tall cultivation; grass; scrubs; prefers damp areas

Pale brown upperparts; whitish supercilium and lores; dark wings and tail; long, graduated tail, with buff tips and white outer feathers; buff-white underbody; tawny flanks and belly. In winter, more rufous above. Sexes alike. Pairs, or several, move about in low growth; skulker, difficult to see; jerky, low flight, soon vanishing into bush; tail often flicked. Similar to Jungle but smaller and with shorter tail.

MOUNTAIN TAILORBIRD

Phyllergates cuculatus Cettiidae

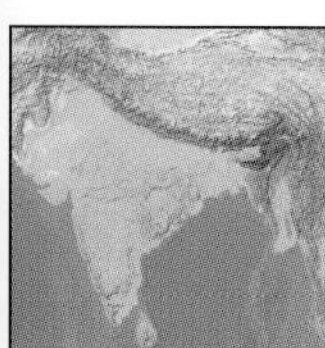

Size 13 cm

Voice Alarm call a *kiz...kiz...kiz*. Song a high, musical whistle

Range E Nepal, Bhutan, Arunachal Pradesh, Assam and S Assam Hills

Habitat Forest undergrowth; bamboo, grass thickets; secondary growth

Brightly-coloured tailorbird, with distinct markings. Rich rufous crown and forehead; dark grey nape and hindcrown; thin white supercilium and eye-ring; yellow above eye; dark grey eye-stripe and lores. Upperparts olive green; yellow belly, flanks and undertail-coverts; grey sides of throat and breast with some mottling; paler grey centre of throat; dark brown tail, edged olive. Solitary, in pairs or small parties. Active in lower forest storeys; occasional aerial sallies. Skulks. Strong, direct, short flights.

COMMON TAILORBIRD

Orthotomus sutorius Cisticolidae

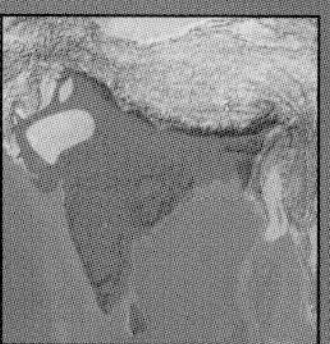

Size 13 cm

Voice Very vocal. Call a loud, familiar *towit...towit*. Song a rapid version of call, with slight change, loud *chuvee... chuvee...chuvee*, uttered for upto seven minutes at a stretch; male sings on exposed perch

Range Subcontinent to about 2,000 m in outer Himalayas

Habitat Forests; cultivation; habitation

breeding

Olive-green above; rust-red forecrown; buffy-white underbody; dark spot on throat sides, best seen in calling male; long, pointed tail, often held erect; central tail feathers about 5 cm longer and pointed in breeding male. Sexes alike. One of India's best-known birds; found usually in pairs; rather common amidst habitation, but keeps to bushes in gardens; remains unseen even when at arm's length, but very vocal; tail often cocked, carried almost to back; clambers up into trees more than other related warblers.

DARK-NECKED TAILORBIRD

Orthotomus atrogularis Cisticolidae

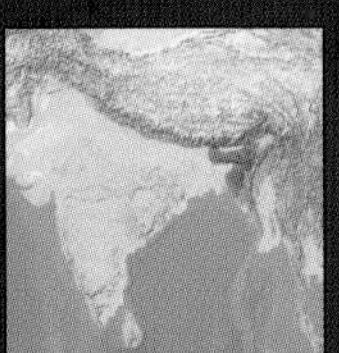

Size 13 cm

Voice Calls include loud, nasal *krrri...krrri... krrri* and *tew*

Range Scarce and local breeding resident in plains and lower hills of NE India and Bangladesh

Habitat Dense scrub; forest undergrowth, edges of forests

Small, greenish warbler with long-tail. Breeding male has dark throat patch and longer tail. Non-breeding male similar to female, but with stronger streaking on throat and breast. Very similar to Common but more extensive chestnut crown and lores; yellow vent and bend of wings. Behaves and nests as Common but much less confiding. Call attracts attention.

CRESTED FINCHBILL

Spizixos canifrons Pycnonotidae

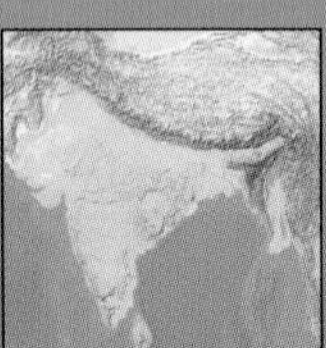

Size 22 cm

Voice Call a long, dry bubbling trill *purr...purr...prruitprruit...prruit.* Long, dry warble

Range Hills of NE India upto 3,000 m

Habitat Secondary growth, thickets; glades

Medium to large bulbul with short, pale, conical bill. Dark grey head, pale grey forehead, chin, throat, mask and hindcrown; dark brown iris; pinkish feet; broad, black terminal band on tail. Yellowish-green underparts. Juvenile has more green tinge to head and shorter greenish crest and brownish breast-band. Noisy, conspicuous. In flocks, in non-breeding season. Forages high in trees, also bushes and undergrowth.

GREY-HEADED BULBUL

Pycnonotus priocephalus Pycnonotidae

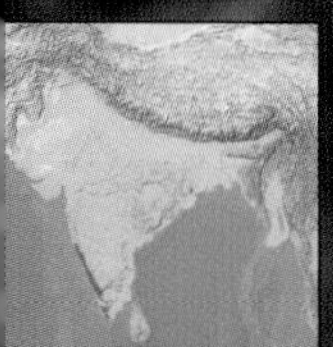

Size 19 cm

Voice Calls include *chalk*, a buzzing *dzee* and high *tweep*

Range Locally common endemic breeding resident of forests of SW India from Goa southwards

Habitat Moist broadleaved evergreen forests with bamboo and dense undergrowth

Overall olive-green bulbul with bluish-grey head and pale yellow bill. Grey forehead; yellow wash on grey cheeks; dark greyish-black chin; similar coloured barring on lower back and rump with broad, pale yellow tips; bluish-grey uppertail-coverts and middle tail feathers; outer-tail feathers broadly edged with grey. Underparts more olive-yellow; grey undertail-coverts. Sexes alike. Juvenile has duller yellow on forehead and dark olive head.

BLACK-HEADED BULBUL

Pycnonotus atriceps Pycnonotidae

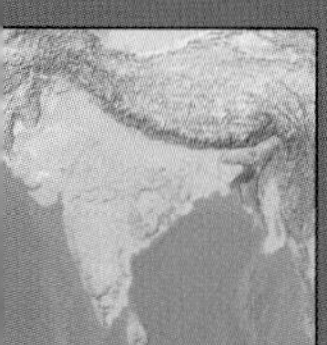

Size 18 cm

Voice Calls include plaintive whistle *whiwhi…tyee* and metallic *chirp*

Range Locally common breeding resident in Bangladesh. Status uncertain in neighbouring parts of NE India and in Andaman Islands

Habitat Open forests; scrubs; gardens

juvenile

adult

Medium-sized bird, more heard than seen. No crest; glossy, black head and throat; broad, yellow tip to tail with dark subterminal band, diagnostic. Dark olive-green upperparts with bright yellowish-green wing patches and uniform yellow underparts. More greyish-yellow in some birds. Pale blue iris. Sexes alike. In pairs, or small flocks of six to eight. Nests low down in thick cover. Feeds on fruits and insects at all levels.

ANDAMAN BULBUL

Pycnonotus (atriceps) fuscoflavescens Pycnonotidae

Small bulbul, similar to Black-headed, but distinguished by dark olive-green head, dull black throat and forehead. Olive-yellow breast and belly; dull olive wings; yellow tip to tail with dark subterminal band. Male has brighter olive upperparts and brighter yellower underparts than female. Juvenile similar to female. Usually in pairs and sometimes in mixed feeding parties; often inconspicuous.

Size 17 cm

Voice Call a penetrating *cherk*. Song a jolting series of unmelodious short piping whistles

Range Andaman Islands

Habitat Evergreen forests, light deciduous forests, edges and thick secondary growth

Nicobar Bulbul

BLACK-CRESTED BULBUL

Pycnonotus (melanicterus) flaviventris Pycnonotidae

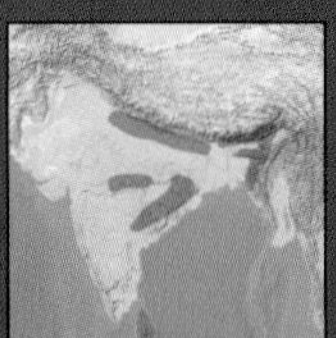

Size 18 cm

Voice Cheerful whistles; also harsh *cburrr* call; 4- to 8-note song

Range The Himalayas, from Himachal Pradesh eastwards; NE India; foothills to about 2,000 m

Habitat Forests; bamboos; clearings; orchards; forest and dense scrub

Distinctive-looking bird with glossy black head, tall, erect crest and black throat; olive-yellow nape and back, graduating to brown on tail; yellow below throat. Sexes alike. In pairs or small parties, sometimes with other birds; arboreal. Sits conspicuously on open perch and calls. Feeds on fruit and insects.

FLAME-THROATED BULBUL

Pycnonotus (melanicterus) gularis Pycnonotidae

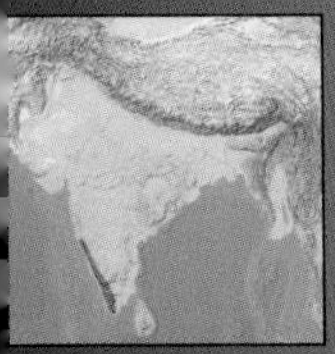

Size 19.5 cm

Voice Song sweet, hurried and rather high-pitched

Range Western Ghats

Habitat Evergreen foothill forests, especially in lower-edge ecotone with drier formations, in thorny bamboo

Slim bulbul, with very short, ragged crest and relatively short, very slightly rounded tail. Glossy black head and crest; olive-green upperparts; bright yellow breast and belly; bright ruby-red throat; indistinct white tips to outer-tail. Juvenile similar but has more brownish and yellow throat. Nest made of dead leaves, held together with cobweb. Feeds on ficus, lantana berries and other fruits, and insects. In small flocks; prefers dense cover.

BLACK-CAPPED BULBUL

Pycnonotus melanicterus Pycnonotidae

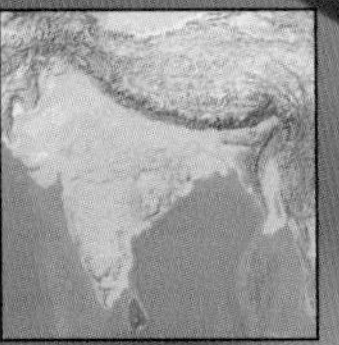

Size 19 cm

Voice Song an ascending *yet…yer…ye* or *wer…wer…we… we*

Range Sri Lanka

Habitat Open forests and woodlands upto 1,300 m, secondary growth. Moist broadleaved forests

Medium-sized, olive-green bulbul with bright yellow underparts, washed pale olive. Lacks crest; broad white tips to outer-tail feathers; yellow underwing-coverts; brownish-olive flight feathers; brown, rounded tail; dull reddish iris. Female has brown iris. Juvenile similar but has more brownish cap. Noisy and conspicuous. In pairs, or small parties. Mainly insectivorous; also eats small berries and seeds.

RED-WHISKERED BULBUL

Pycnonotus jocosus Pycnonotidae

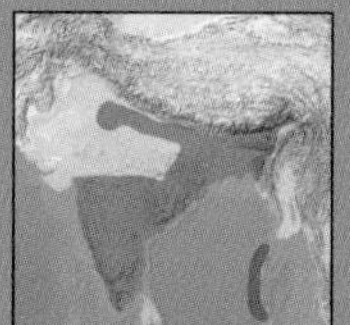

Size 20 cm

Voice Calls include cheerful whistling notes; also harsh, grating alarm notes

Range From Uttarakhand east along the Himalayan foothills to about 1,500 m; most common in south of Satpura mountains in peninsular India; disjunct population in hilly areas of S, SE Rajasthan and N Gujarat

Habitat Forests, clearings, gardens and orchards; vicinity of human habitation

Slim bulbul with prominent, black crest; black crown and nape; black moustachial stripe; prominent white cheeks with red-patch behind eye. Mostly dark brown above. Whitish underparts; buff flanks with white tail-tips and underparts; sometimes broken dark, chest-band; long, brown tail, tipped white; red vent. Sexes alike.

fuscicaudatus

emeria

WHITE-EARED BULBUL

Pycnonotus leucotis Pycnonotidae

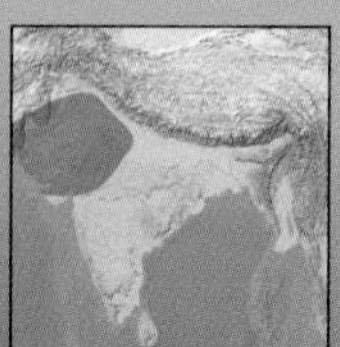

Size 20 cm

Voice Call a liquid *pip…pip.* Usually loud *whichyu… whichyu,* sometimes extended to more phrases

Range Locally common breeding resident in plains of Pakistan and NW India south to Gujarat and east to Delhi and W Uttar Pradesh

Habitat Dry open woodlands and scrubs, often on rocky ground. Also mangroves, urban gardens and parks

Similar to the Himalayan, but smaller, no crest and larger white-patch on cheek; pale, bare eye-ring. Black, slightly domed head; black chin. Brown above; pale buff below; orangish-yellow undertail-coverts; brown tail with white tip. Sexes alike. Juvenile has more brownish head. Feeds at all levels on fruits, nectar and insects. Sociable, confiding, inquisitive and lively, often perching openly. Mixes with other bulbuls. Powerful undulating flight. Nests in low cover.

HIMALAYAN BULBUL

Pycnonotus leucogenys Pycnonotidae

Size 20 cm

Voice Calls include pleasant whistling notes

Range Found in the Himalayas, from the foothills to about 3,400 m

Habitat Open scrub, vicinity of habitation, edges of forests. Breeds in wooded valleys, also bushy hillsides

Medium-sized bulbul with conspicuous curved crest. Brown head; short, white superciliary-stripe; black around eyes, chin and throat; white cheeks with black crescent-shaped patch below; white blaze on neck sides; reddish iris with narrow yellow eye-ring. Upperparts mostly greyish-brown; darker flight feathers; brownish-black tail with some whitish subterminal markings. White underparts with grey-buff wash on breast and belly; bright sulphur yellow undertail-coverts. Black bill and legs. Sexes alike. Juvenile has duller brown head than adult. In pairs or small parties; active birds on the move, attracts attention by their pleasant calls; hawks insects; perches on tops of bushes, shakes tail and calls frequently. Agile flier. Common in the hills, where quite confiding and noisy.

YELLOW-THROATED BULBUL

Pycnonotus xantholaemus Pycnonotidae

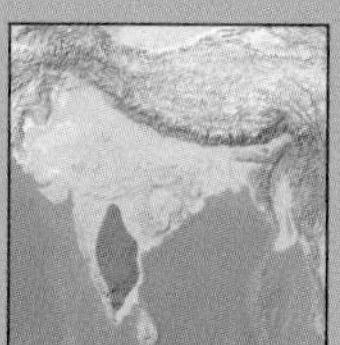

Size 20 cm

Voice Call a lively *whichit woo... ichit wee...wee*

Range Extremely local endemic breeding resident restricted to few hills in S Andhra Pradesh, E Karnataka and Tamil Nadu

Habitat Rocky, scrub-covered hills

One of India's rarest bulbuls with limited distribution. No crest; greenish-grey upperparts; bright yellow throat, vent and tail tip; yellowish-green head and wing edgings; dark greenish-grey tail; dirty-white breast, washed grey; greyish belly and flanks. Sexes alike. Feeds on fruits, insects; usually in pairs, or small groups. Shy, usually hides in scrub, but sometimes perches in open. Nest not well known.

YELLOW-EARED BULBUL

Pycnonotus penicillatus Pycnonotidae

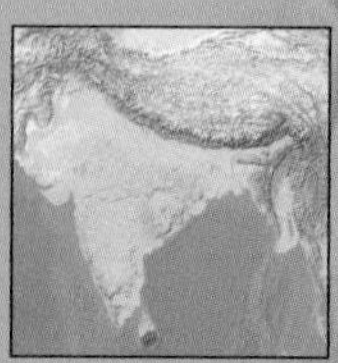

Size 20 cm

Voice Calls include loud, mellow *wheet... wit...wit* and *crr...crr*

Range Common endemic breeding resident restricted to wet zone of Sri Lanka

Habitat Lower and middle levels of wet forests, nearby gardens

Overall olive-green and yellow bulbul with distinctive head pattern. Black crown, eye and moustachial stripes; white tufts in front of eye; yellow-patch below eye; yellow tufts on ear-coverts; white throat. Sexes alike. Feeds mainly on fruits, by entering canopy. Usually in pairs, or small parties but larger flocks congregate on fruiting trees. Rather shy. Cup-shaped nest, made of moss and roots in fork of low trees or on hanging branches.

FLAVESCENT BULBUL

Pycnonotus flavescens Pycnonotidae

Size 22 cm

Voice Harsh alarm call. Song a jolly phrase of usually 3-6 notes

Range Hills of NE India

Habitat Open country with scattered bushes and trees; thick bushes in deserted cultivation and secondary growth

Medium to large-sized, dull-looking bulbul. Stout, black bill; short white supercilium and/or white eye-crescents; black lores; short crest. Olive-brown upperparts tinged greenish; brownish-grey underparts with yellow cast; yellow undertail-coverts; olive-yellow in wings and tail. Juvenile has less prominent supercilium, browner upperparts, rufous edges to flight feathers and paler bill. Rather quiet. Forages inside bushes and trees, rather than perching conspicuously on top. Arboreal. Keeps in flocks of six to 30 birds.

WHITE-BROWED BULBUL

Pycnonotus luteolus Pycnonotidae

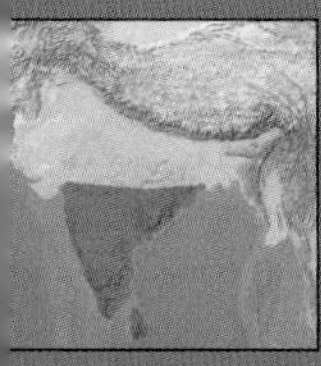

Size 20 cm

Voice Calls include loud, explosive chatter; assortment of bubbling, whistling notes and chuckles

Range Peninsular India, south of line from C Gujarat to S West Bengal; avoids heavy-rainfall hill zones of Western Ghats

Habitat Dry scrub; village habitation; light forests

Sexes alike. Olive plumage, brighter above; whitish forehead and supercilium, explosive calls confirm identity. In pairs, or small parties; not an easy bird to see; skulks in dense, low growth, from where its chattering calls suddenly explode; seen only momentarily when emerges on bush-tops, or flies low from one bush-patch to another; usually does not associate with other birds.

bengalensis

RED-VENTED BULBUL

Pycnonotus cafer Pycnonotidae

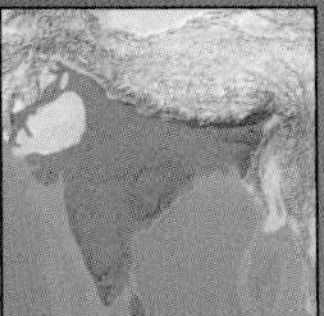

Size 20 cm

Voice Cheerful whistling calls; alarm calls on sighting snake, owl or some other intrusion, serving to alert other birds

Range Subcontinent, to about 1,800 m in the Himalayas

Habitat Light forests; gardens; haunts of man

Dark sooty-brown upperparts; pale edges of feathers on back and breast give scaly appearance; glossy, black head, with slight crest; almost black throat; white rump and bright red vent distinctive; dark tail tipped white; brown breast graduated to white belly. Sexes alike. In pairs or small flocks, but large numbers gather to feed; arboreal, keeps to middle levels of trees and bushes; well-known Indian bird, rather attached to human habitation; pleasantly noisy and cheerful, aggressive and quarrelsome; indulges in dust-bathing; also hunts flycatcher-style.

humayuni

WHITE-THROATED BULBUL

Alophoixus flaveolus Pycnonotidae

Size 22 cm

Voice Variety of nasal calls, variously described as *chi…chack, chi…chack; kake…kake*; etc.

Range Nepal to Myanmar; S Assam Hills

Habitat Dense primary, secondary evergreen hill forests, with heavy undergrowth; open lowland forests

Olive-green, brown-and-yellow bulbul with diagnostic long, untidy, brown crest. Greyish white lores, ear-coverts; brown eye-ring; prominent white throat; olive-green mantle; darker, rufous brown on wings, tail; bright yellow underparts. Seen in small parties when not breeding; arboreal; moves in middle, lower forest storeys, usually in thick undergrowth; sometimes in canopy.

YELLOW-BROWED BULBUL

Acritillas indica Pycnonotidae

Size 20 cm

Voice Noisy. Call a fluty *whit…wee* which is extended into song. Also, harsh *churrs*

Range Common endemic breeding resident in Western Ghats and associated hills south from Maharashtra

Habitat Forest and secondary cover

Overall bright olive-green and bright yellow bulbul. Black bill and eyes; yellow face and throat; slightly decurved bill; bright yellow orbital patch; Upperparts bright olive-green; and underparts bright yellow. Sexes alike. Juvenile duller with rufous in wings. Feeds on berries and invertebrates, often in mixed hunting groups, and usually at middle or lower levels. Lively and not shy. Nests in bushes.

OLIVE BULBUL

Iole virescens Pycnonotidae

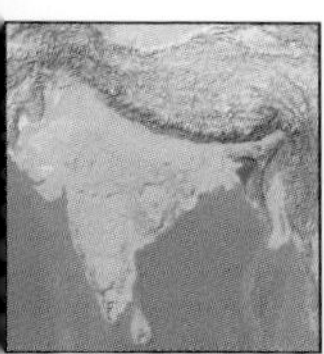

Size 19 cm

Voice Call a disyllabic, musical *whe…ic*

Range NE India (Assam, Manipur, Meghalaya, Mizoram) and Bangladesh

Habitat Dense, moist, broadleaved evergreen forests; secondary growth in deserted cultivation in forests

Small, nondescript bulbul. Yellowish-olive head sides; paler ear-coverts; crown and upperparts strongly tinged olive; pale rufous vent; rufous-brown tail. Brownish horn bill with paler lower mandible. Similar to Flavescent, but smaller, with shorter tail and longer bill. Legs and feet brownish-pink (black on Flavescent).

MOUNTAIN BULBUL

Ixos mcclellandii Pycnonotidae

Size 23 cm

Voice Noisy, with a variety of calls. Most commonly, metallic *tsyi… tsyi* and *cheep…har…lee*

Range Fairly common breeding resident in N mountains from Uttarakhand east to Myanmar border and perhaps Bangladesh. Moves lower down to foothills and even adjacent plains in winter

Habitat Forests and secondary growth with scattered trees

Large, but slim, olive-and-rufous bulbul with shaggy brown crown. Cheeks and breast pale rufous, streaked with buff. Olive-green upperparts. Streaked white throat, often puffed out; buff belly and vent. Long powerful bill. Sexes alike. Usually in pairs, or small groups. Nests high in trees. Feeds mainly on fruits, mostly in canopy.

STRIATED BULBUL

Pycnonotus striatus Pycnonotidae

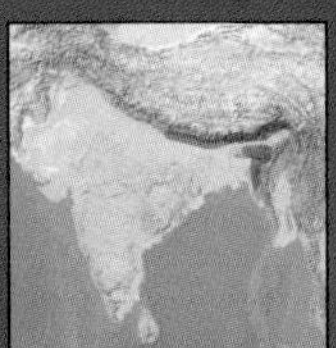

Size 20 cm

Voice Chatters. Calls include *tee… wut, pik…pik* and *chee…tu*

Range Locally common breeding resident in N mountains from C Nepal to Myanmar border. Moves lower down in winter

Habitat Forests

Large, heavily-streaked, long-tailed bulbul. Long, pointed crest; greenish-brown cheeks and crown; yellow lores and eye-ring, chin and vent; heavily streaked whitish on head and mantle; grey and yellow underparts, also heavily streaked. Sexes alike. Often in small parties. Strong flight. Nests in bushes. Feeds mainly on fruits in canopy; also flycatches.

ASHY BULBUL

Hemixos flavala Pycnonotidae

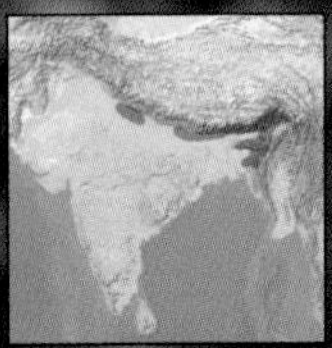

Size 20 cm

Voice Noisy. Calls include liquid, descending *tew…de…de…do…it* and variants

Range Common breeding resident in N foothills from Uttarakhand east to Myanmar border. Also Bangladesh. Winters lower down, sometimes in plains

Habitat Sub-montane forests; plantations

Grey bulbul with large, pale green-patch on wing. Brownish-grey head, face and crown; black, tringle-shaped patch on lores; brown cheeks; white throat. Dark grey outer wings and tail. Whitish underparts, washed grey. Sexes alike. Nests low down. Feeds on fruits, nectar and insects in canopy and middle storey, often in flocks. Flycatches.

BLACK BULBUL

Hypsipetes leucocephalus Pycnonotidae

Ashy-grey plumage; black, loose-looking crest; coral-red beak and legs diagnostic; whitish below abdomen. Sexes alike. Flocks in forest, often dozens together; strictly arboreal, keeps to topmost branches of tall forest trees, rarely comes down into undergrowth; noisy and restless, hardly staying on trees for few minutes; feeds on berries, fruits, but also hunts insects in flycatcher manner.

white-headed

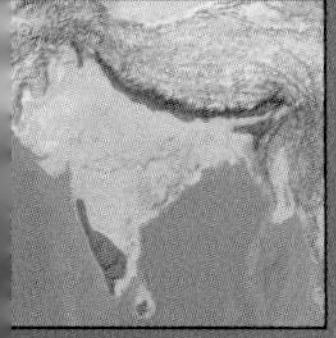

'forked-tailed'

Size 23 cm

Voice Very noisy. Calls include an assortment of whistles and screeches

Range Several races; resident in the Himalayas and NE India. Southern race *H.l. ganeesa* darker with square tail and is found in Western Ghats and Sri Lanka. White-headed races are vagrants to the NE of the region

Habitat Tall forests; hill-station gardens

'squared-tailed'

BRISTLED GRASSBIRD

Chaetornis striata Locustellidae

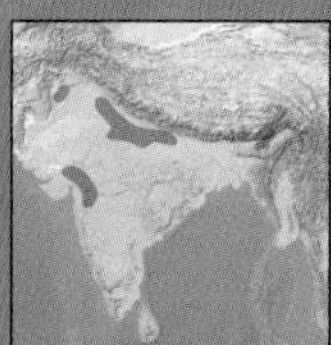

Size 22 cm

Voice Call a soft whistle followed by loud *weee...choo*

Range Globally threatened; endemic breeding resident; very erratically recorded

Habitat Tall, wet, grasslands; reed beds

Large buff-brown warbler, with strong black streaks on upperparts; unmarked underparts; stout blackish bill; no obvious supercilium; indistinct necklace of dark, stiffened feathers on breast; slight streaking on lower throat; prominent rictal bristles; cross-barring on undertail. Similar to Striated, but smaller and less streaked with shorter, graduated tail with pale tips. Sexes alike. Exceptionally furtive. Feeds on invertebrates low in grass.

STRIATED GRASSBIRD

Megalurus palustris Locustellidae

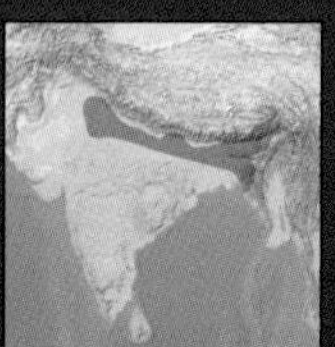

Size 25 cm

Voice Call a metallic, long-drawn whistle, ending in a loud *weee...choo*

Range Locally common to rare resident; NE and C India

Habitat Tall grass; scrubs; reed beds near water

Large warbler with a long, graduated tail and upright posture. Mainly buff upperparts; blackish streaking from crown to rump; some rufous on crown; heavily streaked above; long whitish supercilium; whitish lores; light streaking on whitish-buff underparts; long pale bill and pale legs. In worn plumage, greyer than buff. Sexes alike, but female slightly smaller. Often confused with Striated Babbler. Singly or in pairs. Frequently seen perched on tall grass or reeds. Easier to see during breeding; secretive otherwise. Feeds and nests low down in vegetation, close to ground.

RUFOUS-RUMPED GRASSBIRD

Graminicola bengalensis Locustellidae

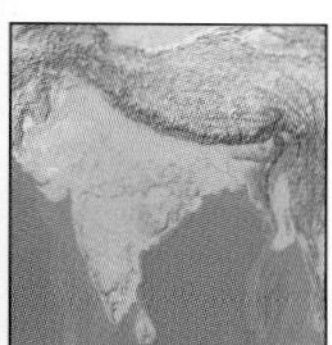

Size 18 cm

Voice Calls *er wit wit wit*. Similar to that of Rusty-rumped Warbler. Song *err wi wi wi*; a buzzzing *wi wi wi yu wuoo…yu wuoo*

Range Rarely seen resident in plains of NE India; scattered records east from Nepal

Habitat Grass and reed beds near water

Large grass warbler with dark rufous-streaked crown, nape and mantle; whitish supercilium; darker rufous-brown streaking on back and lower mantle; rump and wings mostly rufous; long, dark, graduated tail; whitish underparts with rufous-buff breast sides and flanks; pale bill. Sexes similar. Juvenile duller with less dark streaking. Skulks in dense grass and reed beds. Dives back into cover when flushed. Noisy during breeding.

BROAD-TAILED GRASSBIRD

Schoenicola platyurus Locustellidae

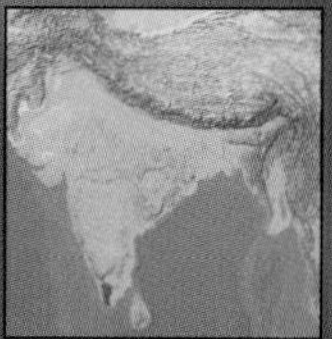

Size 14 cm

Voice Calls include gruff *chak* and sharp *zip*. Breeding male song a lark-like trill

Range Globally threatened; resident or local migrant, S Western Ghats

Habitat Tall grass; reeds on steep, open hillsides

Unstreaked, olive-brown warbler. Identified by stout bill and long, broad, dark, graduated tail. Whitish underparts; buffish supercilium; orangish tint on breast and flanks; tail, rump and uppertail-coverts faintly barred; dark undertail. Smallish head, heavy bill. Sexes alike, but female has brown gape, while male has black. Skulking, except during breeding, when male sings in open with tail fanned. Usually shows at dawn or dusk. Nests in tall grass. Feeding habits not well documented, but probably insects.

CHESTNUT-HEADED TESIA

Oligura castaneocoronata Cettiidae

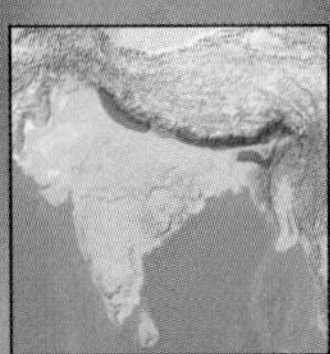

Size 8 cm

Voice Call a high-pitched *si-si-si-si* or loud, piercing *tzit,* repeated when alarmed

Range Resident in the Himalayas, Nepal; hills of NE India, upto 3,900 m. Winters in foothills; lower in non-breeding

Habitat Thick undergrowth in moist forests; dark ravines near streams; moss-covered boulders or logs

Tiny bird with a dumpy, rounded body. Dark olive-green back; bright chestnut-red hood; lemon-yellow chin and throat and breast sides and flanks; rest of upperparts, dull green; underparts olive-washed yellow; small white crescent behind eye; long legs; stubby, short tail, barely extending beyond wings. Pale bill shorter than other tesias. Juvenile has drab olive upperparts and faded yellow underparts with rufous cheeks, flanks and breast-band; chestnut head absent. Singly or in pairs. Shy and elusive, jerks body when calling; keeps to forest floor, hopping around in bushy undergrowth.

GREY-BELLIED TESIA

Tesia cyaniventer Cettiidae

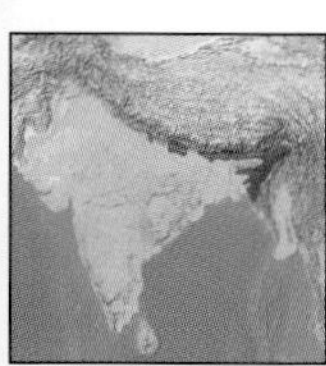

Size 9 cm

Voice Call similar to Slaty-bellied's. Song preceded by soft twitter before 3 trilling notes

Range Resident, altitudinal migrant in the Himalayas from Uttarakhand east to Arunachal Pradesh; hills of NE India and Bangladesh

Habitat Summers in thick undergrowth near small streams or moist ravines in broadleaved forest; winters in shady, broadleaved forests and secondary growth

Plain-looking tesia. Upperparts uniformly olive-green; crown and mantle olive-green; bright green supercilium; pale grey chin, throat and middle of belly; lighter green underwing-coverts; short, square-ended tail; dark bill with white tip. Similar to Slaty-bellied, but has paler grey underparts and stronger black stripe behind eye.

SLATY-BELLIED TESIA

Tesia olivea Cettiidae

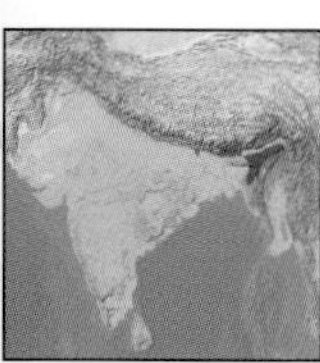

Size 8 cm

Voice Calls *chirik*. Song includes pleasant but tuneless jumbled whistles

Range Himachal Pradesh to Arunachal Pradesh; S Assam Hills

Habitat Dense damp waterside undergrowth, with ferns and nettles in moist subtropical and tropical evergreen forests

Similar to Grey-bellied, but has brighter yellow crown and no prominent supercilium. Upperparts dark olive-green; crown and nape vivid greenish-gold; face and underparts uniform dark slaty grey; long legs; bright orange lower mandible; slender, pointed bill; red inside of mouth; almost tail-less. Juvenile similar to Grey-bellied, but has darker underparts, duller crown and paler bill. Singly, or in pairs. Skulks in undergrowth, hopping around; active; inconspicuous; curious, but shy; rarely emerges from cover.

CHESTNUT-CROWNED BUSH WARBLER

Cettia major Cettiidae

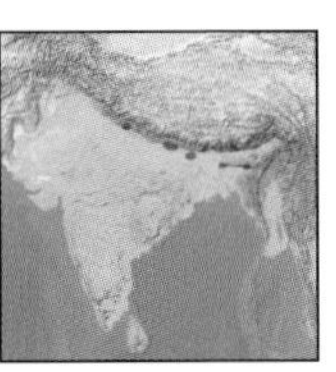

Size 13 cm

Voice Call an explosive bunting-like *pseek*. Song a 6-noted, ascending *wi…wi*

Range Resident: the Himalayas from Uttarakhand east to Arunachal Pradesh; hills of NE India

Habitat Summers in rhododendron, fir and oak forests; winters in lowland reed beds

Dark brown upperparts; whitish underparts; greyish-olive sides of breast; chestnut forehead, crown and nape; brownish-olive flanks; distinct white eye-ring. Distinguished from Grey-sided by larger size, bigger bill, longer supercilium and whiter underparts. Juvenile lacks chestnut on crown and even olive-brown above. The sub-species *C m vafra* is found in Assam and S Assam Hills.

BROWN-FLANKED BUSH WARBLER

Cettia fortipes Cettiidae

Size 11 cm

Voice Loud 3-note call; single note *chak…*or *suck…*

Range Locally common breeding resident: the Himalayas; S Assam Hills; winters lower down to foothills and adjacent plains

Habitat Undergrowth on hillsides; edges of forests; bamboos; tea plantations; grasslands

Small, dark, nondescript warbler. Rounded crown; rufescent olive-brown above; buff eyebrow; dark through eyes; dull whitish below, tinged ashy-brown on throat; buff-brown flanks and undertail; relatively long tail; dark grey bill; pinkish-yellow lower mandible; pale pinkish-brown legs. Sexes alike. Feeds singly, on invertebrates close to the ground. Loner, shy and secretive, sneaking in undergrowth; rarely seen; located by loud distinctive call. Nests low in thick cover.

PALE-FOOTED BUSH WARBLER

Cettia pallidipes Cettiidae

Size 11 cm

Voice Call a series of sharp chirps. Song a loud, explosive *zip…zip… tschuk…o…tschuk*

Range Resident, altitudinal migrant in the lower Himalayas, NE India and S Andaman Islands

Habitat Tall grass and bushes on forest edges

Small, plain-looking bush warbler with short tail; large, rounded head; olivish-brown forehead, crown and nape; whitish supercilium; white chin, throat and middle belly and undertail-coverts; brown tail with indistinct greenish-brown fringe. Distinguished from Brown-flanked by smaller size, paler underparts; brownish-olive breast sides and flanks; more rufescent upperparts; shorter, square-ended tail; pale pinkish legs and feet. The Andaman race *osmastoni* has a bigger bill, with richer brown upperparts.

ABERRANT BUSH WARBLER

Cettia flavolivacea Cettiidae

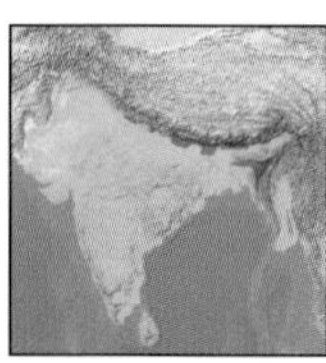

Size 12 cm

Voice Calls *thrit*. Song a loud, tuneful, wavering whistle

Range Altitudinal migrant: S Himalayas from Uttarakhand east to Arunachal Pradesh; S Assam Hills

Habitat Forest edges and clearings; scrubs and long grass; bushes in pine forests

Olive upperparts with yellowish tint; sulphur yellow chin and throat; underparts dull yellow graduating to darker olive-yellow on sides of breast and flanks; greyish-yellow supercilium. Distinguished from Hume's by greenish cast to upperparts, notched tail and more rounded wings. Juvenile similar to adult, but has more yellow-brown underparts. Builds nest of grass and bamboo in bushes.

HUME'S BUSH WARBLER

Cettia brunnescens Cettiidae

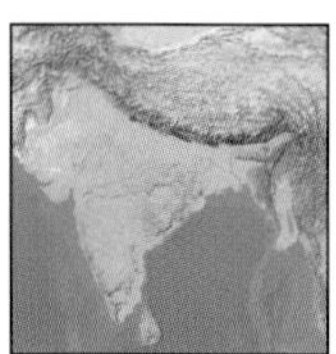

Size 11 cm

Voice Calls *trrrt*. Song comprises ascending 3-4 short whistles

Range Resident: high Himalayas from Uttarakhand east to Arunachal Pradesh; S Assam Hills

Habitat Open forest upto treeline; bamboo thickets

Recently split from Yellowish-bellied. Small bush warbler with thin, long bill. Overall warm brown with greyish-brown wings; creamish supercilium, above a narrow, dark eye-stripe; rufous wash on crown. Warm brown upperparts; cinnamon tips to flight feathers; square-tipped tail; breast and throat creamy-white; rump, belly and flanks have a yellowish wash. Pinkish-grey bill dark-tipped. Juvenile greenish-grey above and pale yellow below.

GREY-SIDED BUSH WARBLER

Cettia brunnifrons Cettiidae

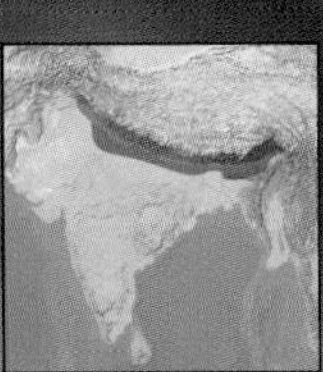

Size 11 cm

Voice Call a soft *tsik...tsik*. Song a repetitive, an extended *whooeeu... whooweeou*

Range Locally common breeding resident in the Himalayas; altitudinal migrant; breeds upto 4,000 m; winters below 2,200 m

Habitat Rhododendrons; shrubberies and bushes on forest edges; open forests; winters in tea gardens

Small warbler with a distinct head pattern. Bright rufous cap; long pale supercilium (well-defined in front of the eye) with bold dark eye-stripe. Uniform rufous-brown upperparts; whitish chin, throat and belly; conspicuous grey breast sides and flanks; vent, olive-brown. Dark grey bill, with pale yellow lower mandible; pinkish wash to grey-brown feet. Juvenile has less distinct head pattern; overall duller, thereby mistaken for other species. Usually remains close to the ground, feeding in the undergrowth. Breeding male flicks and cocks tail. Secretive in breeding. Nests low, in thick cover.

CETTI'S BUSH WARBLER

Cettia cetti Cettiidae

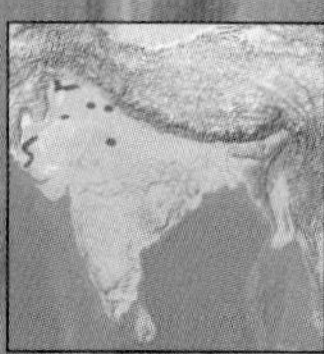

Size 14 cm

Voice Call a loud, metallic *tzit*. Song high-pitched but melodious, uttered continuously

Range Rare winter visitor, passage migrant to Pakistan; NW India. Locally common

Habitat Dense reed beds and tamarisk by streams and in marshes

Medium to large-sized, roundish dull-looking warbler. Dull rufous-brown forehead and nape. Upperparts greyish-brown, more rufous towards lower back; greyish breast sides and flanks; greyish-brown tail, rump and wings; undertail-coverts also grey-brown, tipped whitish; grey eyebrow and cheeks; very white supercilium. Underparts whitish, with white-tipped undertail-coverts. Long, broad graduated tail. Female much smaller than male. Can be confused with Pale-footed, but larger in size, with larger tail and much shorter supercilium. Singly or in pairs. Skulks in dense bush cover, hopping between bushes. Territorial, even in non-breeding. Breeding male sings from open perch. Low, fast flight when flushed.

SPOTTED BUSH WARBLER

Bradypterus thoracicus Locustellidae

Size 13 cm

Voice Call a rhythmic *trick…i…di, tric…i…di* or *tri…tri…tri…tree*. Song a low buzzing drone

Range Altitudinal migrant; breeds locally in the Himalayas from Kashmir to Arunachal Pradesh; winters in foothills, NE Indian plains

Habitat Open, grassy pastures; rhododendron upto treeline; scrubs upto 4,000 m

Small bush warbler, with a distinct song that rings through the Himalayas. Dark olive-brown (with a rufescent cast), unstreaked upperparts; pure white chin and abdomen; ash-brown throat; long, boldly-patterned undertail-coverts with darker brown centres and white tips; unpronounced ashy-brown supercilium; greyish ear-coverts and sides of neck; olive-brown flanks; short, graduated tail. Could be confused with Long-billed, Chinese, Baikal and Russet Bush Warblers, but distinguished by a gorget of numerous spots on breast and throat; shorter tail and ash-brown on the sides of head. Juvenile has more yellowish-green underparts, with darker mottling on breast and flanks.

WEST HIMALAYAN BUSH WARBLER

Bradypterus kashmirensis Locustellidae

Size 13 cm

Voice Call a rhythmic *trick…i…di, tric…i…di* or *tri…tri…tri…tree*

Range Breeds locally in the Himalayas in Kashmir

Habitat Same as Spotted's

Similar to Spotted Bush but has paler throat. Recently split from Spotted. Has two morphs: one paler and duller than the other, which has an obvious supercilium. Yet to be studied closely.

BAIKAL BUSH WARBLER

Locustella davidi Locustellidae

Similar to Spotted Bush, but smaller in size. Recently discovered in the Tinsukia area of Northern Assam, normally breeds in northeast China. Habitat said to be boreal forests. Little is known about its breeding status in India.

BROWN BUSH WARBLER

Bradypterus luteoventris Locustellidae

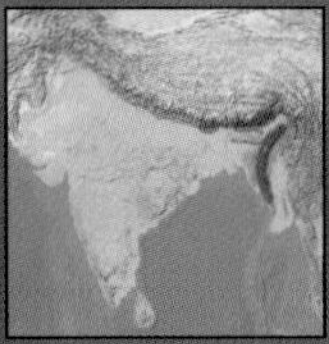

Size 13 cm

Voice Calls include rapid, reeling *tic tic tic tic tic* and *teck teck*

Range E Himalayas upto Arunachal Pradesh; S Assam Hills

Habitat Grassy hillsides; undergrowth in coniferous forests

Rather nondescript bird, narrow whitish eye-ring being the only distinguishing feature. Upperparts reddish-brown; white underparts, with pale brown wash on breast; rufous-buff ear-coverts, sides of neck, breast and flanks; throat, centre of breast and belly whitish; faint rufous-buff supercilium to eye; throat, plain breast and undertail-coverts. Juvenile has yellowish wash to underparts.

RUSSET BUSH WARBLER

Bradypterus mandelli Locustellidae

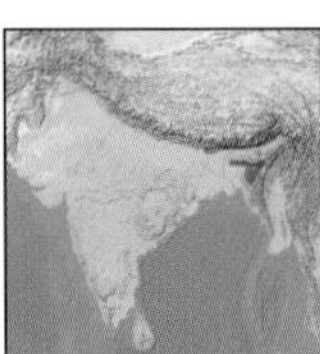

Size 14 cm

Voice Call a hard *shtuk*. Song a 2-note series followed by a sharp *tic*

Range E Himalayas; S Assam Hills

Habitat Edges of forests; secondary growth; shrubby thickets; bamboos

Warm-brown slender-bodied warbler with russet upperparts. Similar to Spotted, but identified by longer and broader tail and plainer undertail-coverts edged with pale buff. Also lacks grey on cheeks. Underparts slightly lighter brown; hint of whitish supercilium (which does not extend beyond the eye); blackish bill and brown ear-coverts; short, rounder wings; long, graduated tail. Some birds have brown spots on lower throat and upper breast, but not as prominent as on Spotted.

LANCEOLATED WARBLER

Locustella lanceolata Locustellidae

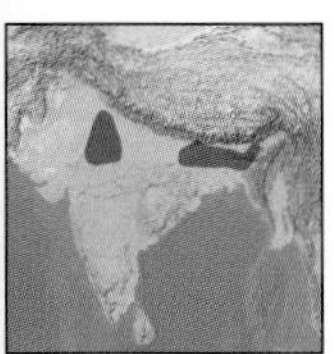

Size 12 cm

Voice Calls include hard *clik* and *chrrr.* Song a far-carrying trill

Range Rare winter visitor mainly to lowlands of Pakistan and N India. Often overlooked

Habitat Dense grass; stubble; thick bushes

Small brown warbler with heavily streaked, brown upperparts; underparts whitish with buff flanks and vent; distinct gorget of fine streaks on lower throat and breast; thin 'lanceolated' streaks on flanks; unstreaked vent; small, short tail; blackish tertials with buff edges. Juvenile duller, less streaked. Feeds on invertebrates. Extremely secretive, scuttles rapidly along ground. Conceals itself in very short grass. Rarely seen in flight.

SRI LANKA BUSH WARBLER

Elaphrornis palliseri Locustellidae

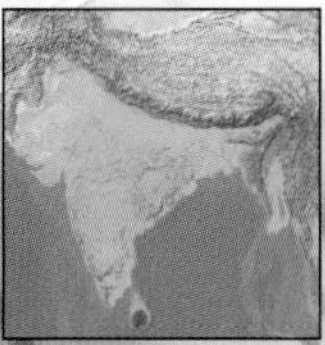

Size 15 cm

Voice Call a high-pitched, repeated *tsick*; sometimes interspersed with a low-pitched *churp*

Range Endemic to Sri Lankan mountains

Habitat Forests with dense undergrowth; prefers vegetation along streams

Large-sized, rather drab warbler. Plain, dark olive-brown upperparts, with rufescent cast to wings and tail; pale grey underparts with olive-yellow wash around belly; ashy-brown ear-coverts and weak pale grey supercilium; broad tail; shortish wings and rufous throat. Juvenile similar, but lacks orange on throat. Sexes alike. Rare and little known. Skulking. Keeps low in vegetation, where it feeds on insects.

GRASSHOPPER WARBLER

Locustella naevia Locustellidae

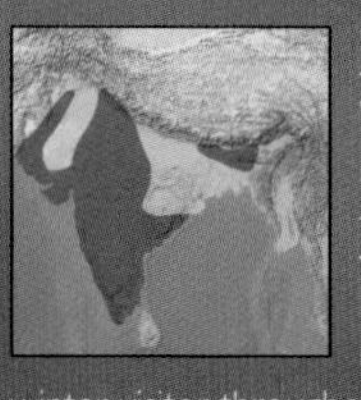

Size 13 cm

Voice Call a sharp *pstt.* Song a rhythmic, insect-like churring. Unlikely to be heard in our region

Range Widespread and much overlooked winter visitor throughout region; most regularly seen in SW India

Habitat Damp grasslands; reed beds and paddy fields

Uniformly olive-brown warbler with short rounded wings. Upperparts streaked darker; head rather plain; whitish or yellowish underparts usually unstreaked; olive-brown crown and mantle; hint of pale supercilium; undertail-coverts long and streaked; long, graduated and rounded tail; pink legs. Sexes alike. Creeps low down feeding on insects. Reluctant flier. Rarely seen unless flushed, then flies low into cover. Crepuscular.

RUSTY-RUMPED WARBLER

Locustella certhiola Locustellidae

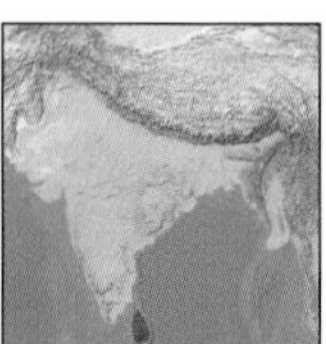

Size 14 cm

Voice Calls include sharp, metallic *pit* and hard, drawn-out, descending rattle *trrrrrrrrr*

Range Winters locally across subcontinent

Habitat Reed beds; paddy fields

Medium-sized warbler. Darkly streaked olive-brown back; darkly streaked crown; whitish grey underparts, unstreaked except on undertail; rufous olive-brown breast sides and flanks. Similar to Grasshopper but larger, with more pronounced supercilium, greyer crown, more heavily streaked mantle with hint of rufous; rump and uppertail-coverts also rufous; narrower fringes on tertials. In flight shows dark, white-tipped tail. Juvenile yellowish below, breast lightly spotted, supercilium fainter, crown and mantle olive-brown with lighter streaking.

THICK-BILLED WARBLER

Phragamaticola aedon Acrocephalidae

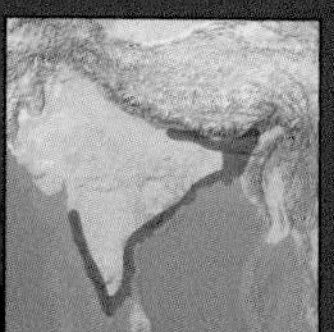

Size 18 cm

Voice Calls include loud *tschack* and *chack*

Range Scarce and local winter visitor mainly to plains of S Nepal, NE, S India, Bangladesh

Habitat All types of low scrubs and grass often, but not exclusively, in wetlands

Large grey-brown warbler. Unstreaked, brown upperparts; buff underparts; short, heavy, pointed bill; small, black eyes; plain face with pale lores and supercilium; rusty rump; long, rounded and graduated tail; short wings. Juvenile a richer buff. Sexes alike. Feeds on invertebrates low down in vegetation, hopping through in a crouched, rather babbler-like fashion with tail held low. Secretive and usually singly.

ORIENTAL REED WARBLER

Acrocephalus orientalis Acrocephalidae

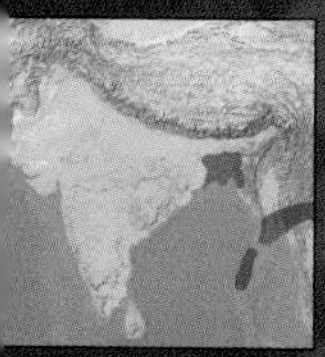

Size 18 cm

Voice Calls include deep *turrr*, harsh *chak*; some croaks and warbling. Noisy

Range Vagrant; winter visitor mainly to NE India

Habitat Reed beds on edges of paddy fields; edges of mangroves; marshes

Largish, olive-brown warbler with paler rump. Whitish supercilium, bordered below by dark indistinct eye-stripe; sides of neck and breast streaked; whitish tips to outer-tail feathers; creamy-white underparts; more brown on flanks and undertail-coverts; streaking on underparts not very visible; narrow greyish streaks on breast and throat; longish, heavy, brownish bill has pink below; grey feet; long, round-tipped tail. Sings from perch on reeds, with puffed throat, usually before spring migration. Very similar to Clamorous Reed but smaller and slimmer with shorter, squarer tail.

BLACK-BROWED REED WARBLER

Acrocephalus bistrigiceps Acrocephalidae

Size 13 cm

Voice Call a soft, repeated *chuc*; churring *currr*. Song prolonged and jumbled, interspersed with mimicry

Range Winter visitor; mainly NE India and Bangladesh

Habitat Reed beds; paddy fields

Medium-sized, dull-coloured, unstreaked warbler. Creamy underparts tinged yellow; short, rounded wings; rounded tail; long undertail-coverts; faint streaking on crown, nape and mantle; pale rump with rufous tinge; prominent buffish-white supercilium extends beyond eye; black eyebrow above and fine eye-stripe below supercilium; black lateral crown-stripe; brown ear-coverts; dark legs and feet. Similar to Paddyfield but has broader supercilium. Perches on tall reeds when singing.

MOUSTACHED WARBLER

Acrocephalus melanopogon Acrocephalidae

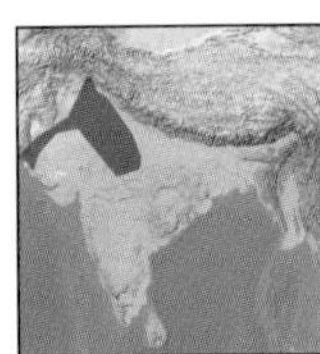

Size 13 cm

Voice Calls include deep *truk* and a short *trik*. Song an ascending rattling trill

Range Scarce but probably overlooked winter visitor to Pakistan and NW India

Habitat Reed beds, particularly typha; waterside bushes. Feeds low down in reeds and also on floating vegetation

Medium-sized, perky warbler with streaked crown. Overall dark, with whitish underparts with rufous-buff wash; short wings; bold, square-ended, creamy supercilium; streaked crown has black border; dark eye-stripe and ear-coverts; greyish cheeks and white throat; unstreaked rusty rump. Sexes alike. Juvenile more heavily streaked. Remains hidden for long periods. Singly, or in pairs. Cocks tail when alarmed. Feeds on invertebrates low down in reed litter and on floating vegetation. Secretive and unobtrusive but will climb to top of reeds to call.

CLAMOROUS REED WARBLER

Acrocephalus stentoreus Acrocephalidae

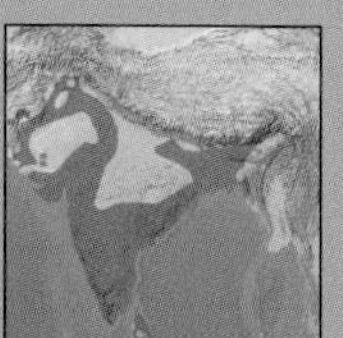

Size 19 cm

Voice Highly vocal. Calls include loud *chack, chakrrr* and *khe* notes; distinctive, loud warbling. Loud, lively song

Range From Kashmir valley, south through country; sporadically breeds in many areas, migrant in others

Habitat Reed beds; mangroves

Upperparts plain uniform brown; distinct pale supercilium; whitish throat, dull buffy-white below; short, rounded wings; at close range, salmon-coloured inside of mouth can be seen; call diagnostic. Sexes alike. Solitary or in pairs; difficult to see but easily heard; keeps low in dense reeds, mangrove and low growth, always around water; does not associate with other species; flies low, immediately vanishes into the vegetation; occasionally emerges on reed or bush-tops, warbling with throat puffed out.

BLUNT-WINGED WARBLER

Acrocephalus concinens Acrocephalidae

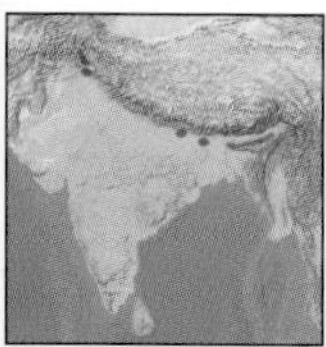

Size 13 cm

Voice Calls include *check* and soft drawn-out *churr*

Range Breeds in W Himalayas; N Pakistan, east to Kashmir; resident in Assam

Habitat Breeds in tall marshes and grass close to water and rivers; in Kashmir

Smallish dull-coloured warbler. Upperparts dark grey-brown; rump and uppertail-coverts marginally darker brown; pale bill has dark tip; breast and flanks pale buff; short, rounded wings; long, rounded tail; pale buff-white underparts; bluish grey soles of feet. Similar to Paddyfield, but distinguished by shorter and less distinct supercilium, which does not extend beyond eye, lack of stripe behind eye and dark border above supercilium. Confiding, except in breeding season.

PADDYFIELD WARBLER

Acrocephalus agricola Acrocephalidae

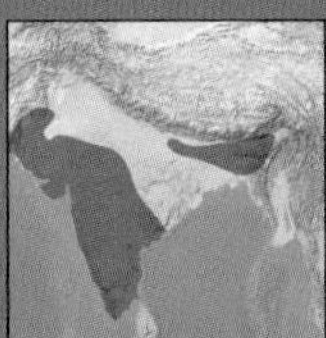

Size 13 cm

Voice Call a rather harsh *chrr… chuck* or single *chack* note

Range Winter visitor; common over most of India, south of and including the Terai

Habitat Damp areas; reed beds; tall cultivation

Medium-sized warbler with rufescent-brown upperparts; brighter on rump; whitish throat and belly; rich buff underparts; short, rounded wings; darker tertials with darker centres and pale edge; short, stubby bill; long cream-coloured supercilium. Sexes alike. Solitary, hopping amidst low growth; rarely seen along with other birds; damp areas, especially reed growth and cultivation are favourite haunts; flies low, but soon vanishes into growth.

BLYTH'S REED WARBLER

Acrocephalus dumetorum Acrocephalidae

Medium-sized warbler with olive, brown-and-grey upperparts and whitish underparts with greyish flanks; long sloping forehead; longish bill; grey legs. Sexes alike. Juvenile more rust above. Feeds on invertebrates at all levels, including canopies, bushes and ground. Rarely in reed beds. Flicks wings and fans tail. Usually singly or in loose groups.

Size 13 cm

Voice Call a loud quick *tchik..* or *tchi..* Rarely, a warbling song

Range Common winter visitor to plains of S India, Bangladesh, NE India. Common passage migrant in N India

Habitat Well-wooded, often quite dry country

LARGE-BILLED REED WARBLER

Acrocephalus orinus Acrocephalidae

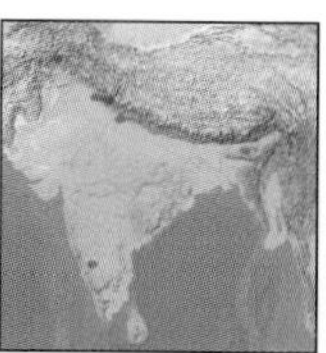

Size 13.5 cm

Voice Call includes scratchy wheezes. Song similar to Blyth's Reed's

Range Rare passage migrant. Scattered records in India and Pakistan. Recently seen after many years in the Kolkata region and the Sunderbans

Habitat Breeds in Afghanistan

Similar to Blyth's Reed, probably not safely identifiable in the field. In fresh plumage, usually less olive, more rufous tinged above than Blyth's Reed; underparts strongly washed with olive-buff, sides more olive-brown, throat creamy olive; longer, stronger and slightly broader bill, which tapers less towards tip; more rounded wings and longer graduated tail with pointed tail feathers. Smaller with weaker bill and feet than Clamorous Reed.

3OOTED WARBLER

'duna caligata Acrocephalidae

ize 13.5 cm

oice Call a strong, but low *chak... ıak...churr*

ange Winters over peninsula, south from unjab to West Bengal

labitat Open country with acacias and :rub; occasionally light forests

ery small warbler with dull olive-brown pperparts; short, pale white supercilium; ale buffy-white below. Dark toes give it a ooted' look, hence its name. Confused with lyth's Reed which is brighter olive-brown ıd mostly frequents bushes. Sexes alike. olitary or two to four birds, sometimes mixed bands of small birds; very active ıd agile; hunts amongst leaves and upper anches; overall behaviour very Leaf Warbler-ke, but calls diagnostic.

SYKES'S WARBLER

Iduna rama Acrocephalidae

Small grey warbler with whitish outer-tail feathers to square-ended tail. Upperparts plain, dull greyish brown. Very similar to, and recently separated from, Booted, but distinguished by shorter wings, longer tail, flatter crown, colder grey above, whiter below and shows less dark edges on crown; does not seem 'booted'. Also similar to Chiffchaff but broader-based bill has pinkish-yellow lower mandible and legs pale pinkish-grey. Sexes similar. Seen in small parties. Feeds very actively on invertebrates and nectar, often in loose parties and at all levels. Flicks tail upwards.

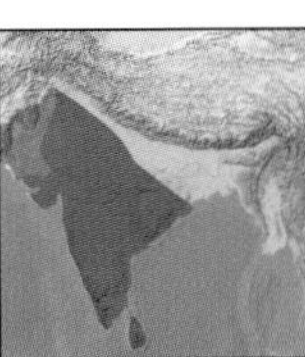

Size 12 cm

Voice Call a clicking *chuk*

Range Common breeding summer visitor to NW India. In winter, spreads to lowlands

Habitat Dry scrub. Breeds in waterside tamarisks and reeds

COMMON CHIFFCHAFF

Phylloscopus collybita Phylloscopidae

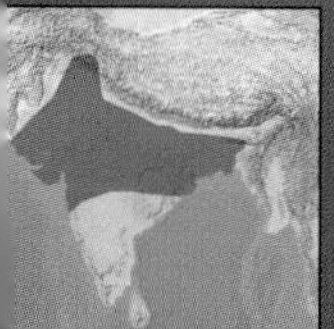

Size 11 cm

Voice Mostly silent but sometimes utters a soft *wheep, zit* or *peeu*

Range Common winter visitor throughout N plains

Habitat All types of wooded country, preferably near water; reed beds and crops

Small, plain dull greyish-brown warbler often with olive wash. Creamish throat, breast and belly; dark eye-stripe; short, whitish supercilium; short rounded wings; long, square-ended tail; tail and flight feathers more brownish, edged olive-yellow; black bill and legs. Sometimes shows very slight wing-bars and, more often, yellow at shoulder. Sexes alike. Feeds actively at all levels foraging in foliage for insects. Approachable and easy to observe.

MOUNTAIN CHIFFCHAFF

Phylloscopus sindianus Phylloscopidae

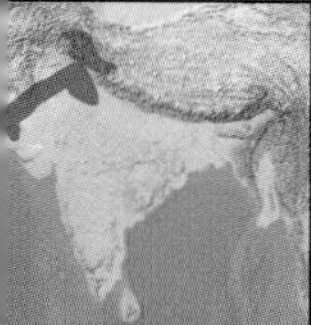

Size 11 cm

Voice Noisier than Common. Call a *tiss…yip* or *swe…eet*

Range Common breeding visitor to N mountains

Habitat Scrubs and open woodlands. Often near water. Usually spends winters close to water. Similar to Common's

Small, roundish warbler, almost identical to Common, but does not show any olive-green or yellow. Upperparts plain greyish-brown; distinct supercilium; deep grey lores; grey-brown ear-coverts; darker flanks; cream underparts washed pale buff. Sexes alike. Similar but smaller; northwestern Plain Warbler *P neglectus* more brown with shorter tail and wings and a tiny bill. Behaviour same as Common.

PLAIN LEAF WARBLER

Phylloscopus neglectus Phylloscopidae

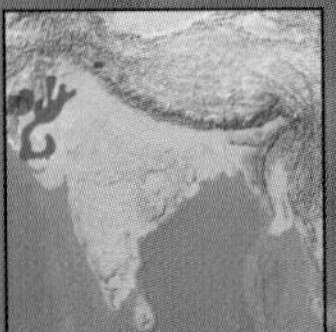

Size 10 cm

Voice Call a hard *tak...tak* or Lesser Whitethroat-like *tshak... tshak*; low-pitched *churr* or *chiip*

Range Rare altitudinal migrant

Habitat Summers in coniferous forests; low bushes. Winters in damp riverine habitats; dry habitats such as roadside trees and acacias

Small, pale warbler. Upperparts plain grey-brown; pale, faint supercilium; small, brownish-black bill; tail very short and square-ended; short, rounded wings; dark legs. Upperparts and wing have no yellow and green tints; in fresh plumage shows pale buffish edges to secondaries which form panel on wing. Singly, or in pairs but seen feeding with other warblers.

DUSKY WARBLER

Phylloscopus fuscatus Phylloscopidae

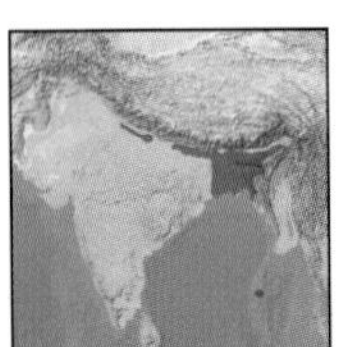

Size 11 cm

Voice Call a strong *chock...chock*

Range Winter visitor; Himalayan foothills; NE India and Bangladesh

Habitat Bushes; long grass

Upperparts, wings and tail vary between dark and pale brownish-grey; whitish underparts with touches of buff on breast sides and flanks; slender, dark legs; broad, dark eye-stripe; whitish-grey eye-ring; greyish lores. Sexes alike. Northeast wintering *P. f weigoldi* darker above, and duskier below, and with touch of yellow on underparts in fresh plumage. Skulking; keeps low in undergrowth, often on ground.

SMOKY WARBLER

Phylloscopus fuligiventer Phylloscopidae

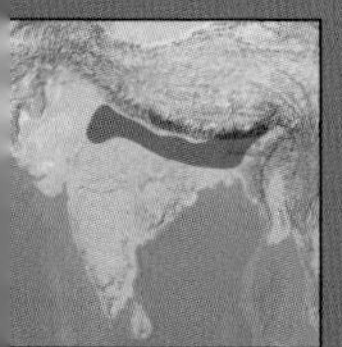

Size 10 cm

Voice Calls include low *tsrrk* and *chup*

Range Rare breeding summer visitor to the Himalayas. Sometimes, spends winters n plains

Habitat Montane scrub and boulder fields in summer

Upperparts, wings and tail dark grey-brown; underparts from dusky-yellow to olive-green; dark eye-stripe; dull yellow lores; short, yellowish or whitish (in eastern race) supercilium; thin, dark legs; dark brown tail; pale base to lower mandible. Similar to Dusky; paler above and whiter below, with bolder supercilium and eye-stripe, pale legs. Confiding; feeds on ground. Spends winters near water. Feeds on invertebrates, close to water. Sometimes, flycatches over water.

TICKELL'S LEAF WARBLER

Phylloscopus affinis Phylloscopidae

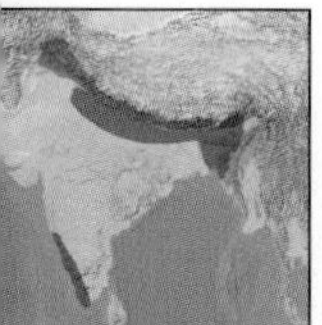

Size 11 cm

Voice Call a strong *chip* or *tsip*

Range Not uncommon breeding summer visitor to N mountains. Winters mainly in Bangladesh, hills of NE and SW India

Habitat Summers in montane scrub. Winters in edges of forests, scrubs and gardens

Small roundish warbler with dark olive-green upperparts; underparts yellow, graduating to buff on sides; no wing-bar; distinct yellow supercilium extends behind crown; pale yellow eye-ring; chin, throat and belly paler buff-yellow; prominent dark eye-stripe; pale legs and lower mandible; long wings; slightly forked tail. Sexes alike. Feeds on invertebrates, close to the ground; flits through the foliage singly or in small parties. Confiding and conspicuous. Nests close to ground.

SULPHUR-BELLIED WARBLER

Phylloscopus griseolus Phylloscopidae

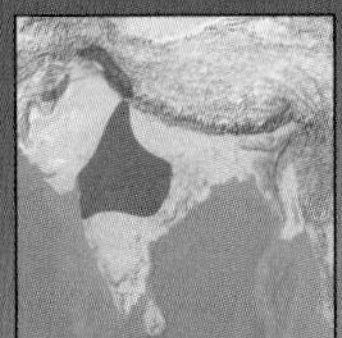

Size 11 cm

Voice Call a soft *dip* or *pik*

Range Locally common breeding summer visitor mainly to N and C India in plains

Habitat Rocky areas with scrubs and scattered trees. Winters in old ruins and open woodland

Small, dark, rotund warbler with prominent bright yellow supercilium that is orangish towards crown; upperparts dark brownish-grey; no wing-bars; underparts pale yellow, with pale green wash, turning olivish towards rump; thin, pale legs; longish wings; short tail. Sexes alike. Sulphur-bellied not as dark above as Smoky or Dusky. Characteristically forages between rocks and tree trunks in wren-like manner for invertebrates, on or close to ground. Singly, or in pairs. Confiding but unobtrusive. Nests in low vegetation.

ASHY-THROATED WARBLER

Phylloscopus maculipennis Phylloscopidae

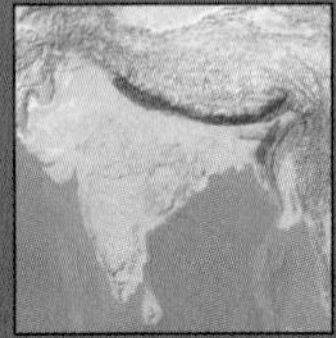

Size 9 cm

Voice Call a loud *zit*, repeated often. Song a rhythmic *sweechu… sweechu*

Range Common breeding resident in N mountains from Himachal to Arunachal Pradesh. Also, hills of NE India. Moves lower down in winter

Habitat Forests and secondary growth

Small, bright yellow and green warbler. Upperparts bright olive-green; distinctive grey face and throat; whitish grey median crown-stripe and supercilium; dark grey crown sides and eye-stripe. Underparts pale yellow; short, rounded wings with a double wing-bar; forked tail; white outer-tail feathers noticeable in flight. Similar to Lemon-rumped and Buff-barred, but has grey head and throat diagnostic. Sexes alike. Feeds on invertebrates, singly or in pairs and in mixed hunting groups in non-breeding season. Often hovers. Nests high in trees.

BUFF-BARRED WARBLER

Phylloscopus pulcher Phylloscopidae

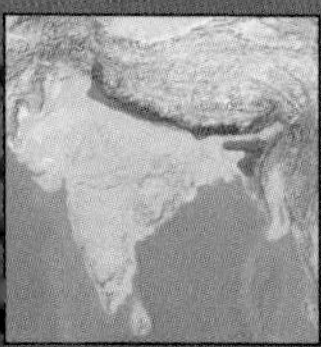

Size 10 cm

Voice Call a strong *swit*

Range Common breeding resident in the Himalayas. Moves lower down in winter

Habitat High-altitude shrubberies and forests in summer. Broadleaved forests in winter

Small, brightly-coloured roundish warbler with diagnostic orangish-buff wing-bars. Upperparts olive-brown; faint grey crown-stripe; indistinct, greyish median crown-stripe; forehead and crown blackish-grey; yellow supercilium; dark eye-stripe; greyish-olive cheeks and ear-coverts. Underparts yellowish; short, rounded wings; touches of white on outer tail; yellow rump; short, spiky, pale bill and pale, slender legs. Sexes alike. Feeds high in canopy on invertebrates, often in mixed hunting groups. Arboreal. Frequently flicks tail open. Rarely hovers. Nests low down.

HUME'S LEAF WARBLER

Phylloscopus humei Phylloscopidae

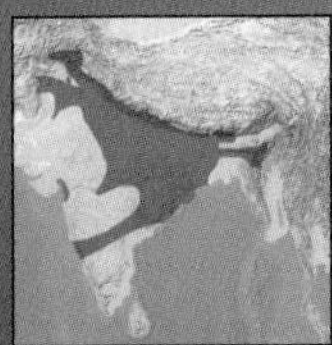

Size 10-11 cm

Voice Calls include disyllabic *whit-hoot* and sparrow-like *chwee.* Song a repeated *wesoo,* often followed by descending high-pitched *zweeeeeeeeoooo*

Range Breeds in the Himalayas. Winters in plains

Habitat Breeds in subalpine forests. Winters in forest and secondary growth

Small, fairly bright warbler. Overall greyish-olive upperparts; yellowish-green mantle and back; brownish crown; indistinct beige supercilium, beige ear-coverts; greyish-green lores and eye-stripe; creamish underparts; short, rounded wings; dark brown tail with greenish edges; poorly-defined median-covert bar but two wing-bars much more obvious; greater-covert wing-bars buffish-white; dark bill and legs. Colours brighter when fresh, duller when worn. Very similar to Yellow-browed, but paler grey above. Singly, or in pairs but often found in mixed feeding parties outside breeding season. Very shy. Arboreal. Feeds in canopy at all levels.

BROOKS'S LEAF WARBLER

Phylloscopus subviridis Phylloscopidae

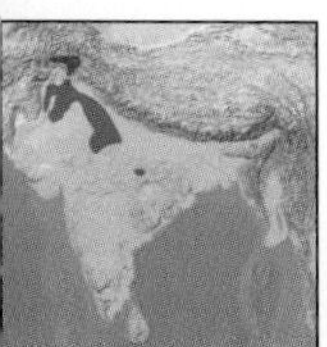

Size 9 cm

Voice Call different from that of Hume's, a monosyllabic, loud and piercing chwee, e.g. *chif… chif…chif*

Range Breeds in the Himalayas in N Pakistan. Winters in plains and hills in N Pakistan and N India

Habitat Summers in coniferous and mixed fir-broadleaved forests. Winters in bushes

Tiny yellowish warbler, with narrow greenish-yellow crown-stripe, golden-yellow supercilium; greyish-olive crown and yellow wash to cheeks and throat; pale rump; underparts have a buffish-yellow wash, in worn, underparts and wing-bars whiter. Square tail; dark, slender legs; short, spiky bill. Singly, or in pairs, but in mixed feeding groups outside breeding season.

YELLOW-BROWED WARBLER

Phylloscopus inornatus Phylloscopidae

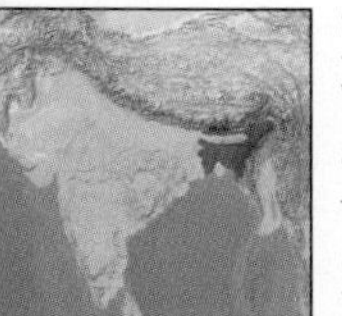

Size 10-11 cm

Voice Call a loud *cheweest*, with a distinct rising inflection, and typically quite different from that of Hume's

Range Winters from C Nepal east to NE India and Bangladesh, and in Kerala, Tamil Nadu, and Andaman and Nicobar Islands

Habitat Gardens, groves and open forests

Small warbler, with well-marked plumage pattern. Overall olive-green above and creamy-white with pale yellow streaking below; yellowish-white supercilium, ear-coverts and wing-bars. Similar to Lemon-rumped, but no yellow rump and has well-defined yellowish-white crown-stripe. In fresh plumage, brighter green above compared with Hume's, in worn plumage, greyer above with whiter supercilium, wing-bars and underparts.

LEMON-RUMPED WARBLER

Phylloscopus chloronotus Phylloscopidae

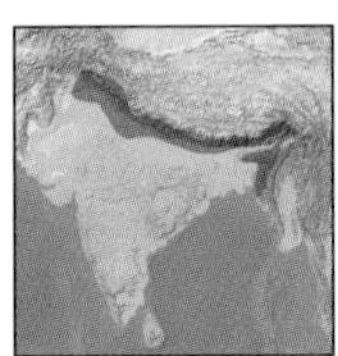

Size 9 cm

Voice Call a high *tsip*. Loud trilling song

Range Breeding resident in N hills of the Himalayas. Winters lower down in NE hills; S Assam Hills

Habitat Hill forests; secondary growth

Small, brightly-coloured warbler. Upperparts olive-green; strong patterning on head; dark lateral crown-stripe; distinct long pale yellow supercilium; broad grey-green eye-stripe and lores; underside whitish, sometimes with a pale yellow wash; pale yellow rump and a dark bill; two yellow wing-bars; short tail; pale legs. Sexes alike. Seen in mixed groups year round. Nests in trees. Feeds on invertebrates at all levels.

LARGE-BILLED LEAF WARBLER

Phylloscopus magnirostris Phylloscopidae

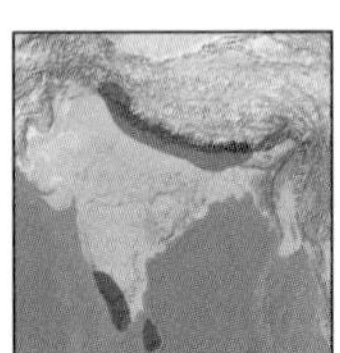

Size 13 cm

Voice Call a distinctive *dir...tee*, the first note slightly lower. Loud, ringing song

Range Breeds in the Himalayas. Spends winters over most of the peninsula, though exact range uncertain

Habitat Forests; groves

Medium-sized, brightly-coloured leaf warbler. Upperparts brown-olive; greenish-grey wash on breast sides and flanks; yellowish supercilium, dark eye-stripe distinctive; one or two faint wing-bars, not always easily seen. Underparts dull-yellow below. Sexes alike. Usually solitary, sometimes in mixed parties of small birds; quite active; spends most time in leafy upper branches of medium-sized trees; not easy to sight, but characteristic call notes help in confirming presence.

TYTLER'S LEAF WARBLER

Phylloscopus tytleri Phylloscopidae

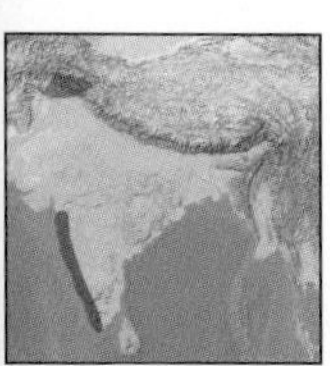

Size 10 cm

Voice Call a long *sooeeet*; also a harsh *huweest*

Range Rare endemic breeding summer visitor restricted to N Pakistan and Kashmir. Winters mainly in Western Ghats; passage records elsewhere

Habitat Forest undergrowth; coniferous forests

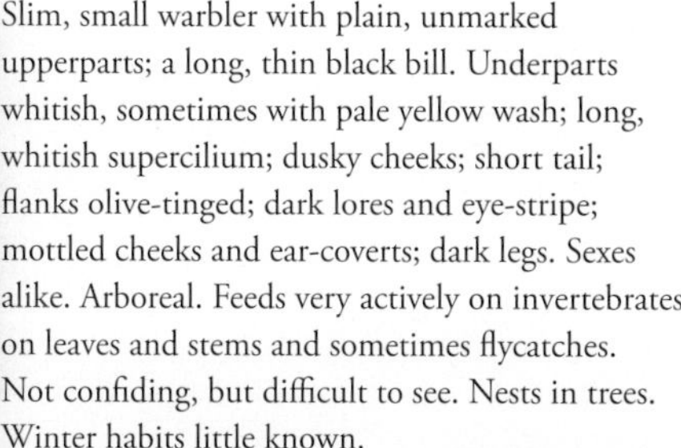

Slim, small warbler with plain, unmarked upperparts; a long, thin black bill. Underparts whitish, sometimes with pale yellow wash; long, whitish supercilium; dusky cheeks; short tail; flanks olive-tinged; dark lores and eye-stripe; mottled cheeks and ear-coverts; dark legs. Sexes alike. Arboreal. Feeds very actively on invertebrates on leaves and stems and sometimes flycatches. Not confiding, but difficult to see. Nests in trees. Winter habits little known.

WESTERN CROWNED WARBLER

Phylloscopus occipitalis Phylloscopidae

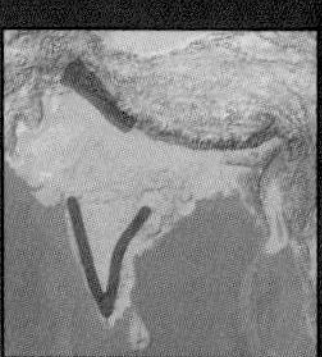

Size 11 cm

Voice Mostly silent. Though sometimes *chit…weei*

Range Summer breeding visitor to N hills upto E Uttarakhand. Winters mainly in Eastern and Western Ghats. Scattered records elsewhere and more widespread in India on passage

Habitat Forests

Stocky warbler with pale central crown-stripe, pale lower mandibles and dark legs. Upperparts greyish-green, with more green on wings and tail; two yellowish wing-bars on each wing; striking yellowish supercilium; underparts white. Sexes alike. Feeds on invertebrates actively in canopy and also in shrub layers. Seen in small parties and mixed hunting groups. Alternately flicks wings half-open. Confiding. Nests low down.

GREENISH WARBLER

Phylloscopus trochiloides Phylloscopidae

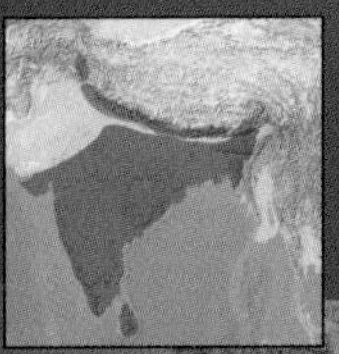

Size 11 cm

Voice Call a loud *tis…lee*

Range Breeding resident in the Himalayas. Winters widely in penisular lowlands and Sri Lanka. Common passage migrant elsewhere

Habitat All types of wooded country, including gardens

Dull greenish-brown bird with cream underparts. Medium-sized; slim; prominent, long, sweeping supercilium; whitish eye-ring; broad eye-stripe; mottled ear-coverts; strong patterning on head; one wing usually visible; brown legs. Sexes alike. Arboreal. Feeds on invertebrates, mainly in the canopy but also lower down. Active and restless. Frequently flycatches. Usually in scattered parties or mixed hunting groups. Nests low down.

YELLOW-VENTED WARBLER

Phylloscopus cantator Phylloscopidae

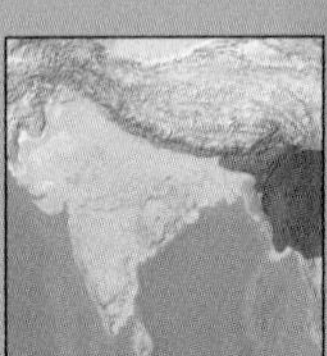

Size 10 cm

Voice Calls *pio…pio*. Long, loud, sweet song

Range E Nepal to rest of region

Habitat Dense, moist broadleaved evergreen forests; light forests

Overall yellowish-green bird, distinguished by bright yellow median crown-stripe and supercilium; dark lateral crown; olive-grey eye-stripe and lores; cheeks and ear-coverts mottled; underparts bright yellow-green; bright yellow chin, upper breast and undertail-coverts; lower breast and belly white; distinct yellow wing-bar on edge of greater covert; thin, pale bill and pale orange legs. Arboreal. Prefers vegetation close to water. Seen singly, or in pairs when breeding; gregarious; joins mixed foraging flocks with other insectivorous species in winter; usually active in lower forest storeys; flicks and fans tail when calling.

GREEN WARBLER

Phylloscopus (trochiloides) nitidus Phylloscopidae

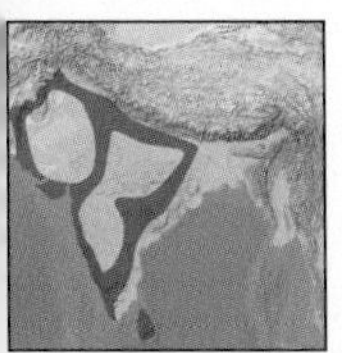

Size 10 cm

Voice Song a prolonged, sweet, thin, tumbling, tinkling, slightly descending, unslurred warble with a few burry notes

Range Passage migrant to Western Ghats and Sri Lanka

Habitat Similar to Greenish's

In fresh plumage, pale yellowish-green above with more prominent lower wing-bar than Greenish, yellowish supercilium, cheek, throat and breast; underparts may be quite yellowish, but not as pure yellow as Tickell's Leaf (more brown above and thinner-billed). In worn plumage, becomes greyer above, whiter below and resembles the fresh viridanus of Greenish, but usually retains some yellow tint to supercilium and cheek.

BLYTH'S LEAF WARBLER

Phylloscopus reguloides Phylloscopidae

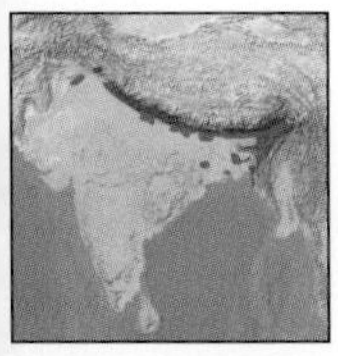

Size 11 cm

Voice Call a *kee…kew…i, see…pit*. Long, trilling song

Range Summer visitor to NW Himalayas. Resident in E Uttarakhand to S Assam hills

Habitat Oak, rhododendron, coniferous; wet evergreen forests; edges of forests; shrubberies

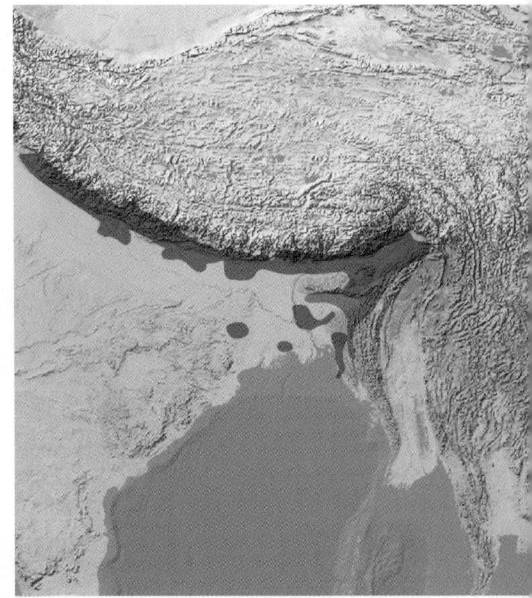

Medium-sized, brightly-coloured leaf warbler. Upperparts almost uniform green; dusky olive crown; whitish-yellow median crown-stripe; yellowish supercilium extends to nape; dark lores and eye-stripe; dark sides to crown; two broad, yellowish wing-bars; underparts range from white to pale yellow, with a grey tint; white edges to outer-tail feathers; racial variations. Habit of alternate flicking of wings distinguishes it from other leaf warblers. Singly, in pairs, sometimes in mixed foraging flocks with other insectivorous species.

CHESTNUT-CROWNED WARBLER

Seicercus castaniceps Phylloscopidae

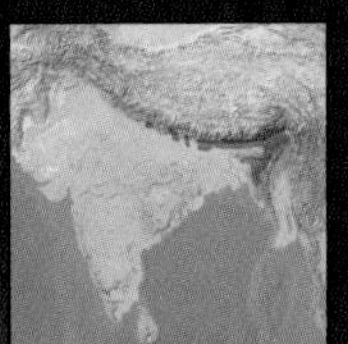

Size 9.5 cm

Voice Call a *tsik; chi…chi; sitsitsit*

Range Nepal to Myanmar; S Assam Hills

Habitat Dense oak, or mixed oak-rhododendron forests

Very colourful warbler with a distinct chestnut crown edged white on hindneck; prominent white eye-ring; face and mantle grey; whitish throat and breast; centre of belly white; rump and flanks bright yellow; mantle and back olive-green; two broad, yellow wing-bars; long, blunt bill and flesh-coloured legs and feet. Similar to Broad-billed but distinguished by dark lateral crown-stripe, absence of white supercilium and dark eye-stripe. Arboreal, seen mostly in mid to upper canopy; highly active. Usually found in pairs, small groups or mixed hunting parties; hovering and making short aerial sallies.

WHITE-SPECTACLED WARBLER

Seicercus affinis Phylloscopidae

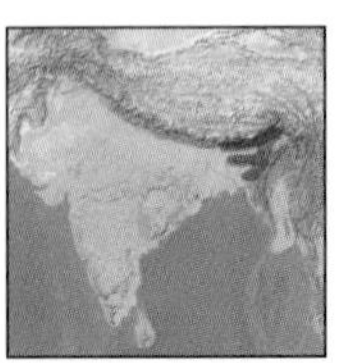

Size 10 cm

Voice Call a strong *che weet*

Range Common breeding resident in NE and S Assam Hills. Winters lower down in foothills and nearby plains

Habitat Undergrowth in dense, damp, broadleaved forests

Small, rounded warbler, with a domed head. Upperparts green and yellow; prominent white eye-ring; dark grey crown, nape and sides of head; darkish lateral crown-stripe; olive-green wings have single yellow wing-bar; broad, blunt bill and pale lower mandible. Very similar to Golden-spectacled, but grey extends down to nape and cheeks greenish. Sexes alike. Similar Grey-cheeked; *S. pologenys* has grey head and lores; white chin with only indistinct crown-stripe. Active in middle storey. Singly, in pairs or small groups.

GREY-CROWNED WARBLER

Seicercus tephrocephalus Phylloscopidae

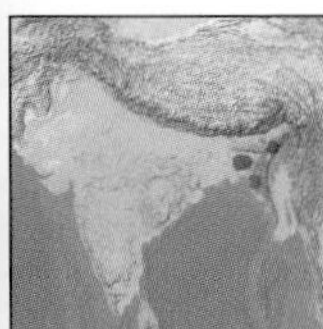

Size 11-12 cm

Voice Song sweet and clear with many trills, rather similar to Green-crowned's but without the slurring, warbling quality of Whistler's

Range Summer visitor; hills of NE India

Habitat Forest understorey

Largish warbler, with obvious grey crown with dark crown-stripe. Underparts bright yellow. Similar to Green-crowned, but crown and supercilium greyer than olive-green. Sides of crown darker than Whistler's; lacks prominent wing-bar; narrower yellow eye-ring. Skulks low in vegetation.

GREY-HOODED WARBLER

Phylloscopus xanthoschistos Phylloscopidae

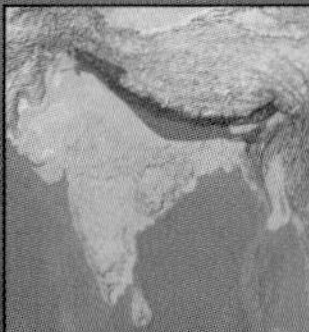

Size 10 cm

Voice Call a double-note *psit, psit…tyee, tyee*; quite vocal; familiar calls in the Himalayan forests. Loud, high-pitched, pleasant, trilling song

Range The Himalayas (900-3,000 m); altitudinal movement in winter

Habitat Himalayan forests; gardens

Plump, rounded warbler. Grey upperparts; crown, nape and back grey; prominent, long pale eyebrow; distinct white eye-rings; dark eye-stripe; dark grey lateral crown-stripe extends up to nape; yellowish rump and wings; bright yellow throat; yellow underparts, merging into olive-green flanks; white in outer-tail seen in flight; long, blunt bill; paler lower mandible. Sexes alike. Juvenile has a paler grey crown, tinted greenish. Arboreal, mainly in middle storey. In pairs or small bands, often along with mixed hunting parties; actively hunts and flits in canopy foliage and tall bushes; highly energetic, making frequent sallies to catch insects.

GREEN-CROWNED WARBLER

Seicercus burkii Phylloscopidae

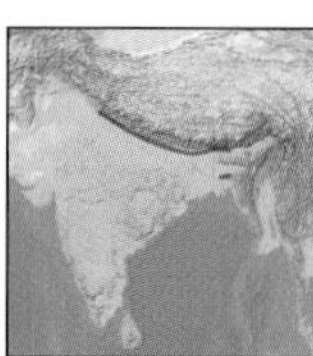

Size 11 cm

Voice Fairly noisy. Calls include sharp *chip…chip* or *cheup… cheup* notes

Range Breeds in the Himalayas. Winters in foothills, parts of C and E peninsula, N Maharashtra, S Madhya Pradesh, NE Andhra Pradesh

Habitat Forest undergrowth

Brightly-coloured warbler with a distinctive yellow eye-ring. Olive-green upperparts; greenish or grey-green eyebrow bordered above with prominent black coronal bands; greyish-green nape and crown; greenish sides of face; completely yellow below; greyish-brown wing-coverts edged with green; orange lower mandible; brownish-yellow legs. Sexes alike. Small, restless flocks, often in association with other small birds; keeps to low bushes and lower branches of trees.

WHISTLER'S WARBLER

Seicercus whistleri Phylloscopidae

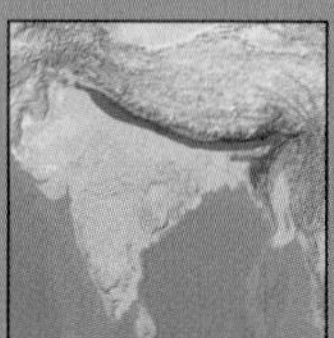

Size 10 cm

Voice Calls *tiu*. Rich, warbling song

Range Resident: the Himalayas: Pakistan to Myanmar. Moves down in winter

Habitat Undergrowth in coniferous, deciduous or evergreen forests

Colourful warbler with green upperparts, bright yellow underparts; domed head, deep olive crown; prominent pale yellow eye-ring; diffused crown-stripe. Similar to Green-crowned but has broad, dark lateral crown-stripe, pale yellow lores and broader eye-ring; upperparts duller, front less distinct, lower mandible pale; breast sides and flanks have touches of green or brown; usually more distinct wing-bar; more white in tail. Usually found in pairs, or in mixed foraging flocks; active in undergrowth. Skulking and secretive. Northwestern race paler plumaged than Eastern.

GREY-CHEEKED WARBLER

Seicercus poliogenys Phylloscopidae

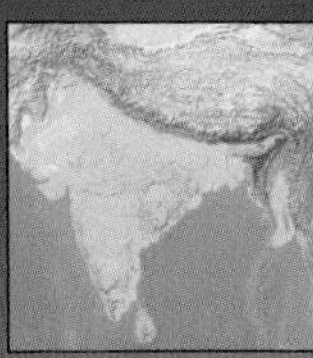

Size 10 cm

Voice Calls *tweest*. Sings *sweetu… sweetu; chewchi…chewchi*

Range C Nepal to Myanmar; S Assam Hills; altitudinal migrant

Habitat Evergreen forests; secondary growth with bamboo

Small, vividly-coloured warbler. Underparts bright yellow; green upperparts; dark grey hood, nape and sides of head; greyish-black lateral crown-stripe; paler cheeks and ear-coverts; pale grey lores and white eye-ring. Underparts bright yellow; whitish chin, throat and tail have olive-green tint; single yellow wing-bar; pale brown legs. Similar to Green-crowned but distinguished by white, not yellow, eye-ring and broader wing-bar. Juvenile has overall less colour intensity than adult. Singly or in pairs; outside breeding season in flocks with other small birds; active, unobtrusive, hovering, fluttering, making short aerial sallies to catch invertebrates.

BLACK-FACED WARBLER

Abroscopus schisticeps Cettiidae

Size 9 cm

Voice Call a buzzing alarm. Trilling song

Range Breeding resident; W Uttarakhand to Arunachal Pradesh; S Assam Hills

Habitat Glades; thick undergrowth in moist broadleaved oak forest with mossy trees

Small, brightly-coloured warbler with distinct broad black mask; prominent broad, yellow brow; yellow supercilium, throat and vent; yellow-green lower mantle and wings; crown, nape, rear ear-coverts, upper mantle grey; underparts mostly white; pinkish bill and pale legs. Similar to Yellow-bellied Fantail, but has white, not yellow belly, short tail and no wing-bar. Eastern race, *flavimentalis*, lacks yellow breast and flanks of the Central Himalayan nominate; yellow only on breast. In small, itinerant bird waves, active in middle storeys or bush-tops.

YELLOW-BELLIED WARBLER

Abroscopus superciliaris Cettiidae

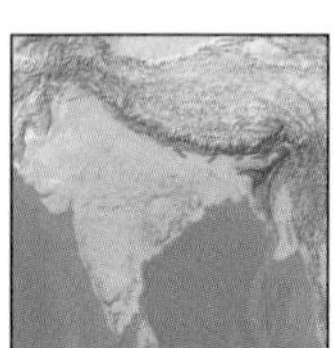

Size 9 cm

Voice Calls *chrrt…chrrt…chrrt.* Song 6-noted, ascending at the end

Range The Himalayas; hills of NE India

Habitat Bamboo forests

Very small warbler with yellowish-olive upperparts and white throat; long, white supercilium; dark crown and eye-stripe; yellowish-olive mantle. Underparts yellow; tail looks pale brownish-buff from below. Similar to Grey-hooded but lacks white in tail. Unlike Phylloscopus, distinguished by long bill, brownish-grey on crown, white throat and yellow underparts, and by narrower tail. Arboreal, keeping to middle and upper storey. Often seen near water. Singly or in pairs, but with other small birds, in non-breeding season.

RUFOUS-FACED WARBLER

Abroscopus albogularis Cettiidae

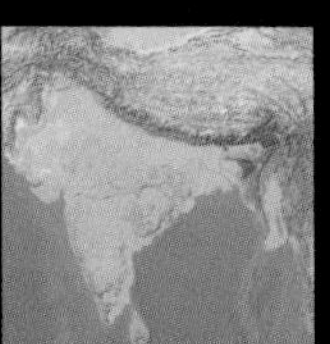

Size 8 cm

Voice Call a high-pitched tittering. Song includes high-pitched whistles and trills

Range E Nepal, Arunachal Pradesh and S Assam Hills

Habitat Edges of moist deciduous and broadleaved forests; bamboos; secondary growth

Tiny warbler with unmistakable rufous face. Buff median crown-stripe; black lateral crown-stripe; upperparts olive-green; throat white with black spotting; yellow breast patch and vent; white belly; pale buff-patch on rump; indistinct eye-ring; broad, blunt bill. Arboreal; usually in pairs when breeding; in small groups or mixed hunting parties; hyperactive; hovers, flutters, makes short aerial sallies. Joins mixed flocks. Calls frequently.

BROAD-BILLED WARBLER

Tickellia hodgsoni Cettiidae

Roundish warbler with rusty crown and forehead. Face grey; whitish supercilium and dark eye-stripe; grey ear-coverts, throat, sides of neck and breast; partial white eye-ring and crown-stripe not so prominent; nape and mantle olive-green; brown wing-coverts edged olive-green. Similar to Chestnut-crowned but belly and vent yellow, no wing-bars or yellow rump. Shorter tail and bill than Mountain Tailorbird. Singly or in pairs. Seen in forest undergrowth; rarely in canopy. Confiding.

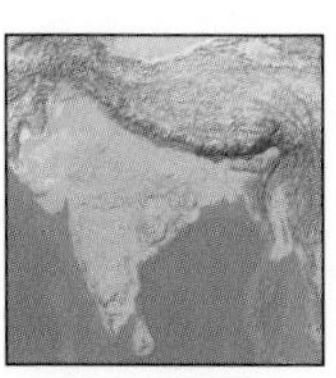

Size 10 cm

Voice Call a high-pitched twittering. Song a series of high-pitched whistled notes

Range Patchily in E Nepal, Bhutan and Arunachal Pradesh; possibly S Assam Hills

Habitat Dense undergrowth with bamboo in broadleaved evergreen forests; forest edge; dense scrub

ORPHEAN WARBLER

Sylvia hortensis Sylviidae

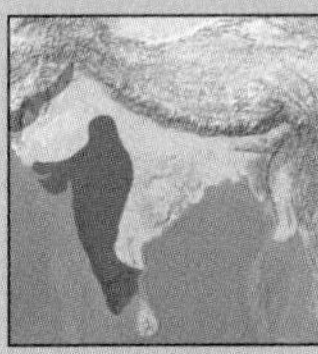

Size 15 cm

Voice Loud warbling song

Range Summer visitor to Pakistan. Winters mainly in India

Habitat Bush-covered hills; winters in scrub, orchards and groves

Medium-sized, dull-coloured warbler with strong markings. Large dark grey head; upperparts mostly grey; pale grey mantle; blackish crown; dark forehead, forecrown and even darker ear-coverts; underparts whitish, tinged pink; dark uppertail with greyish centres; blackish tail with pale fringes to undertail-coverts; long, pointed wings; square-ended tail; pale iris and dark legs. Female overall more brown with a dark brown head; underparts tinged buff rather than pink and more creamy-brown, speckled iris. Mostly singly or in pairs. Very confiding and mostly hidden in thick cover in breeding season. Seen calling from bush-tops or shrubs.

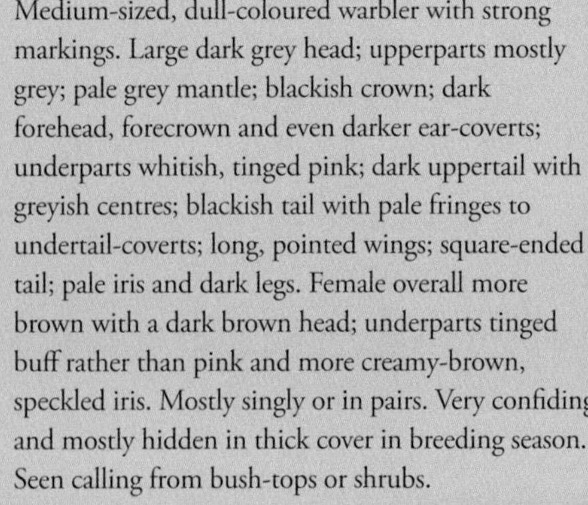

LESSER WHITETHROAT

Sylvia curruca Sylviidac

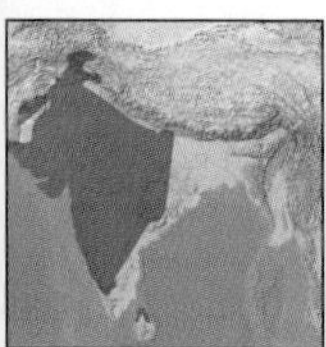

Size 13 cm

Voice Noisy. Call a clicking *tek*; also churrs. Song a flourished rattle

Range Common winter visitor to Pakistan, W peninsula and N India; south to N Tamil Nadu and N Sri Lanka. Absent or rare from most of E and NE India, Bangladesh

Habitat Open woodlands; scrubs

Dull ash-brown warbler with dark cheek patches; grey head; brown mantle and wings; short brown tail with white outer-tail feathers; underparts creamy-white; throat white; grey breast and belly; brownish flanks. Recently split Desert Whitethroat is smaller and paler. Often in loose groups. Horizontal carriage. Confident direct flight. Rather shy. Feeds on insects and nectar, usually high in trees but also in bushes.

DESERT WHITETHROAT

Sylvia (curruca) minula Sylviidac

Size 13 cm

Voice Noisy. Call a clicking *tek*; also *churrs*. Song a flourished rattle

Range Common winter visitor to Pakistan and NW India

Habitat Open woodlands and scrubs, feeding on insects and nectar, usually high in trees but also in bushes

Until recently, considered conspecific with the Lesser; seen as members of a superspecies. Distinguished from Hume's and Lesser by smaller size and smaller bill. Paler grey head lacks the well-marked dark cheeks of Hume's and Lesser, and a lighter grey-brown back; white throat; underparts pale greyish-white. Often in loose groups. Horizontal carriage. Confident direct flight. Rather shy.

HUME'S WHITETHROAT

Sylvia althaea Sylviidae

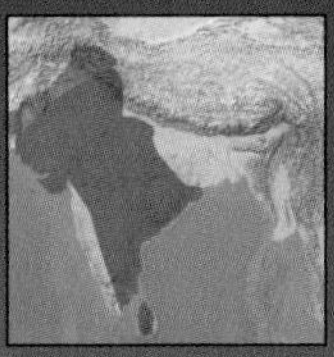

Size 13 cm

Voice Noisy. Similar to Lesser's. Song more bubbling and cheerful

Range Uncommon breeding summer visitor to N hills from W Pakistan east to Kashmir

Habitat Open woodlands and scrubs. Behaviour as Lesser's

Medium-sized, rather dark greyish warbler with even darker cheeks; large head; dark ashy-grey crown; greyish-brown back. Similar to Lesser, but distinguished by slightly larger size, stouter bill, darker top of the head and darker grey-brown back. Underparts white with grey wash on flanks. Sexes alike.

MÉNÉTRIES'S WARBLER

Sylvia mystacea Sylviidae

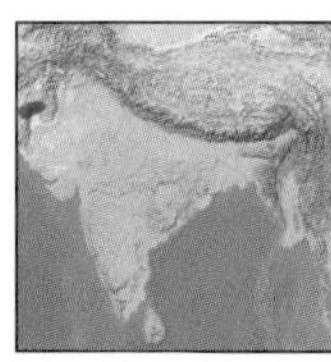

Size 12 cm

Voice Dry, chattering warbling song

Range Summer visitor to Balochistan

Habitat Scrubs in semi-desert

Small, striking-looking warbler with black crown. Distinctive rusty-orange eye-ring; reddish iris; upperparts blue-grey; dark grey lores, cheeks and ear-coverts; white throat and breast tinged pink; white sub-moustachial line; long tail. In some, underparts whitish, head paler grey. Female and juvenile have more plain and ochre-brown upperparts, whitish underparts; iris yellowish-brown. Singly or in pairs; in small flocks during migration. Confiding. Keeps under cover.

ASIAN DESERT WARBLER

Sylvia nana Sylviidae

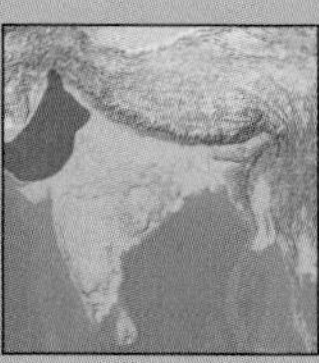

Size 10 cm

Voice Call a chattering *ch…errr.* Jingling song

Range Locally common winter visitor to dry parts of Pakistan and extreme NW India

Habitat Scrubs in sandy or stony deserts; saline flats; rocky hillsides

Drab-looking warbler with brownish-grey upperparts; rufous rump; central tail with broad white edges; underparts creamy-white; indistinct white eye-ring; yellow iris; lower mandible and legs also yellow; short, rounded wings; square-ended tail. Sexes alike. Recently split from paler north African race *S. deserti.* Feeds on invertebrates, mainly on ground, moving with short hops; also feeds in shrubs and occasionally perches in open. Constantly flicks tail. Territorial in breeding. Male often cocks and fans tail when singing.

COMMON WHITETHROAT

Sylvia communis Sylviidae

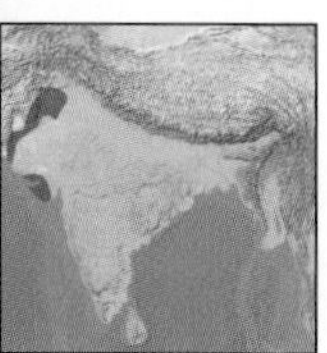

Size 14 cm

Voice Call a grating *charr* and a loud *tak.* Song scratchy and delivered in short song flight

Range Fairly common passage migrant through Pakistan and NW India

Habitat Low scrub; cultivation

Medium-sized warbler with a largish slaty-grey domed head. Pale (not grey) legs. Brown upperparts; darker central tail feathers; diagnostic white throat and pale underparts; white eye-ring; chestnut wing panels. Female has brown head. Feeds mainly on invertebrates and fruits, sometimes in scattered groups. Inquisitive, though skulking. Flight low and laboured. Often perches on bush-tops with raised crown.

SPOT-THROATED BABBLER

Pellorneum albiventre Timaliidae

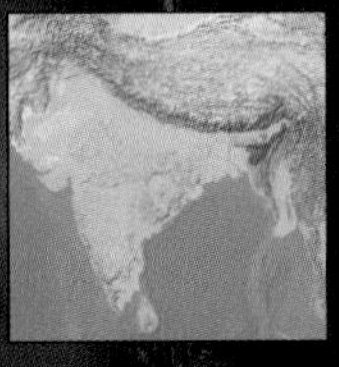

Size 14 cm

Voice Calls include harsh *chrrr-chrrrchrrr...chrrrit* and slightly explosive *tip...tip...tip*

Range The Himalayan foothills in E Bhutan, and hills of NE India and Bangladesh

Habitat Scrubs and thickets of secondary growth or bamboos; avoids dense forests

Dull, almost uniform deep olive-brown babbler. White throat with faint grey mottling; olive-brown breast and flanks; short, rounded tail; rufescent vent. Similar to Abbott, but has smaller head and bill and no rufous on tail. Similar to Buff-breasted in size and shape, but with shorter tail that has more rounded tip. Unlike Abbot's, has no rufous on tail. Skulks in undergrowth, usually in pairs.

MARSH BABBLER

Pellorneum palustre Timaliidae

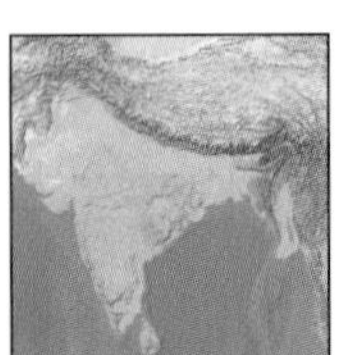

Size 15 cm

Voice Calls include loud, double chirp, *chi...chew;* series of undistinguished, unobtrusive *churrs*

Range Endemic: Subcontinent, NE India and Bangladesh

Habitat Extensive reed beds and tall grasslands at edges of marshes and rivers, bushes in swampy ground

Smallish babbler with rufous-brown crown and uniform olive-brown upperparts. White throat and centre of belly; grey supercilium; blackish streaking on throat, breast and flanks. Thin bill; dark flanks; rufescent vent. Similar to Puff-throated, but less prominent supercilium, lacks rufous crown and smaller in size. Confused with Spot-throated, but distinguished by much bolder streaking and longer, rounded tail. Skulks in undergrowth. Nests in low vegetation.

PUFF-THROATED BABBLER

Pellorneum ruficeps Timaliidae

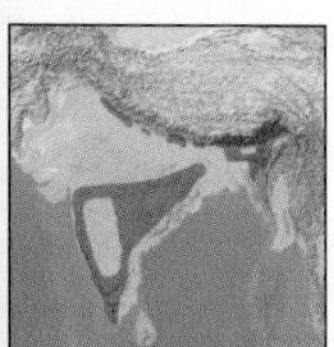

Size 15 cm

Voice Best-known call a 4-note whistle, interpreted as *he...will... beat...you.* Noisy when breeding; mellow whistle, 2, 3, or 4-noted

Range Hilly-forest areas; the Himalayas, to about 1,500 m, east of SE Himachal Pradesh; NE states; S Bihar, Odisha, Satpura range across C India, Eastern and Western Ghats

Habitat Forest undergrowth; bamboos; overgrown ravines; nullahs

ruficebs

mandellii

Small bird with olive-brown upperparts; dark rufous cap; whitish-buff stripe over eye; white throat; dull fulvous-white underbody, boldly streaked blackish-brown on breast and sides. Sexes alike. Solitary, or in pairs; shy, secretive bird of undergrowth; mostly heard, extremely difficult to see; rummages on ground, amidst leaf litter; hops about, rarely ascends into upper branches.

BROWN-CAPPED BABBLER

Pellorneum fuscocapillus Timaliidae

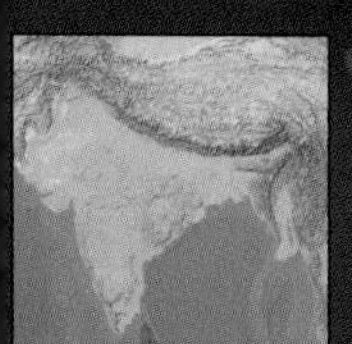

Size 16 cm

Voice Song and call probably similar to Puff-throated's. Noisy when feeding

Range Endemic resident; common in lowlands and hills

Habitat Thick ground cover, such as scrub, low jungles and forest undergrowth

Plain, dull-coloured babbler. Upperparts olive-brown; dark brown-black crown and nape; head sides cinnamon-brown; dark olive-brown wings; short, rounded tail. Underparts more cinnamon brown. Confused with Puff-throated. *P. f. babaulti* (lowlands) has paler ochre-buff sides of head and underparts; paler ash-brown upperparts, wings and tail. Usually in pairs. Forages for insects on ground in dry vegetation and fallen leaves. Nests on ground or holes.

ABBOTT'S BABBLER

Malacocincla abbotti Timaliidae

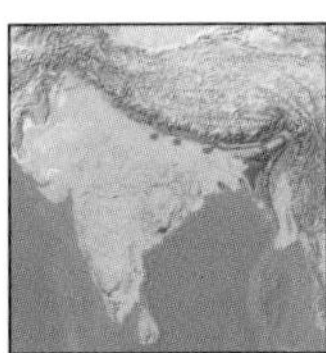

Size 17 cm

Voice Calls include trills, churrs, mews. Whistled song *tchwee…tchu…tchwee*; occasionally, duets

Range Nepal, Bhutan, Assam and Arunachal Pradesh

Habitat Thick undergrowth in moist broadleaved evergreen forests; thickets; streams; tree ferns

Plain, drab, brownish babbler with short tail, thick bill, stocky appearance; light-grey supercilium and lores; greyish or greyish-white throat and breast; olive-brown above; unmarked throat and breast; rufous breast sides; olive-brown flanks; rufous tail, uppertail-coverts; brighter rufous vent and undertail-coverts. Solitary, or in pairs; territorial and site-loyal; terrestrial; forages on or near ground; shy and secretive; stays close to dense cover; rarely flies. Juvenile has dark rufescent-brown crown and upperparts.

BUFF-BREASTED BABBLER

Pellomeum tickelli Timaliidae

Resident in NE Indian hills. Plain-looking, has dark brown underparts; whitish belly. Often confused with Abbott's as well as Spot-throated. Skulks in undergrowth in damp moist forest floors as well as in bamboo thickets. Sharp and loud call often attracts attention.

LARGE SCIMITAR BABBLER

Pomatorhinus hypoleucos Timaliidae

Upperparts overall olive-brown; grey ear-coverts; mottling on sides of neck and supercilium. Lacks strong white supercilium. Underparts grey with rufous wash; white throat; breast streaked white; grey legs and feet; less curved and stouter bill. Juvenile has shorter, dull-coloured bill; more rufous on underparts and less rufous on vent. Usually in pairs or small flocks. Feeds on insects on ground. Usually located by call.

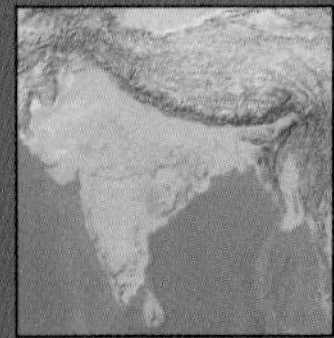

Size 28 cm

Voice Sings with loud, hollow, variable piping notes; with pairs, often calling antiphonally, *i…e… wiu…pu…pu…wup…up*

Range Hills of NE India (Arunachal Pradesh, Assam, Manipur, Meghalaya, Nagaland, Tripura) and Bangladesh

Habitat Canebrakes, bamboo thickets, reeds, elephant grass; dense undergrowth in broadleaved evergreen forests

SPOT-BREASTED SCIMITAR BABBLER

Pomatorhinus erythrocnemis Timaliidae

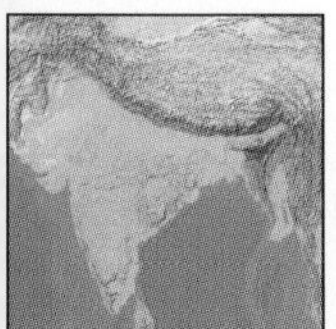

Size 12 cm

Voice Song and call quite low-pitched and persistent, fluty *tfuu…tuu*, first note stressed, followed by higher-pitched *tfuuk*

Range Hills of NE India; Bangladesh

Habitat Undergrowth in forests; scrub jungles; thickets in forest clearings and abandoned cultivation

Medium-sized babbler. Only scimitar babbler with both brown spotting on underparts and no white supercilium. Likely to be confused only with Large Scimitar. Distinguished from that species by smaller size, finer bill, rufous lores and ear-coverts, uniform olive-brown breast sides and flanks, paler olive-brown upperparts, brownish rather than lead-grey legs and feet.

RUSTY-CHEEKED SCIMITAR BABBLER

Pomatorhinus erythrogenys Timaliidae

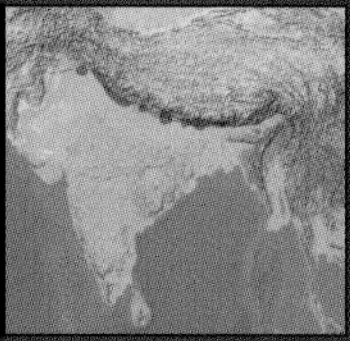

Size 25 cm

Voice Noisy. Call a mellow, fluty whistle, 2-noted *cue…pe…cue…pe*, followed by single (sometimes double) note reply by mate. Also, guttural alarm call and liquid contact note

Range The Himalayan foothills to at least 2,200 m and possibly to 2,600 m

Habitat Forest undergrowth; ravines; bamboos

Olive-brown above; orangish-rufous (rusty) forehead, sides of face, head, thighs and flanks; long, curved 'scimitar' beak; pale eye surrounded by bare, greyish mottled skin. Underparts mostly pure white. Sexes alike. Seen in small bands in forests; hops on jungle floors; turns over leaves or digs with beak; sometimes hops into leafy branches, but more at ease on ground. Juvenile overall paler and duller rufous.

SRI LANKA SCIMITAR BABBLER

Pomatorhinus melaurus Timaliidae

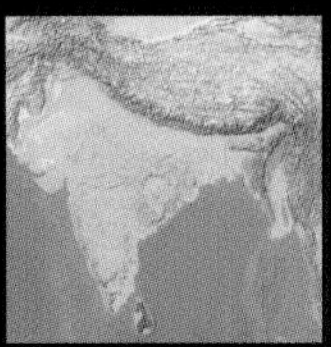

Size 21.5 cm

Voice Calls include a variety of loud, bubbling whistles

Range The only scimitar babbler in Sri Lanka

Habitat Forests; well-wooded areas

Upperparts rich rust-brown; white supercilium extending to nape; black eye-stripe; dark ear-coverts; downcurved yellow bill, white underparts, breast and flanks. Undertail-coverts and vent also white. Sexes alike. In pairs, or small flocks. Feeds on ground.

WHITE-BROWED SCIMITAR BABBLER

Pomatorhinus schisticeps Timaliidae

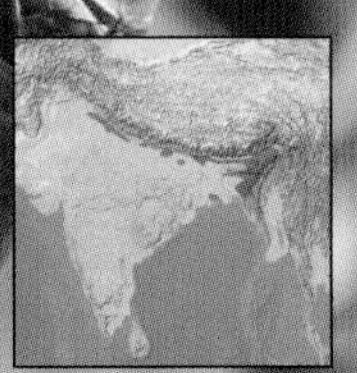

Size 22 cm

Voice Often duets, hoots, whistles

Range Punjab east throughout the region

Habitat Dense forest undergrowth; secondary growth

Largish scimitar babbler, with long, broad white supercilium; variable crown—from grey to rufous-brown, even blackish; dark lores, ear-coverts. Long, sturdy, decurved yellow bill; pale eyes; pure white throat, breast, belly. Chestnut neck sides below, breast, flanks; olive-brown upperparts, tail. Similar to Streak-breasted, smaller with shorter bill, streaked breast. Rusty-cheeked lacks supercilium, black mask; has grey throat. In mixed foraging flocks, with other babblers; bird of mid-storey; hunts in thickets, undergrowth, small trees.

STREAK-BREASTED SCIMITAR BABBLER

Pomatorhinus ruficollis Timaliidae

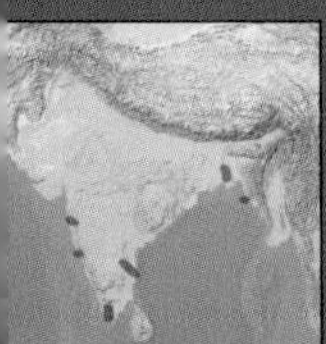

Size 19 cm

Voice Off-and-on duets between males and females *kwee…kwee*

Range Hills of E Uttarakhand to Myanmar

Habitat Forest undergrowth; hillside scrub; secondary growth

Fairly small scimitar babbler. Long, broad white supercilium merging above bill; black mask; decurved yellow bill; dark crown and olive-brown upperparts. Similar to White-browed, but smaller, with shorter bill; chestnut only around nape; olive-brown streaks on breast and belly, and plain olive-brown flanks; white only around chin, throat. In pairs when breeding, otherwise, in small groups. Skulking, secretive; more often heard than seen; forages on ground, moving quickly through dense cover, bounding along in long hops, or flies from bush to bush.

RED-BILLED SCIMITAR BABBLER

Pomatorhinus ochraceiceps Timaliidae

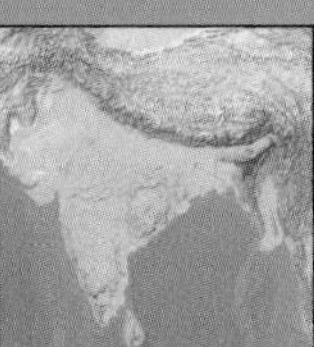

Size 23 cm

Voice Typically, gives hurried, hollow piping, e.g. *wu…wu…wu…* or *wu…wu…whip* or *pu…pu*

Range Uncommon resident in hills of NE India (Arunachal Pradesh, Assam, Manipur, Meghalaya, Mizoram, Nagaland); 1,500-2,400 m, moves lower down to foothills in winter

Habitat Dense undergrowth in broadleaved evergreen forests and bamboo thickets

Medium-sized scimitar babbler. Upperparts ash-brown; orange-red bill curved down; striking white supercilium; sides of neck, flanks and vent dark grey. Underparts pale buff; deep buff lower throat and breast. Similar to Coral-billed which has shorter, thicker bill and broader black mask. In pairs, or small flocks. Feeds on ground, foraging in vegetation for insects. Very secretive.

INDIAN SCIMITAR BABBLER

Pomatorhinus horsfieldii Timaliidae

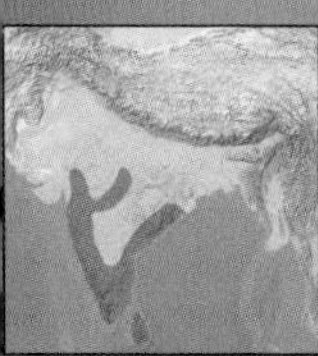

Size 22 cm

Voice Fluty, musical whistle, often followed by bubbling note; often calls in duet

Range Hilly forest regions of peninsular India, with four races

Habitat Mixed forests; scrub; bamboos

Deep olive-brown above; long, white supercilium; broad, black band through eye; white throat, breast and belly centre; diagnostic long, curved yellow 'scimitar' beak with blackish base to upper mandible. Tail long, broad and graduated; short, rounded wings. Sexes alike. Juvenile overall darker, lacks black lateral crown-stripes and has paler bill. In pairs, or small, loose bands in forests; keeps to undergrowth, more often heard than seen. Hops on jungle floors, vigorously rummages through leaf litter, digs with long beak; hops into leafy branches, but not for long; scattered birds keep in touch through calls. Rarely seen flying in open.

CORAL-BILLED SCIMITAR BABBLER

Pomatorhinus ferruginosus Timaliidae

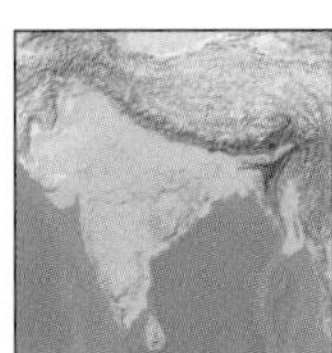

Size 22 cm

Voice Calls include soft, fluty oriole-like whistles; *churrs*

Range E Nepal to Arunachal Pradesh, S Assam Hills

Habitat Dense forest undergrowth; secondary growth; bamboos

Distinctive scimitar babbler with bright coral-red bill; long, white supercilium; long, black mask from bill to mantle; white upper throat. E Himalayan nominate race has black crown, nape; bright chestnut-rufous throat, breast, belly; bristly rufous feathers on forehead, lores. Races south, east of Brahmaputra have brown crown, thin black lateral crown-stripe, buff underparts; confused only with Red-billed, which has longer, more curved bill, white breast, belly. In pairs when breeding, or in small parties; forages on ground, bushes, small trees.

SLENDER-BILLED SCIMITAR BABBLER

Xiphirhynchus superciliaris Timaliidae

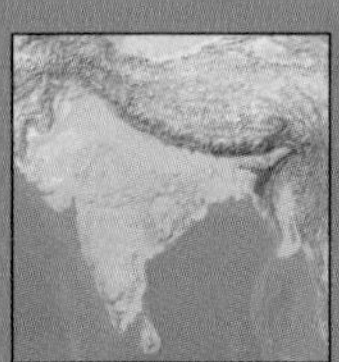

Size 20 cm

Voice Varied calls include series of repeated powerful mellow hoots, uttered rapidly

Range E Himalayas; NE India

Habitat Moist broadleaved forests, bamboo thickets

Medium-sized scimitar babbler with very long, slender, sharply downcurved black bill; small, dark slaty-grey head with long, white, feathery supercilium; grey ear-coverts. Upperparts brown; brighter rufous-brown underparts; whitish throat streaked with grey. Sexes alike. Skulking and secretive; forages in bamboos or in low undergrowth; often in small flocks.

LONG-BILLED WREN BABBLER

Rimator malacoptilus Timaliidae

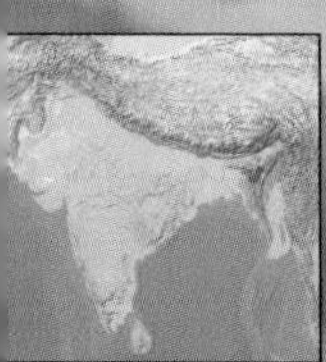

Size 12 cm

Voice Only vocalisation recorded from the subcontinent a sweet chirping whistle. Alarm call includes churring...*prurr...prurr... prrit* etc, or quickly repeated *ker... wickit...ker...wickit*

Range The Himalayas; from Sikkim and West Bengal east to Arunachal Pradesh; NE India

Habitat Forest undergrowth on rocky ground, steep ravines, and overgrown, abandoned clearings

Largish wren babbler with diagnostic narrow, long, dark grey, downcurved bill. Upperparts brown, streaked with paler buff-brown; narrow, dark moustachial stripe; indistinct malar stripe. Underparts buffish-white; throat buff-streaked; brown breast and flanks; and rufous-brown vent and undertail-coverts. Short tail. Secretive. Forages on ground; solitary, or in pairs.

STREAKED WREN BABBLER

Napothera brevicaudata Timaliidae

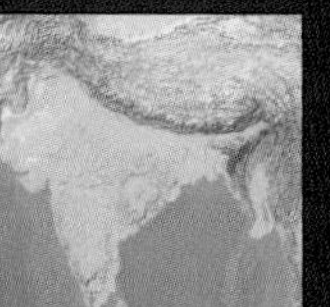

Size 12 cm

Voice Sings with variable, clear, ringing whistled notes *peee...oo, pu...ee, chiu...ree, chewee...ee...,pee...wi* etc, sometimes single *pweeee*

Range Fairly common resident in hills of NE India (Arunachal Pradesh, Assam, Manipur, Meghalaya, Mizoram, Nagaland), subject to some altitudinal movements

Habitat Moist, thick forests on rocky ground on steep slopes and in ravines

Large, untidy-looking wren babbler. Upperparts olive-brown, streaked paler from crown to mantle. Large, heavy bill; grey lores, supercilium and ear-coverts; rufescent-patch below rear ear-coverts; whitish throat streaked grey, olive-brown breast; whitish centre of belly streaked with long shafts of medium-brown. Uppertail, rump and wings uniform brown; prominent tail. Secretive. Feeds on ground.

EYEBROWED WREN BABBLER

Napothera epilepidota Timaliidae

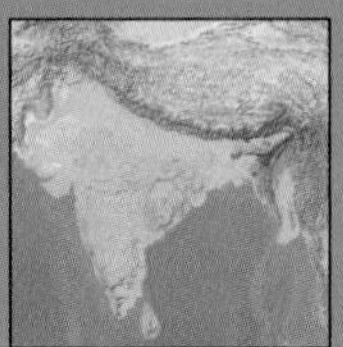

Size 10 cm

Voice Call a plaintive, falling whistle, *cheeeeeu* or *piiiiiu*, repeated at 2-5 second intervals

Range The Himalayas; from E Bhutan eastwards; hills of NE India

Habitat Moss- and fern-covered boulders, fallen logs and stumps in dense, moist shady forest

Smallish wren babbler with strongly marked, ash-brown upperparts. Diagnostic long, pale supercilium; dark eye-stripe; dark ear-coverts; thin bill; wing-coverts spotted white; darkish spotting on breast and throat. Short tail. Sexes alike. *N. e. guttaticollis* of the E Himalayas has whiter supercilium and darker spots on breast and throat. while *N. e. roberti*, south of the Brahmaputra has paler supercilium, sides of throat and breast.

SCALY-BREASTED WREN BABBLER

Pnoepyga albiventer Timaliidae

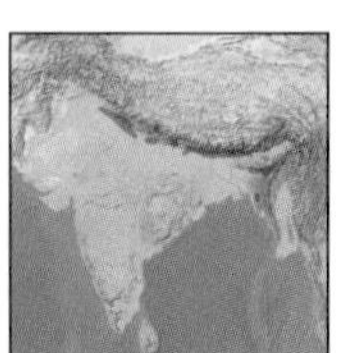

Size 10 cm

Voice Song a fine, strong warble, *tzee…tze…zit…tzu…stu…tzit*, rising and then ending abruptly

Range The Himalayas from W Himachal Pradesh east to Arunachal Pradesh; NE India

Habitat Moist, shady broadleaved forests among ferns and other tall herbage and moss-covered boulders and logs; favours ravines and edges of streams

fulvous morph

Small wren babbler. Underparts boldly scaled; paler buff mottling on lores, sides of neck and ear-coverts. Very short tail and bill. Underparts more boldly scaled in definite scallop pattern. Sexes alike. Juvenile plainer and less distinct above and more marked below. Similar to Pygmy Wren but larger and rounder in shape. Feeds on insects and seeds, skulking amidst stones and tangled vegetation.

white morph

NEPAL WREN BABBLER

Pnoepyga immaculata Timaliidae

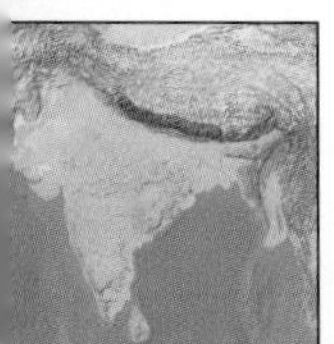

Size 10 cm

Voice Eight high-pitched piercing notes, fairly quickly delivered, sometimes speeding up slightly towards the end, *tsi…tsu…tsitsi… si…tsu…tsi…tsi* or *si…su…si… si…swi*

Range Recently described species, east from Uttarakhand

Habitat Dense scrub

fulvous morph

white morph

Slightly larger than Pygmy Wren. Similar to Scaly-breasted, but longer bill; feathers on less scaly underparts longer, with dark centres and pale fringes; streaked breast. Lacks spotting on crown, mantle and wing-coverts. Longish pale legs; dark bill. Creeps in undergrowth in rodent-like manner.

PYGMY WREN BABBLER

Pnoepyga pusilla Timaliidae

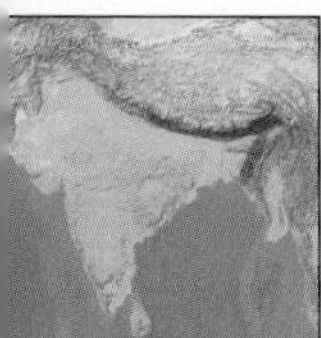

Size 9 cm

Voice Calls *tzook*. Song a repeated drawn-out *tsee…tsu*

Range Fairly common breeding resident in N mountains from W Nepal east to Burmese border and perhaps Bangladesh. Moves lower down in winter. Also occurs in China and SE Asia

Habitat Camp, ferny undergrowth of forests often among mossy boulders and fallen logs near streams

fulvous morph

white morph

Very small and overall brown babbler; extremely short tail. Upperparts dark brown with few paler spots. Underparts beige-white with dark scaling. Unmarked throat; long legs; large, grey bill. Sexes alike. Feeds on invertebrates on ground. Solitary, or in pairs. Secretive, hops away when alarmed. Flicks wings. Nests on mossy ground amidst rocks.

RUFOUS-THROATED WREN BABBLER

Spelaeornis caudatus Timaliidae

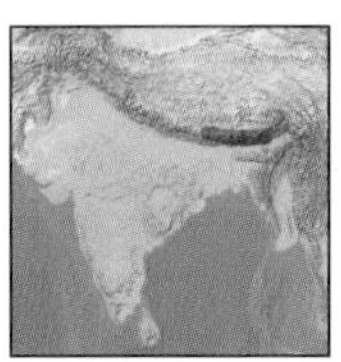

Size 9 cm

Voice Calls include chittering, churring, warbling and chirruping; *dzit…*; *whichoo… whichoo…whichoo*

Range E Nepal, Bhutan; W Arunachal Pradesh

Habitat Undergrowth in moist broadleaved evergreen forests

Small rotund wren babbler. Grey face and whitish chin; unmarked, bright orange-rufous throat, breast and flanks streaked and barred; black-and-white mottled belly; plain brown (with rufous tint) back and wings; almost tail-less. Juvenile has more rufous upperparts and more diffused scaling. Difficult to see in dense ferns, undergrowth and mossy rocks. Territorial. Forages on ground in leaf litter.

RUSTY-THROATED WREN BABBLER

Spelaeornis badeigularis Timaliidae

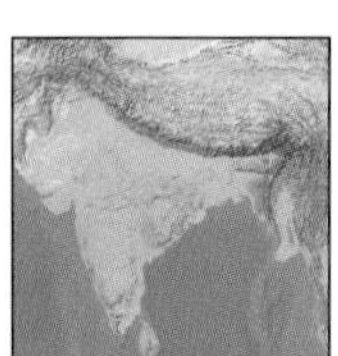

Size 8.5 cm

Voice Evidently, rather like Rufous-throated's

Range Resident in Mishmi Hills, E Arunachal Pradesh

Habitat Moist subtropical forest

Sometimes referred as the Mishmi Wren Babbler. Small, deep brown warbler with distinct rufous-patch on throat. Grey ear-coverts; darkly streaked lower throat; small, whitish-patch on chin. Black-and-white barred lower breast, and belly; flanks and vent dark brown. Small, short tail. Similar to Rufous-throated, except much darker and rufous restricted to throat. Largely terrestrial, foraging in thick undergrowth.

BAR-WINGED WREN BABBLER

Spelaeornis troglodytoides Timaliidae

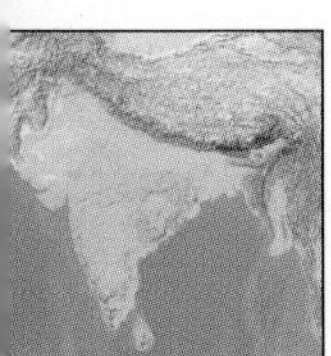

Size 10 cm

Voice Call a soft *churr…cheep*. Mellow warbling song

Range Bhutan; Arunachal Pradesh

Habitat Moist temperate evergreen forests; dense undergrowth

Rufous-brown wren babbler with distinctive markings. Chestnut-rufous crown, with paler spotting; wings and tail finely barred grey; blue-grey lores and around eyes; pale brown ear-coverts; unmarked, white chin, throat and upper breast; flanks and vent rufous-brown. Female has rufous streaking on chin, throat and breast; long tail. Feeds on ground.

LONG-TAILED WREN BABBLER

Spelaeornis chocolatinus Timaliidae

Size 10 cm

Voice Song is a clear *wee-itchy wee-oo*

Range Nagaland

Habitat Not yet distinguished from other Spelaeornis wren-babblers

Sometimes referred to as Naga Wren Babbler. Small, dark brown wren-babbler similar to Tawny-breasted and Grey-bellied (both with grey cheek and blackish stripe), but slightly longer-tailed than either with abundant, prominent white shaft-streaks on flanks. Darker upperparts than Tawny-breasted and browner underparts with fine black flecks below throat; with fine black marks on more fulvous underparts. Said to breed in May, concealing its domed or semi-domed nest on ground amongst leaf litter.

SPOTTED WREN BABBLER

Elachura formosa Timaliidae

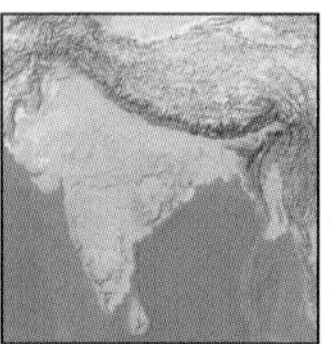

Size 10 cm

Voice Calls *sik*; *put…put*. Song includes high-pitched, stuttering whistles *dit…dit…dit*, etc.

Range Bhutan, Arunachal Pradesh and S Assam Hills

Habitat Moist broadleaved evergreen forests; mossy rocks, dense undergrowth

Very small wren babbler, with mid-length tail; broad dark barring on wings and tail, unlike finer grey-blue barring in Bar-winged; no white throat and breast, or heavy white mottling on crown and nape. Lightly spotted hindcrown, nape and mantle. Heavy speckling and vermiculation on paler underparts; sooty cast to head, mantle, breast; more rufescent on rest of underparts, wings and tail. Habits not well known; shy and skulking; close to ground in low vegetation.

CHIN HILLS WREN BABBLER

Spelaeornis oatesi Timaliidae

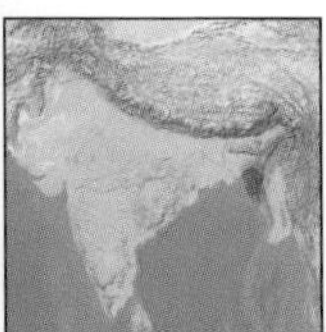

Size 10.5 cm

Voice Song powerful, rather shrill

Range Southern S Assam Hills (Lushai Hills, Mizoram)

Habitat Concealing domed to oval-shaped nest on damp, sloping bank or amongst very low herbage

Small ash-brown wren babbler with plainish brown face; moustachial stripe absent; comparatively longer tail; white throat and breast with dense, extensively flecked black; dull brown flanks also heavily mottled black-and-white. Distinguished from Naga by denser scaling on upperparts. Female has whiter underparts. Behaves as Naga. Breeds in Mar-Jun (Myanmar).

TAWNY-BREASTED WREN BABBLER

Spelaeornis longicaudatus Timaliidae

Warm cinnamon-brown wren babbler. Upperparts scaled in almost same colour; pale grey lores and ear-coverts; pale indistinct streak above eye; unmarked white chin; dark moustachial patch; long tail. Slimmer than other wren babblers. Similar to Long-tailed but has more plain buff underparts without spotting. Juvenile has rufous-brown upperparts, lacking dark scaling. Female has more orange-buff breast. Nests on ground amidst boulders and undergrowth.

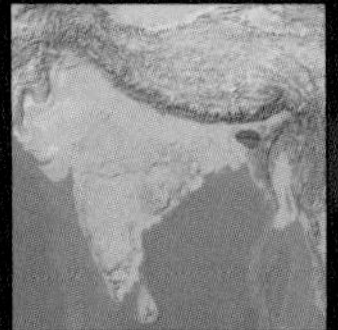

Size 10 cm

Voice Loud, clear whistle; soft churring alarm call

Range Endemic to the subcontinent. Globally threatened. Hills of NE India (Assam, Manipur, Meghalaya, Nagaland), 1,000-2,000 m; current status uncertain

Habitat Deep, moist broadleaved evergreen forests with thick undergrowth, keeping to rocky ravines; steep hillsides with rock outcrops densely-covered with moss, ferns and orchids

HIMALAYAN WEDGE-BILLED WREN BABBLER

Sphenocichla humei Timaliidae

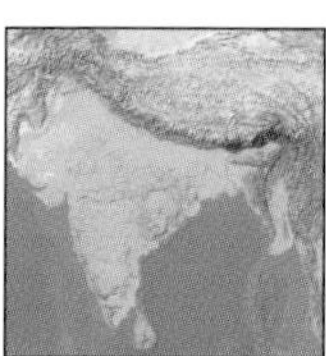

Size 18 cm

Voice Loud melodious whistles

Range The Himalayas of Sikkim, West Bengal and Arunachal Pradesh

Habitat Broadleaved evergreen forests; bamboos

Distinctly-marked babbler. Upperparts dark brown; dark, pointed bill; blackish face mask; indistinct grey supercilium; dense spotting on neck sides. Underparts dark; barred wings and tail; pale buff scales on belly; blackish legs and feet. Forages in undergrowth and along lower parts of tree trunks.

MANIPUR WEDGE-BILLED WREN BABBLER

Sphenocichla roberti Timaliidae

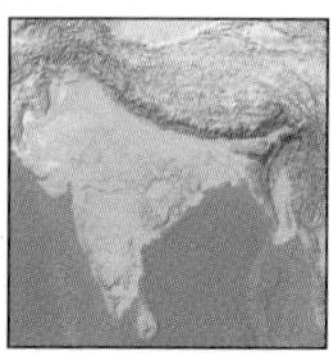

Size 18 cm

Voice Alarm call a subdued, low *hrrrh…hrrrh…hrrrhhrrrit…hrrrh…hrrrh*. Song unknown

Range SE Arunachal Pradesh (Namdapha) and eastern S Assam hills (N Cachar, Nagaland and Manipur)

Habitat Often found in parties of upto 15, working through low vegetation

Large wren babbler with broad dark barring on wings distinct; large white scaling on throat and chest; plain brown cheeks; no visible supercilium; lightly spotted hindcrown, nape and mantle; greyish-brown head, mantle and breast; mid-length tail. Female overall more rufous. Juvenile more rufous with less distinct scaling. Usually seen on tree trunks or rocks in small flocks, in search of insects. Nests on lower parts of tree trunks.

RUFOUS-CAPPED BABBLER

Stachyridopsis ruficeps Timaliidae

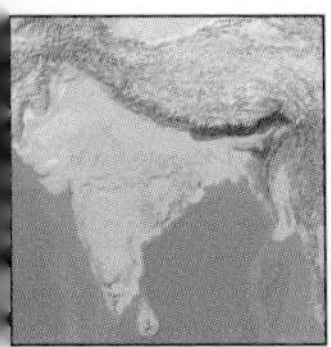

Size 12 cm

Voice Calls *wee...wee...wee... wee*. Song a high-pitched *pi...pi... pi...pi...pi...pi...pi* song

Range E Nepal to Myanmar

Habitat Undergrowth in moist broadleaved evergreen forests; secondary growth; bamboo clumps

Small, buffy-brown and yellowish babbler, with bright rufous cap; very similar to Rufous-fronted, but rufous crown brighter, better defined, and extending to nape. Mantle, wings and tail richer olive; yellowish-buff face, sides of neck and underparts, with faintly streaked yellowish chin and throat. Sharp, pointed bill; pale, diffused eye-ring; in pairs when breeding; rest of the year, usually in bird waves; active in undergrowth or mid-storey trees.

RUFOUS-FRONTED BABBLER

Stachyridopsis rufifrons Timaliidae

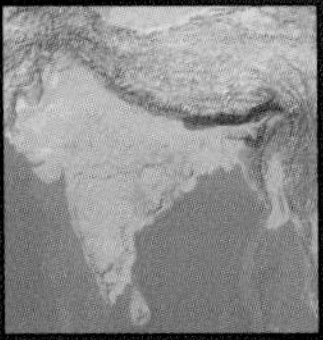

Size 12 cm

Voice Same as Rufous-capped's

Range E Nepal to Myanmar

Habitat Undergrowth in moist broadleaved evergreen forests; secondary growth; bamboos

Often confused with the very similar Rufous-capped. Has white throat, streaked faintly with black. Grey supercilium a good distinguishing feature.

TAWNY-BELLIED BABBLER

Dumetia hyperythra Timaliidae

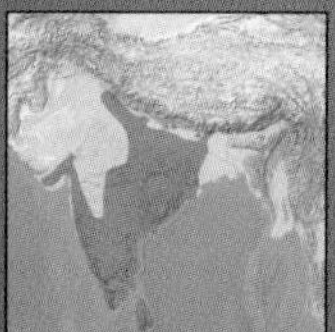

Size 13 cm

Voice Calls include faint *cheep… cheep* contact notes; also, mix of other whistling and chattering notes

Range From SE Himachal Pradesh, east along foothills into peninsular India; absent in arid NW, Punjab plains, extreme NE states

Habitat Scrubs and bamboos, in and around forests

Olivish-brown above; front part of crown reddish-brown; white throat in western and southern races; nominate race has underbody entirely fulvous. Sexes alike. Small, noisy parties in undergrowth; rummages on floor, hopping about, always wary; hardly associates with other birds; great skulkers, difficult to see; any sign of danger and flock disperses amidst noisy chorus of alarm notes but soon reunites.

BLACK-CHINNED BABBLER

Stachyridopsis pyrrhops Timaliidae

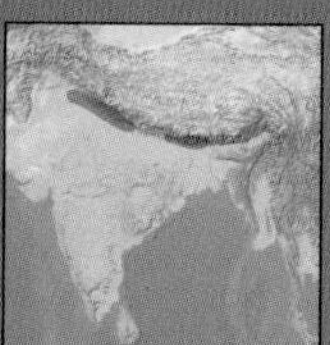

Size 10 cm

Voice Calls include mellow *wit... wit...wit...wit*; soft variable *chirrr*

Range Fairly common endemic breeding resident in N mountains from N Pakistan east to E Nepal. Moves lower down in winter

Habitat Edges of forests and secondary undergrowth, often near streams. Favours bamboos

Tiny, fulvous-brown babbler. Back of crown more olive. Diagnostic black lores and chin. Underparts orange-buff; sides of head more fulvous. Red iris; upper mandible brown; legs, feet and claws pale flesh-brown. Sexes alike. Similar to Dark-fronted *Rhopocichla atriceps* but no black head and mask. Feeds in pairs or small parties on invertebrates, often in mixed hunting groups. Active and not shy. Nests low down.

GREY-THROATED BABBLER

Stachyris nigriceps Timaliidae

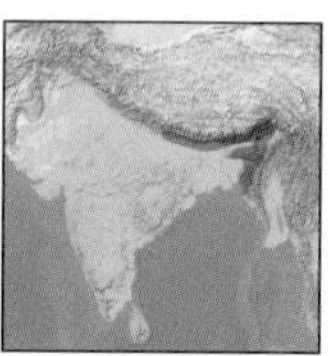

Size 12 cm

Voice Call a distinctive but variable jingling trill

Range Locally common breeding resident from C Nepal east to Burmese border. Also occurs in China and SE Asia

Habitat Undergrowth of forests, particularly with bamboos and near water

Small, plainish-brown babbler. Head marked with black-and-white; pale grey eye-stripe; grey throat; black lateral crown-stripe; underparts more rusty-buff. Sexes alike. Juvenile has less streaked head and underparts have more rufous-buff tint. Similar to Black-chinned but with less distinct black lores and chin. Skulks in undergrowth, feeds on invertebrates, often in mixed hunting groups. Very secretive. Nests low down.

GOLDEN BABBLER

Stachyridopsis chrysaea Timaliidae

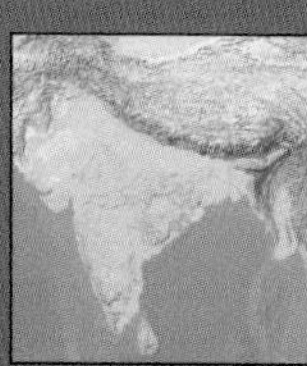

Size 10 cm

Voice Similar to Rufous-capped's, but more paced

Range C Nepal, Bhutan, Arunachal Pradesh, S Assam Hills

Habitat Undergrowth in moist broadleaved evergreen forests; secondary growth

Small babbler with short, sharply pointed bill; gold head, with prominent black streaks from hindcrown to nape; partial black mask; black lores, thin brow line, and black moustachial stripe; olive green-gold upperparts; more golden underparts; dark red eye; nominate race from E Himalayas to Manipur described; *binghami* in southern parts of NE subcontinent has greyer cheeks, duller upper and underparts; in pairs when breeding; otherwise, in mixed hunting parties. Moves constantly.

PIN-STRIPED TIT BABBLER

Macronous gularis Timaliidae

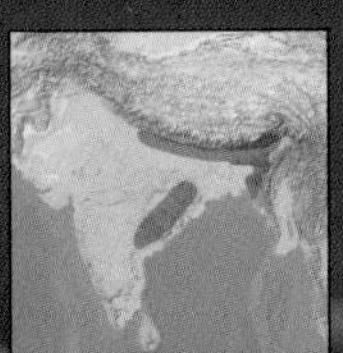

Size 11 cm

Voice Very noisy. Call a loud, regular and repeated barbet-like *chunk… chunk…chunk*. Also, *chrrr*

Range Common breeding resident in N foothills from Uttarakhand east through Nepal to Arunachal Pradesh, NE India and Eastern Ghats

Habitat Forest undergrowth and bamboos, often feeding fairly high but also on ground

Small, brownish babbler; underparts yellow-brown, streaked finely with black; rusty-brown crown; pale yellow lores; plain, rufous-brown wings and tail; mantle more olive; yellowish supercilium; pale iris; dark eye-stripe. Sexes alike. Feeds on invertebrates; in pairs or small parties, often in mixed flocks. Active but furtive, creeping on ground. Nests in undergrowth.

DARK-FRONTED BABBLER

Rhopocichla atriceps Timaliidae

Smallish, rich rufous-brown babbler with black head. Creamy-white breast, throat and belly. Yellow eyes. Square-tipped tail. The typical form with black head is found along Western Ghats from Belgaum to Nilgiris, being replaced in Cochin and Travancore Hills by another race *R. a. bourdilloni* which has the black largely replaced by sooty-brown. A third race *R. a. nigrifrons* is found in Ceylon. Has top of head the same colour as back and black confined to broad band through each eye joining across forehead. All three races occur from sea-level upto 6,000 feet and strictly resident.

Size 13 cm

Voice Calls include unobtrusive *tup*, scolding *churr* and plaintive nasal *mewing*. Also loud, throaty grating

Range Endemic to the subcontinent. Western Ghats in Goa, Karnataka, Kerala, W Tamil Nadu

Habitat Evergreen biotope in dense undergrowth, thickets near streams, reed beds, bamboos, and cardamom cultivation

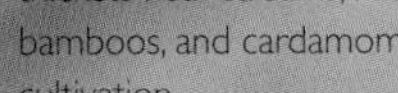

atriceps

nigrifons

CHESTNUT-CAPPED BABBLER

Timalia pileata Timaliidae

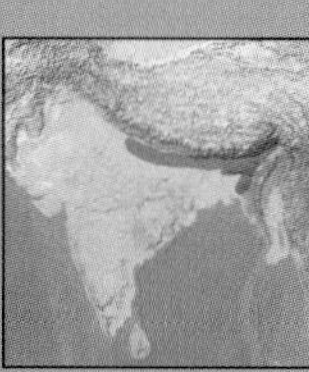

Size 17 cm

Voice Calls *tik…,tik…; chit, chit…*

Range E Uttarakhand to Myanmar; Assam

Habitat Wetlands with tall grass; reed beds; scrub; secondary growth

Rather distinctive babbler, with bright chestnut cap, contrasting with sturdy black bill; black mask, extending only upto eye; white supercilium, forehead, cheeks, chin, throat and breast; finely-streaked lower throat and breast; grey neck sides; drab olive-brown upperparts; mostly olive-buff below; relatively long, scruffy typical babbler tail. In pairs when breeding; otherwise, in small groups. Secretive; skulks in dense vegetation, remaining well hidden; may emerge briefly when singing; forages in low scrub or clambers up tall grass and reeds.

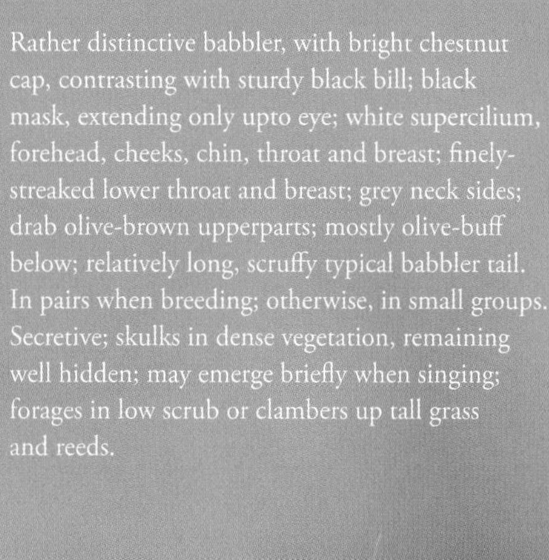

JERDON'S BABBLER

Chrysomma altirostre Timaliidae

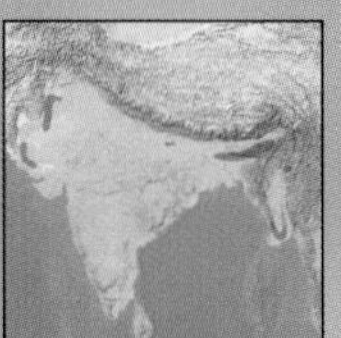

Size 17 cm

Voice Call a piercing *tew...tew... tew...tew...tew,* starting slowly but ending more rapidly and slightly falling in tone

Range Sedentary resident in Indus Plains, Pakistan, C Nepal, Brahmaputra Plains in N West Bengal, Assam, Nagaland and Bangladesh

Habitat Reed beds and extensive tracts of elephant grass

scindicum

griseigulare

Distinguished from Yellow-eyed by paler yellowish-brown bill, brown iris and dull yellowish-green orbital ring, no white lores and supercilium, and fleshy-brown legs and feet. Racial variations. *C. a. altirostre* (Indus plains) olive-brown above with pale grey throat and breast; *C. a. griseigulare* (NE subcontinent) has darker grey throat and breast, richer brown underparts, belly, flanks and vent.

SPINY BABBLER

Turdoides nipalensis Timaliidae

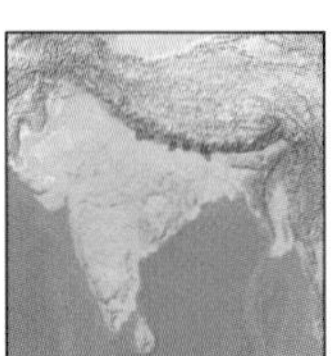

Size 25 cm

Voice Song a distinctive, harsh, ringing whistling *ter...ter...ter...ter... ter...ter*

Range Endemic resident in Nepal

Habitat Dense scrub on hillsides; favours thicker areas, away from cultivation

Upperparts dark rufescent-brown; diagnostic downcurved black bill; white face; pale iris, and strong, fine black streaking on throat and breast; tail has narrow, faint cross-bars. Usually in pairs, feeding on ground. Shy and difficult to observe.

YELLOW-EYED BABBLER

Chrysomma sinense Timaliidae

Sexes alike. Rufous-brown above; whitish lores, short supercilium; yellow iris and orange-yellow eye-rim distinctive at close range; cinnamon wings; long, graduated tail; white below, tinged pale-fulvous on flanks and abdomen. In pairs, or small bands in tall grass and undergrowth; noisy but skulking, suddenly clambers into view for few seconds, before vanishing once again; works its way along stems and leaves, hunts insects; short, jerky flight.

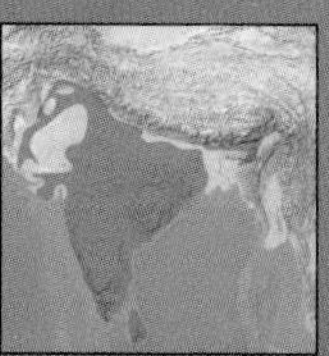

Size 18 cm

Voice Call a mournful *cheep… cheep.* Noisy when breeding (mostly rains); melodious, whistling notes

Range Subcontinent, from the Himalayan foothills south; absent in arid parts of Rajasthan

Habitat Scrub; tall grass; cultivation; edges of forests

STRIATED BABBLER

Turdoides earlei Timaliidae

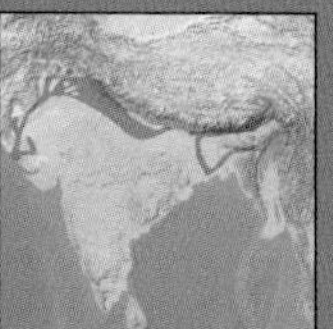

Size 25 cm

Voice Calls include loud, 3-note whistle; also quick-repeated, single whistling note

Range Floodplains of N and NE river systems, especially larger rivers

Habitat Tall grass, reed beds and scrubs

Dull brownish above, streaked darker; long, cross-barred tail; dark streaks on crown; pale supercilium; yellow eye; pale yellow bill has dark tip. Underparts buffy-brown below, with fine dark streaks on throat and breast. Long tail. Sexes alike. Juvenile more orange-brown, with plainer rufous underparts. Sociable; parties of upto 10 birds; keeps to tall grass and reed beds; flies low, rarely drops down to ground.

COMMON BABBLER

Turdoides caudata Timaliidae

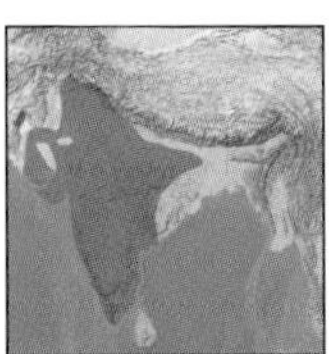

Size 22 cm

Voice Noisy. Calls include pleasant, warbling whistles, often in chorus; squeaky alarm notes. Calls on ground and in low flight

Range Most of N, NW, W and peninsular India, south of outer Himalayas to about 2,000 m; east to West Bengal

Habitat Thorn scrub; open cultivation; grass

Dull brown above, profusely streaked; brown wings; olivish-brown tail, long and graduated, cross-rayed darker; dull white throat; pale fulvous underbody, streaked on breast sides. Sexes alike. Pairs, or small bands in open scrub; skulker, working its way low in bushes or on ground; moves with peculiar bouncing hop on ground, its long, loose-looking tail cocked up; extremely wary, vanishes into scrubs at slightest alarm; weak flight, evident when flock moves from one scrub patch to another, in ones and twos.

LARGE GREY BABBLER

Turdoides malcolmi Timaliidae

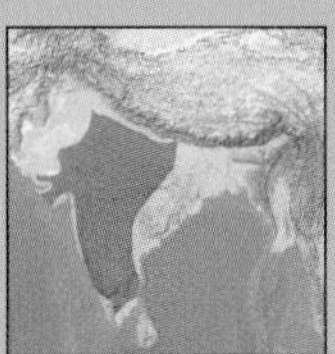

Size 28 cm

Voice Very noisy. Calls include a chorus of squeaking chatter, short alarm note

Range From around E Uttar Pradesh, south through most of peninsula; east to Bihar; abundant in the Deccan

Habitat Scrubs; open country; gardens; vicinity of habitation

Upperparts ash-brown; dark centres to feathers on back give streaked look; greyer forehead; long graduated tail cross-rayed with white outer feathers, conspicuous in flight; fulvous-grey below. Sexes alike. Gregarious; flocks in open country, sometimes seen in dozens; extremely noisy; moves on ground and in medium-sized trees; hops about, turning over leaves on ground; weak flight, never for long; at any sign of danger, flock comes together.

SLENDER-BILLED BABBLER

Turdoides longirostris Timaliidae

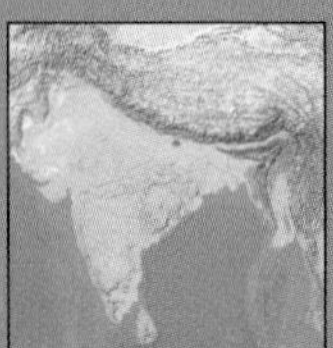

Size 23 cm

Voice Calls include shrill, rather high-pitched, quite strident series of notes, and a rather clear, high-pitched *wiii…wii…jiu…di*

Range C Nepal, NW Bihar, NE India and Bangladesh. In Nepal, recorded only at Chitwan, where locally fairly common

Habitat Tall grass and reeds, especially near water

Rufous-brown babbler with unstreaked upperparts and comparatively long tail. Diagnostic downcurved blackish bill; whitish lores and buff ear-coverts; short eyebrow; whitish throat; unstreaked deep buff underparts; indistinct cross-bars on tail. In pairs, or small flocks. Secretive, staying under cover of tall grass. Feeds on ground. Nests in low bushes.

RUFOUS BABBLER

Turdoides subrufa Timaliidae

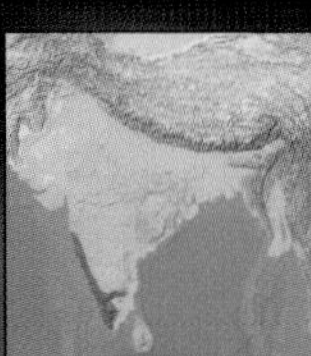

Size 25 cm

Voice Calls include high-pitched shrill, sometimes frenzied squabbling or scolding squeaks

Range Endemic to SW India from C Maharashtra south throughout Western Ghats and east to NC Tamil Nadu

Habitat Thick cover, edges of forest clearings and plantations in broadleaved evergreen, moist deciduous biotope; favours habitats intermixed with tall grass and bamboos

Largish chestnut-brown, unstreaked babbler with rufous underparts. Light grey forehead and forecrown; dark lores; white eyes; upper breast and belly lighter rufous. Black upper mandible and yellow lower mandible. Some show no grey on forehead or forecrown. Juvenile has dark grey iris.

JUNGLE BABBLER

Turdoides striata Timaliidae

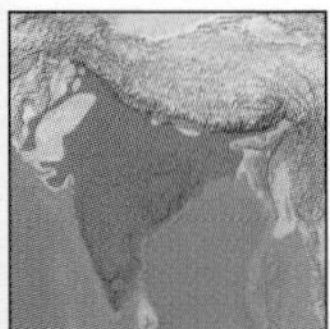

Size 25 cm

Voice Very noisy. Calls include harsh *ke…ke…ke* and hysterical chattering and squeaking in chorus

Range Common endemic breeding resident throughout lowlands and foothills except parts of NE India and Sri Lanka

Habitat Open woodlands; scrub; cultivation; gardens; villages

Overall grey-brown babbler. Light-brown head; whitish iris; stout, yellow bill; short, dark eyebrow; pale lores; dark brown tail. Underparts paler with some greyish streaking on breast. Western race *somervillei* may be separate species, with chestnut tail and dark brown primaries. Extremely noisy. Feeds in groups on insects and seeds, mainly on ground. Confiding and inquisitive. Breeds throughout the year. Nests in bushes.

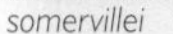

somervillei

orientalis

sindiana

YELLOW-BILLED BABBLER

Turdoides affinis Timaliidae

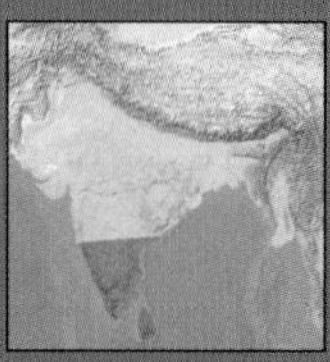

Size 23 cm

Voice Noisy. More musical chatter than the more common Jungle

Range S peninsular India; Karnataka, Andhra Pradesh, Tamil Nadu, Kerala; also Sri Lanka

Habitat Forests; dense growth; neighbourhood of cultivation and habitation; orchards

Rather drab-looking babbler with creamy-white crown; dull brown above, appearing scaly on centre of back; darker wings; ash-brown ear-coverts; cross-barring along tail centre; dark brown throat and breast. Pale blue-grey eyes; pale grey edges to feathers give scaled appearance; yellowish-buff below breast. Sexes alike. In small noisy parties; feeds on ground, turning leaves; if disturbed, moves about in series of short, hopping flights; hops amongst tree branches towards the top, from where travels to adjoining tree after short flight. Similar to Jungle, but has more white on lores, forehead and crown.

ORANGE-BILLED BABBLER

Turdoides rufescens Timaliidae

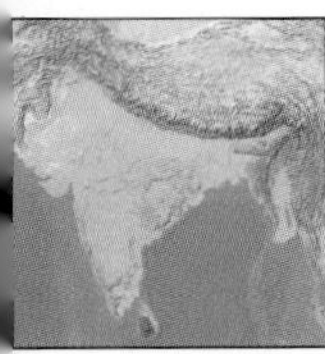

Size 25 cm

Voice Calls include continuous chattering, squeaking and chirping

Range Sri Lanka

Habitat Undisturbed wet-zone forests

Uniform chestnut-rufous babbler with distinctive orange bill and legs. Ash-grey crown; cinnamon-rufous face; pale eyes and lores. Underparts more brownish. Juvenile has greyish chin and browner underparts. Feeds in understorey in large, noisy parties.

CHINESE BABAX

Babax lanceolatus woodi Timaliidae

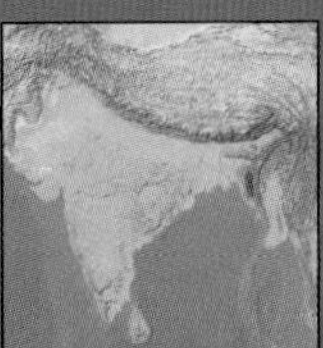

Size 20 cm

Voice Call a short, clear, musical slurred whistle

Range Lushai Hills, Mizoram above 1,200 m. Locally common

Habitat Open broadleaved evergreen forests; edges of forests; secondary growth; scrubs and grass; bamboos

Medium-sized, rather pale and heavily streaked bird. Decurved bill; pale face, pale yellow eyes and black moustache; brown tail. Juvenile has overall more buff with less streaking. Quite shy, occurring in pairs or small parties, mainly on ground and roads, but freely ascends trees.

GIANT BABAX

Babax waddelli Timaliidae

Ash-brown babbler with heavily streaked upperparts; strong downcurved bill; head and mantle darkly streaked. Underparts have less dense streaking. Blackish-brown wings tipped grey similar to Chinese but large in size, darker grey head, and darker streaking. Chinese has sub-moustachial stripe, more downcurved bill, and dark grey tail.

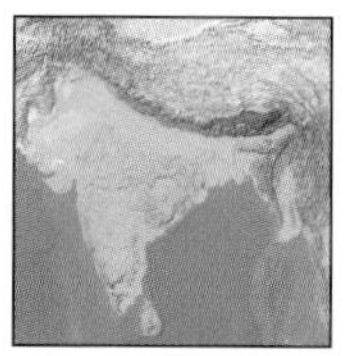

Size 31 cm

Voice Harsh grating call; rapid series of quavering whistles. Pleasant thrush-like song

Range Extreme NE Sikkim

Habitat Dry scrub; favours *Hippophae rhamnoides*

ASHY-HEADED LAUGHINGTHRUSH

Garrulax cinereifrons Timaliidae

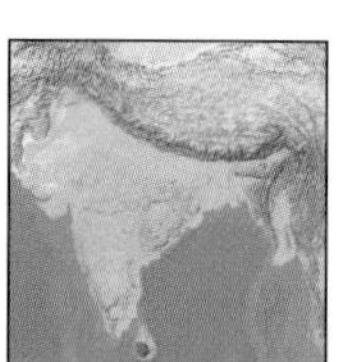

Size 23 cm

Voice Breaks out constantly into harsh chattering, taken up in turn by all members of troop, and ceases just as suddenly

Range Globally threatened. Endemic resident, rare in wet lowlands and adjacent lower hills

Habitat Interior of dense wet forests and bamboo thickets

Overall rufous-brown laughingthrush. Light grey head; white eyes; tawny underparts pinkish-tinged; pale rufous throat; dark bill and legs. Juvenile has brighter rufous underparts, less grey on crown and duller eyes. Small flocks feed together near ground vegetation and leaf litter. Shy and confiding, but noisy when feeding. Only laughingthrush in Sri Lanka.

WHITE-THROATED LAUGHINGTHRUSH

Garrulax albogularis Timaliidae

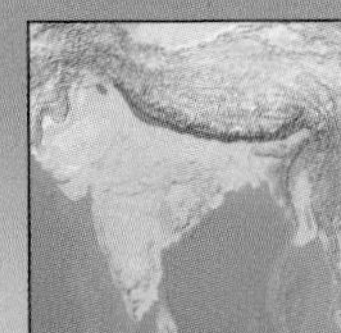

Size 28 cm

Voice Noisy. Alarm call a strident *twitz… tzee*. Lot of squealing, hissing and chattering

Range Locally common breeding resident in N hills from N Pakistan east to Assam. Rarer in E India. Moves lower down in winter

Habitat Undergrowth of forest and scrubs

Large laughingthrush, with uniform sepia-brown upperparts; slight rufous on forehead; distinct white throat and upper breast; graduated tail with white tips; flight feathers more ash-brown; pale rufous vent and belly; white iris and black lores. Sexes alike. Feeds on invertebrates and fruits. Confiding. Usually seen in large groups, often with other species. Nests in shrubs or trees.

WHITE-CRESTED LAUGHINGTHRUSH

Garrulax leucolophus Timaliidae

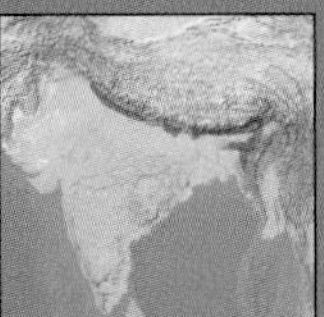

Size 28 cm

Voice Very noisy. Sudden explosive chatter or laughter; also pleasant 2- or 3-note whistling calls

Range The Himalayas, east of N Himachal Pradesh; foothills to height of 2,400 m, most common between 600-1,200 m

Habitat Dense forest undergrowth; bamboos; wooded nullahs

Large, olive-brown laughingthrush. Diagnostic white head, crest, throat, breast and sides of head; black eye mask extending to ear-coverts; pale grey nape; rusty-orange nuchal-collar encircling breast. Juvenile has smaller crest and mask. Moves rapidly in forest undergrowth but also tree foliage branches; makes short sallies between trees; extremely noisy; often seen along with other laughingthrushes, treepies and drongos; hops on ground, rummages in leaf litter.

LESSER NECKLACED LAUGHINGTHRUSH

Garrulax monileger Timaliidae

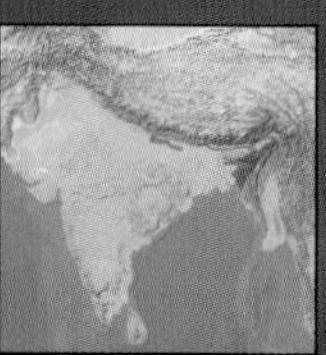

Size 27 cm

Voice Noisy. Calls include subdued *turrrr* and *kaaaaaa*. Song a loud, mellow *tee…too…ka… kew…kew…kew*

Range The Himalayas from WC Nepal east to Arunachal Pradesh; NE India and Bangladesh

Habitat Dense broadleaved evergreen and moist deciduous forests with thick undergrowth, dense secondary growth and bamboo thickets

Large, brown laughingthrush, with black necklace. Centre of breast and belly white; strong, black moustachial stripe, rufous flanks, whitish-grey wing panel; brown-black outer-tail feathers tipped white; white throat, edged rusty-orange; orangish cast above necklace where throat adjoins necklace. Similar to Greater but smaller and slimmer with finer bill and narrower tail. Feeds on ground, foraging for invertebrates.

GREATER NECKLACED LAUGHINGTHRUSH

Garrulax pectoralis Timaliidae

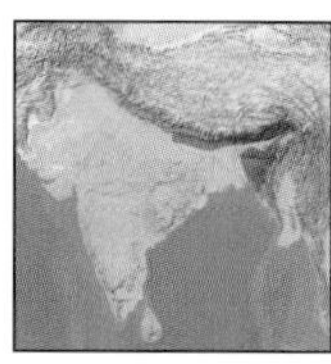

Size 29 cm

Voice Whistles; *week…week… week*. Melodic song

Range W Nepal to Myanmar. Bangladesh and S Assam Hills

Habitat Broadleaved forest undergrowth; secondary scrub; bamboo forests

Large, stocky laughingthrush, with striking black 'necklace'; olive-brown above; rufous flanks, sides of breast, neck; whitish centre of belly; long, graduated white-tipped tail. Similar to Lesser, but has bigger bill, necklace enclosing larger area on whitish breast; throat buff-washed; variable ear-coverts (white, black-and-white or black) completely enclosed by black moustachial stripe joining bill to necklace; black base to primaries; grey legs. In pairs when breeding; otherwise in larger flocks, often with Lesser and White-crested. Wary.

STRIATED LAUGHINGTHRUSH

Grammatoptila striatus Timaliidae

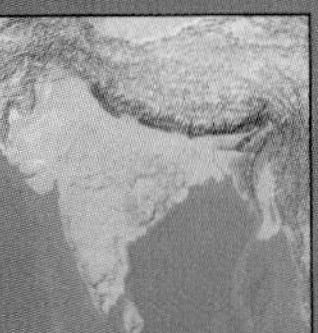

Size 28 cm

Voice Calls include cackling, whistling, chattering

Range Hills from Himachal to Myanmar. Moves lower in winter

Habitat Dense forests; undergrowth

Brown laughingthrush, with bushy, rounded crest; plumage varies from pale to dark rufous-chestnut, darker wings, heavy or fine streaking depending on race; completely streaked from crown, both underparts and upperparts, with buff-white; relatively short stout, black bill; eastern races generally darker than W Himalayan nominate race; intermediate *G. s. cranbrooki* of Arunachal Pradesh has broad, dark supercilium from eye to nape; barely streaked crown; habits similar to other laughingthrushes; more arboreal; upper to lower storeys.

cranbrooki

vibex

CHESTNUT-BACKED LAUGHINGTHRUSH

Garrrulax nuchalis Timaliidae

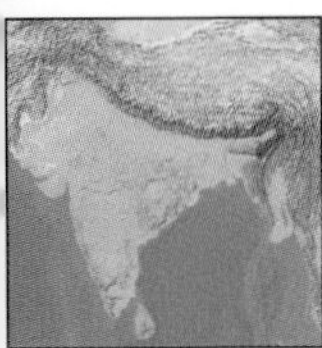

Size 23 cm

Voice Call a soft *chip*. Rich whistled song of 4- or 5-notes; unmistakable *churr* when alarmed

Range Hills of NE India (Assam, Manipur, Nagaland, Arunachal Pradesh)

Habitat Chiefly dense bushes on stony scrub-covered ravines and hills, also tall grass

Medium-sized laughingthrush, with distinctive white ear-coverts and throat sides; white spot on grey forecrown; black face, lores, chin; bright rufous mantle; grey breast; black throat-stripe.

YELLOW-THROATED LAUGHINGTHRUSH

Garrulax galbanus Timaliidae

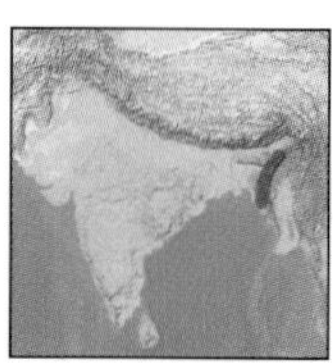

Size 22 cm

Voice Call a frequently uttered feeble

Range Hills of NE India

Habitat Tall grass interspersed with trees and shrubs, open scrub jungles; and margins of dense evergreen broadleaved forests

Small laughingthrush with yellow underparts, black mask, and grey crown and nape. Distinguished from Rufous-vented by greyish-olive flanks and yellowish lower belly and vent, pale olive-brown upperparts. Greyish tail becoming blacker towards tip and with broad, white tips to outer feathers. Noticeable black chin, greyish outer webs of primaries forming indistinct panel on wing, and greyish legs and feet.

WYNAAD LAUGHINGTHRUSH

Garrulax delesserti Timaliidae

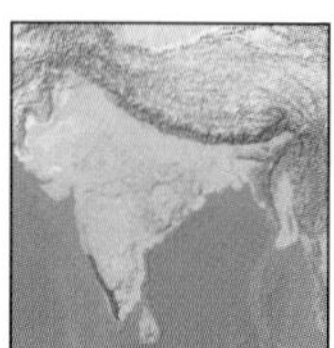

Size 23 cm

Voice Calls include particularly frenzied, discordant series of screeches, squeals and cracked rattles from flock

Range Endemic to Western Ghats, from N Karnataka south to S Kerala and east to W Tamil Nadu

Habitat Humid broadleaved evergreen forests; also cardamom *sholas*; favours patches of dense Strobilanthes undergrowth

Large, ash-brown laughingthrush. Crown and nape lighter grey; black mask; chestnut wing-coverts and back, white throat, greyish breast, blackish tail. Diagnostic yellowish-pink lower mandible. Breast light grey-brown; rufous-wash on belly and darker rufous vent. Skulking. Seen in flocks.

RUFOUS-VENTED LAUGHINGTHRUSH

Garrrulax gularis Timaliidae

ize 23 cm

'oice Call a loud whistle, in addition to cackling laughter

ange Endemic to the subcontinent. The Himalayan oothills from E Bhutan east to E Arunachal Pradesh

Habitat Mainly dense evergreen undergrowth, dense crub and secondary growth; also bamboos and scrub

Jpperparts rufous-brown with grey crown and ape. Prominent black mask; red eye; bare patch of isible grey skin behind eye; long, black bill; rump nd uppertail-coverts brighter rufous. Bright yellow hroat and chin; chestnut-brown belly; grey sides o breast; orange legs. Juvenile similar to adult, but as blackish crown and rufous markings on grey reast. Shy. Forages in flocks on forest floor. Feeds n insects.

'ARIEGATED LAUGHINGTHRUSH

Garrrulax variegatus Timaliidae

Size 25 cm

Voice Noisy. Calls include various whistling and squeaking notes comprising *weet, weer* and *peet weer*

Range Locally common endemic reeding resident in N mountains from N Pakistan east o E Nepal. Moves lower down in winter

abitat Thick forest-edge, undergrowth and secondary owth

verall grey-brown laughingthrush. Rufous orehead; dark mask; dark throat-stripe; grey own; white iris; black chin; grey wings ith black-and-white markings and grey, rufous yellowish-green edgings. Tail dark grey, with aler grey subterminal band; rufous vent. Sexes ike. Juvenile has more rufous cast and less strong arkings. Feeds on invertebrates and fruits close to ound but sometimes seen on lower level of trees. sually in pairs, or small parties.

MOUSTACHED LAUGHINGTHRUSH

Garrrulax cineraceus Timaliidae

Olive-grey laughingthrush. Black forehead and crown; whitish lores; greyish-buff supercilium; black eye-stripe; broad moustachial stripe; streaking on throat sides, white tips to tertials and secondaries, grey panel on wing. Tail olive-grey with white-tipped black subterminal band. Sexes alike. In pairs, or small flocks. Feeds on ground.

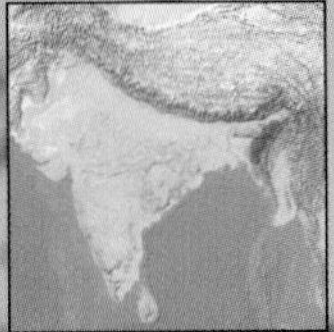

Size 22 cm

Voice Musical call

Range Hills of NE India (Assam, Manipur, Meghalaya, Mizoram, Nagaland), subject to some altitudinal movements. Moves lower in winter

Habitat Dense undergrowth and bushes in moist forests, secondary growth and dense scrub at edges of cultivation

RUFOUS-CHINNED LAUGHINGTHRUSH

Garrrulax rufogularis Timaliidae

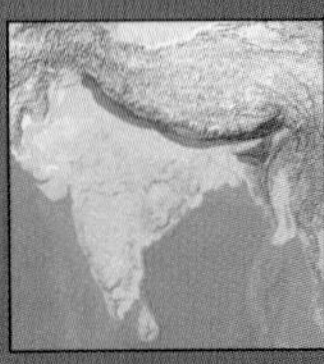

Size 22 cm

Voice Varied calls; squeals and chuckles

Range Hills of Kashmir to Myanmar. Moves lower in winter

Habitat Thick forest undergrowth; scrub; edges of forests; secondary growth

Medium-sized, intricately-patterned laughingthrush; variable rufous on chin, upper throat, ear-coverts; black crown; buff lores; black sub-moustachial area; black, scaly barring on mantle; black bands on wings; black spotting on variable grey or buff-white underparts; bright rufous-chestnut vent and tail edges; black subterminal band on tail. Much racial variation; solitary, in pairs or small flocks; more quiet, shy and wary; near dense cover in lower forest storeys, bushes and undergrowth; forages mostly on ground.

rufog

occidentalis

SPOTTED LAUGHINGTHRUSH

Garrrulax ocellatus Timaliidae

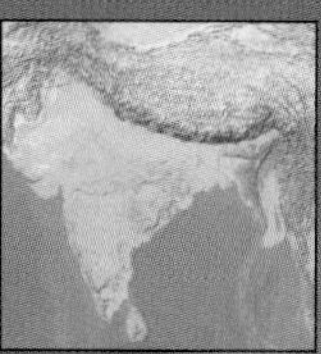

Size 32 cm

Voice Call an arresting *tchu…wee, tchu…wee, tchu…witty…*

Range E Uttarakhand to Arunachal Pradesh

Habitat Undergrowth in mixed broadleaved, coniferous forests; rhododendron

Very large and distinctive laughingthrush, with rufous face, chin, supercilium; dusky throat, ear-coverts; blackish cap; stark white iris; bold black-and-white spotting on rufous-chestnut upperparts. Dense, bold mottling, barring, spotting on buff breast, upper belly; grey-and-black edges to flight feathers; long, chestnut-grey, graduated tail, with black-and-white edges. Can be seen solitary, in pairs or small groups, often with other laughingthrushes; wary but curious. Generally in bushes, undergrowth; forages mostly on ground in leaf litter for insects, berries and seeds.

GREY-SIDED LAUGHINGTHRUSH

Garrrulax caerulatus Timaliidae

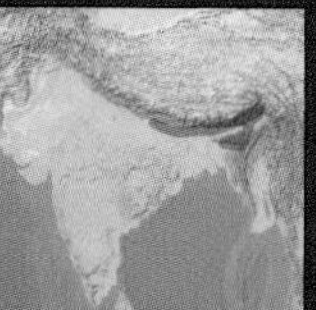

Size 25 cm

Voice Varied calls and songs; mellow whistles; squeals

Range E Nepal, Bhutan and Arunachal Pradesh

Habitat Undergrowth in dense moist evergreen forests; edges of forests; secondary growth; bamboo jungles

Dark rufous-brown, white-and-grey laughingthrush, with variable white cheek patch and slaty-blue orbital patch; rufous-brown cap, with black scaling; black forehead, lores, sub-moustachial stripe and bill. Deep brown upperparts, with rufous cast to wings and tail; white throat, breast and belly; grey flanks and breast sides. Racial variations; solitary, in pairs or small groups; mostly terrestrial; forages on ground in leaf litter.

RUFOUS-NECKED LAUGHINGTHRUSH

Garrrulax ruficollis Timaliidae

Size 23 cm

Voice Varied calls; vast range of trills and whistles, squeals and babbles

Range Nepal, Bhutan, Assam and Arunachal Pradesh

Habitat Open broadleaved forests; edges of forests; undergrowth; bushes; bamboos; tea gardens

Smaller, darker laughingthrush; forecrown, face, throat black; hindcrown, nape grey; red iris; striking rufous-patch down neck, behind ear-coverts; rufous vent and lower belly; rest of plumage olive suffused with rufous; black bill and legs. Like other laughingthrushes; usually in pairs when breeding; larger flocks the rest of the year. Shy and wary; generally near dense cover in lower forest storeys, bushes and undergrowth, or forages on ground in leaf litter.

WHITE-BROWED LAUGHINGTHRUSH

Garrrulax sannio Timaliidae

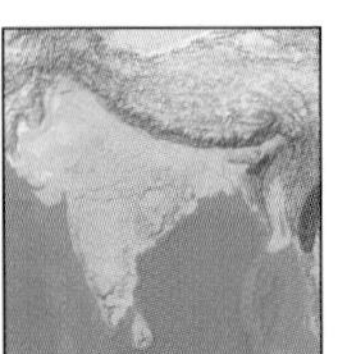

Size 23 cm

Voice Noisy. Calls include harsh, shrill, explosive *tcheu* or *tchow* notes; *tcheu…tcheu…tcheu…* etc. Pairs may call antiphonally

Range Hills of NE India

Habitat Undergrowth in dense forests; secondary growth; bamboo thickets and scrub-covered hillsides

Almost uniform, olive-brown laughingthrush. Crown has brown post-ocular line; nape chestnut-brown, broad supercilium; paler lores and patch on cheek, cinnamon-brown ear-coverts, sides of neck and throat, buff; brown tail. Sexes alike. Underparts more buff-brown; rufous undertail-coverts. Confiding. In small flocks or solitary, or in pairs. Nests in low vegetation.

BLACK-CHINNED LAUGHINGTHRUSH

Garrrulax cachinnans Timaliidae

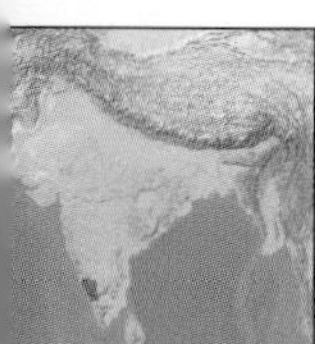

Size 20 cm

Voice Very noisy. Calls include squealing 'laughter' often in chorus; *pee...ko...ko and kee...kee...kee*

Range Globally threatened. Very local but, in places, common endemic breeding resident in Nilgiri Hills of W Tamil Nadu and nearby parts of Kerala

Habitat Forest undergrowth, secondary growth and gardens

Medium-sized, plain, dark brown babbler. Distinctive white feathery eyebrows; dark grey crown; black chin and forehead; broad eye-stripe. Underparts rusty-ochre. Sexes alike. Small parties feed mainly on invertebrates on ground under cover.

cachinnans

jerdoni

KERALA LAUGHINGTHRUSH

Garrulax fairbanki Timaliidae

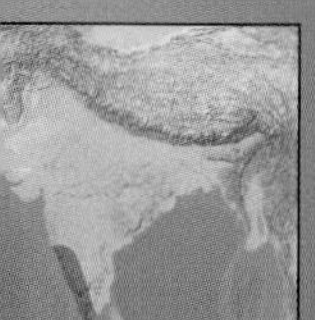

Size 20 cm

Voice Very noisy. Calls include a variety of chattering, squeaking and whistling, including *puwee... puwee...pokee* and *pee...koko*

Range Locally breeding endemic resident in Western Ghats and Palni Hills in W Tamil Nadu, Kerala and S Karnataka

Habitat Undergrowth of forest edges; plantations and gardens; particularly wild raspberry along streamsides

Medium-sized, brown-and-rufous babbler. Dark grey-brown crown; narrow, dark grey eye-stripe with broad white supercilium extending behind eye; breast and neck sides grey or grey-streaked white. Similar to Nilgiri but paler with similar patterning, depending on race. Sexes alike. Feeds on invertebrates and fruits, mainly on or near ground, in small parties or mixed hunting groups. Very shy.

fairbanki

STREAKED LAUGHINGTHRUSH

Garrrulax lineatus Timaliidae

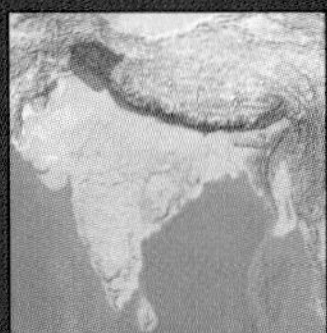

Size 20 cm

Voice Noisy. Constant whistling and squeaking notes including *pitt…wee…err*

Range Common breeding resident in N mountains from W Pakistan east to Arunachal Pradesh. Moves down to foothills in winter

Habitat Low scrub; edges of forests; gardens and roadside grass patches. Often around habitation

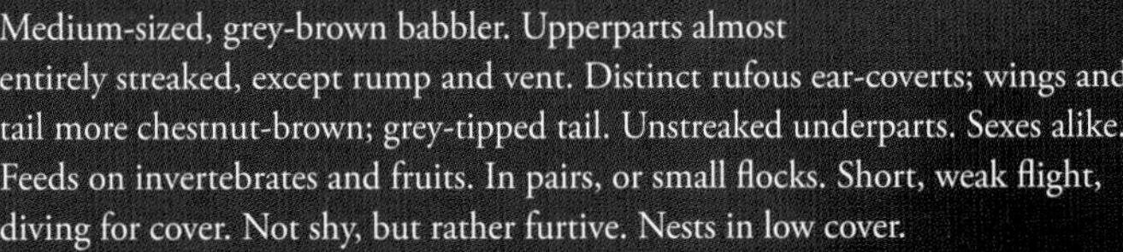

Medium-sized, grey-brown babbler. Upperparts almost entirely streaked, except rump and vent. Distinct rufous ear-coverts; wings and tail more chestnut-brown; grey-tipped tail. Unstreaked underparts. Sexes alike. Feeds on invertebrates and fruits. In pairs, or small flocks. Short, weak flight, diving for cover. Not shy, but rather furtive. Nests in low cover.

BHUTAN LAUGHINGTHRUSH

Garrulax imbricatus Timaliidae

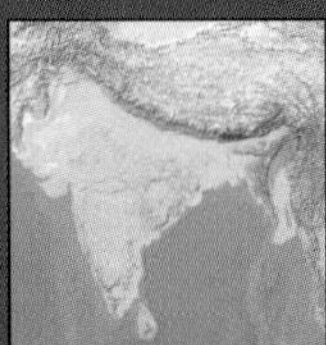

Size 20 cm

Voice Calls *krreerrr; tchu…wee…yuh*

Range Bhutan, straying into W Arunachal Pradesh

Habitat Undergrowth in open forests; secondary growth; hillsides, roadside scrub; gardens

Small, dark russet-brown laughingthrush, once classified as a race of Streaked; distinguished from that species by darker plumage, little or no dark streaking on crown, nape; paler greyish-brown lores, ear-coverts; finer white streaking overall; longer tail. Usually in pairs, or small parties; terrestrial; mostly forages on ground on grassy banks, low bushes, creeping through herbage; will also climb onto mossy walls. Fairly tame; easily seen around habitation, though generally stays near cover.

STRIPED LAUGHINGTHRUSH

Garrrulax virgatus Timaliidae

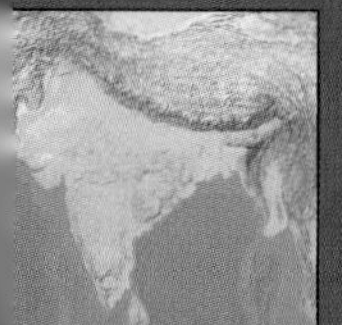

Size 25 cm

Voice Call a plaintive, hurried *chwi...pieu* or *wiwiweu*

Range Hills of NE India

Habitat Dense undergrowth in moist broadleaved evergreen forests; thick secondary growth

Medium-sized laughingthrush with white streaking on upperparts and underparts. Confused with Streaked; easily distinguished by broad, greenish-white supercilium, broad buff-patch on ear-coverts, rufous lores, deep chestnut throat contrasting with rufous-buff breast and belly, chestnut-brown crown and nape, fine but considerably more distinct white shaft streaking on upperparts and underparts, uniform, olive-brown tail.

BROWN-CAPPED LAUGHINGTHRUSH

Garrrulax austeni Timaliidae

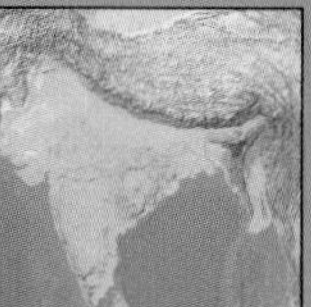

Size 22 cm

Voice Sings with loud, plaintive, jolly phrases, *whit... wee...wiweeoo, whit...wi...chooee, whichi...wi...chooee whiwiwi...weeee...weeoo* etc

Range Hills of NE India

Habitat Undergrowth in oak and rhododendron forests; bushes and bamboo thickets at edges and clearings of forests; ravines

Medium-sized, maroon-brown laughingthrush. Whitish streaks on rufous-brown crown and nape; white, scaled underparts; rufous olive-brown mantle; rufous-brown wings and tail. Greater coverts, tertials and secondaries white-tipped. Tail has narrow white tips to blackish outer feathers, with rufous-brown central feathers. Similar to Chestnut-crowned but has plain brownish face and throat without any grey. In pairs, or small parties. Feeds on ground.

BLUE-WINGED LAUGHINGTHRUSH

Garrulax squamatus Timaliidae

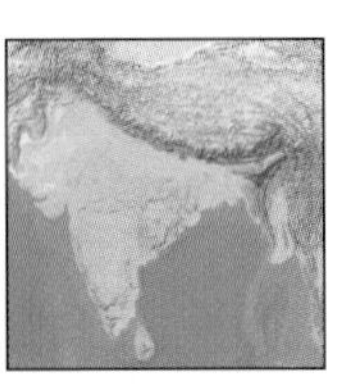

Size 25 cm

Voice Alarm call a scratchy seek. Song a *cur...white...to...go*

Range The Himalayas; NE India

Habitat Dense undergrowth in moist evergreen forests

Overall dark brown, finely-scaled laughingthrush. Black supercilium; rusty-orange and sooty-grey wings; distinct wing panel created by blue-grey outer webs on primaries; rufous wings with darker outer edges; chestnut-brown flanks and vent; chestnut undertail-coverts; black tail with rufous tip. Striking white iris. Female more rufous overall with less scaling. Juvenile even more rufous-red and even less scaling. Similar to Scaly which has yellow rather than rufous on wings. Very shy, hiding in dense undergrowth.

SCALY LAUGHINGTHRUSH

Garrulax subunicolor Timaliidae

Size 23 cm

Voice Normal song a 2- or 3-part wolf-whistle that is buzzy and more slurred than several similar laughingthrush songs

Range The Himalayas from WC Nepal east to Arunachal Pradesh

Habitat Thick undergrowth in moist broadleaved and mixed broadleaved-coniferous forests

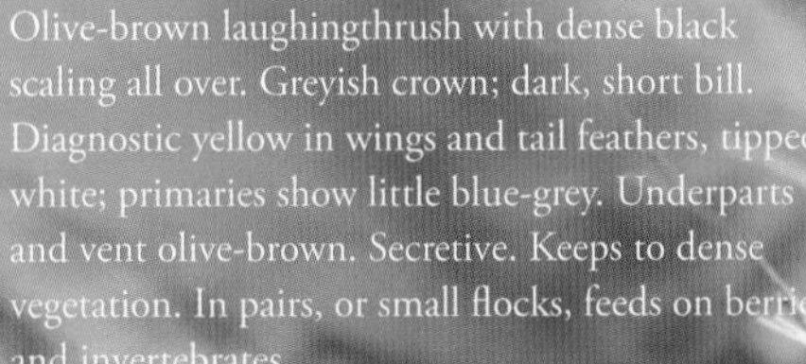

Olive-brown laughingthrush with dense black scaling all over. Greyish crown; dark, short bill. Diagnostic yellow in wings and tail feathers, tipped white; primaries show little blue-grey. Underparts and vent olive-brown. Secretive. Keeps to dense vegetation. In pairs, or small flocks, feeds on berries and invertebrates.

SPOT-BREASTED LAUGHINGTHRUSH

Garrulax merulinus Timaliidae

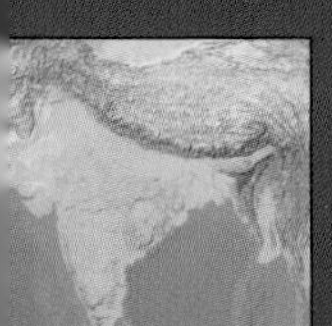

Size 25 cm

Voice Song consists of repetition at intervals of 4-10 seconds, of plaintive phrase, e.g. *wichi…pi…choo* or *whi…pi…choo* or *whi…choo…it*

Range Rare resident in NE Indian hills

Habitat Degraded broadleaved forests

Uniform, dark chestnut-brown laughingthrush with longish bill and short tail. Breast and throat strongly marked with brown spots; very abbreviated supercilium behind eye; wings, flanks, tail olive-brown. Juvenile has paler rufous upperparts, and less prominent streaking on breast and throat. Very shy. In pairs, or small flocks; feeds under dense vegetation.

ELLIOT'S LAUGHINGTHRUSH

Garrrulax elliotii Timaliidae

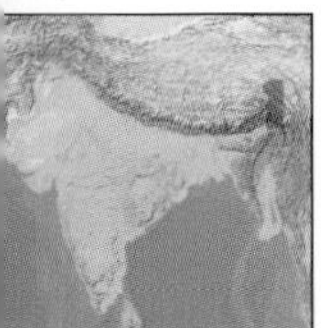

Size 23 cm

Voice Haunting, interrogative, whistled brassy song, *weir…tee…u*, repeated, often for long periods

Range Probably, rare and local resident in NE Arunachal Pradesh

Habitat Mixed temperate forests and adjacent scrubs on edges of forest clearings

Overall grey-brown laughingthrush with no scaling or marking. Forehead lighter brown; darkish face; yellowish-white eyes; whitish fringes to ear-coverts, throat and breast; yellowish-olive edges on secondaries and inner primaries; cinnamon rear flanks and undertail-coverts and yellowish-olive sides to white-tipped grey tail. In pairs, or small flocks. Hops on ground, foraging in vegetation for insects.

ASSAM LAUGHINGTHRUSH

Garrrulax chrysopterum Timaliidae

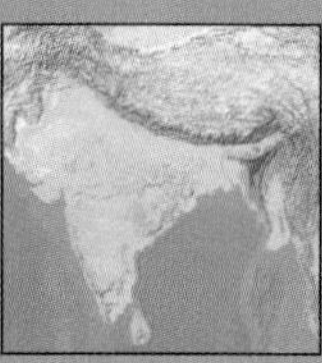

Size 26 cm

Voice Songs differ from Chestnut-crowned's in their lower pitch, mellower quality, and greater complexity and length

Range Hills of NE India

Habitat Forests; bamboos

Largish laughingthrush with bright rufous-patch on crown. Grey supercilium; grey forehead; ear-coverts streaked; rufous breast; mantle shows faintl diffused streaking. Juvenile has lighter brown crow rather than rufous and lighter markings.

BLACK-FACED LAUGHINGTHRUSH

Garrrulax affinis Timaliidae

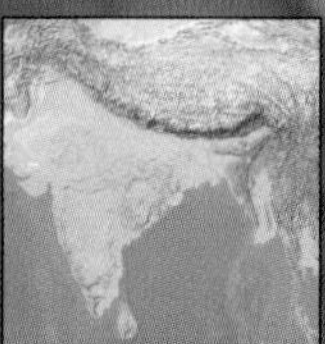

Size 25 cm

Voice Alarm call a rolling *whirrr*. Various high-pitched notes, chuckles. A 4-noted, somewhat plaintive song

Range The Himalayas, from W Nepal eastwards; descends to 1,500 m in winter

Habitat Undergrowth in forests; dwarf vegetation in higher regions

Diagnostic blackish face, throat and part of head and contrasting white malar patches, neck sides and part of eye-ring; rufous-brown above, finely scalloped on back; olive-golden flight feathers tipped grey; rufous-brown below throat, marked grey. Sexes alike. In pairs or small bands, sometimes with other babblers; moves on ground, in low growth; also ascends into middle levels of trees; noisy when disturbed or when snakes or other creatures arouse its curiosity.

BUGUN LIOCICHLA

Liocichla bugunorum Timaliidae

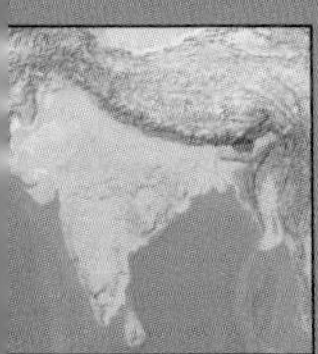

Size 22 cm

Voice Fluty calls on a descending scale, slightly slurred and inflected at the end *weee…keew, yu… weee…keew, wieuu…weei…tuui… tuuuw…tuoow*

Range Globally threatened. Eaglenest Wildlife Sanctuary, Arunachal Pradesh

Habitat Disturbed hillsides with dense shrubberies, small trees and bushes

Olive-brown laughingthrush with black crown. Diagnostic orange-yellow lores; yellow post-ocular spot; grey cheeks; yellow, red and white-patches in wings; black tail with reddish tip, and scarlet red undertail-coverts.

CHESTNUT-CROWNED LAUGHINGTHRUSH

Garrulax erythrocephalus Timaliidae

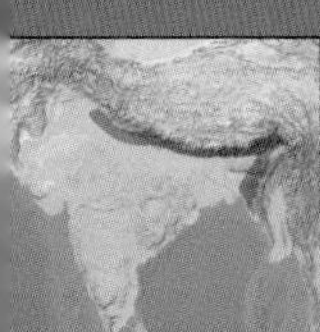

Size 28 cm

Voice Songs quite variable in form, quick, sweet, clear, wiry and emphatic

Range The Himalayas from W Himachal to NE Arunachal Pradesh

Habitat Dense vegetation in broadleaved forests

Variable laughingthrush with brilliant green-gold panel on wings and sides of tail, heavy black spots on upper mantle and scales on breast, chestnut forehead scales and fine black centres on ear-coverts (looking frosted); usually pale eyes. Juvenile has duller crown, more chestnut-tinged upperparts, no spotting or scaling. Nominate racial group has entirely rufous crown, and rufous cheek. In W Himalayas, nominate pale with bright rufous crown, greyish-olive mantle (greyer on scapulars) and pale, dull buff underparts.

nigrimentus

erythrocephalus

RED-FACED LIOCICHLA

Liocichla phoenicea Timaliidae

Distinctive, mainly brown-and-crimson babbler; dark brown upper and underparts; streaked crown; black supercilium; bright red face, ear-coverts, neck sides; large, crimson and orange-patch on primaries; silver and black on secondaries; red undertail-coverts; extensive orange on wing-tips, underside and tips to black tail. Solitary, in pairs when breeding; in small parties or mixed hunting flocks with other species. Shy and secretive; not easily seen; usually forages on ground, or lurks in forest undergrowth; sometimes in mid-storey.

Size 23 cm

Voice Calls include churrs, rattles, mews. Melodious whistled song

Range Bhutan to Myanmar; S Assam Hills; possibly E Nepal

Habitat Thick undergrowth in moist deciduous or evergreen forests; secondary growth

SILVER-EARED MESIA

Mesia argentauris Timaliidae

Size 15 cm

Voice Call a chattering *tiweet…cheweet…cheweet*

Range Hills of Uttarakhand to Myanmar

Habitat Bushes in evergreen forests; edges of forests; secondary growth

Striking, unmistakable babbler, with bright yellow bill, forehead, chin, upper throat; orange-yellow lower throat, breast, upper mantle; black face, crown, partially encircling large, silver-grey ear-covert patch. Crimson wing panel on greenish orange-yellow wings; grey on rest of mantle, back; greenish-yellow on rest of underparts; yellow-edged dark tail. Male has crimson uppertail, undertail-coverts; female duller, paler, with olive-gold uppertail, orange-yellow undertail-coverts. In pairs, or fairly large parties, often in mixed flocks, moving through foliage in lower, middle, sometimes canopy, levels.

RED-BILLED LEIOTHRIX

Leiothrix lutea Timaliidae

Size 13 cm

Voice Quite vocal; often utters a wistful, piping *tee…tee…tee*; mix of sudden explosive notes. Song a musical warble. Noisy

Range The Himalayas, from Kashmir to extreme NE India; 600-2,700 m

Habitat Forest undergrowth; bushy hillsides; plantations

Upperparts olive-grey; dull, buffy-yellow lores and eye-ring; yellow, orange, crimson-and-black in wings; forked-tail, with black tip and edges; yellow throat, orange-yellow breast diagnostic; scarlet beak. Red on wing considerably reduced or absent in the western race *kumaiensis*. Female has yellow, instead of crimson in wings. Small parties or often in mixed hunting parties in forests; rummages in undergrowth, but frequently moves up into leafy branches; lively bird.

HIMALAYAN CUTIA

Cutia nipalensis Timaliidae

Size 20 cm

Voice Calls include toots; squawks; *cheet…cheet*

Range C Nepal to Myanmar; S Assam Hills

Habitat Dense moist broadleaved evergreen, oak and pine forests

Round and unmistakable babbler, with slaty-blue head; male has broad, bluish-black mask, short, sturdy, slightly decurved bill; white underparts, with diagnostic bold, dark barring on buff-washed sides of breast and flanks; blue panels on bluish-black wings; rufous-chestnut mantle, back and long uppertail-coverts; long, buff undertail-coverts, with just tip of black tail visible; orange legs. Female has paler crown, brown mask, mantle streaked brown. Seen in pairs, small groups, or in mixed flocks; arboreal; active on mossy trees.

WHITE-BROWED SHRIKE BABBLER

Pteruthius flaviscapis Timaliidae

Size 16 cm

Voice Churrs in alarm. Song *chyip…chyip…chyip*

Range Pakistan to Myanmar

Habitat Broadleaved evergreen forests; coniferous or mixed forests

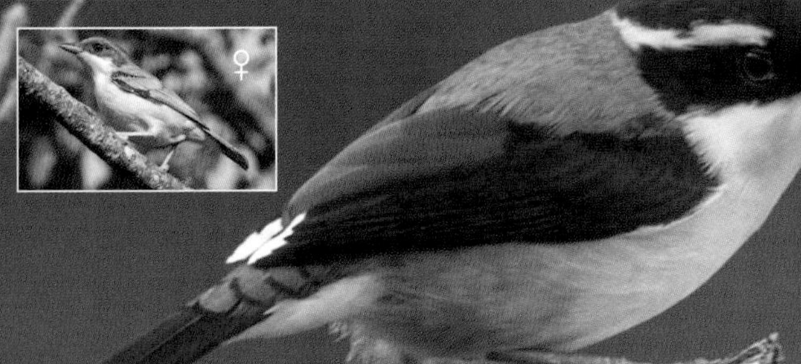

Strikingly-patterned, with short, shrike-like bill, hooked at end; male has broad, white supercilium over and behind eye; bluish-black crown, nape, ear-coverts; grey mantle, back and rump; rufous-chestnut panel on black wings; white-tipped primaries and secondaries; white underparts, with pinkish wash on flanks. Female has pale or no supercilium; grey crown; brownish mantle; rufous wing panel; greenish-yellow wings; buff underparts. Solitary, in pairs, or small parties; arboreal; canopy-feeder.

GREEN SHRIKE BABBLER

Pteruthius xanthochlorus Timaliidae

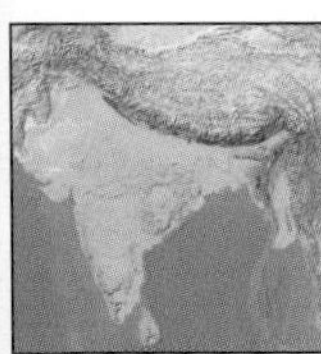

Size 13 cm

Voice Call a harsh *cha; whee...tee, whee...tee*

Range Uttarakhand to Myanmar

Habitat Broadleaved evergreen forests; oak and rhododendron, coniferous and mixed forests

Small, plain and rather drab-looking shrike babbler; warbler-like, but stocky, and with tiny, stubby bill; grey crown and ear-coverts; olive-green mantle, wings, tail; thin, but clear, wing-bar; black-patch on primary coverts; greyish-white underparts; pale yellow belly, and yellowish wash on sides of breast and flanks; white-tipped tail, tertials and secondaries. Female has paler crown. Singly, in pairs, or in mixed hunting parties with other species. Arboreal; forages in most forest storeys; quiet, unobtrusive and not very active. *Occidentalis* is found in the W Himalayas, *zanthochlorus* is resident of E Himalaya while *hybrida* is found south of the River Brahmaputra.

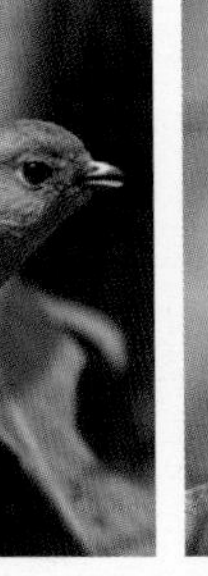

zanthochlorus

occidentalis

hybrida

BLACK-EARED SHRIKE BABBLER

Pteruthius melanotis Timaliidae

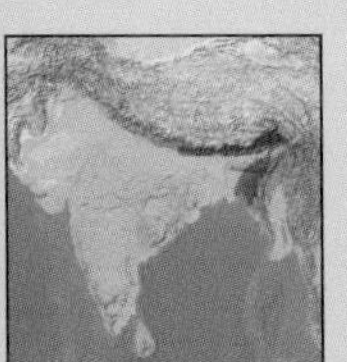

Size 11 cm

Voice Calls *tchew...whee, tchew...whee*

Range W Nepal to Myanmar

Habitat Moist broadleaved evergreen forests

♀

Very small, brightly-coloured shrike babbler; prominent white eye-ring, bordered with black; small, hooked bill; Male has yellow forehead, black lores and eye-stripe curving behind yellow ear-coverts; broad, grey supercilium from behind eye to nape; yellowish-green crown, mantle; two broad, white wing-bars on black wing-coverts; bluish-grey panel on primaries and secondaries; chestnut throat, breast; yellow undersides. Female has chestnut only on malar stripe; duller, with buff wing-bars. Solitary, in pairs, or mixed hunting parties; arboreal; mostly in upper forest storeys; quiet, unobtrusive, slow-moving.

BLACK-HEADED SHRIKE BABBLER

Pteruthius rufiventer Timaliidae

Size 17 cm

Voice Song a bright *pew…pew…peee…ti*, repeated without much variation

Range The Himalayas from WC Nepal east to Arunachal Pradesh; NE India

Habitat Broadleaved forests

Sexes dissimilar. Male has rufous-brown upperparts; black crown and nape; pale grey throat; yellowish-patches on breast sides; rufous-pink belly and vent; rufous-brown rump; grey eyes. Female larger than male; diffused streaking on olive-brown mantle; wings and tail olive-brown; sides of head grey; steel-grey cheeks; black-scaled crown. Juvenile male similar to adult male, but more olive-brown upperparts. Male similar to White-browed but larger and slimmer, and no supercilium. Female distinguished from female White-browed by steely-black crown and nape, olive-brown mantle, sometimes with black markings.

CHESTNUT-FRONTED SHRIKE BABBLER

Pteruthius aenobarbus Timaliidae

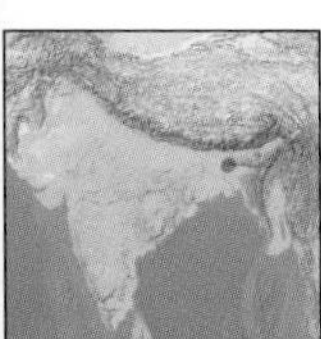

Size 11 cm

Voice Song a monotonous *chip… chip…chip*

Range Meghalaya

Habitat Evergreen forests

Small shrike babbler with distinctive chestnut forehead and bright yellow forecrown. Chestnut throat and upper breast. Similar to Black-eared but both sexes have no black border to ear-coverts; no grey on nape, and silvery-white wing panel. Female not known, but probably similar to female *P a: intermedius* (Burma), which differs from female Black-eared by being duller and with whitish underparts. Nests high in trees.

WHITE-HOODED BABBLER

Gampsorhynchus rufulus Timaliidae

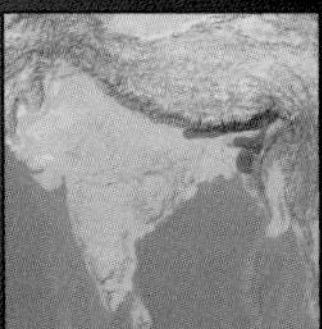

Size 23 cm

Voice Calls include harsh *kaw…ka…yawk*; hard rattling

Range Rather scarce breeding resident in N foothills from extreme eastern Nepal to Burmese border

Habitat Forest undergrowth; bamboo thickets

Large babbler with white head and long tail. Warm brown above and pale rufous-buff below; tail-tip and vent buff; pale iris, bill and legs. Sexes alike. Juvenile has orange crown and nape and buff underparts. Feeds on invertebrates in small parties or mixed hunting groups. Nests in bushes.

STREAK-THROATED BARWING

Actinodura waldeni Timaliidae

Size 22 cm

Voice Contact calls rather nasal, grumbling *grrr…ut…grrr…ut* and *grr…grr…grr…grr…gr* etc.

Range Fairly common resident in hills of NE India (Arunachal Pradesh, Assam, Manipur, Nagaland)

Habitat Mossy, broadleaved evergreen and mixed forests

Two races. *A. w. daflaensis* (E Himalayas) has greyish-white throat, breast and belly diffusely streaked with brownish-grey, and looks like Hoary-throated (although there is no known overlap in ranges). Best distinguished by streaked underparts, lack of bold shaft streaking on crown and nape; no moustachial stripe, and even rufous-brown mantle. *A. w. waldeni* (hills south of the Brahmaputra) has same tawny-brown colouration like Rusty-fronted; best distinguished by lack of rusty 'front' to head.

HOARY-THROATED BARWING

Actinodura nipalensis Timaliidae

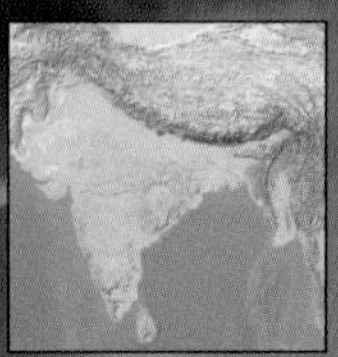

Size 20 cm

Voice Calls *jay…jay…jay; dewit…dewit…dewit*

Range C Nepal to Myanmar; S Assam Hills

Habitat Moist oak, broadleaved evergreen forests; mixed coniferous forests

Mainly grey, buff and brown barwing; feathery grey-brown crest on crown, nape, with pale buff or white shaft streaks; pale grey throat, upper breast, generally unstreaked; grey ear-coverts; diffused dark moustachial stripe; buff or white streaking on mantle, scapulars; grey wing-bar on greater coverts; greyish-buff underparts; more distinctly barred tail than in Rusty-fronted. In pairs, or small parties; often in mixed hunting flocks; arboreal; forages on mossy, epiphytic-covered branches of trees in middle to canopy levels.

RUSTY-FRONTED BARWING

Actinodura egertoni Timaliidae

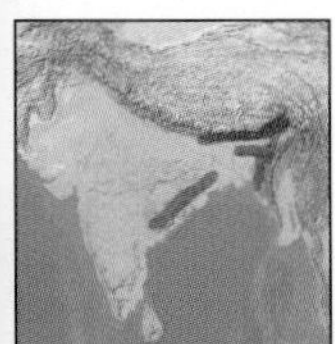

Size 23 cm

Voice Calls include *cheep*; rattles. Song a sweet, whistled *tee… tee…ta*

Range Nepal to Bhutan and W Arunachal Pradesh

Habitat Thick undergrowth, broadleaved evergreen forests; bamboo thickets

Larger, slender barwing, with dark rufous-chestnut forehead, lores and chin; relatively long tail; feathery, unstreaked blue-grey crest, nape, upper mantle and sides of neck; unmarked, rufous-brown lower mantle; unbarred rufous-chestnut on greater coverts and base of primaries; buff-barred primaries and secondaries; blue-grey edge to flight feathers; plain olive-brown below; marked racial variations. In pairs, or small parties. Arboreal; usually in dense bushes and vegetation of lower and mid-storey.

lewisi

egertoni

BLUE-WINGED SIVA

Siva cyanouroptera Timaliidae

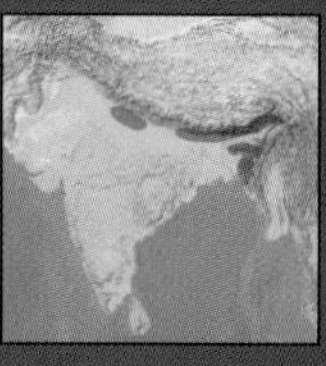

Size 15 cm

Voice Calls *chip…; chik*. Song a loud, high-pitched, whistled *pee… peeoo…; si…seeow*

Range Hills of Uttarakhand to Myanmar. Moves lower in winter

Habitat Broadleaved evergreen forests; mixed broadleaved-coniferous forest; edges of forests; secondary growth

Fairly small, slender, distinctive babbler, with blue crown, wings, tail; deep blue streaks and lateral stripes on blue-grey crown and nape; long, white supercilium; pale, greyish-white face, dark, beady eye and pale, flesh-coloured bill; mauve underparts; brown mantle; blue wings, with grey-blue panel; blue-sided, square-ended tail; usually in small groups.

RED-TAILED MINLA

Minla ignotincta Timaliidae

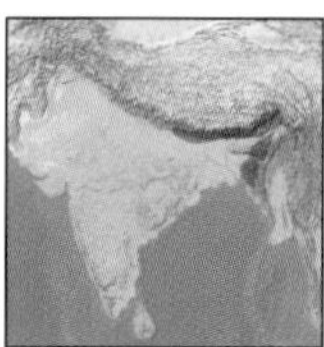

Size 14 cm

Voice Calls include *wi…wi…wi; chik…chik…chik…chik; tsi; chitititit; twiyitwiyuwi*

Range Hills of C Nepal to Myanmar. Moves lower in winter

Habitat Moist, broadleaved evergreen forests; mixed broadleaved, coniferous forests; secondary growth

Small babbler, with black crown, prominent broad, white supercilium and black mask extending to nape; brown mantle and back; pale yellowish underparts; light grey streaks sometimes visible on breast and flanks; white-edged black wing-coverts, secondaries and tertials. Male has red panel on flight feathers; female yellowish-orange; male has chestnut cast to brown mantle; black tail, with red outer-tail and undertail feathers, tip. Arboreal; seen in small mixed flocks.

BAR-THROATED SIVA

Siva strigula Timaliidae

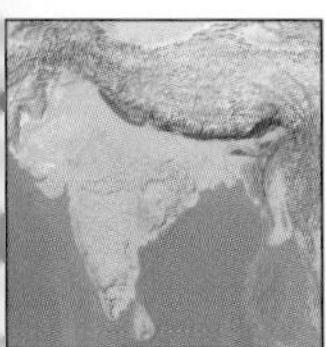

Size 14 cm

Voice Calls include whistling *tsee...tsi...tsay...tsse* and *pseep*

Range Locally common breeding resident in N mountains from Himachal Pradesh east to Burmese border. Moves lower down in winter. Also occurs in China and SE Asia

Habitat Lower canopy; high undergrowth of forests

Small, brightly-coloured babbler with high-domed chestnut crown. Olive-brown above with black, white-and-chestnut-patterned wings and chestnut-centred black tail with yellow edgings. Dusky cheeks and finely black-barred white throat. Feeds actively on invertebrates and fruits in small parties or in mixed hunting groups. Nests low down in cover.

YELLOW-THROATED FULVETTA

Pseudominla cinerea Timaliidae

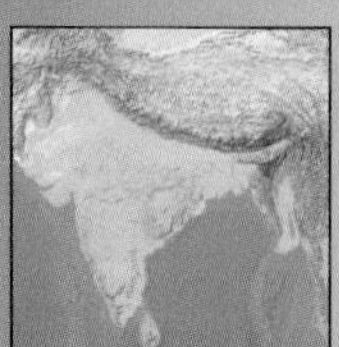

Size 10 cm

Voice Calls include *si…si…si… si…si…si; chrrp…prrp*

Range Hills of NE India

Habitat Understorey in dense, subtropical broadleaved evergreen forests; bamboo thickets; secondary scrub

Small, mainly brown-and-yellow fulvetta; long, broad, yellow supercilium, bordered by dark eye-stripe below and dark lateral crown-stripe above; greyish scaling and mottling on brownish crown; yellowish-brown upperparts. Brown wings; grey streaking on yellowish face; yellow throat and yellowish underparts; dusky flanks and breast sides. Usually in small flocks, often in mixed hunting parties with other insectivorous species; confiding; active in forest understorey; feeding behaviour like leaf warblers.

WHITE-BROWED FULVETTA

Fulvetta vinipectus Timaliidae

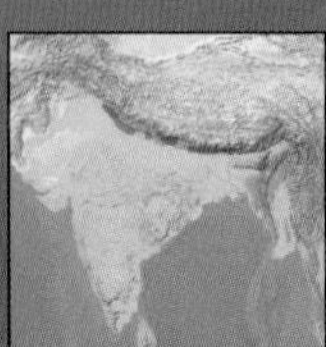

Size 11 cm

Voice Call a fairly sharp *tsuip* or *tship*; also some harsh churring notes, when agitated

Range The Himalayas from W Himachal Pradesh; E Himalayas; NE regions; 1,500-3,500 m, over 4,000 m in some parts; descends to 1,200 m in severe winters

Habitat Scrubs in forest, *ringal* bamboo

austeni

chumbiensis

Brown crown and nape; prominent white eyebrow with black or dark brown line above; blackish sides of face; olive-brown above, washed rufous on wings, rump and tail; some grey in wings; whitish throat and breast; olive-brown below. Sexes alike. Upto 20 birds in low growth or lower branches; energetic, acrobatic; often seen in mixed hunting parties.

RUFOUS-WINGED FULVETTA

Pseudominla castaneceps Timaliidae

Small, rather drab, buff-and-brown fulvetta; dark chestnut-brown crown and nape with pale streaks; long, buff-white supercilium; black eye-stripe, streaked ear-coverts, moustachial stripe; olive-brown mantle; rufous-chestnut edges to primaries forming wing panel; black greater and primary covert panel; dark brown tail; dusty-white underparts, with buff sides of breast and flanks. In fairly large, fast-moving foraging flocks in under- and mid-forest storeys. Characteristic Nuthatch-like behaviour of climbing mossy tree trunks.

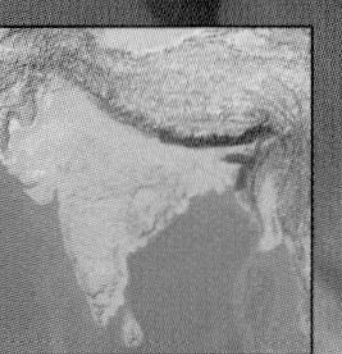

Size 10 cm

Voice Calls include *cheep; tew... twi...twi*

Range Hills of C Nepal to Myanmar. Moves lower in winter

Habitat Undergrowth in broadleaved evergreen forests; secondary growth

RUFOUS-THROATED FULVETTA

Schoeniparus rufogularis Timaliidae

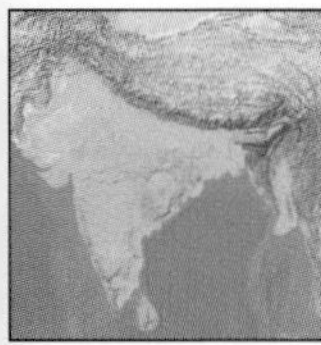

Size 12 cm

Voice Calls include churring, buzzing, cheeping, chattering; *whee...chu whee...chu whee...chu*

Range Patchily in Bhutan and Arunachal Pradesh

Habitat Dense undergrowth in broadleaved forests; secondary growth; bamboo thickets

Slightly larger, mainly brown-and-rufous fulvetta; long, white supercilium; long, black lateral crown-stripe; rufous crown and nape; white throat and upper breast, with distinctive broad rufous gorget; white eye-ring; dark brown ear-coverts; brown wings; whitish centre of underparts; greyish-brown-washed flanks. In pairs, especially when breeding; otherwise, in small flocks; skulks in dense low shrubberies and undergrowth, close to ground, or on ground.

GOLDEN-BREASTED FULVETTA

Lioparus chrysotis Timaliidae

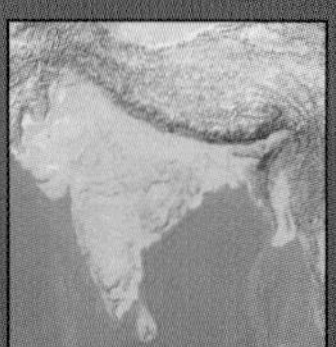

Size 11 cm

Voice Call a twittering *quititit*. High-pitched whistled song

Range Hills of C Nepal to Myanmar; S Assam Hills

Habitat Bamboo growth; understorey in temperate broadleaved evergreen forests; hillside scrub

Very small, striking, golden-yellow, silver grey-and-black babbler. Black face, greyish-black chin and throat; silver-grey cheeks; blackish-grey nape and mantle; golden to orangish-yellow breast and underparts; yellow-and-orange linear panels on black wings; yellow-sided black tail; *albilineata* (of hills south of River Brahmaputra) has prominent white crown-stripe. In pairs, or in large mixed flocks; confiding; active in lower or mid-level forest storeys; acrobatic feeder.

BROWN-THROATED FULVETTA

Fulvetta ludlowi Timaliidae

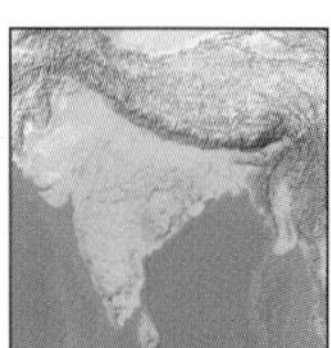

Size 11 cm

Voice Not very well-known. Calls *trrrrt* in alarm, with some see notes

Range Patchily in E Bhutan and Arunachal Pradesh

Habitat Undergrowth in broadleaved, rhododendron and coniferous forests; bamboos

Small, brown and rufous-chestnut fulvetta; lacks supercilium; brown crown, ear-coverts, with rufous hue giving a hooded appearance; brown streaks on whitish throat, breast; grey-brown mantle, upper belly, with pinkish-rufous hue; rufous-orange back, lower belly, vent. Silver grey-and-black wing panels. In pairs, when breeding; otherwise, in small flocks, often with other babblers, warblers, tits; skulks in bushes and undergrowth; occasionally in trees; not often seen.

MANIPUR FULVETTA

Fulvetta manipurensis Timaliidae

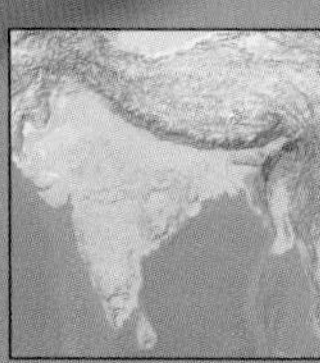

Size 11 cm

Voice Song a repeated, high-pitched *si…swu* or *see…si…wu*

Range Hills of NE India

Habitat Broadleaved evergreen forests, bamboos and bushes

Grey-brown fulvetta with prominent brown lateral crown-stripe and diffused pinkish-brown streaking on throat; grey cheeks; pale upperparts. Similar to White-browed, but lacks supercilium. Distinguished from Brown-throated by greyish ear-coverts, more buff-brown crown, mantle and breast.

BROWN-CHEEKED FULVETTA

Alcippe poioicephala Timaliidae

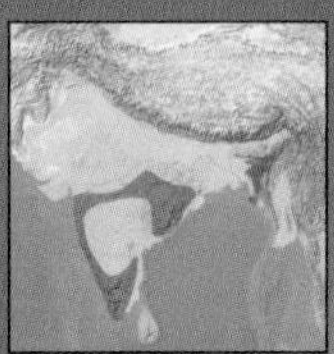

Size 15 cm

Voice Best-known call 4- to 8-syllabled, interpreted as *daddy… give…me…chocolate;* harsh *churrr* notes serve as contact calls

Range Peninsular India, south from S Rajasthan across Pachmarhi (Satpura) to S Bihar and Odisha

Habitat Forests, undergrowth, bamboos; also hill-station gardens in Western Ghats

Sexes alike. Olive-brown above; grey crown and nape distinctive; thin black stripe through eye; rufescent-brown wings and tail; dull fulvous underbody. In pairs or small parties, often along with other birds; moves actively in undergrowth and leafy branches, clinging sideways or springing from perch; rather shy in most areas, but occasionally emerges into open areas.

RUSTY-CAPPED FULVETTA

Schoeniparus dubius Timaliidae

Size 12 cm

Voice Calls include *chu…chi…chiu; chu…witee…wee; chu…witchichu; chu…witchu…chiu; wi…chi…chiu; wi…witu…chu*

Range Hills of NE India

Habitat Bushes and dense undergrowth; especially ferns and brambles; in both thick and open forests; also at edges of forests

Large, rather long-tailed, skulking fulvetta. Has noticeably bright rufous forehead, rufous crown and nape with dark brown scaling; broad, white supercilium contrasting with black lateral crown-stripes, and dark brown ear-coverts and neck sides, latter having prominent buff streaking. Uniform, olive-brown wings help quickly to separate this species from Rufous-winged.

NEPAL FULVETTA

Alcippe nipalensis Timaliidae

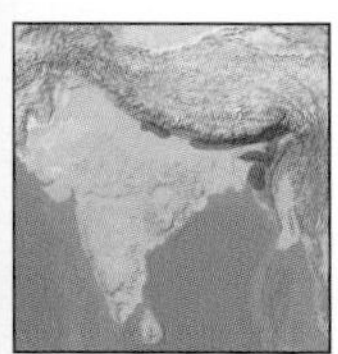

Size 12 cm

Voice Calls include buzzes; trills. Short song *shoo…shoo*

Range W Nepal to Myanmar. S Assam hills

Habitat Forest undergrowth and middle storeys

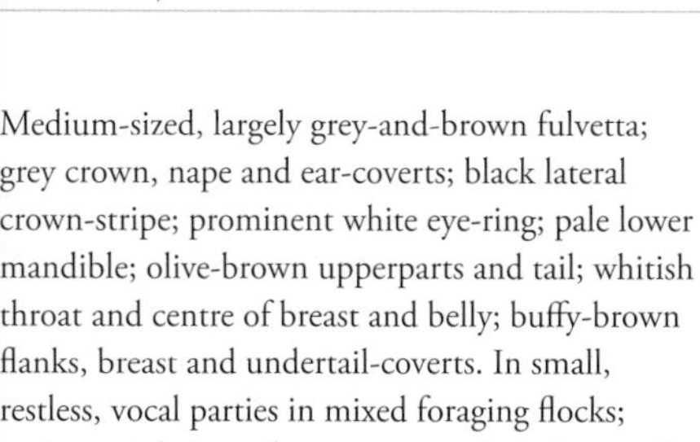

Medium-sized, largely grey-and-brown fulvetta; grey crown, nape and ear-coverts; black lateral crown-stripe; prominent white eye-ring; pale lower mandible; olive-brown upperparts and tail; whitish throat and centre of breast and belly; buffy-brown flanks, breast and undertail-coverts. In small, restless, vocal parties in mixed foraging flocks; active mainly in understorey, sometimes in trees in mid-storey, occasionally descends to ground; shy, and mostly remains hidden from view.

RUFOUS SIBIA

Malacias capistratus Timaliidae

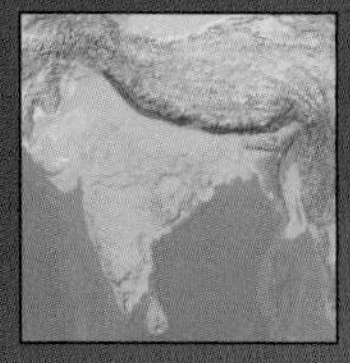

Size 21 cm

Voice Calls includes a wide range of whistling and sharp notes. Rich song of 6- to 8-syllables during the Himalayan summer

Range The Himalayas, 1,500-3,000 m. Sometimes upto about 3,500 m; descends to 600 m in some winters

Habitat Temperate and broadleaved forests

Sexes alike. Rich rufous plumage; grey-brown centre of back (between wings); black crown; slightly bushy crest and sides of head; bluish-grey wings and black shoulder patch; grey-tipped long tail; black subterminal tail-band. Small flocks, sometimes with other birds; active gymnasts, ever on the move; cheerful calls; hunts in canopy and middle-forest storeys, moves amidst moss-covered branches; springs into air after winged insects; sometimes hunts like treecreepers on stems, probing bark crevices.

RUFOUS-BACKED SIBIA

Leioptila annectans Timaliidae

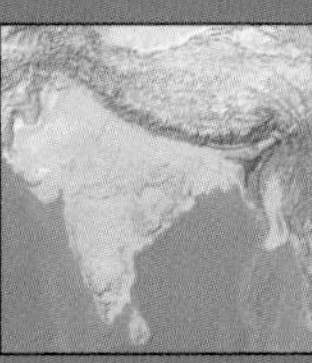

Size 18 cm

Voice Chirrups. Song a loud, cheerful *chew…chew…ee, wheewhee…chee…chewee*

Range E Nepal, Bhutan and Arunachal Pradesh

Habitat Dense, moist subtropical or temperate, broadleaved evergreen forests

Smallest sibia, with relatively shorter tail; black cap, mask and upper mantle; white streaks on black nape; rufous back, rump and uppertail-coverts; mainly black wings with white-edged tertials, silvery panel formed by grey-edged primaries and secondaries, rufous bar on greater coverts; white throat, breast and belly; paler rufous flanks, lower belly and vent; yellow base to bill; yellow legs. Usually in small groups; arboreal; partial to mossy branches.

BEAUTIFUL SIBIA

Malacias pulchellus Timaliidae

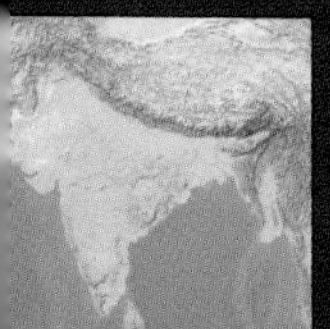

Size 22 cm

Voice Not always vocal. Rattling calls. Loud, whistled song

Range Mostly Arunachal Pradesh

Habitat Moist, broadleaved evergreen forests

Medium-sized blue sibia; pale indigo-blue crown; black ores and variable black on ear-coverts and face; grey-blue upperparts; paler, smoky grey-blue underparts; black greater and primary covert wing patch; silver-grey edges o primaries; grey-blue secondaries; brown tertials; blue, brown-and-grey tail; dark subterminal band. In pairs, during breeding season; otherwise, small parties, larger n winter; arboreal; usually forages on mossy branches at canopy level; moves by hopping upwards on branches.

LONG-TAILED SIBIA

Heterophasia picaoides Timaliidae

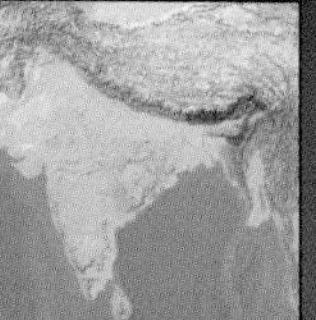

Size 30 cm

Voice Call a ringing *tsip tsip tsip*

Range Locally common breeding resident from E Nepal to Burmese border. Moves lower down in winter

Habitat Upper and middle levels of evergreen forests; edges of forests

Large, brown-grey babbler with long, white-tipped, graduated ail and distinct white wing patch, graduated. Grey head and breast; red iris; slender, slightly downcurved bill; darkish ores. Brownish back, wings and tail. Underparts pale grey. Sexes alike. Juvenile has grey eyes. Arboreal. Feeds on nectar, invertebrates and seeds in pairs or single-species flocks. Confiding, but very active. Nests in tree-ops. Extremely noisy.

GREY SIBIA

Malacias gracilis Timaliidae

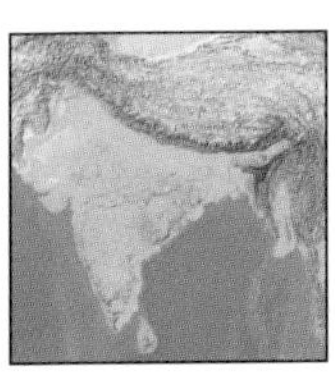

Size 21 cm

Voice Harsh, grating, slightly metallic calls typical of the genus, e.g. *trrit-trrit.* Song loud, strident, far-carrying series of well-spaced high-pitched, shrill whistled notes; *tu…tu…ti…ti…ti…tu; ti…ti…ti… ti…tiu…tu; tiutiu…tiu…tiu…tiu* etc.

Range Hills of NE India

Habitat Deciduous and evergreen broadleaved forests; mainly pine forests in Khasi Hills

Brownish-grey bird, similar to Rufous, but without any rufous. Black crown; no crest; black ear-coverts; brown-grey nape, mantle and back. Underparts white; buff rear flanks and undertail-coverts, black wings, with black edges to grey tertials; grey greater coverts; grey tail with broad, black subterminal band. Arboreal. Feeds in flocks, in trees, outside breeding season. Nests high in trees.

WHISKERED YUHINA

Yuhina flavicollis Timaliidae

Olive-brown above; chocolate-brown crown and crest; white eye-ring and black moustache seen from up close; rufous-yellow nuchal-collar (less distinct in western race *albicollis*); white underbody, streaked rufous-olive on sides of breast and flanks. Sexes alike. Flocks, almost always in association with other small birds; active and restless, flitting about or hunting flycatcher-style; moves between undergrowth and middle-levels of forests; sometimes ascending into canopy; keeps up a constant twitter.

flavicollis

Size 13 cm

Voice Quite vocal. Mix of soft twittering notes and fairly loud titmice-like 2- or 3-note call, *chee...chi...chew*

Range The Himalayas; W Himachal Pradesh to extreme NE India; 800-3,400 m

Habitat Forests

STRIATED YUHINA

Staphida castaniceps Timaliidae

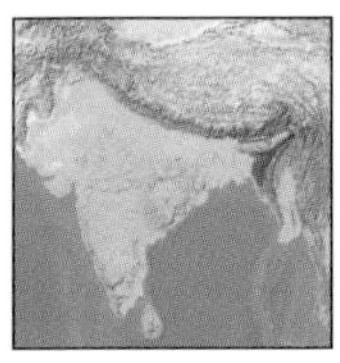

Size 11 cm

Voice Call a loud cheeping or twittering *chir...chit...chir...chit*

Range NE India

Habitat Open and dense broadleaved forests with thick, bushy understorey; secondary growth in tropical and subtropical zones

Not so crested as other yuhinas, and the only one to show white on tail. Main plumage features include very short white supercilium; rufous ear-coverts with fine white streaking, white streaking on greyish-olive mantle, uniform greyish-white underparts, and white tips to graduated tail. Racial variation; three races occur in the subcontinent.

WHITE-NAPED YUHINA

Yuhina bakeri Timaliidae

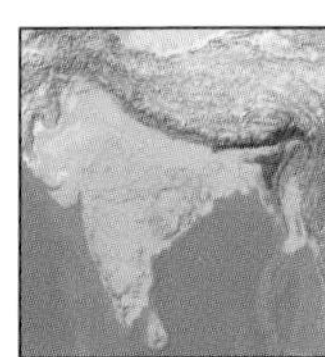

Size 13 cm

Voice Calls *tsit...tsit; zhueh... zhueh*

Range Hills of E Nepal to Myanmar

Habitat Subtropical moist broadleaved evergreen forests; secondary growth

Distinctive rufous-crested yuhina; prominent white nape, better seen when crest raised; short, dark, sturdy bill; rufous crest, face, upper mantle; dark lores, eye-ring; white streaks on ear-coverts; white throat, with no moustachial stripe, as in other yuhinas; olive-brown lower mantle, with white shaft streaks; buff-brown below, with pinkish cast and fine, faint dark streaks. In pairs, when breeding; joins mixed feeding flocks with other babblers and small insectivores; very active in mid-storey trees or bushes in understorey.

STRIPE-THROATED YUHINA

Yuhina gularis Timaliidae

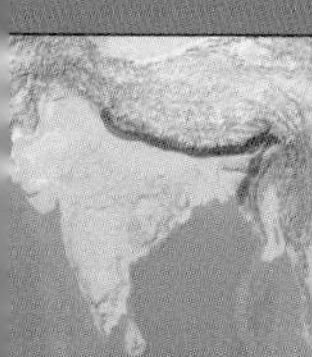

Size 14 cm

Voice Calls *kwee*

Range Hills of Uttarakhand to Myanmar

Habitat Temperate broadleaved, especially oak, rhododendron, forests; coniferous forests; secondary growth

Larger yuhina, with longer, upright, and slightly forward-drooping, grey crest; grey face, mantle; pale pink throat, with black streaks; narrow white eye-ring; patchy rufous-and-buff underparts; more rufous on centre of belly, vent; bright rufous wing patch on secondaries; white-edged black primaries; pale basal two-thirds of lower mandible. As with other yuhinas, in pairs when breeding; otherwise, in small parties, especially with other babblers and small insectivores; usually in taller shrubs or lower branches of trees; partial to flowering trees.

RUFOUS-VENTED YUHINA

Yuhina occipitalis Timaliidae

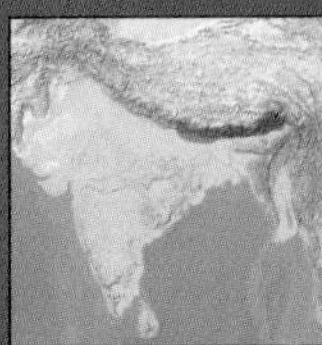

Size 13 cm

Voice Calls include rattling *trr… trr…trr* and *zee…zit*

Range Locally common breeding resident in N mountains from C Nepal to Arunachal Pradesh. Moves lower down in winter. Also occurs in Tibet, Myanmar and China

Habitat Forests, usually quite high in canopy

Upperparts brown with rufous nape and lores. Tall, grey crest; grey neck; forehead has whitish streaks; pale buff sides of head; white eye-ring; black malar stripe. Underparts paler, pink-brown; belly buff; rufous vent; reddish-brown bill and yellow-brown legs. Sexes alike. Juvenile has shorter crest and paler rufous nape and lores. Feeds on invertebrates and nectar in small active parties, often in mixed hunting groups. Nests in small trees in moss or lichen.

BLACK-CHINNED YUHINA

Yuhina nigrimenta Timaliidae

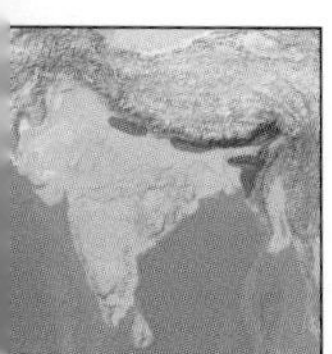

Size 11 cm

Voice Calls include chattering, twittering, buzzing. Whistled song *zeet…zut…zeet…zeet*

Range Hills of Uttarakhand to Myanmar

Habitat Subtropical broadleaved evergreen forests; secondary growth

Small, distinctive, mainly grey, brown-and-black yuhina, with relatively short tail; grey head, ear-coverts, hindneck, upper mantle; black-streaked front to upright grey crest; black lores and chin; slightly curved dark bill, with red-based lower mandible; mostly greyish-brown upperparts; pale, whitish throat, upper breast; mostly buff belly, vent. In pairs, when breeding; in small, noisy, same-species flocks or mixed hunting parties; active from understorey to canopy; acrobatic, tit-like behaviour.

WHITE-BELLIED ERPORNIS

Erpornis zantholeuca Timaliidae

Olive-yellow above and white underparts. Shortish, spiky, olive-yellow crest; light grey lores; black eyes; pale flesh-pink bill and legs. Yellow undertail-coverts and vent. Juvenile duller, with brownish cast to upperparts and shorter crest.

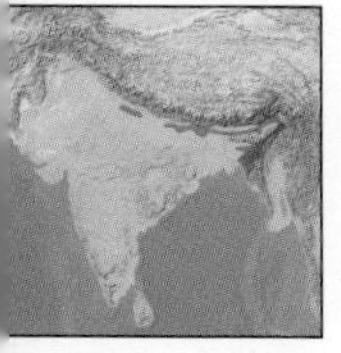

Size 11 cm

Voice Alarm calls include high, subdued, metallic *chit* and *cheaan*; nasal tit-like *na-na*. Sings with a short, high-pitched, descending trill, *si…i…i…i…i…i*

Range The Himalayas from Nepal east to Arunachal Pradesh; NE India and Bangladesh

Habitat Broadleaved forests, especially clearings and edges; secondary growth

GREAT PARROTBILL

Conostoma aemodium Paradoxornithidae

Large parrotbill, with long, rounded, orange-yellow bill; uniform brown, or grey-brown in colour; whitish forecrown; bushy-black lores and brow; no dark lateral crown-stripe; grey primary panel and sides of tail; richer rufous-brown on secondaries, wing-coverts; singly, in pairs, or small flocks; normally concealed in undergrowth, sometimes in foliage of tall trees, occasionally on ground, though not very secretive.

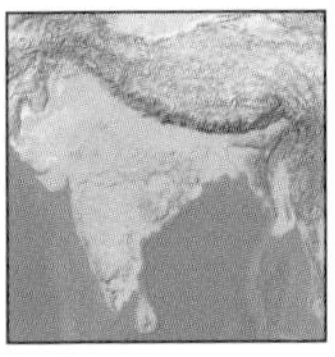

Size 28 cm

Voice Calls include *krarnk; krarnch; wheeoo...whee...wheeoo*

Range Hills of Nepal to Arunachal Pradesh

Habitat Bamboo clumps in or near forests; oak, rhododendron, open or dense broadleaved evergreen, or mixed coniferous, broadleaved forests

BROWN PARROTBILL

Cholornis unicolor Paradoxornithidae

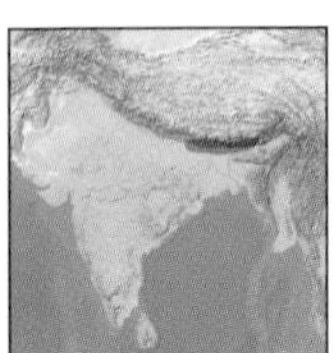

Size 21 cm

Voice Calls include *chrrt...chrrt; wheeoo...wheeoo*

Range Hills of E Nepal to Arunachal Pradesh

Habitat Bamboo stands; dwarf rhododendron shrubberies

Medium-sized parrotbill with small, bulbous, yellow or greyish bill; speckled, greyish-brown crown, sometimes raised in a crest; long, dark lateral crown-stripes; greyish supercilium, extending from behind eye to around ear-coverts; brown ear-coverts speckled with grey; pale eye-ring, broken into two crescents, above and below eye; more brown upperparts, with rich brown wing panel on primaries; greyish throat and breast; brownish belly and flanks; brown tail. Usually in small parties; acrobatic feeder; shy, secretive.

BLACK-BREASTED PARROTBILL

Paradoxornis flavirostris Paradoxornithidae

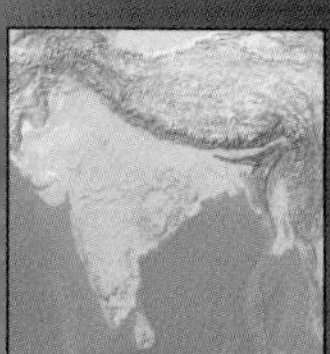

Size 19 cm

Voice Call a striking, whistling *phew…phew…phew…phuit,* ascending in pitch and volume. Also, bleating or mewing cry, and mellow 3-noted warble

Range NE India

Habitat Mixed grass and bamboos in hills, dense reed beds, elephant grass and grasses along riverbanks in lowlands

Medium-sized, stocky parrotbill with rufous-brown head and olive-brown upperparts, black-patch on ear-coverts, and huge orange bill. Likely to be confused only with Spot-breasted, although different distribution. Best distinguished by black breast and solid black chin (with black barring on white throat and malar area), rufous-buff (rather than pale buff) underparts, darker rufous-brown crown and nape, even stouter bill and different call.

SPOT-BREASTED PARROTBILL

Paradoxornis guttaticollis Paradoxornithidae

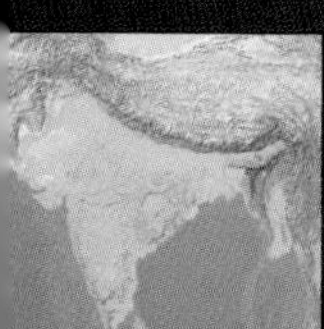

Size 21 cm

Voice Calls include *whit-whit-whit-whit-whit;* or more plaintive series, e.g. *wui…wui…wui…wui* or *whi…whi…whiwhi…whi…whi…whi* or *dri…dri…dri…dri,* etc.

Range Nagaland; Mizoram

Habitat Grass and scrub, bushes and bamboo stands, mainly in subtropical zone

Medium-sized, stocky parrotbill with rufous head and upperparts, black-patch on ear-coverts, and large, orange bill. Likely to be confused only with Black-breasted, although distribution is different. Best distinguished by black arrowhead-shaped spotting on buffish-white throat and breast (lacking bold, black-patch on breast), pale buff (rather than rufous-buff) underparts, brighter rufous crown and nape, less stout bill and different call.

FULVOUS PARROTBILL

Suthora fulvifrons Paradoxornithidae

Small, mainly brown parrotbill, with large head and tiny bill; fulvous crown, olive-brown lateral crown-stripes; feathery, fulvous supercilium, head, neck, throat, lower breast, upper mantle, giving a bushy, large-headed appearance; paler lower belly, vent; buff-white gorget on upper breast; buff-brown lower mantle, rufous wings; silver, black, buff wing panel on flight feathers.

Size 12 cm

Voice Calls include twitters, buzzes

Range Nepal through to Arunachal Pradesh

Habitat Montane bamboo forests

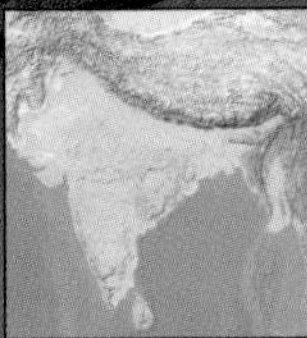

BLACK-THROATED PARROTBILL

Suthora nipalensis Paradoxornithidae

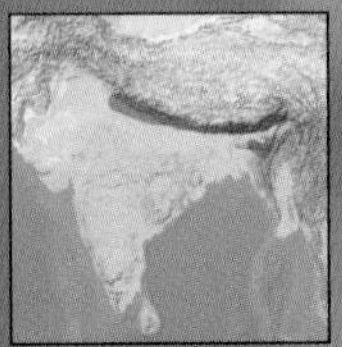

Size 10 cm

Voice Calls include twitters, trills

Range E Uttarakhand to Myanmar

Habitat Bamboos; undergrowth in oak-rhododendron forests

humii

poliotis

Smallest parrotbill in the subcontinent. Large head; tiny, mainly black bill; long, bushy, black lateral crown-stripe to nape; variable black, triangular throat patch; variable white supercilium, face, malar stripe or patch; rufous wings; black primary covert patch; silver, black wing panels; grey to rufous underparts. Western and Central Himalayan races have grey crown, ear-coverts; light rufous underparts; in same-species or mixed flocks; hyperactive, vocal, constantly twittering, moving rapidly through bamboos and bushes.

crocotius

LESSER RUFOUS-HEADED PARROTBILL

Chleuasicus atrosuperciliaris Paradoxornithidae

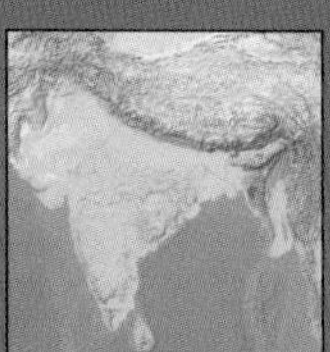

Size 15 cm

Voice Possible song consists of sharp, rapidly repeated chipping *tit…tit…tit…tit…tit…tit…tit*

Range The Himalayas from Nepal and West Bengal east to Arunachal Pradesh; NE India

Habitat Bamboo stands, tall reeds and grass, scrub jungles, mainly in tropical and subtropical zones

Stocky parrotbill with rufous-orange crown and nape and buffish-white underparts, stout pale bill. Distinguished from the similar Greater Rufous-headed by smaller size, smaller and stouter bill, whitish lores and paler buffish-orange ear-coverts. *P. a. oatesi* (E Himalayas) lacks black eyebrow and whiter underparts. Prominent black eyebrow and underparts buff in *P. a. atrosuperciliaris*, which occurs south and east of the Brahmaputra river.

GREATER RUFOUS-HEADED PARROTBILL

Psittiparus ruficeps Paradoxornithidae

Medium-sized, sturdy-looking parrotbill, with large, rounded bill; distinctive, bright rufous-orange crown, nape, face, ear-coverts, sharply contrasting with paler underparts; white, with buff flanks in E Himalayan *ruficeps*; buff in *bakeri* of regions S and E of Brahmaputra; bill has dark upper mandible, pale lower mandible; blue lores, orbital-ring; brown upperparts, tail. In pairs, or small groups; often joins mixed feeding flocks; shy and skulking; prefers to forage in under and lower forest storeys.

Size 18 cm

Voice Calls include chitters, churrs

Range Extreme E Nepal, Bhutan and Arunachal Pradesh; S Assam Hills

Habitat Bamboos; undergrowth in moist broadleaved evergreen forests; reeds; tall grass

GREY-HEADED PARROTBILL

Paradoxornis gularis Paradoxornithidae

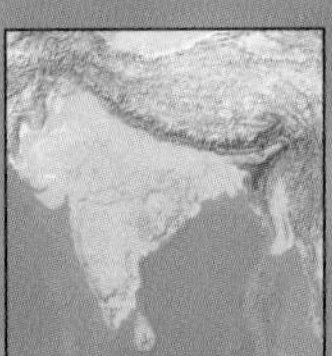

Size 21 cm

Voice Call *jhiew…,jhiew;* rattle. Soft, whistled song

Range Bhutan, Arunachal Pradesh and S Assam Hills

Habitat Bamboo stands; dense and open broadleaved evergreen forests; bushes

Medium-sized parrotbill, with grey crown, nape, ear-coverts and sides of neck; bright orange, bulbous and slightly hooked bill; black lateral crown-stripe, extending from around forehead to nape; white lores, eye-ring and broad malar patch; triangular black throat patch; rufous-brown mantle and upperparts; pinkish-white to pinkish-buff underparts, depending on race. In pairs, or small, same-species flocks; active in bushes in understorey, bamboos, trees in middle storey.

FIRE-TAILED MYZORNIS

Myzornis pyrrhoura Timaliidae

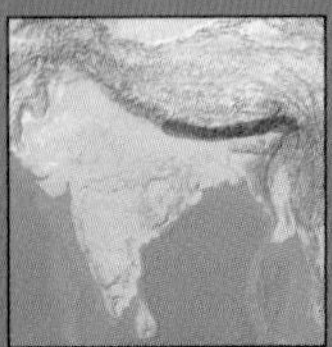

Size 12 cm

Voice Calls include high *tsi…tsi;* rattling *trr…trr*

Range W Nepal to Arunachal Pradesh

Habitat Dwarf juniper, rhododendron shrubberies; mossy oak, rhododendron forests; bamboos

Unmistakable bird; bright, rich, leaf-green above, sometimes washed with gold; slightly paler gold-green below; distinctive black spots on crown; black eye mask; diffused greenish-gold outline around eye mask, on bend of wing; thin, black, slightly downcurved bill; bright red throat and breast; orange-red to centre of underparts below, vent, undertail-coverts; orange-red, white, black wing panels; large white tips to primaries, secondaries; bright red sides to black-tipped tail. Can be spotted solitary, or in small flocks.

EURASIAN WREN

Troglodytes troglodytes Troglodytidae

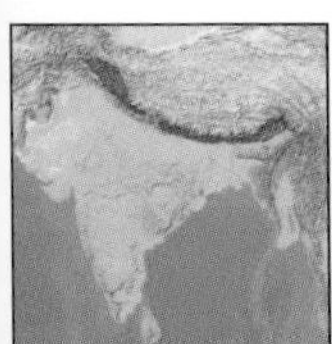

Size 9 cm

Voice Noisy. Calls include angry *zirrr* and *tzit.* Loud, rapid song

Range Locally common breeding resident in N mountains from W Pakistan east to Arunachal Pradesh. Moves lower in winter. Also occurs in Europe, N Africa, W, N, C and E Asia, Myanmar and N America

Habitat Rocky areas with scrubs and low growth in open forests, often near water and habitation

nipalensis

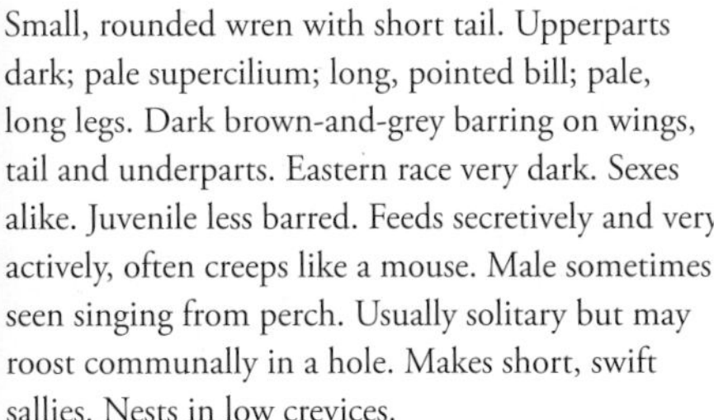

Small, rounded wren with short tail. Upperparts dark; pale supercilium; long, pointed bill; pale, long legs. Dark brown-and-grey barring on wings, tail and underparts. Eastern race very dark. Sexes alike. Juvenile less barred. Feeds secretively and very actively, often creeps like a mouse. Male sometimes seen singing from perch. Usually solitary but may roost communally in a hole. Makes short, swift sallies. Nests in low crevices.

neglectus

YUNNAN NUTHATCH

Sitta yunnanensis Sittidae

Size 12 cm

Voice Call a nasal *nit*

Range Recently found in Arunachal Pradesh; the first record from India

Habitat Open forests of deciduous, broadleaved evergreen and coniferous trees

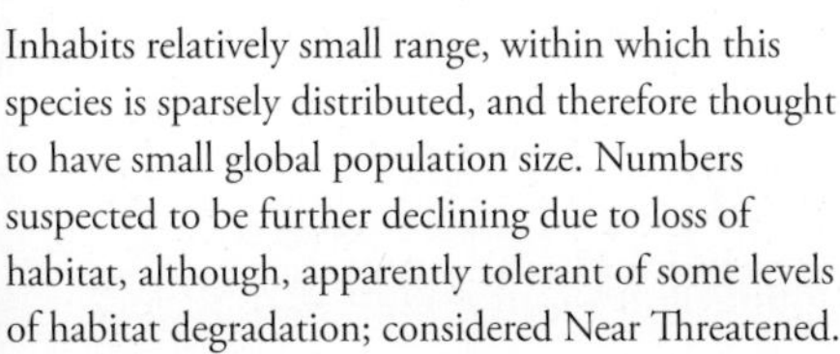

Inhabits relatively small range, within which this species is sparsely distributed, and therefore thought to have small global population size. Numbers suspected to be further declining due to loss of habitat, although, apparently tolerant of some levels of habitat degradation; considered Near Threatened.

CHESTNUT-VENTED NUTHATCH

Sitta nagaensis Sittidae

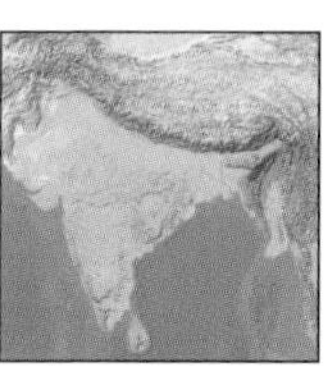

Size 12 cm

Voice Call a distinctive nasal *djeeeep* or *chuueep*. Song a level and vibrating trill, *duiduiduiduiduidui*

Range Common resident in the hills of NE India

Habitat Open forests of deciduous, broadleaved evergreen and coniferous trees

Small to medium-sized bird. Upperparts greyish-blue. Strong, black eye-stripe. Underparts paler grey (variable). Rufous undertail-coverts, with white scallop pattern on side. Female similar to male, but flanks and undertail-coverts paler rufous. Solitary, or in pairs. Appears in mixed hunting parties outside breeding season. Feeds on ground, forages around tree roots and stones for insects.

KASHMIR NUTHATCH

Sitta cashmirensis Sittidae

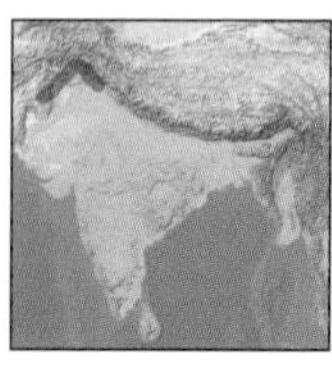

Size 12 cm

Voice Calls *tsip…tsip*

Range Endemic to the subcontinent, N Balochistan and NW Pakistan; the Himalayas from N Pakistan east to Kashmir, NW Nepal

Habitat Deciduous and mixed broadleaved coniferous forests and well-wooded country; more likely at slightly lower altitudes and in deciduous trees than White-cheeked

Medium-sized, bluish-grey bird. Distinct black eye-stripe extends to nape, curving around ear-coverts. Creamy-white chin, cheeks and ear-coverts; buff throat; cinnamon-buff breast; rufous flanks, undertail-coverts and vent. Female similar, but has more buff on cheeks and paler underparts with pinkish tinge on breast. Solitary, or in pairs. Confiding. Forages in lower levels.

CHESTNUT-BELLIED NUTHATCH

Sitta castanea Sittidae

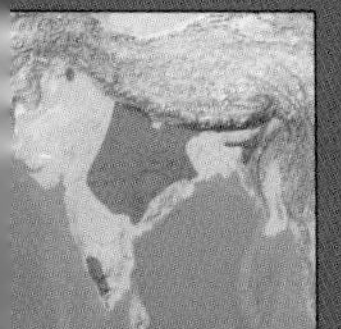

Size 12 cm

Voice Calls include loud *tzsib…*; faint twitter; loud whistle during breeding season

Range Lower Himalayas east of Uttarakhand; to about 1,800 m. Also in hills of peninsular India (race *cinnamoventris*).

Habitat Forests; groves; roadside trees; habitation

Male blue-grey above; black stripe from lores to nape; whitish cheeks and upper throat; all but central tail feathers black, with white markings; chestnut below. Female duller chestnut below. In pairs or several, often with other small birds; restless climber; clings to bark and usually works up the tree stem, hammering with beak; also moves upside-down and sideways; may visit the ground.

♀

WHITE-TAILED NUTHATCH

Sitta himalayensis Sittidae

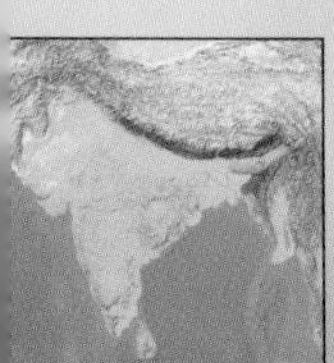

Size 12 cm

Voice Calls *tchip…tchip*. Song a musical *djuwee…djuwee…djuwee*

Range Hills of Himachal Pradesh to Myanmar. Moves lower in winter

Habitat Mixed broadleaved and coniferous forests

Smallish nuthatch, with relatively short bill; bluish-grey upperparts, darker along edges of wing-coverts and tail; diagnostic white central patch at base of tail not always easy to see; pale chin, throat becomes increasingly deeper rufous-buff on breast, belly, flanks and undertail-coverts; bold, black eye-stripe broadens and curves behind ear-coverts; lacks contrasting white throat, scalloping on undertail-coverts of Chestnut-bellied; gregarious; often in pairs; joins mixed-species foraging flocks; arboreal; usually in upper forest storey.

VELVET-FRONTED NUTHATCH

Sitta frontalis Sittidae

Small nuthatch. Male has violet-blue upperparts; jet-black forehead; stripe through eye; white chin and throat, merging into vinous-grey below; coral-red beak. Underparts variable from beige to pinkish-buff. Female lacks black stripe through eye. In pairs, or several in mixed hunting parties; creeps about on stems and branches; fond of moss-covered trees; also clings upside-down; active and agile, quickly moving from tree to tree; calls often, till long after sunset; also checks fallen logs and felled branches.

Size 10 cm

Voice Calls include fairly loud, rapidly repeated, sharp, trilling *chweet…chwit…chwit* whistles

Range From around W Uttarakhand east along lower Himalayas; widespread over hilly, forested areas of C, S and E India; absent in flat and arid regions

Habitat Forests; also tea and coffee plantations

WHITE-CHEEKED NUTHATCH

Sitta leucopsis Sittidae

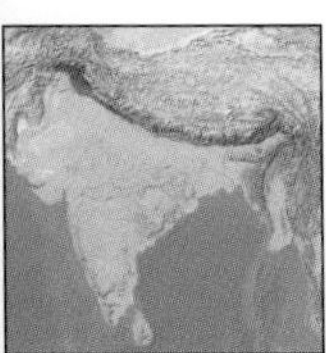

Size 12 cm

Voice Call likened to that of a young goat bleating

Range W Himalayas

Habitat Coniferous and mixed forests

Distinctive nuthatch, with black crown and nape. Upperparts dark blue-grey; large, white cheek patches surrounding eye; white face and throat with beady eyes. Whitish underparts with buffish-wash becoming rufous on rear flanks and undertail-coverts. Juvenile has faint barring on underparts. Forages under tall trees or branches with lichen; solitary, in pairs or mixed flocks.

BEAUTIFUL NUTHATCH

Sitta formosa Sittidae

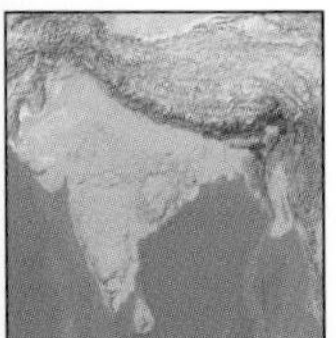

Size 15 cm

Voice Calls include chitters

Range Patchily in E Nepal, Bhutan and Arunachal Pradesh

Habitat Dense primary broadleaved evergreen forests

Unmistakable, but uncommon, large nuthatch with striking, bright blue-and-black pattern on upperparts; blue-and-white streaks down black crown and nape; broad, blue scapular-band across black mantle; prominent bluish-white fringed edging on coverts and tertials; buff-white throat and long, straight supercilium; bright rufous below, paler on breast, vent and undertail-coverts; habits not well-known; gregarious; lives in pairs or small parties; upto 20 reported, often in mixed-species feeding flocks; arboreal; movement heavier, slower; not as agile as other nuthatches.

RUSTY-FLANKED TREECREEPER

Certhia nipalensis Certhiidae

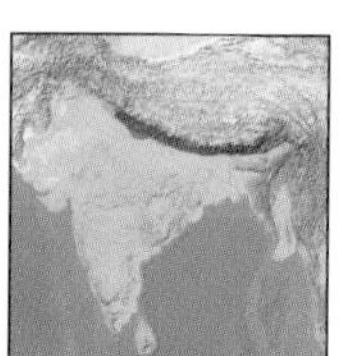

Size 12 cm

Voice Call a thin *sit…sit;…zip*. Song *si…si…ss…srrt…st…ttt*

Range Uttarakhand to Arunachal Pradesh. Moves lower in winter

Habitat Oak, rhododendron, mixed coniferous forests in summer; spends winter in mixed broadleaved forests

More warmly-coloured and distinguished from others by overall darker plumage. Rusty-brown flanks, rump, lower back; warm brown-and-black upperparts streaked with buff; pale buff supercilium encircling dark ear-coverts; shorter bill; tail unbarred; cream breast and belly, rather than whitish of Hodgson's, brownish of Brown-throated; usually solitary; may join other insectivores in mixed hunting parties; quiet and unobtrusive; likely to be missed; climbs vertically around tree trunks; flies to base of next tree; flicks wings constantly.

WALLCREEPER

Tichodroma muraria Tichodromidae

Striking bird, with black, grey-and-crimson plumage; very long, thin, pointed, slightly downcurved bill; breeding male has slaty-grey crown and mantle; bright crimson-patches on black wings; black throat, upper breast; smoky-grey underparts; non-breeding adult has white throat, upper breast; inconspicuous on rock-face till it flies; shows broad, rounded, crimson-and-black wings with two rows of white spots; short, broad black tail with white tips, corners; solitary, in pairs when breeding; shy; uses long toes, strong claws to climb vertical rock-faces, walls.

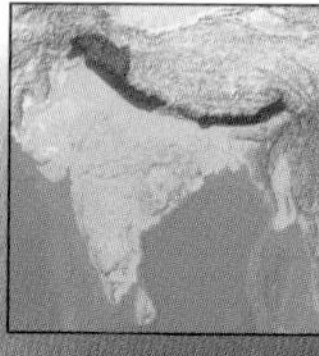

Size 17 cm

Voice Calls *tu…wee*. Whistled song

Range Mountains of Pakistan to Myanmar. Moves lower in winter

Habitat Cliffs; gorges; boulders; earthen banks; ruins; old buildings; quarries

HODGSON'S TREECREEPER

Certhia hodgsoni Certhiidae

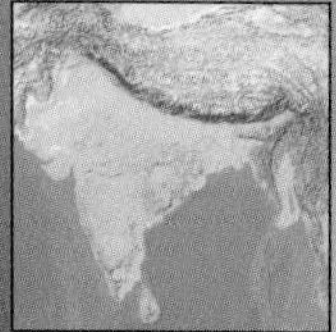

Size 12 cm

Voice Calls *tseep…tseep*

Range Mountains of Pakistan to Myanmar. Moves lower in winter

Habitat Mixed coniferous, birch, oak and rhododendron montane forests

Small, slender, warm brown treecreeper with black-and-white streaked upperparts. White supercilium; plain, long, brown, unbarred, stiff tail; relatively short, decurved bill. Creamy-white (tinged with buff) belly, flanks and vent. Distinguished from Rusty-flanked by pale buff, rather than rusty-brown flanks; paler buff ear-coverts; shorter, less-marked supercilium; distinguished from Brown-throated by whitish rather than brownish throat, breast, belly; more distinct supercilium; usually solitary; joins mixed hunting parties of insectivores in non-breeding season; quiet and inconspicuous; unlike nuthatches, uses tail to support movement on undersides of branches. Not shy. Nests behind loose barks or in tree crevices.

BROWN-THROATED TREECREEPER

Certhia discolor Certhiidae

Size 12 cm

Voice Call a high-pitched *chit…; tsit*. Song a rapid *tchitititit*

Range Nepal to Arunachal Pradesh. S Assam Hills

Habitat Mixed broadleaved oak, oak-coniferous forests

Upperparts mottled brown-and-black, streaked with lighter buff. Distinguished from other treecreepers by brownish rather than whitish throat and breast; paler below; tail unbarred; thin, buff supercilium, extending only to dark ear-coverts, but not around; duller brown on rump, lower flanks than Rusty-flanked; Race *manipurensis* of S Manipur (sometimes separated as Hume's Treecreeper) has brighter rufous on throat and breast, rather than brown of nominate race of the Himalayas; normally solitary; may join mixed hunting parties; quiet and inconspicuous; climbs vertically around lichen-covered tree trunks, uses tail as prop; also undersides of branches, probes barks for insects.

BAR-TAILED TREECREEPER

Certhia himalayana Certhiidae

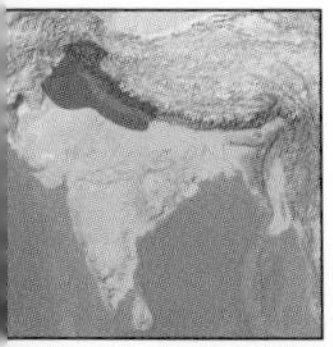

Size 12 cm

Voice Call a long-drawn squeak, somewhat ventriloquial. Loud but short, monotonous song; one of the earliest bird songs, heard much before other birds have begun to sing

Range The Himalayas, east to W Nepal; from about 1,600 m to treeline; descends in winter

Habitat The Himalayan temperate forests

Streaked blackish-brown treecreeper, with fulvous-and-grey upperparts. Pale supercilium; broad fulvous wing-band; white chin and throat; dull ash-brown below; best recognised by dark brown barring on pointed tail. Sexes alike. Solitary, or several in mixed parties of small birds; spends almost entire life on tree trunks; starts climbing from near the base; sometimes creeps on moss-covered rocks and walls.

SPOTTED CREEPER

Salpornis spilonotus Certhiidae

Size 13 cm

Voice Calls include thin *see...ee* and deep *kek...kek...kek.* Whistling song

Range Strangely rare and very local breeding resident in N peninsula from Haryana, Uttar Pradesh and Bihar south to Maharashtra and Andhra Pradesh. Also occurs in Africa, where very local

Habitat Open woodlands and groves, favouring trees with deep-fissured bark such as mangoes and babul

Plump, brown and buff bird with long, curved bill. Broad, white supercilium; dark wings; short, squarish tail, broadly-barred white. Upperparts streaked black-and-white; white throat, fulvous breast, barred and mottled brown. Sexes alike. Feeds usually singly, on invertebrates in bark at all levels in trees. Climbs rapidly up and under tree trunks and branches, often fluttering down to change position. Does not spiral. Nest made of leaves, bark and lichen, usually in branch fork.

SPOT-WINGED STARLING

Saroglossa spiloptera Sturnidae

Size 19 cm

Voice Song similar to that of Rosy, continuous harsh, unmusical jumble of dry, discordant notes and few melodious warbles

Range The Himalayan foothills from W Himachal Pradesh east to Arunachal Pradesh; NE India and Bangladesh

Habitat Open broadleaved forests, edges of forests and clearings; cultivation with groves or scattered trees of Bombax, Erythrina and Salmalia trees, which it favours

Slender, greyish-brown bird. Male has blackish face mask, rufous-brown throat; grey crown and nape; dark patterning on crown and mantle, rufous uppertail-coverts. Underparts whitish with hints of light rusty-orange on breast and flanks. Female overall more brown above and has similar markings. Juvenile like female but more even above. Seen in large flocks. Stays in canopy, rarely descending.

♀

ASIAN GLOSSY STARLING

Aplonis panayensis Sturnidae

tytleri

albris

Size 20 cm

Voice Call consists of sharp, ringing whistles, *tseu… tseu* etc.

Range Partly resident. Breeding visitor to Assam, resident on Andaman and Nicobar Islands, also recorded in Meghalaya, Tripura and Bangladesh

Habitat Coconut groves, forest edges and clearings with large fig trees

Slim, medium-sized starling. Upperparts have greenish-gloss; stout, black bill; short, square tail. Adult glossy greenish-black all over; bright red iris. Blackish primaries with green gloss on edges; secondaries much glossier all over. Bill and legs black. Sexes alike. Juvenile brownish-black above with touches of green; underparts beige, strongly streaked with blackish-brown; eyes lighter yellow. Gregarious.

WHITE-FACED STARLING

Sturnonis albofrontatus Sturnidae

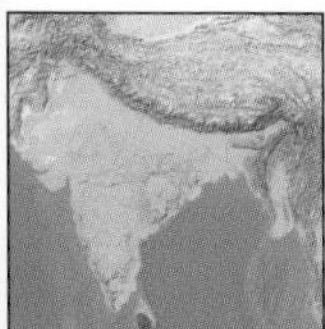

Size 22 cm

Voice Call a starling-type chirp, but generally rather silent

Range Resident in Sri Lanka. Rare in wet zone from foothills upto middle altitudes

Habitat Tall, natural forests

Upperparts dark mauve-grey with faint green gloss; white forehead and face. Underparts paler lavender-grey with fine white shaft streaking. Some individuals have all-white heads. Bluish-brown bill; with plumbeous blue at base of lower mandible. Juvenile has whitish supercilium, ear-coverts and throat, dull brown and dark grey underparts.

GOLDEN-CRESTED MYNA

Ampeliceps coronatus Sturnidae

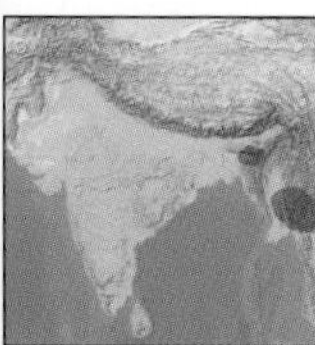

Size 22 cm

Voice Call higher-pitched, more metallic whistle than that of Hill; bell-like note

Range Assam, Manipur and West Bengal

Habitat Open, moist, broadleaved deciduous and evergreen forests; tall trees in cultivated forest clearings

Diagnostic golden throat, crown and forehead. Crown feathers extend to long crest. Overall glossy bluish-black. Sides of face, mantle and breast have more purplish gloss. Wings have yellow-and-white-patches. Naked patch around eye orange-yellow. Pale orange bill and orangish legs. Female similar, but less yellow on crown and throat. Juvenile dark brown with paler underparts; pale yellow lores and throat, and pale yellow-patch on wing.

♂

♂

SRI LANKA HILL MYNA

Gracula ptilogenys Sturnidae

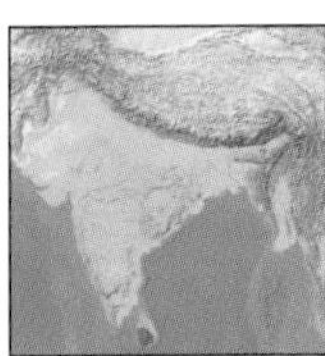

Size 25 cm

Voice Utters various, very loud whistling calls

Range Sri Lanka

Habitat Forests; well-wooded country; plantations; gardens

Black myna with purple gloss. Small tufts of feathers on forehead; pair of yellow wattles behind head; reddish-orange bill with darkish base. Very similar to Lesser Hill but bill stouter and more reddish. Mantle purplish-blue in male and greenish in female. Juvenile has duller bill, smaller, paler yellow wattles and brownish-black underparts. Keeps in canopy, collects in large numbers at fruting trees.

COMMON HILL MYNA

Gracula religiosa Sturnidae

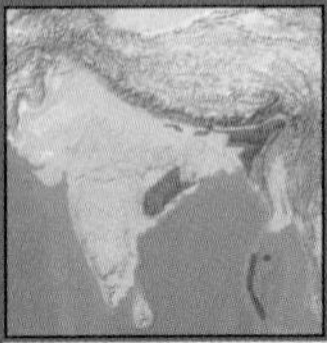

Size 25-29 cm

Voice Amazing vocalist. Calls include a great assortment of whistling, warbling, shrieking notes. Excellent mimic; much sought-after cage bird

Range Lower Himalayas and the Terai, Uttarakhand eastwards; Western Ghats, from N Kanara to extreme South India, and Sri Lanka; ssp. *peninsular* is restricted to Odisha, E Madhya Pradesh and N Andhra Pradesh

Habitat Forests; clearings

Glossy black plumage, with purple-green gloss on crown, nape, mantle and breast; rest of body has greenish gloss; white in flight feathers; orange-red beak; orange-yellow legs, yellow facial skin and fleshy wattles on nape and sides of face. Sexes alike. Small flocks in forests; extremely noisy; mostly arboreal, only occasionally descending into bushes or onto ground; hops amongst branches, and on ground; large numbers gather on fruiting trees, along with barbets, hornbills and green pigeons. Such sights are one of the birdwatching spectacles of the Himalayan foothills.

LESSER HILL MYNA

Gracula (religiosa) indica Sturnidae

Compared with Common, has smaller and finer bill; eye wattles distinctly separated from those on nape (wattles on nape extend upto sides of crown). Bill finer than Sri Lanka Hill, but has no blue at base; wattles on sides of head. Dark eyes, often white in Sri Lanka Hill.

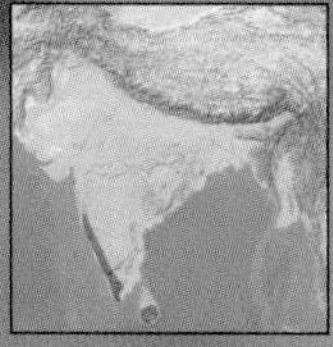

Size 24 cm

Voice Similar to Common Hill's

Range Western Ghats; Sri Lanka

Habitat Moist forests; plantations

GREAT MYNA

Acridotheres cinereus Sturnidae

Size 25 cm

Voice Screeches like Common, but harsher

Range Assam, S Assam Hills and lower Arunachal Pradesh

Habitat Marshes; tall grasslands; wet cultivation; settlements

Glossy, black myna, with frontal crest. Underparts dark grey; white wing patches; white-tipped tail; lemon-yellow bill, legs and feet. Adult could be confused with Jungle, but longer tuft, darker plumage; orange-yellow bill, without dark base; reddish iris; prominent white vent. Female has shorter crest than male. Juvenile browner overall, sometimes lacking tuft and whitish underparts; distinguished in flight by large white vent; in pairs, or small groups; less bold than Common; more wary; follows cattle.

JUNGLE MYNA

Acridotheres fuscus Sturnidae

mahrattensis

Ash-brown myna with small crest at base of bill. Black head; no orbital patch; chin, throat and breast slaty-grey graduating to buffish-white belly; dark blue base to yellow-orange bill; yellow legs and bill; white wing patch and white-tipped tail. Superficially similar to Common and Bank, but distinguished by greyer colour, darker cap not as defined; pale yellow eye, rather than red of Bank; also, white wing patch and tail-tip; gregarious; in pairs, or small groups; larger flocks when not breeding; shyer, less confiding than Common, and less associated with humans; more arboreal. *Mahrattensis* is found in a peninsular India while the nominate *fuscus* is found in N and NE India.

Size 23 cm

Voice Similar to Common's, but higher, more liquid

Range Hills of Pakistan to Arunachal Pradesh

Habitat Edges of forests; wooded areas near cultivation and settlements; plantations; scrubs

fuscus

COMMON MYNA

Acridotheres tristis Sturnidae

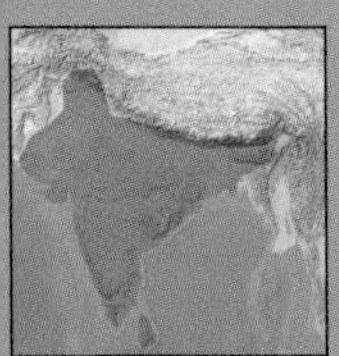

Size 23 cm

Voice Noisy. Calls include a great mix of chattering notes. One of India's most familiar bird sounds

Range Subcontinent, upto about 3,500 m in the Himalayas

Habitat Human habitation; cultivation; light forests

juvenile

Medium-sized bird with rich vinous-brown plumage; black head, neck and upper breast; yellow beak, legs and naked wattle around eyes distinctive; large white spot in dark brown flight feathers, best visible in flight; blackish tail, with broad, white tips to all but central feathers; whitish abdomen. Sexes alike. Seen in solitary, or in scattered pairs or small, loose bands. India's most common and familiar bird; hardly ever strays far from human habitation; rather haughty and confident in looks; aggressive, curious and noisy; struts about on ground, picks out worms; attends to grazing cattle and refuse dumps; enters verandahs and kitchens, sometimes even helping itself on dining tables.

BANK MYNA

Acridotheres ginginianus Sturnidae

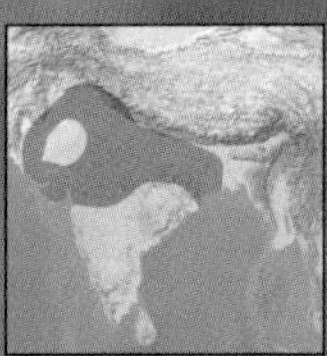

Size 21 cm

Voice Similar to Common's but softer

Range Widespread resident in N and C India

Habitat Human habitation; cultivation; grasslands

Similar to Common but smaller; has bluish-grey neck, mantle and underparts; black head with orange-red wattle around eye; orange-yellow bill, legs and feet yellow; black wings; buff-orange tail-tips and wing patch; grey flanks have cinnamon-brown tinge. Sexes alike. Usually observed in small, scattered groups around human habitation; bold and confiding; often seen along roadside restaurants picking out scraps.

CHESTNUT-TAILED STARLING

Sturnia malabarica Sturnidae

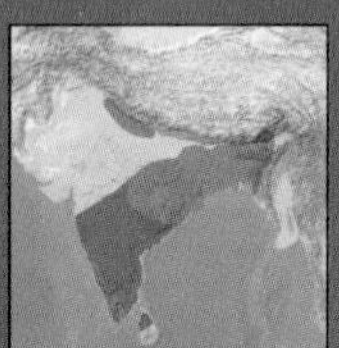

Size 21 cm

Voice Noisy. Metallic, whistling call, becoming a chatter when in flock. Warbling song when breeding

Range India, roughly east and south from S Rajasthan to around W Uttarakhand; upto about 1,800 m in the Himalayan foothills

Habitat Light forests; open country; gardens

Slim bird with silvery-grey upperparts, with faint brownish wash. Dull rufous till breast; brighter below; black-and-grey in wings. Sexes alike. Juvenile more greyish-brown. Sociable; noisy parties in upper branches of trees, frequently along with other birds; incessantly squabbles and moves about, indulging in all manners of acrobatic positions to obtain nectar or reach out to fruits; descends to ground to pick up insects.

ASIAN PIED STARLING

Gracupica contra Sturnidae

juvenile

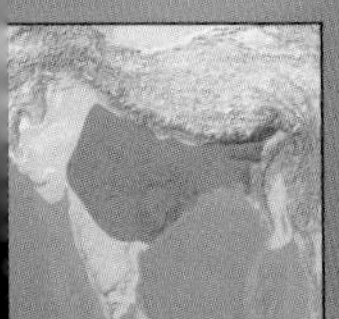

Size 23 cm

Voice Noisy. Calls include a mix of pleasant whistling and screaming notes

Range NC, C and E India, south and east of line roughly from E Punjab, through E Rajasthan, W Madhya Pradesh to Krishna Delta; escaped cage birds have established themselves in several areas out of original range in and around Mumbai

Habitat Open cultivation; orchards; vicinity of habitation

Sexes alike. Black-and-white (pied) plumage distinctive; orange-red beak and orbital skin in front of eyes confirm identity. Sociable; small parties either move on their own or associate with other birds, notably other mynas and drongos; rather common and familiar over its range but keeps distance from human; may make its ungainly nest in garden trees, but never inside houses, nor does it enter houses; bird of open, cultivated areas, preferably where water; attends to grazing cattle; occasionally raids standing crops.

BLYTH'S STARLING

Sturnia (malabarica) blythii Sturnidae

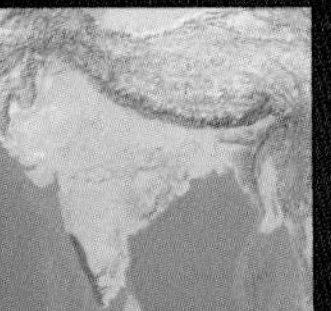

Size 15.5 cm

Voice Song a series of relaxed, short, syncopated, raspy notes

Range S Western Ghats from about S Goa, with few records from N Mumbai

Habitat Light forests; open country; gardens

Larger and longer-billed than Grey-headed but with rufous restricted to vent, darker base of bill, more orange legs. Male's snowy-white hood often extends to mid-belly. Female duller, with white confined to face, greyish breast, pale rufous, abdomen and flanks. Juvenile pale sandy-grey above and greyish-white below, with darker wings and tail, pale bill; outer-tail feathers rufous-tipped.

WHITE-HEADED STARLING

Sturnia erythropygia Sturnidae

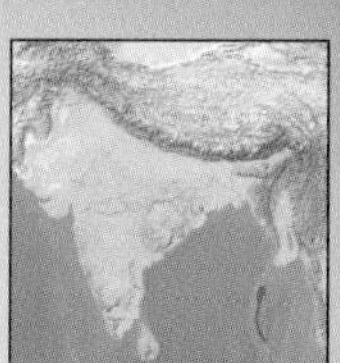

Size 21 cm

Voice Call a grating buzz followed by sharp hiccuping yap, e.g. *grzzzz/kwip!*

Range Resident in Andamans and Nicobars

Habitat Light forests; open country; gardens

Forehead, crown and nape whitish. White upper mantle; lower mantle and upper back grey-tinged purple; narrow white scapular patch; white wing-bars; white bases to black flight feathers; white underwing-coverts; short, yellowish bill with blue base; yellowish legs and feet. Female browner and duller, with no purple. Juvenile like female but duller, with less white on scapulars. In flight, white wing-stripe conspicuous. Seen in both small and large flocks as well as mixed hunting parties. Roosts communally. Gregarious in normal range.

BRAHMINY STARLING

Sturnia pagodarum Sturnidae

Size 20 cm

Voice Quite noisy. Calls include a pleasant mix of chirping notes and whistles, sounds as conversational chatter. Good mimic. Pleasant warbling song of breeding male

Range Subcontinent, to about 2,000 m in W and C Himalayas

Habitat Light forests; gardens; cultivation; vicinity of habitation

Grey, black-and-rufous myna; black crown, nape and forehead, extending to long, black crest; grey back; rich buff sides of head, neck and underbody; black wings and brown tail with white sides and tip distinctive in flight. Sexes similar. Female has slightly smaller crest. Seen in small parties, occasionally collecting into flocks of 20 birds; associates with other birds on flowering trees or on open lands; walks typical myna-style, head held straight up, confident in looks; roosts communally, with other birds.

juvenile

ROSY STARLING

Pastor roseus Sturnidae

Medium-sized starling with rose-pink and black plumage; glossy black head, crest, neck, throat, upper breast, wings and tail; rest of plumage rose-pink, turns brighter with approach of spring migration. Gregarious; flocks often contain juveniles, crestless, dull brown and sooty; often along with other mynas on flowering Erythrina and Bombax trees; causes enormous damage to standing crops; seen also around grazing cattle and damp, open lands; overall aggressive; in huge roosting colonies, resulting in deafening clamour before settling.

juvenile

Size 22 cm

Voice Extremely noisy. Calls include a mix of guttural screams, chattering sounds and melodious whistles

Range Winter visitor to India, most common in W and S India and Sri Lanka. Mainly passage migrant in N India. Arrives end of July and departs mid April to early May

Habitat Open areas; cultivation; orchards; flowering trees amidst habitation

COMMON STARLING

Sturnus vulgaris Sturnidae

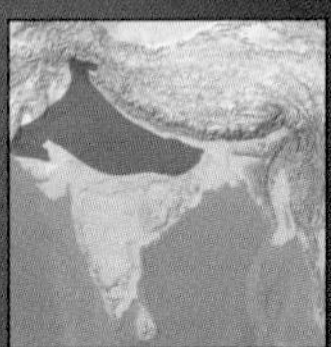

Size 20 cm

Voice Mix of squeaking, clicking notes; other chuckling calls

Range The race *indicus* breeds in Kashmir to about 2,000 m; this including three other races winter over NW and N India, occasionally straying to S Gujarat

Habitat Meadows; orchards; vicinity of habitation; open, fallow lands

Glossy black plumage, with iridescent purple-and-green; plumage spotted with buff-and-white; hackled feathers on head, neck and breast; blackish bill and red-brown legs. Summer (breeding) plumage mostly blackish with yellow bill. Several races winter in N India, with head purple or bronze-green, but field identification of races not very easy in winter. Gregarious, restless; feeds on ground, moves hurriedly, digs with beak in soil; entire flock may often take off from ground; flies around erratically or in circles, but soon settles on trees, or returns to ground.

SRI LANKA WHISTLING THRUSH

Myophonus blighi Turdidae

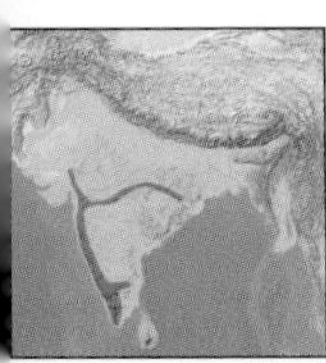

Size 20 cm

Voice Call a shrill whistle, *sreee*

Range Rare and local resident, above 900 m, probably, now confined to the Horton Plains National Park, 1,300-2,300 m

Habitat Mountain streams running through dense, damp montane forests in fern-clad gorges

Blue-black bird with almost flourescent-blue forehead, supercilium and inner wing-coverts. Female brown with blue shoulder patch and rufescent cast to lores, throat and breast. Juvenile similar to female, but with browner upperparts, yellow-brown shaft streaks on head, neck, breast. Smaller than Malabar.

MALABAR WHISTLING THRUSH

Myophonus horsfieldii Turdidae

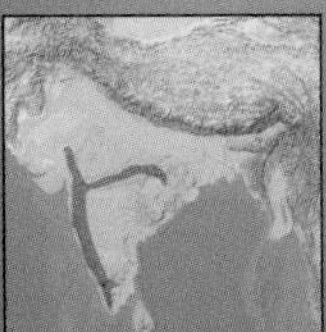

Size 25 cm

Voice Renowned vocalist; especially vocal during rains. Call a harsh, high-pitched *kreeee*; begins to call very early morning. Rich, whistling song, very human in quality, nicknamed 'whistling schoolboy'; fluty notes float over the roar of water

Range Hills of W India, from S Rajasthan, south all along Western Ghats, to about 2,200 m; also, parts of Satpura

Habitat Forest streams; waterfalls; gardens

Large, whistling thrush with deep blue-black plumage, more glistening on wings and tail; bright, cobalt-blue forehead and shoulder patch; black bill and black legs. Sexes alike. Solitary, or in pairs; lively bird of hilly, forested countries; keeps to forest streams and waterfalls; also perches on trees; peculiar stretching of legs and raising of tail; often encountered on roadside culverts, from where it bolts into nullahs or valleys.

PIED THRUSH

Zoothera wardii Turdidae

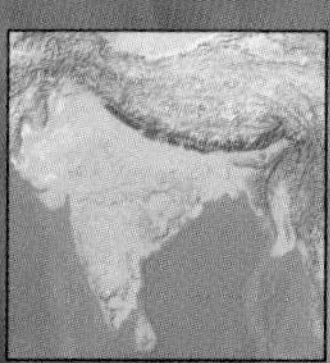

Size 22 cm

Voice Alarm call a spitting *ptz… ptz…ptz…ptz*

Range Breeds in the Himalayas, from E Himachal Pradesh to Arunachal Pradesh, and NE India. Migrates through India to winter in Sri Lanka and Tamil Nadu

Habitat Open broadleaved forests; edges of forests; secondary scrub with scattered trees; thickly-vegetated ravines; undergrowth alongside streams; well-wooded gardens

♀

Adult male mainly black-and-white above, with white supercilium, white wing-bars and white tips to tertials and secondaries; rump has white barring; white belly and flanks, barred with black. Female olive-brown above with buff supercilium, buff wing-bars and tail-tips; spotted olive-brown breast, white belly and flanks, darkly scaled. Juvenile like female, but has streaked mantle and breast.

BLUE WHISTLING THRUSH

Myophonus caeruleus Turdidae

Size 33 cm

Voice Calls include piercing *tzeet* and *zee…zeee*. Rambling, whistling song

Range Common breeding resident in N mountains from E Pakistan to Myanmar border. Moves lower down in winter

Habitat Damp forests and wooded areas, near water

Large, bulky, purple-blue ground thrush with mainly yellow bill. Whole body spotted with spangles of brighter blue. Forehead, shoulders, wing and tail edges bright blue. Sexes alike. Juvenile duller with dusky bill. Noisy, bold, usually approachable. Often close to habitation, even enters buildings. Usually solitary, or in pairs; feeds on insects, crustaceans and amphibians on ground. Nests in rocks, stream-side roots or buildings. Perches on stream boulders and low branches.

ORANGE-HEADED THRUSH

Zoothera citrina Turdidae

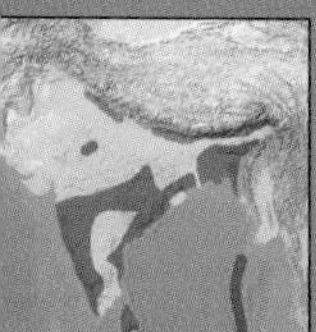

Size 21 cm

Voice Call a shrill, screechy *kreeee*. Loud, rich song, often with mix of other birds' calls thrown in. Noisy in early mornings and late evenings

Range *Cyanotus* peninsular India south of line from S Gujarat across to Odisha; the nominate race *Citrina* breeds in the Himalayas, NE India; winters in foothills, the Terai, parts of E India, Gangetic plains and south along Eastern Ghats. *Albogularis* restricted to Andamans and Nicobar

Habitat Shaded forests; bamboo groves; gardens

citrina

Blue-grey above; orangish-rufous head, nape and underparts; white ear-coverts with two dark brown vertical stripes; white throat and shoulder patch; vent and undertail-coverts white. Orange-headed nominate race has entire head rufous-orange. Usually in pairs; feeds on ground, rummages in leaf litter and under thick growth; flies into leafy branches if disturbed; occasionally associates with laughingthrushes and babblers; vocal and restless when breeding. Feeds on invertebrates in leaf litter. Crepuscular.

cyanotus

SIBERIAN THRUSH

Zoothera sibirica Turdidae

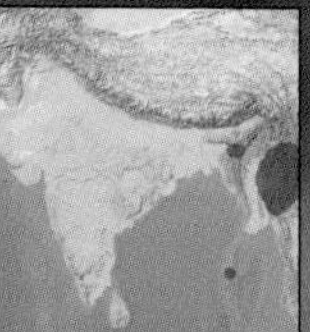

Size 22 cm

Voice Call a soft *stit*

Range Current status uncertain, and no recent published records; recorded in W Maharashtra, Manipur hills upto at least 1,800 m; Andaman Islands

Habitat Broadleaved, evergreen and coniferous forests

Overall slaty-grey thrush with prominent white supercilium, broad white-tipped tail; white-fringed undertail-coverts; white band on underwing tail-coverts visible in flight. Dark bill. Female dark brown with beige supercilium, dark malar stripe, dark olive-brown upperparts, whitish-spotted and scaled underparts. Juvenile similar to adult male, but overall colour paler, supercilium has buff wash.

SPOT-WINGED THRUSH

Zoothera spiloptera Turdidae

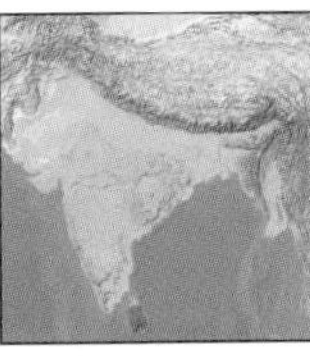

Size 27 cm

Voice Typical, rich, thrush-like song, usually delivered as a series of short, often repeated phrases; each phrase consisting clear and sweet, whistling notes

Range Sri Lanka endemic resident, frequent in lowlands and hills of wet zone

Habitat Dense, damp forests; well-wooded areas; occasionally, gardens near forests

Olive-brown upperparts; white around eye; black-striped face; black crescent near ear. Underparts and flanks white, mottled black; bold, white spots on median and greater coverts. Juvenile less boldly-patterned, though breast scaled, mantle has buff streaking; darker head. Shy. In solitary, or in pairs. Shows at dawn and dusk.

ALPINE THRUSH

Zoothera mollissima Turdidae

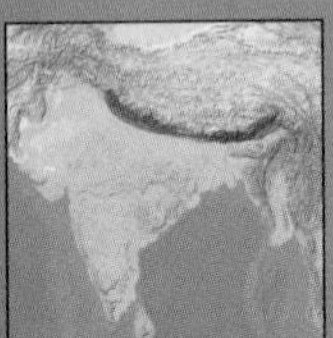

Size 27 cm

Voice Usually silent. Alarm call a rattling *churr*. Song has short mellow, descending phrases

Range Local breeding resident to N mountains from N Pakistan to NE India. Above treeline

Habitat Open woodlands; grassy, fallow, bushy country

Largish, warm brown thrush with prominent black-patch on cheek. Dark face and lores. Heavy barring and streaks on creamish underparts; larger spots on upper throat. Broad, white bands on underwings visible in flight. Sexes alike. Feeds in pairs or small groups on invertebrates on ground. Largely terrestrial. Shy. Flies into trees when disturbed. Sings high, but hidden, in trees. Nests on or near ground. Also see pp 723.

LONG-TAILED THRUSH

Zoothera dixoni Turdidae

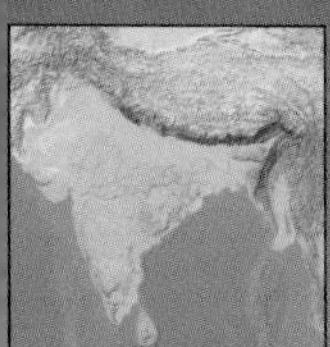

Size 27 cm

Voice Mostly silent; *mollissima* has loud, rattling alarm note

Range The Himalayas, east of C Himachal Pradesh; breeds between 2,000-4,000 m; descends to about 1,000 m in winter

Habitat Treeline forests; scrubs in summer; heavy forests in winter

Plain, olive-brown above; large black-patch around ear; two dull buffy wing-bars and larger wing patch visible in flight; buffy throat, breast and flanks, rest white, boldly spotted dark brown. In pairs, or small groups in winter; feeds on ground; usually difficult to spot till it takes off from somewhere close by; flies up into tree branches if disturbed.

SCALY THRUSH

Zoothera dauma Turdidae

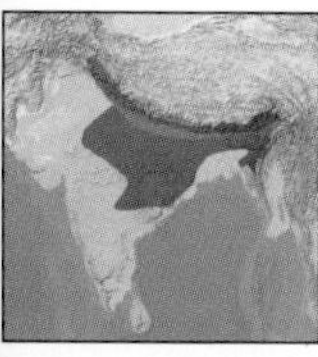

Size 26 cm

Voice Normally silent. Harsh *tchik*; varied, thrush-like song

Range Breeds Kashmir to Myanmar. Winters south to Orissa. See also Nilgiri Thrush on p.572

Habitat Mixed broadleaved and coniferous forests; *sal* and bamboos

Distinctive scaled thrush; distinguished from other thrushes by prominent black or buff-tipped feathers; scales on olive-buff upperparts; black-patch behind ear-coverts; whitish lores; indistinct malar stripe; dark scaling on whitish underparts, heavier on breast, flanks; sturdy bill and legs. Solitary, or in pairs. Mainly terrestrial feeder, forages in leaf litter. Shy and reclusive; flies to low branches or bushes when disturbed; dips and flares tail like most thrushes.

juvenile

SRI LANKA THRUSH

Zoothera imbricata Turdidae

Size 23.5 cm

Voice Song a soft, even, repeated whistle

Range Sri Lanka

Habitat Dense, moist forests

Olive-brown thrush with strong scaling on lower back and rump. Rufous-buff underparts, narrower black scaling upto belly. Face buff-brown with dark lores; pale golden eye-ring and darkish-patch near ear; indistinct malar stripe. Similar to Scaly, but smaller, with shorter tail, and bill proportionately much longer; and head more uniformly marked.

NILGIRI THRUSH

Zoothera dauma neilgherriensis Turdidae

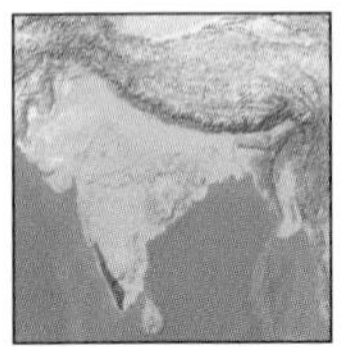

Size 25.5 cm

Voice Apparently unrecorded

Range Western Ghats

Habitat Dense evergreen forests and *sholas*

Medium-sized, heavily-scaled thrush. Underparts also scaled from belly to vent. Dark mottled cheeks with dark patch behind ear; dark, indistinct malar stripe. Two narrow yellowish-buff wing-bars. Similar to Scaly, but darker brown and more even upperparts; mantle and scapulars lack golden-olive subterminal spots. Bill larger and face plainer and black markings more regular. Skulking. Terrestrial.

LONG-BILLED THRUSH

Zoothera monticola Turdidae

Size 28 cm

Voice Rattling alarm call. Pensive whistled song *te…e…uw; tew…tew…tew*

Range Uttarakhand to Arunachal Pradesh

Habitat Dense, moist broadleaved evergreen, coniferous, bamboo forests with thick undergrowth, wet ground, streams

Dark, sturdy thrush; distinctive short tail; very long bill with curved upper mandible, hooked at end; upperparts dark grey-brown; dark brown face, dark malar stripe, small, white throat patch; dense dark spotting on breast; large, dark spots on flanks; less spotting on white belly; brown-and-white-barred vent; strong legs; solitary; shy and seclusive; usually in undergrowth; crepuscular; terrestrial; uses long bill to forage in leaf litter.

DARK-SIDED THRUSH

Zoothera marginata Turdidae

Size 25 cm

Voice Song a thin whistle

Range The Himalayas; NE India

Habitat Dense forests near streams

Rotund, long-billed with rufous-brown upperparts. Sides of dark brown head strongly-patterned; pale, fleshy base to lower mandible; pale lores and black rear patch edged paler; whitish eye-ring; white chin. Underparts paler with bold scaling on breast and flanks; black malar stripe. Short tail; slim, prominent black bill. Wings more rufous-red. Yellowish-brown vent striped with brown. Sexes similar. Juvenile has brighter upperparts with pale shaft streaks and buff tips to wing-coverts. Solitary and crepuscular. Forages on ground amid leaf litter looking for insects. Walks, hops on ground.

TICKELL'S THRUSH

Turdus unicolor Turdidae

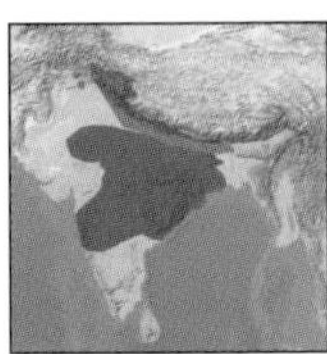

Size 21 cm

Voice A 2-noted alarm call; also some chattering calls. Rich song

Range Breeds in the Himalayas, 1,500-2,500 m, east to C Nepal, and Sikkim; winters along foothills east of Kangra, NE, parts of C and E peninsular India

Habitat Open forests, groves

Light ash-grey bird; duller breast and whiter on belly; rufous underwing-coverts in flight. Female olive-brown above; white throat, streaked on sides; tawny flanks and white belly. Small flocks on ground, sometimes along with other thrushes; hops fast on ground, stopping abruptly, as if to check some underground activity; digs worms from unde soil; flies into trees when approached too close.

BLACK-BREASTED THRUSH

Turdus dissimilis Turdidae

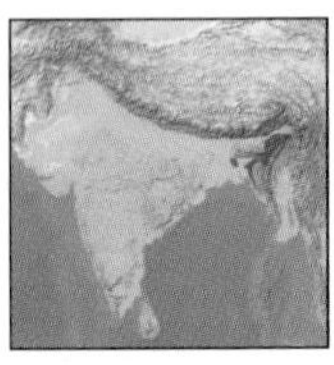

Size 22 cm

Voice Call a resounding *tup… tup…tup…tup tup…tup…tup…*

Range Resident, NE India

Habitat Breeds in moist, shady broadleaved evergreen forests. In winter, also found in scrub jungles and mangroves

Small, compact thrush. Adult male has black head and breast, grey upperparts, orange upper belly and flanks, and white centre to belly and vent Female has dark olive-grey upperparts, plain face (lacking supercilium), prominent dark (streaked) malar stripe and dark spotting across olive-grey upper breast, whitish throat (with variable dark streaking) and sub-moustachial stripe; orange lowe breast and flanks.

GREY-WINGED BLACKBIRD

Turdus boulboul Turdidae

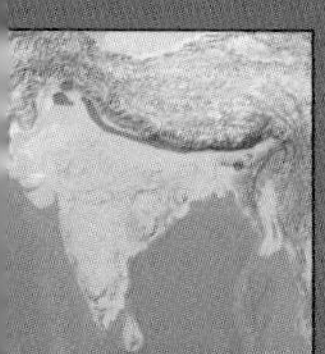

Size 28 cm

Voice Call a deep *chuck… chuck*. Melodious song

Range Hills from Pakistan to Myanmar

Habitat Mixed broadleaved oak, coniferous forests; edges of forests; clearings

Large, dark thrush with longish tail. Adult male black, with contrasting light grey wing panel; bright orange bill, yellowish eye-ring, legs. Juvenile male has white-edged feathers on belly, vent. Female brown, with less distinct, paler brown wing panel, yellow bill. Juvenile similar to White-collared, but has wing panel rather than wing-bars. Solitary, or in pairs; sometimes, in small winter flocks; fairly shy, but emerges onto forest paths to feed. Arboreal and terrestrial; forages on shrubs, trees, forest floor.

WHITE-COLLARED BLACKBIRD

Turdus albocinctus Turdidae

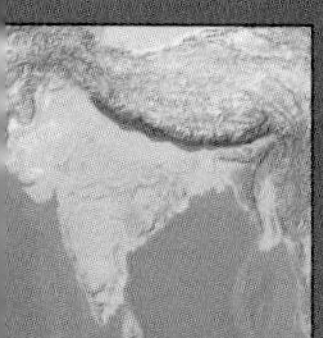

Size 27 cm

Voice Call a deep *chuck…chuck*. Song a whistled *tchew…tchew, tchew…ee*

Range Hills of Uttarakhand to Myanmar

Habitat Mixed broadleaved, coniferous forests; edges of forests; pastures; clearings

Large, distinctive thrush with pale collar. Adult male black, with white collar extending around throat, upper breast, nape and upper mantle; yellow bill, eye-ring, legs; longish tail; female brown, with pale, faintly streaked collar. Juvenile lacks pale collar; dark brown above, with rufous-streaking; two rufous wing-bars; richer rufous-brown below, with dark spotting, giving a mottled appearance. Solitary, or in pairs; sometimes in winter flocks; shy; forages on forest floor, grassy slopes, trees.

INDIAN BLACKBIRD

Turdus (merula) simillimus Turdidae

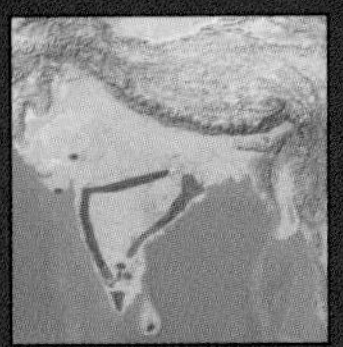

Size 24.5 cm

Voice Loud, melodious song of breeding male; sings from high tree perch; very vocal in evening. Great mimic; screechy *kreeee* during winter. Also, harsh *charrr* note

Range Various races make this a widespread species in the Indian region; hills of W India, from S Rajasthan southwards; Eastern Ghats south of N Odisha

Habitat Forests; ravines; gardens

Upperparts lead-grey, while underparts ash-brown; blackish cap distinctive; darker wings and tail; reddish-orange beak and yellow eye-ring distinctive. Female dark ash-brown above; browner below with grey wash; streaked dark brown on chin and throat. Solitary, or in pairs, sometimes with other birds; rummages on forest floor but also moves up in leafy branches; rather confiding, especially in hill-station gardens.

TIBETAN BLACKBIRD

Turdus (merula) maximus Turdidae

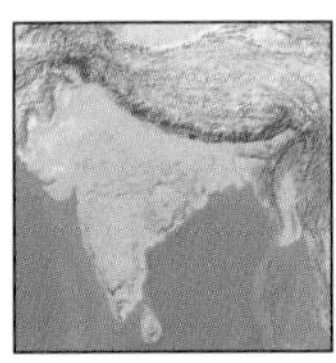

Size 26-29 cm

Voice Call a rattling *chak...chak...chak*. Song a mournful, repeated whistle, *piew...piew*

Range NW Himalayas. From Uttarakhand east to Arunachal Pradesh in winter

Habitat Rocky and grassy slopes with dwarf juniper in summer; juniper stands or shrubs in winter

Large, black bird with long tail without yellow orbital-ring. Female even dark brown. Juvenile has rufous-buff underparts with diffuse dark brown barring and spotting, back and rump variably spotted and barred with rufous-buff; crown and mantle tend to be even dark brown (male) or pale brown (female). Larger than Common with longer wings and tail. Usually quite wary, but can be confiding. Nests on ground or low bushes.

COMMON BLACKBIRD

Turdus merula Turdidae

Size 25-28 cm

Voice Calls *chack...chack*. Song not very melodious

Range Breeding visitor to NW Pakistan

Habitat High-altitude rocky slopes, grassy alpine meadows, dwarf juniper scrub, rhododendron scrub

♀

Large, glossy brown-black thrush with prominent yellow bill. Dark crown; narrow, golden-yellow eye-ring. Similar to White-collared but lacks collar. Distinguished from Grey-winged by lack of wing patch. Female dark brown, with lightly streaked throat and darker bill. Juvenile has paler brown head, rufous underparts; streaked, spotted, barred above and below. In pairs, or small groups when breeding; in small winter flocks with other thrushes; largely, terrestrial feeder.

CHESTNUT THRUSH

Turdus rubrocanus Turdidae

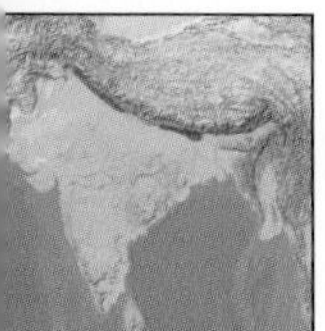

Size 27 cm

Voice Alarm call a *kwik*. Song comprises a series of short phrases, repeated 3-8 times

Range Far W Himalayas. Winters from E Nepal to NE India

Habitat Coniferous and mixed forests in summer; open wooded-areas and orchards in winter

gouldii

Overall rusty-orange thrush with distinct grey head. Buffish-grey collar; blackish wings and tail; yellow bill and legs. Female duller, but very similar; head and hindneck pale brownish-grey, no distinct collar; wings and tail brown. Juvenile has darker head; more white throat; buff shaft streaking above; dark spotting and barring below; back, rump and uppertail-coverts have rusty-orange cast. Sub-species *gouldii* is a rare winter visitor to the extreme NE.

rubrocanus

KESSLER'S THRUSH

Turdus kessleri Turdidae

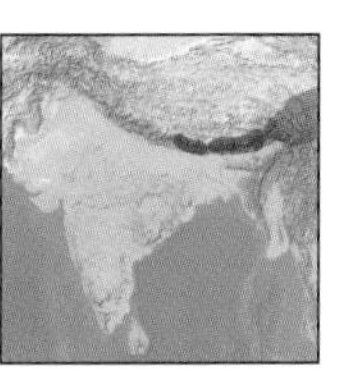

Size 27 cm

Voice Call a soft *dug…dug*

Range Winter visitor, E Himalayas

Habitat Shrubberies and stands of juniper; potato fields

Largish thrush with distinctive brown-black head. Neck and upper breast also black, creamy-white mantle and lower breast; brown-black tail and wings; darkish vent indistinctly scaled. Female's head pattern similar to male's, but duller; head, neck and breast greyish-brown; brown upper breast and rest of underparts more ginger-brown. Terrestrial and gregarious. Feeds on berries in winter.

GREY-SIDED THRUSH

Turdus feae Turdidae

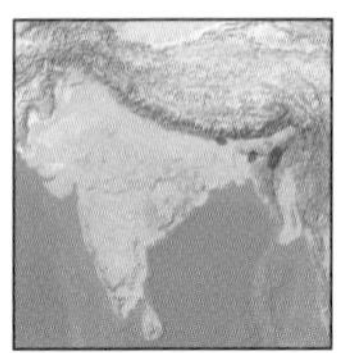

Size 28 cm

Voice Unreported in the region

Range Globally threatened

Habitat Details unknown. Winters in evergreen forests

Smallish thrush which superficially resembles Eyebrowed. Adult male has rufescent-olive upperparts, crown and ear-coverts. Silver-grey throat; grey lower breast with paler belly and vent. White supercilium and white crescent below eye; silver-grey flanks. Female similar to male, but has white throat, also belly whiter; brown-streaked malar stripe; grey of breast and flanks variably washed with orange-buff. Juvenile similar to female, but has whiter throat and pale tips on primaries and tertials. Feeds on nectar, fruits and berries.

RED-THROATED THRUSH

Turdus ruficollis Turdidae

Largish thrush with even, grey upperparts and wings. Sides of tail reddish-orange visible in flight. Red supercilium, throat and breast; grey upperparts; whitish underparts; creamy-white belly and vent. Yellow bill with greyish culmen. Female similar to male, but with more whitish-buff throat, black-streaked malar stripe, mottled orange-red breast. Juvenile male similar to adult female, has white-tipped greater coverts and pale-fringed tertials. First-winter female less heavily marked, and has finely streaked breast and flanks; rufous wash to supercilium and throat, and sometimes breast. Gregarious. Often seen with other thrushes. Feeds on ground and low fruit-bearing bushes.

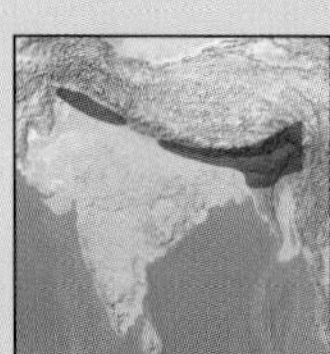

Size 25 cm

Voice Calls include thin see and hard *tack…tack*

Range Winter visitor to the Himalayas, NE India

Habitat Forests; edges of forests; cultivation, pastures with scattered trees

BLACK-THROATED THRUSH

Turdus artogularis Turdidae

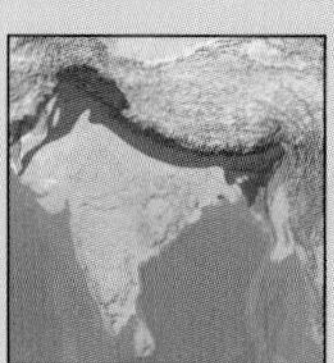

Size 26.5 cm

Voice Calls include shrill rattle in alarm and high-pitched squeaky contacts notes

Range Winter visitor, N subcontinent

Habitat Forests; edges of forests; cultivation, pastures with scattered trees

Adult male has grey upperparts and whitish underparts. Black supercilium, throat and breast; yellow bill with greyish culmen. Female similar, but typically has white or buffish throat and black-streaked malar stripe, black gorget of spotting across breast. First-winter has fine white supercilium and white tips to greater coverts and pale-fringed tertials. First-winter male very similar to adult female. First-winter female less heavily marked, with finely streaked breast and flanks. Feeds on ground. Wary, flies into trees when disturbed. Feeds on berries in winter.

EYEBROWED THRUSH

Turdus obscurus Turdidae

Medium-sized, orange-and-grey thrush with broad, white supercilium and black lores. Male has small, white-patches below eyes, grey head and neck, brownish-grey upperparts. Breast and flanks diagnostic rufous-brown; white belly and vent; lower mandible has yellow cast. Female and immature less grey with blackish-bordered white throat. Small bill with black upper mandible and tip. Feeds on ground on insects, often with other thrushes. Hops. Wary, flushing rapidly into tree canopy.

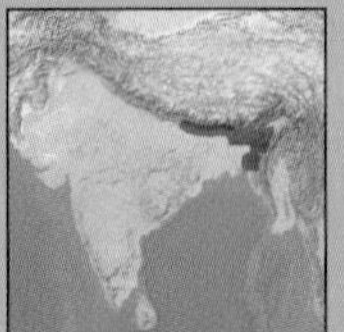

Size 23 cm

Voice Call a thin *teseep…teseep.* Also, chatters

Range Locally common winter visitor to hills of NE India and E Nepal. Rare further south in peninsula India, Bangladesh and Sri Lanka. Also occurs in N, E and SE Asia

Habitat Open forests

DUSKY THRUSH

Turdus eunomus Turdidae

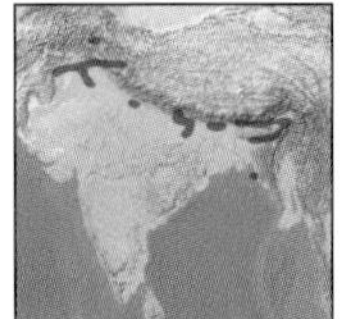

Size 24 cm

Voice Calls include shrill *shrree* and rather harsh *chock…chock*

Range Winter visitor to the Himalayas, NE India

Habitat Open cultivated areas and pastures with scattered trees

Darkish thrush with shades of brown-and-grey in parts. Broad, obvious white supercilium and throat, dark crown and ear-coverts, chestnut-brown wings; rufous-brown mantle with dark feather centres; breast and flanks heavily spotted to form double gorget. Underparts white; dark, scaly breast-band. Female similar to male, but much duller with less distinct marking, but stronger and less prominent supercilium, upperparts greyer, and has duller brown wings. Strong flier. Feeds in open on ground.

FIELDFARE

Turdus pilaris Turdidae

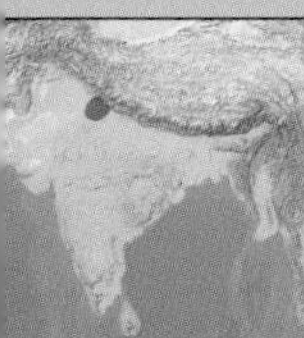

Size 25 cm

Voice Call a hard *shack…shack*, mainly in flight. Also, squeaky *tee*

Range Very rare vagrant from N Asia. Only one record from Uttar Pradesh

Habitat Open cultivation; pastures, orchards

Large, chestnut-and-grey thrush with blue-grey crown, cheeks, nape and rump; indistinct supercilium; black lores; chestnut-brown mantle. Orange-yellow throat and upper breast strongly streaked with dark brown. White lower breast and belly; grey rump. Orange bill. Sexes similar. Feeds on invertebrates in open, hops on ground. Feeds on berries in winter. Rather shy and flies into trees if alarmed. Seen with other thrushes.

REDWING

Turdus iliacus Turdidae

Size 22 cm

Voice Call a softer, twittery, drier, varied burbling *chatter*

Range Winter vagrant, with several sightings in SW and NE Afghanistan, and two earlier records for N Pakistan

Habitat Berry-bearing vegetation

Small thrush with prominent creamy-white supercilium and rusty-red flanks and underwings. Chest, belly and flanks marked with long, dark streaks; bicoloured bill. Sexes similar. First-winter resembles adult, but may retain buff spots on wing-coverts. Almost always in flocks in winter. Roosts communally in thick shrubberies. Nest made of dry grass and clay, lined with fine grass. Feeds on invertebrates, fruits and berries.

MISTLE THRUSH

Turdus viscivorus Turdidae

Large, pale grey-brown thrush. Brownish rump and yellow-brown lower flanks; dark patch on ear-coverts and breast sides. Round spots prominent on otherwise evenly pale underparts. Pale underwings and axillaries. Longish brown tail with white tips often visible on outer-tail feathers. Sexes alike. Similar to Scaly and Long-tailed. Feeds on invertebrates on ground and berries, particularly mistletoe, in trees. Usually solitary, or in pairs. Wary, flying high between food sites. Sings from exposed perch. Nests high in trees.

Size 27 cm

Voice Call a harsh rattle, usually in flight. Song mellow and haunting

Range Fairly common breeding resident in N mountains from W Pakistan to W Nepal. Moves lower down in winter. Also occurs in Europe, W, N and C Asia

Habitat Open mountain forests, grasslands and scrubs

SONG THRUSH

Turdus philomelos Turdidae

Size 23 cm

Voice Calls include quiet, but penetrating *silt*, soft *tit* and hard *tchuk*

Range Vagrant

Habitat Thorn scrub in Pakistan

Medium-sized bird (much smaller than Mistle), with warm brown upperparts, buffy-white underparts, and heavily spotted with black, arrow-shaped spots on breast and flanks; white belly; black bill. Underwings rich buff in colour; yellowish bill and legs and feet pink. Sexes similar. Feeds on ground and flies into trees when alarmed.

GREEN COCHOA

Cochoa viridis Turdidae

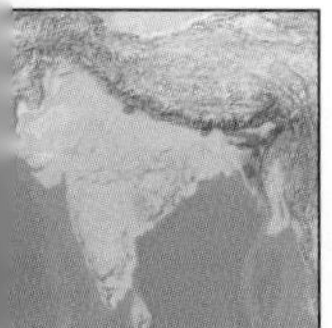

Size 28 cm

Voice Call a pure, drawn-out monotone whistle, thinner and weaker than that of Purple

Range The Himalayas; NE India

Habitat Dense, moist, broadleaved evergreen forests

Overall green with blue crown and nape. Black eyebrow and lores; dark blue ear-coverts; mantle has faint black scaling; wing has pale blue panel; pale blue tail with black tip. Underparts emerald-green with blue wash on throat and belly. Sexes similar. Female has green at base of secondaries and wing. Secondaries stained yellowish-brown instead of blue. Juvenile like adult, white crown with black scales and tawny spotting; upperparts and underparts also darkly scaled.

PURPLE COCHOA

Cochoa purpurea Turdidae

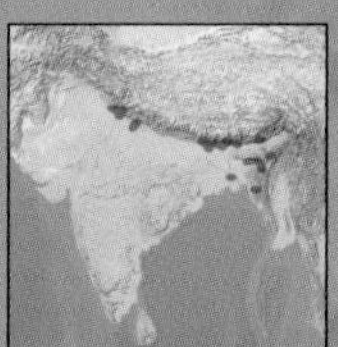

Size 30 cm

Voice Call a low chuckle. Song a flute-like *peeeee*; also *peeee... you...peeee*

Range Summer visitor. The Himalayas, hills of NE India

Habitat Dense, moist broadleaved evergreen forests

Appears dark in the shade, and colours show only in light. Overall greyish-purple; black mask; silvery-blue crown; grey carpal patch at base of black wing feathers and prominent wing patch. Tail silvery-blue with black terminal band. Male has dull purplish-grey secondaries and coverts, body greyish; rufous replaces purple in female. Juvenile has black scaling to crown, indistinct buff streaking and spotting on upperparts, orange-buff underparts with bold, black barring.

RUSTY-BELLIED SHORTWING

Brachypteryx hyperythra Muscicapidae

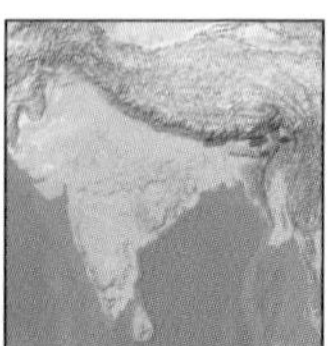

Size 13 cm

Voice Faster, longer and more musical, high-speed warble consists of rather slurred series of notes, distinctly introduced by 2-spaced notes, *tu...tiu* or *wi...tu*

Range The Himalayas in Nepal and from Darjeeling, West Bengal and Sikkim to Arunachal Pradesh and Assam

Habitat Undergrowth in forests, thick secondary scrub and dense thickets of reeds or bamboos in winter

Plum bird with short tail and small wings. Male has rich orange-chestnut underparts that extend upto throat. Upperparts very dark blue, except for conspicuous short, white eyebrow; male's pale bill turns black when breeding; long, pale pink legs. Female lacks rust-coloured belly, slaty-brown above, dark brown face, pale rufous throat, pale belly. Skulking and inconspicuous. Mainly terrestrial.

WHITE-BROWED SHORTWING

Brachypteryx montana Muscicapidae

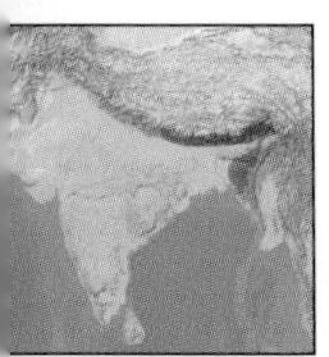

Size 15 cm

Voice Calls include *tak...tak; tt...tt...tt.* Loud warbling song

Range From C Nepal to Arunachal Pradesh

Habitat Damp, mossy forests, undergrowth in forests; near streams; in damp, thickly overgrown gorges

Slightly larger shortwing with long, thin, dark legs and short tail; adult male has distinctive dark blue body, black lores and prominent longish, white supercilium; female has rufous around eyes and forehead; lacks white supercilium; darker brown above, paler below, especially on centre of belly. Immature male like female, but with pale supercilium. Solitary, or in pairs; mainly terrestrial; shy and secretive; usually feeds on damp ground in dense overgrown forest understorey.

GOULD'S SHORTWING

Heteroxenicus stellatus Muscicapidae

Small, round, strikingly-coloured bird with short tail. Adult has black face, bright chestnut upperparts and tail; finely barred, dark slaty-blue-grey underparts with distinctive white triangular spots on belly, flanks, rump. Juvenile duller, streaked rufous above and on breast. Not very shy; often seen in the open and on low, exposed perches; forages on ground in dense undergrowth; not very vocal.

Size 13 cm

Voice Alarm call *tik...tik.* Loud, shrill song consists of *tsi...tsi* notes accelerating into continuous chitter

Range E Uttarakhand to Arunachal Pradesh

Habitat Rocky montane forests above treeline; dwarf rhododendron, juniper scrub; dense undergrowth in moist ravines; forests with fir; bamboos

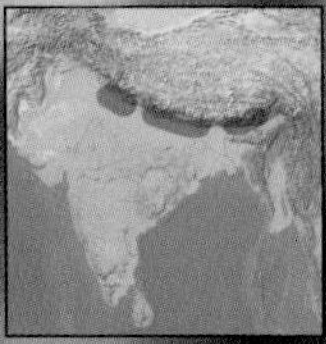

NILGIRI BLUE ROBIN

Myiomela major Muscicapidae

Male has bright blue-grey upperparts, head, neck and throat, dusky lores. Rufous tinge on white lower breast to vent in nominate race (shown). Red iris; long legs and short tail. Sexes alike. Female brown. Usually solitary, or in pairs; feeds on invertebrates on ground. Shy and unobtrusive, creeping on ground in dense undergrowth.

Size 15 cm

Voice Call a piercing whistle *wheep*. Song a varied series of loud whistles

Range Globally threatened. Rare endemic breeding resident of SW Indian hills, in S Karnataka and Nilgiris

Habitat Shady evergreen forests, particularly *sholas*, and ravines

WHITE-BELLIED BLUE ROBIN

Myiomela albiventris Muscicapidae

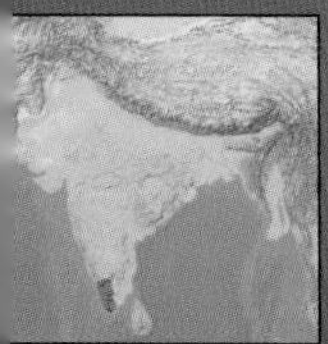

Size 15 cm

Voice Brief, melodious warbling song of about 10- to12-notes, with first note alternating up and down and then accelerating into a rapid jumble

Range Restricted to SW Indian hills of S Kerala and Tamil Nadu, south of Palgat Gap

Habitat Thick undergrowth in damp broadleaved forests and secondary growth

Dark, slaty-blue upperparts, black mask and short, whitish supercilium meet above beak; dark lores. Slaty-blue breast graduates to pale grey belly. Long pinkish-purple legs; dark beak. Short tail and wings. Grey flanks and white vent; centre of belly and vent white. Can be confiding. Sings, perches in undergrowth.

LESSER SHORTWING

Brachypteryx leucophris Muscicapidae

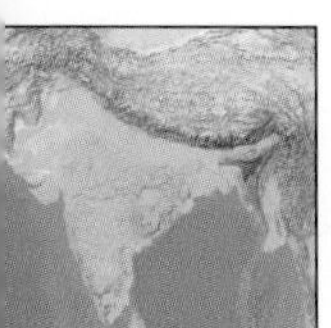

Size 13 cm

Voice Calls include hard *tock… tock* and plaintive whistle

Range The Himalayas; S Assam Hills

Habitat Thick undergrowth in damp broadleaved forests and secondary growth

The Himalayan race *nipalensis* the male is grey-blue above, while the race carolinae, of the South Assam Hills is brown above. Both races have prominent white supercilliam. Pink legs and a very short tail. Female has brownish upperparts, White throat and belly. Rare in the Himalayas, but quite easily found in Nagaland and adjoining hills. Keeps to damp undergrowth, in broadleaved forests, often near water.

BLUETHROAT

Luscinia svecica Muscicapidae

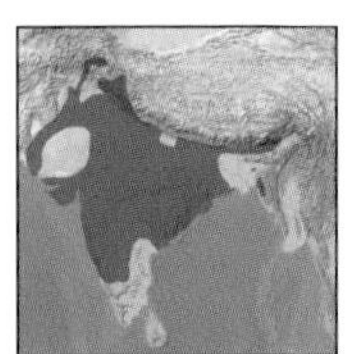

Size 15 cm

Voice Calls *tshik…tshik.* Long, varied song

Range Kashmir to Arunachal Pradesh

Habitat Damp scrub, reed beds and cultivation near water

Adult breeding male has greyish-brown upperparts; whitish underparts; bright blue bib with rufous-patch in middle, bordered below by narrow black-and-white band and broad rufous band. Non-breeding male similar, but has markings on chin, diffused by pale feather-tips. Female has creamy white throat; bordered below by neck-band of darker streaking and mottling; white moustachia stripe. Juvenile more blackish with buffish spots on back; buff underparts mottled dark brown, giving scaly appearance.

pallidogularis

♀

svecica

cyanecula

abbotti

SIBERIAN RUBYTHROAT

Luscinia calliope Muscicapidae

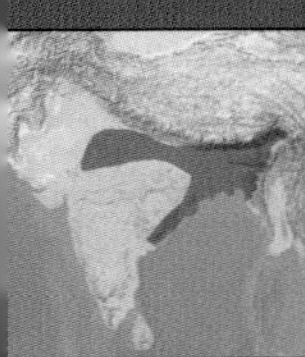

Size 15 cm

Voice Call a *shuk*; *ee… lu*, etc.

Range Uttarakhand to Myanmar

Habitat Dense undergrowth; tall grass, cane, reeds; edges of cultivation

Plumpish, heavy-bodied bird. Breeding male overall olive-brown. Bold, white supercilium and sub-moustachial stripe, edged black; black lores and malar stripe; plain brown rump and tail; ruby-red throat, bordered by thin, black band, varying amounts of grey on breast; greyish-brown underparts; short, unmarked tail. Female uniform brown; buff supercilium, whitish throat, washed grey; grey-brown breast-band. Skulks in dense vegetation; mainly terrestrial; feeds on ground or in low bushes; cocks tail. Feeds singly.

♀

WHITE-TAILED RUBYTHROAT

Luscinia pectoralis Muscicapidae

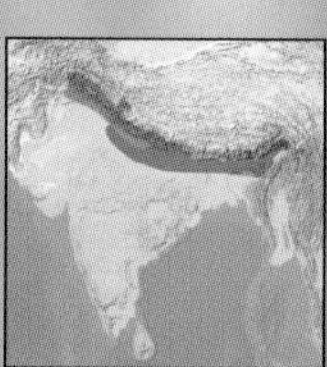

Size 15 cm

Voice Short, metallic call note; short, harsh alarm note. Rich, shrill song

Range Breeds in the Himalayas, 2,700-4,600 m; winters in N, NE India; winter range not properly known

Habitat Dwarf vegetation, rocky hills in summer. In winter, prefers cultivation, damp ground with grass and bushes

Breeding male has slaty upperparts; white supercilium; white in tail; scarlet chin and throat; jet-black throat sides, continuing into broad breast-band; white below, greyer on sides. Non-breeding male more brown rather than grey above with scaly, dirty white breast. Female grey-brown above (greyer than Siberian); white chin and throat; greyish breast; white spots on tips of outer-tail. Juvenile male has white tail base and darker head sides. Solitary; wary, difficult to observe; cocks tail; hops on ground, or makes short dashes; ascends small bush-tops. Breeding male sings all day.

FIRETHROAT

Luscinia pectardens Muscicapidae

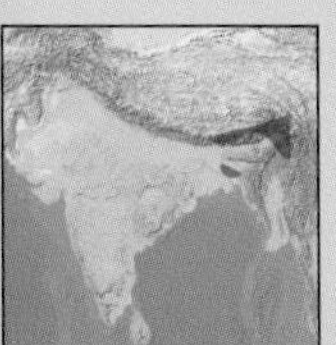

Size 15 cm

Voice Call like that of Orange-flanked Bush Robin

Range Vagrant. Arunachal Pradesh, Meghalaya; West Bengal

Habitat Dense bushes, dense woodlands

Medium-sized bird with thin, short bill. Breeding male has slaty-blue upperparts; black forehead and face; white-patch on neck sides; orange throat and breast bordered black; white on base of blackish tail. Non-breeding male has pale underparts with pale blue, rufous and black breast-bands; broad, pale supercilium; tail and upperparts same as breeding male. First-winter male olive-brown above, with slaty-blue back and wing-coverts; tail similar to adult male's, underparts like adult female's.

INDIAN BLUE ROBIN

Luscinia brunnea Muscicapidae

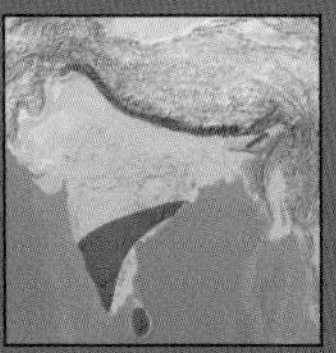

Size 15 cm

Voice Calls include high-pitched *churr* and harsh *tack*... in winter. Trilling song of breeding male, sometimes singing from exposed perch

Range Breeds in the Himalayas, 1,500-3,300 m. Winters in S Western Ghats, Ashambu Hills, and Sri Lanka

Habitat Dense rhododendron, ringal bamboo undergrowth in summer. Evergreen forest undergrowth, coffee estates in winter

Male deep slaty-blue above; white supercilium; blackish lores and cheeks; rich chestnut throat, breast and flanks; white belly centre and undertail. Female brown above; white throat and belly. Solitary, rarely in pairs; great skulker, very difficult to observe; moves amidst dense growth and hops on ground.

SIBERIAN BLUE ROBIN

Luscinia cyane Muscicapidae

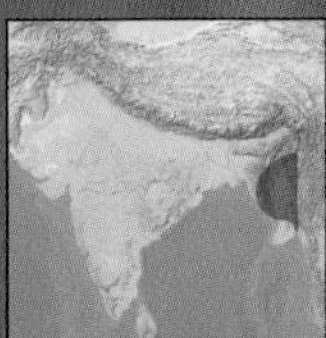

Size 15 cm

Voice Calls include quiet, hard *tuck* and loud *se…ic*

Range Vagrant to our region

Habitat Dense bushes

Male vivid blue above, with black sides to throat and breast, and pure white underparts. Female has olive-brown upperparts, with pale buff throat and breast, scaled with darker brown, rump usually shows blue; some have blue tails. Similar to female Indian Blue, but has orange-buff on breast and flanks. First-winter male like female, with varying amounts of blue on scapulars and mantle; first-winter female like adult female, but no blue on uppertail-coverts and tail. Short tail and long pink legs and feet like Indian Blue's and separate Siberian Blue from other bush robins and rubythroats.

COMMON NIGHTINGALE

Luscinia megarhynchos Muscicapidae

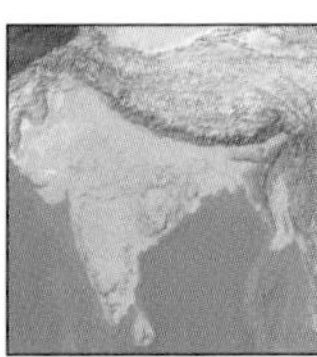

Size 16 cm

Voice Calls include *hweet*, hard *chack*, and deep, throaty *crrer*

Range Vagrant

Habitat Bushes; favours damp places

Rather drab-looking bird known for its beautiful melodious song. Dull brown upperparts graduating to reddish-brown tail; beige-brown breast and remaining underparts dirty white; narrow white eye-ring, indistinct grey eye-stripe; dark bill and flesh-brown legs. Sexes similar. Juvenile has buff spotting on upperparts and buff and indistinct dark scaling on underparts and rust-brown tail. Forages in dense undercover, amongst leaf litter. Also, flycatches insects from low branches. Shy and secretive.

WHITE-BROWED BUSH ROBIN

Tarsiger indicus Muscicapidae

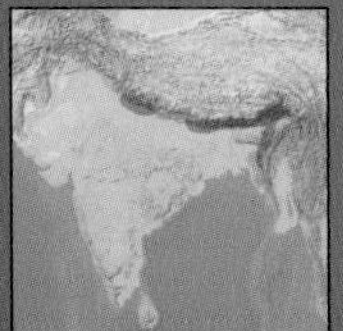

Size 15 cm

Voice Call a churring *trrr*

Range Scarce breeding resident of N hills from Uttarakhand east to Myanmar border. Winters lower down in foothills

Habitat Damp undergrowth of dense forests

Male has slaty-blue face and from forehead to tail with long, white supercilium; yellowish-olive wash to crown; black bill and brown legs; orange throat, breast and flanks. Male similar to Indian Blue but has longer tail with longer supercilium. Much darker above and all orange below. Cheeks black. Female and first-year male have greyish-brown upperparts and orangish-buff underparts and fine, white supercilium. Male displays with drooped wings and flick its tail. Solitary and usually secretive. Sings from small trees. Feeds on invertebrates on ground or in air.

RUFOUS-BREASTED BUSH ROBIN

Tarsiger hyperythrus Muscicapidae

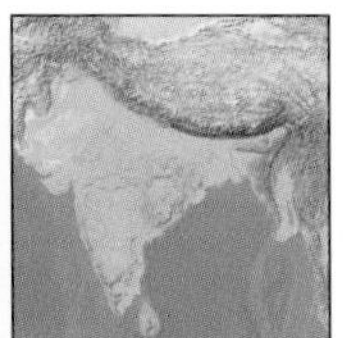

Size 15 cm

Voice Call a *duk…duk…duk…* squeak. Song a lisping warble, *zeew…zee…zwee…zwee*

Range The Himalayas from WC Nepal east to Arunachal Pradesh; winters south to hills of NE India

Habitat Summers in bushes at edges and clearings of dwarf rhododendron, birch forests and in fir-rhododendron forests

Small, blue-and-orange robin. Male dark royal blue above, with blackish face, bright, ultramarine-blue supercilium, shoulder and rump; white undertail-coverts; orange throat, breast and centre of belly. Female olive-brown with bluish cast on tail; no supercilium; olive-brown underparts with rufous wash on flanks. Forages on ground for insects.

GOLDEN BUSH ROBIN

Tarsiger chrysaeus Muscicapidae

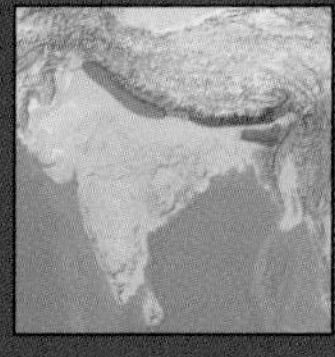

Size 15 cm

Voice Calls *tchek...tchek;...trrrr.* High, thin song

Range Hills from Pakistan to Myanmar

Habitat High-altitude dwarf rhododendron and juniper treeline scrub; scattered shrubs on scree-covered slopes; edges of coniferous forests; dense forest undergrowth, bushes, scrubs

♀

Golden-coloured chat. Male has olive-brown crown; distinct bright yellow supercilium; black stripe running through eye to form cheek patch; golden-yellow scapulars, sides of back and rump; golden-yellow underparts; black-and-golden yellow tail. Female duller yellow-brown above, with indistinct yellow supercilium; paler yellow underparts; long, pale legs. Shy; forages on ground and in low undergrowth, with quick aerial forays.

HIMALAYAN BLUETAIL

Tarsiger (cyanurus) rufilatus Muscicapidae

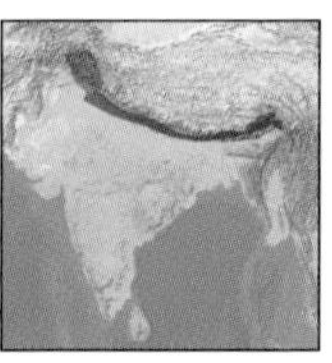

Size 15 cm

Voice Call a deep *tok...tok; weet.* Short, soft song

Range Pakistan to Arunachal Pradesh

Habitat Damp undergrowth in oak, rhododendron, coniferous and evergreen forests

♀

Earlier considered to be a subspecies of the Red-flanked. Longer-tailed chat with diagnostic orange flanks and white throat. Male deep blue above and on breast sides; brighter, glistening blue forehead, supercilium, shoulder, rump; pale grey-blue underparts; blue tail. Female grey-brown above and on breast sides; white throat; orange-washed flanks; blue rump, tail. Hunts and forages aerially, on ground. Male often sings from visible forest perch; flares tail, flicks wings.

RUFOUS-TAILED SCRUB ROBIN

Cercotrichas galactotes Muscicapidae

Size 15 cm

Voice Calls *teck…teck*

Range Rare migrant through Gujarat and Rajasthan

Habitat Dry stony ground and scrubs

Has broad, creamy-white band from behind of eye to beak; whitish 'crescent' below eye; pale brown ear-coverts. Buffish-white underparts; paler chin, centre of belly and undertail-coverts; dark brown flight feathers fringed buff; pale trailing edge; reddish-brown rump; pale brown legs and feet. Juvenile similar but paler sandy-brown. Male's display involves a swoop with lifted wings. Nests in bushes.

ORIENTAL MAGPIE ROBIN

Copsychus saularis Muscicapidae

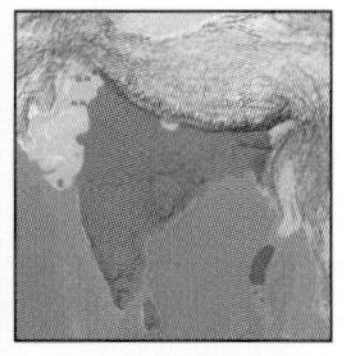

Size 20 cm

Voice Common call a plaintive *sweee…* . One of India's finest songsters; rich, clear song of varying notes and tones; male sings from exposed perches, most frequently between March and June, intermittently year round; also, has harsh *churr* and *chhekh* notes

Range Subcontinent, upto about 1,500 m in the outer Himalayas; absent in extreme W Rajasthan

Habitat Forests; parks; towns

Familiar bird of India. Male glossy blue-black and white; white wing patch and white in outer-tail distinctive; glossy blue-black throat and breast; white below. Female rich slaty-grey, male black. Solitary, or in pairs, sometimes with other birds in mixed parties; hops on ground, prefers shaded areas. Common about human habitation; when perched, often cocks tail; flicks tail often, especially when making short sallies; active at dusk.

WHITE-RUMPED SHAMA

Copsychus malabaricus Muscicapidae

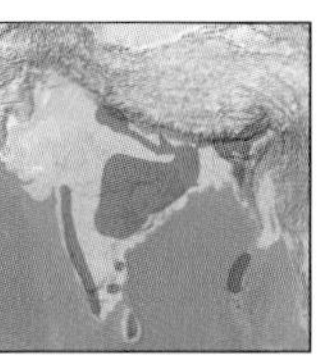

Size 25 cm

Voice Rich songster; melodious, 3- or 4-whistling notes very characteristic. Variety of call notes, including a mix of some harsh notes

Range The Himalayan foothills, the Terai, east of Uttarakhand; NE India; hill forests of Bihar, Odisha, SE Madhya Pradesh, E Maharashtra, south along Eastern Ghats to about Cauvery river; entire Western Ghats

Habitat Forests; bamboos; hill station gardens

Male has glossy black head and back; white rump and sides of graduated tail distinctive; black throat and breast; orange-rufous below. Female grey, male black with shorter tail and duller rufous breast. Arboreal; keeps to shaded areas and foliage, only occasionally emerging in open; launches short sallies.

INDIAN ROBIN

Saxicoloides fulicatus Muscicapidae

Several races in India. Male has dark brown, blackish-brown or glossy blue-back upperbody. Male has white wing patch; glossy blue-black below; chestnut vent and undertail. Female lacks white in wings; duller grey-brown below. Solitary, or in pairs in open country, and often in and around habitation. Rather suspicious and maintains safe distance between man and itself; hunts on ground, hops or runs in short spurts; when on ground, holds head high and often cocks tail, right upto back, flashing chestnut vent and undertail.

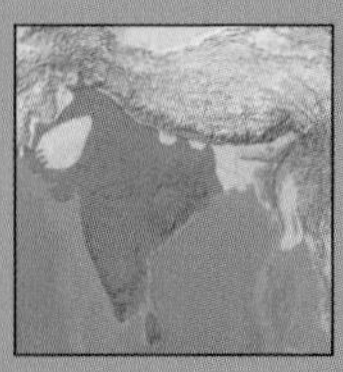

Size 16 cm

Voice Call a long-drawn *sweeeech* or *weeeech*. Warbling song when breeding; also, guttural *charrr*… note

Range Subcontinent, S Himalayan foothills; absent in extreme NE India

Habitat Open country; edges of forests; vicinity of habitation; scrubs

EVERSMANN'S REDSTART

Phoenicurus erythronotus Muscicapidae

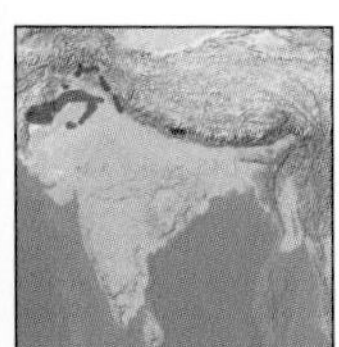

Size 16 cm

Voice Warbling song

Range Pakistan and W Himalayas

Habitat Dry hillsides

Grey, black-and-orange chat, larger than most redstarts. Breeding male has grey crown and broad, black face mask, black wings with white bars and patches; fairly mottled orange body, much paler on belly and vent. Brown tail with orange outer feathers. In winter, turns paler and more mottled. Female brown with orange rump and outer-tail and two beige wing-bars.

BLUE-CAPPED REDSTART

Phoenicurus coeruleocephala Muscicapidae

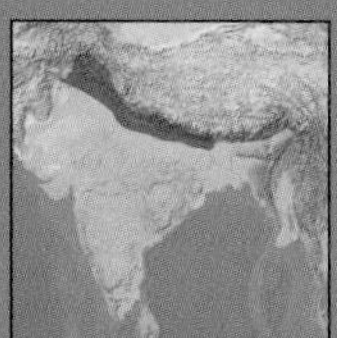

Size 15 cm

Voice Call a soft *tik…tik…tik*. Warbling song

Range Locally common breeding resident in N hills from N Pakistan to Bhutan. Commoner in west. Winters lower down, occasionally moving into N plains as far south as Delhi

Habitat Open forests and scrubs on rocky slopes in summer. Winters in open forests and secondary cover

Adult male has black back, tail, head and breast; white belly and speculum on wing; greyish-blue crown; white belly. Non-breeding male more grey-brown. Female greyish-brown with two buff wing-bars; dark brown tail and chestnut uppertail. Juvenile dark, grey-brown mottled lighter with dark-grey tail and reddish-rufous uppertail; white in wings. Often near water. Feeds on invertebrates on low branches and ground, often dropping from low perch. Shivers and slowly wags tail. Often confiding. Nests on ground.

BLACK REDSTART

Phoenicurus ochruros Muscicapidae

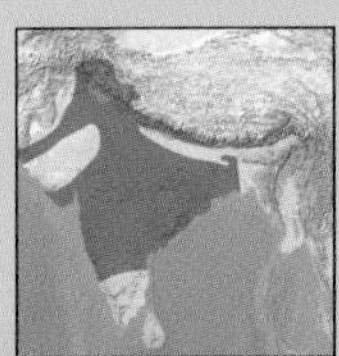

Size 15 cm

Voice Call a squeaking *tictititic*…, often beginning with faint *tsip*… note. Trilling song of breeding male

Range Breeds in the Himalayas, 2,400-5,200 m; winters over much of the subcontinent

Habitat Open country; cultivation

Male black above (marked with grey in winter); grey crown and lower back; rufous rump and tail sides; black throat and breast; rufous below. Female duller brown above; tail similar to male's; dull tawny-brown below. Eastern race *rufiventris* has black crown; common wintering bird of India. Mostly solitary in winter, when common all over India; easy to observe. Perches on overhead wires, poles, rocks and stumps; characteristic shivering of tail and jerky body movements; makes short dashes to ground, soon returning to perch with catch; rather confiding in summer, breeds in houses, under roofs and in wall crevices.

COMMON REDSTART

Phoenicurus phoenicurus Muscicapidae

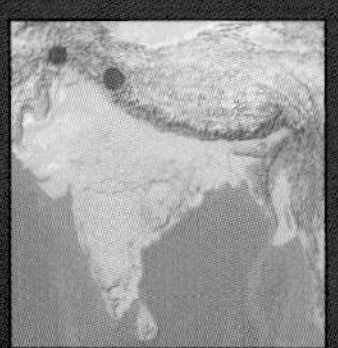

Size 15 cm

Voice Calls include distinctive *hweet*, often followed by loud *tit…tit*

Range Very local and rare spring passage migrant to W borders

Habitat Forests; recorded in the subcontinent in arid areas

Distinctive-coloured redstart with bright orange-rufous rump and tail. Adult male has bluish-grey upperparts; black face and black throat; white forehead and white stripe extending back from above eyes. Rufous breast; buffish-white belly; brownish undertail and wings; blackish-brown central tail feathers; black bill and legs. Female has duller, greyish upperparts, and buff-white underparts, washed and streaked orange; reddish-orange rump and tail; pale eye-ring. Juvenile overall brownish with buff mottling. Characteristic display with quivering tail.

HODGSON'S REDSTART

Phoenicurus hodgsoni Muscipidae

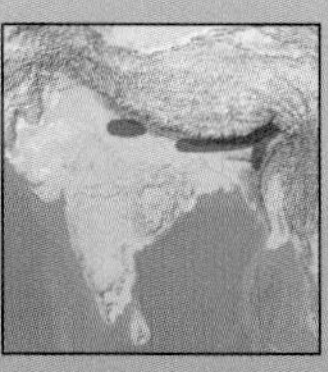

Size 15 cm

Voice Calls include rippling *prtt* and harsh *churrr*

Range Locally common winter visitor to N hills from Uttarakhand east to Myanmar border

Habitat Stony riverbeds; scrubs; open woodlands; grasslands; cultivation

Male has grey upperparts except for rufous tail and rump; small, white wing patch; white forehead; black throat and upper breast; orange underparts. Female overall greyish with rufous tail and vent. Feeds on insects in air and on ground. Behaviour similar to Black's.

WHITE-THROATED REDSTART

Phoenicurus schisticeps Muscicapidae

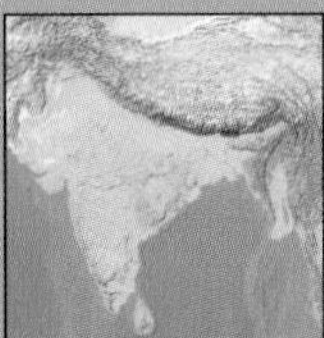

Size 15 cm

Voice Call a drawn-out *zieh*, followed by rattling note. Song undescribed

Range Subject to some attitudinal movements, and winter visitor. Mainly, the Himalayas from W Nepal east to Bhutan

Habitat Summers in open shrubberies on rocky slopes and ridges; also bushes at edges and clearings of open, coniferous and birch forests. Winters in meadows and fallow cultivation and on rocky, bush-covered slopes

Adult male (worn) has blue crown and nape, chin, ear-coverts; mantle black; rufous on scapulars, breast and belly. Adult male (fresh) has rufous fringes to head and upperparts, fringes buff on underparts. Grey-brown on adult female's head and mantle becomes paler on breast, belly buff.

DAURIAN REDSTART

Phoenicurus auroreus Muscicapidae

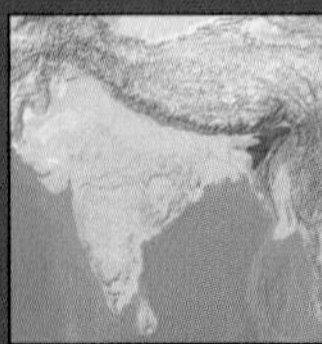

Size 15 cm

Voice Calls include high-pitched *tseep* or *fit*, scolding *tak* or *teck teck* notes in alarm, rapid rattling *tititik*

Range Summer visitor to the Himalayas from E Sikkim to Arunachal Pradesh, hills of NE India. Winters in foothills

Habitat Sparse, open subalpine, riverine thickets. Also, human settlements upto 2,500 m, breeds between 2,800 and 3,700 m

Adult breeding male pale grey from crown to upper mantle; black lower mantle; large, white wing patch; rufous rump and uppertail-coverts; rufous tail with dark central rectrices; black scapulars; blackish wings. Rufous underparts; black face, chin and throat. Non-breeding male more brownish-grey from crown to upper mantle; broad, brown fringe on lower mantle, giving scaly appearance, and pale fringing on breast too. Adult female has brown upperparts and paler underparts; smaller wing patch. Juvenile similar to female but with dark scaling and pale spotting above and below.

BLUE-FRONTED REDSTART

Phoenicurus frontalis Muscicapidae

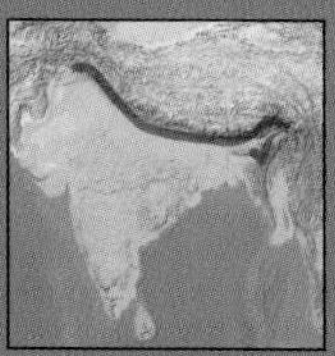

Size 15 cm

Voice Call a squeaking *tik* or *prik*

Range Altitudinal migrant; breeds in the Himalayas upto 5,300 m. Winters in the Himalayan foothills

Habitat Cultivation; open country; gardens

Male has bright blue forehead with darker blue crown and back; orange-chestnut underparts; rufous rump; orange tail with broad, blackish terminal band and central feathers. Female dark olive-brown; yellowish-orange below; rump and tail as in male; tail pattern diagnostic, to separate it from other female redstarts. Mostly solitary, perched on rocks or bushes; drops to the ground to feed; pumps tail.

GULDENSTADT'S REDSTART

Phoenicurus erythrogastrus Muscicapidae

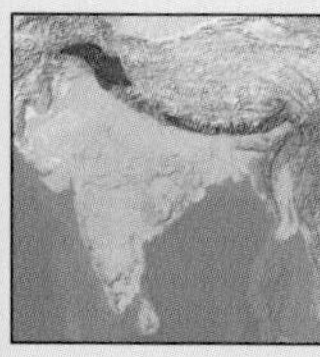

Size 18 cm

Voice Calls include soft *lik* and hard *teek…teek*

Range Locally common breeding resident in N mountains from Pakistan east to Arunachal Pradesh. Winters lower down in foothills

Habitat Stony hillsides, pastures and riverbeds

Big, black, white-and-orange chat with unmarked orange tail. Male has black throat and upperparts with large, white wing patches and crown. Orange underparts, rump and tail. Female brown above and warm buff below with orange rump and tail. Feeds on invertebrates on ground and through aerial sallies. Perches low. Nests among rocks.

WHITE-BELLIED REDSTART

Hodgsonius phoenicuroides Muscicapidae

Size 18 cm

Voice Call a grating *croak*. Also, *chack…chack…chack; teuuh… tiyou…tuh*

Range Altitudinal and short-range migrant. The Himalayas from N Pakistan east to Arunachal Pradesh

Habitat Summers in subalpine dwarf birch, rhododendron and juniper; thickets of *Viburnum* and beds of dense, tall herbs in Pakistan

♀

Male overall dark slaty-blue; white belly and vent; rufous sides to base of tail; two white spots on alula. Distinguished from Blue-fronted Robin by white belly, rufous tail sides and white spots on wing. Female has greenish-brown upperparts; chestnut sides to tail with darker centres, white throat and centre of belly, and reddish-brown flanks and vent. Juvenile similar to female, but spotted above and scaled below.

PLUMBEOUS WATER REDSTART

Rhyacornis fuliginosa Muscicapidae

Size 12 cm

Voice Calls include sharp *kreee…*; also snapping *tzit…tzit*. Rich jingling song of breeding male, infrequently uttered in winter

Range The Himalayas, 800-4,000 m, but mostly 1,000-2,800 m; also breeds south of Brahmaputra River; may descend into foothills, the Terai in winter

Habitat Mountain streams, rivers, rushing torrents

♀

Male has slaty-blue plumage; chestnut tail diagnostic; rufous on lower belly. Female darkish blue-grey-brown above; two spotted wing-bars; white in tail; whitish below, profusely mottled slaty. Juvenile brown, also with white in tail. In pairs on mountain rivers; active, makes short dashes from boulders; moves from boulder to boulder, flying low over roaring waters; tail frequently fanned open and wagged. Hunts late in evening; maintains feeding territories in winter as well as at other times.

WHITE-TAILED ROBIN

Myiomela leucura Muscicapidae

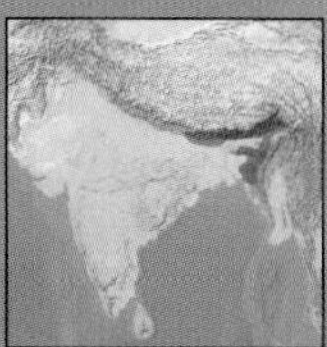

Size 18 cm

Voice Calls include quiet *tuk* and thin whistle. Undulating, rapid song

Range Scarce breeding resident of N hills from Uttarakhand east to Myanmar border. Also, much lower in NE India, Bangladesh. Winters lower down in foothills and rarely in nearby plains

Habitat Damp undergrowth and bamboo clumps in evergreen forests, often near streams or in ravines

Male slaty-blue, with bright blue forehead and shoulders; rufous-chestnut tail and vent; black bill; flesh-coloured legs. Female brown-grey above, with white lower throat patch and brown breast-band. Long, broad, black tail which it lowers and spreads. Shy, keeping close to ground where it feeds on invertebrates. Flies up into trees if disturbed. Solitary, or in pairs. Nests low down.

WHITE-CAPPED REDSTART

Chaimarrornis leucocephalus Muscicapidae

Adult has glossy black head with white crown and upper nape; black back, wings, chin, throat and breast. Rest of underparts and rump rufous; rufous tail with black terminal band; black underwing-coverts mottled chestnut-orange. Bill, eyes, legs and feet blackish. Perches on stones mid-stream, bobbing body and flicking and fanning wings and tail. Flies low over water.

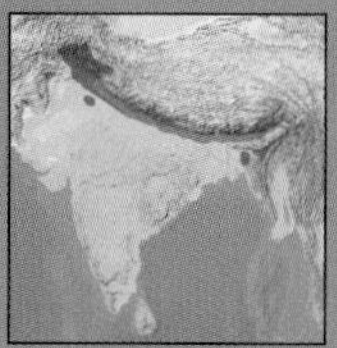

Size 19 cm

Voice Calls include plaintive *tseee* and softer *psst…psst.* Whistling song

Range Common breeding resident to N hills from Pakistan east to Myanmar border. Winters lower down in foothills

Habitat Rocky streams and rivers, fast-flowing water and alpine pastures

BLUE-FRONTED ROBIN

Cinclidium frontale Muscicapidae

Rare blue robin with long legs and longish, dark, graduated tail. Male deep blue; dark lores, shining blue eyebrow, shoulder; sometimes, blotchy white on lower belly, vent. Female rich dusky brown above, paler below; buff-white throat, centre of belly; brown vent streaked white. Shy, elusive; habits little known; mainly terrestrial; usually seen near ground level in dense forest understoreys. Rarely flies; flight only over very short distances; forages by hopping on ground; characteristic horizontal stance; flares tail.

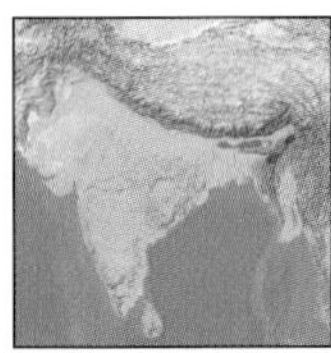

Size 19 cm

Voice Call a soft *tch...tchtch...tch*; alarm *schwik*. Mellow song

Range Small patches in N Bengal, Bhutan and Arunachal Pradesh

Habitat Thick dark, damp gullies; dense forest undergrowth; edges of forests

GRANDALA

Grandala coelicolor Muscicapidae

Size 23 cm

Voice Call a sharp *jeeu…jeeu*. Song an extension of this

Range Locally common breeding resident of high mountains from Kashmir east to Arunachal Pradesh. Descends little lower in winter but always remains in mountain zone

Habitat Rocky hillsides and pastures above treeline

Male glossy purplish-blue all over with blackish wings and tail. Female and immature brownish-grey, heavily streaked with white; white-patches on wings and bluish wash on rump; exceptionally long wing. Usually in flocks, catching invertebrates on wing or on ground. Also eats berries. Rapid and elegant flight.

♀

LITTLE FORKTAIL

Enicurus scouleri Muscicapidae

Size 12 cm

Voice Rather silent except a rarely uttered, sharp *tzittzit* call

Range The Himalayas, W to E. Breeds between 1,200-3,700 m; descends to about 300 m in winter

Habitat Rocky mountain streams, waterfalls, small shaded forest puddles

Adult has bluish-black head, nape and upper back; white forehead; blackish-brown wings with broad, white band; white band also across back; white breast and abdomen; dichromatic, slightly forked tail; black rump patch. Sexes alike. Solitary, or in pairs; energetically moves on moss-covered and wet, slippery rocks; constantly wags and flicks tail; occasionally launches short sallies, but also plunges underwater, dipper style.

BLACK-BACKED FORKTAIL

Enicurus immaculatus Muscicapidae

Medium-sized forktail. Black crown and mantle; broad, white band on forehead extending behind eye; broad white wing-bars; white rump; long, deeply forked black-and-white tail. Black throat, remaining underparts white. Similar to Slaty-backed, but more black and smaller in size.

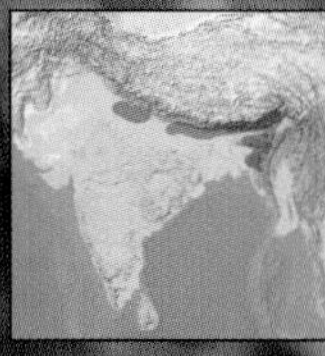

Size 23 cm

Voice Call a short, whistled *tseep...; dew; kurt...see*

Range Foothills from Uttarakhand to Myanmar

Habitat Rushing hill streams in moist tropical forests

Solitary, or in dispersed pairs; forages near water or in rocks at water's edge or mid-stream, occasionally going into water; constantly moves tail up and down; shy; flies along river.

SLATY-BACKED FORKTAIL

Enicurus schistaceus Muscicapidae

Medium-sized forktail with slaty-grey crown and mantle; long, deeply forked black-and-white tail; black throat and wing-coverts; broad, white wing-bars; white rump; narrow, white band across forehead extending behind eye; flesh-pink legs. Juvenile dark brown; adult slaty and has dark streaking on breast. Solitary, or in pairs; always near water; moves restlessly; forages in rocks at water's edge or mid-stream, occasionally going into water; constantly moves tail up and down. Shy.

Size 25 cm

Voice Calls include high-pitched *tsee*; soft *cheet*; metallic *teenk*

Range Mountains from Uttarakhand east

Habitat Rocky forested streams

SPOTTED FORKTAIL

Enicurus maculatus Muscicapidae

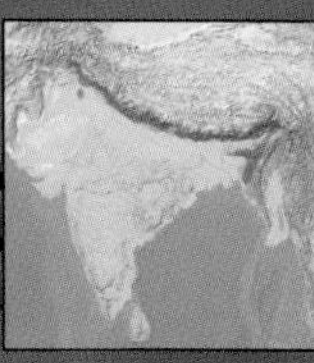

Size 28 cm

Voice Call a shrill, screechy *kree*, mostly in flight; also some shrill, squeaky notes on perch

Range The Himalayas; breeds mostly between 1,200-3,600 m; descends to about 600 m in winter

Habitat Boulder-strewn torrents; forest streams; roadsides

Has white forehead and forecrown; black crown and nape; white-spotted black back; broad, white wing-bar and rump; deeply forked, graduated black-and-white tail; black till breast, white below. Sexes alike. Easily distinguished from other similar-sized forktails in the Himalayas by white-spotted back. Solitary, or in scattered pairs; active, moves on mossy boulders at water's edge or in mid-stream; long, gracefully sways forked tail, almost always kept horizontal.

WHITE-CROWNED FORKTAIL

Enicurus leschenaulti Muscicapidae

Size 28 cm

Voice Call a harsh *scree…scree, chit…chit*. Elaborate, high-pitched whistling song

Range Subject to seasonal movements. The Himalayan foothills from Darjeeling, West Bengal, east to Arunachal Pradesh; hills of NE India

Habitat Fast-flowing streams and rivers in dense, tropical broadleaved evergreen forests

Diagnostic white crown with short crest. Similar to Black-backed but larger, with longer tail. Conspicuous white forehead and forecrown; black throat and breast; unmarked black mantle. Juvenile has brownish-black upperparts, brownish-black throat and breast with white streaking and brown mottling on upper belly, and brown flanks; pink legs. Sometimes seen on rocks mid-stream, constantly flicks tail while foraging.

HODGSON'S BUSHCHAT

Saxicola insignis Muscicapidae

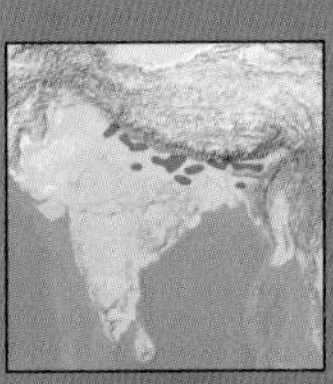

Size 17 cm

Voice Call a metallic *tek…tek*

Range Uttarakhand to Bhutan, Assam

Habitat Dry or wet grasslands, reed beds, cane fields and tamarisks

Largish bushchat with pied upperparts and red-patch on breast. Diagnostic broad, white nuchal-collar on male; white rump. Breeding male has black crown, ear-coverts, mantle, wings and tail; rufous on breast; rufous wash on belly. Female has buff-streaked upperparts; two whitish-buff wing-bars; pale rufous-buff underparts. Solitary, in pairs. Terrestrial hunter. Sometimes dives from perch to catch prey. Upright stance. Territorial in winter.

STOLICZKA'S BUSHCHAT

Saxicola macrorhynchus Muscicapidae

♀

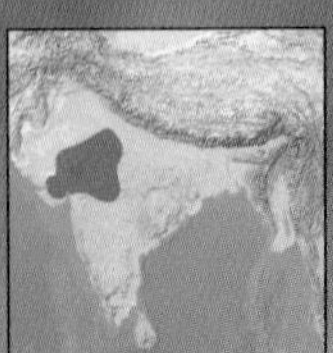

Size 15 cm

Voice Very quiet. Call a soft *prupp… prupp*

Range Globally threatened. Very local. Breeding areas and nest unknown

Habitat Dry semi-desert with grass clumps and scattered bushes

Male has blackish ear-coverts, creamy-white supercilium; white wing patches; white throat. Dark blackish-brown upperparts, paler and more streaked in winter. White in outer-tail feathers. Creamy-white underparts, washed peachy-pink on breast. Long legs and long bill. Female streaked brown with marked supercilium and less white in tail. Territorial in small area. Unique 'puff and roll' display on ground. Often confiding.

COMMON STONECHAT

Saxicola torquatus Muscicapidae

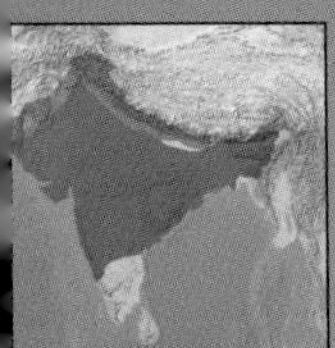

Size 13 cm

Voice Call a double-noted *wheet chat*. Soft, trilling song of breeding male in the Himalayas, occasionally in winter grounds

Range Breeds in the Himalayas, 1,500-3,000 m; all over India in winter, except Kerala and much of Tamil Nadu

Habitat Dry, open areas; cultivation; tidal creeks

breeding

non-breeding

♀

Medium-sized, black, white and rufous chat. Male black above; white rump, wing patch and sides of neck and breast; black throat; orange-rufous breast. In winter, black feathers broadly edged buff-rufous-brown. Female rufous-brown above, streaked darker; unmarked yellowish-brown below; white wing patch and rufous rump. Solitary, or in pairs in open country; perches on small bushes, fence posts and boulders; restless, makes short forays to capture insects, soon returning to perch.

WHITE-TAILED STONECHAT

Saxicola leucurus Muscicapidae

♀

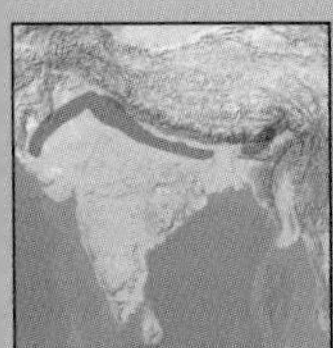

Size 13 cm

Voice Calls include short *pseep* and harder *kek...kek...kek*

Range Local breeding, near-endemic resident in Indus and upper Ganges river systems and the Terai east to Assam, patchily south to N Odisha

Habitat Reed beds and tall grass usually near rivers. Sometimes in adjoining scrubs (often tamarisk) and cultivation. Frequently shares habitat with Common

Small and stocky chat with clearly defined orange breast patch. Black head; white collar. Dark cinnamon-brown back and wings with white on wing-coverts; dark tail shows white on inner webs of outer-tail feathers. Female very similar to Common but greyer, paler below and with greyish in tail. White in tail visible in flight.

PIED BUSHCHAT

Saxicola caprata Muscicapidae

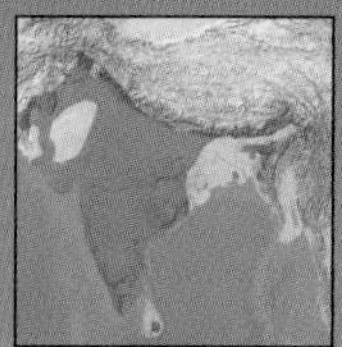

Size 13 cm

Voice Harsh, 2-noted call serves as contact and alarm. Short, trilling song of breeding male

Range Subcontinent, from outer Himalayas to about 1,500 m

Habitat Open country; scrubs; cultivation; ravines

breeding
♀

Breeding male has glossy metallic black plumage; white in wing, rump and belly. Female brown above, paler on lores; darker tail; dull yellow-brown below with rusty wash on breast and belly. Juvenile more grey-brown with yellowish spots and buffy underparts with dark spotting. Solitary, or in pairs; perches on bushes, overhead wires; makes short sallies to prey on ground or carries it to perch; active, sometimes guards feeding territories in winter; flicks and spreads wings.

JERDON'S BUSHCHAT

Saxicola jerdoni Muscicapidae

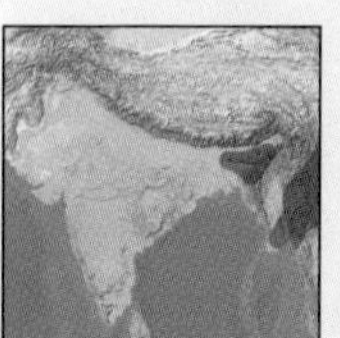

Size 15 cm

Voice Calls include short, plaintive whistle, higher-pitched than that of other chats, and low *chit…churr, chit…churr*

Range Very rare and local breeding resident. Mainly NE India and Bangladesh; Nepal

Habitat Large areas of elephant grass, grass and reeds along river or channel banks

Uniformly black with glossy blue forehead, crown, nape, lores and upperparts. Silky-white chin and throat. Buff wash on belly and breast. White flank feathers edged grey; dull black remiges; glossy black underwing-coverts; black legs, feet and bill. Female has black forehead and crown with rufous-brown streaking; brownish upperparts and white underparts; greyish-brown underwing-coverts; buffy white undertail-coverts; brown feet and legs. Juvenile male has more brownish upperparts, faintly streaked crown and forehead and greyish buff underparts.

GREY BUSHCHAT

Saxicola ferreus Muscicapidae

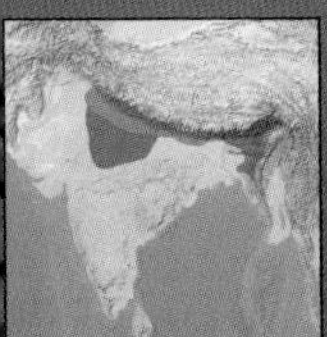

Size 15 cm

Voice Call double-noted; also grating *praee*… .Trilling song of male

Range The Himalayas, 1,400-3,500 m; descends into foothills and adjoining plains, including Gangetic plains, in winter

Habitat Open scrub; edges of forests; cultivation

Male dark grey above, streaked black; black mask; white supercilium, wing patch and outer-tail; white throat and belly; dull grey breast. Female rufous-brown, streaked; rusty rump and outer-tail; white throat; yellow-brown below. Solitary, or in pairs; like other chats, keeps to open country and edges of forests; perches on bush-tops and poles, flits tail often; flies to ground on spotting insects.

ISABELLINE WHEATEAR

Oenanthe isabellina Muscicapidae

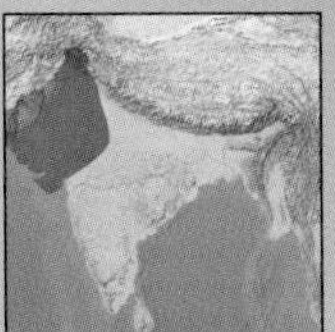

Size 17 cm

Voice Calls include *chak…chak* and *tew*

Range Locally common breeding summer visitor to Balochistan. Fairly common winter visitor to Pakistan and NW India south to Gujarat with scattered records south to Maldives and Sri Lanka and E Sikkim

Habitat Mainly sandy semi-desert and overgrazed pasture

'Isabelline' refers to its pale greyish-yellow or pale fawn overall colouration. Wings slightly darker than body; long, strong, slightly hooked bill; relatively short tail; long body usually held upright; black-and-white tail. Sexes similar. White basal patches on black tail. Looks long-legged because of very upright stance. Paler than female Northern and Desert. More terrestrial than other wheatears, mainly catches prey on ground. Solitary and territorial. Shy. Breeds in rocky gulleys and plateaux. Nests in deep, rodent holes.

NORTHERN WHEATEAR

Oenanthe oenanthe Muscicapidae

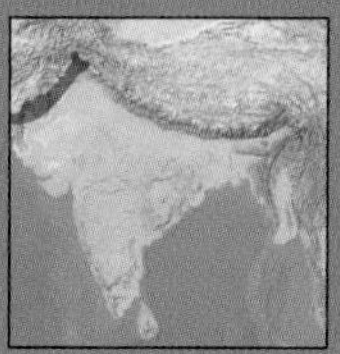

Size 15 cm

Voice Call a hard *chak*, often preceded by *wheet*

Range Scarce passage migrant (may have bred) in W and N Pakistan en route to E Africa. Rare vagrant to N India, Maldives and Nepal

Habitat Open, usually stony, country and cultivation

Small wheatear. Breeding male blue-grey above; black wings; white underparts with rufous cast on breast; white rump; white tail with black central feathers and black terminal band forming T-shaped marking, visible in flight; white forehead; black eye-stripe. Breeding female similar to breeding male, but with pale grey-brown upperparts. Female overall buff-brown. Juvenile similar in appearance to non-breeding female.

RUFOUS-TAILED WHEATEAR

Oenanthe xanthoprymna Muscicapidae

Rather drab-looking wheatear. Male has brownish-grey crown and back; pale supercilium; black lores; rusty-orange tail with black terminal band at end and central black feathers, forming distinctive T-shaped marking. Rusty-orange chin, ear-coverts and breast; black bill. Female has no black lores. more sandy-brown above.

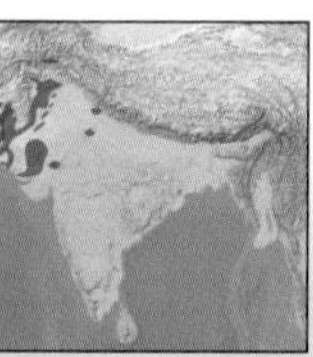

Size 14.5 cm

Voice Low, grating call. Song a loud warbling, with considerable mimicry

Range Breeds in Balochistan, Pakistan; winter visitor to Pakistan and NW India (from Himachal Pradesh south to Gujarat)

Habitat Summers on dry rocky slopes. Winters in semi-desert, on stony or sandy ground with scattered bushes, on low rocky hills and ravines, and at the foot of rocky hillsides

RED-TAILED WHEATEAR

Oenanthe chrysopygia Muscicapidae

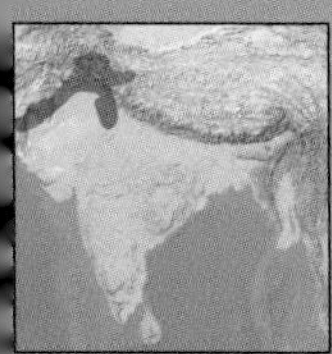

Size 14 cm

Voice Calls include throaty *trrtt* and hard *tak…tak*

Range Locally common breeding summer visitor to N hills from Pakistan east to Himachal Pradesh

Habitat Dry, open, rocky country

Fairly drab-looking bird, mainly grey-brown above and greyish-white below. Faint, pale stripe over eye, rufous tinge to ear-coverts and silvery-white underwing-coverts; rump and bases of outer-tail feathers reddish while rest of tail black forming T-shaped pattern. Sexes similar, but male has black between eye and bill. Territorial. Perches prominently on rocks and buildings from which it preys on aerial and terrestrial invertebrates.

DESERT WHEATEAR

Oenanthe deserti Muscicapidae

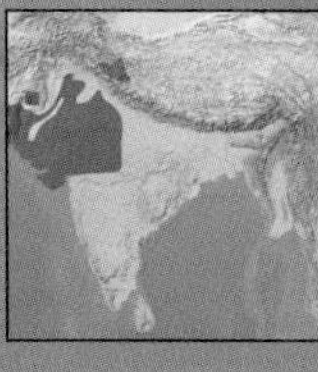

Size 15 cm

Voice Call an occasional *ch…chett* alarm note in winter. Reportedly utters short, plaintive song in winter too

Range Winter visitor over N, C, W India, almost absent south of S Maharashtra and Andhra Pradesh. Tibetan race *oreophila* breeds in Kashmir, Ladakh, Lahaul and Spiti, at about 3,000-5,000 m

Habitat Open, rocky, barren country; sandy areas; fallow lands

Male sandy above, with whitish rump and black tail; black wings; white in coverts; black throat and head sides; creamy-white below. Female has black wings and tail; lacks black throat. Winter male has throat feathers fringed white. Keeps to ground or perches on low bushes or small rocks; has favoured haunts; colouration makes it difficult to spot; makes short sallies to capture insects.

♀

VARIABLE WHEATEAR

Oenanthe picata Muscicapidae

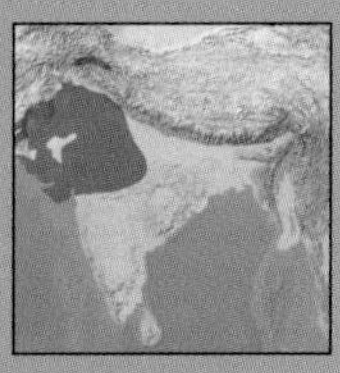

Size 14.5 cm

Voice Calls include hard *chek… chek* and low whistle. Song full of mimicry

Range Common breeding summer visitor to N, W Pakistan. Winters in NW Indian plains. Decidedly rare further east and south

Habitat Dry, open country

capistrata

opistholeuca

picata

Male black with white vent, white breast to vent or white crown and breast to vent. Female also varies but usually grey above and whitish below. Both sexes have extensive white rump and black central tail-bar and black tip. Often perches on low bushes or walls from which it flies to feed on invertebrates on ground or in air. Territorial but rather shy. Usually solitary. Nests in holes in ground. Several sub-species.

HUME'S WHEATEAR

Oenanthe albonigra Muscicapidae

Size 17 cm

Voice Calls include short, sharp whistle and quiet *chit…tit…tit*. Song a loud and cheerful *chew…de…dew…twit*

Range Resident: Gilgit, locally in Sind. Recorded in NW Balochistan and S Makran in winter

Habitat Very barren stony slopes, often with scattered huge boulders and at foot of steep cliffs

PIED WHEATEAR

Oenanthe pleschanka Muscicapidae

Size 15 cm

Voice Calls include throaty *trrtt* and hard *tak…tak*

Range Locally common breeding summer visitor

Habitat Dry, open, rocky country, perches prominently on rocks and buildings from which it preys on aerial and terrestrial invertebrates

BROWN ROCK-CHAT

Cercomela fusca Muscicapidae

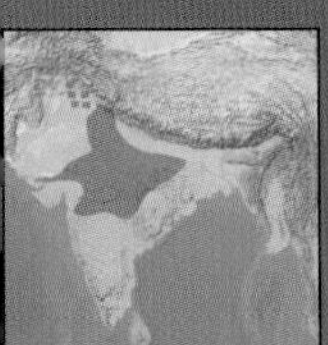

Size 17cm

Voice Calls include harsh *chaeck* and whistling *cheee*. Short, melodious song with mimicry

Range Locally common endemic breeding resident in plains and foothills of NW India from Punjab south to Maharashtra and east to Bihar. Rare in N Pakistan and S Nepal

Habitat Buildings in towns and villages, ruins, quarries, rocky hills and cliffs

Largish chat with brown upperparts and rufous-brown underparts; darker brown wings; dark grey-brown vent; blackish tail. Sexes alike. In pairs; confiding; captures insects on ground; territorial when breeding. Nests in rock clefts. Flicks open wings and tail. Also, slowly raises and fans tail and bobs head. Feeds mainly on insects on ground. Melodious song in breeding season.

HOODED WHEATEAR

Oenanthe monacha Muscicapidae

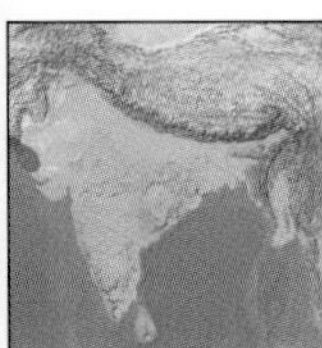

Size 17.5 cm

Voice Song has short, melodious phrases mixed with stone-clacking notes; brief thrush-like warble, infrequently given

Range Rare and local resident in S Balochistan

Habitat Barren desert

Large, slim wheatear with long bill and tail. Breeding male has white crown, black mantle, throat and upper breast; remaining underparts white. Non-breeding male has buffish or greyish wash on crown, while wings, mantle and breast have whitish or buffish fringes. Female paler sandy-grey above with creamy-buff rump, and tail-coverts with dark brown central feathers. Juvenile has pale buff crown, black throat feathers tipped pale; buff wash on flanks, rump and tail sides.

RUFOUS-TAILED ROCK THRUSH

Monticola saxatilis Muscicapidae

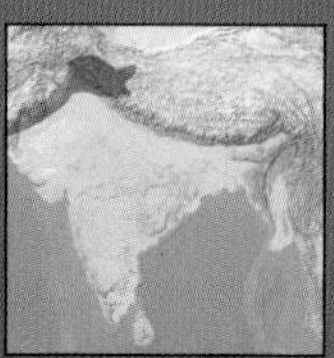

Size 19 cm

Voice Calls include squeaky *whit* and hard *chak…chak*. Song a quiet extended melody, often in flight

Range Scarce breeder in Balochistan. Winters elsewhere in E Pakistan to Ladakh and occasionally Nepal

Habitat Open, dry, rocky hillsides

Breeding male has bluish-grey head and throat; dark chestnut wings; white-patch on back; chestnut underparts and diagnostic, rusty brown tail. Female and winter male dark, scaly brown, paler underparts. Solitary, or in pairs. Shy, but frequently perches on boulders wagging tail. Feeds on ground on insects and seeds. Nests among boulders.

BLUE ROCK THRUSH

Monticola solitarius Muscicapidae

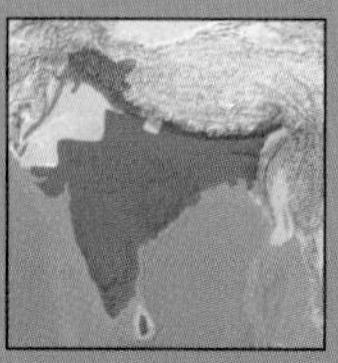

Size 23 cm

Voice Silent in winter. Short, whistling song of breeding male

Range Breeds in the Himalayas, from extreme W to E Nepal; winters from N foothills, NE, S India, throughout the peninsula

Habitat Open, rocky country; cliffs; ravines; ruins; habitation

Male has deep blue plumage; black wings and tail; pale fulvous and black scales more conspicuous in winter; belly whiter in winter. Female duller, grey-brown above; dark shaft-streaks; black barring on rump; dull white below, barred brown. Solitary; has favoured sites, often around habitation; perches on rocks, stumps, rooftops; has rather upright posture; flies on to ground to feed, but sometimes launches short aerial sallies.

CHESTNUT-BELLIED ROCK THRUSH

Monticola rufiventris Muscicapidae

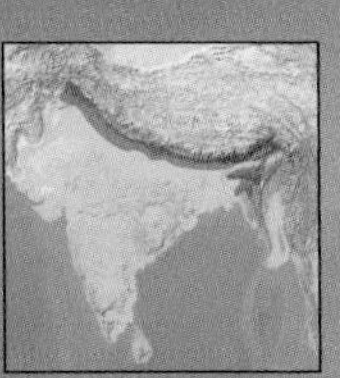

Size 24 cm

Voice Call a harsh rattle. Fluty song

Range The Himalayan forests upto 3,500 m

Habitat Open country, edges of forests, groves on rocky hillsides

Male has deep cobalt-blue head and upperparts with blackish mask; blackish face and head sides; bright blue rump and uppertail-coverts; rich rufous to maroon belly; dark bluish-black tail. Female dull olive-brown with buff throat and lores; heavy scaling on underparts; distinctive face pattern with eye-ring, dark malar stripe and neck patch; brown tail edged brownish-grey. Mostly solitary, or seen in pairs; perches upright.

BLUE-CAPPED ROCK THRUSH

Monticola cinclorhynchus Muscicapidae

Size 17 cm

Voice Mostly silent in winter, except for occasional harsh single or 2-noted call. Rich song of breeding male

Range Breeds in the Himalayas, 1,000-2,500 m, sometimes higher; winters in Western Ghats, from Narmada river

Habitat Shaded forests, groves

Male has blue crown and nape; black back; broad stripe through eyes to ear-coverts; blue throat and shoulder patch; white wing patch and chestnut rump distinctive; chestnut below throat. Back feathers edged fulvous in winter. Female unmarked olive-brown above; buffy-white below, thickly speckled with dark brown. Female Blue Rock *M. solitarius* grey-brown above, has yellow-brown vent and dull wing-bar. Solitary, or in pairs.

DARK-SIDED FLYCATCHER

Muscicapa sibirica Muscicapidae

Small flycatcher with dark greyish-brown upperparts; streaked across breast, flanks; white throat and centre of belly; large, dark eyes with white eye-ring. Similar to Asian Brown, but has smaller, dark bill, less contrasting eye-ring and lores; darker upperparts and breast-bands and flanks; wings and primary projections longer; head and body slimmer.

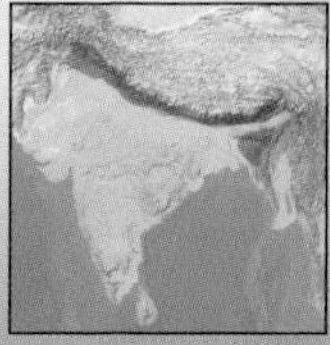

Size 14 cm

Voice Calls *tsee… tsee…tsee*

Range Pakistan to Arunachal Pradesh

Habitat Edges of temperate, or subalpine mixed broadleaved, coniferous forests

SPOTTED FLYCATCHER

Muscicapa striata Muscicapidae

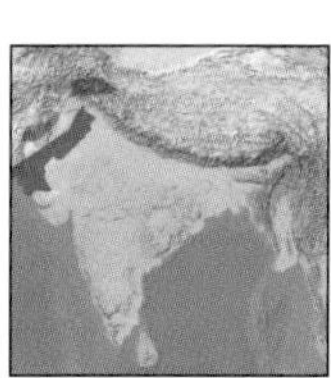

Size 15 cm

Voice Calls include high *zee* and stuttered *zee tic*

Range Local breeding summer visitor to Pakistan mountains. Scarce autumn passage migrant (en route to E Africa) in rest of Pakistan and NW India

Habitat Open forests, groves

Pale ashy-brown flycatcher with large, round head. Lightly streaked crown, throat and breast. Whitish edges to flight feathers. Fairly long, black bill and short, black legs. Long wings and tail. Sexes alike. Juvenile show buff spotting on head and back. Usually solitary. Perches in an alert, upright posture on high perch, launches into air after insects, returning to same perch. Flicks wings and tail when calling.

ASIAN BROWN FLYCATCHER

Muscicapa dauurica Muscicapidae

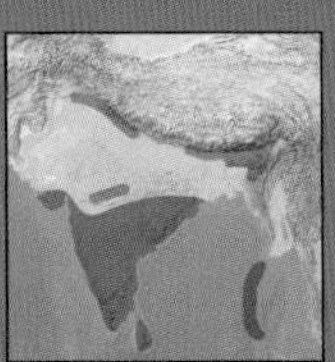

Size 13 cm

Voice Call a thin *tzee*. Whistling song

Range Breeding resident of the Himalayan foothills, with several small disjunct populations resident in the hills of C and peninsular India. Widespread winter visitor in the peninsula

Habitat Open forests; groves; gardens; plantations

juvenile

Nondescript-looking, ashy-brown flycatcher; greyish wash on dirty white breast; short tail; large head with huge eye and prominent eye-ring; pale lores; basal half of lower mandible pale and fleshy; black legs. Sexes alike. Usually solitary; perches upright on lower branches of trees, makes sallies to catch insects and returns to same perch.

BROWN-BREASTED FLYCATCHER

Muscicapa muttui Muscicapidae

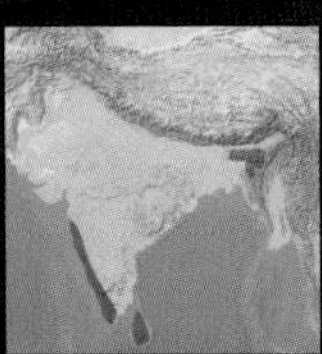

Size 13 cm

Voice Call a thin *zit*. Pleasant song

Range Assam. Distribution little understood in the NE region. Said to be absent in Nepal and Bhutan

Habitat Overgrown thickets in hill forests

Small, rich brown flycatcher, with largish head and large eyes with white eye-ring; sub-moustachial stripe; darker malar stripe. Crown slightly darker than mantle; whitish lores; lower mandible almost entirely yellowish; yellowish legs. Creamy underparts; warm brown breast-band; white throat; brownish-grey wash on flanks; generally warmer rufous tinge to wings, rump, tail; in some plumages, rufous-orange wing-bar. Solitary; shy and unobtrusive; partly crepuscular; prefers to perch in lower forest storeys; hunts aerially.

RUSTY-TAILED FLYCATCHER

Muscicapa ruficauda Muscicapidae

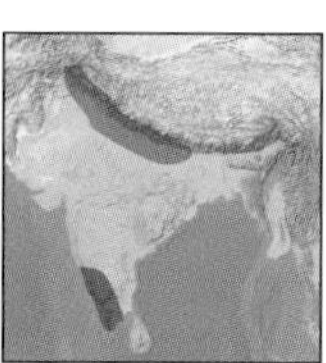

Size 14 cm

Voice Call a plaintive *peu…peu.* Also, churrs

Range Fairly common endemic breeding summer visitor to N mountains from N Pakistan east to E Nepal. Winters mainly in SW India but widespread passage records from elsewhere in India

Habitat Open forests, clearings and edges

Medium to small-sized flycatcher with flattish head. Warm brown upperparts; dark brownish from throat to breast, whitish belly to vent; large eye; ill-defined supercilium and eye-ring. Rump and notched tail bright rufous. Lower mandible pale orange. Sexes alike. Juvenile dark brownish above with buffy streaks and pale buff-brownish-spotted underparts.

FERRUGINOUS FLYCATCHER

Muscicapa ferruginea Muscicapidae

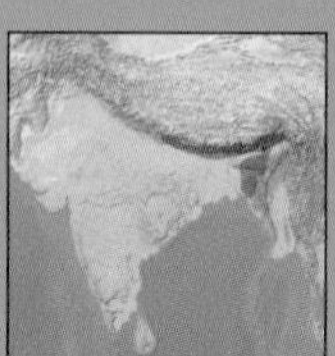

Size 13 cm

Voice Usually quiet. High-pitched trilling song

Range Scarce and local breeding summer visitor to hills of NE India, E Himalayas from C Nepal. Winters probably in SE Asia

Habitat Dense cover of hill forests

Small to medium-sized flycatcher with large head and short bill. Dark grey head; dark rufous upperparts; white throat and belly; rufous breast and flanks; more orange on rump, tail and on prominent wing-bars. Prominent white eye-rings. Pale legs. Sexes alike. Juvenile spotted rufous-orange. Usually seen solitary, low down in bushes, feeds on insects both in foliage and by aerial sorties. Not shy. Perches in understoreys of forests, flying out to catch insects. Crepuscular and unobtrusive. Nests in moss-covered trees.

YELLOW-RUMPED FLYCATCHER

Ficedula zanthopygia Muscicapidae

Size 13 cm

Voice Call a slow, unobtrusive, dry, rattled *tr…r…r…t*, lower-pitched than Red-throated

Range Vagrant

Habitat Luxuriant vegetation and dense undergrowth along rivers and streams

Male has black upperparts with bold, white supercilium; large, white wing patch; white streak on inner secondaries; bright yellow rump diagnostic. Bright citrine yellow underparts; white undertail-coverts; long wings. Female has olive-brown upperparts and yellow rump, narrower wing-bar and inner secondaries. Pale buffy-yellow underparts with darkish scaling on breast and throat; white orbital skin; pale lores. Juvenile similar to female, but has black tail. Solitary; prefers upper storeys of forests, but comes down to feed.

♀

SLATY-BACKED FLYCATCHER

Ficedula hodgsonii Muscicapidae

Size 13 cm

Voice Short and abrupt, flute-like meandering song of whistled notes in a rapid, generally descending series: *per…ip…it…u…or… per…ip…it…tu*

Range The Himalayas from WC Nepal east to Arunachal Pradesh; NE India

Habitat Breeds in oak-rhododendron, fir and pine forests; winters in damp broadleaved forests, shrubberies and bamboos

Male deep blue above and bright orange below, whiter belly; black tail has white-patches at base. Matt-blue plumage and tail separate from male Cyornis flycatchers. Female olive-brown above and greyish-olive below with poorly-defined whitish throat, lores and eye-ring. Olive-brown uppertail-coverts and tail, distinguished from female Slaty-blue. Confused with female Pale Blue, but smaller and has no rufous to tail. Juvenile has buff spotting on upperparts and dark scaling on buff underparts with whitish throat. First-winter male resembles adult female, often breeds in this plumage.

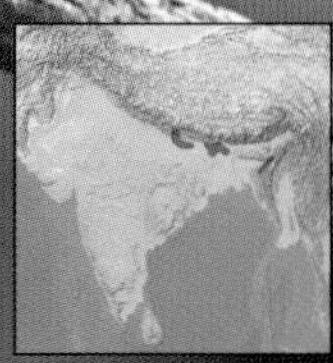

RUFOUS-GORGETED FLYCATCHER

Ficedula strophiata Muscicapidae

Size 14 cm

Voice Calls include metallic *pink*, harsh *trrt*

Range Uncommon resident in the Himalayas and hills of NE India

Habitat Forest clearings and edges

Male has dark olive-brown upperparts; blackish face and throat; conspicuous white forehead and eyebrow; diagnostic rufous-orange gorget, not always visible; grey breast; white sides to black tail. Female similar but duller, has less distinct eyebrow and gorget. Frequently seen perched quietly in shaded areas or dense canopy. Like all flycatchers, hawks insects but sometimes feeds on ground.

TAIGA FLYCATCHER

Ficedula albicilla Muscicapidae

Size 12 cm

Voice Noisy. Calls include trilled *trrr* and hard *tik...tik*

Range Common winter visitor through most of India, Nepal and Bangladesh. Passage migrant only in Pakistan. Rare in Sri Lanka and extreme S India

Habitat Open wooded country; groves; parks; gardens

Small to medium-sized flycatcher with distinct face pattern; rufous-patch on breast strongly demarcated from creamy-buff on lower breast and belly; white-patches at base of tail; blackish face; whitish eyebrow. Female overall much duller. Juvenile has rich buff spots above and blackish scales below. Usually solitary, or in pairs. Forages in undergrowth, occasionally on ground. Active but often rather shy. Best located by calls.

KASHMIR FLYCATCHER

Ficedula subrubra Muscicapidae

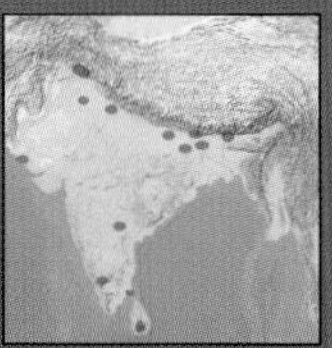

Size 13 cm

Voice Song a short, sweet phrase, *sweet…eat, sweet…eat…didhe*

Range Endemic to the subcontinent. Breeds in NW Himalayas in Neelum valley, Pakistan, Kashmir and Pir Panjal Range, India. Winters in Sri Lanka

Habitat Deciduous forests. Winters in gardens, tea estates and edges of forests

Male has ashy-brown upperparts; deep rufous throat, breast, upper belly and flanks; black-bordered throat and breast; black tail with white panel in outer-tail feathers. Female and first-winter male usually more rufous-orange on throat and breast; grey sides to neck and breast. Juvenile has tail pattern as adult, but has dark brown-spotted upperparts and buffish underparts scaled with dark brown.

RED-BREASTED FLYCATCHER

Ficedula parva Muscicapidae

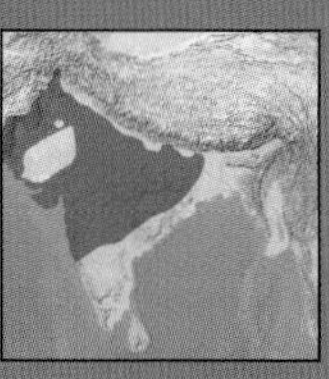

Size 13 cm

Voice Sharp clicking sound. Call a double *tick…tick*

Range Winter visitor, arrives by early September; all over India, south of the Himalayan foothills

Habitat Forests; gardens

Male dull-brown above with greyish-brown head; bright rufous-orange bib; whitish below. Bold, white basal patches to black tail, diagnostic. Female has pale cinnamon upperparts; white throat; pale buff breast; narrow, white eye-ring; no bib. Shy when breeding. Solitary, or in scattered pairs in shaded areas; may descend to ground, but prefers low and middle branches; launches short aerial sallies; hunts till late in the evening; calls often. Feeds in foliage in warbler-like manner.

WHITE-GORGETED FLYCATCHER

Anthipas monileger Muscicapidae

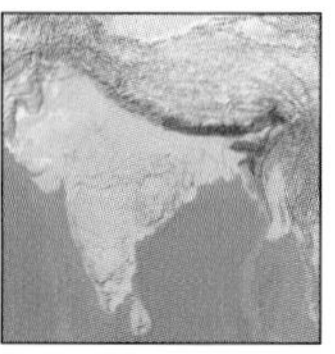

Size 11 cm

Voice Calls include short *tik*, rattle and thin whistle. Wheezy, short song

Range Rare breeding resident from W Nepal east to Arunachal Pradesh. Eastern race rather more frequent in hills of NE India to Myanmar border

Habitat Dense undercover of mountain forests

Small, large-headed, olive-brown flycatcher with short tail. Pristine white throat patch bordered black. Paler brown underparts. Western race has whitish supercilium, eastern has warm buff. Large head and bill, short tail and pink legs. Sexes alike. Juvenile darker above with pale buff streaks. Feeds on invertebrates on or close to ground. Flycatches and flits tail open but usually shy and difficult to observe. Nests near ground.

SNOWY-BROWED FLYCATCHER

Ficedula hyperythra Muscicapidae

♀

Very small, short-tailed flycatcher with rounded head. Small bill. Male has dark slaty-blue upperparts; short, white supercilium; deep orange from chin to breast, paler below; white-patches at base of tail. Female has olive-brown upperparts; rich rusty supercilium, face and breast. Both sexes have pink legs. Feeds on insects unobtrusively on or near ground. Nests in low tree holes.

Size 11 cm

Voice Calls include thin, repeated *sip* and *tsit*. Also *sit…si…sii* song

Range Locally common breeding resident in N mountains from E Uttarakhand to Myanmar border. Moves lower down in winter

Habitat Bushy undergrowth of forests, particularly favouring bamboos and ravines

LITTLE PIED FLYCATCHER

Ficedula westermanni Muscicapidae

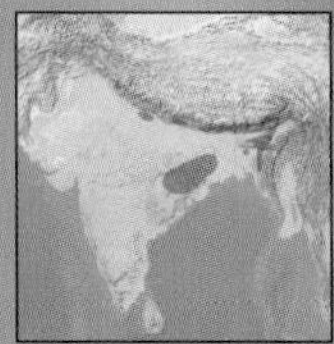

Size 11 cm

Voice Call a *tweet…*; *churr.* High-pitched song

Range Patchily distributed from Himachal Pradesh to Myanmar

Habitat Broadleaved deciduous and evergreen forests; open woodlands, scrubs, orchards

♀

Tiny flycatcher with very short tail. Male has glossy black upperparts; broad, white supercilium; white wing-bar and white-edged black tail, diagnostic. White underparts, sometimes washed grey. Female has pale greyish-blue and brownish upperparts and greyish-white underparts; reddish-brown cast on uppertail and rump. Female of eastern race *australorientis* has more rufous on rump and tail. Juvenile spotted brown and buff.

ULTRAMARINE FLYCATCHER

Ficedula superciliaris Muscicapidae

♀

Male deep blue above; sides of head, neck and breast, forming broken breast-band; long, white eyebrow; white in tail; white below. Female dull-slaty above and grey-white below. Eastern race *aestigma* lacks white over eye and in tail. Solitary, or in pairs; seen in mixed parties during winter; active, hunts in characteristic flycatcher-style; rarely ventures into open.

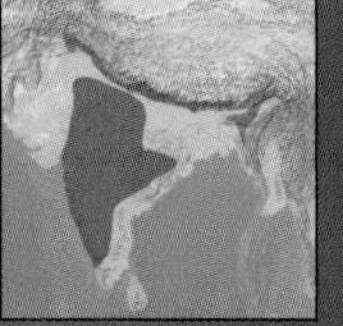

Size 10 cm

Voice Call a faint *tick…tick…* in winter; a *chrrr* alarm note. Three-syllabled song in the Himalayas

Range Breeds in the Himalayas, 1,800-3,200 m. Winters in N and C India, south to Karnataka and N Andhra Pradesh

Habitat Forests; groves; orchards; gardens

SLATY-BLUE FLYCATCHER

Ficedula tricolor Muscicapidae

Size 13 cm

Voice Call a faint *tick...tick*

Range Breeds in the Himalayas, 1,800-2,600 m. Winters in foothills

Habitat Forest undergrowth, reeds, bushes, grass

Male slaty-blue above; greyish-white (The Himalayas) or buff (S Assam hills) below; black mask; white-patch at base of black tail. Female has brown upperparts; warm brownish-buff flanks; rufescent rump and tail. Slim, long-tailed flycatcher; usually solitary or in pairs; feeds near ground with tail cocked.

♀

SAPPHIRE FLYCATCHER

Ficedula sapphira Muscicapidae

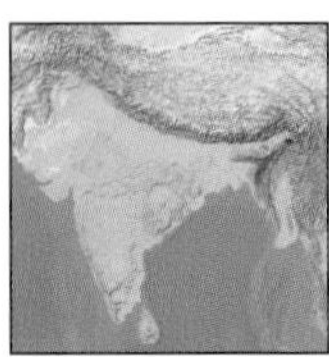

Size 11 cm

Voice Call a low *tit...it...it... it* rattle, deeper than that of other small flycatchers except Ultramarine; dry, rattled call, *trrrt*

Range NE India, Nepal, Bangladesh

Habitat Moist evergreen broadleaved forests

♀

Small, slim flycatcher. Breeding male has bright, glossy blue crown. Bright blue rump and uppertail-coverts, bright blue upperparts, sides of head, neck and breast; orange throat and breast centre; belly and undertail-coverts white. Crown and mantle of immature and some males brown, sides of head, neck and breast also brownish. Female has olive-brown upperparts and orange throat and breast. Distinguished from female Slaty-backed and Slaty-blue by shorter tail, orange throat and breast, white belly and vent. Juvenile spotted above and scaled on breast.

BLACK-AND-ORANGE FLYCATCHER

Ficedula nigrorufa Muscicapidae

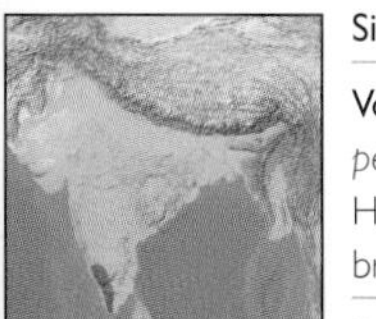

Size 13 cm

Voice Call note a soft, gloomy *pee…*; sharp *zit…zit* alarm call. High-pitched, metallic song when breeding

Range Very local; restricted to Nilgiris and associated hills in S Western Ghats, most common above 1,500 m

Habitat Dense evergreen forests; undergrowth; bamboos

Male has rich orangish-rufous plumage; blackish crown, nape, sides of face and wings. Female similar to male, but has deep olive-brown head; pale eye-ring. Usually solitary, but pairs often close by. Keeps to dense, shaded undergrowth, either hopping low or making short flycatcher-like sallies from low perch; in its restricted range, quite tame and confiding once spotted.

DULL-BLUE FLYCATCHER

Eumyias sordidus Muscicapidae

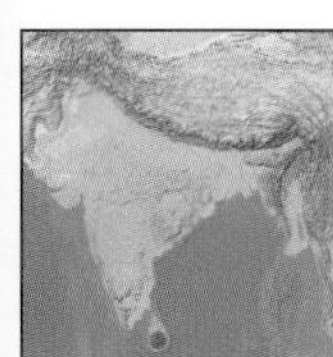

Size 15 cm

Voice Call a series of 4- or 5-chip notes. Song a sweet phrase of 6- to 8-notes, often with slide in each note giving a mournful effect

Range Endemic resident in Sri Lanka, common in higher hills

Habitat Edges of forests and well-wooded areas; shady wooded gardens

Adult dull, ashy-blue with brighter blue forehead; greyish-white belly, flanks and undertail-coverts; dark lores and chin bordered pale blue; brownish-grey tail and flight feathers. Sexes alike, but female overall duller. Juvenile has buff spotting and diffuse black scaling on brown upperparts; black scaling on beige throat and breast; wings and tail like adult, but with buff tips to coverts.

VERDITER FLYCATCHER

Eumyias thalassinus Muscicapidae

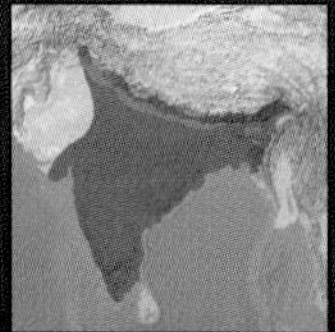

Size 16 cm

Voice Silent in winter, except a rare, faint *chwe...* call. Rich, trilling notes and song during the Himalayan summer

Range The Himalayas, 1,200-3,200 m. Winters in Indian plains, hill forests of C, E and S India

Habitat Open forests; orchards

Male has verditer-blue plumage, darker in wings and tail; black lores. Female duller, greyer overall, has short bill and longish tail. Solitary, or in pairs in winter, sometimes with other birds; restless, flicks tail; rather more noticeable than other flycatchers because of its continuous movement and habit of perching in open-exposed positions, like bare twigs on tree-tops.

juvenile

NILGIRI FLYCATCHER

Eumyias albicaudatus Muscicapidae

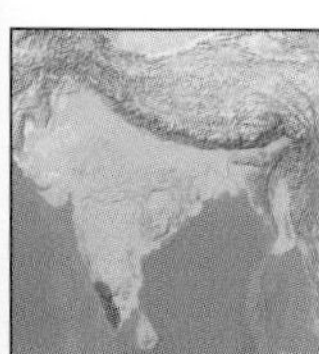

Size 15 cm

Voice Call *tsik…tsik,…chip…chip.* Song a slow, hesitant warble of upto 10 notes

Range Globally near-threatened but fairly common endemic breeding resident restricted to Western Ghats from S Karnataka southwards

Habitat Evergreen forests and edges of forests, often near streams. Also, well-grown plantations

Small to medium-sized, long-tailed flycatcher. Male has slaty-indigo upperparts; forehead and supercilium have faint reddish-purple cast; greyer on belly, with white scaling on vent; small, white basal spots on tail. Female dark greenish-grey. Both much darker than similar species. In pairs; feeds on insects which it catches in aerial sorties, mostly from canopy.

PALE BLUE FLYCATCHER

Cyornis unicolor Muscicapidae

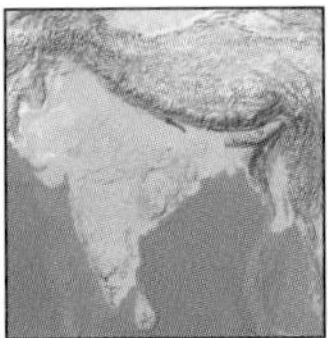

Size 18 cm

Voice Song rich and melodious, loud and thrush-like with descending sequences, *chi…, chuchichu…chuchichu…chucchi*, usually ending with harsh *chizz*

Range The Himalayas in N Uttar Pradesh and from WC Nepal east to Arunachal Pradesh; NE India

Habitat Moist, dense broadleaved forests, bamboos and secondary growth

Similar to the Verditer, but has longer bill and whitish-grey underparts; white vent; vivid blue forecrown and dusky lores. Female pale brown above with reddish-brown uppertail-coverts and tail; greyish underparts. Distinguished by larger size and longer tail, brownish-grey upperparts, and even greyish underparts with greyish-white centre of belly and dark buff undertail-coverts.

♀

HILL BLUE FLYCATCHER

Cyornis banyumas Muscicapidae

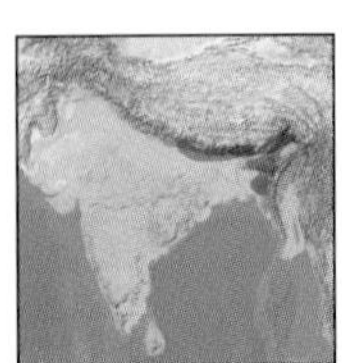

Size 15 cm

Voice Calls include hard *tak* and short rattle. Warbling song more complex than Tickell's

Range Rare breeding resident in N mountains from C Nepal east to Myanmar border. Moves lower in winter

Habitat Thick forests

Male very similar to Tickell's but distinguished by sharp demarcation between rufous-breast and creamy-white underparts; larger and deeper blue above with more black on cheeks. Female dark brown above with rusty tail and warm buff below. Both have rather long, black bill and pinkish-brown (not black) legs. Juvenile has cinnamon-brown upperparts with buffish spotting. Flycatches. Nests low down.

♀

PALE-CHINNED FLYCATCHER

Cyornis poliogenys Muscicapidae

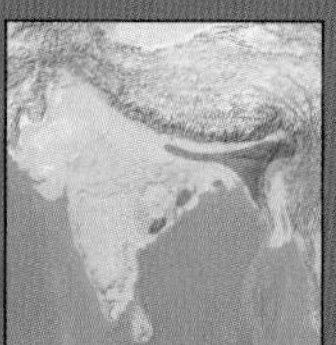

Size 18 cm

Voice Calls include hard clicks and rattles *tick…tick…, etc.* Song a high-pitched series of notes *chee…chee, chit…chit…*, etc.

Range C Nepal to Arunachal Pradesh; S Assam Hills

Habitat Bushes, undergrowth, low trees in open broadleaved forests of foothills; open country in the plains

Medium to large-sized, fairly plain-looking flycatcher. Warm brown upperparts; has varying degrees of grey on crown and face depending on the race; buff lores and eye-ring; buff or creamy-white throat; pale rufous-orange breast and flanks, creamy-white belly with pale rufous wash; rufous rump and tail; mostly arboreal; prefers hunting for insects in forest understoreys, sometimes trees, though will also descend to ground.

WHITE-BELLIED BLUE FLYCATCHER

Cyornis pallipes Muscicapidae

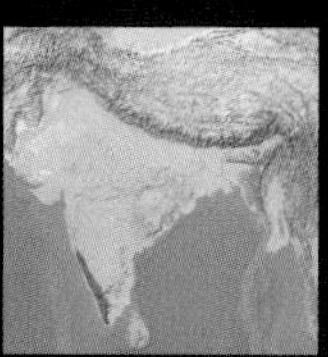

♀

Size 15 cm

Voice Soft 2-noted call. Longish, squeaky song when breeding. Rather silent for most part of the year

Range Western Ghats, south of C Maharashtra, around the latitude of Pune

Habitat Dense forest undergrowth

Male indigo-blue above; black lores; bright blue forehead, supercilium; indigo-blue throat and breast; white lower breast. Female deep olive-brown above; greyish on head; chestnut tail; rufous-orange till breast, whiter below. Juvenile has brown back, scaly head and chest; whitish belly. Solitary, rarely in pairs; sometimes in mixed parties; mostly silent and unobtrusive, hence overlooked; hunts in low growth, often flicks tail.

TICKELL'S BLUE FLYCATCHER

Cyornis tickelliae Muscicapidae

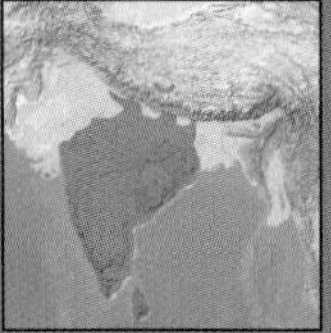

Size 14 cm

Voice Clear, metallic song of 6-notes, sometimes extending to 9 or 10; often uttered in winter too

Range All over India, south roughly of a line from Kutch to W Uttarakhand east along the Terai; absent in extreme N, NW India

Habitat Shaded forests; bamboos; gardens

Male dark indigo-blue above; bright blue on forehead and supercilium; darker, almost appearing black on face sides; rufous-orange throat and breast; whitish below. Female duller overall. Usually in pairs in shaded areas, often in mixed hunting parties; flits about intermittently or launches short sorties; has favourite perches; often breaks into fluty song.

BLUE-THROATED BLUE FLYCATCHER

Cyornis rubeculoides Muscicapidae

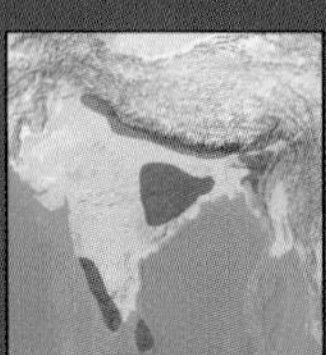

Size 14 cm

Voice Calls include harsh *chrr* and hard *tak...tak*. Rapidly delivered warbling song

Range Locally breeding summer visitor to N hills from N Pakistan east to Myanmar border. Winters in foothills

Habitat Damp forests, particularly overgrown ravines

Small flycatcher with blue throat. Male bright blue; has glossy blue forehead; orange upper breast (sometimes extending onto flanks); white belly to vent. Distinguished from Tickell's by blue throat. Female brown above, more rufous on rump and tail with pale orange throat and upper breast. Lores, belly and vent white. Female Tickell's bluish above. Feeds on invertebrates at lower levels.

RUFOUS-BELLIED NILTAVA

Niltava sundara Muscicapidae

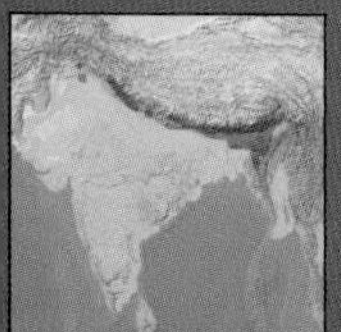

Size 15 cm

Voice Calls include squeaky, churring notes; occasionally sharp *psi...psi*; also some harsh notes and squeaks

Range The Himalayas, NE India; 1,500-3,200 m. Winters in foothills, adjoining plains

Habitat Dense forest undergrowth; bushes

Deep blue and orange niltava. Male has deep purple-blue back and throat; dark blue mask; black forehead; brilliant blue crown, shoulder and rump; chestnut-rufous underbody. Female more olive-brown overall; pale greyish-brown underparts; rufescent tail; white on lower throat diagnostic. Mostly solitary; keeps to undergrowth; highly unobtrusive, seldom seen; often flicks wings like redstart, and bobs body.

VIVID NILTAVA

Niltava vivida Muscicapidae

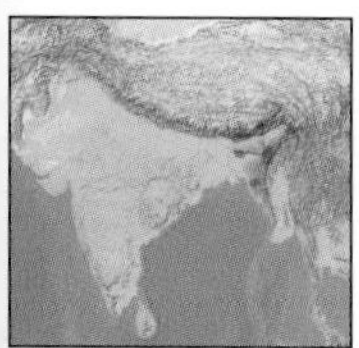

Size 18 cm

Voice Simple, slow song of upto 10 mellow whistles, usually interspersed with scratchier notes, *heu...wee...riu...chrt... trrt...heu...wee...tiu...wee...u*

Range Hills of NE India

Habitat Broadleaved, evergreen and mixed forests

Male cobalt-blue above with blue head and orange below, brighter blue forecrown, rump and tail. Similar to Rufous-bellied, but larger with longer wings, and often has peaked crown. Unlike Rufous-bellied, lacks gleaming blue crown and nape, also, orange of breast extends onto lower throat. Female lacks well-defined oval-shaped patch on lower throat like female Rufous-bellied, and typically has peaked crown. Juvenile as Rufous-bellied, but lacks buff throat patch. More arboreal and spotted away from dense cover.

SMALL NILTAVA

Niltava macgrigoriae Muscicapidae

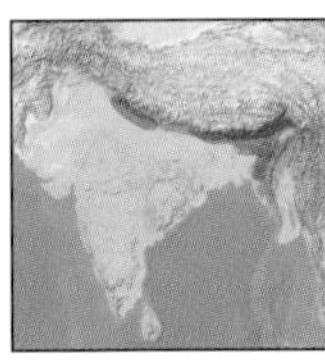

Size 13 cm

Voice Call a high-pitched see… *see; chrrr.* Song *twee…twee-tee…twee*

Range Uttarakhand to Myanmar

Habitat Bushes, undergrowth, paths, forest clearings; lowland reeds, grass jungles

Very small flycatcher, similar to Large, but almost half its size. Male has greyish-blue underparts; very dark blue-black head sides; glistening pale blue forehead reaching to eye, rump and patch on neck; white vent. Female brown with orangish-brown wings and tail; small, glossy blue neck patch. Fairly shy, difficult to see; remains hidden in dense foliage of forest understoreys, making occasional aerial sallies for insects; partly crepuscular.

LARGE NILTAVA

Niltava grandis Muscicapidae

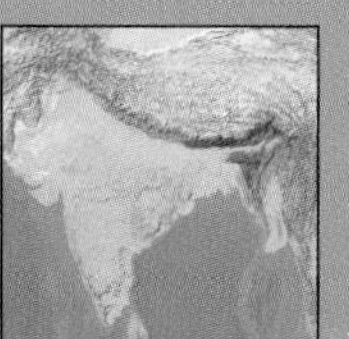

Size 21 cm

Voice Call a harsh rattle; nasal *ju...ee*. Song a pleasant whistle *do...remi*

Range C Nepal to Arunachal Pradesh; S Assam Hills

Habitat Dense, moist evergreen forests and streams

Very large flycatcher with dark bill and legs. Male dark blue with black face, chin; slightly crested, has blue crown, shoulder, neck patches, rump. Female fairly rich brown above; rufous wings, tail; rufous-buff forehead, streaked face; small, buff throat patch; blue shoulder patch; pale blue wash on nape, hindcrown; streaked buff-brown underparts. Juvenile rufous-brown; streaked above, scaled below. Almost, totally arboreal; prefers middle, lower storeys in forest interiors; on perch longer during day, hunts more actively in twilight.

PYGMY BLUE FLYCATCHER

Muscicapella hodgsoni Muscicapidae

Size 10 cm

Voice Calls include *tchurr...*; weak *tseep...*. Song soft, very high-pitched

Range WC Nepal to Arunachal Pradesh

Habitat Dense, moist broadleaved forests; thick secondary growth

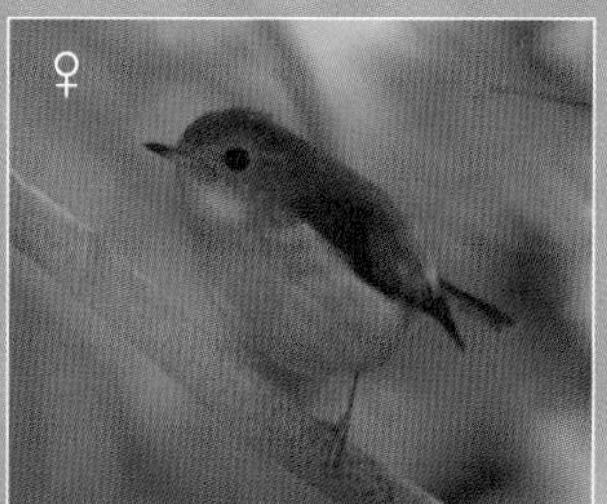

Tiny flycatcher. Male has cobalt-blue upperparts and more vivid, glossy blue crown; bluish-black lores; dark greyish-blue wings and tail and pale orange underparts. Female has olive-brown upperparts; bright orange rump and uppertail; white underparts washed with orange on throat, breast and belly. Distinguished from other flycatchers by tiny size, small, fine bill and short tail. Arboreal; flits restlessly through foliage; often droops wings and cocks tail. Solitary, or in pairs. Prefers middle and lower storeys.

GREY-HEADED CANARY FLYCATCHER

Culicicapa ceylonensis Muscicapidae

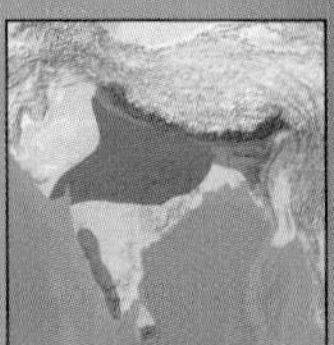

Size 9 cm

Voice Vocal. High-pitched 2- or 3-syllabled calls, *whi…chichee… whi…chichee*. Longer, trilling song; also chattering notes

Range Commonly breeds in the Himalayas, 1,500-3,000 m; possibly in some of the hill forests of C India and Eastern Ghats. Common in winter over much of the subcontinent

Habitat Forests, gardens, orchards

Has ashy-grey hood, throat and breast; darker crown; squarish crest; yellow-green back and yellow rump; yellow in browner wings and tail; bright canary-yellow below breast. Sexes alike. Solitary, or in pairs, occasionally several in vicinity, especially in mixed parties; forest bird, typical flycatcher; excitedly flitting about, launching aerial sallies, calling aloud and generally on the move; wherever this bird is, its cheerful unmistakable calls are heard.

WHITE-THROATED DIPPER

Cinclus cinclus Cinclidae

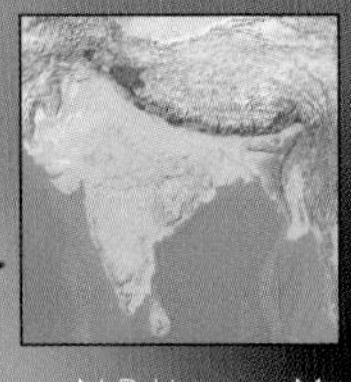

Size 20 cm

Voice Call a loud, piercing *dzittz*, mainly in flight and audible above sound of running water

Range Locally common breeding resident of N mountains from N Pakistan to Myanmar border. Scarce in S Himalayan ranges. Moves lower down in winter

Habitat Higher altitude fast-flowing streams; waterfalls; glacial lakes

Similar to Brown, but has large patch of pristine white from chin to breast, diagnostic. Brown head, mantle and belly, rest of upperparts blackish-brown. Short tail often cocked. Rare brown morph *sordidus* darker than Brown. Long legs. Sexes alike. Juvenile shows dark brown scales on upperparts; greyish streaks below. Active and territorial. Walks on stream bed, forages. Flies fast and low. Bobs and sways on boulders. Nests low in rock face.

sordidus

juvenile

BROWN DIPPER

Cinclus pallasii Cinclidae

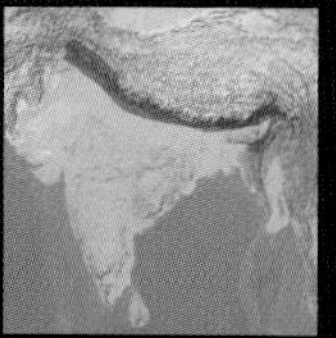

Size 20 cm

Voice Calls *dzit, dzit*. Rich song

Range Mountains throughout the region

Habitat Shallow, fast-flowing, high-altitude rocky streams; mountain lakes

Largish, uniform, dark brown dipper. Small, stocky body; grey-brown mantle, wings and tail; short, stubby tail, often cocked. Brown iris. Sexes alike. Juvenile shows some pale spotting on both upper and underparts. Solitary, in pairs, or small groups. Commonly seen in mountain streams; perches on mid-stream boulders, bobbing up and down; flies low over water; dives and swims underwater, often walking on riverbed; floats downstream briefly on emerging from water. Whirrs wings in display.

BLUE-WINGED LEAFBIRD

Chloropsis cochinchinensis Chloropseidae

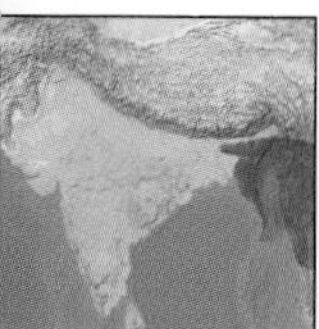

Size 20 cm

Voice Typical song with loud drongo-like chatty phrases, much mimicry plus varied whistles

Range Hills of NE India and Bangladesh

Habitat Edges of forests, groves, open forests, gardens, isolated large trees near villages or in cultivation

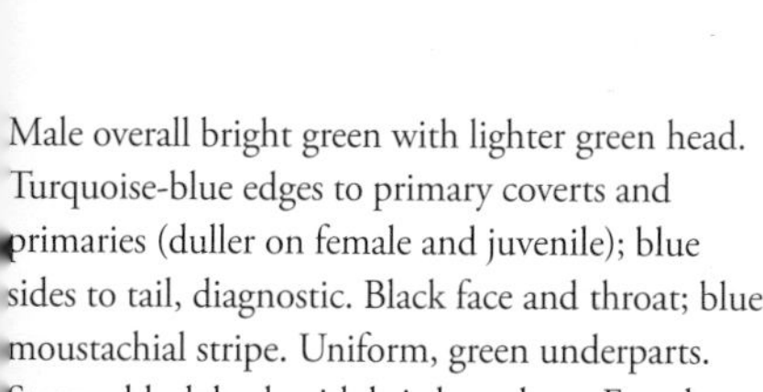

Male overall bright green with lighter green head. Turquoise-blue edges to primary coverts and primaries (duller on female and juvenile); blue sides to tail, diagnostic. Black face and throat; blue moustachial stripe. Uniform, green underparts. Strong, black beak with bristles at base. Female greener on head; has turquoise blue throat patch. Juvenile like female, but no blue on throat.

ORANGE-BELLIED LEAFBIRD

Chloropsis hardwickii Chloropseidae

Size 20 cm

Voice Wide variety of harsh and whistling notes; mimics other birds

Range Himachal to the entire NE region

Habitat Broadleaved evergreen, deciduous forests, secondary growth

Dramatically-coloured leafbird with bright orange lower breast and belly. Bright leaf-green back; yellowish-green forehead, crown and nape; broad, iridescent blue moustachial band; blue-patch over throat and chest; blue edges to outer wing-coverts, primaries, tail sides; blue shoulder patches. Female greener; less extensive orange on undersides. Solitary, in pairs or mixed parties; arboreal; usually in canopy or upper forest storeys.

♀

GOLDEN-FRONTED LEAFBIRD

Chloropsis aurifrons Chloropseidae

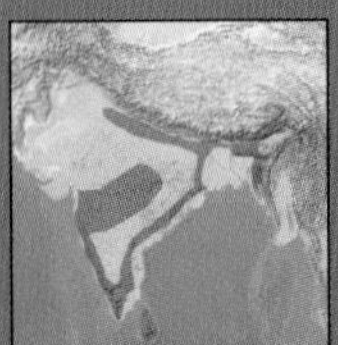

Size 19 cm

Voice Most common call a drongo or shikra-like *che... chwe*. Noisy; wide assortment of whistling notes, including imitations of several species

Range Upto about 1,600 m in Uttarakhand Himalayas; east to Bihar, Odisha, south along Eastern Ghats and up the Western Ghats and adjoining areas

Habitat Forests

Medium-sized, vivid leaf-green bird. Male has golden-orange forehead; glossy blue 'flash' on shoulder; bluish-black chin and cheeks; black lores; orangish ear-coverts, continuing as loop around blue throat. Female duller. Black chin and throat absent in juvenile; green crown. Usually in pairs; favours canopy. Hunts actively; rather aggressive, and territorial.

♀

JERDON'S LEAFBIRD

Chloropsis jerdoni Chloropseidae

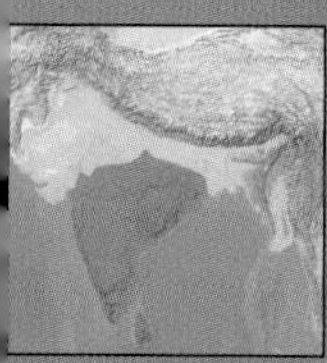

Size 20 cm

Voice As Blue-winged's

Range Peninsular India and Sri Lanka

Habitat As Blue-winged's

Distinguished immediately from Golden-fronted by lack of orange-gold crown. Male has black throat patch that continues to eye; black cheeks; blue moustache; greenish-yellow forehead. Bluish-green lesser wing-coverts. Underparts softer green. Female has greenish-blue throat and cheeks; blue moustache. Juvenile uniform leaf-green. Prefers canopy, well-camouflaged in foliage.

THICK-BILLED FLOWERPECKER

Dicaeum agile Dicaeidae

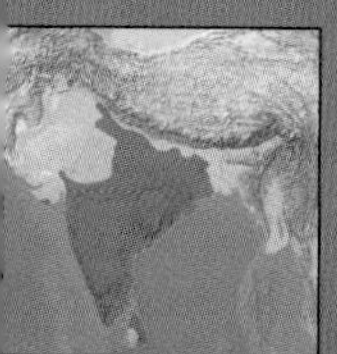

Size 9 cm

Voice Call a loud, sharp *chik…chik*

Range S India, including the Himalayan foothills; absent over arid parts of NW India and large tracts of Tamil Nadu

Habitat Forests, orchards, gardens

Small flowerpecker. Adult has olive-washed brownish-grey upperparts; more olive-brown rump; short, white-tipped tail; whitish spots on undertail-coverts; dull whitish-grey underparts, streaked brown; breast more densely streaked; orangish-red eyes and thick, blue-grey beak. Sexes alike. Juvenile has less streaked underparts. Solitary, or in pairs in canopy foliage; arboreal, restless; flicks tail often while hunting under leaves or along branches; frequents parasitic clumps of *Loranthus* and *Viscum*.

YELLOW-VENTED FLOWERPECKER

Dicaeum chrysorrheum Dicaeidae

Bright olive-green flowerpecker, heavily streaked; pale yellow underparts. Black moustache; white lores; large, decurved bill; red iris. Dark tail shows white-patches; chrome-yellow undertail-coverts; olive-brown wings. Sexes alike. Feeds mainly on *Loranthus* in pairs or singly. Flies strongly, covering considerable distances to favourite feeding trees. Nests high in trees.

Size 9 cm

Voice Call a harsh, repeated *tzreep*

Range Common breeding resident in extreme NE India to Myanmar border. Rare in Nepal and Bangladesh

Habitat Canopy of forests and orchard trees

YELLOW-BELLIED FLOWERPECKER

Dicaeum melanoxanthum Dicaeidae

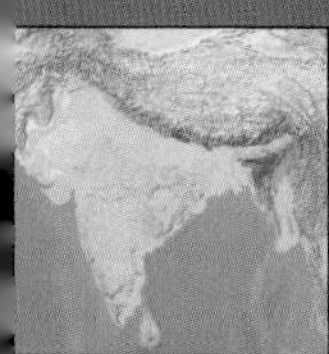

Size 13 cm

Voice Call an agitated *zit... zit...zit...zit*

Range The Himalayas from N Uttar Pradesh and from C Nepal east to Arunachal Pradesh; hills of NE India

Habitat Broadleaved forests, both open forests and clearings, edges of dense forests

Male blackish above with white-patch on throat and breast; yellow underparts. Bright red iris. Female duller with olive-brown or olive-grey upperparts; belly and vent pale yellow. Both have white spots at tip of undertail. Juvenile male similar to female, but has brighter yellow underparts. Legge's similar to Yellow-bellied, but smaller, lacks dark sides to breast, and is found only in Sri Lanka.

LEGGE'S FLOWERPECKER

Dicaeum vincens Dicaeidae

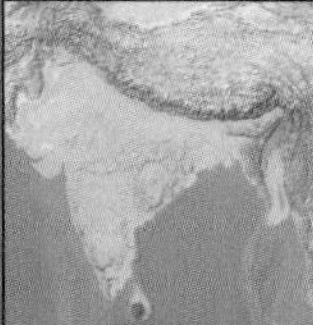

Size 10 cm

Voice Call a weak *tze...tze...tze*

Range Common endemic in Sri Lanka. Resident in wet lowlands and adjacent low hills, below 900 m

Habitat Forests; wooded gardens close to forests

Small, rounded flowerpecker similar to Yellow-bellied. Male bluish-black above with white throat, upper breast and undertail-coverts; yellow lower breast and belly, white tips to outer-tail feathers. Female duller overall; underparts similar to male; blue-grey crown, ear-coverts and nape, turning dark olive on mantle and back. Juvenile similar to female, but yellowish throat, which blends with rest of underparts. Upperparts more uniform olive-brown.

♀

PLAIN FLOWERPECKER

Dicaeum c minullum Dicaeidae

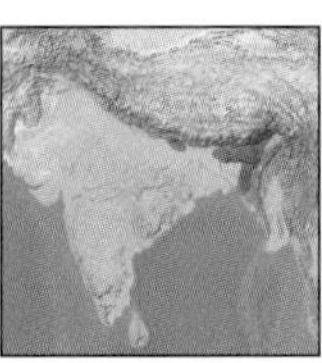

Size 8 cm

Voice Calls include sharp repeated *chik* and *pseep*, particularly in flight. Extended as song

Range Locally common breeding resident in N foothills from C Nepal east to Myanmar border, parts of Bangladesh, Andaman Islands

Habitat Forest canopy, orchards, gardens and mangroves

Tiny, olive-brown arboreal bird with short, dark, decurved bill. Pale supercilium and lores; yellowish-white underparts. Juvenile has paler bill. Southwestern race darker above and whiter below. Andamans' race greener above and yellowish on belly. Sexes similar. Feeds in pairs or small groups, mainly on *Loranthus* berries. Flies strongly and noisily from site to site over large area. Very lively. Nests high in trees.

PALE-BILLED FLOWERPECKER

Dicaeum erythrorynchos Dicaeidae

Rather plain-looking flowerpecker with olive-brown upperparts and uniform greyish-white underparts; pinkish flesh and yellow-brown, markedly downcurved beak. Sexes alike. Solitary, or two to three birds in canopy; frequents parasitic *Loranthus* and *Viscum;* flits from clump to clump; strictly arboreal, restless; territorial even when feeding.

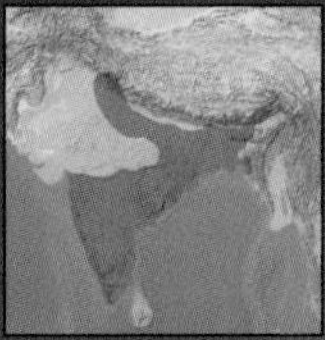

Size 8 cm

Voice Call a sharp, loud *chik...chik*

Range From E Kangra along foothills to NE India; peninsular India south of a line from W Gujarat to S Bihar

Habitat Light forests, groves

ORANGE-BELLIED FLOWERPECKER

Dicaeum trigonostigma Dicaeidae

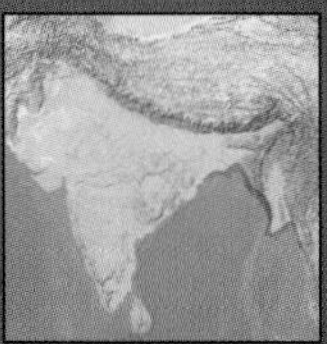

Size 9 cm

Voice Call a repeated metallic *zip*. Song a descending *tsi…si…si…si…sew*

Range Local breeding resident restricted to coastal Bangladesh and probably neighbouring parts of India

Habitat Mainly edges of forests, mangroves

♀

Male has bluish-grey head, upper back, wings and tail; darker tail; grey throat and upper breast; orange underparts from lower mantle to rump. Female overall dull olive with dull orange undertail-coverts and belly; greyish throat and breast. Feeds mainly in canopy but also close to ground. Uneven, whirring flight between feeding sites. Very active and confiding.

NILGIRI FLOWERPECKER

Dicaeum concolor Dicaeidae

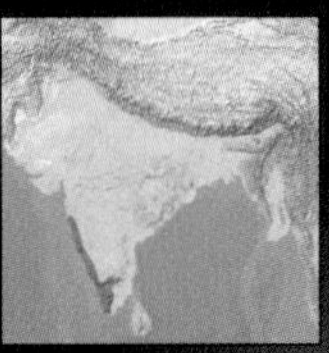

Size 9 cm

Voice Songs include very high, thin, short, trilled and repeated *tseep...tsip...tsip* and very short, more rapid, descending, trilled *tse...ee...ep*

Range Western Ghats

Habitat Edges of broadleaved forests, well-wooded areas, especially fond of mistletoe berries, like many flowerpeckers

Formerly, a subspecies of plain flowerpecker; more brown than olive with slightly thicker and less decurved bill. Tiny bird with medium-brown upperparts, pale greyish-white underparts; whitish eyebrow. Faint yellowish-buff wash on breast and belly. Distinguished from Pale-billed by dark bill and darker brown upperparts and more pronounced supercilium. Sexes alike. Like others of the group, feeds predominantly on nectar and fruits. Prefers forest canopy.

FIRE-BREASTED FLOWERPECKER

Dicaeum ignipectus Dicaeidae

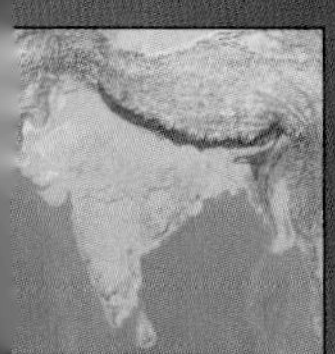

Size 7 cm

Voice Call a sharp, metallic *chip…chip* note. High-pitched, clicking song

Range The Himalayas, Kashmir to extreme E India

Habitat Forests, orchards

Male metallic blue-green-black above; buffy below with scarlet breast patch and black stripe down centre of lower breast and belly. Female olive-green above, yellowish on rump; bright buff below; flanks and sides tinged olive. Mostly solitary; arboreal and active; flits about in foliage canopy, attending to *Loranthus* clumps; may be encountered in restless, mixed hunting bands of small birds in the Himalayan forests. Nests high in trees.

SCARLET-BACKED FLOWERPECKER

Dicaeum cruentatum Dicaeidae

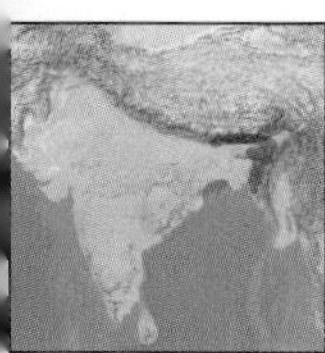

Size 7 cm

Voice Noisy. Call a penetrating *chip…chip*. Song a repeated *tissit…tissit*

Range Scarce breeding resident in N hills from E Nepal (where rare), NE India and Bangladesh

Habitat Open forests, secondary growth and orchards, wherever there is *Loranthus*

Very small flowerpecker; bright red from crown to back. Black head sides; black cheeks; glossy blue-black upperwing; short, black tail. Greyish-white underparts; darker grey flanks. Longish, slender bill. Female brownish above and buff below with red rump and black tail. Juvenile has hint of red on uppertail-coverts and red bill. Feeds on nectar, berries and insects. Usually solitary, in pairs or small parties. Noisily flies from clump to clump high in canopy. Pouch-shaped nest high up in trees.

RUBY-CHEEKED SUNBIRD

Chalcoparia singalensis Nectariniidae

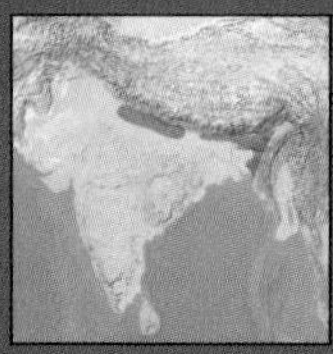

Size 11 cm

Voice Calls *chwee…eest*

Range Uttarakhand to Arunachal Pradesh; S Assam Hills

Habitat Open broadleaved evergreen forests; secondary growth

Distinctive, medium-sized sunbird with short, rather straight bill, orange throat and breast, yellow over rest of underparts. Male has iridescent emerald green upperparts; deep ruby-red lores and ear-coverts, edged below with purplish moustachial stripe. Female yellowish-olive-green above, with duller orange throat and breast and no ruby cheek; distinguished from other female sunbirds by orange breast, yellow underparts and short bill; more gregarious than other sunbirds; sometimes in small flocks when not breeding; actively forages in foliage in lower half of trees and shrubs.

PURPLE-RUMPED SUNBIRD

Leptocoma zeylonica Nectariniidae

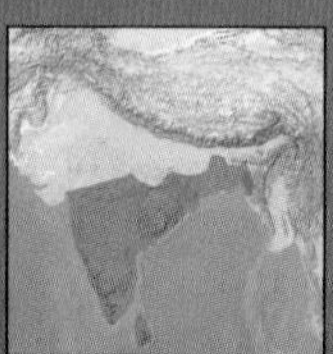

Size 10 cm

Voice Calls *tsiswee…tsiswee…*. Sharp, twittering song of breeding male, much lower in tone and volume than that of Purple Sunbird

Range Peninsular India south of a line from around Mumbai, C Madhya Pradesh, S Bihar and West Bengal

Habitat Open forests, gardens, orchards; common in towns

Male has deep chestnut-crimson back; metallic green crown and shoulder patch; metallic purple rump and throat; maroon collar below throat; yellow underparts. Female ash-brown above, with rufous in wings; whitish throat; yellow underparts. Usually in pairs; very active, flits from flower to flower; occasionally descends into flowering garden bushes.

CRIMSON-BACKED SUNBIRD

Leptocoma minima Nectariniidae

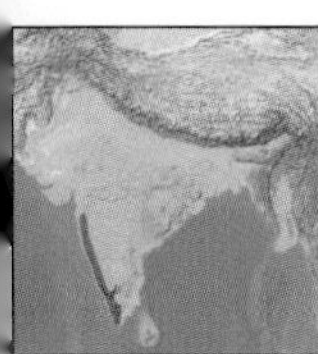

Size 8 cm

Voice Call a stereotypical *tsee... sit...see...su...tse...sit...swee...*

Range Endemic to the Western Ghats and adjacent hills

Habitat Evergreen biotope, chiefly in foothills; forests, sholas, gardens, and flowering shade trees in tea and coffee plantations

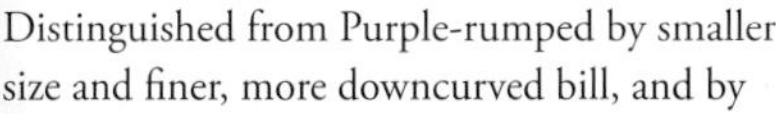

Distinguished from Purple-rumped by smaller size and finer, more downcurved bill, and by flowerpecker-like call. Male similar to Purple-rumped, has metallic green crown, purple rump and purple throat. Distinguished by broad, crimson breast-band restricted to belly, crimson sides of head and mantle, and lack of metallic green shoulder patch. Eclipse male as female, but has metallic purple rump and crimson scapulars and back. Female distinguished from other female sunbirds by combination of small size, crimson rump, olive-green upperparts and edges to wings, uniformly yellowish underparts. Juvenile male appears to be similar to eclipse male, but with duller greyish underparts.

PURPLE-THROATED SUNBIRD

Leptocoma sperata Nectariniidae

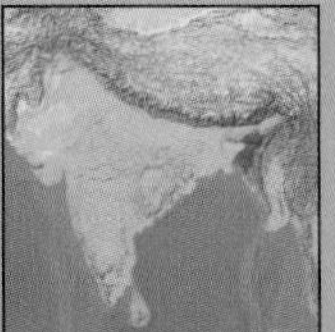

Size 10 cm

Voice Call a weak *chip...chip*

Range Very local breeding resident in Bangladesh north to plains in adjoining Indian states

Habitat Open forests, edges of forests, secondary growth and gardens

Small, fairly short-billed, dark sunbird. Male has purple throat, dark red breast and upper belly and black vent; metallic green crown and metallic blue-green-and-black above. Female greenish-olive above and dark buff below, often with reddish wash on throat. Feeds actively on nectar and insects, usually high in canopy. Solitary, or in pairs. Nest suspended from trees.

OLIVE-BACKED SUNBIRD

Cinnyris jugularis Nectariniidae

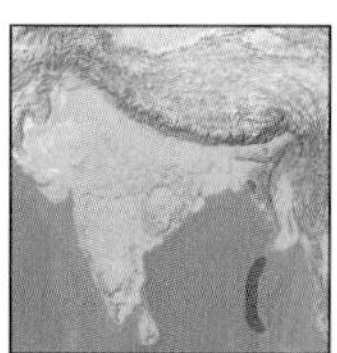

Size 11 cm

Voice Sweet call. Rapid, chattering song

Range Common breeding resident restricted to Andaman and Nicobar Islands

Habitat Forests, scrubs, gardens, mangroves

Medium-sized, olive-green sunbird. Male has metallic blue-green throat and breast which has narrow, chestnut band. Rest of underparts bright yellow. Female yellow from throat to vent. Both have dark tail. Eclipse male has dark, central throat-stripe. Some sub-specific variation on islands. Feeds, often quite low down, on nectar and insects; solitary, or in pairs. Confiding. Nest suspended from grass stems or shrubs.

klossi

PURPLE SUNBIRD

Cinnyris asiaticus Nectariniidae

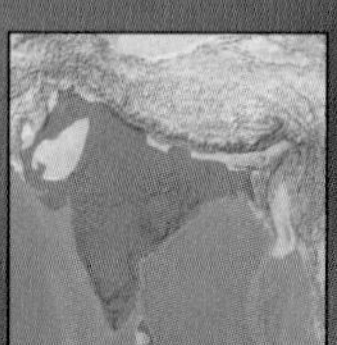

Size 10 cm

Voice Noisier than other sunbirds. Calls include loud *chweet…* notes

Range Subcontinent, south from the Himalayan foothills to about 1,500 m

Habitat Open forests, gardens, groves

Male metallic purple-blue above, and on throat and breast; dark purplish-black belly; narrow, chestnut-maroon band between breast and belly; yellow and scarlet pectoral tufts, normally hidden under wings. Female olive-brown above; pale yellow below (*zeylonica* female has whitish throat). Non-breeding male similar to female but with broad, purple-black stripe down centre of throat to belly. Solitary, or in pairs; important pollinating agent, almost always seen around flowering trees and bushes; displays amazing agility and acrobatic prowess when feeding; sometimes hunts flycatcher-style.

♀

MRS GOULD'S SUNBIRD

Aethopyga gouldiae Nectariniidae

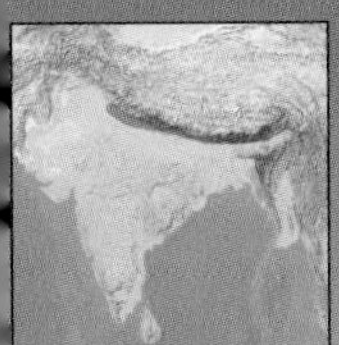

Size Male 15 cm; Female 10 cm

Voice Call a sharp *tzit...tzit*

Range The Himalayas, hills of NE India

Habitat Rhododendrons, forests, gardens, scrubs

♀

Male a strikingly-coloured sunbird with rich red mantle and back; bright yellow underparts; purplish-blue crown and throat; metallic blue tail; yellow rump. Female olive-brown with yellow belly, vent and rump-band; grey crown and throat. Mostly solitary; sometimes in groups with Green-tailed.

LOTEN'S SUNBIRD

Cinnyris lotenia Nectariniidae

Size 13 cm

Voice Call a hard *tchit...tchit.* Measured song *titti...titu chewit...chewit*

Range Fairly common endemic breeding resident to S peninsular India and Sri Lanka, south of Mumbai and S Andhra Pradesh

Habitat Open wooded country including gardens

♀

Large, dark sunbird with diagnostic, long, steeply-curved bill. Male metallic blackish-purple on head and upperparts with more black wings and tail and sooty brown belly. Maroon breast-band and yellow breast tufts. Eclipse male similar to female but with blackish stripe from chin to belly. Female dark olive-green above and pale yellow below with white tail-tips.

GREEN-TAILED SUNBIRD

Aethopyga nipalensis Nectariniidae

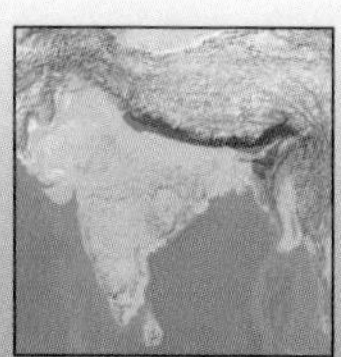

Size Male 14 cm; Female 10 cm

Voice Call a sharp *zig…zig*

Range The Himalayas

Habitat Oak and rhododendron forests, scrubs, gardens

Male has dark metallic blue-green head and nape, bordered by maroon mantle; olive-green back and wings; metallic blue-green tail (appears dark); underparts bright yellow with red-streaked breast; yellow rump not always visible. NW Himalayan race *horsfieldi* has less maroon on mantle. Female olive-green with greyish-olive throat; yellowish-olive on belly; rump slightly yellower than upperparts; pale tail-tips.

BLACK-THROATED SUNBIRD

Aethopyga saturata Nectariniidae

Very dark, mainly black, crimson and greyish-olive sunbird. Distinctive male looks mostly black, with dark, iridescent purple crown, nape, malar stripe, long tail; black throat, breast, face and wings; crimson mantle and sides of neck and throat; underparts greyish-olive. Smaller female has yellow band across back, and no yellow on plain, greyish-olive-green underparts; whitish flanks; ill-defined, pale supercilium around eye; solitary, or in pairs when breeding; normally forages in flowering shrubs, bushes and low branches of trees.

♀

Size Male 15 cm; Female 10 cm

Voice Calls *tzit…tswi…ti…ti…ti…ti*

Range Hills of E Uttarakhand to Myanmar. Moves lower in winter

Habitat Edges of dense forests, scattered bushes, secondary growth, shrubs

VIGORS'S SUNBIRD

Aethopyga siparaja vigorsii Nectariniidae

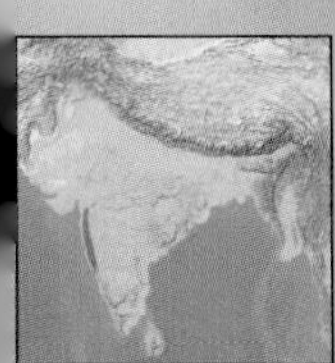

Size 11 cm

Voice Like Crimson's

Range Endemic to the Western Ghats

Habitat Evergreen forests, gardens

Originally considered a subspecies of the Crimson Sunbird with elongated central tail missing. Adult male has crimson breast with yellow streaks and maroon back. Yellow rump; olive belly. Drab-looking female sports dark olive-green back, yellowish breast with white tips to outer-tail feathers.

CRIMSON SUNBIRD

Aethopyga siparaja Nectariniidae

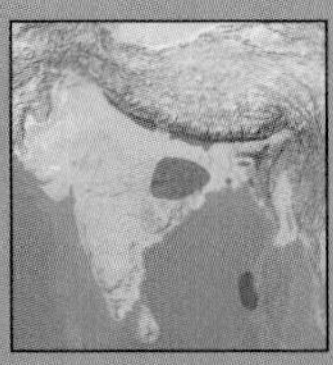

Size Male 15 cm; Female 10 cm

Voice Sharp, clicking call notes. Pleasant chirping song of breeding male (June-August)

Range The Himalayas, hills of NE India. Winters in the Himalayan plains

Habitat Forests, gardens

Male has metallic green crown and long tail; deep crimson back and neck sides; yellow rump not commonly seen; bright scarlet chin and breast; olive-yellow belly. Female has olive plumage; yellow underparts. Solitary, or in pairs; active gymnast, hanging upside-down and sideways as it probes flowers; also hovers; moves in forests, between tall bushes and canopy.

FIRE-TAILED SUNBIRD

Aethopyga ignicauda Nectariniidae

Larger sunbird with very long, red tail streamers, uppertail-coverts of male distinctive. Male has dark purple cap, face, chin, throat; bright red nape, sides of head, neck, and mantle; yellow band on back; yellow breast and belly have orange wash; paler yellow to greyish flanks, vent; brown wings. Smaller female has olive upperparts with more brown wings; olive-yellow on rump; olive underparts; orange-yellow on centre of belly; typical sunbird; seen in small parties when not breeding.

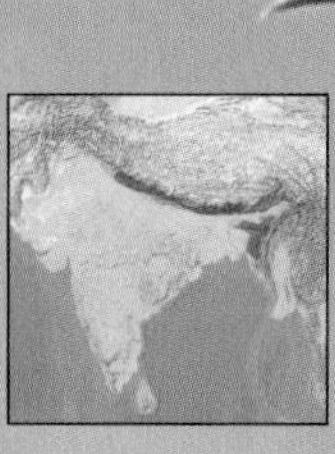

Size Male 16 cm; Female 11 cm

Voice Calls *zizi…zizizi*

Range High mountains of Himachal Pradesh to Myanmar

Habitat Summers in open fir, pine forests; dwarf rhododendrons, junipers. Winters in broadleaved or mixed forests

♀

LITTLE SPIDERHUNTER

Arachnothera longirostra Nectariniidae

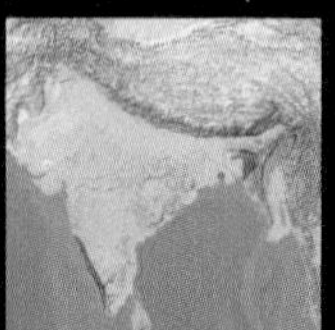

Size 14 cm

Voice Call a high-pitched *chee… chee*. Song a loud *which… which…*, sounding somewhat like tailorbird's

Range Disjunct; found in Western Ghats and Eastern Ghats, foothills from SE Nepal eastwards, E Himalayas and much of NE states

Habitat Forests, secondary growth; nullahs, sholas

Sexes alike. Olive-green above; dark tail, tipped white; greyish-white throat, merging into yellow-white below; orangish pectoral tufts. Very long, curved beak diagnostic. Usually solitary; sometimes two or three birds in vicinity; active, moving considerably between bush and canopy; favours wild banana blossoms, clings upside-down on bracts; long, curved beak especially adapted to nectar diet.

STREAKED SPIDERHUNTER

Arachnothera magna Nectariniidae

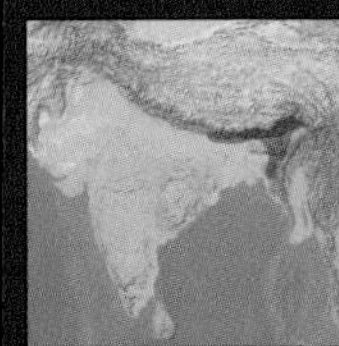

Size 18 cm

Voice Calls include harsh chirruping; short *chik* notes

Range E Nepal to Arunachal Pradesh, Bangladesh and Assam

Habitat Wild bananas and dense undergrowth in moist deciduous and evergreen forests; secondary forests

Fairly unmistakable spiderhunter. Distinguished from Little by large size, exceptionally long bill, and streaking; dusky olive above with fine, dark streaking on face and head, broader streaking on mantle; pale, diffused eye-ring; yellowish-white underparts with bold, dark streaking, yellower vent; prominent sturdy pinkish-orange legs. Solitary, or in pairs; sometimes in mixed-species hunting flocks, moving constantly and rapidly through upper storeys of forests.

HOUSE SPARROW

Passer domesticus Passeridae

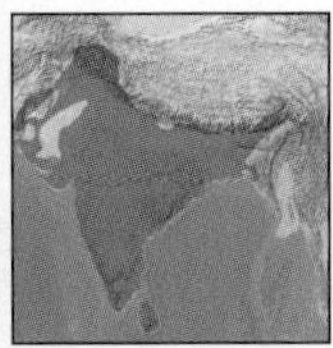

Size 15 cm

Voice Noisy; medley of chirping notes; richer notes of breeding male; double- and triple-brooded

Range Subcontinent, to about 4,000 m in the Himalayas

Habitat Habitation, cultivation

Male has grey crown and rump; chestnut sides of neck and nape; black streaks on chestnut-rufous back; black chin, centre of throat and breast; white ear-coverts. Female dull grey-brown above, streaked darker; dull whitish-brown below. Seen in small parties to large gatherings; mostly commensal on human habitation, feeds and nests in and around habitation, including most crowded localities; also feeds in cultivation; hundreds roost together.

SPANISH SPARROW

Passer hispaniolensis Passeridae

Breeding male has deep chestnut crown and nape; white cheeks; white supercilium; black eye-stripe; boldly black-streaked back and whitish-chestnut wings; black spots extending to belly. Colours fade in non-breeding season and bill turns yellow. Female similar to House but with marked supercilium and lightly streaked underparts. Feeds on seeds in large flocks, often mixing with House.

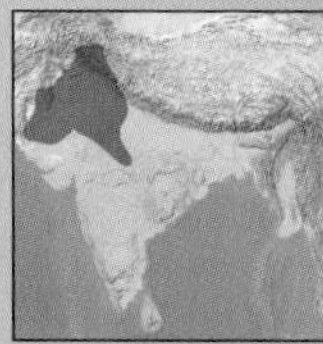

Size 16 cm

Voice Noisy. Call a more metallic chirping than House's

Range Locally common but erratic winter visitor to plains of Pakistan and N India mainly east to Haryana and south to Rajasthan. Vagrant to Uttar Pradesh and Nepal

Habitat Arable cultivation, semi-desert and reed beds

non-breeding

SIND SPARROW

Passer pyrrhonotus Passeridae

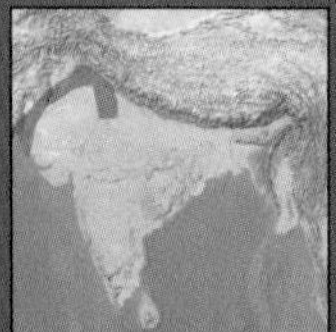

Size 12 cm

Voice Noisy. Call a distinct, rocking *cheepa…cheepa* with periodic *tsweep* note

Range Local breeding near endemic restricted range species in Indus Valley extending into Indian Punjab and recently colonising Haryana via canal systems

Habitat Restricted to babuls and other rivers, canals and lakeside trees, nearby grass and reed beds

Small sparrow with pale grey crown and nape; sides of head and crown deep chestnut-red; whitish cheeks; chestnut upperparts including rump and mantle; back and scapulars heavily streaked black. Female similar to House but with bolder supercilium, grey cheeks, buff underparts and lesser wing-coverts. Roosts in thickets, scrubs or tamarisks.

RUSSET SPARROW

Passer rutilans Passeridae

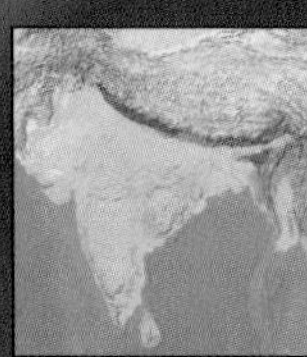

Size 15 cm

Voice Chirping notes *swee*...; Indian Robin-like call

Range The Himalayas; NE India; breeds 1,200-2,600 m, higher to about 4,000 m in NE India; descends in winter

Habitat Cultivation, edges of forests, mountain habitation

Male has rufous-chestnut upperparts streaked black on back; whitish wing-bars; black chin and centre of throat, bordered with dull yellow. Female brown above, streaked darker; pale supercilium and wing-bars; dull ash-yellow below. Gregarious mountain bird; mostly feeds on ground, picking seeds; may associate with other finches; often perches on dry branches and overhead wires.

♀

EURASIAN TREE SPARROW

Passer montanus Passeridae

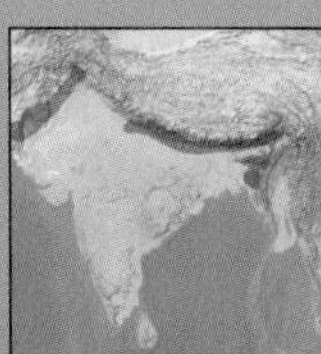

Size 14 cm

Voice Call a *chip...chip; tet...et... et... tsveet*

Range Uttarakhand east to Myanmar; S Assam Hills

Habitat Cities, towns or habitation; cultivation; village groves; orchards

Fairly distinctive sparrow; distinguished from all other *Passer* species by prominent black spots on white ear-coverts, white collar between nape and mantle, cinnamon-chestnut crown; black lores and small throat patch; darkly streaked, buff-brown upperparts; warm rufous-brown wing panel; two well-defined wing-bars; female slightly paler, with smaller throat and ear-covert patches; buff-washed flanks; racial variations; gregarious.

ROCK SPARROW

Petronia petronia Passeridae

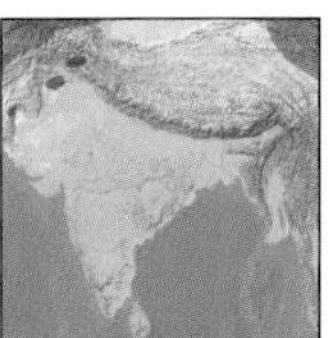

Size 17 cm

Voice Calls include nasal *waip* or *uee…*, a *kriep…*, and metallic *zveeh…vu*. Song a drawn-out, sibilant *vee…viep*

Range Local winter visitor; fairly common in the Gilgit main valley. Vagrant to Gujarat

Habitat Dry stony ground in mountain regions, especially near cliffs

Plumpish sparrow with short tail, and distinctly patterned head. Buffy-white forehead and crown; broad, whitish supercilium; dark brown lateral crown-stripe and eye-stripe; pale central crown-stripe; buffish-white-striped mantle; streaked breast and flanks; yellow throat patch; white-tipped tail and patch at base of primaries obvious in flight. Juvenile similar to adult, but has more brown upperparts and lacks throat patch.

CHESTNUT-SHOULDERED PETRONIA

Gymnoris xanthocollis Passeridae

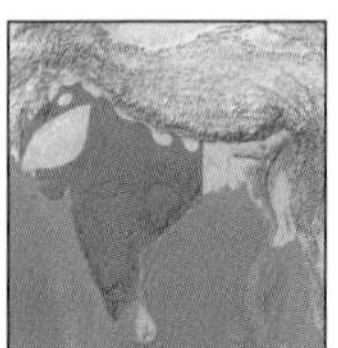

Size 14 cm

Voice Noisy. Calls include *cheellup* and *cheep*. Song a rather high *cheep…cheep*

Range Locally common resident and local migrant throughout most of Indian plains and hills except extreme NW and NE India. Summer visitor to Pakistan. Vagrant to Sri Lanka; unknown in Bangladesh

Habitat Open woodlands, forests and thorn-scrub, often near cultivation

Uniformly grey bird with bold chestnut shoulder patches. Prominent yellow-patch on chin and throat; broad, white tips to median coverts; narrower white tips on greater coverts. Underparts pale buff-grey. Female similar with duller throat patch. Breeding male has yellow bill, black in non-breeding male. Short, notched tail. Long, slender bill. Feeds on invertebrates, leaves and nectar. Difficult to spot in foliage.

♀

WHITE-WINGED SNOWFINCH

Montifringilla nivalis Passeridae

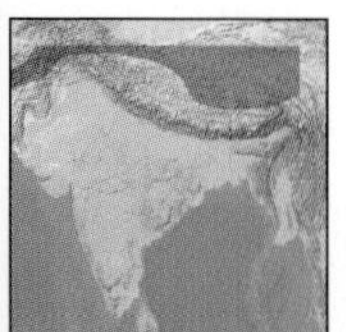

Size 17 cm

Voice Creaky calls. Chattering song, trills

Range Local winter visitor; fairly common in the Gilgit main valley

Habitat Dry stony ground in mountain regions, especially near cliffs

Large, rotund finch with snowy-white underparts and slaty-grey head. Rich brown mantle, scapulars and upper back with pale brown edges to feathers; lower back, rump and uppertail-coverts sooty grey, edged black; long tail with black central feathers and white outer feathers tipped black. Black wings with large, white wing panels, and white-edged black tail seen in flight. Breeding male has more black bill and black bib. Sexes alike. In pairs, or small flocks in breeding and very large flocks outside.

TIBETAN SNOWFINCH

Montifringilla adamsi Passeridae

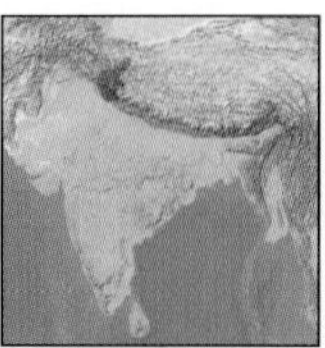

Size 17 cm

Voice Calls include hard *pink... pink* and soft mewing

Range Breeding resident in N Himalayas at higher altitudes above 3,600 m

Habitat High-altitude scrubs, meadows, rocky bushy slopes, hillsides

Sexes alike. Dull grey-brown above with some streaking on back (less pronounced in juvenile and fresh plumage); blackish wings with white-panel in wing-coverts; male has greyish-black bib (not usually seen in female); breeding male has black bill; in flight, shows obvious white wing patch; white tail with black central feathers and narrow, black terminal band. Gregarious and often seen in large flocks or around human habitation. Runs on ground like a lark. Swift, undulating flight. Courtship flight particularly impressive.

WHITE-RUMPED SNOWFINCH

Onychostruthus taczanowskii Passeridae

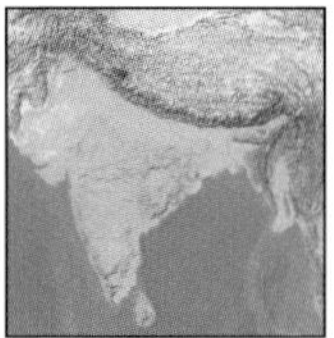

Size 17 cm

Voice Simple, weak song of clipped notes, asthmatic *wheezes* and more pleasant whistles

Range Winter visitor; N Himalayas in Ladakh, N Sikkim and NW Nepal and N India

Habitat Stony plateaux in Tibetan steppe country

Sexes alike. Forehead and supercilium to nape and hindneck whitish-buff; grey crown and nape; black lores become thin, dark eye-stripe behind eye. Pale greyish upperparts, streaked mantle and scapulars; white throat; white on sides of tail and diffused white-panel at base of secondaries and inner primaries. Pale stout. Yellow bill darkly tipped. White rump, conspicuous in flight. Juvenile warmer brown on mantle and wings with buffish breast.

RUFOUS-NECKED SNOWFINCH

Pyrgilauda ruficollis Passeridae

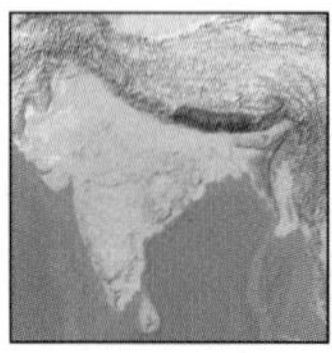

Size 15 cm

Voice Song an erratic repetition of simple sparrow-like notes, *dishu…tchelu…tischu…delu*

Range N Himalayas in N Nepal, N Sikkim and Darjeeling, West Bengal

Habitat Barren, stony Tibetan steppe and grassy plateaux

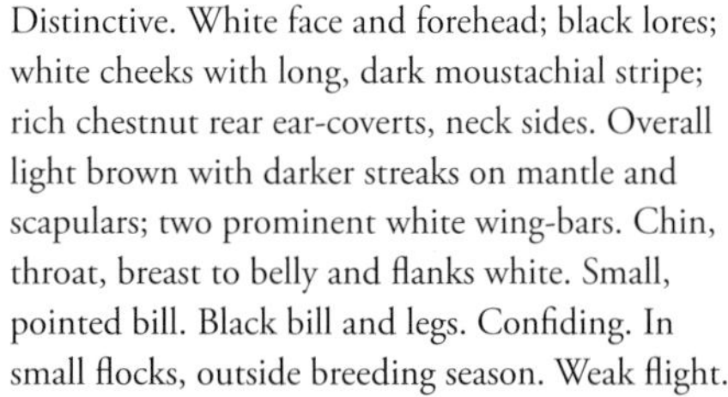

Distinctive. White face and forehead; black lores; white cheeks with long, dark moustachial stripe; rich chestnut rear ear-coverts, neck sides. Overall light brown with darker streaks on mantle and scapulars; two prominent white wing-bars. Chin, throat, breast to belly and flanks white. Small, pointed bill. Black bill and legs. Confiding. In small flocks, outside breeding season. Weak flight.

BLANFORD'S SNOWFINCH

Pyrgilauda blanfordi Passeridae

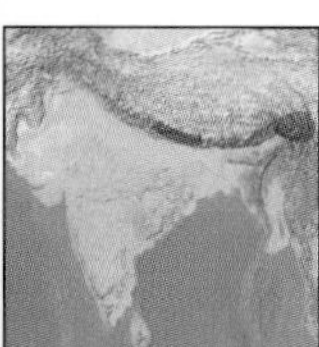

Size 15 cm

Voice Poorly described; flocks give rapid, twittering calls on ground and in flight

Range Tibetan steppe country

Habitat Winter visitor to Pakistan, N Nepal, N Sikkim, near Darjeeling, West Bengal and Ladakh

Sexes alike. Whitish forehead to forecrown; black spur from base of bill to forecrown; black lores; thin eye-stripe across ear-coverts; pale brown supercilium; white cheeks and ear-coverts. Light brown mantle, back and scapulars. Chin, upper throat black; rest of underparts creamy-white. Brown central tail feathers; outer feathers blotched grey with black tips. Dark, conical bill. Juvenile duller with no head pattern. Silent and confiding. Very sparrow-like behaviour. Plainer than juvenile Rufous-necked and has white cheeks.

BLACK-BREASTED WEAVER

Ploceus benghalensis Ploceidae

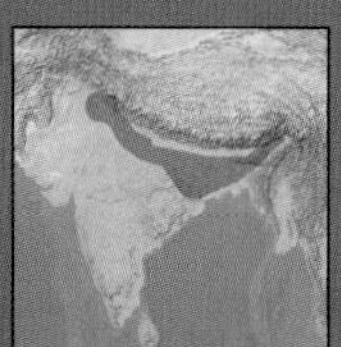

Size 15 cm

Voice Calls *chit...chit.* Song a quiet, repeated *tsik...tsik...tsik*

Range Plains from Punjab to Arunachal Pradesh

Habitat Marshes; reed beds; irrigated fields

Mainly yellow, black, brown and whitish weaver, distinguished from other weavers by pale blue-grey bill. Breeding male has bright yellow crown and broad, black breast-band; ear-coverts, throat may be whitish or brownish, irrespective of region; whitish or pale underparts with weak streaking on flanks; upperparts streaked brown. Non-breeding male has black cap, yellow supercilium, throat, under-eye crescent; black eye-stripe and malar stripe; sometimes broken breast-band; female, juvenile somewhat similar; gregarious even when breeding; colonial nester.

juvenile

BAYA WEAVER

Ploceus philippinus Ploceidae

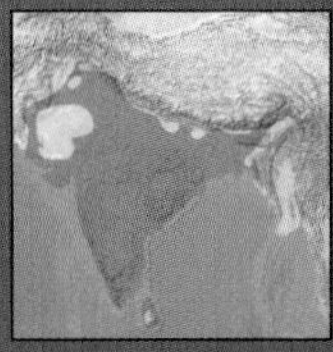

Size 15 cm

Voice Chirping and high-pitched wheezy notes of breeding male. Very noisy at nesting colony (monsoons)

Range Most of India upto about 1,000 m in outer Himalayas; absent in Kashmir

Habitat Open country, tree- and palm-dotted cultivation

Breeding male has bright yellow crown; dark brown above streaked yellow; dark brown ear-coverts and throat; yellow breast. Female buffy-yellow above streaked darker; pale supercilium and throat, turning buffy-yellow on breast, streaked on sides. Non-breeding male has bolder streaking than female; male of eastern race *burmanicus* has yellow restricted to crown. Gregarious; one of the most familiar and common birds of India, best known for its nest; keeps to cultivated areas, interspersed with trees; feeds on ground and in standing crops.

STREAKED WEAVER

Ploceus manyar Ploceidae

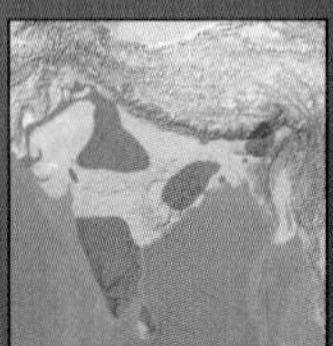

Size 15 cm

Voice Calls include high-pitched chirping, wheezy notes and chatter, much like Baya's

Range Most of India, south of the Himalayas; absent in parts of Rajasthan and NW regions

Habitat Reed beds, tall grass in well-watered areas, marshes

Male has yellow crown; blackish head sides; fulvous streaks on dark brown back; heavily streaked lower throat and breast. Female and non-breeding male have streaks above; yellow stripe over eye continues to behind ear-coverts; very pale below, boldly streaked on throat and breast. Gregarious; prefers tall grass and reed beds in well-watered areas; often nests close to other weavers. Eastern race *peguensis* darker and much more rufous above.

burmanicus ♂

♀ burmanicus

philippinus

FINN'S WEAVER

Ploceus megarhynchus Ploceidae

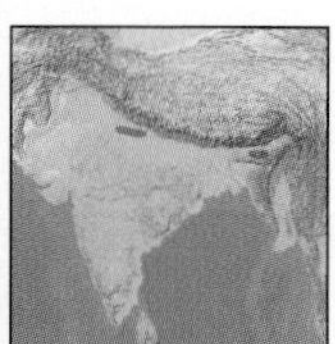

Size 17 cm

Voice Call a harsh *twit...twit*

Range Endemic to India and Nepal

Habitat Similar to Baya's

Unlike other weavers, breeding male has bright yellow head with dark brown ear-coverts, golden-yellow underparts, yellow rump and uppertail-coverts. Streaked mantle and back; dark patches on breast. Yellow in breeding female and first-year male paler; mantle has dark streaking. No yellow on non-breeding adult and immature, but plumage similar to Baya's. Roosts in tall grass and sugarcane stands.

♀

GREEN AVADAVAT

Amandava formosa Estrildidae

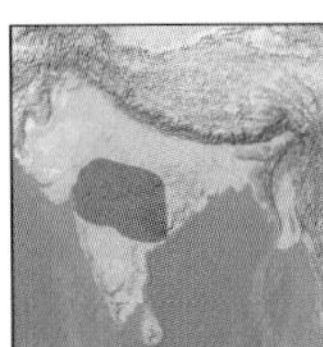

Size 10 cm

Voice Call a quiet *swee…swee*

Range Globally threatened; endemic and rare breeding resident known only from a few sites in NC peninsular India, from Rajasthan east to Odisha, and south to Andhra Pradesh. Scattered records from elsewhere, probably relate to escaped or released cage birds

Habitat Grass, scrubs and sugarcane often near water

Tiny, green weaver with distinct striped flanks. Upperparts green, with black tail; yellow underparts, paler throat. Female has more brown in upperparts. Red bill. Feeds on small seeds or invertebrates on ground. Small flocks. Nests in thick cover.

RED AVADAVAT

Amandava amandava Estrildidae

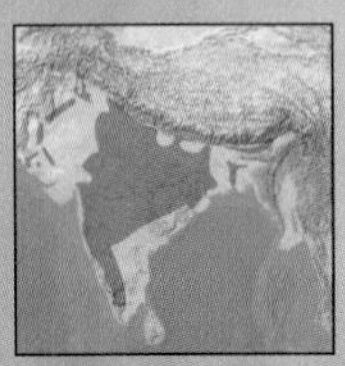

Size 10 cm

Voice Calls include shrill and high-pitched notes, also uttered in flight

Range Subcontinent, south of the Himalayan foothills

Habitat Tall grass, reeds, sugarcane, scrubs, gardens

Breeding male crimson and brown, spotted white on wings and flanks; white-tipped tail. Female brown above, spotted on wings; crimson rump; dull white throat; buffy-grey breast, yellow brown below. Non-breeding male similar to female, but has greyer throat; upper breast distinctive. In small flocks, often with other weavers; partial to tall grass and scrubs, preferably around well-watered areas; active and vibrant, rather confiding; huge numbers captured for bird markets.

INDIAN SILVERBILL

Euodice malabarica Estrildidae

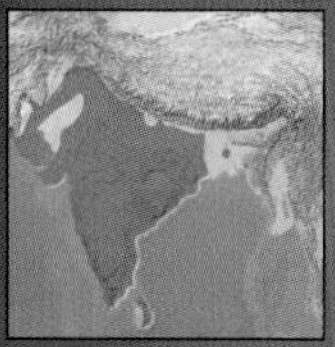

Size 10 cm

Voice Calls include faint *tee… tee…* notes; also, whistling note sometimes

Range Subcontinent to about 1,500 m in the Himalayas, chiefly the outer ranges

Habitat Prefers dry areas; cultivation, scrub and grass; sometimes light, open forests

Overall rather 'dull' bird, both in colour and demeanour. Sexes alike. Dull-brown above with white rump; very dark, almost black wings; pointed tail; pale buffy-white below with some brown on flanks; thick, grey-blue or slaty beak striking. Gregarious; mostly keeps to scrubs in open country; feeds on ground and on standing crops, especially millet.

SCALY-BREASTED MUNIA

Lonchura punctulata Estrildidae

Size 10 cm

Voice Common call a double-noted *ki…tee…ki…tee*

Range Most of India, to about 1,500 m in parts of the Himalayas; absent in much of Punjab, NW regions and W Rajasthan

Habitat Open scrub, cultivation, especially where interspersed with trees; gardens

Chocolate-brown upperparts; olive-yellow, pointed tail; white bars on rump; chestnut sides of face, chin and throat. Silvery-white underparts, thickly speckled with very dark brown on breast, flanks and part of belly (speckles may be absent during winter and much of summer). Sexes alike. Sociable, moves in flocks of six to several dozen birds, often with other munias and weavers; feeds on ground and low bushes, rests in trees.

WHITE-RUMPED MUNIA

Lonchura striata Estrildidae

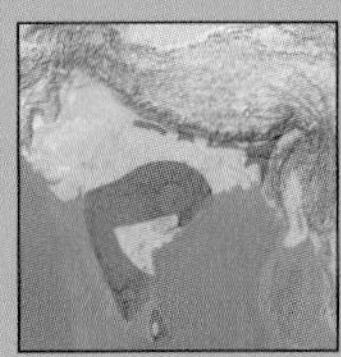

Size 10 cm

Voice Call a weak up and down twittering

Range Foothills of Uttarakhand to Arunachal Pradesh; Bangladesh

Habitat Light wooded areas, scrubs, fields, grasslands

Slim, dark munia with short, thick, conical beak; dark brown head, throat, upper breast, mantle, wings, tail, vent, with shaft streaking; white-patch on lower back; white belly; short, wedge-shaped tail. *Acuticauda* of the Himalayan foothills of N India, Nepal, Bhutan and NE subcontinent has more rufous brown on face, neck, breast. In small family parties when breeding; otherwise, larger flocks; communal rooster; usually associated with other munias and weavers. Forages on ground or on stalks and stems of seed-bearing grass and crops.

BLACK-THROATED MUNIA

Lonchura kelaarti Estrildidae

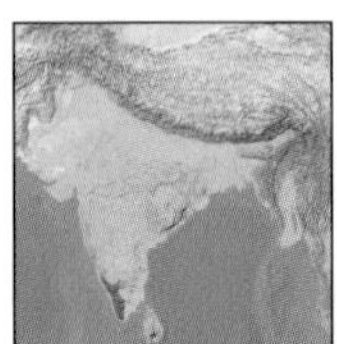

Size 12 cm

Voice Calls include *tay* and *chirp*

Range Hills of SW and E India

Habitat Forest clearings; scrub lands

Brown-black head, more brownish on crown, nape and mantle; brown-black rump spotted or finely barred white; blackish face, throat and centre of breast; lower breast, belly, flanks creamy-white spotted with deep brown. Short, stout bill with dark upper mandible and paler lower mandible with dark tip; long, black tail. Gregarious. Feeds mainly on seeds. Sexes alike.

BLACK-HEADED MUNIA

Lonchura malacca Estrildidae

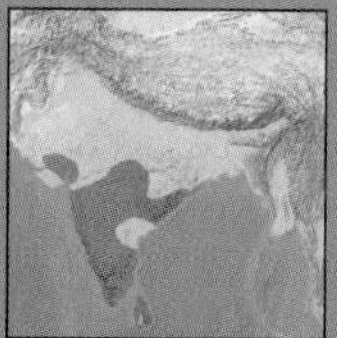

Size 10 cm

Voice Call a faint *pee…pee…*

Range Foothills; the Terai from SE Punjab eastwards; most of NE India, N Odisha; peninsular India south from Mumbai to S Madhya Pradesh

Habitat Reed beds, paddy, grass and scrubs

Male has black head, throat, breast, centre of belly and thighs; rufous-chestnut back, deeper chestnut on rump; white upper belly and sides of underbody. Female similar to male, but has deep brown undertail-coverts. Gregarious, except when breeding; prefers reed beds and cultivation, especially where flooded; during breeding season (monsoons), often seen along with Streaked; feeds on ground.

CHESTNUT MUNIA

Lonchura (malacca) atricapilla Estrildidae

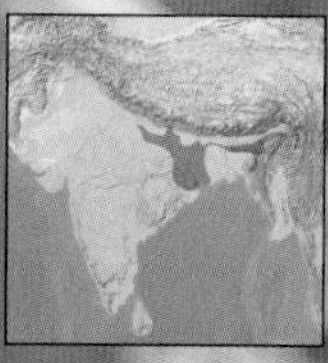

Size 10 cm

Voice Call a soft *pee…pee*. Some racial variations

Range Locally common breeding resident in hills and plains from Uttarakhand east to NE India and Bangladesh. Also in N, W and S peninsula and Sri Lanka. Absent from Pakistan and much of NW India. Localised pockets probably originate from captive birds

Habitat Reed beds, paddy, tall grass and grassy scrubs

Small munia with black head, nape, crown, throat and upper breast. Striking silvery-blue bill. Chestnut upperparts; rusty-orange rump and tail. Sexes alike. Feeds actively in flocks, often mixed with other seed-eaters, on seeds and invertebrates on ground and plants. Often very confiding. Nests in reeds.

ALPINE ACCENTOR

Prunella collaris Prunellidae

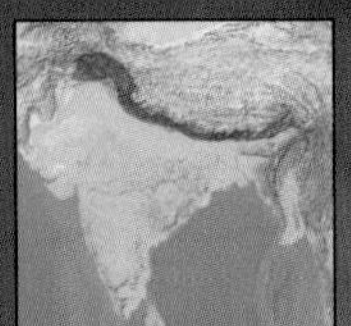

Size 17 cm

Voice Calls *chirrirrip*. Mellow song

Range High mountains from Pakistan to Arunachal Pradesh

Habitat High-altitude scree, moraine; alpine pastures. Mountain villages in winter

Largest accentor with unmarked grey head, nape, upper mantle, sides of neck and throat, breast, centre of belly; white throat patch with fine, black barring; thin, pale supercilium mark; buff and brown streaked mantle; black wing-covert panel with white tips; diffused rufous-chestnut streaking on flanks, wings; rufous-chestnut uppertail-coverts; darkly streaked undertail-coverts; forages on ground on rocky or grassy slopes.

ALTAI ACCENTOR

Prunella himalayana Prunellidae

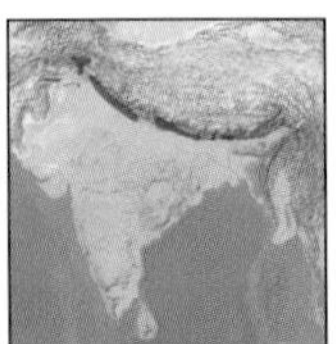

Size 16 cm

Voice Calls *tee…tee*

Range Winter visitor. The Himalayas

Habitat Grassy slopes

Superficially resembles House Sparrow with its back streaked brown, but adult has grey head and red-brown spotting on underparts. Has an insectivore's finely pointed bill. Sexes similar, though male may be contrasted in appearance. Juvenile has more brown head and underparts.

ROBIN ACCENTOR

Prunella rubeculoides Prunellidae

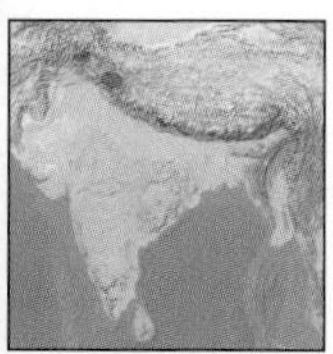

Size 17 cm

Voice Call a sharp trilling note; also, *tszi…tszi…* . Short, chirping song

Range Higher reaches of the Himalayas; breeds 3,200-5,300 m; descends in winter to about 2,000 m, rarely below 1,500 m

Habitat Tibetan facies; damp grass, scrubs; high-altitude habitation

Sexes alike. Pale brown above, streaked darker on back; grey head and throat; two whitish wing-bars; rufous breast and creamy-white belly; streaks on flanks. Flocks in winter, occasionally, along with other accentors, pipits and sparrows; rather tame and confiding around high-altitude habitation; hops on ground; flies into bushes if intruded upon beyond a point.

BROWN ACCENTOR

Prunella fulvescens Prunellidae

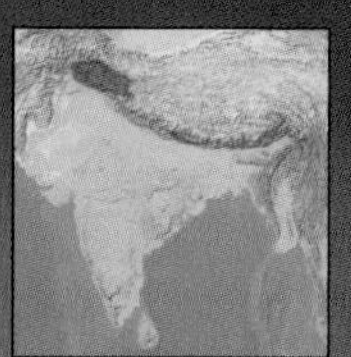

Size 15 cm

Voice Call a thin *zit…zit…zit*; also, thin rattle

Range Locally common breeding resident at or above treeline in N mountains from E Pakistan to Nepal. Moves lower in winter

Habitat Montane scrubs. Around fallow and villages in winter

Small, pale brown-and-buff accentor with prominent white supercilium and black cheeks. Crown and upperparts streaked light brown. Rich buff from chin to vent, usually completely unstreaked. Sexes alike. Feeds on ground in pairs or small groups on invertebrates and seeds. Unobtrusive. Nests on or near ground.

RUFOUS-BREASTED ACCENTOR

Prunella strophiata Prunellidae

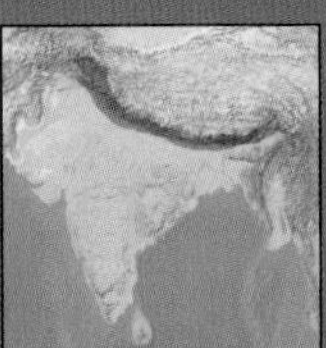

Size 15 cm

Voice Calls include sharp, trilling notes; also, *twitt...twitt...* . Short, chirping song

Range The Himalayas; breeds between 2,700-5,000 m; descends to about 1,200 m in summer, rarely below 600 m

Habitat Montane scrub, high-altitude habitation; descends lower in winter

Sexes alike. Small chestnut-and-brown accentor; heavily streaked throat; brown-streaked crown and upperparts; orange supercilium with white in front of eyes and buffy-white moustache.

BLACK-THROATED ACCENTOR

Prunella atrogularis Prunellidae

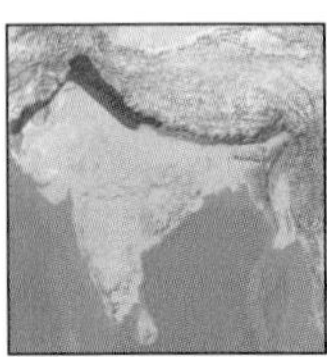

Size 15 cm

Voice Call a soft *trrrt*

Range Locally common winter visitor to foothills of N mountains from E Pakistan to W Nepal

Habitat Bushes, dry scrub and orchards

Small, streaked accentor with black throat, cheeks and crown sides. Similar to Brown but much brighter and more heavily streaked above and brighter orange-buff below with some streaking. Supercilium and moustache orange-buff. Black throat, sometimes obscured. Sexes alike. Confiding but unobtrusive, although will perch on bush-tops. Feeds on ground, on invertebrates and seeds, in loose groups, often with other passerines.

MAROON-BACKED ACCENTOR

Prunella immaculata Prunellidae

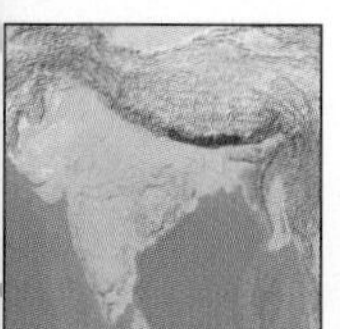

Size 15 cm

Voice Calls *zeh...dzit*

Range Scarce; presumed breeding resident in N mountains from C Nepal east to Arunachal Pradesh. Moves lower in winter

Habitat Ground beneath rhododendrons, coniferous forest undergrowth, edges of forests, nearby cultivation

Small, dark, uniquely-coloured accentor with white iris. Grey head, breast and wing panel with white scaling on crown. Maroon-brown upperparts and belly, darker on wings and tail. Pale legs. Sexes alike. Juvenile heavily streaked. Feeds on invertebrates and seeds on ground. Difficult to observe. Usually in small parties. Nest not known.

FOREST WAGTAIL

Dendronanthus indicus Motacillidae

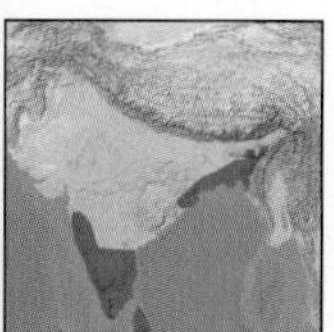

Size 17 cm

Voice Calls *pink; zi...fi zi...fi or zi...chu zi...chu*

Range C Nepal to entire NE India

Habitat Paths, clearings in forests

Distinctive wagtail with relatively short tail; olive or grey-brown upperparts; whitish throat, underparts; two broad, black 'half-necklace' breast-bands; white supercilium, patch below ear-coverts. Broad, white median coverts, barred greater wing-coverts; white-patches on primaries, secondaries; white-edged grey-brown tail; pale pinkish legs. Solitary, or in pairs when breeding; wags tail, hindquarters from side to side, rather than up and down like other wagtails. Walks, and runs along openings, paths in forests; also walks along horizontal branches.

CITRINE WAGTAIL

Motacilla citreola Motacillidae

Size 17 cm

Voice Ordinary call note a wheezy *tzzeep*

Range Winter visitor over most of India

Habitat Marshes, wet cultivation, edges of jheels

♀

Grey back; diagnostic yellow head, sides of face, complete underbody; white in dark wings. The race *calcarata* has deep black back and rump; yellow of head may be paler in female; plumage of races often confusing. Sociable, often with other wagtails; shows marked preference for damp areas; sometimes moves on floating vegetation on pond surfaces; either walks cautiously or makes short dashes.

♂ *calcarata*

♂ *calcarata*

♂ *citreola*

YELLOW WAGTAIL

Motacilla flava Motacillidae

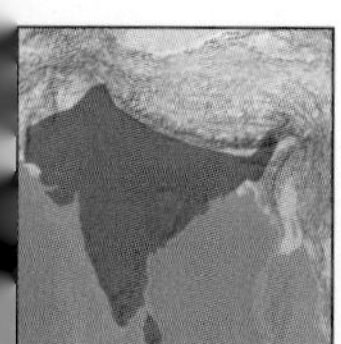

Size 17 cm

Voice Calls include *swee…ip; zhrreep*

Range Lowlands throughout the region. Said to be absent in Bhutan

Habitat Marshy pastures; flooded fields; edges of waterbodies

Very variable, mainly greenish-and-yellow wagtail; many races and hybrids occur; only wagtail with olive-green or brownish mantle, back, and rump (brownish-backed Forest Wagtail has unmistakable wing, breast pattern). Relatively shorter tail; yellow underparts, vent (Citrine has white vent); two wing-bars. Breeding male has greenish-yellow to dark grey crown and ear-coverts. Non-breeding and female brownish with straight, pale supercilium (Citrine has curved); whitish or yellow-washed underparts; very gregarious in winter; less undulating wagtail flight.

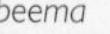

beema

lutea

thunbergi

taivana

feldegg

superciliaris

WHITE WAGTAIL

Motacilla alba Motacillidae

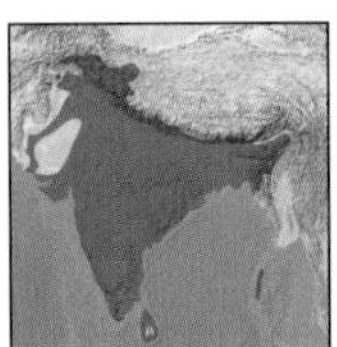

Size 18 cm

Voice Calls include *chee…cheep; cheesik*

Range Throughout the region

Habitat Summers in upland meadows or open areas near streams. Winters in wet fields; often near water

alba

Very variable, black, white and/or grey wagtail; for purposes of ID, races characterised as black-backed or grey-backed; all the several races of White have white foreheads. Breeding bird has extensive black on throat and/or breast. Non-breeding adult generally has white throat; variable wing pattern. Solitary, or in pairs when breeding; sometimes in loose, scattered flocks; communal rooster. Forages on ground; sits prominently on exposed perches; calls while perched, in flight, or on ground.

baicalensis

alboides

personata

dukhunensis

ocularis

leucopsis

WHITE-BROWED WAGTAIL

Motacilla maderaspatensis Motacillidae

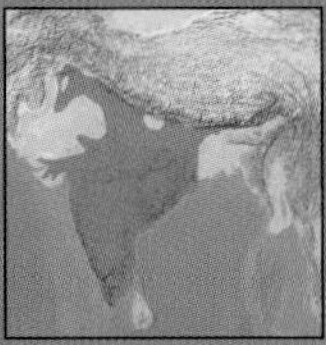

Size 21 cm

Voice Call a sharp *tzizit* or *cheezit*.... Pleasant whistling song of breeding male

Range Most of India; south of the Himalayan foothills to about 1,200 m; only resident wagtail in the Indian plains, breeding upto 2,000 m in peninsula mountains

Habitat Rocky streams, rivers, ponds, tanks; may enter wet cultivation

Black above; prominent white supercilium and large wing-band; black throat and breast; white below. Female usually more brown, male black. Mostly in pairs, though small parties may feed together in winter; bird of flowing waters, especially fond of rock-strewn rivers. Feeds at edges of water, frequently wags tail; also rides on ferry boats plying rivers.

GREY WAGTAIL

Motacilla cinerea Motacillidae

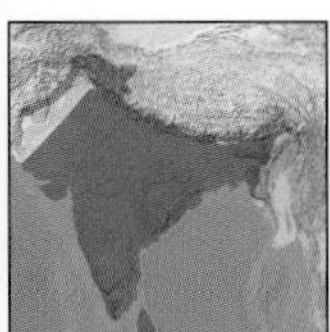

Size 19 cm

Voice Call a sharp *tzitsi*..., uttered on the wing. Pleasant song and display flight of breeding male

Range Breeds in the Himalayas, from N Balochistan east to Nepal, 1,200-4,300 m; winters from foothills south throughout India

Habitat Rocky mountain streams in summer. Open areas, forest clearings, watersides in winter

breeding

Breeding male grey above with white supercilium; brownish wings with yellow-white band; yellow-green at base of tail; blackish tail with white outer-tail feathers; black throat and white malar stripe; yellow below. Wintering male and female have whitish throat (sometimes mottled black in breeding female); paler yellow below. Mostly solitary, or in pairs; typical wagtail, feeds on ground, incessantly wags tail; settles on house roofs and overhead wires.

BLYTH'S PIPIT

Anthus godlewskii Motacillidae

Size 17 cm

Voice Calls include buzzing *spzeeu* and *chup...chup*

Range Probably widespread and fairly common winter visitor to most of Indian plains, but identification problems make status uncertain. Very rare in Pakistan and Sri Lanka; rare in Bangladesh and Nepal

Habitat Short, open grasslands, cultivation, fallow and marshes; similar to Paddyfield's, wetter than Tawny and drier than Richard's, although all four can occur together

Similar to Richard's, but has shorter bill, tail, legs and hind claws; also, more buff below. Adult has squared centres to median coverts. Penultimate outer-tail feathers have white edges. Powerful flight. Feeds in loose groups, on ground, on insects and seeds. Can be rather furtive.

PADDYFIELD PIPIT

Anthus rufulus Motacillidae

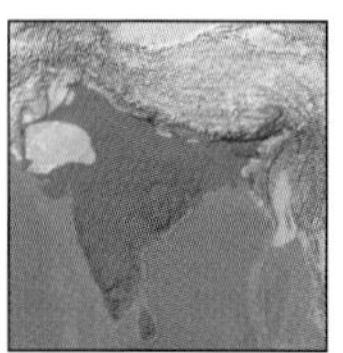

Size 15 cm

Voice Call a thin *tsip, tseep* and *tsip...tseep...* . Trilling song of breeding male

Range Upto about 2,000 m in outer Himalayas, south throughout India

Habitat Grasslands, marshy ground, cultivation

Sexes alike. Fulvous-brown above with dark brown central feathers, giving a distinctive appearance; dark brown tail with white outer-tail feathers, easily seen in flight; dull fulvous below, streaked dark brown on sides of throat, neck and entire breast. In pairs, or several scattered on ground; runs in short spurts; when disturbed, utters feeble note as it takes off; singing male perches on grass tufts and small bushes.

TAWNY PIPIT

Anthus campestris Motacillidae

Size 16 cm

Voice Calls *tseep* or *chulp*

Range Common winter visitor mainly to Pakistan and NW India but scattered records throughout lowlands. Rare in Nepal and Bangladesh

Habitat Dry open country including semi-desert, fallow and plough

Plain, medium-sized sandy pipit with dark lores. Adult plain sandy-brown above with streaking only on crown and breast sides. Juvenile streaked above and spotted on breast and easily confused with other streaked pipits. Long, pale supercilium and indistinct moustache. Obvious white-edged, black median coverts. Outer-tail feathers buff. Hind claws short. Horizontal wagtail-like carriage.

LONG-BILLED PIPIT

Anthus similis Motacillidae

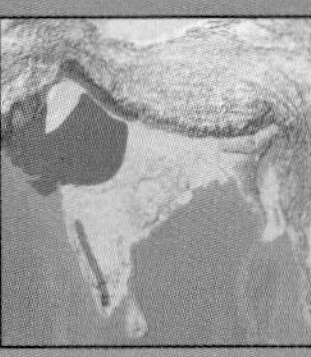

Size 20 cm

Voice Call a deep *chup*. Rather slow song

Range Common breeding resident and summer visitor in N hills from W Pakistan east to W Nepal

Habitat Breeds in dry, rocky, grassy uplands. Winters in dry grasslands, open scrub, woodlands and fallow cultivation

Largest pipit. Greyish-brown with rufous edges to wings, dark lores. Northern races greyest and plainest with barely streaked, whitish-buff or rufous-buff underparts. Southern races more heavily streaked above and more lightly streaked on breast with rufous-buff underparts. Powerful thrush-like bill, short legs and upright stance. Bounding flight; pumps and fans tail upwards.

RICHARD'S PIPIT

Anthus richardi Motacillidae

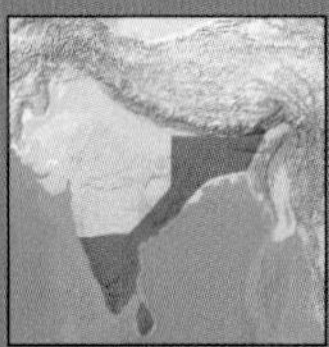

Size 18 cm

Voice Call a loud, grating *shreep*

Range Fairly common winter visitor to E lowlands including Bangladesh and Sri Lanka

Habitat Often wet grasslands and cultivation

Streaked pipit with strong thrush-like bill. Sandy or greyish-buff upperparts streaked dark brown. Well-streaked breast. Warm buff flanks contrast with white belly. Pale lores, dark moustache bordering white throat. Long hind claws, legs and tail; has upright stance.

TREE PIPIT

Anthus trivialis Motacillidae

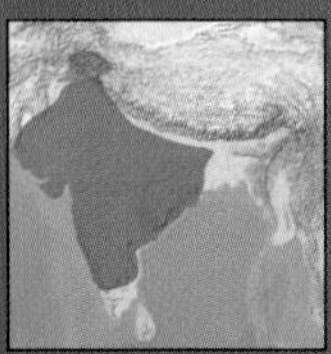

Size 15 cm

Voice Call a sibilant, piercing *beeze*, usually louder than Olive-backed's. Loud trilling song

Range Local breeding summer visitor to N mountains from Pakistan to Himachal Pradesh. Winters widely in lowlands except extreme S and E India. Commonest in N and C areas. Vagrant to Bangladesh. Unknown in Sri Lanka

Habitat Breeds on grassy mountain slopes. Winters in open wooded areas, cultivation and village margins with trees

trivialis

Small, brown pipit, heavily streaked above, especially crown, though rump plain. Buffish edgings to wing feathers and buff-washed breast and flanks, white belly. Indistinct whitish lores and supercilium. Sometimes shows white spots on ear-coverts. Pink legs and bill base. Horizontal stance.

haringtoni

OLIVE-BACKED PIPIT

Anthus hodgsoni Motacillidae

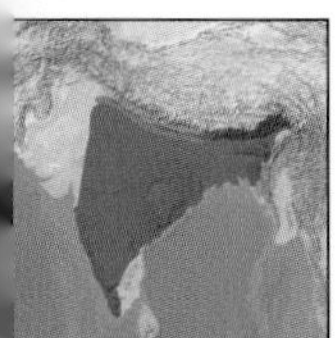

Size 15 cm

Voice Call a faint *tseep*... . Lark-like song of breeding male

Range Breeds in the Himalayas, east from W Himachal Pradesh; above 2,700 m, to timberline; winters in foothills and almost across India, except arid NW, Kutch

Habitat Forests, grassy slopes

Sexes alike. Olive-brown above, streaked dark brown; dull white supercilium, two wing-bars; pale buff-white below, profusely streaked dark brown on entire breast and flanks. Gregarious in winter; spends considerable time on ground, runs briskly; if disturbed, flies with *tseep*... calls into trees; descends in few minutes.

ROSY PIPIT

Anthus roseatus Motacillidae

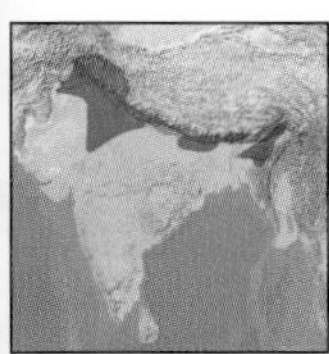

Size 15 cm

Voice Call a short, thin *seep*... *seep*

Range Common breeding summer visitor to N mountains from Pakistan east to Arunachal Pradesh. Winters in N plains south to Rajasthan, Odisha and Bangladesh

Habitat Breeds in high-altitude meadows. Winters in marshes and damp cultivation

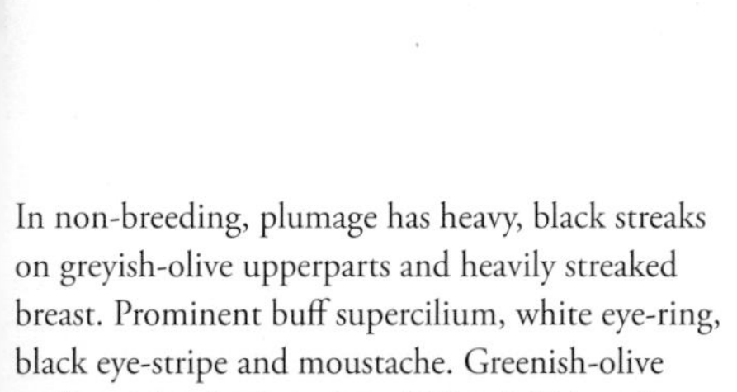

In non-breeding, plumage has heavy, black streaks on greyish-olive upperparts and heavily streaked breast. Prominent buff supercilium, white eye-ring, black eye-stripe and moustache. Greenish-olive wash to wing feather edges. Light pinkish wash on underparts when breeding. Similar to Red-throated.

RED-THROATED PIPIT

Anthus cervinus Motacillidae

Size 15 cm

Voice Call a characteristic *psii*

Range Winter visitor to N subcontinent

Habitat Mountains, marshland and tundra

Small pipit. Adult easily identified in breeding season by brick-red face and throat. Difficult to identify in non-breeding plumage. Heavily streaked brown upperparts with whitish mantle-stripes. Strong flight.

Non-breeding

BUFF-BELLIED PIPIT

Anthus rubescens Motacillidae

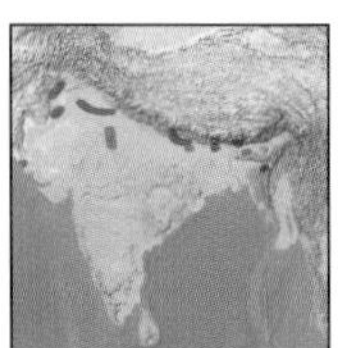

Size 15 cm

Voice Calls *seep…seep*

Range Winter visitor to N subcontinent

Habitat Marshes, lightly vegetated areas and grasslands

Undistinguished-looking species which can usually be seen running around on ground. Has lightly streaked grey-brown upperparts. Buff breast and flanks diffusely streaked. Whitish belly; bill and legs dark with reddish hue.

WATER PIPIT

Anthus spinoletta Motacillidae

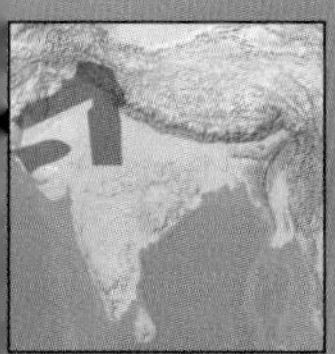

Size 15 cm

Voice Call a thin *tsiip* similar to Rosy's

Range Scarce winter visitor to lowlands and foothills of Pakistan and N India, South to Rajasthan

Habitat Marshes, wet cultivation, edges of freshwater

Greyish, dark-legged pipit. Prominent supercilium and pale lores. Grey head in breeding plumage, more brown back and plain, pinkish-white underparts. In non-breeding, plumage lightly streaked below, greyer above. Less heavily streaked than Rosy and Red-throated. Similar to Buff-bellied but less streaked. Feeds in loose groups.

NILGIRI PIPIT

Anthus nilghiriensis Motacillidae

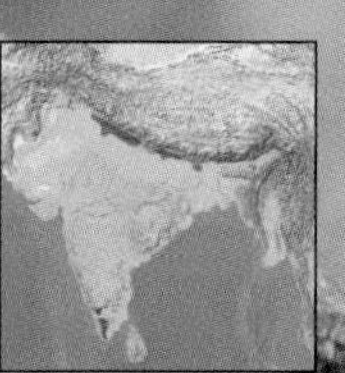

Size 15 cm

Voice Calls see…*see*

Range Hills of SW India

Habitat Short, montane grasslands

Distinctive species of pipit, endemic to high-altitude hills of southern India. Richer brown than other pipits in the region; non-migratory; tends to fly into low trees when disturbed.

UPLAND PIPIT

Anthus sylvanus Motacillidae

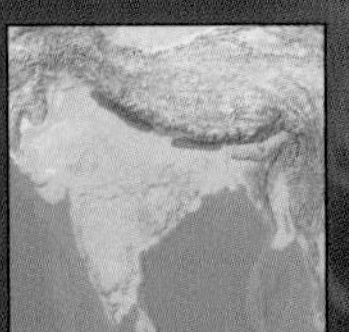

Size 17 cm

Voice Calls include short *chirp* and *zip…zip*. Double whistling song *wee…chee…we…chee*

Range Locally common breeding resident in N foothills from Pakistan east to West Bengal, including Nepal. Moves lower down in winter

Habitat Open woodlands, scrubby grassy slopes and abandoned cultivation

Large, heavily streaked pipit with short, broad bill. Dark buff or grey-brown with very heavy, blackish streaking on upperparts and breast. Prominent buff supercilium, blackish lores and moustache. Pink legs. Thin, pointed tail feathers. Flicks tail. Feeds solitary or in pairs, on invertebrates and seeds on ground. Often rather furtive but will perch prominently, particularly when singing.

COMMON CHAFFINCH

Fringilla coelebs Fringillidae

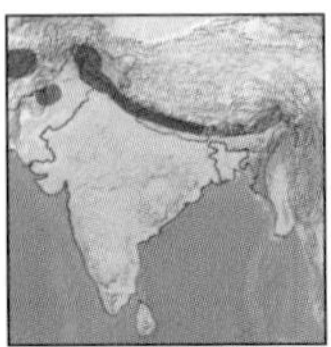

Size 16 cm

Voice Calls *chink*. Strong voice

Range Rare winter visitor to hills of Pakistan and N India

Habitat Open woodlands

Rounded, medium-sized finch with brightly-coloured slaty-blue cap, nape and crown. Face rusty pink and rusty red underparts; mantle and back chestnut-brown. Black wings edged white. Female much dull in colour, but both sexes have two contrasting white wings-bars and white tail sides. Male sings from exposed perch. Shuffles and nods head when walking on ground.

♀

BRAMBLING

Fringilla montifringilla Fringillidae

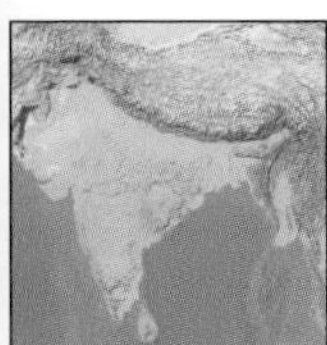

Size 16 cm

Voice Call a loud *zweee*

Range Rare winter visitor to hills of Pakistan and N India

Habitat High-altitude fields

Distinctive-looking bird, particularly in breeding. Black head, nape, cheeks, mantle and upper back; rusty orange scapulars; sooty-grey uppertail-coverts; orange breast and white belly. Jet-black tail. Female similar to non-breeding male but more brown rather than black. In pairs, or small parties. Strong, undulating flight. Feeds on ground, but makes frequent forays into trees.

RED-FRONTED SERIN

Serinus pusillus Fringillidae

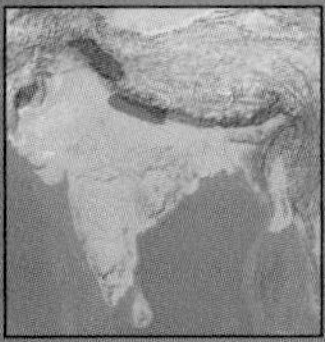

Size 12 cm

Voice Pleasant twittering *chrr... chrr*; faint *tree...tree...* call note

Range W Himalayas, extreme west to Uttarakhand

Habitat Rocky, bush-covered mountainsides

juvenile

Small finch with bright scarlet-orange forehead. Blackish-grey crown; buffy back streaked dark; yellow-orange rump and shoulder; yellow wing edges and whitish wing-bars; sooty-brown underparts; dull yellow-buff belly and flanks, streaked brown. Female similar, but has duller and smaller patch of red on forehead. Gregarious and active; feeds on flower-heads and on ground; drinks and bathes often; spends considerable time in bushes and low trees.

TIBETAN SERIN

Serinus thibetanus Fringillidae

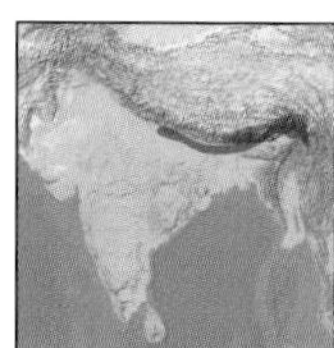

Size 12 cm

Voice Call a wheezy *twang*

Range C and E Himalayas

Habitat Temperate forests

Adult male has bright olive crown, olive-greenish upperparts, yellow underparts, yellowish-green rump, yellow supercilium and border behind ear-coverts. Wing and tail feathers broadly differentiated by yellowish-green colour. Female has black streaking on darker greyish-green upperparts, more clearly defined wing-bars and paler, yellowish throat and black-flanked breast with streaking. Juvenile duller green, tinged brownish-buff on upperparts, with duller rump, buff fringes to greater coverts and heavily streaked underparts.

EURASIAN SISKIN

Carduelis spinus Fringillidae

Size 12 cm

Voice Call a wheezy *toolee*

Range Vagrant to Nepal and N India

Habitat Coniferous forests

♀ juvenile

Male black from forehead to hindcrown with long, yellow supercilium beginning above eye and extending behind ear-coverts and neck sides. Narrow, black eye-stripe; olive-green lores, cheeks and ear-coverts. Lower nape, back mantle and scapulars, deep olive-green; bright yellow rump. Short, notched tail. Black median coverts broadly-tipped with greenish-yellow; greater coverts also black-tipped, pale green. Underparts yellow around chin and breast turning greenish towards belly. Female overall greenish-brown; duller supercilium; heavily streaked upperparts and dull yellow underparts. Gregarious. In mixed feeding parties with other finches. Undulating flight. Feeds high in trees.

BLACK-HEADED GREENFINCH

Carduelis ambigua Fringillidae

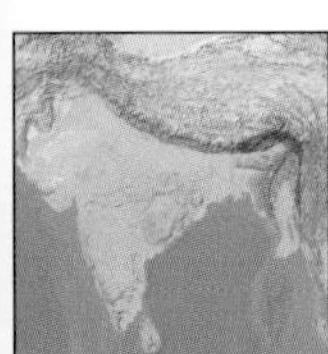

Size 12 cm

Voice Call a thin, high-pitched, metallic twitter

Range NE Arunachal Pradesh

Habitat High-altitude fields

Male has diagnostic black head and yellow base to primaries and secondaries forming broad panel across wing; dull greenish nape and mantle; greenish rump and grey uppertail-coverts; yellow sides to base of tail. Underparts olive-green, mottled yellow towards throat; pale belly and thighs; pale yellow undertail-coverts. Female has brownish-grey crown and mantle, with indistinct dark streaking; grey ear-coverts. Juvenile overall buff-brown and darkly streaked; bright yellow in wings and yellow underparts streaked brown.

YELLOW-BREASTED GREENFINCH

Carduelis spinoides Fringillidae

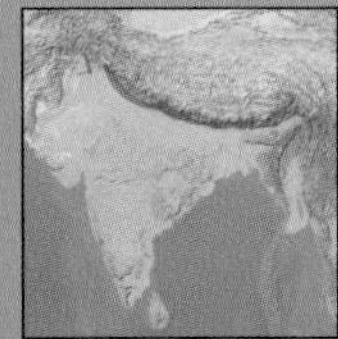

Size 14 cm

Voice Noisy. Calls include *tzweee...* and *weeee...chu.* Also twitters and extends calls into song, often uttered in flight

Range Locally common breeding resident in N mountains from Pakistan to Myanmar border. Moves lower down in winter

Habitat Edges of forests, cultivation, meadows, gardens and scrubs

Medium-sized finch with bright yellow forehead, lores and stout, pink bill; yellow supercilium extends below eye and around cheeks; greenish-black sub-moustachial stripe. Upperparts blackish-brown with olive-brown mantle. Yellow bars on wings, rump and base of tail. Female duller. Prefers trees. In small flocks. Feeds on seeds, berries and sometimes insects. Active and sometimes confiding. Undulating flight. Nests in trees.

EUROPEAN GOLDFINCH

Carduelis carduelis Fringillidae

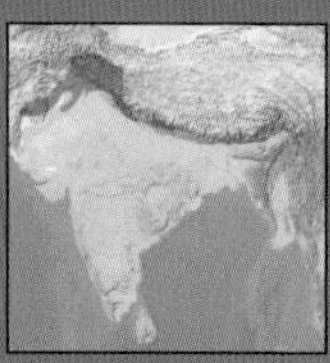

juvenile

Size 13 cm

Voice Ordinary call note a somewhat liquid *witwit…witwit…*

Range The Himalayas, extreme west to around C Nepal

Habitat Open coniferous forests, orchards, cultivation, scrubs

Distinctive-looking bird with bright crimson forehead; black lores; greyish-brown upperparts with large, white rump patch; black-and-yellow wings striking, at rest and in flight. Sexes alike. Juvenile has streaked upperparts. Sociable; flock size ranges from four to several dozen together, sometimes along with other finches; forages on ground; also attends to flower-heads; undulating, somewhat dancing flight.

TWITE

Carduelis flavirostris Fringillidae

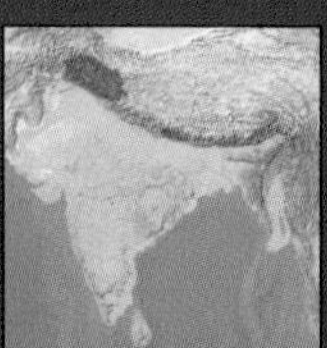

Size 13 cm

Voice Calls include nasal, drawn-out *tweet* and twittering *ditoo… di…dowit*

Range Locally common breeding resident from N Pakistan east to N Nepal. Moves lower down in winter

Habitat Dry, open, montane, stony plateaux and scrubby slopes above treeline

Medium-sized bird with dark brown crown and forehead; plain, buff supercilium and face. Streaked brown upperparts, breast and flanks; pinkish rump; whitish wing-bars and whitish edges to flight and tail feathers. Often spotted in flocks mixed with other passerines; undulating, erratic flight. Deeply notched tail. Feeds on ground on seeds and invertebrates. Often in flocks with other ground feeders. Nests low down. Perches on rocks and low bushes.

EURASIAN LINNET

Carduelis cannabina Fringillidae

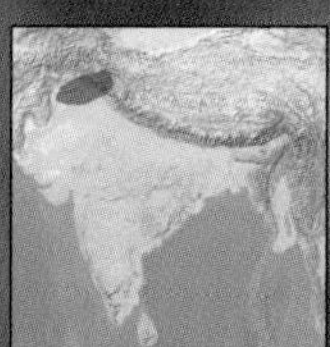

Size 13 cm

Voice Call a dry *teet…eet…eet…eet*

Range Erratic winter visitor to N Pakistan and Kashmir hills. Vagrant elsewhere in N India and Nepal

Habitat Open stony country and fallow

Male has crimson forehead and creamy-beige lower forehead. Grey face, head and neck; cinnamon-brown back and scapulars; back and rump paler; black uppertail-coverts have whitish tips; deeply notched tail, pale creamy chin and breast streaked brown; crimson breast in breeding season. Female grey-brown, streaked brown with greyer head; creamy-white rump. Feeds on ground on seeds and invertebrates; perches on bushes and trees. In flocks with other seed-eaters. Fast, undulating flight.

PLAIN MOUNTAIN FINCH

Leucosticte nemoricola Fringillidae

Grey-brown upperparts streaked dark brown; greyer on rump; pale-buffy bar and markings in dark brown wings; dull grey-brown below, streaked more brown on breast sides and flanks. Finches with plenty of white in wings, and generally found in the high Tibetan country of the Himalayas, are snowfinches. Sexes alike. Gregarious; good-sized flocks on ground, amidst stones; sometimes associates with other finches and buntings; calls often when feeding.

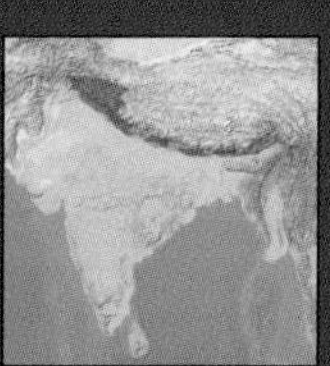

Size 15 cm

Voice Twittering and chattering notes, rather Sparrow-like in tone; calls frequently

Range High Himalayas, breeds between 3,200-4,800 m (above timberline); descends in winter, occasionally to as low as 1,000 m

Habitat Open meadows, dwarf scrub, cultivation

BRANDT'S MOUNTAIN FINCH

Leucosticte brandti Fringillidae

breeding

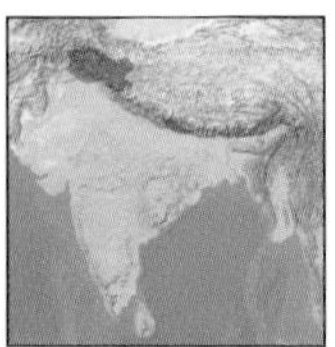

Size 18 cm

Voice Call a *twitt...twitt...twee... ti...ti...it...peek...peek.* Also, *churrs*

Range Locally common breeding resident in N mountains from N Pakistan east to Sikkim. Moves lower down in winter

Habitat Stony slopes and montane meadows, favours edges of snowmelt

Male has sooty grey forehead and crown with grey nape and ash-brown mantle. Upperparts a mix of shades from dark grey to brown; tail tipped whitish; rump washed pink. Underparts pale grey graduating to buff around belly. In non-breeding season, head more brown. Female similar to male, but duller. Juvenile paler with dark wing edging. In pairs, or flocks. Feeds on seeds and invertebrates.

SPECTACLED FINCH

Callacanthis burtoni Fringillidae

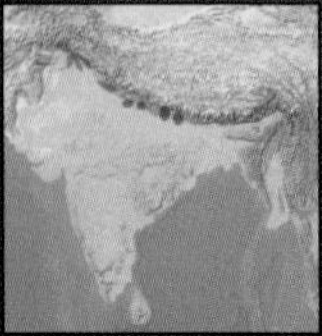

Size 18 cm

Voice Call a loud whistle

Range Resident; the Himalayas

Habitat Open mixed forests

Reddish-brown bird with diagnostic broad, red or yellow around eye. Male has red forehead and lores; crown, nape and neck sides finely streaked with grey; black wings have distinct white tips. Ash-brown chin; black throat, mottled scarlet towards breast. Female more olive-brown with paler head with yellow 'spectacles', olive-brown mantle, and buffish-brown underparts with yellowish wash to breast. Juvenile has buff eye patch. In pairs, or small flocks; shy, keeps to undergrowth.

TRUMPETER FINCH

Bucanetes githagineus Fringillidae

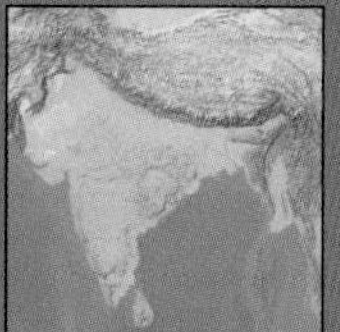

Size 18 cm

Voice Call an abrupt *chee* or *chit*; flight call a soft *weechp*. Song a drawn-out buzzing *cheeeee*, rising on scale

Range Subject to local movements in Pakistan; winter visitor to NW India

Habitat Dry rocky hills and stony semi-desert

Uniformly sandy-brown finch with largish head and long wings. Breeding male has grey head with red-tipped feathers; moustachial region and neck sides washed pink; pale brown upperparts; short, thick, bright bill; breast, rump and tail pink. Tail has dark terminal feathers. Non-breeding male, female and juvenile much duller version of breeding male. Largly terrestrial. Shuffles and hops on ground foraging for seeds. Also found in drinking pools especially at dusk. Fast, undulating flight.

MONGOLIAN FINCH

Eremopsaltria mongolica Fringillidae

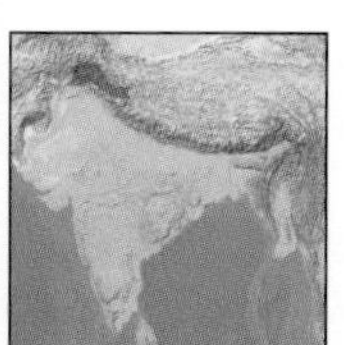

Size 15 cm

Voice Call a loud, liquid *djou*. Measured *do mi sol mi song*

Range Locally common breeding resident in N Pakistan and Ladakh. Moves lower down and, rarely, east to Nepal in winter. Rather nomadic

Habitat Dry stony and gravely hillsides

Plain-looking, medium-sized finch with stout, yellow bill. Forehead and upper crown sandy grey-brown; pale beige eye-ring; faded pink lores and supercilium. Upperparts streaked beige; black-edged pink and white in wings and tail. Black eyes and brown legs. Breeding male has pink supercilium and flanks. Female has pale buff supercilium and underparts. Feeds on seeds on ground and low growth. Usually in pairs, or small parties. Confiding. Strong, bounding flight, particularly to water sources. Nests on ground.

♀

BLANFORD'S ROSEFINCH

Carpodacus rubescens Fringillidae

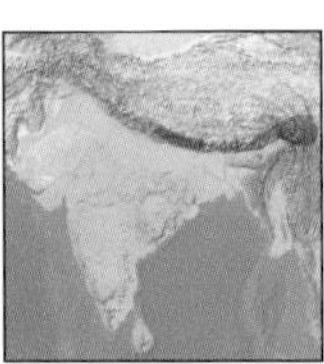

Size 15 cm

Voice Calls *sip…sip*

Range C and E Himalayas

Habitat Meadows in mixed forests

Male has bright crimson head and deeper crimson upperparts. Unstreaked, pinkish-red underparts; crimson double wing-bars; dusky lores; chin, throat and lower breast lighter pinkish-red; rump and uppertail-coverts reddish-crimson with slightly paler edges. Dark brown tail with crimson edging, slightly notched. Female has reddish-brown crown; unstreaked underparts and plain khaki-brown upperparts. Juvenile similar to female. Feeds on ground.

DARK-BREASTED ROSEFINCH

Carpodacus nipalensis Fringillidae

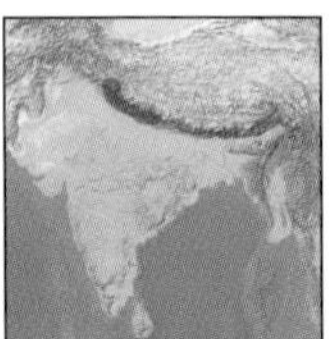

Size 17 cm

Voice Twittering, churring, monotonous chipping song

Range Kashmir to Arunachal Pradesh

Habitat Oak, rhododendrons, fir forests; alpine pastures, shrubberies; grassy slopes; clearings; fields

Dark rosefinch with brown upperparts washed with crimson; slender bill; dark brownish-maroon mantle, wings, flanks, breast-band, rump; broad eye-stripe; rose-pink forehead, forecrown, supercilium, throat, belly; diffusely streaked mantle; pale scaling on undertail-coverts. Female darker than most female rosefinches; unstreaked underparts; two buffish wing-bars, tips to tertials; paler throat; normally lacks supercilium; streaked mantle. In pairs, or small flocks. Feeds on ground, bushes, trees; wary.

♀

BEAUTIFUL ROSEFINCH

Carpodacus pulcherrimus Fringillidae

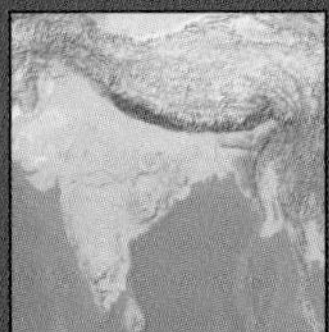

Size 14 cm

Voice Calls *trip, trillip* or *cheet cheet*

Range Very local breeding resident in N mountains from Uttarakhand east to Arunachal Pradesh (where the only recent Indian records come from). Common in Nepal. Moves lower down in winter

Habitat Scrubs, above treeline in summer. Often near cultivation in winter

Medium-sized rosefinch with broad, pale pink supercilium. Pinkish-brown upperparts darkly streaked; upper forehead, nape and crown greyish-streaked with dark brown; dark eye-stripe and dark brown around base of pale bill; pink, unstreaked rump. Female has heavily brown-streaked white underparts. Feeds on seeds and buds on ground or in low bushes. In small groups, or pairs. Sits quietly, especially after being disturbed. Nests low down.

♀

COMMON ROSEFINCH

Carpodacus erythrinus Fringillidae

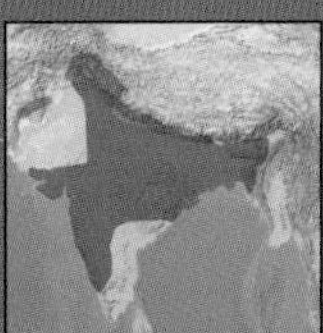

Size 15 cm

Voice Call a double-noted, questioning, *twee…ee*. Rather quiet in winter. Pleasant song of upto 8 notes; may sing before departure from wintering grounds

Range Breeds in the Himalayas, 2,700-4,000 m; winters over most of India

Habitat Cultivation, open forests, gardens, bushes

non-breeding

breeding

Grey-brown finch streaked red. Bright red head and breast; dark eye-stripe; brown wing panel washed crimson; rump and underbody crimson, fading into dull rose-white belly; brown, notched tail. Female buff-brown above, streaked dark; two pale wing-bars; dull buff below, streaked, except on belly. In small flocks; feeds on bushes and crops; often descends to ground; associates with other birds.

PINK-BROWED ROSEFINCH

Carpodacus rodochroa Fringillidae

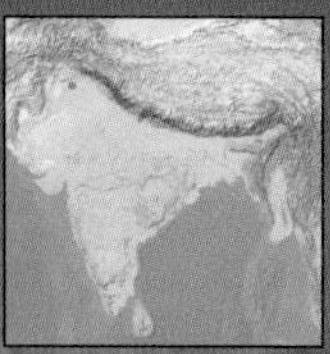

Size 15 cm

Voice Calls include *swe…eet perle* and *chew…eee*

Range Locally common breeding resident in N mountains from N Pakistan east to Nepal. Moves lower down in winter

Habitat Open forests and scrubs. Winters in oak forests and scrubs, sometimes near villages

Bright pink rosefinch with distinct broad, pink supercilium. Male has dark-streaked, pinkish-brown upperparts; unstreaked, reddish-brown crown with pink wing-bars. Dark crimson-brown eye-stripe; pink rump. Underparts uniformly dark pink with indistinct streaking. Female has whitish supercilium; heavily streaked rusty-buff, above and below; whitish throat streaked brown, unstreaked rump. In small flocks in non-breeding season. Forages in low bushes or on ground.

♀

DARK-RUMPED ROSEFINCH

Carpodacus edwardsii Fringillidae

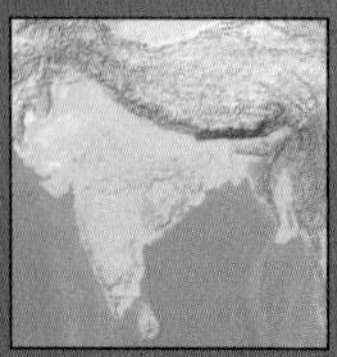

Size 17 cm

Voice Calls include sharp *twink* and *chreewee*

Range Scarce breeding resident in N mountains from C Nepal east to Arunachal Pradesh. Moves lower down in winter

Habitat Montane scrubs

♀

Male has dark brown forehead, crown and nape; distinct pink supercilium; dark pink lores; pale pink cheeks and lower ear-coverts; indistinct pink wing-bars and reddish-brown lower breast-band; brown rump; dark brown tail, slightly notched. Female paler and more streaked below with buff wing-bars. Solitary, in pairs or small parties. Skulks; shy. Feeds on rhododendrons, bushes close to ground, on seeds and nectar. Nest not known.

THREE-BANDED ROSEFINCH

Carpodacus trifasciatus Fringillidae

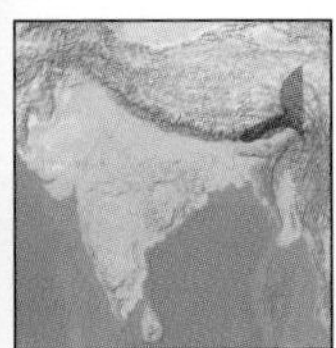

Size 20 cm

Voice Unknown

Range Vagrant

Habitat Temperate forests

Male has white forehead edged crimson, dark grey, red-tinged upperparts; red rump, black tail and wings. Sides of neck, crown and nape very dark, almost black. Cheeks, lores and ear-coverts black with crimson edges; throat and chin brownish-black; darkish wing panel with white wing-bars. Female overall deep grey, streaked with black; yellowish-brown throat. Underparts, breast and flanks white. Black tail. Juvenile similar to adult female but overall darker brown. Feeds on ground, mostly on seeds and in bushes. Seen hopping on ground.

SPOT-WINGED ROSEFINCH

Carpodacus rodopeplus Fringillidae

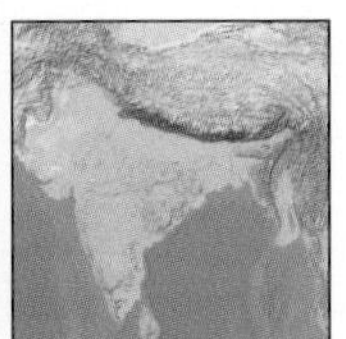

Size 16 cm

Voice Calls include *chirp* and *schwee*

Range Very local breeding resident in N mountains from Himachal Pradesh east to Arunachal Pradesh. Rare in India, less so in Nepal

Habitat Rhododendron shrubs and meadows, bamboo thickets in winter

Distinctive finch with deep crimson-and-brown upperparts. Prominent pale pink supercilium; bright pink lores, cheeks and ear-coverts; dark eye-stripe; dark median and greater coverts spotted pink. Pale pink throat; deep pink breast and belly mottled towards outer edges. Female darkly streaked brown, more so on underparts; buffish-white supercilium and blackish cheeks; buff wing-bars. Large, conical bill. Shy. Nest not known.

WHITE-BROWED ROSEFINCH

Carpodacus thura Fringillidae

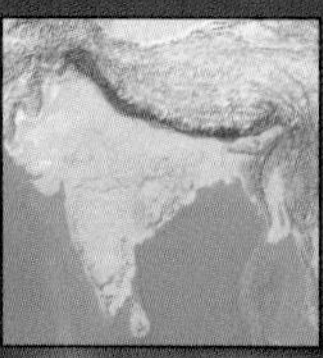

Size 17 cm

Voice Calls often when feeding on ground, a fairly loud *pupuepipi*...

Range The Himalayas, breeds at 3,000-4,000 m; winters to about 1,800 m

Habitat Treeline forests, fir, juniper, rhododendrons; open mountainsides and bushes in winter

Male rich brown above, streaked blackish; pink-and-white forehead and deep pink supercilium; dark eye-stripe; rose-pink rump and double wing-bars. Underparts uniformly pale pink; brownish flanks. Female streaked brown; broad, whitish supercilium and single wing-bar; yellow rump; buffy below, streaked. White in supercilium easily identifies this species. In small flocks, either by themselves or with other finches; mostly feeds on ground, but settles on bushes and small trees.

♀

RED-MANTLED ROSEFINCH

Carpodacus rhodochlamys Fringillidae

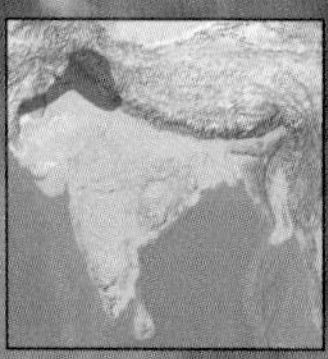

Size 18 cm

Voice Calls include *wheezy... quwee* and sharp *wir*

Range Locally common breeding resident in N mountains from W Pakistan east to Uttarakhand. Moves lower down in winter

Habitat Dry montane forests and shrubs

♀

Largish finch with greyish-brown washed pink upperparts and indistinct streaking. Upper forehead and crown deep pink; broad, rose-pink supercilium. Underparts white-streaked pink. Female ash-brown and heavily streaked. Both sexes have strong, pale bill. Feeds mainly on or near ground on seeds, berries and buds. Solitary, in pairs or small flocks. Confiding. Powerful, undulating flight.

GREAT ROSEFINCH

Carpodacus rubicilla Fringillidae

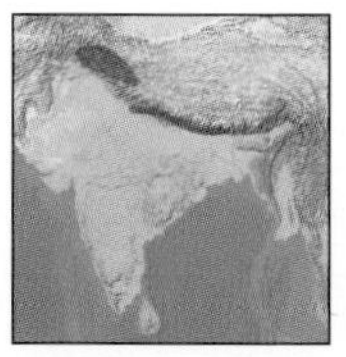

Size 19 cm

Voice Varied calls, including a drawn-out *weeep* and *twink*

Range Generally scarce breeding resident in N mountains from N Pakistan east to Sikkim. Moves lower down in winter

Habitat Dry, rocky and bushy mountainous country

Large-billed rosefinch. Male has crimson-red forehead, crown, lores, cheeks, nape and ear-coverts, streaked or spotted white and pale pink; pale brown tinged with crimson back and mantle with mild streaking; deep pink rump; notched tail darker brown. Chin and throat crimson; rest of underparts pale with crimson wash and spotted. Female pale brown-grey, finely streaked, darker red and brown. Juvenile similar to female, but more sandy-brown. Solitary, in pairs or in small flocks, often with other rosefinches, feeds on ground on seeds and berries. Strong, undulating flight. Nests on ground.

STREAKED ROSEFINCH

Carpodacus rubicilloides Fringillidae

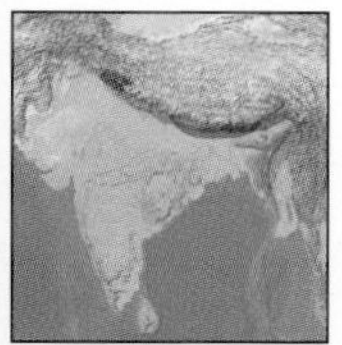

Size 19 cm

Voice Calls include *twink…sip* and *doid…doid*

Range Locally common breeding resident in N mountains

Habitat Dry stony country

Large-billed rosefinch. Bright crimson face; forehead and crown less deep pink-crimson, finely streaked; nape, lores, cheeks and ear-coverts bright crimson. Back and mantle brown-washed with crimson; pink rump; dark brown notched tail. Female overall grey-brown, streaked darker. Solitary, in pairs or small flocks. Feeds on ground on seeds.

RED-FRONTED ROSEFINCH

Carpodacus puniceus Fringillidae

♀

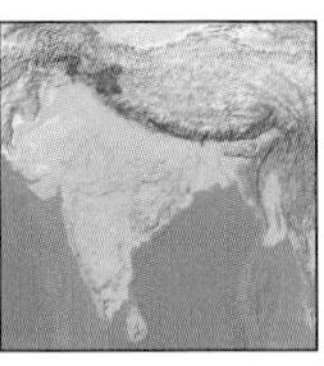

Size 20 cm

Voice Call a cheerful *wistle*

Range The Himalayas

Habitat High-altitude slopes, above treeline, rock screes, cliffs and meadows

Large, brown high-altitude finch. Red forehead extends above eye; crown, nape and mantle brown with streaks; short supercilium; chin, breast and rump also crimson; lower breast slightly duller crimson; brown belly streaked with black; notched dark brown tail with lighter brown edging; dark brown wing panels; pink undertail-coverts. Female similar to male, but slightly smaller and olive-brown, with narrower and paler supercilium. In small flocks; fairly approachable but wary, flying into trees when disturbed. Hops on ground foraging for seeds.

CRIMSON-BROWED FINCH

Propyrrhula subhimachala Fringillidae

Size 19-20 cm

Voice Calls include pleasant chirping; warbling

Range Patchily from Nepal to Bhutan. Rarer East

Habitat Montane shrubberies, dense undergrowth in open forests

Large, stocky, overall grey-brown finch. Bright crimson forehead and throat; upper breast crimson, mottled pink-and-white; dark eye-stripe; red rump and unstreaked, greyish belly, smallish bill and long tail. Female has olive-yellow forehead, brow and breast; streaked grey throat, grey face, nape, belly and greenish-brown upperparts. Solitary, or in pairs when breeding; shy and quiet; forages in bushes, moving slowly in undergrowth.

♀

SCARLET FINCH

Haematospiza sipahi Fringillidae

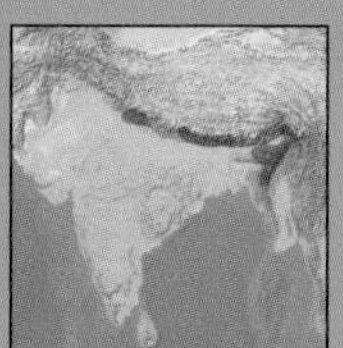

Size 18 cm

Voice Call a pleasant *tu…wee; quee…i…eu*

Range Uttarakhand to Arunachal Pradesh

Habitat Coniferous, oak forests; streamsides, ravines, clearings

Bright scarlet bird from head to uppertail. Slightly brown from lower forehead to lores; dark wings and tail edged scarlet; short, square-ended tail edged dark red. Large, strong bill with upper and lower mandible curving towards tip. Female has olive-green upperparts with dark scaling on crown, nape, mantle and finer scaling on throat and breast; greyish underparts; rump bright yellow. Juvenile male similar to female, but overall more brownish with orange rump. Solitary, in pairs or small flocks; vocal; forages on ground, in bushes and canopy levels.

♀

RED CROSSBILL

Loxia curvirostra Fringillidae

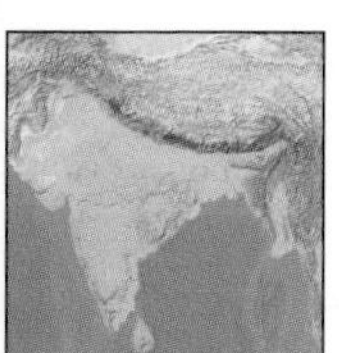

Size 16 cm

Voice Noisy. Call a distinctive *chip… chip*

Range Scarce and erratic visitor or breeding resident in N mountains from N Pakistan east to Bhutan

Habitat Coniferous forests

Medium-sized bird with large head and crossed mandibles. Red head and nape, cheeks and ear-coverts (varies to orange-red); brown lores. Upperparts duller brown, mottled darker. Upperwings washed red; bright red-pink rump; wings edged reddish. Female dull greenish-brown with yellower rump and darker wings and tail. Juvenile heavily streaked and mandibles not crossed. Feeds noisily on seeds of cones high in canopy. In small flocks. Restless with bounding flight. Frequently drinks out of pools. Nests colonially.

♀

BROWN BULLFINCH

Pyrrhula nipalensis Fringillidae

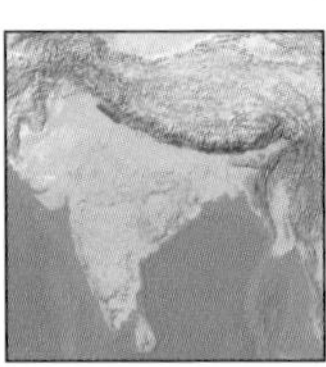

Size 17 cm

Voice Call a mellow *per…lee*

Range Resident with small altitudinal movements. The Himalayas

Habitat Dense moist forests or thick undergrowth in fir, oak and rhododendron forests

Smallish bullfinch with ash-brown back, head, nape and breast, mottled darker. Forehead, lores, and edge of chin edged grey-black; dark patch surrounding eye; white cheek. Thick, short, dark grey bill. Centre of belly white and undertail-coverts; black wings with ash-brown bars; deeply notched, black tail. White rump seen in flight. Female very similar to male, but with small, whitish-yellow wing edgings. In pairs, or small flocks. Confiding.

ORANGE BULLFINCH

Pyrrhula aurantiaca Fringillidae

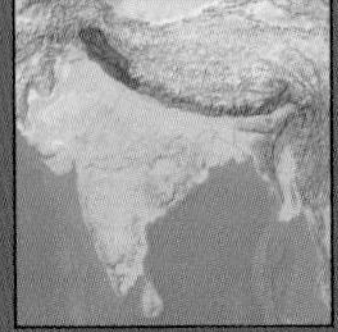

Size 14 cm

Voice Call a rising *tew* or *tewtya*

Range Local endemic breeding resident in N mountains from N Pakistan east to Uttarakhand

Habitat Open coniferous forests

Distinctive orange-and-black finch. Male has black forehead, lores, upper cheek and chin; rich orange crown, mantle and back; white base to uppertail-coverts; white rump and vent; broad, orange wing-bars; thick, stubby bill. Female has lighter orange-and-grey head. Similar to Red-headed but has smaller and yellow rather than grey mantle. Juvenile similar to adult female, but crown and forehead more tawny-brown. Feeds singly, in pairs or groups. Nests low in trees.

RED-HEADED BULLFINCH

Pyrrhula erythrocephala Fringillidae

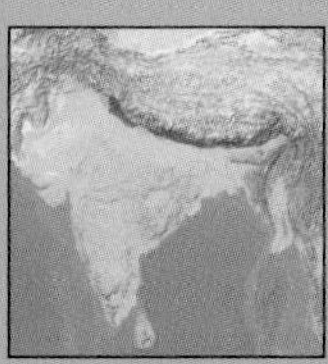

Size 17 cm

Voice Call a single or double-noted *pheu...pheu...*

Range The Himalayas, Kashmir to extreme E India; breeds at 2,400-4,000 m; descends in winter to about 1,200 m

Habitat Forests, bushes

Exotically-coloured finch. Male has black around base of beak and eye; brick-red crown; grey back; white rump; glossy purple-black wings; forked tail; black chin; rusty red below; ash-white belly. Female similar to male, but has olive-yellow crown; grey-brown back and underbody. Seen in small parties, occasionally with other birds; feeds in low bushes, sometimes on ground; rather quiet and secretive.

♀

GREY-HEADED BULLFINCH

Pyrrhula erythaca Fringillidae

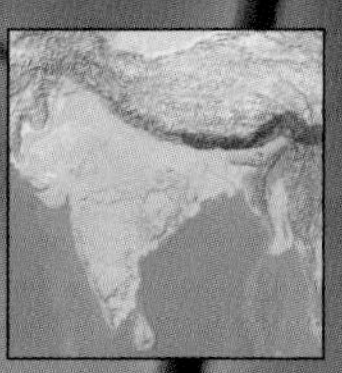

Size 17 cm

Voice Call a soft *soo...ee* or *poo...ee*

Range Resident, subject to altitudinal movements. Darjeeling Himalayan Hill region, West Bengal, east to Arunachal Pradesh

Habitat Coniferous, rhododendron forests

♀

Male has black forehead, lores and chin. Dove-grey back, head and nape; rusty orange breast; black wings and tail. Greater coverts have broad, pale grey tips, greyish-white wing-bar and white rump conspicuous in flight. Female brown below, darker grey on head and nape. Feeds on seeds and cones, and usually found in small flocks in winter.

WHITE-WINGED GROSBEAK

Mycerobas carnipes Fringillidae

Size 22 cm

Voice Loud 3- or 4-noted calls, usually from tree-tops; harsh note sometimes

Range The Himalayas, extreme W to E India; breeds at 1,500-4,000 m, but mostly above 2,500 m, even in winter. *M melanozanthos* descends much lower in winter

Habitat Dwarf juniper above timberline; high forests; may be seen in bamboos and pine during winter

♀

Sooty black grosbeak with long tail. Male black above, on throat and breast; olive-yellow rump, belly and wing spots; larger, white wing patch. Square-ended tail. Female brownish-grey, male black; streaks on ear-coverts. Juvenile similar to adult female, but more brown than black and parts of wing olive-yellow and tipped. Seen in small flocks, often with other grosbeaks; active and noisy; mostly feeds in higher branches.

BLACK-AND-YELLOW GROSBEAK

Mycerobas icterioides Fringillidae

♀

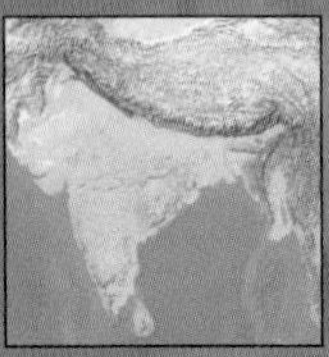

Size 22 cm

Voice Call a loud 2- or 3-noted *whistle*. Familiar bird call of W Himalayas; loud *chuck…chuck* note when feeding. Rich song of male. Rather noisy

Range W Himalayas up to C Nepal

Habitat Mountain forests

Male has black head, throat, wings, tail and thighs; yellow collar, back and underbody below breast; thick, finch-like bill. Female grey above with buff rump and belly. Seen in small parties in tall coniferous forests; also feeds on ground and bushes, but spends considerable time in higher branches, where it is difficult to spot.

COLLARED GROSBEAK

Mycerobas affinis Fringillidae

Size 22 cm

Voice Noisy. Calls include ringing *ki…ki…ki…kiw* and *pip…pip…pip…pip…ugh*

Range Locally common breeding resident in N mountains from Himachal Pradesh to Arunachal Pradesh. Moves lower down in winter.

Habitat Similar to Black and Yellow's, though also found in mixed forests

Large grosbeak with glossy black crown and throat. Hindneck and sides of lower neck bright golden-yellow, creating a collar. Rest of upperparts black; tail black with glossy black central feathers. Underparts golden-yellow. Female has grey head, greenish-grey upperparts and greenish-yellow underparts. Nest not known.

SPOT-WINGED GROSBEAK

Mycerobas melanozanthos Fringillidae

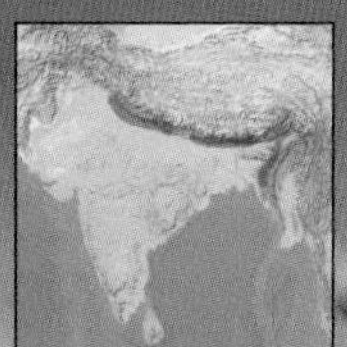

Size 22 cm

Voice Call a *teew…teew; krrrk*

Range Pakistan to Myanmar

Habitat Mixed broadleaved and coniferous forests

Large finch with very large, stout bill, and relatively short tail; white spots on greater wing-coverts, secondaries, tertials. Male has greyish-black hood, mantle, tail, rump, including nape and throat; breast, belly, vent bright yellow; black on flanks. Female heavily streaked on yellow upper and underparts, with dark eye- and malar stripe; yellow supercilium; white-spotted dark wings. In pairs, or fairly large groups; feeds at all levels, usually on fruiting trees; strong bill used for opening fruit stones for kernels.

♀

GOLD-NAPED FINCH

Pyrrhoplectes epauletta Fringillidae

Size 15 cm

Voice Call a *fuweet; teeew...; pi... pi...pi...pi*

Range Nepal to Arunachal Pradesh

Habitat Dense forests, undergrowth in oak, rhododendrons, bamboos; edges of forests

Small, distinctive finch, almost completely black except for bright yellow-orange crown, wing, nape and white edges to tertials. Short, dark bill. Female has olive-yellow crown, nape and face. Upperparts grey and rufous; black wings; pinkish-orange underparts. Juvenile similar to adult female, but duller. Solitary, in pairs when breeding; sometimes in winter mixed-species flocks; forages at lower levels, within bushes or on ground; quiet and inconspicuous.

♀

CRESTED BUNTING

Melophus lathami Emberizidae

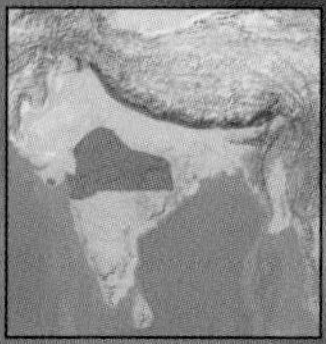

Size 15 cm

Voice Call a faint *chip*… . Pleasant, though somewhat monotonous song of breeding male

Range Resident in India, from the outer Himalayas to about 1,800 m

Habitat Open, bush and rock-covered mountainsides, open country; sometimes also cultivation

juvenile

Glossy black bunting with long, pointed crest and chestnut wings and tail. Female also crested; olive-brown above, streaked darker; rufous in wings; buffy-yellow below, darkly streaked on breast; darkish moustachial stripe. Juvenile overall duller with streaked upperparts. In small flocks, often spread wide over an area; feeds on ground, paths, meadows and tar roads, especially along mountainsides; perches on ruins, walls, stones and low bushes.

CORN BUNTING

Emberiza calandra Emberizidae

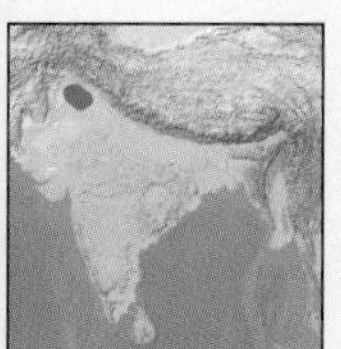

Size 18 cm

Voice Calls include *thick…tik* and *tsritt*. Jangling song

Range Vagrant to N Pakistan, India

Habitat Cultivation and stubble

Large bunting with prominent pale bill and short tail. Grey-brown upperparts streaked with brown. Whitish underparts more sparsely streaked. Spots converge to form dark patch on breast centre. Darkish malar stripe. Pale flesh-yellow legs and feet. Feeds on ground on seeds. Most likely to be found with other seed-eaters. Sexes alike. Strong but heavy, undulating flight. Flies with dangling legs. Nests on ground in grass or herbage.

YELLOWHAMMER

Emberiza citrinella Emberizidae

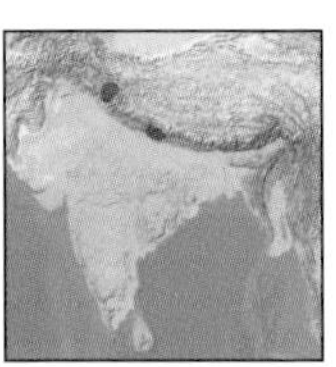

Size 17 cm

Voice Call a *tzik*. Wheezing song

Range Vagrant or rare winter visitor to N India and Nepal

Habitat Upland fallow and stubble fields or scrubs

Has distinct yellow head and underparts. Plain face; narrow, black streak above supercilium and blackish ear-coverts. Rufous breast darker towards wings. Olive-brown mantle streaked brown-black; streaked flanks; white in outer-tail feathers. Upperparts streaked brown; plain rump. Female also heavily streaked with yellow head. Sometimes interbreeds with Pine. Juvenile much duller with less yellow, pale yellow underparts and less distinct streaking. Nests on ground beneath shrubs. Gregarious. Seen in flocks of hundreds.

PINE BUNTING

Emberiza leucocephalos Emberizidae

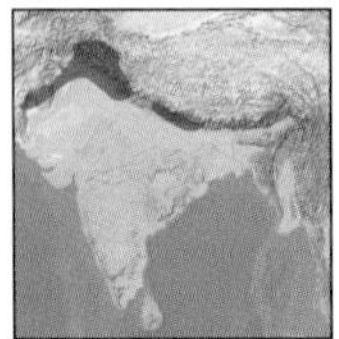

Size 17 cm

Voice Call a *pit...*, *trp* or *dzee*

Range Fairly common but erratic winter visitor to N hills from E Baluchistan. Very scarce in E India

Habitat Hill cultivation

Identified by distinct head patterning. White crown and cheeks edged black; narrow, lateral crown-stripe; broad chestnut, brown supercilium; rufous-brown scapulars boldly streaked with black; rufous-mottled breast and white belly. Female has dark moustache; pale spot on rear cheeks; streaking on chestnut-brown upperparts, rufous rump and underparts; white outer-tail feathers. Rather shy. Feeds in flocks on seeds on ground. Nests on ground in shallow depressions. Seen in large flocks with other buntings and finches.

ROCK BUNTING

Emberiza cia Emberizidae

Size 16 cm

Voice Squeaky *tsip…tsip…* note; calls often. Common bird call of W Himalayas. Squeaky song of several notes

Range The entire Himalayas between 1,500-4,200 m; most common in W Himalayas; winters in foothills

Habitat Grassy, rocky hillsides in open forests; cultivation, scrubs

Male has blue-grey head with prominent black lateral stripes. Black eye-stripe, lores and moustachial stripe; whitish supercilium and cheeks; pale chestnut-brown back, streaked dark. Unmarked rump; white outer sides of dark tail distinct; blue-grey throat and breast; rufous-chestnut below. Female duller. Solitary, or in small parties; active and restless; mostly feeds on ground, meadows, paths and roads; flicks tail often; regularly settles on bushes and trees.

GODLEWSKI'S BUNTING

Emberiza godlewskii Emberizidae

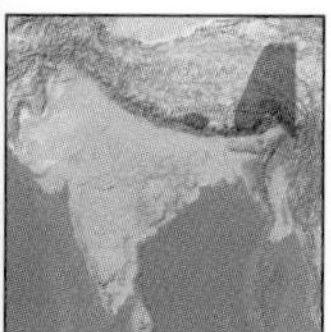

Size 16 cm

Voice Unknown

Range N Arunachal Pradesh

Habitat Dry slopes with bushes and rocks

Largish bunting with grey head, neck, and breast. Prominent chestnut-brown lateral crown-stripes; black moustachial stripe. Grey breast sharply separated from rufous belly. Underparts and rump have buff. Back streaked orange-and-black. Black tail with some orange above and white below. Beak black above and pale below. Legs and feet light pink.

WHITE-CAPPED BUNTING

Emberiza stewarti Emberizidae

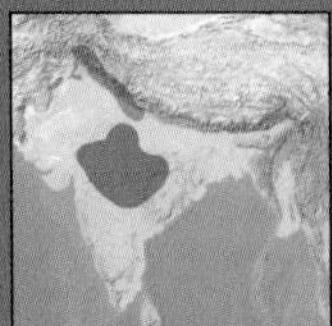

Size 15 cm

Voice Call a faint but sharp *tsit*… or *chit*… note

Range Breeds in W Himalayas, extreme west to Uttarakhand, 1,500-3,500 m; winters in W Himalayan foothills, and over extensive parts of W and C India, south to Maharashtra

Habitat Open, grass-covered, rocky hillsides, scrubs

Male has pale grey top of head; black eye-stripe; whitish cheeks; blackish supercilium; black chin and upper throat distinctive; chestnut back and rump; white outer-tail; white breast with chestnut gorget below; dull fulvous below, chestnut flanks. Female lacks black-and-white head pattern of male; brown above, streaked; rufous-chestnut rump; fulvous-buff below with rufous breast. Seen in small flocks, often with other buntings and finches; feeds on ground; rests in bushes and trees.

GREY-NECKED BUNTING

Emberiza buchanani Emberizidae

Size 15 cm

Voice Call a faint, single note

Range Winter visitor; quite common

Habitat Open, rocky grassy country, scrubs

Bunting of drier regions. Male has bluish-grey head with white eye-ring; buffish sub-moustachial stripe; pale grey nape and head sides; sandy-brown mantle with diffused streaking; brown back with faint rufous wash and dark streaks; white edges to dark tail; not easily visible; pale rufous-chestnut below. Female somewhat duller than male; has more prominent moustachial stripe. Seen in small flocks; feeds mostly on ground, sometimes along with other birds; quite active.

ORTOLAN BUNTING

Emberiza hortulana Emberizidae

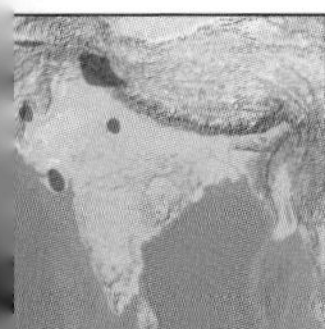

Size 16 cm

Voice Song *tsie…tsie…tsie…tsie, truh…truh…truh*

Range Vagrant

Habitat Orchards, grassy slopes

Identified by uniformly ash-olive-green head, nape and chin upto breast. Prominent buff eye-ring; pale yellow sub-moustachial stripe; boldly streaked, brown mantle; rufous belly and flanks; flesh-coloured bill. Female similar to male, but more washed-out with dark streaking on crown and nape, streaked malar stripe and dark streaking on greyish-yellow breast. Very similar to Grey-necked with rather plain head. More insectivorous than other buntings, catches insects in flight.

STRIOLATED BUNTING

Emberiza striolata Emberizidae

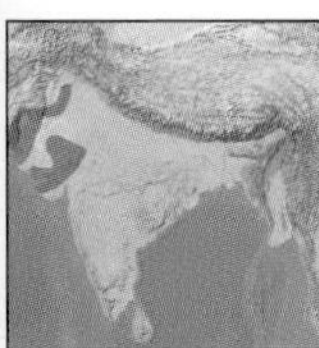

Size 14 cm

Voice Calls include nasal *chwer* and *tzwee*. Song a *witch…witch weech…witchy…witch*

Range Locally common breeding resident in lowland Pakistan, W Rajasthan and Gujarat

Habitat Scrubby hillsides, semi-desert and ruins, but not usually near human habitation

Nondescript-looking bird with fine, darkly streaked crown. Upperparts sandy-brown, narrowly streaked with rufous-washed wings. Pale grey cheeks; dark eye and moustachial stripes; pale supercilium and diagnostic darkly streaked, grey throat. Female lighter. Yellow lower mandible. Similar to Rock but with paler mantle streaked grey and rufous in wings. Nests in crevices or on ground.

♀

CHESTNUT-EARED BUNTING

Emberiza fucata Emberizidae

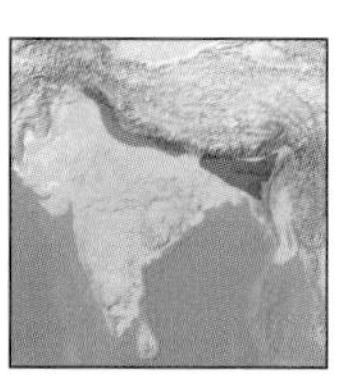

Size 16 cm

Voice Calls include loud *pzik…*, *zii* and *chutt*

Range Uncommon breeding resident in N hills from N Pakistan east to C Nepal. Winters in nearby foothills and plains

Habitat Rocky, grassy and bushy hillsides

Large bunting with distinctive chestnut cheeks and lower breast. Grey mottled crown and nape; creamy-white throat and upper breast; black moustache extends to upper breast forming a broad gorget of spots; buffish flanks and belly. Upperparts buff, heavily streaked russet; rufous rump; white outer-tail feathers. Female very dull and more brown. Nests in dry patches in marshy lands. Never seen in large flocks.

YELLOW-BREASTED BUNTING

Emberiza aureola Emberizidae

Chestnut brown-and-yellow bunting with diagnostic bright yellow chin, throat and belly. Breeding plumage male dark chestnut-brown above with striking white wing-bars. Face and throat black; chestnut collar. Non-breeding male paler and more streaked with dusky cheeks. Female similar but with black-edged pale cheeks and no breast-bar. Feeds on seeds, inconspicuously on ground, usually in large flocks. Confiding. Perches in trees and bushes when disturbed.

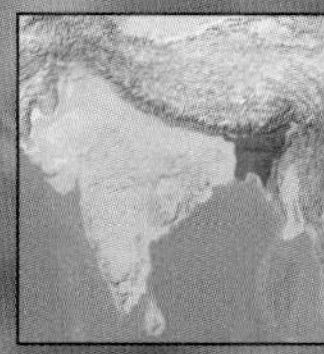

Size 15 cm

Voice Calls *tzip…tzip*

Range Common winter visitor to plains of Nepal, NE India and Bangladesh. Rare further W India

Habitat Cultivation and grasslands, often near wetlands

LITTLE BUNTING

Emberiza pusilla Emberizidae

Size 13 cm

Voice Call a clicking *zik*

Range Nepal to Arunachal Pradesh

Habitat Grass, stubble, fields, orchards, gardens

Tiny bunting with a small, pointed bill and rufous-chestnut face. Breeding male has rufous-chestnut crown-stripe; dark blackish-brown lateral crown-stripes; rufous-chestnut face; pale eye-ring; broad, buffish-white sub-moustachial stripe curving around behind ear-covert stripe; dark brown malar stripe; buffish-white chin and throat; dark streaking on rufescent-brown upperparts; two pale wing-bars; whitish underparts with prominent streaking on breast and flanks. Seen in small parties; forages on ground; flies into bushes or trees when flushed.

RED-HEADED BUNTING

Emberiza bruniceps Emberizidae

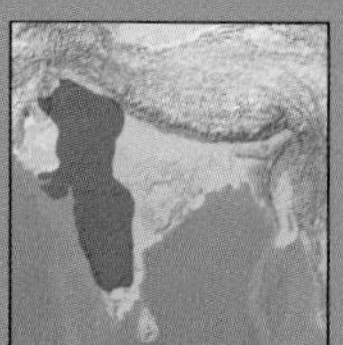

Size 17 cm

Voice Call a high-pitched *tzeett...*

Range Common winter visitor over most of the country, south of the Himalayas; absent in extreme south and along E coastal regions

Habitat Open cultivated areas

Male has rufous-chestnut crown, throat, breast; olive-yellow back streaked blackish; unmarked yellow underparts and rump; whitish wing-bars; yellow neck sides, underbody below breast. Female pale-brown above, has yellowish rump. Highly gregarious winter visitor; appears in huge numbers, frequently along with Black-headed; causes considerable damage to crops.

CHESTNUT BUNTING

Emberiza rutila Emberizidae

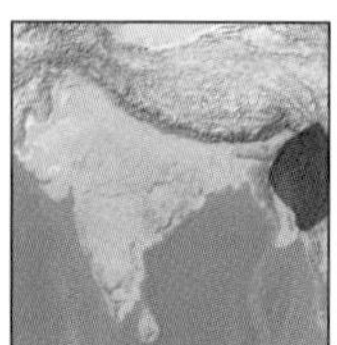

Size 15 cm

Voice Call a short *zick*

Range S Assam Hills

Habitat Rice fields, forest clearings, open forests

Fairly small bunting with uniformly chestnut-brown head, breast and upperparts; yellow belly; primary coverts, primaries and secondaries brown; dusky streaking on flanks; short, pointed tail. Brownish bill and pale brown tarsus. Breeding male has bright chestnut-brown upperparts and head. Yellow breast and belly with streaks on sides. Female mostly dull brown with dark streaks above, while underparts pale yellow; rufous rump; buffish throat. Feeds on ground, flees into trees when disturbed. Relatively shy.

BLACK-HEADED BUNTING

Emberiza melanocephala Emberizidae

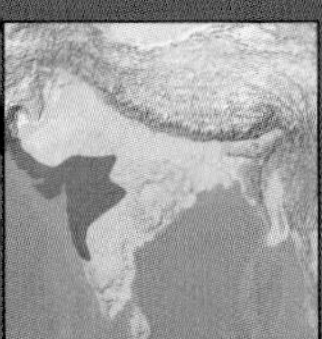

Size 18 cm

Voice Call note a musical *tzeett…*; faint chip occasionally

Range Common in winter over wide parts in W and C India; Gujarat, Rajasthan, W and C Madhya Pradesh, Maharashtra, parts of Karnataka

Habitat Open cultivation

Male has black head; thin, yellow collar and rufous-chestnut back. Bright yellow underparts with some rufous on breast sides and wing-bars. Female has brown upperparts, streaked; yellowish rump; pale buff-yellow below; very similar to female Red-Headed. Often seen in large flocks with other buntings, notably the Red-headed; feeds on crops and ground; bold, not easily driven away from croplands; in most areas, yellow males seen in greater numbers.

BLACK-FACED BUNTING

Emberiza spodocephala Emberizidae

Size 15 cm

Voice Calls *zit…; sip…; zii*

Range Nepal to Arunachal Pradesh

Habitat Tall grass, stubble, fields, paddy fields

Distinctive small bunting with greyish-olive-green head; black lores and chin; pale brown mantle streaked black; grey-brown lesser coverts; median coverts brown-black-tipped buff; grey-brown greater coverts tipped pale buff. Unstreaked grey rump. Upperparts pale yellow; white on outer-tail feathers. Female and non-breeding male have duller head with yellowish supercilium; yellowish sub-moustachial stripe around ear-coverts; yellowish throat; streaked breast; olive rump. Solitary, in pairs, or small flocks; normally feeds on ground Shy.

COMMON REED BUNTING

Emberiza scholeniclus Emberizidae

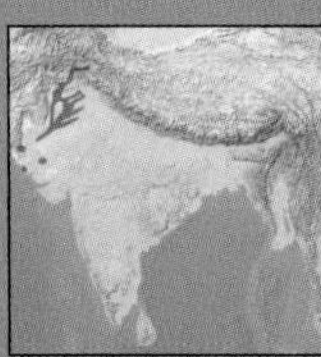

Size 15 cm

Voice Calls include *teesu* and *chirp*

Range Winter visitor to Pakistan, NW India

Habitat Reed beds

Medium-sized bird with black head and throat. Prominent sub-moustachial stripe; white collar; grey-brown mantle streaked with darker brown-and-black; rufous wings have indistinct wing-bars. Whitish underparts; dark streaking on flanks; pure white outer-tail feathers; small, sturdy bill. Female much duller with streaked brown head, and streaked underparts. Juvenile has chestnut crown streaked black; buff sub-moustachial stripe and throat. Flicks tail on perch. Hops on ground, foraging for insects.

SEE-SEE PARTRIDGE *Ammoperdix griseogularis*

Similar to Chukar but has grey head with black eye-stripe and lacks black throat gorget. Sandy-brown above with wavy white and brown flank stripes. Resident in Pakistan.

CHESTNUT-BREASTED PARTRIDGE *Arborophila mandellii*

Male similar to Black Francolin male, but has orange-buff crown sides; white throat without chestnut collar, and black upperparts. Resident in Manipur, NE India.

TIBETAN EARED PHEASANT *Crossoptilon harmani*

Reported sporadically from Arunachal Pradesh. Said to be tame around monastries in Tibet. More studies needed in the region.

SNOW GOOSE *Anser caerulescens*

Mid-sized white goose with black wing-tips. No definite records from the area. Recent record from Kathiawar considered escapee. Often mistaken for domestic geese.

MUTE SWAN *Cygnus olor*

Large long-necked swan, similar to Whooper. Bill orange with black knob. Winter vagrant to Pakistan and NW India. Rare and mostly silent. Mostly seen singly, or in pairs in large lakes and rivers.

TUNDRA SWAN *Cygnus columbianus*

Smaller than the Whooper with shorter neck. Bill yellow and black. Noisier than Whooper. Rare winter vagrant to Pakistan and NW India. Few recent records.

WHOOPER SWAN *Cygnus cygnus*

Large elegant swan with long neck and broad breast. Has been recorded in Pakistan, Nepal and India. In February 2013, a pair was seen in Pong Dam in Himachal Pradesh after almost a century.

RED-BREASTED GOOSE *Branta ruficollis*

Few earlier records, but seen and photographed near Delhi in 2014. Said to be gregarious and was indeed seen grazing with a large group of Greylags.

MANDARIN DUCK *Aix galericulata*

Strikingly-coloured, spectacular duck with breeding male sporting red bill, brown-crested crown and broad, white supercilium. Very rare but recorded from Bangladesh, Nepal and NE India.

LONG-TAILED DUCK *Clangula hyemalis*

A sea duck with long neck, also recorded in large freshwater bodies. Male has long, pointed and elongated tail. Vagrant, but scattered records from Pakistan, Nepal and NW India. Recent records from Gajaldoba in West Bengal and Pangong Tso in Ladakh.

RED-THROATED DIVER *Gavia stellata*

Upturned bill and rounded head. Several once reported from the Makran coast in Pakistan in November. Few other records and recently seen in SE Nepal. Vagrant.

BLACK-THROATED DIVER *Gavia arctica*

Straight bill and square head. Early reports from the Ambala region but recently seen and photographed on the Jia Bhorelli River in Nameri, Assam.

SOOTY SHEARWATER *Puffinus griseus*

Ocean-faring bird, often mistaken for Short-tailed Shearwater. Vagrant. Few unconfirmed sightings from N Sri Lankan coast.

BARAU'S PETREL *Pterodroma baraui*

Distinctive grey-and-white petrel with white forehead and dark cap, heavy black bill and grey-patches on side of whitish breast. Summer visitor to Indian Ocean.

LONG-TAILED SKUA *Stercorarius longicaudus*

Small and elegant Skua often seen around the coast of Sri Lanka. Recently seen on the eastern coast of India after a violent cyclone.

WHITE-HEADED PETREL *Pterodroma lessonii*

Large grey-and-white petrel with distinctive white head and underbody that contrasts with dark underwings. Fast swooping flight. Single possible sighting off Sri Lankan coast.

SWINHOE'S STORM PETREL *Oceanodroma monorhis*

Fully dark storm-petrel with pale bar on upperwing-coverts. Fast and weaving flight with short glides. Recent records from pelagics conducted off SW coast of India.

BLACK-BELLIED STORM PETREL *Fregetta tropica*

Similar to Wilson's Storm-petrel but has rounded tail, and white on underwing and flanks, with black band running down the centre of white underbody. Erratic, weaving flight.

WHITE-BELLIED STORM-PETREL *Fregetta grallaria*

Similar to Black-bellied but with completely white underbody. Vagrant to the subcontinent.

CHRISTMAS ISLAND FRIGATEBIRD *Fregata andrewsi*

Black below except for narrow, white path on belly. Female has white breast and belly, with 'spurs' extending to underwing. Vagrant to the subcontinent.

PYGMY CORMORANT *Phalacrocorax pygmeus*

Very difficult to differentiate from Little Cormorant, so probably overlooked. Records from Pakistan and Afghanistan. Vagrant.

RED KITE *Milvus milvus*

Rufous-brown body with very deeply forked-tail, has white primary flight feathers contrasting with black wing-tips and dark secondaries. Winter vagrant in the subcontinent.

ROUGH-LEGGED BUZZARD *Buteo lagopus*

Similar to White-eyed Buzzard but with grey cheek, barred underwing and tail seen in flight. Unconfirmed records from Andaman and Nicobar Islands.

GREY-FACED BUZZARD *Butastur indicus*

Similar to White-eyed Buzzard but with grey cheek, barred underwing and tail seen in flight. Unconfirmed records from Andaman and Nicobar Islands.

GREAT BUSTARD *Otis tarda*

Huge bustard. Winter vagrant to Afghanistan, Baluchistan and NW Pakistan. Hunted for its meat. Wary and difficult to circumvent.

LITTLE BUSTARD *Tetrax tetrax*

Small, sandy-brown bustard with grey face, black-and-white pattern on neck and breast. Rare winter visitor to Pakistan and N India.

LITTLE CRAKE *Porzana parva*

Similar to Baillon's Crake, but with little or no white on upperparts, and less extensive barring on underparts. Uncommon winter visitor to Pakistan and W India.

RED-LEGGED CRAKE *Rallina fasciata*

Similar to Slaty-legged Crake but with coral-red legs, black-and-white barring on wings and red eye. Recorded from NE India, but no recent records.

CORN CRAKE *Crex crex*

Middle-sized crake. Very secretive and difficult to see. Probably overlooked. Records from Afghanistan, Kashmir and Sri Lanka. Fall passage migrant. Globally threatened.

HOODED CRANE *Grus monacha*

Small, dark grey crane with white neck and head. Forecrown black and red. Early records from NE India. No recent records from the subcontinent.

EURASIAN DOTTEREL *Charadrius morinellus*

Similar to Sociable Plover but larger. Vagrant, but recently reordered in Baluchistan.

GREAT SNIPE *Gallinago media*

Large snipe with barred flanks. Winter vagrant to S India and Sri Lanka. Also reported from the Andaman Islands, but no recent records.

LONG-BILLED DOWITCHER *Limnodromus scolopaceus*

Similar to Asian Dowitcher but smaller in size with shorter legs. Recorded from Bharatpur in Rajasthan. Recent records from Sultanpur National Park near Delhi.

EASTERN CURLEW *Numenius madagascariensis*

Similar to Eurasian Curlew but with buff underparts. Status uncertain in the region. Two unconfirmed sight records, one from near Kabul and the other from Cox's Bazaar in Bangladesh.

CASPIAN PLOVER *Charadrius asiaticus*

Few reliable records, from W Indian coast, Maldives and Sri Lanka mostly in winter, when presumably on passage.

GREY-TAILED TATTLER *Tringa brevipes*

Stocky wader with prominent supercilium. Recorded several times in spring from Bangladesh. Also reported from Goa in the month of February.

PECTORAL SANDPIPER *Calidris melanotos*

Similar to Sharp-tailed Sandpiper but has sharply demarcated, darkly streaked breast-band. Vagrant. Reported from Harike in Punjab, and recently from Kannur in Kerala. Probably overlooked.

SHARP-TAILED SANDPIPER *Calidris acuminata*

Big, slender, long-necked wader vagrant to the region. Single records from Gilgit in Kashmir and another from Sri Lanka.

BUFF-BREASTED SANDPIPER *Tryngites subruficollis*

Brown-breasted sandpiper recorded earlier from Sri Lanka and Goa. Recently photographed in Kannur, Kerala in November 2011.

BLACK-FRONTED DOTTEREL *Elseyornis melanops*

Plover with black band through eyes, and another from bill upto forehead. Unmistakeable red bill and eye-ring. Vagrant to the subcontinent. No recent records.

ORIENTAL PLOVER *Charadrius veredus*

Very similar to Caspian, but larger. Few unconfirmed records mostly from Sri Lanka and Andaman Islands. Probably overlooked.

LITTLE GULL *Hydrocoloeus minutus*

Diminutive tern-like gull known from one specimen from Ladakh. Several unconfirmed sight reports from Gujarat, especially from Bhavnagar in Kutch.

LESSER BLACK-BACKED GULL *Larus fuscus*

White gull with black upperparts, yellow legs and small, white 'mirrors' at wing-tips. May not occur in the subcontinent.

LONG-TAILED SKUA *Stercorarius longicaudus*

Tern-like bird, smaller and slimmer than other skuas. Pale underbody with uniformly dark underwing. Sometimes, has long wispy tail-streamers. May not occur in the subcontinent.

LICHTENSTEIN'S SANDGROUSE *Pterocles lichtensteinii*

Small, heavily barred sandgrouse. Male has two black bands across forehead, and yellowish-buff band across chest. Female grey-and-white barred all over. Resident in SW Pakistan.

STOCK DOVE *Columba oenas*

Rare vagrant, earlier known from two old records from Kabul but recently recorded in Nameri in Assam.

EUROPEAN TURTLE DOVE *Streptopelia turtur*

Smaller and slimmer than Oriental Turtle Dove. Summer visitor to Afghanistan and sometimes strays into Pakistan. Reported in Ladakh as well as Maldives.

SNOWY OWL *Bubo scandiacus*

Large, white owl with no ear-tufts. Known from a record from NW Pakistan.

SIND WOODPECKER *Dendrocopos assimilis*

Black-and-white woodpecker. Similar to Himalayan Woodpecker but smaller, lacks black cheek-bar and has broad, white barring on wings and white shoulder patch. Widespread resident in Pakistan.

GREAT GREY SHRIKE *Lanius excubitor*

Similar to Southern Grey Shrike but darker, with white rump and broad, white band at base of secondaries. Resident in Pakistan.

WOODCHAT SHRIKE *Lanius senator*

Black-and-white shrike, but with chestnut nape and hindcrown. Juvenile heavily scaled, similar to juvenile of Red-backed Shrike. Pakistan. One unconfirmed recent record from Maharashtra.

AZURE TIT *Cyanistes cyanus*

Small, long-tailed tit with short bill. White head with dark eye-stripe, white underparts and grey mantle. Vagrant to Pakistan.

ROCK MARTIN *Ptyonoprogne fuligula*

Similar to Eurasian Crag Martin but smaller and paler, with plain, buffish-white throat. Scarce resident in C and S Pakistan.

ASIAN STUBTAIL *Urosphena squameiceps*

Similar to Pale-footed Bush Warbler but with very short tail and long legs, reminiscent of wren-babbler or tesia. Vagrant to E Nepal and NE India. One recent record from Kolkata.

LONG-BILLED BUSH WARBLER *Bradypterus major*

Similar to Spotted Bush Warbler but larger with long, fine bill. Olive-brown upperparts, whiter underparts, has variable spotting on throat and upper breast. Breeds in the W Himalayas, Kashmir.

MANCHURIAN BUSH WARBLER *Cettia canturians*

Large, plain bush warbler with long tail and heavy bill. Similar to Thick-billed warbler but has pale supercilium, blackish eye-stripe and whiter underparts. Vagrant in NE India.

GREAT REED WARBLER *Acrocephalus arundinaceus*

Like Clamorous Reed Warbler, but larger with more distinct supercilium and very long primary projection. No recent records.

SEDGE WARBLER *Acrocephalus schoenobaenus*

Similar to Moustached Warbler but paler above, with less striking head pattern and some streaking on crown and mantle. Rare passage migrant through Ladakh in India.

EURASIAN REED WARBLER *Acrocephalus scirpaceus*

Very similar to Blyth's Reed but with longer primary projection and indistinct supercilium. No recent records from the subcontinent.

BUFF-THROATED WARBLER *Phylloscopus subaffinis*

Very similar to Tickell's Leaf Warbler but with shorter supercilium, more uniformly yellowish, and buff-yellow underparts.

RADDE'S WARBLER *Phylloscopus schwarzi*

Similar to Dusky Warbler but larger with longer, brownish-white supercilium, becoming white at the rear, and dark eye-stripe. Stout bill and pale legs. Rare winter visitor to Nepal and India.

ARCTIC WARBLER *Phylloscopus borealis*

Very similar to Greenish Warbler, but larger in size and has stouter bill with dark tip to pale lower mandible. Very rare winter visitor to Andaman Islands in India. No recent records.

WILLOW WARBLER *Phylloscopus trochilus*

Similar to Common Chiffchaff but slimmer, with pale lower mandible ending in dark tip. Distinctive warbling song. Could occur in the subcontinent as passage/winter vagrant.

GARDEN WARBLER *Sylvia borin*

Stocky warbler with plain, olive-brown upperparts; greyish-white underparts and short, stout, greyish bill. Rare passage migrant in Ladakh in India. No recent records.

BARRED WARBLER *Sylvia nisoria*

Large warbler with long tail, dark grey barring on white underparts; brownish-grey upperparts and stout, pointed bill. Rare passage migrant through Pakistan and Jammu & Kashmir in India.

BEARDED REEDLING *Panurus biarmicus*

Small orange-brown bird with long tail and small yellow bill. Male has grey head with black moustache, while female has plain, brownish head. Rare/vagrant in Pakistan.

WHITE-SHOULDERED STARLING *Sturnia sinensis*

Grey body with black-and-white wings. Female more brown, with little white on wings. Black tail with greyish-white sides. Vagrant in NE India, bordering Myanmar.

DAURIAN STARLING *Agropsar sturninus*

Small, grey starling with short tail, purplish upperparts and hindcrown patch. Vagrant to Pakistan, India and Sri Lanka, with some recent records from Andaman and Nicobar Islands.

COLLARED MYNA *Acridotheres albocinctus*

Dark grey, with large white-patches on neck sides. Pale blue eyes, and white tips to grey undertail-coverts. Resident in Manipur and Assam in NE India.

EUROPEAN ROBIN *Erithacus rubecula*

Large robin with orange-red face, throat and breast. Rare/vagrant in Pakistan. No recent records.

FINSCH'S WHEATEAR *Oenanthe finschii*

Similar to Pied Wheatear but has creamy-buff to white mantle and back (black in Pied Wheatear). Female has more contrasting mantle and rufous ear-coverts than female Pied. Winter visitor to W Pakistan.

JAVA SPARROW *Lonchura oryzivora*

Adult has black head with white cheek, bright pinkish-red bill and eye-ring; grey upperparts and pink belly. Introduced species, feral populations may exist.

SIBERIAN ACCENTOR *Prunella montanella*

Brown streaked upperparts, yellowish throat, breast and supercilium, grey nape and crown with dark centre stripe. May not occur in the subcontinent.

VINACEOUS ROSEFINCH *Carpodacus vinaceus*

Male uniformly deep crimson, with bright pink supercilium. Female streaked, with no supercilium or wing-bars. Rare resident of high Himalayas, from Himachal Pradesh to Nepal.

JAPANESE GROSBEAK *Eophona personata*

Typical grosbeak, with large, bright yellow bill. Adult has black head with pale whitish-grey neck sides. Grey back with black wings and tail. Possible vagrant to NE India.

HAWFINCH *Coccothraustes coccothraustes*

Stocky, tawny-brown finch with huge, pinkish bill. Black chin and lores, white shoulder, and broad, white tip on short tail. Female duller. Very rare winter visitor to Pakistan and parts of Kashmir.

PALLAS'S REED BUNTING *Emberiza pallasi*

Similar to Common Reed Bunting but has smaller bicoloured bill and less rufous wings. Breeding male dark-mantled with prominent white wing-bars. Rare/vagrant in Nepal.

RUSTIC BUNTING *Emberiza rustica*

Male has distinctive black-and-white head pattern, rusty hindneck and rufous streaking on breast and flanks and white belly. Rare/vagrant in Nepal.

HIMALAYAN FOREST THRUSH *Zoothera salimalii*

Subrato Sanyal

Scientists have described a new species of thrush in the lowland forests of Northeast India called the Himalayan Forest Thrush. The researchers observed that the erstwhile Plain-backed Thrush *Zoothera mollissima* sang with harsh and scratchy notes in the alpine regions whereas, below the treeline, its song was much more musical. The differences in songs were corroborated with comparisons of specimens from 15 museums and by performing DNA analysis, which left no doubt that the Plain-backed Thrush actually contained in it two separate species from India. Scientists have now named the species found above the treeline as 'Alpine Thrush' *Zoothera mollissima* (*see pp 570*) and that below the treeline as 'Himalayan Forest Thrush' *Zoothera salimalii*; in honour of the late Dr. Salim Ali.

ACKNOWLEDGEMENTS

The authors and Om Books International would like to thank the following photographers for so generously contributing their photographs. If any names have inadvertently been omitted, please contact us at biks.grewal@gmail.com and we will rectify it in the next edition.

A D Wilson CC
A P Zaibin
A V Prassana
Aameesh Patel
Abhay Kewat
Abhilash Arjunan
Abhinash Dhal
Abhishek Das
Abhishek Varma
Abrar Ahmed
Adesh Shivkar
Adrain Pingstone CC
Agnij Sur
Akshay Charegaonkar
Aleksey Levashkin
Alka Vaidya
Amano Samarpan
Amar Jyoti Saikia
Ameya Joshi
Amish Patel
Amit Gupta
Amit Thakurta
Anand Arya
Anand Israel
Ananda Bannerjee
Ananta Singh
Anantha Murthy
Andre Karwath CC
Andrea Trepte CC
Anirban Chatterjee
Ankur Patel
Antony Grossy
Anuj Gande
Anup Dutt
Anushree Bhattacharya
Arka Sarkar
Arpit Bansal
Arpit Deomurari
Ashish Imamdar
Ashok Chaudhary
Atanu Mondal
Ateeb Hussain
Atul Jain
Avinash Adappa
Avinash Khemka
Barsha Gogoi
Bhanu Singh
Bharat Rughani
Bhaskar Das
Bhavita Toliya
Bhilhotra Dips
Bijoy KI
Biju P B
Bikram Grewal
Bishan Monappa
Biswapriya Rahut
Bjorn Johansson
Brian Patteson
Chandima Jayaweera
Charles J Sharp CC
Charles Lam CC
Chewang Bonpo Phempu Lhasung
Chinmay Rahane
Clement M Francis
Dant Mante CC
Dave Curtis CC
David Iliff CC
Debapratim Saha
Deboshree Gogoi
Deepak Sahu
Devashish Deb
Devindra Dadhwal
Devojit Deb
Devon Pike CC
Dhananjay Joshi
Dhanu Paran
Dhanushka Senadheera
Dharuman Nanjan
Dhritiman Hore
Dhritiman Mukkerjee
Dibyendu Ash
Dileep Kumar Pushpangadhan
Dipaknkar Ghosh
Dolly L Bhardwaj
Donna Dewhurst CC
Dr Tanmoy Das
Dr Vaibhav
Dr. Nagraj
Duncan Wright CC
Dushyant Prashar
Eash Hoskote
Esha Munshi
Falguna Shah
Francis C Franklin CC
Francis Yap CC
Frank Schulenburg CC
Frankie Chu CC
Franky Boy CC
Ganesh Adhikari
Garima Bhatia
Gaurav Bhatnagar
Gaurav Deshmukh
Gaurav Kataria
Gaurika Wijeratne
Gayathri and Mansoor
Gertrud and Helmut Denzau
Girish Ketkar
Gopal Chandra Rao
Gopi Sundar
Gopinath Kollur
Gunjan Arora
Gurum Eklaya
Guruprasad Kambar
Gururaj Moorching
Hardik Pala
Harish Narasimhamurty
Harmenn Ningthoucha
Harshvardhan
HB Varun
Hilary Chambers CC
Hiyashi Haka CC
Igor Karyakin

Ingo Waschkies
J M Garg CC
Jainy Maria Kurikose
James Eaton
James Merrill
James Perdue CC
Jan W van Besten
Jason L Buberal CC
Jaysukh Parekh
Jerry Strzelecki CC
Jignesh
Jitendra Bhatia
JJ Harrison CC
Joanna Van Gruisen
John and Jemi Holmes
Jugul Tiwari
Jyotendra Thakuri
Jyotimoy Dev,
K Ramesh
K Uschel Gurung
Kallol Mukkerjee
Kalyan Varma
Karthik R
Kartik Patel
Kedar Potnis
Kim Rogers CC
Kim Yip Ho CC
Koshy Koshy
Kshounish Shankar Ray
Kulashekara Chakravarthy
Kuldeep Shukla
Kunan Naik
L J Tim CC
Lieven De Temmerman
M Savitha Ravi
Mahesh Reddy
Maitreyee Das
Manjeet Jadeja
Manjula Mathur
Manoj Sharma
Marjolein De Weirdt
Masood Hussain
Maurice van Bruggen CC
MC Sajin
MD Imran
Meg Roy Choudhury
Megna Bannerjee
Michael J Braid CC
Misha Desai
Mital Patel
Mitash Biswas
Mohamed Mothi
Mohan Munivenkatapa
Mohanram Kemparaju
Mousumi Datta
MV Shreeram
N Shiva Kumar
Nandhini Raveendaran
Narbir Singh Kalhon
Natalia Parlina and Christan Orden
Navendu Lad
Nayan Khanolkar
Nikhil Bhopale
Nikhil Devasar
Nilay Desai
Ninaad Kulkarni
Niraj Mistry
Niranjan Sant
Nirmala Sridhar
Nitin Bhardwaj
Nitin Srinivasamurthy
Olivier Klein CC
Otto Pfister
Panchami Manoo Ukil
Paramanand Chikane
Parashuram Lad
Partha Sen
Parvinder S Anand
Pema Bhutia
Peter Kaestner
Porag Jyoti Phukan
Prabhakar Manjunath
Prakash Ramakrishnan
Pranesh Kodancha
Pranjal J Saikia
Prasad Basavaraj
Prashant Kotian
Prashant Poojary
Prassana Parab
Prosenjit Singa Deo
Puja Sharma
Pushpal Goswami
R K Pai
R Kartik
Raghavendra M
Rahul Sachdeva
Raj Kamal Phukan
Raj Phukan
Rajeev Kumar
Rajesh Dhareshwar
Rajesh Panwar
Rajneesh Suvarna
Rakesh Kalra
Ramakrishna Prakash
Ramanan RR
Ramesh Anantharaman
Ramki Sreenivasan
Ranand Israel
Ranjan Barthakur
Ranjan K Das
Rathika Ramasami
Ratna Ghosh
Ravi Chand
Ravindar Musalcol
Rayees Rahman
Remi Bigonneau CC
Rohit Naniwadekar
Rohit Sant
Ron Knight CC
Ronald Haldar
Roon Bhuyan
Roshan Kamath
Rosy Chaudhary
S Krishnamurthy
S N Ragavendra
S Rajeshkumar
Saandip Nandagudi
Saandip Nandangudi
Sachin Rai
Salim Ali
Sameer Khan
Saminathan Babu
Saminathan Babu
Samyak Kaninde
Samyak Kaninde
Sangameshwar Ghattargi
Sanjay Dutt Tiwari
Santosh Gujjar
Sarthak Awhad
SarwanDeep Singh
Satish Chettri Kutwal
Satisha Sarakki
Satyendra Sharma

Savio Fonseca
Savitha Ravi
Sayan U Choudhury
Shahnawaz Khan
Sharad Agrawal
Sharad Sridhar
Shashank Dalvi
Shiva Shankar
Shiva Shankar
Shreya Singha Roy
Shyam Ghate
Sidharth Bramhankar
Sidharth Damle
Simon Cook CC
Sitara Kartikeyan
Solomon Sampath Kumar
Soma Jha
Sonu Anand
Sonu Arora
Soumayjit Nandy
Steve Ryan CC
Subharanjan Sen
Subharghaya Das
Subhasis Roy
Suboranjan Sen
Subramaniam Mani
Subranangshu Ghosh
Subroto Sanyal
Sudeep Dhatre
Sudhir Garg
Sudhir Shivaraman
Sudipto Roy
Sugata Goswami
Sujan Chatterjee
Sumit Das
Sumit K Sen
Supriya Dam
Supriya Das
Supriyo Samanta
Surendra Chouhan
Suresh K Rathod
Suresh Kamath
Suru Nair
Susan Myers
Sushmita
Swethadri Doraiswamy
T Saburaj
Tapas Misra
Tejinder Singh Rawal
Tejus Naik
Tim Loseby
Udayan Borthakur
Udayan Rao Pawar,
Umesh Srinivasan
Urmil Jhaveri
Uttan Mahata
Vaibhav Dalal
Vaibhav Deshmukh
Vaibhav Mishra
Vaidehi Gunjal
Venu Gopal
Vijay Anand Ishmavel
Vijay Cavale
Vijay Sachan
Vijay Sethi
Vishvatej Nair
Vishwatej Pawar
Vitraag Shah
Vivek Tiwari
VK Gupta
Waler Siegmund CC
Yoav Perelmen
Yograj Jadeja

Hundreds of birdwatchers, photographers and friends helped in the creation of this book. We are specially grateful to the following for providing advice and friendship: Aasheesh Pittie, Ajay Mago, Alpa Sheth, Arijit Banerjee, Arjun Sen, Bhavita Toliya, Bill Harvey, Bishan Monappa, Bittu Sahgal, Caesar Sen, Hemlata Pradhan , Krishna Kumari, Lavanya Khare, Meena Subramaniam, Nigel Redman, Om Mago, Prakash Muduli, Pritam Barua, Priyasha Ukil, Prosenjit Singa Deo, Raghuvir Khare, Ramki Sreenivasan, Ranjan K Das, Ranjeet Ranade, Ravi Singh, Rayika Sen, Rohan Chakravarty, Rohit Chakravarty, Samiha Grewal, Sanjay Mago, Sudhir Vyas, Sushama Durve, Tanaji Chakravorty and TV Prabhakar.

Special thanks to Tim and Carol Inskipp for so generously sparing time to write the introduction and helping in all departments.

Above all, we would like to thank Alpana Khare and her team—Neeraj Aggarwal, Ajmal Nayab Siddiqui and Raj Kishore Beck—for designing this book; and Ipshita Mitra, Shoili Sarkar-Seth and Dipa Chaudhuri for treating *Birds of India* as their own.

BIBLIOGRAPHY

Ali, S. & Abdulali, H. (1941) *The Birds of Bombay and Salsette*. Bombay: Prince of Wales Museum.

Ali, S. (1941) *The Book of Indian Birds*. Bombay: BNHS.

Ali, S. (1945) *The Birds of Kutch*. London: OUP.

Ali, S. (1949) *Indian Hill Birds*. Bombay: OUP.

Ali, S. (1953) *The Birds of Travancore and Cochin*. Bombay: OUP.

Ali, S. (1956) *The Birds of Gujarat*. Bombay: Gujarat Research Society.

Ali, S. (1960) *A Picture Book of Sikkim Birds*. Gangtok : Government of Sikkim.

Ali, S. (1962) *The Birds of Sikkim*. Delhi: OUP.

Ali, S. & Ripley, D. (1964-74) *Handbook of the Birds of India & Pakistan* (Vols. 1-10). Bombay: OUP.

Ali, S. & Futehally, L. (1967) Common Birds. New Delhi: NBT.

Ali, S. (1968) *Common Indian Birds, A Picture Album*. New Delhi: NBT.

Ali, S. (1969) *Birds of Kerala*. Madras: OUP.

Ali, S. (1977) *Field Guide to the Birds of the Eastern Himalayas*. Bombay: OUP.

Ali, S. (1979) *Bird Study in India: Its History and its Importance*. New Delhi: ICCR.

Ali, S. & Ripley, D. (1983) *A Pictorial Guide to the Birds of the Indian Subcontinent*. Bombay: OUP.

Ali, S. (1985) *Fall of a Sparrow*. Bombay: OUP.

Ali, S. (1996) *The Book of Indian Birds*. (12th ed.) New Delhi: BNHS & OUP.

Ali, S., Biswas, B. & Ripley, D. (1996) *Birds of Bhutan*. Calcutta: ZSI.

Ara, J. (1970) *Watching Birds*. New Delhi: NBT.

BNHS. (1996) *Dr. Salim Ali Centenary Issue* (Vol. 93, No.3). Bombay: BNHS.

Baker, E.C.S. (1908) *The Indian Ducks and Their Allies*. Bombay: BNHS.

Baker, E.C.S. (1913) *Indian Pigeons and Doves*. London: Witherby & Co.

Baker, E.C.S. (1921-30) *Game-Birds of India, Burma & Ceylon*. (Vols. I-3). London: John Bale.

Baker, E.C.S. (1922-31) *Fauna of British India*: Birds. (Vols. 1-8). London: *Taylor & Francis*.

Baker, E.C.S. (1923) *A Handlist of the Genera and Species of Birds of the Indian Empire*. Bombay: BNHS.

Baker, E.C.S. (1923) *Handlist of the Birds of the Indian Empire*. Bombay: RO Spence.

Baker, E.C.S. (1932-35) *The Nidification of Birds of the Indian Empire*. (Vols.1-4) London: Taylor & Francis.

Baker, H.R. & Inglis, C.M. (1930) *The Birds of Southern India: Madras, Malabar, Travancore, Cochin, Coorg and Mysore*. Madras: Govt. Press.

Bannerjee, A. (2008) *Common Birds of the Indian Subcontinent*. New Delhi, Rupa

Barnes, H.E. (1885) *Handbook to the Birds of the Bombay Presidency*. Calcutta: Calcutta Central Press.

Bates, R.S.P. (1931) *Bird Life in India*. Madras: Madras Diocesan Press.

Bates, R.S.P. & Lowther, E.H.N. (1952) *Breeding Birds of Kashmir*. Bombay: OUP.

Beebe, W. (1927, 1994) *Pheasant Jungles*. Reading: WPA.

Besten, J, W den. (2004) *Birds of Kangra, Dharmsala*: Moonpeak Publishers

Besten, J, W den. (2008) *Birds of India*, New Delhi: Mosaic Books

BirdLife International (2001): *Threatened Birds of Asia: BirdLife International Red Data Book*. Cambridge: BirdLife International

Blyth, E. (1849-52) *Catalogue of the Birds in the Museum of Asiatic Society*. Calcutta: J. Thomas Baptist Mission Press.

Choudhury, A. (2001) *Birds of Assam*, Guwahati: Gibbon Books.

Choudhury, A. (2006) *A Pocket Guide to the Birds of Arunachal Pradesh*, Guwahati: The Rhino Foundation

Choudhury, A. (2003) *A Pocket Guide to the Birds of Nagaland*, Guwahati: Gibbon Books

Daniels, J.C. & Ugra, G. (2003) *Petronia*, Mumbai: BNHS

Daniels, R. (1992). *Birds of Urban South India*. Bangalore: *Indian Institute of Science*.

Daniels, R. (1996) *Fieldguide to the Birds of Southwest India*. New Delhi: OUP.

Dave, K.N. (1985) *Birds in Sanskrit Literature*. Delhi: Motilal Banarsidass.

Dewar, D. (1909) *Birds of the Plains*. London: John Lane.

Dewar, D. (1915) *Birds of the Indian Hills*. London: The Bodley Head.

Dewar, D. (1916) *A Bird Calendar for Northern India*. London: Thacker.

Dewar, D. (1923) *Himalayan and Kashmiri Birds*. London: J. Lane.

Dewar, D. (1923) *Indian Birds*. London: John Lane the Bodley Head.

Dewar, D. (1923) *Birds at the Nest*. London: John Lane

Dewar, D. (1923-25) *The Common Birds of India*. Vols.I-2. Calcutta: Thacker and Spink.

Dewar, D. (1925) *Indian Bird Life*. London: John Lane The Bodley Head Limited.

Dewar, D. (1928) *Game Birds*. London: Chapman & Hall.

Dharmakumarsinhji, R.S. (1954) *Birds of Saurashtra. Bombay:* TOI Press.

Dharmakumarsinhji, R.S. & Lavkumar, K.S. (1972) *Sixty Indian Birds*. New Delhi: Ministry of Information and Broadcasting.

EHA Introduction by Ali, S. (1947) *The Common Birds of India*. Bombay: Thacker & Co. Ltd.

Finn, F. (1901) *How to Know the Indian Ducks*. Calcutta: Thacker, Spinks & Co.

Finn, F. (1916) *Game Birds of India & Asia*. Calcutta: Thacker, Spink & Co.

Finn, F. (1917) *The Birds of Calcutta*. Calcutta: Thacker, Spink & Co.

Finn, F. (1920) *How to Know the Indian Waders*. Calcutta: Thacker, Spink & Co.

Finn, F. (1920) *Indian Sporting Birds*. London: F. Edwards.

Finn, F. (1921) *The Water Fowl of India & Asia*. Calcutta & Simla: Thacker, Spink & Co.

Finn, F. (1950) *Garden & Aviary Birds of India*. Calcutta: Thacker, Spink & Co.

Fleming, R.L. Sr. & Fleming, R. Jr. (1970) *Birds of Kathmandu and Surrounding Hills Kathmandu*: Jore Ganesh Press.

Fleming, R.L. Sr. et al. (1984) *Birds of Nepal: With reference to Kashmir and Sikkim*. Nepal: Nature Himalayas.

Futehally, L. (1959) *About Indian Birds*. Bombay: Blackie & Son (India) Ltd.

Futehally, L., Ali, S. & Devasar N (2008) *About Indian Birds*: New Delhi, Wisdom Tree

Futehally, Z. (ed) (2006) *India Through Its Birds*, Bangalore, Dronequill Publishers Pvt. Ltd

Gandhi, T. (ed) (2007) *A Bird's Eye View: The Collected Essays and Shorter Writings of Salim Ali* (two Vols.) New Delhi: *Permanent Black*.

Ganguli, U. (1975) *A Guide to the Birds of the Delhi Area*. New Delhi: ICHR.

Gould, J. (1832) *A Century of Birds from the Himalayan Mountains*. London: Published by the author.

Gould, J. (1850-73) *Birds of Asia*. Vols. I-6. London: Published by the author.

Grewal, B. (1995) *Birds of the Indian Subcontinent*. Hong Kong: *The Guidebook Company Limited*.

Grewal, B. (1995, 2008) *Birds of the India & Nepal*. London: New Holland.

Grewal, B. (1995) *Threatened Birds of India*. New Delhi.

Grewal, B. (ed) (1995) *The Avifauna of the Indian Subcontinent Part 1*. Bombay: Sanctuary (Vol XV No. 5).

Grewal, B. (ed) (1995) *The Avifauna of the Indian Subcontinent Part 2*. Bombay: Sanctuary (Vol. XV No. 6).

Grewal, B. (1998) *A Photographic Guide to the Birds of the Himalayas*. London: New Holland.

Grewal, B. & Mahajan, J. (2001) *Splendid Plumage, British Bird Painters in India*, Hong Kong: Local Colour.

Grewal, B., Pfister, O. & Harvey, B. (2002) *A Photographic Guide to the Birds of India, and the Indian Subcontinent including Pakistan, Nepal, Bhutan, Bangladesh, Sri Lanka and the Maldives,* Singapore: Periplus

Grewal, B., Sen S. & Sreenivasan. (2012) *Birds of Nagaland*, Kohima: Nagaland Govt.

Grewal, B., Sen S. & Sreenivasan. (2012) A Companion to the *Birds of Nagaland*, Kohima: Nagaland Govt.

Grimmet, R. Inskipp, T., & Inskipp, C. (1998) *Birds of the Indian Subcontinent*. UK: A&C Black.

Grimmet, R. Inskipp, T., & Inskipp, C. (1999) *Field Guide to the Birds of Bhutan*; UK: A&C Black

Grimmet, R. Inskipp, T., & Inskipp, C. (2000) *Field Guide to the Birds of Nepal*; UK: A&C Black

Grimmet, R. & Inskipp, T. (2003) *Birds of*

Northern India New Delhi: OUP. (Available also in Gujarati, Urdu & Hindi)

Grimmet, R. & Inskipp, T. (2005) *Birds of Southern India New Delhi*, OUP: (Available also in Marathi, Kannada, Malayalam, Telugu & Tamil)

Grimmet, R. Inskipp, T., & Roberts, T. (2008) *Birds of Pakistan*, London: Christopher Helm

Harris, P. (1996) Goa, *The Independent Birder?s Guide*. Lowestoft UK: Eastern Publications.

Harrison, J. (1999) *A Field Guide to The Birds of Sri Lanka*, New Delhi: OUP

Harvey, W.G. (1990) *Birds in Bangladesh*. Dhaka: University Press Limited.

Harvey, B., Devasar, N. & Grewal, B. (2006) *Atlas of the Birds of Delhi and Haryana*, New Delhi: Rupa & Co

Hassan, M. (2001) *Birds of the Indus*, Karachi: OUP

Henry, G.M. (1927) *Birds of Ceylon*. London: The Ceylon Government.

Henry, G.M. (1953) *A Picture Book of Ceylon Birds*. Dept. of Information. Ceylon.

Henry, G.M. (1955) *A Guide to the Birds of Ceylon*. London: OUP.

Holmer, M.R.N. (1923) *Indian Bird life*. London: OUP.

Holmer, M.R.N. (1926) *Bird Study in India*. London: OUP.

Hume, A.O. (1869) *My Scrap Book: or Rough Notes on Indian Oology and Ornithology.* Calcutta: C.B. Lewis, Baptist Mission Press.

Hume, A.O. (1873) *Contributions to Indian Ornithology*. London: L. Reeve & Co.

Hume, A.O. (ed) (1873-83) *Stray Feathers*
(Vols. 1-12) Published by the Editor.

Hume, A.O. & Marshall (1879-81) *The Game Birds of India, Burmah, and Ceylon*. Vols. I-3. London: John Bale.

Hume, A.O. & Oates (1889) *Hume?s Nests & Eggs of Indian Birds*. (Vol. I-3) London: R.H. Porter.

Hutson, Major-General H.P.W. (1954) *The Birds About Delhi*. The Delhi Bird Watching Society.

Inglis, C.M. (undated) *Sixty-eight Indian Birds*. Darjeeling: Natural History Museum.

Inskipp, C. (1988) A Birdwatchers? *Guide To Nepal*. England: Prion.

Inskipp, T. & Inskipp, C. (1991) *A Guide to The Birds of Nepal*. London: Christopher Helm.

Inskipp, C. & Inskipp, T. (undated) *An Introduction to Birdwatching in Bhutan. Thimpu*, Bhutan: WWF.

Inskipp, T. et al. (1996) *An Annotated Checklist of the Birds of the Oriental Region*. Sandy, UK: OBC.

Inskipp, C. (1989) *Nepal?s Forest Birds: Their Status and Conservation*. Cambridge: UK.

Islam, MZ ur and Rahmani, A. (eds) (2004) *A Important Bird Areas in India: Priority Sites for Conservation* Mumbai: BNHS

Islam, MZ ur and Rahmani, A. (2005) *Threatened Birds of India*, Mumbai, BNHS

Jerdon, T.C. (1845-1847) *Illustrations of Indian Ornithology*. Madras.

Jerdon, T.C. (1862-64) *The Birds of India: A Natural History*. Vols. I-3. Calcutta: The Military Orphan Press.

Jerdon, T.C. (1864) *The Game Birds and Wildfowl of India*. London: The Military Orphan Press.

Jonathan, J.K., & Kulkarni. (1989) *Beginners' Guide to Field Ornithology*. Calcutta: ZSI.

Jones, A.E. (undated) *The Common Birds of Simla. Simla:* Liddell's Printing Works.

Kaul, S.C. (1939) *Birds of Kashmir. Srinagar*: The Normal Press.

Kazmierczak, K. & Singh, R. (2001) *A Bird Watchers Guide to India*. Delhi: OUP

Kazmierczak, K. & van Perlo, B. (2000) *A Field-Guide to the Birds of the Indian Subcontinent*. UK: Pica Press

Kershaw, C. (1925) *Familiar Birds of Ceylon*. Colombo: H.W. Cave & Co.

Kershaw, C. (1949) *Bird Life in Ceylon*.

Khacher, L. (undated) *Birds of the Indian Wetland*. New Delhi: *Department of Environment*.

King, B. et al. (1991) *A Field Guide to the Birds of South East Asia*. London: Collins.

Kotagama, S., & Jinasama, J (2000) *Endemic Birds of Sri Lanka*, Colombo, Wild Heritage Trust

Kotagama, S., & Fernando, P. (1994) *A Field Guide to the Birds of Sri Lanka*. Colombo: The Wildlife Heritage Trust of Sri Lanka.

Kothari, A. & Chhapgar, B.F. (eds.) (1996) *Salim Ali's India*. New Delhi: OUP & BNHS.

Lal, R. (2003) *Birds of Delhi*. New Delhi: OUP

Lal, R. (2006) *Water Birds New Delhi*: Rupa.

Lainer, H. (2004) *Birds of Goa*, Goa: The Other

India Bookstore

Lester, C.D. (undated) *The Birds of Kutch.*

Lister, M.D. (1954) *A Contribution to the Ornithology of the Darjeeling Area.* Bombay: BNHS.

Lowther, E.H.N. (1949) *A Bird Photographer in India.* London: OUP.

Lushington, C. (1949) *Bird Life in Ceylon.* Colombo: Times of Ceylon Ltd.

MacDonald, M. (1960) *Birds in My Indian Garden.* London: Jonathan Cape.

MacDonald, M. (1962) *Birds in The Sun*: Some Beautiful Birds of India. London: D.B. Taraporevala & Sons.

Mackintosh, L.J. (1915) *Birds of Darjeeling and India*: Part I. Calcutta: J.N. Banerjee & Son.

Monga, S. (2003) *Birds of Mumbai*, Mumbai, India Book House

Monga, S. (2004) *Birds of the Sanjay Gandhi National Park, Mumbai*, BNHS

Mookherjee, K. (1995) *Birds and Trees of Tolly.* Calcutta: Tollygunge Club.

Mukherjee, A.K. (1992) *Birds of Goa.* Calcutta: ZSI.

Mukherjee, A.K. (1995) *Birds of Arid & Semi Arid Tracts.* Calcutta: ZSI.

Mukherjee, K. (1994) *Narendrapur Wildlife Sanctuary.* Calcutta: K. Dey.

Murray, J.A. (1888) *Indian Birds or the Avifauna of British India.* Vols. I-2. London: Trubner & Co.

Murray, J.A. (1889) *The Edible and Game Birds of British India with its Dependencies and Ceylon.* London: Trubner.

Murray, J.A. (1890) *The Avifauna of the Island of Ceylon.* Bombay: Educational Society Press.

Naoroji, R (2006) *Birds of Prey of the Indian Subcontinent*, London: Christopher Helm

Neelakantan, K.K., Sashikumar & Venugopalan (1993) *A Book of Kerala Birds.* Trivandrum: WWF.

Oates, E.W. (1883) *Handbook of the Birds of British Burma.* (Vols.1-2). London: R.H. Porter.

Oates, E.W. & Blandford (1889-98) *Fauna of British India Birds.* (Vols.1-4). London: Taylor & Francis.

Oates, E.W. (1898) *A Manual of the Game Birds of India, Land Birds.* Bombay: Messrs. A.J. Combridge.

Oates, E.W. (1899) A *Manual of the Game Birds of India*: *Game Birds.* Bombay: A.J. Combridge.

Pande, S., Tambe, S., Clement, Francis & Sant, N. (2003) *Birds of Western Ghats, Konkan and Malabar Mumbai*: BNHS

Pfister, O. (2004) *Birds and Mammals of Ladakh.* New Delhi: OUP.

Phillips, W.W.A. (1949-1961) *Birds of Ceylon*: (Vols.1-4). Colombo: Ceylon Daily News Press, Lake House.

Phillips, W.W.A. (1953) *Revised Checklist of the Birds of Ceylon.* National Museums of Ceylon.

Phillips, W.W.A. (1978) *Annotated Checklist of the Birds of Ceylon.* Colombo: Ceylon Bird Club.

Pittie, A. (1995) *A Bibliographic Index to the Ornithology of the Indian Region. Part 1.* Hyderabad: Published by the author

Pittie, A. (2010) *Birds in Books.* New Delhi: Permanent Black

Prasad, A. (2006) *Birds of Western Maharashtra, A Reference Guide,* Goa, The Other India Bookstore

Pyhala, M. (2001) *Birds of Islamabad*: *Status and Seasonality,* WWF Pakistan

Rahmani, A. (2005) *Common Birds of India New Delhi*: Publications Division.

Rahmani, A. & Ugra, G. (2005) *Birds of Wetlands and Grasslands.* Mumbai: BNHS

Rangaswami, S. & Sridhar, S. (1993) *Birds of Rishi Valley.* Andhra Pradesh.

Rasmussen, P. & Anderton, J. (2005) *Birds of South Asia*: *The Ripley Guide*, Barcelona: Lynx Editions.

Ripley, D. (1952) *Search for the Spiny Babbler.* Boston: Houghton Mifflin.

Ripley, D. (1978) *A Bundle of Feathers.* London: OUP.

Ripley, D. (1982) *A Synopsis of the Birds of India and Pakistan.* Bombay: BNHS.

Roberts, T.J. (1991-92) *The Birds of Pakistan.* Vols. I-2. Karachi: OUP.

Samarpan, A. (2006) *Birds of India*: *Including Nepal, Sri Lanka, Bhutan, Pakistan and Bangladesh,* New Delhi: Wisdom Tree.

Shrestha, T.K. (1998) *The Spiny Babbler, An Endemic Bird of Nepal (?)*

Sinclair, I., & Langard, O (1998) *Birds of the Indian Ocean*, Struik

Smythies, B.E. (1953) *The Birds of Burma. London*: Oliver and Boyd.

Snilloc. (1945) *Mystery Birds of India*. Bombay: Thacker & Company Limited.

Sondhi, A. (2001) *Birds of Pune*, New Delhi: Kalpavriksh

Sonobe, K. (ed) (1993) *A Field Guide to the Waterbirds of Asia*. Tokyo.

Spierenburg, P. (2005) *Birds in Bhutan: Status and Distribution*, Sandy: OBC

Tikader, B.K. (1984) *Birds of Andaman & Nicobar Islands*. Calcutta: ZSI.

Urfi, A.J. (2004) *Birds: Beyond Watching*. Hyderabad: Universities Press.

Urfi, A.J. (2007) *Birds of India: A Literary Anthology*. New Delhi. OUP

Vaurie, Charles. (1972) *Tibet and its Birds*. London: H.F. & G. Witherby Ltd.

Wait, W.E. (1925) *Birds of Ceylon*. London: Dualu & Co.

Ward, Geoff. (1994) *Islamabad Birds*. Islamabad: Asian Study Group.

Whistler, Hugh. (1928) *Popular Handbook of Indian Birds*. London: Gurney and Jackson.

Wijeyeratne, S., Warakagoda, D. & Zylva T.S. (2000) *A Photographic Guide to the Birds of Sri Lanka*, London: New Holland.

Woodcock, M. (1980) *Collins Handguide to the Birds of the Indian Subcontinent*. London: Collins.

Wright, R.C & Dewar, D. (1925) *The Ducks of India*. London: H.F. & G. Witherby.

SOUND GUIDES

Barucha, E. (1999) *Indian Bird Calls*, Bombay: BNHS

Breil, F., & Roche, J.C. (2000) *Birding in India and Nepal*. Sittelle Editions

Connop, S. (1993) *Birdsongs of Nepal*. New York: Turaco.

Connop, S. (1995) *Birdsongs of the Himalayas*. Toronto: Turaco.

Warakagoda, *Bird Sounds of Sri Lanka*

Roche, J., & Walker, A. *Jungles of Sri Lanka*

Jannes, H (2002) *Bird Sounds of Goa and South India, Wildsounds*

Sivaprasad, P.S. (1994) *An Audio Guide to the Birds of South India*. London: OBC.

Smith, Steve (1995) *Bird Recordings from Sri Lanka (Privately Produced)*

Surat Nature Club *Call of Indian Birds* (4 Vols) Surat

Rymer, M. (2002) *Birding Goa* (2 Vols). (Privately Produced)

Rymer, M. (1999) *Birding in Sri Lanka* (Privately Produced)

Warakagoda, D. (2002) *The Bird Sounds of Sri Lanka, Drongo*

White, T. (1984) *A Field Guide to the Bird Songs of South East Asia*. London: British Library.

DESCRIPTIVE PARTS OF A BIRD

eye-ring
lores
culmen
supercillium
upper mandible
eye-strip
lower mandible
moustachial stripe
submoustachial stripe
malar stripe

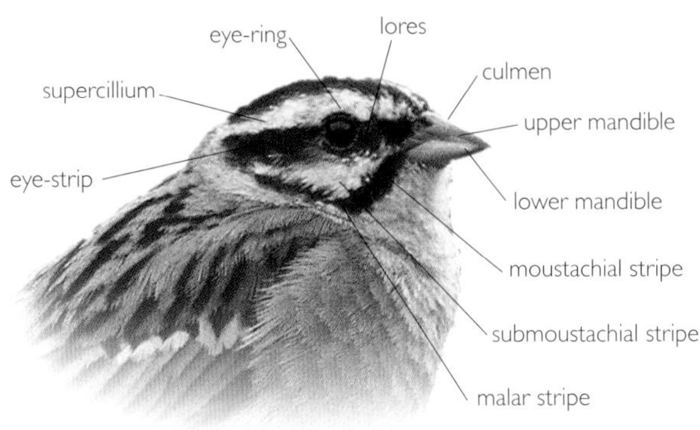

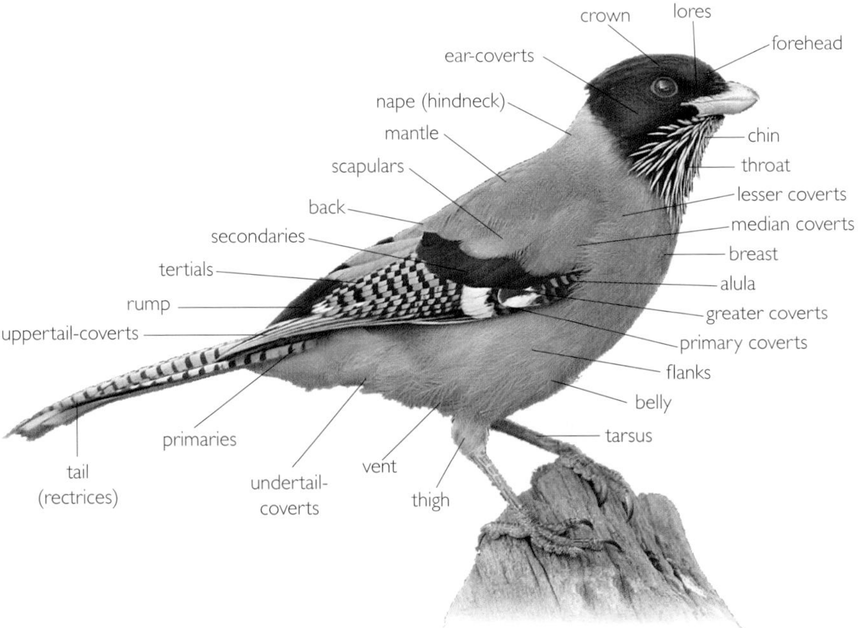
crown
lores
forehead
ear-coverts
nape (hindneck)
mantle
chin
throat
scapulars
back
lesser coverts
median coverts
secondaries
breast
tertials
alula
rump
greater coverts
uppertail-coverts
primary coverts
flanks
belly
tarsus
primaries
tail
(rectrices)
undertail-
coverts
vent
thigh

A GLOSSARY OF ORNITHOLOGICAL TERMS

Aberrant Abnormal or unusual
Accidental Vagrant
Adult Mature, Capable of breeding
Aerial Making use of the open sky
Allopatric Relating to two or more related species whose range do not overlap
Altitudinal migrant Moving between high mountains and lower foothills
Altricial Blind and helpless when hatched
Apical Outer extremities, particularly of the tail
Aquatic Living on or in water
Arboreal Living in trees
Ashy Greyish Colour
Axillaries Underwing feathers at the base of the wings, forming 'armpits'
Back Loosely applied to the mantle scapulars and rump
Banyan Type of fig tree
Barring 'Sideway' lines such as on tail or breast
Basal Innermost extremities, particularly of the tail or bill
Bheel Shallow lake or wetland
Biosphere The part of earth that is inhabited by life
Biotope Area of uniform environment, flora and fauna
Bristles Sensory feathers near beak
Brood Young hatched from a single clutch
Brood Parasitism Depositing of eggs by one species in the nest of an another
Buff Yellowish white with a hint of pale brown
Bund Man-made mud embankment
Canopy Leafy foliage of treetops
Cap Upper part of head
Carpal Bend of a closed wing, sometimes called shoulder
Casque Growth above bill of hornbills
Cere Patch of bare skin on upper base of bill of raptors
Cheek Term loosely applied to sides of head, below the eye or on ear-coverts
Chevrons V-shaped contrasting marks on wings or bands across breast
Cinnamon Light yellowish-brown colour
Clutch Complete set of eggs laid by a single female
Collar Distinctive band of colour that encircles or partly encircles the neck
Colonial Roosting or nesting in groups
Confiding Not shy
Commensal Living together with man for mutual benefit
Coverts Small feathers on wings and base of tail
Covey Small group of partridges and allied species
Crepuscular Active at dusk (twilight) and dawn
Crest Extended feathers on head
Crop Pouch-like enlargement of gullet in some birds where food is partially digested
Crown Upper part of head
Crown-stripe Distinct line from forehead along centre of crown
Cryptic Hidden - having protective colouring and/ or behaviour
Culmen Ridge on upper mandible of bill
Cursorial Ground running
Deciduous Trees that shed their leaves annually
Decurved Curving downwards
Diagnostic Sufficient to identify a species or sub-species
Dimorphic Having two forms of plumage
Distal Terminal or the outer end
Diurnal Active during daytime
Down Small soft feathers close to body of chicks
Drake Male duck
Drumming Rhythmic territorial hammering on trees by woodpeckers
Duars Forested areas south of eastern Himalayas
Ear-coverts Feathers covering the ear opening. Often distinctly coloured
Ear tufts Feathers protruding near ears
Echolocate Navigate by sound
Eclipse Plumage New dull plumage after breeding season, especially in ducks
Endemic Indigenous and confined to a place
Endangered Species facing high risk of extinction
Eurasian Of both Europe and Asia
Evergreen Forests that always have leaves
Eye-ring Contrasting ring around the eye
Eye-stripe Stripe through eye
Extinct No longer in existence
Extirpated Locally extinct
Extralimital Not existing in the region
Facial Disc Heart-shaped arrangement of feathers as in some owls and harriers
Fallow Cultivated land after cultivation and before ploughing
Family Specified group of genera
Forage Search for food
Ferruginous Rusty-brown colour
Feral Escaped, and living and breeding in the wild
Filoplume Hair-like feathers like in breeding egrets
Flank Side of body
Fledged Having just acquired feathers and ready to leave nest
Fledglings Young birds which have just acquired feathers
Flight feathers Primary and secondary wing feathers
Flushed When disturbed into flight at close quarters
Foreneck The lower throat
Form Sub-species
Frons Forehead
Frugivorous Fruit-eating

Fulvous Brownish-yellow
Game birds Pheasants, partridges and allied species
Gape Basal part of the beak (mainly for young birds and raptors)
Genera Plural of genus
Genus Group of related species
Ghats Hills parallel to the east and west coast of India
Gorget Band across upper chest
Granivorous Grain-eating
Gregarious Sociable living in communities or flocks
Gular pouch Loose area of skin extending from throat as in pelicans and hornbills
Gular stripe Narrow and often dark stripe running down from the centre of throat
Guttural From the throat
Hackles Long and pointed neck feathers
Hawking Capturing insects in flight
Hepatic Rust or liver coloured plumage phase, mainly in female cuckoos
Hood Dark-coloured head and throat
Hunting party Group of birds usually of different species, seeking food
Hybridisation Cross-breeding between two different species
Immature Plumage phases prior to adult
Incubate Giving warmth for eggs to hatch
Iris Coloured eye membrane surrounding pupil
Irruption Mass movement of a population from one place to another
Jheel Shallow lake or wetland
Jizz Essence or striking characteristics of a species;
Juvenile Immature bird immediately after leaving nest
Lamellae Small stiff comb-like membrane on inner edge of bill used for sieving food
Lanceolate Lance-shaped. Slim and pointed
Lantana Invasive aggressive shrub introduced to the region
Leading edge Front edge of wing
Lek Sociable courtship gatherings
Lobe Fleshy extensions to side-edges of toes of some birds
Local Unevenly distributed with a region
Loranthus Parasitical bush that grows on tress and frequented by flowerpeckers
Lores Area between eye and bill base
Lump Treatment of one or more forms previously treated as distinct species as race of a single species
Malar Stripe on side of throat
Mandible Each of the two parts of bill
Mangrove Coastal salt-resistant trees or bushes
Mantle Back, between wings
Mask Dark plumage round eye and ear-coverts
Mesial Stripe Central throat stripe
Migration Seasonal movement between distant places
Mirror White spots in wing-tips, mainly of gulls
Monotypic Of a single form with no subspecies
Montane Pertaining to mountains
Monsoon Rainy season in India
Morph One of several distinct types of plumage in the same species
Moult Seasonal shedding of plumage
Nail Hook on tip of upper mandible
Nape Back of neck
Nares Nostril openings
Necklace Narrow line round neck
Nictitating Membrane Transparent fold of skin forming a third eyelid
Nidicolous Chicks that remain in nests for a long duration after hatching
Nidifugous Chicks that leave the nests soon after hatching
Nidification Relating to nests or nesting
Nocturnal Active at night
Nomadic Species without specific territory except when breeding
Nominate First sub-species to be formally named
Non-passerine All order of birds except for Passerines
Notch Indentations in outline of feathers, wing or tail
Nuchal Crest Crest along back of neck
Nullah Dry or wet stream bed or ditch
Nuptial Plumage Breeding plumage
Ocelli Brightly-coloured 'eye-like' spots as on peacocks
Occipital Back of head
Oology Study of bird's eggs
Orbital ring Narrow ring of skin or feathers round the eye
Order Group of related families
Paddy-fields Rice fields often flooded
Paleartic Old world and arctic zone
Parasitic Deriving sustenance or taking advantage of others, like cuckoos laying eggs in other bird's nest
Passerines Perching and song birds
Pectoral Breast area
Pelagic Ocean-going
Pellet Indigested material regurgitated by owls
Phase Colour form of a species
Pied Black and white
Plumage Feathers of a bird
Plumes Long, showy feathers, acquired during the breeding season
Polyandrous Female having more than one mate
Polygamous Male with more than one mate
Polymorphic Taking several forms
Postocular Area behind the eye
Precocial Young hatched sighted and down-covered, e.g. ducklings
Predator Who feeds on other birds or animals
Primaries Outer flight feathers in wing
Race Sub-species

Rachis Central shaft of a feather
Range Geographical area or areas inhabited by a species
Raptors Birds of prey and Vultures, excluding owls
Record Published, or otherwise broadcast, occurrence
Rectrices Tail feathers
Remiges The primaries and secondaries combined
Rictal Around the bill
Resident Non-migratory and breeding in same place
Riparian Along creeks, streams, rivers and waterways
Roost Resting or sleeping space
Rufescent Inclining to redness
Rufous Reddish brown
Rump Lower back
Sal Dominant tree of North Indian forests
Sallies Short flights and returning to perch as in bee-eaters and flycatchers
Salt pans Shallow reservoirs for drying out salt
Savanna Open flat land with grass and scattered bushes
Sedentary Staying in the same area throughout the year
Scalloped Curved markings on edges of feathers
Scapulars Feathers along edge of mantle
Scrape Shallow depression made by birds to serve as nest
Secondaries Inner wing feathers
Sedentary Confined with a particular area
Shaft Central stem of a feather, often hidden
Shank Bare parts of a leg
Sholas Small forests in SW Indian valleys
Shoulder Where the wing meets the body
Shorebird Long-legged bird living near water
Skins Bird specimens prepared for scientific studies
Skulker Bird that mostly remains within vegetation cover
Slaty Dull bluish-grey
Soar Rising flight on still extending wings using thermals
Speculum Area of colour on secondary feathers of wings
Streamers Long extensions to feathers, usually of tail
Spangles Distinctive white or shimmering spots in plumage
Species Groups of birds reproductively isolated from other such groups
Speculum Shiny, colourful patch on secondary feathers of the wing of some ducks
Storey Level of the tree or forest
Spur Sharp horny growth on legs of some birds
Straw Pale yellow colour
Streaks 'Lengthwise' lines on breasts or tail
Streamers Long extension of tail feathers
Striated Marked with fine streaks
Sooty Blackish Colour
Sub-adult Immature moulting into adult plumage
Sub-montane Hills below highest mountains
Sub-song Subdued version of normal territorial song
Sub-species Distinct form that does not have specific status
Sub-terminal Band Broad band on outer part of feather
Supercilia Plural of supercilium
Supercilium Streak above eye
Symbiotic Interdependence between different species
Tail Streamers Elongated ribbon-like tail feathers
Talons Strong sharp claws used to seize or kill prey
Tank Water reservoir
Tarsus Lower part of a bird's legs
Taxonomy Science of classifying organisms
Teak Dominant tree of South Indian forests
Terai Alluvial strech of land south of the Himalayas
Terminal band Broad band on tip of feather or tail
Terrestrial Living on the ground
Tertials Innermost wing coverts, often covering secondaries
Totipalmate All four toes connected to a single web
Trailing edge Rear edge of wing
Underparts Under surface of a bird from throat to vent
Underwing Undersurface of a wing including the linings and flight feathers
Upperparts Upper surface of a bird including wings, back and tail
Upperstorey Canopy of a tree
Vagrant Accidental, irregular
Vent Undertail area
Ventral Undersurface of body
Vermiculations Wavy (worm-like) markings
Vinaceous Red wine coloured warm pink
Vocal mimicry Imitating the sounds of other birds
Waders Shorebirds. Usually, the smaller, long-legged waterbirds
Washed Suffused with a particular colour
Wattle Bare skin, often coloured, on part of head
Web Skin stretched between toes
Wildfowl Ducks and geese
Wing-bar visible line of colour at tip on wing-coverts
Wing-coverts Small feathers on wing at base of primaries and secondaries
Wing-span Length from one wing tip to the other when fully extended
Winter plumage Plumage seen during the non-breeding winter months
Zygodactylous Having two toes directed forward and two backwards

CHECKLIST: BIRDS OF THE INDIAN SUBCONTINENT

as per classification and nomenclature in **Pamela C. Rasmussen & John C. Anderton's *Birds of South Asia: The Ripley Guide* 2nd Edition 2012**

Red-throated Diver *Gavia stellata*
Black-throated Diver *Gavia arctica*
Little Grebe *Tachybaptus ruficollis*
Red-necked Grebe *Podiceps grisegena*
Great Crested Grebe *Podiceps cristatus*
Horned Grebe *Podiceps auritus*
Black-necked Grebe *Podiceps nigricollis*
Barau's Petrel *Pterodroma baraui* ?
Bulwer's Petrel *Bulweria bulwerii* ?
Jouanin's Petrel *Bulweria fallax* ?
Streaked Shearwater *Calonectris leucomelas*
Wedge-tailed Shearwater *Ardenna pacifica*
Flesh-footed Shearwater *Ardenna carneipes*
Audubon's Shearwater *Puffinus lherminieri*
Persian Shearwater *Puffinus persicus*
Wilson's Storm-petrel *Oceanites oceanicus*
Black-bellied Storm-petrel *Fregetta tropica*
Swinhoe's Storm-petrel *Oceanodroma monorhis* ?
White-tailed Tropicbird *Phaethon lepturus*
Red-billed Tropicbird *Phaethon aethereus*
Red-tailed Tropicbird *Phaethon rubricauda* ?
Great White Pelican *Pelecanus onocrotalus*
Spot-billed Pelican *Pelecanus philippensis*
Dalmatian Pelican *Pelecanus crispus*
Masked Bobby *Sula dactylatra* ?
Brown Bobby *Sula leucogaster*
Red-footed Bobby *Sula sula*
Little Cormorant *Microcarbo niger*
Indian Shag *Phalacrocorax fuscicollis*
Great Cormorant *Phalacrocorax carbo*
Oriental Darter *Anhinga melanogaster*
Lesser Frigatebird *Fregata ariel*
Great Frigatebird *Fregata minor*
Christmas Island Frigatebird *Fregata andrewsi* ?
Little Egret *Egretta garzetta*
Western Reef-heron *Egretta gularis*
Pacific Reef-heron *Egretta sacra*
Great Egret *Egretta alba*
Intermediate Egret *Egretta intermedia*
Grey Heron *Ardea cinerea*
Goliath Heron *Ardea goliath*
White-bellied Heron *Ardea insignis*
Purple Heron *Ardea purpurea*
Eastern Cattle Egret *Bubulcus coromandus*
Indian Pond-heron *Ardeola grayii*
Chinese Pond-heron *Ardeola bacchus*
Striated Heron *Butorides striata*
Black-crowned Night-heron *Nycticorax nycticorax*
Malayan Night-heron *Gorsachius melanolophus*
Little Bittern *Ixobrychus minutus*
Yellow Bittern *Ixobrychus sinensis*
Chestnut Bittern *Ixobrychus cinnamomeus*
Black Bittern *Dupetor flavicollis*
Eurasian Bittern *Botaurus stellaris*
Painted Stork *Mycteria leucocephala*
Asian Openbill *Anastomus oscitans*
Black Stork *Ciconia nigra*
Wooly-necked Stork *Ciconia episcopus*
White Stork *Ciconia ciconia*
Black-necked Stork *Ephippiorhynchus asiaticus*
Lesser Adjutant *Leptoptilos javanicus*
Greater Adjutant *Leptoptilos dubius*
Glossy Ibis *Plegadis falcinellus*
Black-headed Ibis *Threskiornis melanocephalus*
Indian Black Ibis *Pseudibis papillosa*
Eurasian Spoonbill *Platalea leucorodia*
Greater Flamingo *Phoenicopterus roseus*
Lesser Flamingo *Phoenicopterus minor*
Fulvous Whistling-duck *Dendrocygna bicolor*
Lesser Whistling-duck *Dendrocygna javanica*
White-headed Duck *Oxyura leucocephala*
Mute Swan *Cygnus olor* ?
Whooper Swan *Cygnus cygnus* ?
Bewick's Swan *Cygnus bewickii* ?
Bean Goose *Anser fabalis*
Greater White-fronted Goose *Anser albifrons*
Lesser White-fronted Goose *Anser erythropus*
Greylag Goose *Anser anser*
Bar-headed Goose *Anser indicus*
Ruddy Shelduck *Tadorna ferruginea*
Common Shelduck *Tadorna tadorna*
White-winged Duck *Asarcornis scutulata*
Knob-billed Duck *Sarkidiornis melanotos*
Cotton Teal *Nettapus coromandelianus*
Mandarin Duck *Aix galericulata* ?
Gadwall *Mareca strepera*
Falcated Duck *Mareca falcata*
Eurasian Wigeon *Mareca penelope*
Mallard *Anas platyrhynchos*
Indian Spot-billed Duck *Anas poecilorhyncha*
Chinese Spot-billed Duck *Anas zonoryncha*
Northern Shoveler *Spatula clypeata*

Andaman Teal *Anas albogularis*
Northern Pintail *Anas acuta*
Garganey *Querquedula querquedula*
Baikal Teal *Sibrionetta formosa*
Common Teal *Anas crecca*
Marbled Duck *Marmaronetta angustirostris*
Pink-headed Duck *Rhodonessa caryophyllacea* (Extinct)
Red-crested Pochard *Netta rufina*
Common Pochard *Aythya ferina*
Ferruginous Duck *Aythya nyroca*
Baer's Pochard *Aythya baeri*
Tufted Duck *Aythya fuligula*
Greater Scaup *Aythya marila*
Long-tailed Duck *Clangula hyemalis*
Common Goldeneye *Bucephala clangula*
Smew *Mergellus albellus*
Red-breasted Merganser *Mergus serrator*
Common Merganser *Mergus merganser*
Jerdon's Baza *Aviceda jerdoni*
Black Baza *Aviceda leuphotes*
Oriental Honey-buzzard *Pernis ptilorhyncus*
Black-winged Kite *Elanus caeruleus*
Black Kite *Milvus migrans*
'Black-eared' Kite *Milvus (migrans) lineatus*
Brahminy Kite *Haliastur indus*
White-bellied Sea-eagle *Haliaeetus leucogaster*
Pallas's Fish-eagle *Haliaeetus leucoryphus*
White-tailed Eagle *Haliaeetus albicilla*
Lesser Fish-eagle *Icthyophaga humilis*
Grey-headed Fish-eagle *Icthyophaga ichthyaetus*
Bearded Vulture *Gypaetus barbatus*
Egyptian Vulture *Neophron percnopterus*
White-rumped Vulture *Gyps bengalensis*
Indian Vulture *Gyps indicus*
Slender-billed Vulture *Gyps tenuirostris*
Himalayan Vulture *Gyps himalayensis*
Griffon Vulture *Gyps fulvus*
Cinereous Vulture *Aegypius monachus*
Red-headed Vulture *Aegypius calvus*
Short-toed Eagle *Circaetus gallicus*
Crested Serpent-eagle *Spilornis cheela*
Greater Nicobar Serpent-eagle *Spilornis klossi*
Andaman Serpent-eagle *Spilornis elgini*
Western Marsh Harrier *Circus aeruginosus*
Eastern Marsh Harrier *Circus spilonotus* ?
Hen Harrier *Circus cyaneus*
Pallid Harrier *Circus macrourus*
Pied Harrier *Circus melanoleucos*
Montagu's Harrier *Circus pygargus*
Crested Goshawk *Accipiter trivirgatus*
Shikra *Accipiter badius*
Nicobar Sparrowhawk *Accipiter butleri*
Chinese Sparrowhawk *Accipiter soloensis*
Japanese Sparrowhawk *Accipiter gularis*
Besra Sparrowhawk *Accipiter virgatus*
Eurasian Sparrowhawk *Accipiter nisus*
Northern Goshawk *Accipiter gentilis*
White-eyed Buzzard *Butastur teesa*
Himalayan Buzzard *Buteo burmanicus*
Long-legged Buzzard *Buteo rufinus*
Upland Buzzard *Buteo hemilasius*
Black Eagle *Ictinaetus malayensis*
Indian Spotted Eagle *Clanga hastata*
Greater Spotted Eagle *Clanga clanga*
Tawny Eagle *Aquila rapax*
Steppe Eagle *Aquila nipalensis*
Eastern Imperial Eagle *Aquila heliaca*
Golden Eagle *Aquila chrysaetos*
Bonelli's Eagle *Aquila fasciata*
Booted Eagle *Hieraaetus pennatus*
Rufous-bellied Eagle *Lophotriorchis kienerii*
Changeable Hawk-eagle *Nisaetus limnaeetus*
Crested Hawk-eagle *Nisaetus cirrhatus*
Mountain Hawk-eagle *Nisaetus nipalensis*
Legge's Hawk-eagle *Nisaetus kelaarti*
Western Osprey *Pandion haliaetus*
Collared Falconet *Microhierax caerulescens*
Pied Falconet *Microhierax melanoleucos*
Lesser Kestrel *Falco naumanni*
Common Kestrel *Falco tinnunculus*
Red-headed Falcon *Falco chicquera*
Amur Falcon *Falco amurensis*
Merlin *Falco columbarius*
Eurasian Hobby *Falco subbuteo*
Oriental Hobby *Falco severus*
Laggar Falcon *Falco jugger*
Saker Falcon *Falco cherrug*
Peregrine Falcon *Falco peregrinus*
Barbary Falcon *Falco pelegrinoides*
Nicobar Megapode *Megapodius nicobariensis*
Himalayan Snowcock *Tetraogallus himalayensis*
Tibetan Snowcock *Tetraogallus tibetanus*
Chukar Partridge *Alectoris chukar*
Black Francolin *Francolinus francolinus*
Painted Francolin *Francolinus pictus*
Chinese Francolin *Francolinus pintadeanus*
Grey Francolin *Francolinus pondicerianus*
Swamp Francolin *Francolinus gularis*
Tibetan Partridge *Perdix hodgsoniae*
Common Quail *Coturnix coturnix*
Japanese Quail *Coturnix japonica*
Rain Quail *Coturnix coromandelica*
Blue-breasted Quail *Excalfactoria chinensis*
Jungle Bush-quail *Perdicula asiatica*
Rock Bush-quail *Perdicula argoondah*

Painted Bush-quail *Perdicula erythrorhyncha*
Manipur Bush-quail *Perdicula manipurensis*
Mountain Bamboo Partridge *Bambusicola fytchii*
Snow Partridge *Lerwa lerwa*
Common Hill-partridge *Arborophila torqueola*
Rufous-throated Hill-partridge *Arborophila rufogularis*
White-cheeked Hill-partridge *Arborophila atrogularis*
Chestnut-breasted Hill-partridge *Arborophila mandellii*
Red Spurfowl *Galloperdix spadicea*
Painted Spurfowl *Galloperdix lunulata*
Himalayan Quail *Ophrysia superciliosa* (extinct)
Blood Pheasant *Ithaginis cruentus*
Western Tragopan *Tragopan melanocephalus*
Satyr Tragopan *Tragopan satyra*
Blyth's Tragopan *Tragopan blythii*
Temminck's Tragopan *Tragopan temminckii*
Koklass Pheasant *Pucrasia macrolopha*
Himalayan Monal *Lophophorus impejanus*
Sclater's Monal *Lophophorus sclateri*
Red Junglefowl *Gallus gallus*
Grey Junglefowl *Gallus sonneratii*
Kalij Pheasant *Lophura leucomelanos*
Cheer Pheasant *Catreus wallichii*
Mrs Hume's Pheasant *Syrmaticus humiae*
Grey Peacock-pheasant *Polyplectron bicalcaratum*
Indian Peafowl *Pavo cristatus*
Small Buttonquail *Turnix sylvaticus*
Yellow-legged Buttonquail *Turnix tanki*
Barred Buttonquail *Turnix suscitator*
Siberian Crane *Leucogeranus leucogeranus* ?
Sarus Crane *Grus antigone*
Demoiselle Crane *Grus virgo*
Common Crane *Grus grus*
Black-necked Crane *Grus nigricollis*
Andaman Crake *Rallina canningi*
Slaty-legged Crake *Rallina eurizonoides*
Slaty-breasted Rail *Gallirallus striatus*
European Water Rail *Rallus aquaticus*
Eastern Water Rail *Rallus indicus*
Corn Crake *Crex crex*
Brown Crake *Porzana akool*
Black-tailed Crake *Porzana bicolor*
Little Crake *Porzana parva*
'Eastern' Baillon's Crake *Porzana pusilla*
Spotted Crake *Porzana porzana*
Ruddy-breasted Crake *Porzana fusca*
Watercock *Gallicrex cinerea*
Grey-headed Swamphen *Porphyrio poliocephalus*
Common Moorhen *Gallinula chloropus*
Eurasian Coot *Fulica atra*
Masked Finfoot *Heliopais personatus*
Little Bustard *Tetrax tetrax ?*
Great Indian Bustard *Otis nigriceps*
Macqueen's Bustard *Chlamydotis macqueenii*
Bengal Florican *Houbaropsis bengalensis*
Lesser Florican *Sypheotides indicus*
Pheasant-tailed Jacana *Hydrophasianus chirurgus*
Bronze-winged Jacana *Metopidius indicus*
Greater Painted-snipe *Rostratula benghalensis*
Eurasian Oystercatcher *Haematopus ostralegus*
European Golden Plover *Pluvialis apricaria*
Pacific Golden Plover *Pluvialis fulva*
Grey Plover *Pluvialis squatarola*
Eurasian Dotterel *Charadrius morinellus*
Common Ringed Plover *Charadrius hiaticula*
Long-billed Plover *Charadrius placidus*
Little Ringed Plover *Charadrius dubius*
Kentish Plover *Charadrius alexandrinus*
Lesser Sand Plover *Charadrius mongolus*
Greater Sand Plover *Charadrius leschenaultii*
Caspian Plover *Charadrius asiaticus*
Oriental Plover *Charadrius veredus*
Northern Lapwing *Vanellus vanellus*
Yellow-wattled Lapwing *Vanellus malabaricus*
River Lapwing *Vanellus duvaucelii*
Grey-headed Lapwing *Vanellus cinereus*
Red-wattled Lapwing *Vanellus indicus*
Sociable Plover *Vanellus gregarius*
White-tailed Lapwing *Vanellus leucurus*
Eurasian Woodcock *Scolopax rusticola*
Solitary Snipe *Gallinago solitaria*
Wood Snipe *Gallinago nemoricola*
Pintail Snipe *Gallinago stenura*
Swinhoe's Snipe *Gallinago megala*
Common Snipe *Gallinago gallinago*
Great Snipe *Gallinago media*
Jack Snipe *Lymnocryptes minimus*
'Western' Black-tailed Godwit *Limosa limosa*
'Eastern' Black-tailed Godwit *Limosa (limosa) melanuroides*
Bar-tailed Godwit *Limosa lapponica*
Eurasian Whimbrel *Numenius phaeopus*
Eurasian Curlew *Numenius arquata*
Spotted Redshank *Tringa erythropus*
Common Redshank *Tringa totanus*
Common Greenshank *Tringa nebularia*
Spotted Greenshank *Tringa guttifer*
Marsh Sandpiper *Tringa stagnatilis*
Green Sandpiper *Tringa ochropus*
Wood Sandpiper *Tringa glareola*
Terek Sandpiper *Xenus cinereus*
Common Sandpiper *Actitis hypoleucos*
Grey-tailed Tattler *Tringa brevipes*

Ruddy Turnstone *Arenaria interpres*
Long-billed Dowitcher *Limnodromus scolopacea*
Asian Dowitcher *Limnodromus semipalmatus*
Great Knot *Calidris tenuirostris*
Red Knot *Calidris canutus*
Sanderling *Ereunetes alba*
Little Stint *Ereunetes minuta*
Rufous-necked Stint *Ereunetes ruficollis*
Temminck's Stint *Ereunetes temminckii*
Long-toed Stint *Ereunetes subminuta*
Pectoral Sandpiper *Ereunetes melanotos*
Dunlin *Ereunetes alpina*
Curlew Sandpiper *Erolia ferruginea*
Spoon-billed Sandpiper *Eurynorhynchus pygmeus*
Buff-breasted Sandpiper *Tryngites subruficollis*
Broad-billed Sandpiper *Limicola falcinellus*
Ruff *Philomachus pugnax*
Ibisbill *Ibidorhyncha struthersii*
Black-winged Stilt *Himantopus himantopus*
Pied Avocet *Recurvirostra avosetta*
Red-necked Phalarope *Phalaropus lobatus*
Red Phalarope *Phalaropus fulicarius*
Crab-plover *Dromas ardeola*
Indian Stone-curlew *Burhinus indicus*
Great Thick-knee *Esacus recurvirostris*
Beach Thick-knee *Esacus magnirostris*
Jerdon's Courser *Rhinoptilus bitorquatus*
Cream-coloured Courser *Cursorius cursor*
Indian Courser *Cursorius coromandelicus*
Collared Pratincole *Glareola pratincola*
Oriental Pratincole *Glareola maldivarum*
Small Pratincole *Glareola lactea*
Brown Skua *Stercorarius antarctica*
South Polar Skua *Stercorarius maccormicki* ?
Pomarine Jaeger *Stercorarius pomarinus*
Parasitic Jaeger *Stercorarius parasiticus* ?
Sooty Gull *Ichthyaetus hemprichii* ?
Mew Gull *Larus canus*
Heuglin's Gull *Fuscus heuglini*
'Steppe' Gull *Larus heuglini barabensis*
Great Black-headed Gull *Ichthyaetus ichthyaetus*
Brown-headed Gull *Chroicocephalus brunnicephalus*
Common Black-headed Gull *Chroicocephalus ridibundus*
Slender-billed Gull *Chroicocephalus genei*
Little Gull *Hydrocoloeus minutus*
Black-legged Kittiwake *Rissa tridactyla* ?
Gull-billed Tern *Gelochelidon nilotica*
Caspian Tern *Hydroprogne caspia*
Lesser Crested Tern *Thalasseus bengalensis*
Greater Crested Tern *Thalasseus bergii*
Sandwich Tern *Thalasseus sandvicensis*
River Tern *Sterna aurantia*
Roseate Tern *Sterna dougallii*
Black-naped Tern *Sterna sumatrana*
Common Tern *Sterna hirundo*
Arctic Tern *Sterna paradisaea* ?
Little Tern *Sternula albifrons*
Saunders's Tern *Sternula saundersi*
White-cheeked Tern *Sterna repressa*
Black-bellied Tern *Sterna acuticauda*
Bridled Tern *Onychoprion anaethetus*
Sooty Tern *Onychoprion fuscata*
Whiskered Tern *Chlidonias hybrida*
White-winged Tern *Chlidonias leucopterus*
Whiskered Tern *Chlidonias hybrida*
Brown Noddy *Anous stolidus*
Black Noddy *Anous minutus* ?
Lesser Noddy *Anous tenuirostris* ?
White Tern *Gygis alba* ?
Indian Skimmer *Rynchops albicollis*
Tibetan Sandgrouse *Syrrhaptes tibetanus*
Pallas's Sandgrouse *Syrrhaptes paradoxus* ?
Pin-tailed Sandgrouse *Pterocles alchata*
Chestnut-bellied Sandgrouse *Pterocles exustus*
Spotted Sandgrouse *Pterocles senegallus*
Black-bellied Sandgrouse *Pterocles orientalis*
Painted Sandgrouse *Pterocles indicus*
Snow Pigeon *Columba leuconota*
Rock Pigeon *Columba livia*
Hill Pigeon *Columba rupestris*
Yellow-eyed Pigeon *Columba eversmanni*
Common Woodpigeon *Columba palumbus*
Speckled Woodpigeon *Columba hodgsonii*
Ashy Woodpigeon *Columba pulchricollis*
Nilgiri Woodpigeon *Columba elphinstonii*
Ceylon Woodpigeon *Columba torringtoniae*
Pale-capped Woodpigeon *Columba punicea*
Andaman Woodpigeon *Columba palumboides*
European Turtle-dove *Streptopelia turtur*
Oriental Turtle-dove *Streptopelia orientalis*
Laughing Dove *Spilopelia senegalensis*
Spotted Dove *Spilopelia chinensis*
Red Collared-dove *Streptopelia tranquebarica*
Eurasian Collared-dove *Streptopelia decaocto*
Barred Cuckoo-dove *Macropygia unchall*
Andaman Cuckoo-dove *Macropygia rufipennis*
Emerald Dove *Chalcophaps indica*
Nicobar Pigeon *Caloenas nicobarica*
Orange-breasted Green-pigeon *Treron bicinctus*
Grey-fronted Green-pigeon *Treron affinis*
Ashy-headed Green-pigeon *Treron phayrei*
Andaman Green-pigeon *Treron chloropterus*
Yellow-footed Green-pigeon *Treron phoenicopterus*
Thick-billed Green-pigeon *Treron curvirostra*
Pin-tailed Green-pigeon *Treron apicauda*

Wedge-tailed Green-pigeon *Treron sphenurus*
Pied Imperial-pigeon *Ducula bicolor*
Mountain Imperial-pigeon *Ducula badia*
Green Imperial-pigeon *Ducula aenea*
Nicobar Imperial-pigeon *Ducula nicobarica*
Vernal Hanging Parrot *Loriculus vernalis*
Alexandrine Parakeet *Psittacula eupatria*
Rose-ringed Parakeet *Psittacula krameri*
Himalayan Parakeet *Psittacula himalayana*
Finsch's Parakeet *Psittacula finschii*
Plum-headed Parakeet *Psittacula cyanocephala*
Rosy-headed Parakeet *Psittacula roseata*
Malabar Parakeet *Psittacula columboides*
Red-breasted Parakeet *Psittacula alexandri*
Nicobar Parakeet *Psittacula caniceps*
Long-tailed Parakeet *Psittacula longicauda*
Greater Coucal *Centropus sinensis*
'Southern' Coucal *Centropus (sinensis) parroti*
Andaman Coucal *Centropus (sinensis) andamanensis*
Lesser Coucal *Centropus bengalensis*
Sirkeer Malkoha *Taccocua leschenaultii*
Blue-faced Malkoha *Phaenicophaeus viridirostris*
Green-billed Malkoha *Phaenicophaeus tristis*
Chestnut-winged Cuckoo *Clamator coromandus*
Jacobin Cuckoo *Clamator jacobinus*
Asian Koel *Eudynamys scolopaceus*
Asian Emerald Cuckoo *Chrysococcyx maculatus*
Violet Cuckoo *Chrysococcyx xanthorhynchus*
Banded Bay Cuckoo *Cacomantis sonneratii*
Plaintive Cuckoo *Cacomantis merulinus*
Grey-bellied Cuckoo *Cacomantis passerinus*
'Square-tailed'Drongo Cuckoo *Surniculus lugubris*
'Forked-tailed' Drongo Cuckoo *Surniculus (lugubris) dicruroides*
Large Hawk-cuckoo *Hierococcyx sparverioides*
Common Hawk-cuckoo *Hierococcyx varius*
Whistling Hawk-cuckoo *Hierococcyx nisicolor*
Small Cuckoo *Cuculus poliocephalus*
Indian Cuckoo *Cuculus micropterus*
Himalayan Cuckoo *Cuculus saturatus*
Horsfield's Cuckoo *Cuculus opatus*
Common Cuckoo *Cuculus canorus*
Common Barn Owl *Tyto alba*
Andaman Barn Owl *Tyto deroepstroffi*
Eastern Grass Owl *Tyto longimembris*
Oriental Bay Owl *Phodilus badius*
Andaman Scops Owl *Otus balli*
Mountain Scops Owl *Otus spilocephalus*
Pallid Scops Owl *Otus brucei*
Eurasian Scops Owl *Otus scops*
Walden's Scops Owl *Otus modestus*
Nicobar Scops Owl *Otus alius*
Indian Scops Owl *Otus bakkamoena*
Collared Scops Owl *Otus lettia*
Eurasian Eagle Owl *Bubo bubo*
Snowy Owl *Bubo scandiacus ?*
Indian Eagle Owl *Bubo bengalensis*
Dusky Eagle Owl *Bubo coromandus*
Forest Eagle Owl *Ketupa nipalensis*
Brown Fish Owl *Ketupa zeylonensis*
Tawny Fish Owl *Ketupa flavipes*
Buffy Fish Owl *Ketupa ketupu*
Mottled Wood Owl *Strix ocellata*
Brown Wood Owl *Strix leptogrammica*
Tawny Wood Owl *Strix aluco*
Himalayan Wood Owl *Strix nivicolum*
Collared Owlet *Glaucidium brodiei*
Asian Barred Owlet *Glaucidium cuculoides*
Jungle Owlet *Glaucidium radiatum*
Chestnut-backed Owlet *Glaucidium casstanotum*
Little Owl *Athene noctua*
Spotted Owl *Athene brama*
Forest Owlet *Hetroglaux blewitti*
Boreal Owl *Aegolius funereus* ?
Brown Hawk Owl *Ninox scutulata*
Hume's Hawk Owl *Ninox obscura*
Andaman Hawk Owl *Ninox affinis*
Northern Long-eared Owl *Asio otus*
Short-eared Owl *Asio flammeus*
Ceylon Frogmouth *Batrachostomus moniliger*
Hodgson's Frogmouth *Batrachostomus hodgsoni*
Great Eared-nightjar *Lyncornis macrotis*
Indian Jungle Nightjar *Caprimulgus indicus*
Grey Nightjar *Caprimulgus jotaka*
European Nightjar *Caprimulgus europaeus*
Syke's Nightjar *Caprimulgus mahrattensis*
Large-tailed Nightjar *Caprimulgus macrurus*
Jerdon's Nightjar *Caprimulgus atripennis*
Andaman Nightjar *Caprimulgus andamanicus*
Indian Little Nightjar *Caprimulgus asiaticus*
Savanna Nightjar *Caprimulgus affinis*
White-bellied Swiftlet *Collocalia esculenta*
Indian Swiftlet *Aerodramus unicolor*
Himalayan Swiftlet *Aerodramus brevirostris*
Edible-nest Swiftlet *Aerodramus fuciphagus*
Indian White-rumped Spinetail *Zoonavena sylvatica*
White-throated Needletail *Hirundapus caudatus*
Silver-backed Needletail *Hirundapus cochinchinensis*
Brown-throated Needletail *Hirundapus giganteus*
Asian Palm-swift *Cypsiurus balasiensis*
Alpine Swift *Tachymarptis melba*
Blyth's Swift *Apus leuconyx*
Salim Ali's Swift *Apus salimali*
Common Swift *Apus apus*
Pacific Swift *Apus pacificus*
Dark-rumped Swift *Apus acuticauda*

Little Swift *Apus affinis*
Crested Treeswift *Hemiprocne coronata*
Malabar Trogon *Harpactes fasciatus*
Red-headed Trogon *Harpactes erythrocephalus*
Ward's Trogon *Harpactes wardi*
Blyth's Kingfisher *Alcedo hercules*
Common Kingfisher *Alcedo atthis*
Blue-eared Kingfisher *Alcedo meninting*
Black-backed Dwarf Kingfisher *Ceyx erithaca*
Rufous-backed Dwarf Kingfisher *Ceyx rufidorsa* ?
Stork-billed Kingfisher *Pelargopsis capensis*
Brown-winged Kingfisher *Pelargopsis amauroptera*
Ruddy Kingfisher *Halcyon coromanda*
White-throated Kingfisher *Halcyon smyrnensis*
Black-capped Kingfisher *Halcyon pileata*
Collared Kingfisher *Todiramphus chloris*
Himalayan Pied Kingfisher *Ceryle lugubris*
Lesser Pied Kingfisher *Ceryle rudis*
Blue-bearded Bee-eater *Nyctyornis athertoni*
Little Green Bee-eater *Merops orientalis*
Blue-cheeked Bee-eater *Merops persicus*
Blue-tailed Bee-eater *Merops philippinus*
European Bee-eater *Merops apiaster*
Chestnut-headed Bee-eater *Merops leschenaulti*
European Roller *Coracias garrulus*
Indian Roller *Coracias benghalensis*
Dollarbird *Eurystomus orientalis*
Common Hoopoe *Upupa epos*
Malabar Grey Hornbill *Ocyceros griseus*
Indian Grey Hornbill *Ocyceros birostris*
Malabar Pied Hornbill *Anthracoceros coronatus*
Oriental Pied Hornbill *Anthracoceros albirostris*
Great Pied Hornbill *Buceros bicornis*
White-throated Brown Hornbill *Anorrhinuis austeni*
Rufous-necked Hornbill *Aceros nipalensis*
Wreathed Hornbill *Rhyticeros undulatus*
Narcondam Hornbill *Rhyticeros narcondami*
Great Barbet *Megalaima virens*
Brown-headed Barbet *Megalaima zeylanica*
Lineated Barbet *Megalaima lineata*
White-cheeked Barbet *Megalaima viridis*
Golden-throated Barbet *Megalaima franklinii*
Blue-throated Barbet *Megalaima asiatica*
Blue-eared Barbet *Megalaima australis*
Malabar Barbet *Xantholaema malabarica*
Ceylon Small Barbet *Xantholaema rubicapillus*
Coppersmith Barbet *Xantholaema haemacephalus*
Yellow-rumped Honeyguide *Indicator xanthonotus*
Eurasian Wryneck *Jynx torquilla*
Speckled Piculet *Vivia innominata*
White-browed Piculet *Sasia ochracea*
Indian Pygmy Woodpecker *Dendrocopos nanus*
Grey-capped Pygmy Woodpecker *Dendrocopos canicapillus*
Brown-fronted Pied Woodpecker *Dendrocopos auriceps*
Fulvous-breasted Pied Woodpecker *Dendrocopos macei*
Spot-breasted Pied Woodpecker *Dendrocopos analis*
Stripe-breasted Pied Woodpecker *Dendrocopos atratus*
Yellow-fronted Pied Woodpecker *Dendrocopos mahrattensis*
Crimson-breasted Pied Woodpecker *Dendrocopos cathpharius*
Darjeeling Pied Woodpecker *Dendrocopos darjellensis*
Great Spotted Woodpecker *Dendrocopos major*
Sind Pied Woodpecker *Dendrocopos assimilis*
Himalayan Pied Woodpecker *Dendrocopos himalayensis*
Rufous-bellied Woodpecker *Hypopicus hyperythrus*
Rufous Woodpecker *Micropternus brachyurus*
White-bellied Woodpecker *Dryocopus javensis*
Andaman Woodpecker *Dryocopus hodgei*
Lesser Yellownape *Picus chloropus*
Greater Yellownape *Chrysophlegma flavinucha*
Steak-breasted Woodpecker *Picus viridanus*
Steak-throated Woodpecker *Picus xanthopygaeus*
Scaly-bellied Woodpecker *Picus squamatus*
Grey-faced Woodpecker *Picus canus*
Himalayan Flameback *Dinopium shorii*
Common Flameback *Dinopium javanense*
Black-rumped Flameback *Dinopium benghalense*
Greater Flameback *Chrysocolaptes guttacristatus*
White-naped Flameback *Chrysocolaptes festivus*
Malabar Flameback *Chrysocolaptes socialis*
Pale-headed Woodpecker *Gecinulus grantia*
Bay Woodpecker *Blythipicus pyrrhotis*
Heart-spotted Woodpecker *Hemicircus canente*
Great Slaty Woodpecker *Mulleripicus pulverulentus*
Silver-breasted Broadbill *Serilophus lunatus*
Long-tailed Broadbill *Psarisomus dalhousiae*
Blue-naped Pitta *Hydrornis nipalensis*
Blue Pitta *Hydrornis cyaneus*
Hooded Pitta *Pitta sordida*
Indian Pitta *Pitta brachyura*
Mangrove Pitta *Pitta megarhyncha*
Singing Bushlark *Mirafra cantillans*
Indian Bushlark *Mirafra erythroptera*
Jerdon's Bushlark *Mirafra affinis*
Bengal Bushlark *Mirafra assamica*
Ashy-crowned Finch-lark *Eremopterix griseus*
Black-crowned Finch-lark *Eremopterix nigriceps*
Rufous-tailed Lark *Ammomanes pheonicura*

Desert Lark *Ammomanes deserti*
Bimaculated Lark *Melanocorypha bimaculata*
Tibetan Lark *Melanocorypha maxima*
Greater Short-toed Lark *Calandrella brachydactyla*
Hume's Short-toed Lark *Calandrella acutirostris*
Lesser Short-toed Lark *Calandrella rufescens*
Sand Lark *Calandrella raytal*
Crested Lark *Galerida cristata*
Malabar Lark *Galerida malabarica*
Sykes's Lark *Galerida deva*
Eurasian Skylark *Alauda arvensis*
Oriental Skylark *Alauda gulgula*
Horned Lark *Eremophila alpestris*
Greater Hoopoe Lark *Alaemon alaudipes*
Common Sand-martin *Riparia riparia*
Pale Sand-martin *Riparia diluta*
Grey-throated Sand-martin *Riparia chinensis*
Eurasian Crag-martin *Ptyonoprogne rupestris*
Pale Crag-martin *Ptyonoprogne obsoleta* ?
Dusky Crag-martin *Ptyonoprogne concolor*
Barn Swallow *Hirundo rustica*
House Swallow *Hirundo tahitica*
Hill Swallow *Hirundo domicola*
Wire-tailed Swallow *Hirundo smithii*
Red-rumped Swallow *Cecropis daurica*
Ceylon Swallow *Cecropis hyperythra*
Striated Swallow *Cecropis striolata*
Streak-throated Swallow *Petrochelidon fluvicola*
Nepal House-martin *Delichon nipalense*
Asian House-martin *Delichon dasypus*
Northern House-martin *Delichon urbicum*
Forest Wagtail *Dendronanthus indicus*
White Wagtail *Motacilla alba*
White-browed Wagtail *Motacilla maderaspatensis*
Citrine Wagtail *Motacilla citreola*
Western Yellow Wagtail *Motacilla flava*
Grey Wagtail *Motacilla cinerea*
Richard's Pipit *Anthus richardi*
Paddyfield Pipit *Anthus rufulus*
Tawny Pipit *Anthus campestris*
Blyth's Pipit *Anthus godlewskii*
Long-billed Pipit *Anthus similis*
Tree Pipit *Anthus trivialis*
Olive-backed Pipit *Anthus hodgsoni*
Meadow Pipit *Anthus pratensis* ?
Red-throated Pipit *Anthus cervinus*
Rosy Pipit *Anthus roseatus*
Water Pipit *Anthus spinoletta*
Buff-bellied Pipit *Anthus rubescens*
Nilgiri Pipit *Anthus nilghiriensis*
Upland Pipit *Anthus sylvanus*
Large Cuckooshrike *Coracina macei*
Andaman Cuckooshrike *Coracina dobsoni*
Black-winged Cuckooshrike *Lalage melaschistos*
Black-headed Cuckooshrike *Lalage melanoptera*
Pied Triller *Lalage nigra*
Rosy Minivet *Pericrocotus roseus*
Ashy Minivet *Pericrocotus divaricatus*
Small Minivet *Pericrocotus cinnamomeus*
White-bellied Minivet *Pericrocotus erythropygius*
Grey-chinned Minivet *Pericrocotus solaris*
Long-tailed Minivet *Pericrocotus ethologus*
Short-billed Minivet *Pericrocotus brevirostris*
Scarlet Minivet *Pericrocotus specious*
Orange Minivet *Pericrocotus flammeus*
Pied Flycatcher-shrike *Hemipus picatus*
Large Woodshrike *Tephrodornis gularis*
Malabar Woodshrike *Tephrodornis sylvicola*
Common Woodshrike *Tephrodornis pondicerianus*
Bohemian Waxwing *Bombycilla garrulus* ?
Grey Hypocolius *Hypocolius ampelinus*
Indian Paradise Flycatcher *Terpsiphone paradisi*
Black-naped Blue Monarch *Hypothymis azurea*
Mangrove Whistler *Pachycephala cinerea*
White-browed Fantail *Rhipidura aureola*
White-spotted Fantail *Rhipidura albogularis*
White-throated Fantail *Rhipidura albicollis*
Yellow-bellied Fantail *Rhipidura hypoxantha*
Crested Finchbill *Pycnonotus canifrons*
Striated Bulbul *Pynconotus striatus*
Grey-headed Bulbul *Microtarsus priocephalus*
Black-headed Bulbul *Microtarsus atriceps*
Andaman Bulbul *Microtarsus fuscoflavescens*
Black-crested Bulbul *Pynconotus flaviventris*
Flame-throated Bulbul *Pynconotus gularis*
Red-whiskered Bulbul *Pynconotus jocosus*
White-eared Bulbul *Pynconotus leucotis*
Himalayan Bulbul *Pynconotus leucogenys*
Red-vented Bulbul *Pynconotus cafer*
Yellow-throated Bulbul *Pynconotus xantholaemus*
Flavescent Bulbul *Pynconotus flavescens*
White-browed Bulbul *Pynconotus luteolus*
White-throated Bulbul *Alophoixus flaveolus*
Olive Bulbul *Iole virescens*
Yellow-browed Bulbul *Acritillas indica*
Yellow-eared Bulbul *Kelaartia penicillata*
Ashy Bulbul *Hemixos flavala*
Mountain Bulbul *Ixos mcclellandi*
Himalayan Black Bulbul *Hypsipetes leucocephalus*
Square-tailed Black Bulbul *Hypsipetes ganeesa*
Nicobar Bulbul *Ixos nicobariensis*
Common Iora *Aegithina tiphia*
Marshall's Iora *Aegithina nigrolutea*
Gold-fronted Leafbird *Chloropsis aurifrons*
Blue-winged Leafbird *Chloropsis cochinchinensis*
Jerdon's Leafbird *Chloropsis jerdoni*

Orange-bellied Leafbird *Chloropsis hardwickii*
Red-backed Shrike *Lanius collurio*
Isabelline Shrike *Lanius isabellinus*
Brown Shrike *Lanius cristatus*
Burmese Shrike *Lanius collurioides*
Bay-backed Shrike *Lanius vittatus*
Long-tailed Shrike *Lanius schach*
Grey-backed Shrike *Lanius tephronotus*
Great Grey Shrike *Lanius excubitor lathora/ pallidirostris?*
Southern Grey Shrike *Lanius meridionalis*
Brown Dipper *Cinclus pallasii*
White-throated Dipper *Cinclus cinclus*
Eurasian Wren *Troglodytes troglodytes*
Alpine Accentor *Prunella collaris*
Altai Accentor *Prunella himalayana*
Robin Accentor *Prunella rubeculoides*
Rufous-breasted Accentor *Prunella strophiata*
Brown Accentor *Prunella fulvescens*
Black-throated Accentor *Prunella atrogularis*
Maroon-backed Accentor *Prunella immaculata*
Pied Thrush *Geokichla wardii*
Orange-headed Thrush *Geokichla citrina*
Siberian Thrush *Geokichla sibirica*
Spot-winged Thrush *Geokichla spiloptera*
AlpineThrush *Zoothera mollissima*
Himalayan Forest Thrush *Zoothera salimalii*
Long-tailed Thrush *Zoothera dixoni*
Small-billed Scaly Thrush *Zoothera dauma*
Nilgiri Thrush *Zoothera neigherriensis*
Long-billed Ground-thrush *Zoothera monticola*
Dark-sided Ground-thrush *Zoothera marginata*
Tickell's Thrush *Turdus unicolor*
Black-breasted Thrush *Turdus dissimilis*
White-collared Blackbird *Turdus albocinctus*
Grey-winged Blackbird *Turdus boulboul*
Tibetan Blackbird *Turdus maximus*
Indian Blackbird *Turdus simillimus*
Chestnut Thrush *Turdus rubrocanus*
Kessler's Thrush *Turdus kessleri* ?
Grey-sided Thrush *Turdus feae*
Eyebrowed Thrush *Turdus obscurus*
Red-throated Thrush *Turdus ruficollis*
Black-throated Thrush *Turdus atrogularis*
Dusky Thrush *Turdus eunomus*
Song Thrush *Turdus philomelos*
Mistle Thrush *Turdus viscivorus*
Malabar Whistling-thrush *Myophonus horsfieldii*
Blue Whistling-thrush *Myophonus caeruleus*
Purple Cochoa *Cochoa purpurea*
Green Cochoa *Cochoa viridis*
Nicobar Jungle Flycatcher *Cyornis nicobaricus*
Spotted Flycatcher *Muscicapa striata*
Dark-sided Flycatcher *Muscicapa sibirica*
Asian Brown Flycatcher *Muscicapa dauurica*
Rusty-tailed Flycatcher *Muscicapa ruficauda*
Brown-breasted Flycatcher *Muscicapa muttui*
Ferruginous Flycatcher *Muscicapa ferruginea*
Yellow-rumped Flycatcher *Ficedula zanthopygia*
Slaty-backed Flycatcher *Ficedula sordida*
Orange-gorgeted Flycatcher *Ficedula strophiata*
Red-breasted Flycatcher *Ficedula parva*
Red-throated Flycatcher *Ficedula albicilla*
Kashmir Flycatcher *Ficedula subrubra*
White-gorgeted Flycatcher *Anthipes monileger*
Snowy-browed Flycatcher *Ficedula hyperythra*
Little Pied Flycatcher *Ficedula westermanni*
Ultramarine Flycatcher *Ficedula superciliaris*
Slaty-blue Flycatcher *Ficedula tricolor*
Sapphire Flycatcher *Ficedula sapphira*
Black and Orange Flycatcher *Ficedula nigrorufa*
Verditer Flycatcher *Eumyias thalassinus*
Dusky Blue Flycatcher *Eumyias sordidus*
Nilgiri Flycatcher *Eumyias albicaudatus*
Large Niltava *Niltava grandis*
Small Niltava *Niltava macgrigoriae*
Rufous-bellied Niltava *Niltava sundara*
Vivid Niltava *Niltava (vivida) oatesi*
White-tailed Blue Flycatcher *Cyornis concretus*
White-bellied Blue Flycatcher *Cyornis pallipes*
Pale-chinned Flycatcher *Cyornis poliogenys*
Pale Blue Flycatcher *Cyornis unicolor*
Blue-throated Flycatcher *Cyornis rubeculoides*
Large Blue Flycatcher *Cyornis magnirostris*
Hill Blue Flycatcher *Cyornis banyumas*
Tickell's Blue Flycatcher *Cyornis tickelliae*
Pygmy Blue Flycatcher *Ficedula hodgsoni*
Grey-headed Canary-flycatcher *Culicicapa ceylonensis*
Rufous-tailed Rock-thrush *Monticola saxatilis*
Chestnut-bellied Rock-thrush *Monticola rufiventris*
Blue-headed Rock-thrush *Monticola cinclorhynchus*
Asian Rock-thrush *Monticola philippensis*
Grandala *Grandala coelicolor*
Gould's Shortwing *Hetroxenicus stellatus*
Rusty-bellied Shortwing *Brachypteryx hyperythra*
Lesser Shortwing *Brachypteryx leucophris*
White-browed Shortwing *Brachypteryx montana*
Siberian Rubythroat *Calliope calliope*
Himalayan Rubythroat *Calliope pectoralis*
Bluethroat *Luscinia svecica*
Firethroat *Calliope pectardens*
Indian Blue Robin *Larvivora brunnea*
Siberian Blue Robin *Larvivora cyane*
Himalayan Red-flanked Bush-robin *Tarsiger rufilatus*

Northern Red-flanked Bush-robin *Tarsiger cyanurus* ?
Golden Bush-robin *Tarsiger chrysaeus*
White-browed Bush-robin *Tarsiger indicus*
Rufous-breasted Bush-robin *Tarsiger hyperythrus*
Rufous-tailed Scrub-robin *Cercotrichas galactotes*
Oriental Magpie-robin *Copsychus saularis*
White-rumped Shama *Copsychus malabaricus*
Andaman Shama *Copsychus albiventris*
Indian Black Robin *Copsychus fulicatus*
Eversmann's Redstart *Phoenicurus erythronotus*
Black Redstart *Phoenicurus ochruros*
Common Redstart *Phoenicurus phoenicurus* ?
Hodgson's Redstart *Phoenicurus hodgsoni*
White-throated Redstart *Phoenicurus schisticeps*
Daurian Redstart *Phoenicurus auroreus*
White-winged Redstart *Phoenicurus erythrogastus*
Blue-fronted Redstart *Phoenicurus frontalis*
Blue-capped Redstart *Phoenicurus coeruleocephala*
White-capped River-chat *Phoenicurus leucocephalus*
Plumbeous Water-redstart *Phoenicurus fuliginosus*
Hodgson's Blue Robin *Hodgsonius phaenicuroides*
White-tailed Blue Robin *Myiomela leucura*
White-bellied Blue Robin *Myiomela albiventris*
Nilgiri Blue Robin *Myiomela major*
Blue-fronted Blue Robin *Cinclidium frontale*
Little Forktail *Enicurus scouleri*
Black-backed Forktail *Enicurus immaculatus*
Slaty-backed Forktail *Enicurus schistaceus*
White-crowned Forktail *Enicurus leschenaulti*
Spotted Forktail *Enicurus maculatus*
White-browed Bushchat *Saxicola macrorhynchus*
White-throated Bushchat *Saxicola insignis*
Siberian Bushchat *Saxicola maurus*
White-tailed Bushchat *Saxicola leucurus*
Pied Bushchat *Saxicola caprata*
Jerdon's Bushchat *Rhodophila jerdoni*
Grey Bushchat *Rhodophila ferrea*
Hume's Wheatear *Oenanthe albonigra*
Finsch's Wheatear *Oenanthe finschii* ?
Variable Wheatear *Oenanthe picata*
Pied Wheatear *Oenanthe pleschanka*
Rufous-tailed Wheatear *Oenanthe xanthoprymna*
Red-tailed Wheatear *Oenanthe chrysopygia*
Desert Wheatear *Oenanthe deserti*
Isabelline Wheatear *Oenanthe isabellina*
Brown Rock-chat *Oenanthe fusca*
White-throated Laughingthrush *Garrulax albogularis*
White-crested Laughingthrush *Leucodioptron leucolophum*
Lesser Necklaced Laughingthrush *Garrulax monileger*
Greater Necklaced Laughingthrush *Garrulax pectoralis*
Striated Laughingthrush *Grammatoptila striata*
Chestnut-backed Laughingthrush *Dryonastes nuchalis*
Yellow-throated Laughingthrush *Dryonastes galbanus*
Wynaad Laughingthrush *Dryonastes delesserti*
Rufous-vented Laughingthrush *Dryonastes gularis*
Rufous-necked Laughingthrush *Dryonastes ruficollis*
White-browed Laughingthrush *Dryonastes sannio*
Grey-sided Laughingthrush *Dryonastes caerulatus*
Spot-breasted Laughingthrush *Stactocichla merulina*
Ashy Laughingthrush *Ianthocincla cineracea*
Rufous-chinned Laughingthrush *Ianthocincla rufogularis*
Spotted Laughingthrush *Ianthocincla ocellata*
Brown-capped Laughingthrush *Ianthocincla austeni*
Variegated Laughingthrush *Trochalopteron variegatum*
Kerala Laughingthrush *Strophocincia fairbanki*
Black-chinned Laughingthrush *Trochalopteron cachinnans*
Streaked Laughingthrush *Trochalopteron lineatum*
Bhutan Laughingthrush *Trochalopteron imbricatum*
Striped Laughingthrush *Trochalopteron virgatum*
Blue-winged Laughingthrush *Trochalopteron squamatum*
Scaly Laughingthrush *Trochalopteron subunicolor*
Black-faced Laughingthrush *Trochalopteron affine*
Red-headed Laughingthrush *Trochalopteron erythrocephalum*
Assam Laughingthrush *Trochalopteron chrysopterum*
Red-faced Liocichla *Liocichla phoenicea*
Bugun Liocichla *Liocichla bugunorum*
Himalayan Cutia *Cutia nipalensis*
Abbott's Babbler *Malacocincla abbotti*
Buff-breasted Babbler *Pellorneum tickelli*
Spot-throated Babbler *Pellorneum albiventre*
Marsh Babbler *Pellorneum palustre*
Puff-throated Babbler *Pellorneum ruficeps*
Large Scimitar Babbler *Megapomatorhinus hypoleucos*
Spot-breasted Scimitar Babbler *Megapomatorhinus mcclellandi*
Rusty-cheeked Scimitar Babbler *Megapomatorhinus erythrogenys*
Indian Scimitar Babbler *Pomatorhinus horsfieldii*
Ceylon Scimitar Babbler *Pomatorhinus melanurus*
White-browed Scimitar Babbler *Pomatorhinus schisticeps*
Streak-breasted Scimitar Babbler *Pomatorhinus ruficollis*
Long-billed Scimitar Babbler *Pomatorhinus*

ochraceiceps
Black-crowned Scimitar Babbler *Pomatorhinus ferruginosus*
Phayre's Scimitar Babbler *Pomatorhinus phayrei*
Slender-billed Scimitar Babbler *Xiphirhynchus superciliaris*
Long-billed Wren Babbler *Rimator malacoptilus*
Streaked Wren Babbler *Napothera brevicaudata*
Eyebrowed Wren Babbler *Napothera epilepidota*
Scaly-breasted Wren Babbler *Pnoepyga albiventer*
Pygmy Wren Babbler *Pnoepyga pusilla*
Nepal Wren Babbler *Pnoepyga immaculata*
Rufous-throated Wren Babbler *Cyanoderma rufifrons*
Mishmi Wren Babbler *Spelaeornis badeigularis*
Bar-winged Wren Babbler *Spelaeornis troglodytoides*
Spotted Wren Babbler *Elachura formosa*
Naga Wren Babbler *Spelaeornis chocolatinus*
Grey-bellied Wren Babbler *Spelaeornis reptatus* ?
Chin Hills Wren Babbler *Spelaeornis oatesi*
Tawny-breasted Wren Babbler *Spelaeornis longicaudatus*
Sikkim Wedge-billed Babbler *Sphenocichla humei*
Cachar Wedge-billed Babbler *Sphenocichla roberti*
Rufous-fronted Babbler *Stachyris rufifrons*
Rufous-capped Babbler *Cyanoderma ruficeps*
Black-chinned Babbler *Stachyris pyrrhops*
Golden Babbler *Cyanoderma chrysaeum*
Grey-throated Babbler *Stachyris nigriceps*
Snowy-throated Babbler *Stachyris oglei*
Tawny-bellied Babbler *Dumetia hyperythra*
Dark-fronted Babbler *Rhopocichla atriceps*
Pin-striped Tit Babbler *Mixornis gularis*
Chestnut-capped Babbler *Timalia pileata*
Yellow-eyed Babbler *Chrysomma sinense*
Jerdon's Babbler *Chrysomma altirostre*
Common Babbler *Turdoides caudata*
Striated Babbler *Turdoides earlei*
Slender-billed Babbler *Turdoides longirostris*
Large Grey Babbler *Turdoides malcolmi*
Indian Rufous Babbler *Turdoides subrufa*
Jungle Babbler *Turdoides striata*
Yellow-billed Babbler *Turdoides affinis*
Mount Victoria Babax *Babax (lanceolatus) woodi*
Silver-eared Mesia Leiothrix *Leiothrix argentauris*
Red-billed Leiothrix *Leiothrix lutea*
Indian White-hooded Babbler *Gampsorhynchus rufulus*
Rusty-fronted Barwing *Actinodura egertoni*
Hoary-throated Barwing *Ixops nipalensis*
Streak-throated Barwing *Ixops waldeni*
Blue-winged Minla *Siva cyanouroptera*
Bar-throated Minla *Chrysominla strigula*
Red-tailed Minla *Minla ignotincta*
Golden-breasted Fulvetta *Lioparus chrysotis*
Yellow-throated Fulvetta *Pseudominla cinerea*
Rufous-winged Fulvetta *Pseudominla castaneceps*
White-browed Fulvetta *Fulvetta vinipectus*
Chinese Fulvetta *Fulvetta striaticollis*
Manipur Fulvetta *Fulvetta manipurensis*
Brown-throated Fulvetta *Fulvetta ludlowi*
Rufous-throated Fulvetta *Choeniparus rufogularis*
Rusty-capped Fulvetta *Choeniparus dubius*
Brown-cheeked Fulvetta *Alcippe poioicephala*
Nepal Fulvetta *Alcippe nipalensis*
Rufous-backed Sibia *Leioptila annectens*
Rufous Sibia *Malacias capistratus*
Grey Sibia *Malacias gracilis*
Beautiful Sibia *Malacias pulchellus*
Long-tailed Sibia *Heterophasia picaoides*
Striated Yuhina *Staphida castaniceps*
White-naped Yuhina *Yuhina bakeri*
Whiskered Yuhina *Yuhina flavicollis*
Stripe-throated Yuhina *Yuhina gularis*
Rufous-vented Yuhina *Yuhina occipitalis*
Black-chinned Yuhina *Yuhina nigrimenta*
Fire-tailed Myzornis *Myzornis pyrrhoura*
Great Parrotbill *Conostoma oemodium*
Brown Parrotbill *Paradoxornis unicolor*
Grey-headed Parrotbill *Paradoxornis gularis*
Black-breasted Parrotbill *Paradoxornis flavirostris*
Spot-breasted Parrotbill *Paradoxornis guttaticollis*
Fulvous Parrotbill *Suthora fulvifrons*
Black-throated Parrotbill *Suthora nipalensis*
Pale-billed Parrotbill *Paradoxornis atrosuperciliaris*
White-breasted Parrotbill *Paradoxornis ruficeps*
Rufous-headed Parrotbill *Paradoxornis bakeri*
Black-headed Shrike Babbler *Pteruthius rufiventer*
Blyth's Shrike Babbler *Pteruthius aeralatus*
Green Shrike Babbler *Pteruthius xanthochlorus*
Black-eared Shrike Babbler *Pteruthius melanotis*
Clicking Shrike Babbler *Pteruthius intermedius aenobarbus*
White-bellied Erpornis *Erpornis zantholeuca*
Zitting Cisticola *Cisticola juncidis*
Bright-headed Cisticola *Cisticola exilis*
Rufous-vented Prinia *Prinia burnesii*
Swamp Prinia *Prinia cinerascens*
Striated Prinia *Prinia crinigera*
Black-throated Prinia *Prinia atrogularis*
Hill Prinia *Prinia superciliaris*
Rufous-fronted Prinia *Prinia buchanani*
Grey-crowned Prinia *Prinia cinereocapilla*
Rufescent Prinia *Prinia rufescens*
Grey-breasted Prinia *Prinia hodgsonii*
Graceful Prinia *Prinia gracilis*

Yellow-belied Prinia *Prinia flaviventris*
Ashy Prinia *Prinia socialis*
Jungle Prinia *Prinia sylvatica*
Plain Prinia *Prinia inornata*
Mountain Tailorbird *Phyllergates cuculatus*
Common Tailorbird *Orthotomus sutorius*
Black-necked Tailorbird *Orthotomus atrogularis*
Chestnut-headed Tesia *Oligura castaneocoronata*
Slaty-bellied Tesia *Tesia olivea*
Yellow-browed Tesia *Tesia cyaniventer*
Pale-footed Bush-warbler *Urosphena pallidipes*
Large Bush-warbler *Oligura major*
Grey-sided Bush-warbler *Oligura brunnifrons*
Korean Bush-warbler *Horornis canturians* ?
Strong-footed Bush-warbler *Horornis fortipes*
'Himalayan' Aberrant Bush-warbler *Horornis flavolivaceus*
'Manipur' Aberrant Bush-warbler *Horornis flavolivaceus weberi*
Hume's Bush-warbler *Horornis brunnescens*
Cetti's Bush-warbler *Cettia cetti*
Spotted Bush-warbler *Locustella thoracica*
West Himalayan Bush-warbler *Locustella kashmirensis*
Long-billed Bush-warbler *Locustella major*
Chinese Bush-warbler *Locustella tacsanowskia*
Brown Bush-warbler *Locustella luteoventris*
Russet Bush-warbler *Locustella mandelli*
Lanceolated Warbler *Locustella lanceolata*
Grasshopper Warbler *Locustella naevia*
Rusty-rumped Warbler *Locustella certhiola*
Moustached Warbler *Acrocephalus melanopogon*
Paddyfield Warbler *Acrocephalus agricola*
Blunt-winged Reed-warbler *Acrocephalus concinens*
Blyth's Reed-warbler *Acrocephalus dumetorum*
Great Reed-warbler *Acrocephalus arundinaceus* ?
Oriental Reed-warbler *Acrocephalus orientalis*
Indian Reed-warbler *Acrocephalus (stentoreus) brunnescens*
Large-billed Reed-warbler *Acrocephalus orinus*
Thick-billed Reed-warbler *Phragamaticola aedon*
Sykes's Warbler *Iduna rama*
Booted Warbler *Iduna caligata*
Eastern Olivaceous Warbler *Iduna pallida*
Siberian Chiffchaff *Phylloscopus (collybita) tristis*
Mountain Chiffchaff *Phylloscopus sindianus*
Plain Leaf-Warbler *Phylloscopus neglectus* ?
Dusky Warbler *Phylloscopus fuscatus*
Smoky Leaf-warbler *Phylloscopus fuligiventer*
Tickell's Leaf-warbler *Phylloscopus affinis*
Buff-throated Leaf-warbler *Phylloscopus subaffinis*
Sulphur-bellied Warbler *Phylloscopus griseolus*
Orange-barred Leaf-warbler *Phylloscopus pulcher*
Grey-faced Leaf-warbler *Phylloscopus maculipennis*
Lemon-rumped Leaf-warbler *Phylloscopus chloronotus*
Brook's Leaf-warbler *Phylloscopus subviridis*
Yellow-browed Leaf-warbler *Phylloscopus inornatus*
Mandelli's Leaf-warbler *Phylloscopus (humei) mandellii*
Hume's Leaf-warbler *Phylloscopus humei*
Arctic Warbler *Phylloscopus borealis* ?
Greenish Warbler *Phylloscopus trochiloides*
Bright-green Warbler *Phylloscopus nitidus*
Pale-legged Leaf-warbler *Phylloscopus tenellipes* ?
Large-billed Leaf-warbler *Phylloscopus magnirostris*
Tytler's Leaf-warbler *Phylloscopus tytleri*
Western Crowned Warbler *Phylloscopus occipitalis*
Eastern Crowned Warbler *Phylloscopus coronatus* ?
Blyth's Leaf-warbler *Phylloscopus reguloides*
Yellow-vented Warbler *Phylloscopus canator*
Grey-hooded Warbler *Phylloscopus xanthoschistos*
Green-crowned Warbler *Seicercus burkii*
Whistler's Warbler *Seicercus whistleri*
Grey-crowned Warbler *Seicercus tephrocephalus*
White-spectacled Warbler *Seicercus affinis*
Grey-cheeked Warbler *Seicercus poliogenys*
Chestnut-crowned Warbler *Seicercus castaniceps*
Broad-billed Warbler *Tickellia hodgsoni*
Rufous-faced Warbler *Abroscopus albogularis*
Black-faced Warbler *Abroscopus schisticeps*
Yellow-bellied Warbler *Abroscopus superciliaris*
Striated Grassbird *Megalurus palustris*
Bristled Grassbird *Chaetornis striata*
Indian Grassbird *Graminicola bengalensis*
Indian Broad-tailed Grass-warbler *Schoenicola platyurus*
Barred Warbler *Sylvia nisoria*
Lesser Whitethroat *Sylvia curruca*
Desert Whitethroat *Sylvia minula*
Hume's Whitethroat *Sylvia althaea*
Eastern Orphean Warbler *Sylvia crassirostris*
Common Whitethroat *Sylvia communis*
Asian Desert Warbler *Sylvia nana*
White-browed Tit-warbler *Leptopoecile sophiae*
Goldcrest *Regulus regulus*
White-throated Tit *Aegithalos niveogularis*
Red-headed Tit *Aegithalos iredalei*
Black-throated Tit *Aegithalos concinnus*
Rufous-fronted Tit *Aegithalos iouschistos*
White-crowned Penduline Tit *Remiz coronatus*
Fire-capped Tit *Cephalopyrus flammiceps*
Rufous-naped Tit *Periparus rufonuchalis*
Rufous-vented Tit *Periparus rubidiventris*
'Spot-winged' Coal Tit *Periparus ater melanolophus*
Coal Tit *Parus ater aemodius*

Grey-crested Tit *Lophophanes dichrous*
Cinerous Tit *Parus cinereus*
Green-backed Tit *Parus monticolus*
White-naped Tit *Parus nuchalis*
Black-lored Yellow Tit *Parus xanthogenys*
Indian Yellow Tit *Parus aplonotus*
Black-spotted Yellow Tit *Parus spilonotus*
Sultan Tit *Melanochlora sultanea*
Yellow-browed Tit *Sylviparus modestus*
Willow Tit *Poecile montanus*
Ground-tit *Pseudopodoces humilis*
Chestnut-vented Nuthatch *Sitta nagaensis*
Kashmir Nuthatch *Sitta cashmirensis*
Indian Nuthatch *Sitta castanea*
Neglected Nuthatch *Sitta neglecta*
White-tailed Nuthatch *Sitta himalayensis*
White-cheeked Nuthatch *Sitta leucopsis*
Velvet-fronted Nuthatch *Sitta frontalis*
Beautiful Nuthatch *Sitta formosa*
Wallcreeper *Tichodroma muraria*
Hodgson's Treecreeper *Certhia hodgsoni*
Bar-tailed Treecreeper *Certhia himalayana*
Rusty-flanked Treecreeper *Certhia nipalensis*
Sikkim Treecreeper *Certhia discolor*
Manipur Treecreeper *Certhia manipurensis*
Indian Spotted Creeper *Salpornis spilonotus*
Thick-billed Flowerpecker *Pachyglossa agilis*
Modest Flowerpecker *Pachyglossa obsoleta*
Yellow-vented Flowerpecker *Pachyglossa chrysorrhea*
Yellow-bellied Flowerpecker *Pachyglossa melanoxantha*
Legge's Flowerpecker *Pachyglossa vincens*
Orange-bellied Flowerpecker *Dicaeum trigonostigma*
Pale-billed Flowerpecker *Dicaeum erythrorynchos*
Nicobar Flowerpecker *Dicaeum concolor*
Plain Flowerpecker *Dicaeum minullum*
Andaman Flowerpecker *Dicaeum virescens*
Fire-breasted Flowerpecker *Dicaeum ignipectus*
Scarlet-backed Flowerpecker *Dicaeum cruentatum*
Ruby-cheeked Sunbird *Chalcoparia singalensis*
Purple-rumped Sunbird *Leptocoma zeylonica*
Small Sunbird *Leptocoma minima*
Van Hasselt's Sunbird *Leptocoma brasiliana*
Olive-backed Sunbird *Cinnyris jugularis*
Purple Sunbird *Cinnyris asiaticus*
Loten's Sunbird *Cinnyris lotenius*
Mrs Gould's Sunbird *Aethopyga gouldiae*
Green-tailed Sunbird *Aethopyga nipalensis*
Black-breasted Sunbird *Aethopyga saturata*
Crimson Sunbird *Aethopyga siparaja*
Vigors's Sunbird *Aethopyga vigorsii*
Fire-tailed Sunbird *Aethopyga ignicauda*
Little Spiderhunter *Arachnothera longirostra*
Streaked Spiderhunter *Arachnothera magna*
Oriental White-eye *Zosterops palpebrosus*
Crested Bunting *Emberiza lathami*
Yellowhammer *Emberiza citrinella* ?
Pine Bunting *Emberiza leucocephalus*
Rock Bunting *Emberiza cia*
Grey-necked Bunting *Emberiza buchanani*
Ortolan Bunting *Emberiza hortulana*
White-capped Bunting *Emberiza stewarti*
Striolated Bunting *Emberiza striolata*
Chestnut-eared Bunting *Emberiza fucata*
Little Bunting *Emberiza pusilla*
Yellow-breasted Bunting *Emberiza aureola*
Chestnut Bunting *Emberiza rutila*
Black-headed Bunting *Emberiza melanocephala*
Red-headed Bunting *Emberiza bruniceps*
Black-faced Bunting *Emberiza spodocephala*
Reed Bunting *Emberiza schoeniclus*
Corn Bunting *Emberiza calandra*
Common Chaffinch *Fringilla coelebs*
Brambling *Fringilla montifringilla* ?
Fire-fronted Serin *Serinus pusillus*
Himalayan Greenfinch *Chloris spinoides*
Black-headed Greenfinch *Chloris ambigua* ?
Eurasian Siskin *Spinus spinus*
Tibetan Siskin *Spinus thibetanus*
Eurasian Goldfinch *Chloris hloris*
European Linnet *Linaria cannabina* ?
Twite *Linaria flavirostris* ?
Plain Mountain-finch *Leucosticte nemoricola*
Brandt's Mountain-finch *Leucosticte brandti*
Red-browed Finch *Callacanthis burtoni*
Trumpeter Finch *Bucanetes githagineus*
Mongolian Finch *Bucanetes mongolicus*
Blandford's Rosefinch *Agraphospiza rubescens*
Dark-breasted Rosefinch *Procarduelis nipalensis*
Common Rosefinch *Erythrina erythrina*
Red-fronted Rosefinch *Carpodacus puniceus*
Himalayan Beautiful Rosefinch *Carpodacus pulcherrimus*
Vinaceous Rosefinch *Carpodacus vinaceus*
Pink-browed Rosefinch *Carpodacus rodochroa*
Dark-rumped Rosefinch *Carpodacus edwardsii*
Spot-winged Rosefinch *Carpodacus rodopeplus*
Blyth's Rosefinch *Carpodacus grandis*
Himalayan White-browed Rosefinch *Carpodacus thura*
Streaked Great Rosefinch *Carpodacus rubicilloides*
Spotted Great Rosefinch *Carpodacus severtzovi*
Red-fronted Rosefinch *Carpodacus punicea*
Crimson-browed Finch *Carpodacus subhimachalus*
Scarlet Finch *Haematospiza sipahi*
Red Crossbill *Loxia curvirostra*

Brown Bullfinch *Pyrrhula nipalensis*
Orange Bullfinch *Pyrrhula aurantiaca*
Red-headed Bullfinch *Pyrrhula erythrocephala*
Grey-headed Bullfinch *Pyrrhula erythaca*
Gold-naped Finch Pyrrhoplectes *epauletta*
Hawfinch *Coccothraustes coccothraustes* ?
Black and Yellow Grosbeak *Mycerobas icterioides*
Collared Grosbeak *Mycerobas affinis*
Spot-winged Grosbeak *Mycerobas melanozanthos*
White-winged Grosbeak *Mycerobas carnipes*
Red Avadavat *Amandava amandava*
Green Avadavat *Amandava formosa*
Indian Silverbill *Euodice malabarica*
White-rumped Munia *Lonchura striata*
Black-throated Munia *Lonchura kelaarti*
Scaly-breasted Munia *Lonchura punctulata*
Chestnut Munia *Lonchura atricapilla*
Tricoloured Munia *Lonchura malacca*
House Sparrow *Passer domesticus*
Spanish Sparrow *Passer hispaniolensis*
Sind Sparrow *Passer pyrrhonotus*
Cinnamon Sparrow *Passer rutilans*
Eurasian Tree Sparrow *Passer montanus*
Yellow-throated Sparrow *Gymnoris xanthocollis*
Rock Sparrow *Petronia petronia ?*
Black-winged Snowfinch *Montifringilla adamsi*
White-rumped Snowfinch *Onychostruthus taczanowskii*
Rufous-necked Snowfinch *Pyrgilauda ruficollis*
Plain-backed Snowfinch *Pyrgilauda blanfordi*
Black-breasted Weaver *Ploceus benghalensis*
Streaked Weaver *Ploceus manyar*
Baya Weaver *Ploceus philippinus*
Finn's Weaver *Ploceus megarhynchus*
Asian Glossy Starling *Aplonis panayensis*
Spot-winged Starling *Saroglossa spiloptera*
Grey-headed Starling *Sturnia malabarica*
Malabar White-headed Starling *Sturnia blythii*
Andaman White-headed Starling *Sturnia erythropygia*
Daurian Starling *Agrospar sturninus*
Brahminy Starling *Sturnia pagodarum*
Rosy Starling *Pastor roseus*
Common Starling *Sturnus vulgaris*
White-faced Starling *Sturnornis albofrontatus*
Asian Pied Starling *Gracupica contra*
Common Myna *Acridotheres tristis*
Bank Myna *Acridotheres ginginianus*
Jungle Myna *Acridotheres fuscus*
White-vented Myna *Acridotheres grandis*
Collared Myna *Acridotheres albocinctus*
Gold-crested Myna *Ampeliceps coronatus* ?
Common Hill Myna *Gracula religiosa*
Lesser Hill Myna *Gracula indica*
European Golden Oriole *Oriolus oriolus*
Indian Golden Oriole *Oriolus kundoo*
Black-naped Oriole *Oriolus chinensis*
Slender-billed Oriole *Oriolus tenuirostris*
Black-hooded Oriole *Oriolus xanthornus*
Maroon Oriole *Oriolus traillii*
Asian Fairy Bluebird *Irene puella*
Black Drongo *Edolius macrocercus*
Ashy Drongo *Edolius leucophaeus*
White-bellied Drongo *Edolius caerulescens*
Crow-billed Drongo *Dicrurus annectans*
Bronzed Drongo *Chaptia aenea*
Lesser Racket-tailed Drongo *Dicrurus remifer*
Hair-crested Drongo *Dicrurus hottentottus*
Andaman Drongo *Dicrurus andamanensis*
Greater Racket-tailed Drongo *Dicrurus paradiseus*
Ashy Woodswallow *Artamus fuscus*
White-breasted Woodswallow *Artamus leucorynchus*
Eurasian Jay *Garrulus glandarius*
Black-headed Jay G*arrulus lanceolatus*
Yellow-billed Blue Magpie *Urocissa flavirostris*
Red-billed Blue Magpie *Urocissa erythrorhyncha*
Common Green Magpie *Cissa chinensis*
Rufous Treepie *Dendrocitta vagabunda*
Grey Treepie *Dendrocitta formosae*
White-bellied Treepie *Dendrocitta leucogastra*
Collared Treepie *Dendrocitta frontalis*
Andaman Treepie *Dendrocitta bayleii*
Eurasian Magpie *Pica pica*
Larger-spotted Nutcracker *Nucifraga multipunctata*
Spotted Nutcracker *Nucifraga caryocatactes*
Kashmir Nutcracker *Nucifraga multipunclata*
Red-billed Chough *Pyrrhocorax pyrrhocorax*
Yellow-billed Chough *Pyrrhocorax graculus*
Eurasian Jackdaw *Coloeus monedula*
House Crow *Corvus splendens*
Rook *Corvus frugilegus*
Carrion Crow *Corvus corone*
Hooded Crow *Corvus (corone) cornix*
Large-billed Crow *Corvus (macrorynchos) japonensis*
Eastern Jungle Crow *Corvus (macrorynchos) levaillantii*
Indian Crow *Corvus (macrorynchos) culminatus*
Common Raven *Corvus corax*

CHECKLIST: BIRDS OF INDIA

This is a definitive Checklist of birds of India ('the India Checklist') in a modern taxonomy. We have reviewed all the past records of bird species from within the political boundaries of the Republic of India and have included only those species whose occurrence within the country is well corroborated. In this process, we follow *'The Howard and Moore Complete Checklist of the Birds of the World'* (4th Edition) for taxonomy and species sequence. In total, the India Checklist acknowledges inclusion of 1263 species of birds out of which 61 (4.8%) are endemic to India. Taxonomically, it covers 23 orders, 107 families, and 498 genera. We hope that the India Checklist—a systematic, peer-reviewed baseline data for the country's avifauna—will standardise the taxonomy, and nomenclature, of Indian birds and will streamline communications in Indian ornithology. We also plan to regularly update the India Checklist online, which will be freely available to all users at http://www.indianbirds.in/india/.

[Source: Praveen J., Jayapal, R., & Pittie, A., 2016. A checklist of the birds of India. Indian BIRDS 11 (5&6): 113–172A.]

English Name	Scientific Name	Alternative Name(s)
Anseriformes (Anatidae)		
Fulvous Whistling Duck	*Dendrocygna bicolor*	Large Whistling Teal
Lesser Whistling Duck	*Dendrocygna javanica*	Lesser Whistling Teal, Tree Duck
White-headed Duck	*Oxyura leucocephala*	White-headed Stiff-tailed Duck
Mute Swan	*Cygnus olor*	
Tundra Swan	*Cygnus columbianus*	Bewick's Swan C. [c.] bewickii
Whooper Swan	*Cygnus cygnus*	
Red-breasted Goose	*Branta ruficollis*	
Bar-headed Goose	*Anser indicus*	
Greylag Goose	*Anser anser*	
Bean Goose	*Anser fabalis*	[Tundra Bean Goose, Taiga Bean Goose]
Greater White-fronted Goose	*Anser albifrons*	
Lesser White-fronted Goose	*Anser erythropus*	
Long-tailed Duck	*Clangula hyemalis*	
Common Goldeneye	*Bucephala clangula*	
Smew	*Mergellus albellus*	
Common Merganser	*Mergus merganser*	Goosander
Common Shelduck	*Tadorna tadorna*	
Ruddy Shelduck	*Tadorna ferruginea*	Brahminy Duck
Marbled Teal	*Marmaronetta angustirostris*	Marbled Duck
White-winged Wood Duck	*Asarcornis scutulata*	White-winged Duck
Red-crested Pochard	*Netta rufina*	
Common Pochard	*Aythya ferina*	
Baer's Pochard	*Aythya baeri*	
Ferruginous Duck	*Aythya nyroca*	White-eyed Pochard
Tufted Duck	*Aythya fuligula*	Tufted Pochard
Greater Scaup	*Aythya marila*	
Pink-headed Duck	*Rhodonessa caryophyllacea*	
Garganey	*Spatula querquedula*	
Northern Shoveler	*Spatula clypeata*	
Baikal Teal	*Sibirionetta formosa*	
Falcated Duck	*Mareca falcata*	Falcated Teal
Gadwall	*Mareca strepera*	
Eurasian Wigeon	*Mareca penelope*	
Chinese Spot-billed Duck	*Anas zonorhyncha*	Eastern Spot-billed Duck
Indian Spot-billed Duck	*Anas poecilorhyncha*	Spotbill Duck (incl. A. zonorhyncha)
Mallard	*Anas platyrhynchos*	
Andaman Teal	*Anas gibberifrons albogularis*	[Grey Teal, Sunda Teal]
Northern Pintail	*Anas acuta*	
Common Teal	*Anas crecca*	Green-winged Teal, Eurasian Teal
Comb Duck	*Sarkidiornis melanotos*	Knob-billed Duck, African Comb Duck
Mandarin Duck	*Aix galericulata*	
Cotton Teal	*Nettapus coromandelianus*	Cotton Pygmy Goose
Galliformes (Megapodiidae)		
Nicobar Megapode	*Megapodius nicobariensis*	Nicobar Scrubfowl
Galliformes (Phasianidae)		
Common Hill Partridge	*Arborophila torqueola*	Hill Partridge
Galliformes (Phasianidae)		

English Name	Scientific Name	Alternative Name(s)
Rufous-throated Hill Partridge	*Arborophila rufogularis*	Rufous-throated Partridge
White-cheeked Hill Partridge	*Arborophila atrogularis*	White-cheeked Partridge
Chestnut-breasted Hill Partridge	*Arborophila mandellii*	Chestnut-breasted Partridge
Indian Peafowl	*Pavo cristatus*	Blue Peafowl, Common Peafowl
Green Peafowl	*Pavo muticus*	Burmese Peafowl
Grey Peacock Pheasant	*Polyplectron bicalcaratum*	
Common Quail	*Coturnix coturnix*	Grey Quail
Japanese Quail	*Coturnix japonica*	
Rain Quail	*Coturnix coromandelica*	Black-breasted Quail
Blue-breasted Quail	*Synoicus chinensis*	King Quail, Asian Blue Quail
Himalayan Snowcock	*Tetraogallus himalayensis*	
Tibetan Snowcock	*Tetraogallus tibetanus*	
Chukar Partridge	*Alectoris chukar*	Chukor
Snow Partridge	*Lerwa lerwa*	
Jungle Bush Quail	*Perdicula asiatica*	
Rock Bush Quail	*Perdicula argoondah*	
Painted Bush Quail	*Perdicula erythrorhyncha*	
Manipur Bush Quail	*Perdicula manipurensis*	
Himalayan Quail	*Ophrysia superciliosa*	Mountain Quail
Black Francolin	*Francolinus francolinus*	Black Partridge
Painted Francolin	*Francolinus pictus*	Painted Partridge
Chinese Francolin	*Francolinus pintadeanus*	Burmese Francolin
Grey Francolin	*Francolinus pondicerianus*	Grey Partridge
Swamp Francolin	*Francolinus gularis*	Swamp Partridge
Mountain Bamboo Partridge	*Bambusicola fytchii*	Bamboo Partridge
Red Junglefowl	*Gallus gallus*	
Grey Junglefowl	*Gallus sonneratii*	
Himalayan Monal	*Lophophorus impejanus*	Impeyan Monal, Impeyan Monal Pheasant
Sclater's Monal	*Lophophorus sclateri*	
Western Tragopan	*Tragopan melanocephalus*	Western Horned Pheasant
Satyr Tragopan	*Tragopan satyra*	Crimson Horned Pheasant
Blyth's Tragopan	*Tragopan blythii*	Grey-bellied Tragopan
Temminck's Tragopan	*Tragopan temminckii*	Chinese Crimson Horned Pheasant
Mrs Hume's Pheasant	*Syrmaticus humiae*	Mrs Hume's Barred-back Pheasant
Cheer Pheasant	*Catreus wallichii*	
Kalij Pheasant	*Lophura leucomelanos*	Kaleej Pheasant
Tibetan Partridge	*Perdix hodgsoniae*	
Red Spurfowl	*Galloperdix spadicea*	
Painted Spurfowl	*Galloperdix lunulata*	
Koklass Pheasant	*Pucrasia macrolopha*	Koklas Pheasant
Blood Pheasant	*Ithaginis cruentus*	
Phoenicopteriformes (Phoenicopteridae)		
Greater Flamingo	*Phoenicopterus roseus*	
Lesser Flamingo	*Phoeniconaias minor*	
Phoenicopteriformes (Podicipedidae)		
Little Grebe	*Tachybaptus ruficollis*	Dabchick
Red-necked Grebe	*Podiceps grisegena*	
Great Crested Grebe	*Podiceps cristatus*	
Horned Grebe	*Podiceps auritus*	Slavonian Grebe
Black-necked Grebe	*Podiceps nigricollis*	Eared Grebe
Columbiformes (Columbidae)		
Rock Pigeon	*Columba livia*	Rock Dove, Blue Rock Pigeon
Hill Pigeon	*Columba rupestris*	
Snow Pigeon	*Columba leuconota*	
Yellow-eyed Pigeon	*Columba eversmanni*	Pale-backed Pigeon, Eastern Stock Pigeon
Common Wood Pigeon	*Columba palumbus*	Wood Pigeon, Eastern Wood Pigeon
Speckled Wood Pigeon	*Columba hodgsonii*	Speckled Pigeon
Ashy Wood Pigeon	*Columba pulchricollis*	Ashy Pigeon
Nilgiri Wood Pigeon	*Columba elphinstonii*	Nilgiri Pigeon
Pale-capped Pigeon	*Columba punicea*	Purple Wood Pigeon
Andaman Wood Pigeon	*Columba palumboides*	Andaman Pigeon
European Turtle Dove	*Streptopelia turtur*	Turtle Dove

English Name	Scientific Name	Alternative Name(s)
Oriental Turtle Dove	*Streptopelia orientalis*	Rufous Turtle Dove
Eurasian Collared Dove	*Streptopelia decaocto*	Indian Ring Dove
Red Collared Dove	*Streptopelia tranquebarica*	Red Turtle Dove
Spotted Dove	*Streptopelia chinensis*	[Western Spotted Dove, Eastern Spotted Dove]
Laughing Dove	*Streptopelia senegalensis*	Little Brown Dove, Senegal Dove
Barred Cuckoo Dove	*Macropygia unchall*	Bar-tailed Cuckoo Dove
Andaman Cuckoo Dove	*Macropygia rufipennis*	
Orange-breasted Green Pigeon	*Treron bicinctus*	
Pompadour Green Pigeon	*Treron pompadora*	[Grey-fronted Green Pigeon, Andaman Green Pigeon, Ashy-headed Green Pigeon]
Thick-billed Green Pigeon	*Treron curvirostra*	
Yellow-legged Green Pigeon	*Treron phoenicopterus*	Yellow-footed Green Pigeon
Pin-tailed Green Pigeon	*Treron apicauda*	
Wedge-tailed Green Pigeon	*Treron sphenurus*	Kokla
Nicobar Pigeon	*Caloenas nicobarica*	
Emerald Dove	*Chalcophaps indica*	
Green Imperial Pigeon	*Ducula aenea*	[Nicobar Imperial Pigeon]
Mountain Imperial Pigeon	*Ducula badia*	Maroon-backed Imperial Pigeon D. b. cuprea & D. b. insignis, Grey-headed Imperial Pigeon D. b. griseicapilla; [Nilgiri Imperial Pigeon]
Pied Imperial Pigeon	*Ducula bicolor*	
Pterocliformes (Pteroclidae)		
Tibetan Sandgrouse	*Syrrhaptes tibetanus*	
Pallas's Sandgrouse	*Syrrhaptes paradoxus*	
Pin-tailed Sandgrouse	*Pterocles alchata*	Large Pintail Sandgrouse
Chestnut-bellied Sandgrouse	*Pterocles exustus*	Common Indian Sandgrouse, Indian Sandgrouse
Spotted Sandgrouse	*Pterocles senegallus*	
Black-bellied Sandgrouse	*Pterocles orientalis*	Imperial Sandgrouse
Painted Sandgrouse	*Pterocles indicus*	Close-barred Sandgrouse (incl. P. lichtensteinii)
Phaethontiformes (Phaethontidae)		
Red-billed Tropicbird	*Phaethon aethereus*	Short-tailed Tropicbird
Red-tailed Tropicbird	*Phaethon rubricauda*	
White-tailed Tropicbird	*Phaethon lepturus*	White Tropicbird
Caprimulgiformes (Podargidae)		
Sri Lanka Frogmouth	*Batrachostomus moniliger*	
Hodgson's Frogmouth	*Batrachostomus hodgsoni*	
Caprimulgiformes (Caprimulgidae)		
Great Eared Nightjar	*Lyncornis macrotis*	
Grey Nightjar	*Caprimulgus indicus*	[Jungle Nightjar/Indian Jungle Nightjar]
European Nightjar	*Caprimulgus europaeus*	Eurasian Nightjar
Sykes's Nightjar	*Caprimulgus mahrattensis*	
Jerdon's Nightjar	*Caprimulgus atripennis*	
Large-tailed Nightjar	*Caprimulgus macrurus*	Long-tailed Nightjar (incl. C. atripennis & C. andamanicus)
Andaman Nightjar	*Caprimulgus andamanicus*	
Indian Nightjar	*Caprimulgus asiaticus*	Common Indian Nightjar, Indian Little Nightjar
Savanna Nightjar	*Caprimulgus affinis*	Franklin's Nightjar, Allied Nightjar
Caprimulgiformes (Apodidae)		
Crested Treeswift	*Hemiprocne coronata*	
White-rumped Spinetail	*Zoonavena sylvatica*	White-rumped Needletail, White-rumped Spinetail Swift
White-throated Needletail	*Hirundapus caudacutus*	White-throated Spinetail Swift
Silver-backed Needletail	*Hirundapus cochinchinensis*	Cochinchina Spinetail Swift
Brown-backed Needletail	*Hirundapus giganteus*	Brown-throated Needletail, Large Brown-throated Spinetail Swift
Glossy Swiftlet	*Collocalia esculenta*	White-bellied Swiftlet
Himalayan Swiftlet	*Aerodramus brevirostris*	
Indian Swiftlet	*Aerodramus unicolor*	Indian Edible-nest Swiftlet
Edible-nest Swiftlet	*Aerodramus fuciphagus*	Andaman Grey-rumped Swiftlet, White-nest Swiftlet
Asian Palm Swift	*Cypsiurus balasiensis*	
Alpine Swift	*Tachymarptis melba*	

English Name	Scientific Name	Alternative Name(s)
Dark-rumped Swift	*Apus acuticauda*	Khasi Hills Swift
Pacific Swift	*Apus pacificus*	Fork-tailed Swift, Large White-rumped Swift; [Blyth's Swift]
Nepal House Swift	*Apus nipalensis*	
Indian House Swift	*Apus affinis*	Little Swift, House Swift (incl. A. nipalensis)
Common Swift	*Apus apus*	Swift
Cuculiformes (Cuculidae)		
Greater Coucal	*Centropus sinensis*	Crow-pheasant; [Andaman Coucal]
Lesser Coucal	*Centropus bengalensis*	
Sirkeer Malkoha	*Taccocua leschenaultii*	Sirkeer Cuckoo
Blue-faced Malkoha	*Phaenicophaeus viridirostris*	Small Green-billed Malkoha
Green-billed Malkoha	*Phaenicophaeus tristis*	Large Green-billed Malkoha
Pied Cuckoo	*Clamator jacobinus*	Pied Crested Cuckoo, Jacobin Cuckoo
Chestnut-winged Cuckoo	*Clamator coromandus*	Red-winged Crested Cuckoo
Asian Koel	*Eudynamys scolopaceus*	Common Koel
Asian Emerald Cuckoo	*Chrysococcyx maculatus*	
Violet Cuckoo	*Chrysococcyx xanthorhynchus*	
Banded Bay Cuckoo	*Cacomantis sonneratii*	Bay-banded Cuckoo
Plaintive Cuckoo	*Cacomantis merulinus*	Rufous-bellied Plaintive Cuckoo
Grey-bellied Cuckoo	*Cacomantis passerinus*	Indian Plaintive Cuckoo
Drongo Cuckoo	*Surniculus lugubris*	[Fork-tailed Drongo Cuckoo, Square-tailed Drongo Cuckoo]
Large Hawk Cuckoo	*Hierococcyx sparverioides*	
Common Hawk Cuckoo	*Hierococcyx varius*	Brainfever Bird
Whistling Hawk Cuckoo	*Hierococcyx nisicolor*	Hodgson's Hawk Cuckoo (with H. fugax)
Indian Cuckoo	*Cuculus micropterus*	
Common Cuckoo	*Cuculus canorus*	Eurasian Cuckoo
Himalayan Cuckoo	*Cuculus saturatus*	Oriental Cuckoo (incl. C. optatus)
Lesser Cuckoo	*Cuculus poliocephalus*	Small Cuckoo
Gruiformes (Rallidae)		
Andaman Crake	*Rallina canningi*	Andaman Banded Crake
Slaty-legged Crake	*Rallina eurizonoides*	Slaty-legged Banded Crake
Western Water Rail	*Rallus aquaticus*	Water Rail (incl. R. indicus)
Eastern Water Rail	*Rallus indicus*	Brown-cheeked Rail
Slaty-breasted Rail	*Lewinia striata*	Blue-breasted Banded Rail
Corncrake	*Crex crex*	
Spotted Crake	*Porzana porzana*	
Ruddy-breasted Crake	*Zapornia fusca*	Ruddy Crake
Brown Crake	*Zapornia akool*	
Little Crake	*Zapornia parva*	
Baillon's Crake	*Zapornia pusilla*	
Black-tailed Crake	*Zapornia bicolor*	Elwes's Crake
White-breasted Waterhen	*Amaurornis phoenicurus*	
White-browed Crake	*Amaurornis cinerea*	
Watercock	*Gallicrex cinerea*	Kora
Purple Swamphen	*Porphyrio porphyrio*	Purple Moorhen, Grey-headed Swamphen P. [p.] poliocephalus
Common Moorhen	*Gallinula chloropus*	Eurasian Moorhen, Indian Moorhen
Common Coot	*Fulica atra*	Eurasian Coot
Gruiformes (Heliornithidae)		
Masked Finfoot	*Heliopais personatus*	
Gruiformes (Gruidae)		
Siberian Crane	*Leucogeranus leucogeranus*	
Sarus Crane	*Antigone antigone*	
Demoiselle Crane	*Grus virgo*	
Common Crane	*Grus grus*	
Black-necked Crane	*Grus nigricollis*	
Otidiformes (Otididae)		
Great Indian Bustard	*Ardeotis nigriceps*	Indian Bustard
Little Bustard	*Tetrax tetrax*	
Bengal Florican	*Houbaropsis bengalensis*	
Lesser Florican	*Sypheotides indicus*	Leekh, Likh

English Name	Scientific Name	Alternative Name(s)
Macqueen's Bustard	*Chlamydotis macqueenii*	Asian Houbara, Houbara Bustard (with C. undulata)
Gaviiformes (Gaviidae)		
Red-throated Diver	*Gavia stellata*	Red-throated Loon
Black-throated Diver	*Gavia arctica*	Black-throated Loon, Arctic Loon
Procellariiformes (Oceanitidae)		
Wilson's Storm-petrel	*Oceanites oceanicus*	
White-faced Storm-petrel	*Pelagodroma marina*	
Black-bellied Storm-petrel	*Fregetta tropica*	Dusky-vented Storm-petrel
Procellariiformes (Hydrobatidae)		
Swinhoe's Storm-petrel	*Hydrobates monorhis*	Fork-tailed Storm-petrel
Procellariiformes (Procellariidae)		
Cape Petrel	*Daption capense*	
Barau's Petrel	*Pterodroma baraui*	
Wedge-tailed Shearwater	*Ardenna pacifica*	
Short-tailed Shearwater	*Ardenna tenuirostris*	Slender-billed Shearwater
Flesh-footed Shearwater	*Ardenna carneipes*	Pink-footed Shearwater (incl. A. creatopus)
Streaked Shearwater	*Calonectris leucomelas*	White-fronted Shearwater
Cory's Shearwater	*Calonectris borealis*	
Tropical Shearwater	*Puffinus bailloni*	[Persian Shearwater]
Jouanin's Petrel	*Bulweria fallax*	Jouanin's Gadfly Petrel
Pelecaniformes (Ciconiidae)		
Greater Adjutant	*Leptoptilos dubius*	Adjutant Stork
Lesser Adjutant	*Leptoptilos javanicus*	
Painted Stork	*Mycteria leucocephala*	
Asian Openbill	*Anastomus oscitans*	Openbill Stork, Open-billed Stork
Black Stork	*Ciconia nigra*	
Woolly-necked Stork	*Ciconia episcopus*	Asian Woollyneck C. e. episcopus, White-necked Stork
European White Stork	*Ciconia ciconia*	
Black-necked Stork	*Ephippiorhynchus asiaticus*	
Pelecaniformes (Pelecanidae)		
Great White Pelican	*Pelecanus onocrotalus*	Rosy Pelican
Spot-billed Pelican	*Pelecanus philippensis*	Grey Pelican
Dalmatian Pelican	*Pelecanus crispus*	
Pelecaniformes (Ardeidae)		
Eurasian Bittern	*Botaurus stellaris*	Great Bittern
Little Bittern	*Ixobrychus minutus*	
Yellow Bittern	*Ixobrychus sinensis*	
Cinnamon Bittern	*Ixobrychus cinnamomeus*	Chestnut Bittern
Black Bittern	*Ixobrychus flavicollis*	
Malayan Night Heron	*Gorsachius melanolophus*	Malay Bittern, Tiger Bittern
Black-crowned Night Heron	*Nycticorax nycticorax*	
Striated Heron	*Butorides striata*	Little Green Heron
Indian Pond Heron	*Ardeola grayii*	Paddybird
Chinese Pond Heron	*Ardeola bacchus*	
Cattle Egret	*Bubulcus ibis*	
Grey Heron	*Ardea cinerea*	
White-bellied Heron	*Ardea insignis*	
Goliath Heron	*Ardea goliath*	Giant Heron
Purple Heron	*Ardea purpurea*	
Great Egret	*Ardea alba*	Large Egret
Intermediate Egret	*Ardea intermedia*	Median Egret, Smaller Egret
Little Egret	*Egretta garzetta*	
Western Reef Egret	*Egretta gularis*	Western Reef Heron, Indian Reef Heron
Pacific Reef Egret	*Egretta sacra*	Pacific Reef Heron, Eastern Reef Egret, Eastern Reef Heron
Pelecaniformes (Threskiornithidae)		
Black-headed Ibis	*Threskiornis melanocephalus*	White Ibis, Oriental White Ibis
Eurasian Spoonbill	*Platalea leucorodia*	
Indian Black Ibis	*Pseudibis papillosa*	Red-naped Ibis
Glossy Ibis	*Plegadis falcinellus*	

English Name	Scientific Name	Alternative Name(s)
Pelecaniformes (Fregatidae)		
Lesser Frigatebird	*Fregata ariel*	Least Frigatebird
Great Frigatebird	*Fregata minor*	Lesser Frigatebird (vide HBK)
Christmas Island Frigatebird	*Fregata andrewsi*	Christmas Frigatebird
Pelecaniformes (Sulidae)		
Red-footed Booby	*Sula sula*	
Brown Booby	*Sula leucogaster*	
Masked Booby	*Sula dactylatra*	
Pelecaniformes (Phalacrocoracidae)		
Little Cormorant	*Microcarbo niger*	
Great Cormorant	*Phalacrocorax carbo*	Large Cormorant
Indian Cormorant	*Phalacrocorax fuscicollis*	Indian Shag
Pelecaniformes (Anhingidae)		
Oriental Darter	*Anhinga melanogaster*	Snake-bird
Charadriiformes (Burhinidae)		
Eurasian Thick-knee	*Burhinus oedicnemus*	Eurasian Stone-curlew; [Indian Thick-knee]
Great Thick-knee	*Esacus recurvirostris*	Great Stone-curlew, Great Stone Plover
Beach Thick-knee	*Esacus magnirostris*	Beach Stone-curlew, Australian Stone Plover
Charadriiformes (Haematopodidae)		
Eurasian Oystercatcher	*Haematopus ostralegus*	
Ibisbill	*Ibidorhyncha struthersii*	
Charadriiformes (Recurvirostridae)		
Pied Avocet	*Recurvirostra avosetta*	Avocet
Black-winged Stilt	*Himantopus himantopus*	[White-headed Stilt, Pied Stilt]
Charadriiformes (Charadriidae)		
Grey Plover	*Pluvialis squatarola*	Black-bellied Plover
Eurasian Golden Plover	*Pluvialis apricaria*	European Golden Plover, Golden Plover
Pacific Golden Plover	*Pluvialis fulva*	Eastern Golden Plover
Common Ringed Plover	*Charadrius hiaticula*	Eastern Ringed Plover
Long-billed Plover	*Charadrius placidus*	Long-billed Ringed Plover
Little Ringed Plover	*Charadrius dubius*	
Kentish Plover	*Charadrius alexandrinus*	[White-faced Plover]
Lesser Sand Plover	*Charadrius mongolus*	Mongolian Plover
Greater Sand Plover	*Charadrius leschenaultii*	Large Sand Plover
Caspian Plover	*Charadrius asiaticus*	Caspian Sand Plover
Oriental Plover	*Charadrius veredus*	Eastern Sand Plover
Northern Lapwing	*Vanellus vanellus*	Peewit
River Lapwing	*Vanellus duvaucelii*	Spur-winged Lapwing/Spur-winged Plover (with V. spinosus)
Yellow-wattled Lapwing	*Vanellus malabaricus*	
Grey-headed Lapwing	*Vanellus cinereus*	
Red-wattled Lapwing	*Vanellus indicus*	
Sociable Lapwing	*Vanellus gregarius*	Sociable Plover
White-tailed Lapwing	*Vanellus leucurus*	
Charadriiformes (Rostratulidae)		
Greater Painted-snipe	*Rostratula benghalensis*	
Charadriiformes (Jacanidae)		
Pheasant-tailed Jacana	*Hydrophasianus chirurgus*	
Bronze-winged Jacana	*Metopidius indicus*	
Charadriiformes (Scolopacidae)		
Whimbrel	*Numenius phaeopus*	
Eurasian Curlew	*Numenius arquata*	
Bar-tailed Godwit	*Limosa lapponica*	
Black-tailed Godwit	*Limosa limosa*	
Ruddy Turnstone	*Arenaria interpres*	Turnstone
Great Knot	*Calidris tenuirostris*	Eastern Knot
Red Knot	*Calidris canutus*	Knot
Ruff	*Calidris pugnax*	
Broad-billed Sandpiper	*Calidris falcinellus*	
Sharp-tailed Sandpiper	*Calidris acuminata*	Asian Pectoral Sandpiper
Curlew Sandpiper	*Calidris ferruginea*	
Temminck's Stint	*Calidris temminckii*	

English Name	Scientific Name	Alternative Name(s)
Long-toed Stint	*Calidris subminuta*	
Spoon-billed Sandpiper	*Calidris pygmaea*	
Red-necked Stint	*Calidris ruficollis*	Rufous-necked Stint, Eastern Little Stint
Sanderling	*Calidris alba*	
Dunlin	*Calidris alpina*	
Little Stint	*Calidris minuta*	
Buff-breasted Sandpiper	*Calidris subruficollis*	
Pectoral Sandpiper	*Calidris melanotos*	
Asian Dowitcher	*Limnodromus semipalmatus*	Snipe-billed Godwit
Long-billed Dowitcher	*Limnodromus scolopaceus*	
Eurasian Woodcock	*Scolopax rusticola*	
Solitary Snipe	*Gallinago solitaria*	
Wood Snipe	*Gallinago nemoricola*	
Pintail Snipe	*Gallinago stenura*	
Swinhoe's Snipe	*Gallinago megala*	
Great Snipe	*Gallinago media*	
Common Snipe	*Gallinago gallinago*	Fantail Snipe
Jack Snipe	*Lymnocryptes minimus*	
Terek Sandpiper	*Xenus cinereus*	
Common Sandpiper	*Actitis hypoleucos*	
Green Sandpiper	*Tringa ochropus*	
Spotted Redshank	*Tringa erythropus*	Dusky Redshank
Common Greenshank	*Tringa nebularia*	Greenshank
Common Redshank	*Tringa totanus*	
Wood Sandpiper	*Tringa glareola*	Spotted Sandpiper
Marsh Sandpiper	*Tringa stagnatilis*	
Red-necked Phalarope	*Phalaropus lobatus*	
Red Phalarope	*Phalaropus fulicarius*	Grey Phalarope
Charadriiformes (Turnicidae)		
Small Buttonquail	*Turnix sylvaticus*	Common Buttonquail, Little Bustard-quail
Yellow-legged Buttonquail	*Turnix tanki*	Yellow-legged Bustard-quail
Barred Buttonquail	*Turnix suscitator*	Common Bustard-quail
Charadriiformes (Dromadidae)		
Crab-plover	*Dromas ardeola*	
Charadriiformes (Glareolidae)		
Jerdon's Courser	*Rhinoptilus bitorquatus*	Double-banded Courser
Cream-coloured Courser	*Cursorius cursor*	
Indian Courser	*Cursorius coromandelicus*	
Collared Pratincole	*Glareola pratincola*	Collared Swallow-plover, Swallow-plover
Oriental Pratincole	*Glareola maldivarum*	Large Indian Swallow-plover, Large Indian Pratincole
Little Pratincole	*Glareola lactea*	Small Pratincole, Small Indian Pratincole, Small Indian Swallow-plover
Charadriiformes (Stercorariidae)		
Long-tailed Skua	*Stercorarius longicaudus*	Long-tailed Jaeger
Arctic Skua	*Stercorarius parasiticus*	Parasitic Jaeger
Pomarine Skua	*Stercorarius pomarinus*	Pomarine Jaeger
South Polar Skua	*Stercorarius maccormicki*	
Brown Skua	*Stercorarius antarcticus*	Antarctic Skua, Southern Skua
Charadriiformes (Laridae)		
Brown Noddy	*Anous stolidus*	Noddy Tern
Lesser Noddy	*Anous tenuirostris*	
Black Noddy	*Anous minutus*	
White Tern	*Gygis alba*	Fairy Tern
Indian Skimmer	*Rynchops albicollis*	
Black-legged Kittiwake	*Rissa tridactyla*	
Sabine's Gull	*Xema sabini*	
Slender-billed Gull	*Chroicocephalus genei*	
Brown-headed Gull	*Chroicocephalus brunnicephalus*	
Black-headed Gull	*Chroicocephalus ridibundus*	Common Black-headed Gull
Little Gull	*Hydrocoloeus minutus*	
Franklin's Gull	*Leucophaeus pipixcan*	

English Name	Scientific Name	Alternative Name(s)
Sooty Gull	*Ichthyaetus hemprichii*	
Pallas's Gull	*Ichthyaetus ichthyaetus*	Great Black-headed Gull
Mew Gull	*Larus canus*	
Lesser Black-backed Gull	*Larus fuscus*	[Heuglin's Gull, Steppe Gull, Taimyr Gull]
Caspian Gull	*Larus cachinnans*	
Mongolian Gull	*Larus smithsonianus mongolicus*	[Herring Gull, American Herrring Gull, Vega Gull]
Sooty Tern	*Onychoprion fuscatus*	
Bridled Tern	*Onychoprion anaethetus*	Brown-winged Tern
Little Tern	*Sternula albifrons*	White-shafted Ternlet S. a. pusilla
Saunders's Tern	*Sternula saundersi*	Black-shafted Ternlet
Gull-billed Tern	*Gelochelidon nilotica*	
Caspian Tern	*Hydroprogne caspia*	
Whiskered Tern	*Chlidonias hybrida*	
White-winged Tern	*Chlidonias leucopterus*	White-winged Black Tern
Black Tern	*Chlidonias niger*	
River Tern	*Sterna aurantia*	
Roseate Tern	*Sterna dougallii*	Rosy Tern
Black-naped Tern	*Sterna sumatrana*	
Common Tern	*Sterna hirundo*	
White-cheeked Tern	*Sterna repressa*	
Arctic Tern	*Sterna paradisaea*	
Black-bellied Tern	*Sterna acuticauda*	
Lesser Crested Tern	*Thalasseus bengalensis*	
Sandwich Tern	*Thalasseus sandvicensis*	
Greater Crested Tern	*Thalasseus bergii*	Large Crested Tern
Accipitriformes (Pandionidae)		
Osprey	*Pandion haliaetus*	
Black-winged Kite	*Elanus caeruleus*	Black-shouldered Kite
Oriental Honey Buzzard	*Pernis ptilorhynchus*	Crested Honey Buzzard
Jerdon's Baza	*Aviceda jerdoni*	Brown Lizard Hawk
Black Baza	*Aviceda leuphotes*	Black-crested Baza, Black-crested Lizard Hawk
Bearded Vulture	*Gypaetus barbatus*	Lammergeier
Egyptian Vulture	*Neophron percnopterus*	Scavenger Vulture, White Scavenger Vulture
Crested Serpent Eagle	*Spilornis cheela*	[Central Nicobar Serpent Eagle]
Nicobar Serpent Eagle	*Spilornis klossi*	Great Nicobar Serpent Eagle
Andaman Serpent Eagle	*Spilornis elgini*	Andaman Dark Serpent Eagle
Short-toed Snake Eagle	*Circaetus gallicus*	Short-toed Eagle
Red-headed Vulture	*Sarcogyps calvus*	King Vulture, Black Vulture, Pondicherry Vulture
Himalayan Vulture	*Gyps himalayensis*	Himalayan Griffon
White-rumped Vulture	*Gyps bengalensis*	White-backed Vulture
Indian Vulture	*Gyps indicus*	Long-billed Vulture (incl. G. tenuirostris)
Slender-billed Vulture	*Gyps tenuirostris*	
Griffon Vulture	*Gyps fulvus*	Eurasian Griffon
Cinereous Vulture	*Aegypius monachus*	Black Vulture
Mountain Hawk Eagle	*Nisaetus nipalensis*	[Legge's Hawk Eagle, Hodgson's Hawk Eagle]
Changeable Hawk Eagle	*Nisaetus cirrhatus*	[Crested Hawk Eagle]
Rufous-bellied Eagle	*Lophotriorchis kienerii*	Rufous-bellied Hawk Eagle
Black Eagle	*Ictinaetus malaiensis*	
Indian Spotted Eagle	*Clanga hastata*	Lesser Spotted Eagle (with C. pomarina)
Greater Spotted Eagle	*Clanga clanga*	
Tawny Eagle	*Aquila rapax*	
Steppe Eagle	*Aquila nipalensis*	
Eastern Imperial Eagle	*Aquila heliaca*	
Golden Eagle	*Aquila chrysaetos*	
Bonelli's Eagle	*Aquila fasciata*	Bonelli's Hawk Eagle
Booted Eagle	*Hieraaetus pennatus*	Booted Hawk Eagle
Western Marsh Harrier	*Circus aeruginosus*	Eurasian Marsh Harrier (incl. C. spilonotus)
Eastern Marsh Harrier	*Circus spilonotus*	Striped Harrier
Hen Harrier	*Circus cyaneus*	Northern Harrier
Pallid Harrier	*Circus macrourus*	Pale Harrier
Pied Harrier	*Circus melanoleucos*	

English Name	Scientific Name	Alternative Name(s)
Montagu's Harrier	*Circus pygargus*	
Crested Goshawk	*Accipiter trivirgatus*	
Shikra	*Accipiter badius*	
Nicobar Sparrowhawk	*Accipiter butleri*	
Chinese Sparrowhawk	*Accipiter soloensis*	Horsefield's Sparrowhawk
Japanese Sparrowhawk	*Accipiter gularis*	Eastern Sparrowhawk
Besra	*Accipiter virgatus*	
Eurasian Sparrowhawk	*Accipiter nisus*	
Northern Goshawk	*Accipiter gentilis*	
White-bellied Sea Eagle	*Haliaeetus leucogaster*	
Pallas's Fish Eagle	*Haliaeetus leucoryphus*	Ring-tailed Fishing Eagle
White-tailed Sea Eagle	*Haliaeetus albicilla*	
Lesser Fish Eagle	*Icthyophaga humilis*	Himalayan Grey-headed Fishing Eagle
Grey-headed Fish Eagle	*Icthyophaga ichthyaetus*	Grey-headed Fishing Eagle
Brahminy Kite	*Haliastur indus*	
Red Kite	*Milvus milvus*	
Black Kite	*Milvus migrans*	Pariah Kite, Black-eared Kite M. m. lineatus
White-eyed Buzzard	*Butastur teesa*	White-eyed Buzzard Eagle
Grey-faced Buzzard	*Butastur indicus*	
Common Buzzard	*Buteo buteo*	Eurasian Buzzard, Steppe Buzzard/Desert Buzzard B. b. vulpinus
Himalayan Buzzard	*Buteo refectus*	
Long-legged Buzzard	*Buteo rufinus*	
Upland Buzzard	*Buteo hemilasius*	
Strigiformes (Tytonidae)		
Bay Owl	*Phodilus badius*	[Oriental Bay Owl, Sri Lanka/Ceylon Bay Owl]
Eastern Grass Owl	*Tyto longimembris*	Australasian Grass Owl
Andaman Barn Owl	*Tyto deroepstorffi*	Andaman Masked Owl
Common Barn Owl	*Tyto alba*	Barn Owl, Western Barn Owl
Strigiformes (Strigidae)		
Brown Hawk Owl	*Ninox scutulata*	Brown Boobook; [Hume's Hawk Owl]
Andaman Hawk Owl	*Ninox affinis*	Andaman Boobook
Collared Owlet	*Glaucidium brodiei*	Collared Pygmy Owlet
Asian Barred Owlet	*Glaucidium cuculoides*	Barred Owlet
Jungle Owlet	*Glaucidium radiatum*	Barred Jungle Owlet
Spotted Owlet	*Athene brama*	
Little Owl	*Athene noctua*	
Forest Owlet	*Heteroglaux blewitti*	Forest Spotted Owlet, Blewitt's Owl
Boreal Owl	*Aegolius funereus*	Tengmalm's Owl
Andaman Scops Owl	*Otus balli*	
Mountain Scops Owl	*Otus spilocephalus*	Spotted Scops Owl
Eurasian Scops Owl	*Otus scops*	European Scops Owl
Pallid Scops Owl	*Otus brucei*	Striated Scops Owl
Oriental Scops Owl	*Otus sunia*	Scops Owl; [Walden's Scops Owl]
Nicobar Scops Owl	*Otus alius*	
Collared Scops Owl	*Otus bakkamoena*	[Indian Scops Owl]
Northern Long-eared Owl	*Asio otus*	Long-eared Owl
Short-eared Owl	*Asio flammeus*	
Mottled Wood Owl	*Strix ocellata*	
Brown Wood Owl	*Strix leptogrammica*	
Tawny Owl	*Strix aluco*	[Himalayan Owl]
Eurasian Eagle Owl	*Bubo bubo*	Great Horned Owl (incl. B. bengalensis)
Indian Eagle Owl	*Bubo bengalensis*	Rock Eagle-Owl
Spot-bellied Eagle Owl	*Bubo nipalensis*	Forest Eagle Owl
Dusky Eagle Owl	*Bubo coromandus*	Dusky Horned Owl
Brown Fish Owl	*Ketupa zeylonensis*	
Tawny Fish Owl	*Ketupa flavipes*	
Buffy Fish Owl	*Ketupa ketupu*	Malay Fish Owl
Trogoniformes (Trogonidae)		
Malabar Trogon	*Harpactes fasciatus*	
Red-headed Trogon	*Harpactes erythrocephalus*	
Ward's Trogon	*Harpactes wardi*	

English Name	Scientific Name	Alternative Name(s)
Bucerotiformes (Bucerotidae)		
Great Hornbill	*Buceros bicornis*	Great Pied Hornbill, Great Indian Hornbill
Malabar Pied Hornbill	*Anthracoceros coronatus*	
Oriental Pied Hornbill	*Anthracoceros albirostris*	Indian Pied Hornbill
Austen's Brown Hornbill	*Ptilolaemus austeni*	Godwin Austen's Brown Hornbill, White-throated Brown Hornbill
Malabar Grey Hornbill	*Ocyceros griseus*	
Indian Grey Hornbill	*Ocyceros birostris*	Common Grey Hornbill
Rufous-necked Hornbill	*Aceros nipalensis*	
Narcondam Hornbill	*Rhyticeros narcondami*	
Wreathed Hornbill	*Rhyticeros undulatus*	
Bucerotiformes (Upupidae)		
Common Hoopoe	*Upupa epops*	Eurasian Hoopoe
Piciformes (Indicatoridae)		
Yellow-rumped Honeyguide	*Indicator xanthonotus*	Orange-rumped Honeyguide
Piciformes (Picidae)		
Eurasian Wryneck	*Jynx torquilla*	Wryneck, Northern Wryneck
White-browed Piculet	*Sasia ochracea*	Rufous Piculet
Speckled Piculet	*Picumnus innominatus*	
Heart-spotted Woodpecker	*Hemicircus canente*	
Himalayan Golden-backed Woodpecker	*Dinopium shorii*	Himalayan Flameback, Himalayan Golden-backed Three-toed Woodpecker
Common Golden-backed Woodpecker	*Dinopium javanense*	Common Flameback, Indian Golden-backed Three-toed Woodpecker
Lesser Golden-backed Woodpecker	*Dinopium benghalense*	Black-rumped Flameback
Pale-headed Woodpecker	*Gecinulus grantia*	
Rufous Woodpecker	*Micropternus brachyurus*	
Greater Yellow-naped Woodpecker	*Chrysophlegma flavinucha*	Greater Yellownape, Yellow-naped Woodpecker
Lesser Yellow-naped Woodpecker	*Picus chlorolophus*	Lesser Yellownape, Small Yellow-naped Woodpecker
Streak-throated Woodpecker	*Picus xanthopygaeus*	Little Scaly-bellied Green Woodpecker
Grey-headed Woodpecker	*Picus canus*	Grey-faced Woodpecker, Black-naped Green Woodpecker
Scaly-bellied Woodpecker	*Picus squamatus*	Scaly-bellied Green Woodpecker, Large Scaly-bellied Green Woodpecker
Great Slaty Woodpecker	*Mulleripicus pulverulentus*	
White-bellied Woodpecker	*Dryocopus javensis*	Great Black Woodpecker
Andaman Woodpecker	*Dryocopus hodgei*	Andaman Black Woodpecker
Bay Woodpecker	*Blythipicus pyrrhotis*	Red-eared Bay Woodpecker
Greater Golden-backed Woodpecker	*Chrysocolaptes lucidus*	[Greater Flameback, Large Golden-backed Woodpecker, Malabar Flameback]
White-naped Woodpecker	*Chrysocolaptes festivus*	Black-backed Woodpecker
Brown-capped Pygmy Woodpecker	*Dendrocopos moluccensis*	Indian Pygmy Woodpecker D. [m.] nanus
Grey-capped Pygmy Woodpecker	*Dendrocopos canicapillus*	Grey-crowned Pygmy Woodpecker
Fulvous-breasted Pied Woodpecker	*Dendrocopos macei*	Fulvous-breasted Woodpecker; [Spot-breasted Woodpecker, Freckle-breasted Woodpecker]
Stripe-breasted Pied Woodpecker	*Dendrocopos atratus*	Stripe-breasted Woodpecker
Brown-fronted Pied Woodpecker	*Dendrocopos auriceps*	Brown-fronted Woodpecker
Yellow-fronted Pied Woodpecker	*Dendrocopos mahrattensis*	Yellow-crowned Woodpecker, Mahratta Woodpecker
Crimson-breasted Pied Woodpecker	*Dendrocopos cathpharius*	Scarlet-breasted Woodpecker, Crimson-breasted Woodpecker
Darjeeling Pied Woodpecker	*Dendrocopos darjellensis*	Darjeeling Woodpecker
Himalayan Pied Woodpecker	*Dendrocopos himalayensis*	Himalayan Woodpecker
Sind Pied Woodpecker	*Dendrocopos assimilis*	Sind Woodpecker
Great Spotted Woodpecker	*Dendrocopos major*	
Rufous-bellied Woodpecker	*Dendrocopos hyperythrus*	Rufous-bellied Sapsucker
Piciformes (Ramphastidae)		
Great Barbet	*Psilopogon virens*	Great Hill Barbet, Hill Barbet
Brown-headed Barbet	*Psilopogon zeylanicus*	Large Green Barbet
Lineated Barbet	*Psilopogon lineatus*	
White-cheeked Barbet	*Psilopogon viridis*	Small Green Barbet
Golden-throated Barbet	*Psilopogon franklinii*	

English Name	Scientific Name	Alternative Name(s)
Blue-throated Barbet	*Psilopogon asiaticus*	
Blue-eared Barbet	*Psilopogon australis*	
Malabar Barbet	*Psilopogon malabaricus*	Crimson-throated Barbet (with P. rubricapillus)
Coppersmith Barbet	*Psilopogon haemacephalus*	Crimson-breasted Barbet
Coraciiformes (Meropidae)		
Blue-bearded Bee-eater	*Nyctyornis athertoni*	
Green Bee-eater	*Merops orientalis*	Small Green Bee-eater, Little Green Bee-eater
Chestnut-headed Bee-eater	*Merops leschenaulti*	
Blue-tailed Bee-eater	*Merops philippinus*	
Blue-cheeked Bee-eater	*Merops persicus*	
European Bee-eater	*Merops apiaster*	
Coraciiformes (Coraciidae)		
Indian Roller	*Coracias benghalensis*	[Indochinese Roller]
European Roller	*Coracias garrulus*	Kashmir Roller
Dollarbird	*Eurystomus orientalis*	Broad-billed Roller
Coraciiformes (Alcedinidae)		
Oriental Dwarf Kingfisher	*Ceyx erithaca*	[Rufous-backed Dwarf Kingfisher, Black-backed Dwarf Kingfisher]
Blue-eared Kingfisher	*Alcedo meninting*	
Blyth's Kingfisher	*Alcedo hercules*	
Common Kingfisher	*Alcedo atthis*	Small Blue Kingfisher
Crested Kingfisher	*Megaceryle lugubris*	Himalayan Pied Kingfisher
Pied Kingfisher	*Ceryle rudis*	Lesser Pied Kingfisher
Stork-billed Kingfisher	*Pelargopsis capensis*	Brown-headed Stork-billed Kingfisher
Brown-winged Kingfisher	*Pelargopsis amauroptera*	Brown-winged Stork-billed Kingfisher
Ruddy Kingfisher	*Halcyon coromanda*	
White-throated Kingfisher	*Halcyon smyrnensis*	White-breasted Kingfisher
Black-capped Kingfisher	*Halcyon pileata*	
Collared Kingfisher	*Todiramphus chloris*	White-collared Kingfisher
Falconiformes (Falconidae)		
Collared Falconet	*Microhierax caerulescens*	Red-thighed Falconet, Red-breasted Falconet
Pied Falconet	*Microhierax melanoleucos*	White-legged Falconet
Lesser Kestrel	*Falco naumanni*	
Common Kestrel	*Falco tinnunculus*	Eurasian Kestrel
Red-necked Falcon	*Falco chicquera*	Red-headed Falcon, Red-headed Merlin
Amur Falcon	*Falco amurensis*	
Merlin	*Falco columbarius*	
Eurasian Hobby	*Falco subbuteo*	
Oriental Hobby	*Falco severus*	
Laggar Falcon	*Falco jugger*	
Saker Falcon	*Falco cherrug*	
Peregrine Falcon	*Falco peregrinus*	Shaheen Falcon F. p. peregrinator; [Barbary Falcon]
Psittaciformes (Psittaculidae)		
Grey-headed Parakeet	*Psittacula finschii*	Finsch's Parakeet, Eastern Slaty-headed Parakeet
Slaty-headed Parakeet	*Psittacula himalayana*	Himalayan Parakeet, Himalayan Slaty-headed Parakeet
Blossom-headed Parakeet	*Psittacula roseata*	Eastern Blossom-headed Parakeet, Rosy-headed Parakeet
Plum-headed Parakeet	*Psittacula cyanocephala*	Blossom-headed Parakeet
Red-breasted Parakeet	*Psittacula alexandri*	
Lord Derby's Parakeet	*Psittacula derbiana*	Derbyan Parakeet
Long-tailed Parakeet	*Psittacula longicauda*	Red-cheeked Parakeet
Malabar Parakeet	*Psittacula columboides*	Blue-winged Parakeet
Alexandrine Parakeet	*Psittacula eupatria*	Large Indian Parakeet
Rose-ringed Parakeet	*Psittacula krameri*	
Nicobar Parakeet	*Psittacula caniceps*	Blyth's Nicobar Parakeet
Vernal Hanging Parrot	*Loriculus vernalis*	Indian Lorikeet
Passeriformes (Pittidae)		
Blue-naped Pitta	*Pitta nipalensis*	
Blue Pitta	*Pitta cyanea*	
Indian Pitta	*Pitta brachyura*	

English Name	Scientific Name	Alternative Name(s)
Blue-winged Pitta	*Pitta moluccensis*	
Mangrove Pitta	*Pitta megarhyncha*	
Hooded Pitta	*Pitta sordida*	Green-breasted Pitta
Passeriformes (Eurylaimidae)		
Long-tailed Broadbill	*Psarisomus dalhousiae*	
Silver-breasted Broadbill	*Serilophus lunatus*	Collared Broadbill
Passeriformes (Campephagidae)		
White-bellied Minivet	*Pericrocotus erythropygius*	
Small Minivet	*Pericrocotus cinnamomeus*	
Grey-chinned Minivet	*Pericrocotus solaris*	Yellow-throated Minivet
Short-billed Minivet	*Pericrocotus brevirostris*	
Long-tailed Minivet	*Pericrocotus ethologus*	
Scarlet Minivet	*Pericrocotus flammeus*	[Orange Minivet]
Ashy Minivet	*Pericrocotus divaricatus*	
Swinhoe's Minivet	*Pericrocotus cantonensis*	Brown-rumped Minivet
Rosy Minivet	*Pericrocotus roseus*	
Large Cuckooshrike	*Coracina javensis*	
Andaman Cuckooshrike	*Coracina dobsoni*	Barred Cuckooshrike/Bar-bellied Cuckooshrike (with C. striata)
Pied Triller	*Lalage nigra*	Pied Cuckooshrike
Black-winged Cuckooshrike	*Lalage melaschistos*	Dark Grey Cuckooshrike
Black-headed Cuckooshrike	*Lalage melanoptera*	
Passeriformes (Pachycephalidae)		
Mangrove Whistler	*Pachycephala cinerea*	Grey Thickhead
Passeriformes (Vireonidae)		
Black-headed Shrike-babbler	*Pteruthius rufiventer*	Rufous-bellied Shrike-babbler
Himalayan Shrike-babbler	*Pteruthius ripleyi*	
Blyth's Shrike-babbler	*Pteruthius aeralatus*	Red-winged Shrike-babbler (incl. P. ripleyi)
Green Shrike-babbler	*Pteruthius xanthochlorus*	
Black-eared Shrike-babbler	*Pteruthius melanotis*	Chestnut-throated Shrike-babbler
Clicking Shrike-babbler	*Pteruthius intermedius*	Chestnut-fronted Shrike-babbler (with P. aenobarbus)
White-bellied Erpornis	*Erpornis zantholeuca*	White-bellied Yuhina
Passeriformes (Oriolidae)		
Maroon Oriole	*Oriolus traillii*	
Black-hooded Oriole	*Oriolus xanthornus*	Black-headed Oriole
Eurasian Golden Oriole	*Oriolus oriolus*	Golden Oriole (incl. O. kundoo)
Indian Golden Oriole	*Oriolus kundoo*	
Black-naped Oriole	*Oriolus chinensis*	
Slender-billed Oriole	*Oriolus tenuirostris*	
Passeriformes (Artamidae)		
White-breasted Woodswallow	*Artamus leucoryn*	White-breasted Swallow-shrike
Ashy Woodswallow	*Artamus fuscus*	Ashy Swallow-shrike
Passeriformes (Vangidae)		
Bar-winged Flycatcher-shrike	*Hemipus picatus*	Pied Flycatcher-shrike
Large Woodshrike	*Tephrodornis virgatus*	[Malabar Woodshrike]
Common Woodshrike	*Tephrodornis pondicerianus*	
Passeriformes (Aegithinidae)		
Common Iora	*Aegithina tiphia*	
Marshall's Iora	*Aegithina nigrolutea*	White-tailed Iora
Passeriformes (Dicruridae)		
Black Drongo	*Dicrurus macrocercus*	
Ashy Drongo	*Dicrurus leucophaeus*	Grey Drongo
White-bellied Drongo	*Dicrurus caerulescens*	
Crow-billed Drongo	*Dicrurus annectens*	
Bronzed Drongo	*Dicrurus aeneus*	
Lesser Racket-tailed Drongo	*Dicrurus remifer*	
Hair-crested Drongo	*Dicrurus hottentottus*	Spangled Drongo
Andaman Drongo	*Dicrurus andamanensis*	
Greater Racket-tailed Drongo	*Dicrurus paradiseus*	
Passeriformes (Rhipiduridae)		
White-browed Fantail	*Rhipidura aureola*	White-browed Fantail-flycatcher

English Name	Scientific Name	Alternative Name(s)
White-throated Fantail	*Rhipidura albicollis*	White-throated Fantail-flycatcher; [White-spotted Fantail, Spot-breasted Fantail]
Passeriformes (Laniidae)		
Brown Shrike	*Lanius cristatus*	Philippine Shrike L. c. lucionensis, Japanese Shrike L. c. superciliosus
Red-backed Shrike	*Lanius collurio*	
Red-tailed Shrike	*Lanius phoenicuroides*	Turkestan Shrike, Rufous Shrike
Isabelline Shrike	*Lanius isabellinus*	Pale Brown Shrike, Rufous-tailed Shrike (incl. L. phoenicuroides)
Burmese Shrike	*Lanius collurioides*	Chestnut-rumped Shrike
Bay-backed Shrike	*Lanius vittatus*	
Long-tailed Shrike	*Lanius schach*	Rufous-backed Shrike
Grey-backed Shrike	*Lanius tephronotus*	Tibetan Shrike
Lesser Grey Shrike	*Lanius minor*	
Great Grey Shrike	*Lanius excubitor*	[Southern Grey Shrike, Steppe Grey Shrike]
Woodchat Shrike	*Lanius senator*	
Passeriformes (Corvidae)		
Rufous Treepie	*Dendrocitta vagabunda*	Indian Treepie
Grey Treepie	*Dendrocitta formosae*	Himalayan Treepie
White-bellied Treepie	*Dendrocitta leucogastra*	Southern Treepie
Collared Treepie	*Dendrocitta frontalis*	Black-browed Treepie
Andaman Treepie	*Dendrocitta baileii*	
Red-billed Chough	*Pyrrhocorax pyrrhocorax*	
Yellow-billed Chough	*Pyrrhocorax graculus*	Alpine Chough
Yellow-billed Blue Magpie	*Urocissa flavirostris*	Gold-billed Magpie
Red-billed Blue Magpie	*Urocissa erythroryncha*	Blue Magpie
Common Green Magpie	*Cissa chinensis*	
Eurasian Jay	*Garrulus glandarius*	Red-crowned Jay
Black-headed Jay	*Garrulus lanceolatus*	Black-throated Jay
Eurasian Magpie	*Pica pica*	Black-billed Magpie (incl. P. hudsonia)
Eurasian Nutcracker	*Nucifraga caryocatactes*	[Large-spotted Nutcracker, Kashmir Nutcracker, Spotted Nutcracker]
Eurasian Jackdaw	*Corvus monedula*	Western Jackdaw, Jackdaw
Rook	*Corvus frugilegus*	
Common Raven	*Corvus corax*	Northern Raven
Carrion Crow	*Corvus corone*	[Hooded Crow]
House Crow	*Corvus splendens*	
Large-billed Crow	*Corvus macrorhynchos*	[Jungle Crow, Indian Jungle Crow, Eastern Jungle Crow]
Passeriformes (Monarchidae)		
Black-naped Monarch	*Hypothymis azurea*	Black-naped Monarch Flycatcher, Black-naped Flycatcher
Blyth's Paradise-flycatcher	*Terpsiphone affinis*	Oriental Paradise-flycatcher
Indian Paradise-flycatcher	*Terpsiphone paradisi*	Asian Paradise-flycatcher (incl. T. affinis)
Passeriformes (Dicaeidae)		
Yellow-bellied Flowerpecker	*Dicaeum melanozanthum*	
Yellow-vented Flowerpecker	*Dicaeum chrysorrheum*	
Thick-billed Flowerpecker	*Dicaeum agile*	[Modest Flowerpecker]
Pale-billed Flowerpecker	*Dicaeum erythrorhynchos*	Tickell's Flowerpecker
Plain Flowerpecker	*Dicaeum concolor*	[Andaman Flowerpecker, Nilgiri Flowerpecker]
Scarlet-backed Flowerpecker	*Dicaeum cruentatum*	
Fire-breasted Flowerpecker	*Dicaeum ignipectus*	
Passeriformes (Nectariniidae)		
Little Spiderhunter	*Arachnothera longirostra*	
Streaked Spiderhunter	*Arachnothera magna*	
Ruby-cheeked Sunbird	*Chalcoparia singalensis*	Rubycheek
Purple-rumped Sunbird	*Leptocoma zeylonica*	
Crimson-backed Sunbird	*Leptocoma minima*	Small Sunbird
Purple-throated Sunbird	*Leptocoma sperata*	Van Hasselt's Sunbird
Purple Sunbird	*Cinnyris asiaticus*	
Olive-backed Sunbird	*Cinnyris jugularis*	
Loten's Sunbird	*Cinnyris lotenius*	Long-billed Sunbird, Maroon-breasted Sunbird

English Name	Scientific Name	Alternative Name(s)
Fire-tailed Sunbird	*Aethopyga ignicauda*	Fire-tailed Yellow-backed Sunbird
Black-throated Sunbird	*Aethopyga saturata*	Black-breasted Sunbird
Green-tailed Sunbird	*Aethopyga nipalensis*	Nepal Yellow-backed Sunbird
Mrs Gould's Sunbird	*Aethopyga gouldiae*	
Vigors's Sunbird	*Aethopyga vigorsii*	Vigors's Yellow-backed Sunbird
Crimson Sunbird	*Aethopyga siparaja*	Yellow-backed Sunbird (incl. A. vigorsii)
Passeriformes (Irenidae)		
Asian Fairy-bluebird	*Irena puella*	
Golden-fronted Leafbird	*Chloropsis aurifrons*	Gold-fronted Chloropsis, Golden-fronted Chloropsis
Jerdon's Leafbird	*Chloropsis jerdoni*	Jerdon's Chloropsis
Orange-bellied Leafbird	*Chloropsis hardwickii*	Orange-bellied Chloropsis
Blue-winged Leafbird	*Chloropsis cochinchinensis*	Gold-mantled Chloropsis
Passeriformes (Prunellidae)		
Altai Accentor	*Prunella himalayana*	Himalayan Accentor, Rufous-streaked Accentor
Alpine Accentor	*Prunella collaris*	
Maroon-backed Accentor	*Prunella immaculata*	
Robin Accentor	*Prunella rubeculoides*	
Rufous-breasted Accentor	*Prunella strophiata*	
Brown Accentor	*Prunella fulvescens*	
Black-throated Accentor	*Prunella atrogularis*	
Passeriformes (Ploceidae)		
Black-breasted Weaver	*Ploceus benghalensis*	Bengal Weaver, Black-throated Weaver
Streaked Weaver	*Ploceus manyar*	
Baya Weaver	*Ploceus philippinus*	Indian Baya
Finn's Weaver	*Ploceus megarhynchus*	Yellow Weaver, Finn's Baya
Passeriformes (Estrildidae)		
Red Munia	*Amandava amandava*	Red Avadavat
Green Munia	*Amandava formosa*	Green Avadavat
Indian Silverbill	*Euodice malabarica*	White-throated Munia
White-rumped Munia	*Lonchura striata*	White-backed Munia
Scaly-breasted Munia	*Lonchura punctulata*	Spotted Munia
Black-throated Munia	*Lonchura kelaarti*	Rufous-bellied Munia
Black-headed Munia	*Lonchura malacca*	[Chestnut Munia, Tricoloured Munia]
Passeriformes (Passeridae)		
House Sparrow	*Passer domesticus*	
Spanish Sparrow	*Passer hispaniolensis*	
Sind Sparrow	*Passer pyrrhonotus*	Sind Jungle Sparrow
Russet Sparrow	*Passer cinnamomeus*	Cinnamon Tree Sparrow, Cinnamon Sparrow
Eurasian Tree Sparrow	*Passer montanus*	Tree Sparrow
Pale Rock Sparrow	*Carpospiza brachydactyla*	Pale Rockfinch
Eurasian Rock Sparrow	*Petronia petronia*	Rock Petronia
Yellow-throated Sparrow	*Gymnoris xanthocollis*	Chestnut-shouldered Petronia
Black-winged Snowfinch	*Montifringilla adamsi*	Tibetan Snowfinch
White-rumped Snowfinch	*Onychostruthus taczanowskii*	Mandelli's Snowfinch, Taczanowski's Snowfinch
Rufous-necked Snowfinch	*Pyrgilauda ruficollis*	Red-necked Snowfinch
Blanford's Snowfinch	*Pyrgilauda blanfordi*	Plain-backed Snowfinch
Passeriformes (Motacillidae)		
Forest Wagtail	*Dendronanthus indicus*	
Tree Pipit	*Anthus trivialis*	Eurasian Tree Pipit
Olive-backed Pipit	*Anthus hodgsoni*	Indian Tree Pipit
Red-throated Pipit	*Anthus cervinus*	
Rosy Pipit	*Anthus roseatus*	Vinaceous-breasted Pipit
Buff-bellied Pipit	*Anthus rubescens*	American Pipit
Water Pipit	*Anthus spinoletta*	
Upland Pipit	*Anthus sylvanus*	
Nilgiri Pipit	*Anthus nilghiriensis*	
Richard's Pipit	*Anthus richardi*	
Paddyfield Pipit	*Anthus rufulus*	
Blyth's Pipit	*Anthus godlewskii*	
Tawny Pipit	*Anthus campestris*	
Long-billed Pipit	*Anthus similis*	Brown Rock Pipit

English Name	Scientific Name	Alternative Name(s)
Western Yellow Wagtail	*Motacilla flava*	
Grey Wagtail	*Motacilla cinerea*	
Citrine Wagtail	*Motacilla citreola*	Yellow-headed Wagtail
White-browed Wagtail	*Motacilla maderaspatensis*	Large Pied Wagtail
White Wagtail	*Motacilla alba*	Pied Wagtail
Passeriformes (Fringillidae)		
Common Chaffinch	*Fringilla coelebs*	Eurasian Chaffinch
Brambling	*Fringilla montifringilla*	
Black-and-yellow Grosbeak	*Mycerobas icterioides*	
Collared Grosbeak	*Mycerobas affinis*	Allied Grosbeak
Spot-winged Grosbeak	*Mycerobas melanozanthos*	
White-winged Grosbeak	*Mycerobas carnipes*	
Hawfinch	*Coccothraustes coccothraustes*	
Common Rosefinch	*Erythrina erythrina*	
Scarlet Finch	*Haematospiza sipahi*	
Streaked Rosefinch	*Carpodacus rubicilloides*	Eastern Great Rosefinch, Streaked Great Rosefinch
Great Rosefinch	*Carpodacus rubicilla*	Spotted Great Rosefinch
Red-fronted Rosefinch	*Carpodacus puniceus*	Red-breasted Rosefinch
Crimson-browed Finch	*Carpodacus subhimachalus*	Red-headed Rosefinch
Himalayan White-browed Rosefinch	*Carpodacus thura*	
Blyth's Rosefinch	*Carpodacus grandis*	Red-mantled Rosefinch (with C. rhodochlamys)
Himalayan Beautiful Rosefinch	*Carpodacus pulcherrimus*	Beautiful Rosefinch (incl. C. waltoni)
Dark-rumped Rosefinch	*Carpodacus edwardsii*	Large Rosefinch
Pink-browed Rosefinch	*Carpodacus rodochroa*	
Spot-winged Rosefinch	*Carpodacus rodopeplus*	
Vinaceous Rosefinch	*Carpodacus vinaceus*	
Brown Bullfinch	*Pyrrhula nipalensis*	
Orange Bullfinch	*Pyrrhula aurantiaca*	
Red-headed Bullfinch	*Pyrrhula erythrocephala*	
Grey-headed Bullfinch	*Pyrrhula erythaca*	
Trumpeter Finch	*Bucanetes githagineus*	Trumpeter Bullfinch
Mongolian Finch	*Eremopsaltria mongolica*	Mongolian Desert Finch
Blanford's Rosefinch	*Agraphospiza rubescens*	Crimson Rosefinch
Spectacled Finch	*Callacanthis burtoni*	Red-browed Finch
Gold-naped Finch	*Pyrrhoplectes epauletta*	Gold-headed Black Finch
Dark-breasted Rosefinch	*Procarduelis nipalensis*	Dark Rosefinch, Nepal Dark Rosefinch
Plain Mountain Finch	*Leucosticte nemoricola*	Plain-coloured Mountain Finch, Hodgson's Mountain Finch
Brandt's Mountain Finch	*Leucosticte brandti*	Black-headed Mountain Finch
Sillem's Mountain Finch	*Leucosticte sillemi*	Tawny-headed Mountain Finch
Yellow-breasted Greenfinch	*Chloris spinoides*	Himalayan Greenfinch
Black-headed Greenfinch	*Chloris ambigua*	Tibetan Greenfinch
Twite	*Linaria flavirostris*	
Common Linnet	*Linaria cannabina*	Eurasian Linnet, Eastern Linnet, European Linnet
Red Crossbill	*Loxia curvirostra*	Crossbill
European Goldfinch	*Carduelis carduelis*	
Fire-fronted Serin	*Serinus pusillus*	Red-fronted Serin, Gold-fronted Finch
Tibetan Siskin	*Spinus thibetanus*	Tibetan Serin
Eurasian Siskin	*Spinus spinus*	
Passeriformes (Emberizidae)		
Striolated Bunting	*Fringillaria striolata*	House Bunting
Crested Bunting	*Melophus lathami*	
Red-headed Bunting	*Granativora bruniceps*	
Black-headed Bunting	*Granativora melanocephala*	
Chestnut-eared Bunting	*Emberiza fucata*	Grey-headed Bunting
Godlewski's Bunting	*Emberiza godlewskii*	
Rock Bunting	*Emberiza cia*	
Grey-necked Bunting	*Emberiza buchanani*	Grey-hooded Bunting
Ortolan Bunting	*Emberiza hortulana*	
White-capped Bunting	*Emberiza stewarti*	Chestnut-breasted Bunting

English Name	Scientific Name	Alternative Name(s)
Yellowhammer	*Emberiza citrinella*	
Pine Bunting	*Emberiza leucocephalos*	
Eurasian Reed Bunting	*Schoeniclus schoeniclus*	Common Reed Bunting
Black-faced Bunting	*Schoeniclus spodocephala*	
Chestnut Bunting	*Schoeniclus rutilus*	
Little Bunting	*Schoeniclus pusillus*	
Yellow-breasted Bunting	*Schoeniclus aureolus*	
Tristram's Bunting	*Schoeniclus tristrami*	
Passeriformes (Stenostiridae)		
Yellow-bellied Fairy-fantail	*Chelidorhynx hypoxanthus*	Yellow-bellied Fantail, Yellow-bellied Fantail-flycatcher
Grey-headed Canary-flycatcher	*Culicicapa ceylonensis*	Grey-headed Flycatcher
Passeriformes (Paridae)		
Fire-capped Tit	*Cephalopyrus flammiceps*	
Yellow-browed Tit	*Sylviparus modestus*	
Sultan Tit	*Melanochlora sultanea*	
Coal Tit	*Periparus ater*	Spot-winged Tit/Crested Black Tit P. [a.] melanolophus
Rufous-naped Tit	*Periparus rufonuchalis*	Black-breasted Tit, Dark-grey Tit, Simla Black Tit
Rufous-vented Tit	*Periparus rubidiventris*	Rufous-bellied Crested Tit, Black Crested Tit
Grey-crested Tit	*Lophophanes dichrous*	Brown Crested Tit, Fulvous Tit, Grey Crested Tit
Azure Tit	*Cyanistes cyanus*	Blue Tit
Ground Tit	*Pseudopodoces humilis*	Tibetan Ground Tit, Hume's Ground Chough, Hume's Groundpecker, Groundpecker
Green-backed Tit	*Parus monticolus*	
Cinereous Tit	*Parus cinereus*	Grey Tit/Great Tit (with P. major)
White-naped Tit	*Machlolophus nuchalis*	White-winged Black Tit
Black-lored Tit	*Machlolophus xanthogenys*	Yellow-cheeked Tit (incl. M. spilonotus); [Indian Tit, Indian Black-lored Tit, Himalayan Black-lored Tit, Black-lored Yellow Tit]
Yellow-cheeked Tit	*Machlolophus spilonotus*	Black-spotted Yellow Tit
Passeriformes (Remizidae)		
White-crowned Penduline Tit	*Remiz consobrinus*	Eastern Penduline Tit, Penduline Tit
Passeriformes (Alaudidae)		
Greater Hoopoe Lark	*Alaemon alaudipes*	Large Desert Lark
Rufous-tailed Lark	*Ammomanes phoenicura*	Rufous-tailed Finch Lark
Desert Lark	*Ammomanes deserti*	Desert Finch Lark
Black-crowned Sparrow Lark	*Eremopterix nigriceps*	Black-crowned Finch Lark
Ashy-crowned Sparrow Lark	*Eremopterix griseus*	Ashy-crowned Finch Lark
Singing Bushlark	*Mirafra cantillans*	
Bengal Bushlark	*Mirafra assamica*	Rufous-winged Bushlark (incl. M. affinis)
Indian Bushlark	*Mirafra erythroptera*	Red-winged Bushlark
Jerdon's Bushlark	*Mirafra affinis*	
Lesser Short-toed Lark	*Alaudala rufescens*	[Asian Short-toed Lark]
Sand Lark	*Alaudala raytal*	Indian Short-toed Lark
Bimaculated Lark	*Melanocorypha bimaculata*	Eastern Calandra Lark
Tibetan Lark	*Melanocorypha maxima*	Long-billed Calandra Lark
Hume's Short-toed Lark	*Calandrella acutirostris*	Hume's Lark
Greater Short-toed Lark	*Calandrella brachydactyla*	
Horned Lark	*Eremophila alpestris*	
Eurasian Skylark	*Alauda arvensis*	Skylark
Oriental Skylark	*Alauda gulgula*	Small Skylark
Crested Lark	*Galerida cristata*	
Malabar Lark	*Galerida malabarica*	Malabar Crested Lark
Sykes's Lark	*Galerida deva*	Tawny Lark, Deccan Crested Lark, Sykes's Crested Lark
Passeriformes (Cisticolidae)		
Zitting Cisticola	*Cisticola juncidis*	Streaked Fantail Warbler
Golden-headed Cisticola	*Cisticola exilis*	Bright-capped Cisticola, Red-headed Cisticola C. e. erythrocephalus, Yellow-headed Cisticola C. e. tytleri
Striated Prinia	*Prinia crinigera*	Brown Hill Warbler

English Name	Scientific Name	Alternative Name(s)
Hill Prinia	*Prinia atrogularis*	Black-throated Hill Warbler; [Black-throated Prinia]
Grey-crowned Prinia	*Prinia cinereocapilla*	Hodgson's Wren Warbler
Rufous-fronted Prinia	*Prinia buchanani*	Rufous-fronted Wren Warbler
Rufescent Prinia	*Prinia rufescens*	Rufous Wren Warbler
Grey-breasted Prinia	*Prinia hodgsonii*	Franklin's Wren Warbler, Ashy-grey Wren Warbler
Graceful Prinia	*Prinia gracilis*	Streaked Wren Warbler
Jungle Prinia	*Prinia sylvatica*	Jungle Wren Warbler
Yellow-bellied Prinia	*Prinia flaviventris*	Yellow-bellied Wren Warbler
Ashy Prinia	*Prinia socialis*	Ashy Wren Warbler
Plain Prinia	*Prinia inornata*	Plain Wren Warbler
Common Tailorbird	*Orthotomus sutorius*	
Dark-necked Tailorbird	*Orthotomus atrogularis*	Black-necked Tailorbird
Passeriformes (Locustellidae)		
Rusty-rumped Warbler	*Locustella certhiola*	Pallas's Grasshopper Warbler
Lanceolated Warbler	*Locustella lanceolata*	Streaked Grasshopper Warbler
Brown Bush Warbler	*Locustella luteoventris*	
Chinese Bush Warbler	*Locustella tacsanowskia*	
Long-billed Bush Warbler	*Locustella major*	Large-billed Bush Warbler
Grasshopper Warbler	*Locustella naevia*	
Baikal Bush Warbler	*Locustella davidi*	David's Bush Warbler
West Himalayan Bush Warbler	*Locustella kashmirensis*	
Spotted Bush Warbler	*Locustella thoracica*	
Russet Bush Warbler	*Locustella mandelli*	
Striated Grassbird	*Megalurus palustris*	Striated Marsh Warbler
Broad-tailed Grassbird	*Schoenicola platyurus*	Broad-tailed Grass Warbler
Bristled Grassbird	*Chaetornis striata*	Bristled Grass Warbler
Passeriformes (Acrocephalidae)		
Thick-billed Warbler	*Arundinax aedon*	
Booted Warbler	*Iduna caligata*	Siberian Booted Tree Warbler
Sykes's Warbler	*Iduna rama*	Indian Booted Tree Warbler
Black-browed Reed Warbler	*Acrocephalus bistrigiceps*	
Moustached Warbler	*Acrocephalus melanopogon*	Moustached Sedge Warbler
Sedge Warbler	*Acrocephalus schoenobaenus*	
Large-billed Reed Warbler	*Acrocephalus orinus*	
Blyth's Reed Warbler	*Acrocephalus dumetorum*	
Paddyfield Warbler	*Acrocephalus agricola*	
Blunt-winged Warbler	*Acrocephalus concinens*	Blunt-winged Paddyfield Warbler, Blunt-winged Reed Warbler
Great Reed Warbler	*Acrocephalus arundinaceus*	Eurasian Great Reed Warbler
Oriental Reed Warbler	*Acrocephalus orientalis*	Eastern Great Reed Warbler
Clamorous Reed Warbler	*Acrocephalus stentoreus*	Indian Reed Warbler / Indian Great Reed Warbler A. s. brunnescens
Passeriformes (Pnoepygidae)		
Nepal Wren Babbler	*Pnoepyga immaculata*	Immaculate Cupwing
Pygmy Wren Babbler	*Pnoepyga pusilla*	Brown Wren Babbler, Pygmy Cupwing
Scaly-breasted Wren Babbler	*Pnoepyga albiventer*	Scaly-breasted Cupwing
Passeriformes (Hirundinidae)		
Northern House Martin	*Delichon urbicum*	Common House Martin, European House Martin
Asian House Martin	*Delichon dasypus*	
Nepal House Martin	*Delichon nipalense*	
Streak-throated Swallow	*Petrochelidon fluvicola*	Indian Cliff Swallow
Red-rumped Swallow	*Cecropis daurica*	Striated Swallow (incl. C. striolata)
Striated Swallow	*Cecropis striolata*	
Pacific Swallow	*Hirundo tahitica*	[Hill Swallow, House Swallow]
Wire-tailed Swallow	*Hirundo smithii*	
Barn Swallow	*Hirundo rustica*	Common Swallow
Eurasian Crag Martin	*Ptyonoprogne rupestris*	Crag Martin
Dusky Crag Martin	*Ptyonoprogne concolor*	
Plain Martin	*Riparia paludicola*	Grey-throated Sand Martin/Grey-throated Martin R. [p.] chinensis

English Name	Scientific Name	Alternative Name(s)
Sand Martin	*Riparia riparia*	Collared Sand Martin (incl. R. diluta), Bank Swallow, Common Sand Martin
Pale Martin	*Riparia diluta*	Pale Sand Martin
Passeriformes (Pycnonotidae)		
White-throated Bulbul	*Alophoixus flaveolus*	
Olive Bulbul	*Iole viridescens*	
Ashy Bulbul	*Hemixos flavala*	Brown-eared Bulbul
Nicobar Bulbul	*Ixos nicobariensis*	
Mountain Bulbul	*Ixos mcclellandii*	Rufous-bellied Bulbul
Black Bulbul	*Hypsipetes leucocephalus*	[Square-tailed Bulbul, Himalayan Black Bulbul]
Crested Finchbill	*Spizixos canifrons*	Finch-billed Bulbul
Striated Bulbul	*Pycnonotus striatus*	Striated Green Bulbul
Black-crested Bulbul	*Pycnonotus melanicterus*	[Flame-throated Bulbul, Ruby-throated Bulbul]
Red-whiskered Bulbul	*Pycnonotus jocosus*	
Himalayan Bulbul	*Pycnonotus leucogenis*	White-cheeked Bulbul (incl. P. leucotis)
White-eared Bulbul	*Pycnonotus leucotis*	
Red-vented Bulbul	*Pycnonotus cafer*	
Yellow-throated Bulbul	*Pycnonotus xantholaemus*	
Flavescent Bulbul	*Pycnonotus flavescens*	Blyth's Bulbul
White-browed Bulbul	*Pycnonotus luteolus*	
Black-headed Bulbul	*Brachypodius atriceps*	
Andaman Bulbul	*Brachypodius fuscoflavescens*	Andaman Black-headed Bulbul
Grey-headed Bulbul	*Brachypodius priocephalus*	
Yellow-browed Bulbul	*Acritillas indica*	
Passeriformes (Phylloscopidae)		
Chinese Leaf Warbler	*Abrornis yunnanensis*	
Brooks's Leaf Warbler	*Abrornis subviridis*	
Yellow-browed Warbler	*Abrornis inornatus*	Yellow-browed Leaf Warbler
Hume's Leaf Warbler	*Abrornis humei*	Hume's Warbler, Mandelli's Leaf Warbler A. [h.] mandellii
Lemon-rumped Warbler	*Abrornis chloronotus*	Pale-rumped Warbler, Pallas's Leaf Warbler (with A. proregulus)
Buff-barred Warbler	*Abrornis pulcher*	Orange-barred Leaf Warbler
Ashy-throated Warbler	*Abrornis maculipennis*	Grey-faced Leaf Warbler
Dusky Warbler	*Phylloscopus fuscatus*	Dusky Leaf Warbler
Smoky Warbler	*Phylloscopus fuligiventer*	Smoky Leaf Warbler
Buff-throated Warbler	*Phylloscopus subaffinis*	Buff-throated Leaf Warbler
Common Chiffchaff	*Phylloscopus collybita*	Siberian Chiffchaff P. [c.] tristis
Kashmir Chiffchaff	*Phylloscopus sindianus*	Mountain Chiffchaff (incl. P. lorenzii)
Plain Leaf Warbler	*Phylloscopus neglectus*	
Tytler's Leaf Warbler	*Phylloscopus tytleri*	
Sulphur-bellied Warbler	*Phylloscopus griseolus*	Olivaceous Leaf warbler
Tickell's Leaf Warbler	*Phylloscopus affinis*	
White-spectacled Warbler	*Seicercus affinis*	Allied Flycatcher Warbler, White-spectacled Leaf Warbler
Grey-cheeked Warbler	*Seicercus poliogenys*	Grey-cheeked Flycatcher Warbler, Grey-cheeked Leaf Warbler
Green-crowned Warbler	*Seicercus burkii*	Golden-spectacled Warbler/Black-browed Flycatcher Warbler (incl. S. whistleri & S. tephrocephalus), Green-crowned Leaf Warbler
Grey-crowned Warbler	*Seicercus tephrocephalus*	Grey-crowned Leaf Warbler
Whistler's Warbler	*Seicercus whistleri*	Whistler's Leaf Warbler
Chestnut-crowned Warbler	*Seicercus castaniceps*	Chestnut-headed Flycatcher Warbler, Chestnut-crowned Leaf Warbler
Green Leaf Warbler	*Seicercus nitidus*	Bright-green Leaf Warbler
Greenish Leaf Warbler	*Seicercus trochiloides*	
Two-barred Leaf Warbler	*Seicercus plumbeitarsus*	
Arctic Warbler	*Seicercus borealis*	Arctic Leaf Warbler
Pale-legged Leaf Warbler	*Seicercus tenellipes*	
Large-billed Leaf Warbler	*Seicercus magnirostris*	
Yellow-vented Leaf Warbler	*Seicercus cantator*	Black-browed Leaf Warbler, Yellow-faced Leaf Warbler, Yellow-vented Warbler
Claudia's Leaf Warbler	*Seicercus claudiae*	

English Name	Scientific Name	Alternative Name(s)
Blyth's Leaf Warbler	*Seicercus reguloides*	
Western Crowned Leaf Warbler	*Seicercus occipitalis*	Large Crowned Leaf Warbler
Grey-hooded Leaf Warbler	*Seicercus xanthoschistos*	Grey-headed Flycatcher Warbler
Passeriformes (Scotocercidae)		
Slaty-bellied Tesia	*Tesia olivea*	Slaty-bellied Ground Warbler
Grey-bellied Tesia	*Tesia cyaniventer*	Yellow-browed Tesia, Yellow-browed Ground Warbler
Chestnut-crowned Bush Warbler	*Cettia major*	Large Bush Warbler
Grey-sided Bush Warbler	*Cettia brunnifrons*	Rufous-capped Bush Warbler
Chestnut-headed Tesia	*Cettia castaneocoronata*	Chestnut-headed Ground Warbler
Cetti's Warbler	*Cettia cetti*	Cetti's Bush Warbler
Pale-footed Bush Warbler	*Hemitesia pallidipes*	
Asian Stubtail	*Urosphena squameiceps*	Stub-tailed Bush Warbler
Yellow-bellied Warbler	*Abroscopus superciliaris*	Yellow-bellied Flycatcher Warbler
Rufous-faced Warbler	*Abroscopus albogularis*	White-throated Flycatcher Warbler
Black-faced Warbler	*Abroscopus schisticeps*	Black-faced Flycatcher Warbler
Mountain Tailorbird	*Phyllergates cucullatus*	Golden-headed Tailorbird, Leafworker
Broad-billed Warbler	*Tickellia hodgsoni*	Broad-billed Flycatcher Warbler
Brownish-flanked Bush Warbler	*Horornis fortipes*	Strong-footed Bush Warbler, Brown-flanked Bush Warbler
Hume's Bush Warbler	*Horornis brunnescens*	Yellowish-bellied Bush Warbler (with H. acanthizoides)
Aberrant Bush Warbler	*Horornis flavolivaceus*	
Manchurian Bush Warbler	*Horornis canturians*	Chinese Bush Warbler, Korean Bush Warbler
Passeriformes (Aegithalidae)		
White-browed Tit Warbler	*Leptopoecile sophiae*	Stoliczka's Tit Warbler
Crested Tit Warbler	*Leptopoecile elegans*	
Black-throated Tit	*Aegithalos concinnus*	Black-throated Bushtit; [Red-headed Tit]
White-cheeked Tit	*Aegithalos leucogenys*	White-cheeked Bushtit
White-throated Tit	*Aegithalos niveogularis*	White-throated Bushtit
Black-browed Tit	*Aegithalos iouschistos*	Black-browed Bushtit; [Rufous-fronted Tit, Rufous-fronted Bushtit]
Passeriformes (Sylviidae)		
Garden Warbler	*Sylvia borin*	
Asian Desert Warbler	*Curruca nana*	
Barred Warbler	*Curruca nisoria*	
Eastern Orphean Warbler	*Curruca crassirostris*	
Lesser Whitethroat	*Curruca curruca*	[Hume's Whitethroat, Desert Whitethroat, Small Whitethroat]
Common Whitethroat	*Curruca communis*	Greater Whitethroat
Fire-tailed Myzornis	*Myzornis pyrrhoura*	
Golden-breasted Fulvetta	*Lioparus chrysotis*	Golden-breasted Tit Babbler
Yellow-eyed Babbler	*Chrysomma sinense*	
Jerdon's Babbler	*Chrysomma altirostre*	
White-browed Fulvetta	*Fulvetta vinipectus*	White-browed Tit Babbler
Ludlow's Fulvetta	*Fulvetta ludlowi*	Brown-throated Fulvetta, Himalayan Brown-headed Tit Babbler
Streak-throated Fulvetta	*Fulvetta cinereiceps*	Manipur Brown-headed Tit Babbler/Manipur Fulvetta F. [c.] manipurensis, Grey-hooded Fulvetta
Black-breasted Parrotbill	*Paradoxornis flavirostris*	Black-throated Parrotbill, Gould's Parrotbill
Spot-breasted Parrotbill	*Paradoxornis guttaticollis*	White-throated Parrotbill
Greater Rufous-headed Parrotbill	*Psittiparus ruficeps*	[Rufous-headed Parrotbill, White-breasted Parrotbill]
Grey-headed Parrotbill	*Psittiparus gularis*	
Great Parrotbill	*Conostoma aemodium*	
Brown Parrotbill	*Cholornis unicolor*	
Fulvous Parrotbill	*Suthora fulvifrons*	Fulvous-fronted Parrotbill
Black-throated Parrotbill	*Suthora nipalensis*	Black-fronted Parrotbill S. n. humii, Ashy-eared Parrotbill S. n. nipalensis, Orange Parrotbill S. n. poliotis
Lesser Rufous-headed Parrotbill	*Chleuasicus atrosuperciliaris*	Pale-billed Parrotbill, Lesser Red-headed Parrotbill C. a. oatesi, Black-browed Parrotbill C. a. atrosuperciliaris

English Name	Scientific Name	Alternative Name(s)
Passeriformes (Zosteropidae)		
Striated Yuhina	*Yuhina castaniceps*	White-browed Yuhina, Chestnut-headed Yuhina
Black-chinned Yuhina	*Yuhina nigrimenta*	
Stripe-throated Yuhina	*Yuhina gularis*	
Whiskered Yuhina	*Yuhina flavicollis*	Yellow-naped Yuhina
Rufous-vented Yuhina	*Yuhina occipitalis*	Slaty-headed Yuhina
White-naped Yuhina	*Yuhina bakeri*	
Oriental White-eye	*Zosterops palpebrosus*	
Passeriformes (Timaliidae)		
Rufous-throated Wren Babbler	*Spelaeornis caudatus*	Tailed Wren Babbler
Mishmi Wren Babbler	*Spelaeornis badeigularis*	Rusty-throated Wren Babbler
Bar-winged Wren Babbler	*Spelaeornis troglodytoides*	Spotted Long-tailed Wren Babbler
Naga Wren Babbler	*Spelaeornis chocolatinus*	Streaked Long-tailed Wren Babbler
Chin Hills Wren Babbler	*Spelaeornis oatesi*	Chin Hills Long-tailed Wren Babbler
Grey-bellied Wren Babbler	*Spelaeornis reptatus*	
Tawny-breasted Wren Babbler	*Spelaeornis longicaudatus*	Long-tailed Wren Babbler
Spotted Wren Babbler	*Elachura formosa*	Spotted Elachura, Spotted Short-tailed Wren Babbler
Red-billed Scimitar Babbler	*Pomatorhinus ochraceiceps*	Long-billed Scimitar Babbler
Coral-billed Scimitar Babbler	*Pomatorhinus ferruginosus*	[Phayre's Scimitar Babbler, Black-crowned Scimitar Babbler]
Slender-billed Scimitar Babbler	*Pomatorhinus superciliaris*	
Indian Scimitar Babbler	*Pomatorhinus horsfieldii*	
White-browed Scimitar Babbler	*Pomatorhinus schisticeps*	Slaty-headed Scimitar Babbler (incl. P. horsfieldii)
Streak-breasted Scimitar Babbler	*Pomatorhinus ruficollis*	Rufous-necked Scimitar Babbler
Large Scimitar Babbler	*Erythrogenys hypoleucos*	
Rusty-cheeked Scimitar Babbler	*Erythrogenys erythrogenys*	
Spot-breasted Scimitar Babbler	*Erythrogenys erythrocnemis*	
Grey-throated Babbler	*Stachyris nigriceps*	Black-throated Babbler
Wedge-billed Babbler	*Stachyris humei*	[Chevron-breasted Babbler, Blackish-breasted Babbler, Cachar Wedge-billed Babbler, Sikkim Wedge-billed Babbler]
Snowy-throated Babbler	*Stachyris oglei*	Austen's Spotted Babbler
Tawny-bellied Babbler	*Dumetia hyperythra*	Rufous-bellied Babbler D. h. hyperythra, White-throated Babbler D. h. albogularis & D. h. abuensis
Dark-fronted Babbler	*Rhopocichla atriceps*	Black-headed Babbler
Chestnut-capped Babbler	*Timalia pileata*	Red-capped Babbler
Striped Tit Babbler	*Mixornis gularis*	Yellow-breasted Babbler, Pin-striped Tit Babbler
Golden Babbler	*Cyanoderma chrysaeum*	Golden-headed Babbler
Black-chinned Babbler	*Cyanoderma pyrrhops*	Red-billed Babbler
Rufous-capped Babbler	*Cyanoderma ruficeps*	Red-headed Babbler
Buff-chested Babbler	*Cyanoderma ambiguum*	Rufous-fronted Babbler/Red-fronted Babbler (with C. rufifrons)
Passeriformes (Pellorneidae)		
White-hooded Babbler	*Gampsorhynchus rufulus*	White-headed Shrike Babbler
Rusty-capped Fulvetta	*Schoeniparus dubius*	Rufous-headed Tit Babbler
Rufous-throated Fulvetta	*Schoeniparus rufogularis*	Red-throated Tit Babbler
Yellow-throated Fulvetta	*Schoeniparus cinereus*	Dusky Green Tit Babbler, Yellow-throated Tit Babbler
Rufous-winged Fulvetta	*Schoeniparus castaneceps*	Chestnut-headed Tit Babbler
Long-tailed Grass Babbler	*Laticilla burnesii*	Rufous-vented Prinia L. [b.] burnesii, Swamp Prinia L. [b.] cinerascens
Puff-throated Babbler	*Pellorneum ruficeps*	Spotted Babbler
Marsh Babbler	*Pellorneum palustre*	Marsh Spotted Babbler
Spot-throated Babbler	*Pellorneum albiventre*	Brown Babbler
Buff-breasted Babbler	*Trichastoma tickelli*	Tickell's Babbler
Abbott's Babbler	*Malacocincla abbotti*	
Streaked Wren Babbler	*Turdinus brevicaudatus*	
Eyebrowed Wren Babbler	*Napothera epilepidota*	Small Wren Babbler
Long-billed Wren Babbler	*Rimator malacoptilus*	
Rufous-rumped Grass Babbler	*Graminicola bengalensis*	Indian Grassbird, Rufous-rumped Grassbird, Large Grass Warbler

English Name	Scientific Name	Alternative Name(s)
Passeriformes (Leiothrichidae)		
Quaker Tit Babbler	*Alcippe poioicephala*	Brown-cheeked Fulvetta, Quaker Babbler
Nepal Tit Babbler	*Alcippe nipalensis*	Nepal Fulvetta, Nepal Quaker Babbler
Striated Laughingthrush	*Grammatoptila striata*	
Cutia	*Cutia nipalensis*	Nepal Cutia, Himalayan Cutia
Large Grey Babbler	*Argya malcolmi*	
Rufous Babbler	*Argya subrufa*	Indian Rufous Babbler
Striated Babbler	*Argya earlei*	
Common Babbler	*Argya caudata*	Scrub Babbler
Slender-billed Babbler	*Chatarrhaea longirostris*	
Jungle Babbler	*Turdoides striata*	
Yellow-billed Babbler	*Turdoides affinis*	White-headed Babbler
Spot-breasted Laughingthrush	*Garrulax merulinus*	
Lesser Necklaced Laughingthrush	*Garrulax monileger*	Necklaced Laughingthrush
White-crested Laughingthrush	*Garrulax leucolophus*	
Spotted Laughingthrush	*Garrulax ocellatus*	White-spotted Laughingthrush
Moustached Laughingthrush	*Garrulax cineraceus*	Ashy Laughingthrush
Rufous-chinned Laughingthrush	*Garrulax rufogularis*	
White-browed Laughingthrush	*Garrulax sannio*	
Chestnut-backed Laughingthrush	*Garrulax nuchalis*	
Greater Necklaced Laughingthrush	*Garrulax pectoralis*	Black-gorgeted Laughingthrush
Chinese Babax	*Garrulax lanceolatus*	Mount Victoria Babax
White-throated Laughingthrush	*Garrulax albogularis*	
Grey-sided Laughingthrush	*Garrulax caerulatus*	
Rufous-necked Laughingthrush	*Garrulax ruficollis*	
Yellow-throated Laughingthrush	*Garrulax galbanus*	
Wynaad Laughingthrush	*Garrulax delesserti*	
Rufous-vented Laughingthrush	*Garrulax gularis*	Yellow-breasted Laughingthrush
Scaly Laughingthrush	*Trochalopteron subunicolor*	Plain-coloured Laughingthrush
Brown-capped Laughingthrush	*Trochalopteron austeni*	
Blue-winged Laughingthrush	*Trochalopteron squamatum*	
Streaked Laughingthrush	*Trochalopteron lineatum*	[Bhutan Laughingthrush]
Kerala Laughingthrush	*Trochalopteron fairbanki*	Grey-breasted Laughingthrush, White-breasted Laughingthrush, Palani Laughingthrush T. [f.] fairbanki, Travancore Laughingthrush T. [f.] meridionale
Black-chinned Laughingthrush	*Trochalopteron cachinnans*	Nilgiri Laughingthrush / Rufous-breasted Laughingthrush T. [c.] cachinnans, Banasura Laughingthrush / Coorg White-breasted Laughingthrush T. [c.] jerdoni
Striped Laughingthrush	*Trochalopteron virgatum*	Manipur Streaked Laughingthrush
Variegated Laughingthrush	*Trochalopteron variegatum*	
Black-faced Laughingthrush	*Trochalopteron affine*	
Elliot's Laughingthrush	*Trochalopteron elliotii*	
Chestnut-crowned Laughingthrush	*Trochalopteron erythrocephalum*	Red-headed Laughingthrush; [Assam Laughingthrush]
Long-tailed Sibia	*Heterophasia picaoides*	
Beautiful Sibia	*Heterophasia pulchella*	
Rufous Sibia	*Heterophasia capistrata*	Black-capped Sibia
Grey Sibia	*Heterophasia gracilis*	
Silver-eared Mesia	*Leiothrix argentauris*	
Red-billed Leiothrix	*Leiothrix lutea*	
Rufous-backed Sibia	*Leioptila annectens*	Chestnut-backed Sibia
Red-tailed Minla	*Minla ignotincta*	
Red-faced Liocichla	*Liocichla phoenicea*	Crimson-winged Laughingthrush
Bugun Liocichla	*Liocichla bugunorum*	
Hoary-throated Barwing	*Sibia nipalensis*	Hoary Barwing
Streak-throated Barwing	*Sibia waldeni*	
Blue-winged Minla	*Siva cyanouroptera*	Blue-winged Siva
Chestnut-tailed Minla	*Chrysominla strigula*	Bar-throated Siva, Bar-throated Minla
Rusty-fronted Barwing	*Actinodura egertoni*	
Passeriformes (Regulidae)		
Goldcrest	*Regulus regulus*	

English Name	Scientific Name	Alternative Name(s)
Passeriformes (Bombycillidae)		
Bohemian Waxwing	*Bombycilla garrulus*	Waxwing
Passeriformes (Hypocoliidae)		
Grey Hypocolius	*Hypocolius ampelinus*	
Passeriformes (Certhiidae)		
Rusty-flanked Treecreeper	*Certhia nipalensis*	Nepal Treecreeper
Sikkim Treecreeper	*Certhia discolor*	Brown-throated Treecreeper
Manipur Treecreeper	*Certhia manipurensis*	Hume's Treecreeper
Bar-tailed Treecreeper	*Certhia himalayana*	Himalayan Treecreeper
Hodgson's Treecreeper	*Certhia hodgsoni*	Eurasian Treecreeper (with C. familiaris)
Passeriformes (Sittidae)		
Chestnut-vented Nuthatch	*Sitta nagaensis*	Naga Nuthatch
Kashmir Nuthatch	*Sitta cashmirensis*	
Chestnut-bellied Nuthatch	*Sitta castanea*	[Indian Nuthatch]
White-tailed Nuthatch	*Sitta himalayensis*	
Yunnan Nuthatch	*Sitta yunnanensis*	
White-cheeked Nuthatch	*Sitta leucopsis*	
Velvet-fronted Nuthatch	*Sitta frontalis*	
Beautiful Nuthatch	*Sitta formosa*	
Indian Spotted Creeper	*Salpornis spilonota*	Spotted Treecreeper, Spotted Grey Creeper
Wallcreeper	*Tichodroma muraria*	
Passeriformes (Troglodytidae)		
Eurasian Wren	*Troglodytes troglodytes*	Winter Wren
Passeriformes (Sturnidae)		
Common Starling	*Sturnus vulgaris*	European Starling
Rosy Starling	*Pastor roseus*	Rosy Pastor
Purple-backed Starling	*Agropsar sturninus*	Daurian Myna, Daurian Starling
Chestnut-cheeked Starling	*Agropsar philippensis*	
Asian Pied Starling	*Gracupica contra*	Pied Myna
Brahminy Starling	*Sturnia pagodarum*	Black-headed Myna, Brahminy Myna
Chestnut-tailed Starling	*Sturnia malabarica*	Grey-headed Myna; [Malabar Starling, Malabar White-headed Starling]
White-headed Starling	*Sturnia erythropygia*	Andaman White-headed Starling, White-headed Myna
Common Myna	*Acridotheres tristis*	Indian Myna
Bank Myna	*Acridotheres ginginianus*	
Jungle Myna	*Acridotheres fuscus*	
Collared Myna	*Acridotheres albocinctus*	
Great Myna	*Acridotheres grandis*	White-vented Myna, Orange-billed Jungle Myna
Spot-winged Starling	*Saroglossa spilopterus*	Spotted-winged Stare
Hill Myna	*Gracula religiosa*	[Southern Hill Myna, Lesser Hill Myna, Common Hill Myna]
Golden-crested Myna	*Ampeliceps coronatus*	
Asian Glossy Starling	*Aplonis panayensis*	Glossy Stare
Passeriformes (Cinclidae)		
White-throated Dipper	*Cinclus cinclus*	White-breasted Dipper
Brown Dipper	*Cinclus pallasii*	
Passeriformes (Muscicapidae)		
Rufous-tailed Scrub Robin	*Cercotrichas galactotes*	Rufous Chat
Indian Robin	*Saxicoloides fulicatus*	Indian Black Robin
Oriental Magpie Robin	*Copsychus saularis*	
White-rumped Shama	*Kittacincla malabarica*	[Andaman Shama]
Spotted Flycatcher	*Muscicapa striata*	
Dark-sided Flycatcher	*Muscicapa sibirica*	Sooty Flycatcher
Asian Brown Flycatcher	*Muscicapa dauurica*	
Brown-breasted Flycatcher	*Muscicapa muttui*	
Rusty-tailed Flycatcher	*Muscicapa ruficauda*	Rufous-tailed Flycatcher
Ferruginous Flycatcher	*Muscicapa ferruginea*	
Pale Blue Flycatcher	*Cyornis unicolor*	
White-bellied Blue Flycatcher	*Cyornis pallidipes*	
Pale-chinned Flycatcher	*Cyornis poliogenys*	Brooks's Flycatcher, Pale-chinned Blue Flycatcher
Large Blue Flycatcher	*Cyornis magnirostris*	Large-billed Blue Flycatcher

English Name	Scientific Name	Alternative Name(s)
Hill Blue Flycatcher	*Cyornis banyumas*	
Tickell's Blue Flycatcher	*Cyornis tickelliae*	Tickell's Red-breasted Blue Flycatcher
Blue-throated Flycatcher	*Cyornis rubeculoides*	Blue-throated Blue Flycatcher
White-tailed Blue Flycatcher	*Cyornis concretus*	
Nicobar Jungle Flycatcher	*Cyornis nicobaricus*	Olive Flycatcher
White-gorgeted Flycatcher	*Anthipes monileger*	
Rufous-bellied Niltava	*Niltava sundara*	
Vivid Niltava	*Niltava vivida*	Rufous-bellied Blue Flycatcher
Large Niltava	*Niltava grandis*	
Small Niltava	*Niltava macgrigoriae*	
Blue-and-white Flycatcher	*Cyanoptila cyanomelana*	
Verditer Flycatcher	*Eumyias thalassinus*	
Nilgiri Flycatcher	*Eumyias albicaudatus*	Nilgiri Verditer Flycatcher
White-browed Shortwing	*Brachypteryx montana*	
Lesser Shortwing	*Brachypteryx leucophris*	
Rusty-bellied Shortwing	*Brachypteryx hyperythra*	
White-bellied Shortwing	*Brachypteryx major*	[Rufous-bellied Shortwing, Nilgiri Shortwing, White-bellied Blue Robin, Nilgiri Blue Robin]
Gould's Shortwing	*Heteroxenicus stellatus*	
Indian Blue Robin	*Larvivora brunnea*	Indian Blue Chat
Siberian Blue Robin	*Larvivora cyane*	Siberian Blue Chat
Bluethroat	*Luscinia svecica*	
Hodgson's Blue Robin	*Luscinia phaenicuroides*	White-bellied Redstart, Hodgson's Shortwing
Little Forktail	*Enicurus scouleri*	
Black-backed Forktail	*Enicurus immaculatus*	
Slaty-backed Forktail	*Enicurus schistaceus*	
White-crowned Forktail	*Enicurus leschenaulti*	Leschenault's Forktail
Spotted Forktail	*Enicurus maculatus*	
Blue-fronted Robin	*Cinclidium frontale*	
Malabar Whistling Thrush	*Myophonus horsfieldii*	
Blue Whistling Thrush	*Myophonus caeruleus*	
Firethroat	*Calliope pectardens*	
White-tailed Rubythroat	*Calliope pectoralis*	Himalayan Rubythroat
Siberian Rubythroat	*Calliope calliope*	Rubythroat
White-tailed Robin	*Myiomela leucura*	White-tailed Blue Robin
White-browed Bush Robin	*Tarsiger indicus*	
Golden Bush Robin	*Tarsiger chrysaeus*	
Red-flanked Bush Robin	*Tarsiger cyanurus*	Red-flanked Bluetail, Japanese Blue Chat, Northern Red-flanked Bush Robin
Himalayan Bush Robin	*Tarsiger rufilatus*	Orange-flanked Bush Robin (with T. cyanurus), Himalayan Bluetail, Himalayan Red-flanked Bush Robin
Rufous-breasted Bush Robin	*Tarsiger hyperythrus*	Rufous-bellied Bush Robin
Kashmir Flycatcher	*Ficedula subrubra*	Kashmir Red-breasted Flycatcher
Red-breasted Flycatcher	*Ficedula parva*	
Taiga Flycatcher	*Ficedula albicilla*	Red-throated Flycatcher
Snowy-browed Flycatcher	*Ficedula hyperythra*	Rufous-breasted Blue Flycatcher
Rufous-gorgeted Flycatcher	*Ficedula strophiata*	Orange-gorgeted Flycatcher
Ultramarine Flycatcher	*Ficedula superciliaris*	White-browed Blue Flycatcher F. s. superciliaris, Little Blue-and-white Flycatcher F. s. aestigma
Little Pied Flycatcher	*Ficedula westermanni*	
Mugimaki Flycatcher	*Ficedula mugimaki*	
Yellow-rumped Flycatcher	*Ficedula zanthopygia*	Korean Flycatcher
Slaty-blue Flycatcher	*Ficedula tricolor*	
Black-and-orange Flycatcher	*Ficedula nigrorufa*	Black-and-rufous Flycatcher
Pygmy Blue Flycatcher	*Ficedula hodgsoni*	
Slaty-backed Flycatcher	*Ficedula sordida*	Rusty-breasted Blue Flycatcher
Sapphire Flycatcher	*Ficedula sapphira*	Sapphire-headed Flycatcher
Blue-fronted Redstart	*Adelura frontalis*	
White-throated Redstart	*Adelura schisticeps*	
Blue-capped Redstart	*Adelura coeruleocephala*	Blue-headed Redstart
Eversmann's Redstart	*Adelura erythronota*	Rufous-backed Redstart

English Name	Scientific Name	Alternative Name(s)
Plumbeous Water Redstart	*Rhyacornis fuliginosa*	Plumbeous Redstart
White-capped Water Redstart	*Chaimarrornis leucocephalus*	River Chat, White-capped Redstart
Hodgson's Redstart	*Phoenicurus hodgsoni*	
Common Redstart	*Phoenicurus phoenicurus*	White-fronted Redstart
Black Redstart	*Phoenicurus ochruros*	
Daurian Redstart	*Phoenicurus auroreus*	
White-winged Redstart	*Phoenicurus erythrogastrus*	Güldenstädt's Redstart
Blue-capped Rock Thrush	*Monticola cinclorhyncha*	Blue-headed Rock Thrush
Chestnut-bellied Rock Thrush	*Monticola rufiventris*	
Rufous-tailed Rock Thrush	*Monticola saxatilis*	Common Rock Thrush, Rock Thrush
Blue Rock Thrush	*Monticola solitarius*	[Asian Rock Thrush]
Stoliczka's Bushchat	*Saxicola macrorhynchus*	White-browed Bushchat
Hodgson's Bushchat	*Saxicola insignis*	White-throated Bushchat
Siberian Stonechat	*Saxicola maurus*	Collared Bushchat, Eastern Stonechat, Common Stonechat (with S. torquatus)
White-tailed Stonechat	*Saxicola leucurus*	
Pied Bushchat	*Saxicola caprata*	
Jerdon's Bushchat	*Saxicola jerdoni*	
Grey Bushchat	*Saxicola ferreus*	Dark-grey Bushchat
Northern Wheatear	*Oenanthe oenanthe*	Wheatear
Isabelline Wheatear	*Oenanthe isabellina*	Isabelline Chat
Desert Wheatear	*Oenanthe deserti*	
Pied Wheatear	*Oenanthe pleschanka*	Pleschanka's Chat
Brown Rock Chat	*Oenanthe fusca*	Indian Chat
Variable Wheatear	*Oenanthe picata*	Pied Chat
Hume's Wheatear	*Oenanthe albonigra*	Hume's Chat
Red-tailed Wheatear	*Oenanthe chrysopygia*	Rusty-tailed Wheatear, Red-tailed Chat
Passeriformes (Turdidae)		
Grandala	*Grandala coelicolor*	Hodgson's Grandala
Long-tailed Thrush	*Zoothera dixoni*	Long-tailed Mountain Thrush
Alpine Thrush	*Zoothera mollissima*	Plain-backed Mountain Thrush/Plain-backed Thrush (incl. Z. salimalii)
Himalayan Forest Thrush	*Zoothera salimalii*	
Dark-sided Thrush	*Zoothera marginata*	Lesser Brown Thrush, Dark-sided Ground Thrush
Long-billed Thrush	*Zoothera monticola*	Large Brown Thrush, Long-billed Ground Thrush
Scaly Thrush	*Zoothera dauma*	Scaly Mountain Thrush, Small-billed Mountain Thrush/Small-billed Scaly Thrush Z. d. dauma; [Nilgiri Thrush]
Purple Cochoa	*Cochoa purpurea*	
Green Cochoa	*Cochoa viridis*	
Siberian Thrush	*Geokichla sibirica*	White-browed Ground Thrush
Pied Thrush	*Geokichla wardii*	Pied Ground Thrush
Orange-headed Thrush	*Geokichla citrina*	Orange-headed Ground Thrush, White-throated Ground Thrush G. c. cyanota
Chinese Thrush	*Otocichla mupinensis*	
Mistle Thrush	*Turdus viscivorus*	
Song Thrush	*Turdus philomelos*	
Grey-winged Blackbird	*Turdus boulboul*	
Indian Blackbird	*Turdus simillimus*	
Black-breasted Thrush	*Turdus dissimilis*	
Tickell's Thrush	*Turdus unicolor*	
Eyebrowed Thrush	*Turdus obscurus*	Dark Thrush
Grey-sided Thrush	*Turdus feae*	Fea's Thrush
Kessler's Thrush	*Turdus kessleri*	White-backed Thrush
Tibetan Blackbird	*Turdus maximus*	
Fieldfare	*Turdus pilaris*	
White-collared Blackbird	*Turdus albocinctus*	
Chestnut Thrush	*Turdus rubrocanus*	Grey-headed Thrush
Dusky Thrush	*Turdus eunomus*	
Black-throated Thrush	*Turdus atrogularis*	
Red-throated Thrush	*Turdus ruficollis*	Dark-throated Thrush (incl. T. atrogularis)

INDEX

D

G

H

I

J

K

L

M

N

O

P

Q

R

U

V

W

X

Y

Z

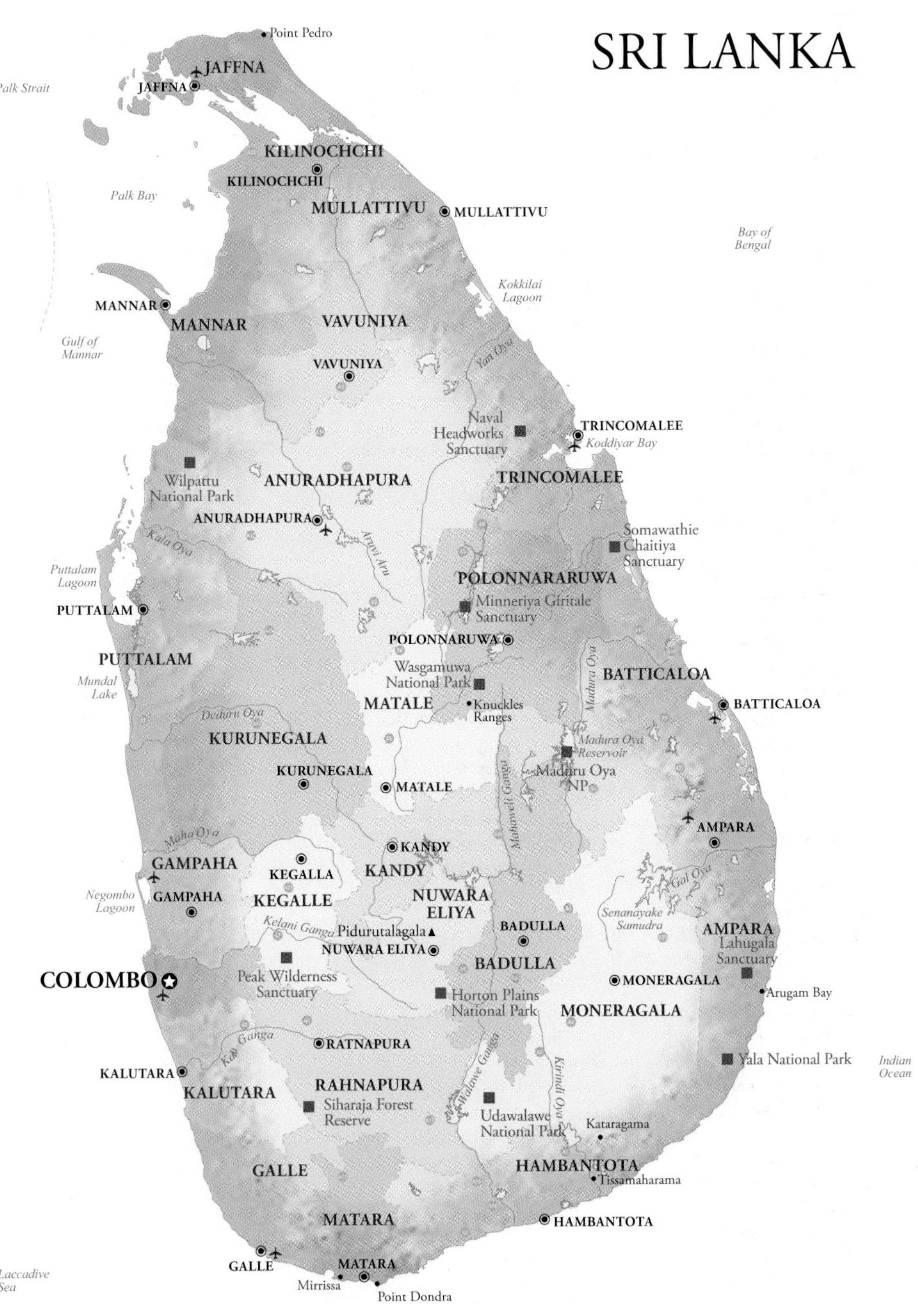

The external boundary as shown in these maps, as depicted here may not be authentic or exact.

INDIA

AFGHANISTAN
TAJIKISTAN
KABUL
ISLAMABAD
PAKISTAN
CHINA
Tibet
NEPAL
KATHMANDU
BHUTAN
THIMPHU
BANGLADESH
DHAKA
MYANMAR
BAY
JAMMU AND KASHMIR
K2
Gasherbum
Nanga Parbat
Dachigam
SRINAGAR
Lamayuru
Leh
Ladakh
Lahul
Chamba
Dalhousie
Dharamshala
HIMACHAL PRADESH
Spiti
Great Himalayan NP
SHIMLA
PUNJAB
Amritsar
CHANDIGARH
HARYANA
DELHI
UTTARAKHAND
DEHRADUN
Rajaji NP
Corbett NP
UTTAR PRADESH
Dudwa NP
LUCKNOW
Fatehpur Sikri
Agra
Gwalior
Jhansi
Sarnath
Varanasi
Kushinagar
RAJASTHAN
GREAT INDIAN DESERT
Bikaner
Jaisalmer
Desert NP
Osiyan
Mandor
Jodhpur
Ranakpur
Kumbhalgarh
Udaipur
Mount Abu
Pushkar
Ajmer
JAIPUR
Sariska
Keoladev Ghana
Ranthambore NP
Chittaurgarh
Shivpuri
Madhav NP
GUJARAT
RANN OF KACHCHH
Bhuj
Dhangadhra WLS
Modhera
Patan
GANDHINAGAR
Ahmedabad
Vadodara
Nal Sarovar
Velavadar
Palitana
Junagadh
Sasan Gir NP
DIU
DAMAN
DADRA AND NAGAR HAVELI
MADHYA PRADESH
BHOPAL
Khajuraho
Panna
Bandhavgarh NP
Kanha NP
Pench NP
Melghat NP
Satpura NP
Omkareshwar
Mandu
Maheshwar
Ajanta
CHHATTISGARH
RAIPUR
BIHAR
PATNA
Nalanda
Bodh Gaya
JHARKHAND
RANCHI
Hazaribagh WLS
Palamau WLS
WEST BENGAL
KOLKATA
Shanti Niketan
Sundarbans NP
Similipal NP
ODISHA
Mt. Everest
Gauri Shankar
Kunchenjunga
SIKKIM
GANGTOK
Darjeeling
Kalimpong
Siliguri
Jaldapara
Manas NP
ARUNACHAL PRADESH
ITANAGAR
Namdapha NP
Dibru Saikowa
Nameri NP
Sonai Rupa
Orang
Kaziranga NP
ASSAM
DISPUR
MEGHALAYA
SHILLONG
NAGALAND
KOHIMA
MANIPUR
IMPHAL
Keibul Lamjao NP
MIZORAM
AIZAWL
Dampa WLS
TRIPURA
AGARTALA

The external boundary as shown in this map, as depicted here may not be authentic or exact.

BHUTAN
CHINA
INDIA
Kula Gangri
Tsendagang
Masagang
Terigang
Table Mountain
Zongophu Gang
Gangla Karchung
Jejekangphu Gang
Gangkhar Puensum
Chisangang
GASA
Bhutanese Traditional Dwellings
Jechu Drake
Jumolhari
Jigme Dorj National Park
Rinchen Zoe La
Punakha Dzong
Talo Gompa
KENCHO
LHUENTSE
Kulong Chu Wildlife Sanctuary
SHINGBE
SHABLING
NASPE
BUMTHANG
TRASHI YANGTSE
PARO
DOTANANG
PUNAKHA
PUNAKHA
Taktsang Gompa
THIMPHU
Gangtey Gompa
Jakar
PARO
WANGDUE-PHODRANG
Tongsa Dzong
LAMTI
SANGKARI
SAWAPHU
TRONGSA
Torsa Strict Nature Resere
HA
GETTA DZONG
Longsho Gompa
Thrumshingla National Park
MONGAR
TRASHIGANG
Sakteng Wildlife Sanctuary
Simtokha Dzong
Black Mountain National Park
SHIUIJI
CHUKHA
CHALAIKA
KENGA
KANGPAR
DAGANA
TSIRANG
DHAJE
SARPANG
ZHEMGANG
PANKA
PEMAGATSHEL
TUNGKA LA
SAMTSE
CHHUKHA
BHURGAON
Phuentsholing
GEDU
Phipsoo Wildlife Sanctuary

NEPAL
CHINA
INDIA
Rara National Park
MAHAKALI
SETI
KARNALI
Shey Phosundo National Park
DADELDHURA
SILGHADI
JUMLA
Royal Suklaphanta National Park
BHERI
Dhorpatan Hunting Reserve
Annapurna Area Conservation Project
Royal Bardia National Park
Dhaulagiri
Annapurna
Manaslu
RAPTI
DHAULAGIRI
GANDAKI
Langtang National Park
TULSIPUR
BAGLUNG
POKHARA
BAGMATI
Sagarmatha National Park
Cho Oyu
Mt. Everest
Lhotse
NEPALGUNJ
KATHMANDU
Lukla
BUTWAL
Makalu-Barun National Park and Conservation Area
Kanchanju
LUMBINI
HETAUDA
Royal Chitwan National Park
Parsa Wildlife Reserve
SINDJULIMADI
MECHI
JANAKPUR
KOSHI
ILAM
NARAYANI
SAGARMATHA
Koshi Tappu Wildlife Reserve
DHARAN
RAJBIRAJ